Donated by
Friends of Neva Lomason Memorial Library
2012

Delish

COOKING SCHOOL

Delish

COOKING SCHOOL

TRIPLE TESTED · SUCCESS EVERY TIME!

LEARNING TO COOK
STEP-BY-STEP

HEARST BOOKS
New York

contents

Whether you cook every once in a while or every day, love being in the kitchen or worry that preparing a meal is simply too challenging, you'll come to rely on the *Delish Cooking School.* With triple-tested recipes, easy-to-follow instructions on how to handle the ingredients, clearly explained cooking methods, beautiful photographs and simple serving suggestions, *Delish Cooking School* helps home cooks at every level prepare delicious dishes with ease.

What makes this cookbook so vital?

Our recipes come from talented, dedicated people with various backgrounds; some are chefs, some teachers, others caterers or simply food-lovers. The result is a wide assortment of recipes that are all excellent and easy to make.

The recipes provide a list of ingredients in the order in which they are used, clear guidelines on measuring and weighing, logical directions on how to prepare, step-by-step photos to help guide you along the way, useful notes on proper bowl, pan or dish sizes, and all the nutritional information you need to plan healthy meals for your family. There are no tricks, no use of fake ingredients, no gimmicks; just good food cooked properly, presented well.

We're not only cooks, we're food shoppers too, so this book will show you how much of an ingredient you need to use in a recipe as well as how much you'll need to buy. We choose ingredients that can be found in most major supermarkets, but also we offer ideas for simple substitutions.

Our goal is to help you serve terrific meals without confusion, stress, or hassle. From dinners for one to parties for dozens, appetizers to dessert and everything in between, *Delish Cooking School* shows you exactly what you need to know to make your meals wonderful, and inspires you to cook even more. And be sure to visit delish.com for thousands of other recipes, cooking videos and an on-line community of home cooks.

Elizabeth Shepard
Executive Director
Delish

RECIPES TO KNOW BY HEART

Recipes to know by heart

Anyone can cook, but to be a good cook–a passionate cook, and a confident cook–takes particular care and attention. Cooking is both an art and a science, requiring equal amounts of creativity and technical know-how. You should be aware that there is a reason for every instruction you read in a recipe: when the butter cake recipe warns against overbeating, for example, it's not just on a whim, it's because overbeating can make the mixture "tough" and can effect the cooking result, and so on.

Like all of life's worthwhile endeavors, cooking requires time, dedication and persistence to do it well, but the rewards are many. The ability to confidently cook a delicious dinner for family and friends is deeply satisfying and so is turning out a perfect cake.

KEEP IT SIMPLE AND BUILD YOUR REPERTOIRE

THE BASICS

Use the freshest and best-quality ingredients: try to visit a farmers' market if you can and buy the freshest, preferably organic, produce available.

Invest in some good-quality cooking utensils: a couple of quality saucepans, a quality, heavy-based frying pan, a wok, a roasting dish and a range of different-shaped cake pans are good starting points.

Read the recipe thoroughly, a couple of times, before starting to cook and follow it carefully.

Make sure you have all the required ingredients ahead of time. Use measuring equipment, not just your own estimates, and be precise with measurements.

It's important to grasp the basics before you start getting too ambitious: a well-cooked roast chicken, for example, is much nicer than a badly cooked coq au vin.

In this chapter we have assembled a selection of recipes that, collectively, encompass a range of cooking methods you would be wise to learn.

From an easy Sunday night meal of a fluffy omelette through to a mid-week pork and vegetable stir-fry and a traditional roast chicken, these are recipes to commit to your memory's hard drive.

If you follow these recipes carefully, and learn them, then you're on your way to being a good cook.

COOKING TECHNIQUES

SOME COOKING TERMS ARE INTERCHANGEABLE ("ROAST" AND "BAKE" ARE THE SAME, FOR EXAMPLE, WHEN TALKING ABOUT MEATS, CHICKEN AND VEGETABLES) WHILE OTHERS SEEM TO OVERLAP IN MEANING: BROWNING, SEARING AND "LIGHT PAN-FRYING", FOR EXAMPLE, CAN CAUSE CONFUSION. HERE IS A QUICK SNAPSHOT OF SOME OF THE COOKING TECHNIQUES YOU'LL NEED IN THIS CHAPTER AND THAT YOU'LL EMPLOY IN ANY AVERAGE WEEK IN THE KITCHEN:

BROILING Using the humble broiler found in every wall oven and under some stove tops, broiling produces an even and tasty browned surface on everything from lamb chops to an omelette and is a healthy way to cook because the fats and juices drip into the tray.

PAN-FRYING (Also called shallow frying, encompasses browning and searing) refers to cooking foods in a shallow amount of cooking oil in the frying pan on the stove top. The idea is to brown the food, cooking one side first and then turning once. Heat the oil first and when it is giving off a haze, place the food in the pan. Variations in the amount of oil used and in the stove top temperature setting will produce different results: searing uses the tiniest amount of oil and a quick cooking time; pan-frying a steak or cutlet requires more oil and a medium-high heat. See the chapter on pan-frying on page 456.

DEGLAZING This is the term used when you add liquid (water, wine or stock) to a hot frying pan or baking dish after the meat or poultry has been removed. This liquid is then stirred over moderate-hot heat to blend all the leftover cooking juices into the liquid to create a sauce that can be added to other ingredients.

STIR-FRYING This fast cooking method involves cooking meat and vegetables in oil, tossing them in a wok, over a high heat. See the chapter on stir-fry, page 334.

ROASTING The words "roast" and "bake" are both used to describe foods (meats, chicken and vegetables) cooked uncovered in the oven. The vessel in which we cook these roasted items can be called a roasting pan or a baking dish. Most ovens have a "hot spot"—that is, the oven doesn't heat up evenly, with the heat concentrating in one area. Many are also hotter towards the back, so you'll need to check on your roast once or twice during cooking and turn the pan around, if necessary, to even out the cooking.

RESTING After cooking, all meat and poultry needs to "stand" or rest in a warm place (the oven turned off). Joints of meat or whole birds should stand for 15 minutes; smaller pieces of meat and poultry require 5 minutes. This makes the meat more succulent by allowing the juices to settle into the tissues.

BULB BASTER This looks like a giant eye-dropper with a metal stem and a rubber bulb. It makes it easy to suck up pan juices and distribute them over the food as it cooks.

STEWING A favorite technique in cold weather, stewing is a type of slow-cooking that involves submerging meat and vegetables in liquid (water, stock or wine or a combination of the three) and cooking slowly in a large pot on the stove top, until the meat is tender.

herb omelette

The idea of cooking beaten eggs with butter in a pan dates back to ancient times, yet today omelettes are still one of the simplest, most nutritious meals you can whip up in the kitchen. Getting it right, though, requires you to follow a few basic steps.

Chives The smallest member of the onion family, chives are a source of beneficial antioxidants. But their real value to the home cook is the wonderful savory flavor and vibrant color they can add to the most basic dish.

Parsley Fresh parsley is very fragile so it should always be washed right before using. The flat-leaf variety has a stronger flavor than curly parsley, so it holds up better to cooking. For this reason, it is best to use flat-leaf parsley for hot dishes such as this omelette.

Eggs A large number of eggs on the supermarket shelf today are labeled free range. However, many of these are actually cage or barn-laid eggs. To ensure you are buying true free-range eggs, look for a certification logo from a free-range association.

Sharp knife Chopping herbs to the right size can help blend in their flavors. You'll chop faster, more precisely and more safely with a very sharp chef's knife.

The right pan If you don't want your omelette to resemble a dish of scrambled eggs, equip your kitchen with a cast-iron omelette pan. This makes it easy to neatly fold the omelette in half and slide it out of the frying pan without breaking it.

Water Unlike scrambled eggs, omelettes require water, not milk to give them their lightness. The water turns to steam in the pan, producing a light, airy omelette.

Chopping board A wooden cutting surface is just as safe as plastic if cleaned properly. Scrub it after every use with hot, soapy water, rinse, dry and stand it in a dish rack to air completely. Alternatively, use a paste of baking soda and water to clean and deodorize your board.

Use a clean steel or glass bowl. Crack eggs into the bowl and beat lightly with a balloon whisk or fork, taking care not to overbeat. Stir in seasoning, if using, water and any flavoring, such as herbs. We used a combination of fresh flat-leaf parsley, chervil, chives and tarragon for this omelette.

In a small omelette pan, over medium-high heat, add enough butter and oil to cover the base of the pan. As all stove tops vary, adjust temperature if necessary. Cook butter mixture until it starts to foam.

When the butter mixture foams, add a quarter of the egg mixture, gently tilting the pan to cover the base. This ensures even cooking of eggs. Continue cooking over medium heat.

herb omelette

PREP + COOK TIME 20 MINS • SERVES 4

12 eggs
2 tablespoons finely chopped fresh flat-leaf parsley
2 tablespoons finely chopped fresh chervil
2 tablespoons finely chopped fresh chives
1 tablespoon finely chopped fresh tarragon
⅓ cup water
2 tablespoons butter
1 tablespoon olive oil

TIPS

• Use room temperature eggs for an omelette.

• Overbeating eggs will make the omelette tough.

• Using a mixture of butter and oil to cook the omelette stops the butter from burning.

• Using an omelette pan makes it easier to fold and remove the omelette from the pan.

• Do not wash omelette pan with soapy water, just wipe out with a damp cloth. Washing it will make it lose its non-stick surface.

Using a palette, small spatula or fork, draw sides of eggs towards the center of the pan, allowing the uncooked mixture to run underneath. Continue pulling the eggs from the sides until eggs are set underneath but still slightly runny on top. This also gives the omelette a plump, "crinkled" effect.

Once set, carefully flip the side of the omelette towards the center, using a spatula, to form a neat crescent shape. Remove pan from heat.

Gently slide the cooked omelette onto a warmed serving plate. Repeat steps 1 to 6 (wiping out the pan after each omelette), until you have made four omelettes. Serve omelettes while still hot.

Use free range eggs where possible for an omelette that is richer not only in color and flavor, but also in nutrients.

1 Lightly whisk eggs, herbs and water in large bowl until just combined.

2 Heat a quarter of the butter and 1 teaspoon of the oil in small omelette pan. When butter is just bubbling, add a quarter of the egg mixture; tilt pan to cover base with egg mixture. Cook over medium heat until omelette is just set. Use a spatula to lift and fold omelette in half; cook further 30 seconds. Carefully slide omelette onto serving plate.

3 Repeat with remaining butter, oil and egg mixture (wiping out the pan after each omelette), to make a total of four omelettes. Serve immediately.

nutritional count per serving 24.4g total fat (8.2g saturated fat); 300 cal; 0.6g carbohydrate; 20.1g protein; 0.2g fiber

roast chicken with herb stuffing

Its high-protein, healthy image and sheer affordability has driven chicken to the top of the meat menu in most households, while roasting it whole gets the most votes for the tastiest method.

Herb stuffing We used a fresh herb stuffing, which can be made up to one day ahead. Store in an airtight container in the refrigerator until needed. Stuff the chicken just before you are ready to cook it, otherwise there is a risk of bacteria forming.

Serving platter Always preheat the serving dish before placing the chicken on it so it stays warm. When you have removed the stuffing from the chicken's cavity, transfer the stuffing to a separate serving dish–and let everyone help themselves.

Potatoes Perfect baked potatoes are an essential side to roast chicken. In an ovenproof dish, toss unskinned new or young potatoes in 1-2 tablespoons of extra virgin olive oil and season lightly. Roast on the bottom oven rack until golden and crispy on the outside and tender inside.

Crispy skin The key to achieving a crispy, golden-brown skin on the chicken is keeping the skin and flesh intact during roasting. Exposed flesh creates steam in the oven, so avoid cutting up the chicken until roasted.

Vegetables Steam your favorite seasonal vegetables and serve with the chicken. Or, instead of cooking the chicken on a rack, tuck root vegetables around the chicken in a baking dish. This method allows the vegetables to pick up the wonderful roasting juices from the chicken.

Carving tools A well-sharpened carving knife and serving fork will take the effort out of carving chicken. Removing the legs and wings first also makes carving easier. These darker meat areas are more likely to stay moist if cut first, unlike the drier white meat parts of the chicken.

Insert the herb stuffing into the body cavity, being careful not to tear the skin. Avoid overfilling the cavity because the stuffing will expand during cooking due to the absorption of the juices from the chicken. Never stuff the cavity in advance because this will increase the risk of bacteria growth.

Pull the skin flaps back into place to enclose the cavity. Seal in the stuffing by stitching 2 to 3 wooden toothpicks through the edges of the opening, like a needle in a tapestry. This will help hold the stuffing in while the chicken is cooking.

Truss the chicken with kitchen string. Hold one end of the string in each hand, loop the center of the string around the legs and secure a knot.

roast chicken with herb stuffing

PREP + COOK TIME 2 HOURS 15 MINS • SERVES 4

3-pound whole chicken
1 tablespoon butter, melted

herb stuffing
1½ cups stale bread crumbs
1 stalk celery, trimmed, chopped finely
1 small white onion, chopped finely
2 teaspoons finely chopped fresh sage leaves
1 tablespoon finely chopped fresh flat-leaf parsley
1 egg, beaten lightly
2 tablespoons butter, melted

TIPS

• Drying the chicken thoroughly results in a crisper skin.

• Tying the chicken's legs together helps it to keep its shape during roasting.

• Placing the chicken on a rack prevents it from sticking to the pan and causing the skin to tear.

• The water in the baking dish creates steam, keeping the chicken moist.

• Basting the chicken during baking helps the skin to brown and keeps the chicken moist.

Place chicken, breast-side up, on a greased oven rack in a large baking dish. Always use a heavy-based baking dish so it doesn't wobble during cooking. Half-fill the dish with water to prevent any fat from burning and creating odors.

Spoon the pan juices all over the chicken as it cooks in the oven. Occasional basting adds great flavor and can help the chicken brown evenly.

Check whether chicken is done by piercing the thigh with a wooden skewer and inspecting the juices for any signs of pinkness (blood). If there is no sign of pink juices, the chicken is done. You can also check by tugging the drumstick–if the thigh joint feels loose, the chicken is fully cooked through.

A note on hygiene:
Raw chicken contains harmful bacteria that can cause salmonella. In light of this, it is important to be extra careful when handling raw chicken. To avoid cross-contamination, be sure to wash all utensils that have been in contact with the raw meat, especially chopping boards.

A thermometer is an easy way to check whether the chicken (and stuffing) has been cooked through. A temperature of 165°F will ensure the chicken flesh will be white and its juices run clear.

1 Preheat oven to 400°F/350°F fan-forced.

2 Make herb stuffing.

3 Remove and discard any fat from cavity of chicken. Rinse chicken inside and out with water. Pat dry cavity and skin with absorbent paper. Fill cavity of chicken with stuffing, fold over skin to enclose stuffing; secure with toothpicks. Tie legs together with kitchen string.

4 Place chicken on greased rack in large baking dish. Half-fill dish with water– it should not touch the chicken. Brush chicken with butter; roast 15 minutes.

5 Reduce oven to 350°F/320°F fan-forced. Bake for another 1½ hours or until chicken is cooked through, basting occasionally with pan juices. Stand 10 minutes before breaking or cutting into serving-sized pieces.

herb stuffing Combine ingredients in medium bowl.

nutritional count per serving 35.9g total fat (14.4g saturated fat); 583 cal; 19.4g carbohydrate; 45g protein; 1.9g fiber

pork and vegetable stir-fry

The stir-fry has become one of our favorite mid-week meals. It gives meat and poultry more flavor, adds a spark to vegetables and lures time-poor cooks into the kitchen again.

Rice The Chinese always cook more rice than is needed for the meal. Leftovers are often used for making a perfect fried rice the following day as cooked rice that has been chilled for a day works better for this classic dish than freshly cooked rice. Store in a covered container and chill.

Table etiquette If you struggle getting enough grains into your mouth with chopsticks, you'll be glad to know how the Chinese do it. The socially-acceptable method is to bring the bowl close to your mouth and quickly scoop the rice into your mouth with chopsticks.

Balanced ingredients Chinese dishes offer contrast in taste, texture and color. But it's not only to satisfy our senses. It is believed that harmonizing our taste sensations (sour, sweet, salty, bitter and piquant) is a way to keep the body balanced and maintain good health.

Vegetables The trick to shiny, crunchy vegetables is to have all the ingredients ready before you start cooking. Stir-fries happen so fast and once you have started you won't have time to peel the onions or delve in the cupboard for the soy sauce. Keep everything close at hand.

Tea Traditionally, the Chinese do not drink tea with their meal. It is served as a post-meal digestif. Three main types of tea are used. These come from the same plant but are processed to produce black tea (fermented), oolong tea (semi-fermented) or green tea (unfermented).

Essential condiments For those who like to add extra heat, salty zing or a little sweetness to their dish, place condiment servers of hot chili oil, soy, hoisin and sweet chili sauces on the table. All these condiments, except the chili oil, must be refrigerated once opened.

Chopsticks Not all chopsticks are alike–those from China are different from the ones used in Japan, Korea and other Asian countries. In Chinese chopsticks, the end held in the hand is squared off, while the other end is round and blunt. They are also longer–about 10 inches in length.

Pork Some cuts of pork, such as tenderloin filet, are as low or lower in fat than chicken, and more than half of the fat is unsaturated. Tenderloin is an elongated, tender muscle from the loin. It is the most tender part of the pig. Tenderloin filet is the ideal cut for stir-fries.

On a clean chopping surface, cut the pork filet into thin slices with a sharp chef's knife. Always cut pork across the grain for stir-fries as this will keep the meat tender during cooking.

Remove the stem and base of the peppers with a sharp knife. Stand upright on a chopping surface and cut down the length of the pepper to open. Cut into wedges. Place cut-side up and cut along the inside to remove the seeds and membrane.

Cut the onion in half from top to root and rest one of the halves, flat-side down, on the chopping board. Holding a sharp knife parallel to the cutting surface, thinly slice the onion from head to the root. Repeat for the remaining onion half.

pork and vegetable stir-fry

PREP + COOK TIME 30 MINS • SERVES 4

2 tablespoons peanut oil

1¼ pounds pork filets, sliced

1 large brown onion, sliced thinly

1 clove garlic, crushed

10 ounces asparagus, trimmed, cut into 2-inch lengths

2 medium red peppers, sliced thinly

½ cup plum sauce

2 tablespoons light soy sauce

TIPS

• Make sure all your ingredients are prepared and easy to access before starting to stir-fry.

• Heat the wok to very hot before adding the oil, then tilt the wok to coat it all over in oil.

• Cook food in batches so the heat of the wok does not reduce.

• Toss food constantly so it doesn't stick to the base of the wok.

• A wok chan is used to keep food moving and turning constantly. The angle and curved edge of a chan's wide, shovel-like blade are designed to fit the curve of the wok.

Swirl the oil in a very hot wok. Add the pork, in batches, to avoid overcrowding as this reduces the wok's heating capacity, stewing the meat instead of stir-frying it. Adjust the temperature up or down as needed. To allow pork to brown, wait a few seconds before tossing with a wok chan. When the pork is browned, remove from the wok and set aside.

Add vegetables according to density–the onion and garlic should be stirred in first, followed by the peppers and asparagus. Move vegetables around immediately and continuously with the chan.

Return the pork to the wok once the vegetables are almost cooked. This prevents the meat from overcooking and allows the vegetables and meat to retain their individual flavors. Form a "well" in the center by pushing ingredients up the sides of the wok, add sauces in the center and stir to thicken. When stir-fry is cooked, taste and adjust seasonings.

Make sure you cut all your veggies into similar size pieces–strips or bite-sized pieces work well. This ensures that they all cook at the same rate. If you cut your vegetables on the diagonal, it not only improves the attractiveness of the dish, it maximizes their exposure to the heat.

You could use chicken, beef or seafood in this recipe instead of pork.

1 Heat 1 tablespoon of the oil in wok; stir-fry pork, in batches, until browned. Remove pork from wok.

2 Heat remaining oil in wok; stir-fry onion and garlic 1 minute. Add asparagus and peppers; stir-fry until softened.

3 Return pork to wok with combined sauces; stir-fry until pork is cooked as desired.

nutritional count per serving 13.2g total fat (2.9g saturated fat); 394 cal; 30g carbohydrate; 37g protein; 2.9g fiber

serving idea boiled or steamed rice.

glazed meatloaf

A comfort food that nurtured so many of us through the fifties and sixties, meatloaf has made a return. It's a traditional dish but invites innovation, so you can try your own creative turn on the classic. As for the potential with leftovers, you'll be covered for a whole week.

Vegetable mixture By adding grated or pureed vegetables to your mixture, you are adding more moisture to the meatloaf. Not only does this make your final product juicier, it also adds lots of extra flavor and nutrients. Try grated carrot, zucchini or spinach and herbs.

Meat selections Ground beef is the standard for meatloaf as it has the right percentage of meat to fat ratio (80:20) for juicy, but not greasy, results. You can experiment with various combinations such as pork, veal and chicken, as well as Italian sausage.

Bread filler For a very tender, lighter-textured meatloaf, you can replace stale bread crumbs with cubes of fresh white bread. Beat 1 egg and ⅔ cup milk together in a small bowl, pour over bread cubes and soak for 15 minutes, before mashing into small chunks with a fork.

The essential egg Should you add beaten eggs or not? Eggs help bind the loaf and also add richness. Another option is to hard-boil the egg, slice or chop it and combine it with the other ingredients, as well as parmesan cheese, for an extra tasty, high-protein meatloaf.

Matching drinks Think about the flavors in the meatloaf and glaze before pairing with drinks. Our meatloaf is lightly seasoned, so it goes well with almost any full-bodied red wine such as cabernet sauvignon. Tomato juice and mineral water make good non-alcoholic choices.

Accompaniments Meatloaf goes with most vegetables, from a winter potato mash and steamed spinach or broccoli to blanched green beans and asparagus in summer. Salads can offset the flavors of the loaf too–try arugula with tomato, tabbouleh or a robust pasta salad.

Leftovers Meatloaf is so easy to make, it's worth doubling up on the recipe and making two. A little meatloaf goes a long way. Leftovers can be sliced for wraps or sandwiches, or crumbled in a red pasta sauce, Mexican chili bean dish or even a casserole for a quick weeknight meal.

The glaze Coating the meatloaf with a glaze does more than just enhance its presentation. It adds wonderful flavor, which you can vary by using different ingredients. Both savory and sweet glazes work well. Glazing also helps keep the meatloaf moist during cooking.

Lightly brush a loaf pan with oil, once you have preheated the oven to 350°F/320°F fan-forced. This is the ideal temperature for a moist meatloaf. Too hot an oven might reduce the cooking time, but it will also dry out the meat. Keep the temperature at moderate.

Combine the mixture until just mixed. Wet your hands with cold water beforehand to prevent mixture from sticking. A common mistake is to overmix the ingredients. Overmixing produces a compressed mixture, which will squeeze out liquid during baking, resulting in a drier meatloaf. Remember the loaf will be handled again, when it is pressed into the pan.

Press the mixture into the pan, after you have wet your hands again with cold water. Smooth the top of the loaf to remove any cracks, which can cause a loss of moisture during cooking.

glazed meatloaf

PREP + COOK TIME 1 HOUR • SERVES 4

1½ pounds ground beef

1 cup stale bread crumbs

1 medium brown onion, chopped finely

1 egg

2 tablespoons tomato sauce

1 tablespoon Worcestershire sauce

6-ounce can evaporated milk

2 teaspoons mustard powder

1 tablespoon brown sugar

½ teaspoon mustard powder, extra

¼ cup tomato sauce, extra

Invert the loaf pan onto a foil-lined oven tray, leaving the pan in place. Bake for 15 minutes. Meanwhile, prepare the meatloaf glaze, combining the sugar, extra mustard and extra tomato sauce in a small bowl. Set the glaze aside until needed.

Remove the loaf from the oven after 15 minutes and carefully remove the pan. Take care not to break the meatloaf when you are lifting off the pan.

Brush the meatloaf generously with the glaze. Make sure you spread the glaze evenly over the top, then brush the sides lightly with the glaze. Return the meatloaf to the oven for another 45 minutes or until well browned and cooked through. Remove the meatloaf from the oven and allow it to rest for 10 to 15 minutes before slicing and serving.

Let the meatloaf stand for 10 to 15 minutes before serving. This allows it to set and makes it much easier to slice.

Leftover meatloaf is delicious sliced cold as a sandwich filling and is a perfect addition to a picnic basket. It can also be crumbled into pasta sauces or stir-fries.

1 Preheat oven to 350°F/320°F fan-forced. Oil 5½-inch x 8¼-inch loaf pan.
2 Combine beef, bread crumbs, onion, egg, sauces, milk and mustard in medium bowl. Press mixture into pan. Turn pan upside-down onto a foil-lined oven tray; leave pan in place. Bake 15 minutes.
3 Meanwhile, combine sugar, extra mustard and extra tomato sauce in small bowl.
4 Remove loaf from oven; remove pan. Brush loaf well with glaze, return loaf to oven; bake 45 minutes or until well browned and cooked through.
5 Serve meatloaf, if desired, with arugula leaves and tomato wedges.
nutritional count per serving 19.9g total fat (10g saturated fat); 475 cal; 29.1g carbohydrate; 45.8g protein; 1.8g fiber
serving ideas arugula and tomato salad or steamed vegetables.

steak with pepper sauce

Food fads come and go but beef-eaters have never lost their taste for steak with pepper sauce. A good steak is juicy and flavorful–and expensive, so you want to get it right every time. And a creamy pepper sauce is just the right accompaniment, along with some perfectly cooked fries.

The marbling advantage The key to tenderness, flavor and juiciness in a cut is marbling (when fat is distributed evenly throughout the muscle instead of being concentrated in one area). The small flecks of fat deposits dissolve and distribute throughout the meat.

Prime steak cuts For a great steakhouse-style steak at home, consider rib-eye, tenderloin, New York strip (boneless sirloin), t-bone and rump. All can be pan-fried, broiled or barbecued. But rib-eye is prized for its marbling effect.

Judging a rare steak If you like your steak rare, simply make a circle with your index finger and thumb, and apply pressure to the ball on the palm side of your thumb. It will feel very soft when pressed with the back of tongs. Press the center of the steak. If it has the same texture, it is rare.

Resting the meat Never serve steak right after it is cooked. Meat is all tensed up from the heat of the cooking, so it needs to "rest" for about 10 minutes to let the juices move back into the meat. It is best if you cover it loosely and keep it at room temperature–not in the oven.

Steakhouse fries Use floury, low-moisture potatoes like idaho (russets). Cut lengthways into ½-inch slices; cut each slice lengthways into ½-inch-wide sticks. Stand in bowl of cold water for 30 minutes. Drain; pat dry with absorbent paper. Heat peanut oil in deep frying pan; cook fries, in three batches, 4 minutes each or until just soft but not browned. Drain on absorbent paper; stand 10 minutes. Heat oil; cook fries, in three batches, until crisp and golden brown. Drain on absorbent paper. Season lightly.

Best steak pans Only by having contact with really intense heat can you cook a steak hot enough and fast enough to replicate a steakhouse-style steak. To achieve this, you need a basic heavy-based frying pan or cast-iron pan, as these can hold the heat.

Pan deglazing sauce Cooking meat or vegetables in oil, then adding wine, stock, even water to the same pan is the first step to making a deglazing sauce. The idea is to loosen up the bits that have stuck to the pan and incorporate them into the liquid because they are full of flavor.

Grinding pepper Pulverizing ingredients with a mortar and pestle releases flavor essence and oils. Place peppercorns inside the mortar (bowl). Sit the pestle on top of the peppercorns; apply downward pressure and grind using a circular motion. This force pulverizes it.

Add half the oil to the pan over high heat. Before adding the steak, make sure the oil is hot and smoking. Mono-unsaturated oils, such as olive oil, are best for cooking steaks. Unlike butter, it won't burn and it is also low in saturated fats.

Make sure the meat is dry before adding it to the pan. Place the steaks in the pan and cook for 2 minutes or until browned. Turn over and cook until done to your liking. As the pan sears the meat's surface, it begins melting the fat, causing splattering, smoke and sometimes flames, so be careful. This process caramelizes the meat, making it sweet and flavorful. Remove meat, cover and allow it to rest.

Heat the remaining oil in the same pan. Add the onion and celery, and stir well to combine. Cook, stirring all the time, until the vegetables are tender.

steak with pepper sauce

PREP + COOK TIME 25 MINS • SERVES 4

1 tablespoon olive oil

4 x 7-ounce boneless rib-eye steaks

1 stalk celery, trimmed, chopped finely

1 medium brown onion, chopped finely

½ cup dry white wine

1¼ cups cream

1 tablespoon mixed peppercorns, crushed

1 tablespoon coarsely chopped fresh thyme

TIPS

• Make sure the pan is hot before adding the steaks, this helps seal in the juices.

• Cook presentation side of steak first, to get the correct color and then turn to cook the other side to desired doneness.

• Only turn steaks once during pan-frying. Continual turning will result in dry, tough steaks.

• Cook the vegetables in the same pan and then add the wine, which "deglazes" the pan. This picks up all the color and flavor from cooking the steak, resulting in a rich sauce.

Pour the liquid in all at once. We used dry white wine, but stock or water can be used. Scrape the brown bits on the bottom of the pan loose with a wooden spoon. Keep deglazing in this way, scraping and reducing. Cook until the liquid in the pan is reduced by half.

Add the cream and mixed peppercorns and bring the mixture to the boil. Reduce heat and simmer, uncovered, stirring occasionally, for about 5 minutes.

Once sauce has thickened slightly, remove the pan from the heat and stir in fresh thyme. Serve immediately with prepared steak.

1 Heat half the oil in large frying pan; cook steaks, in batches, until cooked as desired. Remove from pan; cover to keep warm.

2 Heat remaining oil in same pan; cook celery and onion, stirring, until vegetables soften. Add wine; stir until liquid is reduced by half. Add cream and peppercorns; bring to a boil. Reduce heat; simmer, uncovered, stirring occasionally, about 5 minutes or until sauce thickens slightly. Remove from heat; stir in thyme.

3 Serve steaks drizzled with sauce.

nutritional count per serving 46.7g total fat (26.3g saturated fat); 636 cal; 5g carbohydrate; 44.2g protein; 1.4g fiber

serving idea steakhouse fries (see page 28).

chicken, mushroom and leek fricassee

A famous French dish, using vegetables, white meat and a creamy sauce, you will find yourself making fricassee for guests over and over again. It even makes a great base for other meals. Its virtue is not only wonderful flavor but simplicity. Once the fricassee is in the oven, you can walk away for a while and join the party.

Adding lean flavor Sometimes chicken fricassee refers to the way the chicken is cut. The French classic recipe calls for a whole chicken, which is cut into eight pieces. We've used leaner thigh filets and given the dish an instant flavor boost with the addition of bacon.

Easy entertainer Aside from the chicken, the only items to have on hand for fricassee are some aromatic vegetables and liquids in which to braise the chicken. This can simply be the wine you didn't finish the other night, the leftover stock and that carton of cream lurking in the refrigerator.

A sauté or stew? Fricassee actually uses both these cooking methods. The chicken is cooked in oil (sautéed), then wine, stock and cream are added, and the chicken is stewed. Our recipe departs from the French classic at times but the results are still the same—a perfect fricassee.

Base to many meals A quick alternative to a slow-cooked ragout, fricassee can be served with pasta, such as tagliatelle or pappardelle. In Louisiana's Cajun country, the dish is often served with rice and kidney beans, while the Tunisians use it as a filling for a fried sandwich.

Food safety Make sure you wash all surfaces that have been used to prepare the chicken. Also wash your hands with hot, soapy water before you handle other food or utensils. When braising the chicken, don't remove it from the pan until it is cooked all the way through.

Mushrooms We used button mushrooms for this recipe but you can use cremini for a richer taste. For extra flavor, try using soaked, dried wild mushrooms such as porcini, chanterelle or a mix, and incorporate the soaking water into the stock mixture.

Choosing the one pot As this fricassee is finished off in the oven, you will need a flameproof baking dish. Both enamel and metal dishes work well. Heavy cast-iron dutch ovens are also a good choice because they conduct heat well on all stove tops, as well as in the oven.

Cut the chicken thigh filets into quarters on a clean, dry surface. Make sure you have dried the chicken thoroughly beforehand by patting each filet with absorbent paper.

Heat oil in a heavy-based flameproof dish. Cook the chicken in batches, turning every minute, for 3 to 4 minutes, until the meat has stiffened slightly and is browned all over. Remove chicken from dish.

Cook the bacon in the same dish, stirring until browned slightly. Add the butter and leek, and cook, stirring occasionally, until leek softens.

chicken, mushroom and leek fricassee

PREP + COOK TIME 50 MINS • SERVES 6

2 tablespoons olive oil
3 pounds chicken thigh filets, quartered
3 strips bacon, chopped coarsely
3 tablespoons butter
3 medium leeks, trimmed, sliced thinly
3 stalks celery, trimmed, sliced thinly
3 cloves garlic, crushed
¼ cup loosely packed fresh thyme sprigs
2 bay leaves
2 tablespoons all-purpose flour
1½ cups dry white wine
1½ cups chicken stock
12 ounces button mushrooms
¼ cup cream
½ cup coarsely chopped fresh flat-leaf parsley

Stir in the celery, garlic, thyme and bay leaves. Sprinkle the flour into the vegetable and bacon mixture, and stir well to combine. By adding the flour you create a roux-like base for the dish.

Stir in the wine and stock to cover the ingredients. Bring to a boil, stirring constantly. Stir in chicken and mushrooms. Transfer dish to oven and cook for 20 minutes or until chicken is cooked through.

Return the dish to the stove top, discard bay leaves then gradually stir in the cream. Add fresh parsley and simmer, uncovered, until fricassee is heated through. Garnish with fresh thyme leaves just before serving.

This flavorsome fricassee makes a fantastic pie filling. Place the warm chicken mixture in a 9½-inch pie dish, top with a sheet of puff pastry and trim around the edge. Bake at 400°F/350°F fan-forced for 25 minutes or until the pastry is browned and crisp.

1 Preheat oven to 325°F/275°F fan-forced.

2 Heat oil in large heavy-based flameproof dish; cook chicken, in batches, until browned all over. Remove from pan.

3 Cook bacon in same dish, stirring, until browned lightly.

4 Add butter and leek to dish; cook, stirring occasionally, until leek softens. Stir in celery, garlic, thyme and bay leaves. Stir in flour, then wine and stock; bring to the boil, stirring. Stir in chicken and mushrooms.

5 Transfer dish to oven; cook about 20 minutes or until chicken is cooked through and sauce has thickened slightly. ·

6 Return dish to stove top, discard bay leaves; stir in cream and parsley. Simmer, uncovered, until fricassee is heated through. Garnish with fresh thyme leaves.

nutritional count per serving 39.2g total fat (14.6g saturated fat); 671 cal; 8.6g carbohydrate; 59.1g protein; 6.2g fiber

featherlight sponge cake

Few things can impress more than a whisked-up sponge cake that's light, airy—and 4 inches high. The secret is a little patience, a light hand and these expert tips.

Preventing a flop Fresh ingredients are a must for a well-risen sponge. When baking, position cakes so the tops of the pans are in the oven center; remove any upper shelves. If using two shelves, swap positions halfway through baking. Opening the oven gently won't affect the cakes at this point.

Getting it light To achieve a fine texture, we used superfine sugar instead of granulated white sugar. Triple-sifting dry ingredients combines them and aerates them.

When is it cooked? When the sponge appears to begin to shrink from the side of the pan, you'll know the cake is ready. It should also feel slightly springy to the touch. Shake the pan gently to make sure the cake is free–turn it out immediately onto a wire rack covered with parchment paper, then turn it up the right way to prevent the wire from forming marks on the cake.

Better baking Shiny aluminium pans are ideal for cake-baking because they reflect heat away from the cake and produce a tender, light brown crust. If you use a pan with a dark, non-stick surface, you need to reduce the oven temperature by 25°F as these pans absorb more heat.

The adaptable sponge You can make the sponge and simply fill it with jam and cream, as we have, or cream and either lemon curd, fresh or stewed fruit.

Deep-sided cake pans give the best results as the high sides protect the delicate sponge mixture and prevent a crisp crust developing. Grease the cake pans using a pastry brush dipped in melted butter. Sprinkle the pans with flour, tap and turn the pans to coat the surface evenly. Tap the pans upside down over the sink to discard excess flour.

Triple-sift the dry ingredients. Sifting three times mixes the ingredients thoroughly and aerates them, which produces a lighter, finer textured cake. Hold the sifter up high to incorporate as much air as possible into the flour.

In the bowl of an electric mixer, beat the eggs and sugar together until the sugar is dissolved and the mixture is thick and creamy. If the mixer has two beaters, use a small narrow-topped bowl to get the maximum volume.

featherlight sponge cake

PREP + COOK TIME 40 MINS • SERVES 10

4 eggs

¾ cup superfine sugar

⅔ cup cake flour

¼ cup custard powder or powdered instant vanilla pudding mix

1 teaspoon cream of tartar

½ teaspoon baking soda

⅓ cup apricot jam

1¼ cups heavy cream, whipped

TIPS

• Cake pans are best greased evenly with melted butter.

• Beating the eggs and sugar can take up to 10 minutes to get the correct volume. Using a narrow-topped bowl will allow the beaters to give volume to the egg and sugar mixture.

• Fold the flour into the cake mixture in a gentle, light circular motion for a lighter texture.

• Store unfilled sponges, wrapped well, in the freezer for up to 2 months.

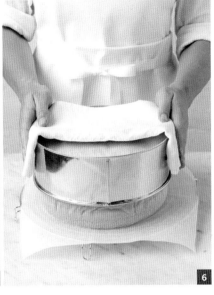

Quickly transfer the mixture to a larger, wide-topped bowl–if using a small bowl–to make it easier to fold the ingredients gently together. Use a metal spoon, a knife, or a plastic or rubber spatula. Fold in triple-sifted dry ingredients.

Divide mixture between the pans, gently spreading it to the edge. The mixture will not spread once it is in the oven. The last scrapings from the bowl should be placed around the edge of the pan. If placed in the center, a dark patch will form. To break large air bubbles, run a knife through mixture a few times.

When cooked, remove cakes from oven. Turn cakes immediately onto wire racks lined with parchment paper, and then turn up the right way. This will prevent the wire racks from marking the cakes.

Sponge cakes rely heavily on eggs for their fluffiness and structure. The quality and age of the eggs used can affect the success of your sponge. Ideally, eggs are at their best for sponge-making at 2 days old.

The sugar will dissolve slightly faster if room-temperature eggs are used.

Use good quality raspberry or plum jam for a more tart filling.

1 Preheat oven to 350°F/325°F fan-forced. Grease and flour two deep 8-inch round cake pans.

2 Beat eggs and sugar in small bowl with electric mixer until thick, creamy and sugar is dissolved. Transfer mixture to large bowl; fold in triple-sifted dry ingredients. Divide mixture between pans.

3 Bake sponges about 20 minutes. Turn, top-side up, onto parchment-covered wire rack to cool.

4 Sandwich sponges with jam and cream.

nutritional count per serving 13.3g total fat (8g saturated fat); 286 cal; 37.2g carbohydrate; 3.8g protein; 0.7g fiber

VARIATIONS

ginger fluff sponge Omit custard powder, increase cake flour to ¾ cup and add 1 teaspoon cocoa powder, 2 teaspoons ground ginger and ½ teaspoon ground cinnamon. Fill sponge with whipped cream.

slab sponge Sponge can be baked in 10-inch square cake pan for 20-25 minutes.

basic butter cake

A good butter cake should be flavorful, yet not overly sweet, tender and somewhat dense in texture, but certainly not dry. It should be able to stand on its own, or be filled and iced, or decorated lavishly. It should become one of your "every occasion" cakes. A butter cake can be the beginning of many great desserts.

Sifting Flours are pre-sifted these days, but it's still best to sift dry ingredients especially when there is more than one–the sifting mixes the ingredients together, as well as aerates them. Use either a sifter or a fine wire or plastic strainer.

Icing the cake If you want to ice the cake, place it on a wire rack over a sheet of parchment paper. Elevating the cake stops the icing from pooling around the bottom of the cake, while the paper catches any drips.

Essence or extract? Vanilla extract has a far superior flavor to vanilla essence. When buying, make sure it is labelled "pure". Imitation vanilla is made with synthetic vanilla and can leave a bitter aftertaste. The extract may be more expensive but you only need to use half as much.

Greasing the pan Cake pans need greasing–even non-stick surfaces–to prevent the cake from sticking. You can use either cooking oil spray or melted butter. It is best to use a pastry brush to coat the base and side(s) of the pans evenly.

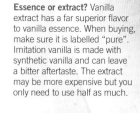

Butter Using butter at room temperature makes it easier to work with and aids aeration. If you have forgotten to take the butter out of the fridge, coarsely grate it or soften it in the microwave for 10 seconds.

Cupcakes The recipe for butter cake makes the perfect mixture for cupcakes. Pour mixture into two 12-hole muffin tins lined with paper cases until two-thirds full. Bake for 20 minutes. Turn cakes, top-side up, onto wire racks to cool completely. Top cakes with icing of your choice.

Have your cake A butter cake is so versatile. Serve it plain or slightly warmed (20 seconds in a microwave oven) with fresh fruit, lightly toasted with ice cream on the side, iced, or spread with jam or cream.

Grease and line the base and side(s) of a pan with parchment paper, extending the paper a little above the edge of the pan. Always use the pan size specified in the recipe. A deep 8-inch square or 9-inch round cake pan is best for this recipe. If you use a pan that is too large, the cake will not rise properly or brown evenly. If the pan is too small, the mixture is likely to dome and crack, or worse, run over the top of the pan.

Beat the softened butter, vanilla extract and sugar at medium speed in an electric mixer or until fluffy and light in color. Scrape down the sides of the bowl with a rubber spatula several times during the mixing.

Add the eggs, one at a time, with the mixer on low speed and beat for several seconds between each addition. Overbeating will soften the butter too much and will cause curdling.

basic butter cake

PREP + COOK TIME 1 HOUR 30 MINS • SERVES 12

2 sticks butter, softened

1 teaspoon vanilla extract

1¼ cups superfine sugar

3 eggs, at room temperature

2¼ cups self-rising flour

¾ cup milk, at room temperature

TIPS

• When beating in eggs, ensure each egg is combined well in butter mixture before adding the next egg. Do this quickly to avoid curdling.

• Add any flavoring such as extracts, essences, citrus rinds etc. with the butter. The resulting flavor of the baked cake will be better than if flavorings were added with the flour and milk.

• Store butter cake at room temperature, in an airtight container for 2 days, or it can be frozen for 2 months.

 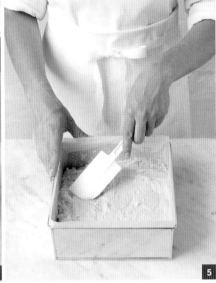 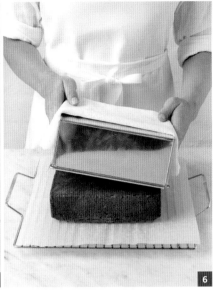

Stir in half the sifted flour and half the milk, gently stir the ingredients together using a wooden spoon; the mixture will look a little lumpy. Add the remaining flour and milk, gently stir until the ingredients combine. Still using the wooden spoon, beat the mixture quickly and firmly for a few seconds to smooth the mixture.

Spread the mixture evenly into the pan and bake in the preheated oven. You may need to rotate the pan to ensure even baking. Check the cake about 5 minutes before the end of baking time. If it feels firm and is browned evenly, test the cake by inserting a fine metal skewer in the center. If the skewer is clean– free from cake mixture–the cake is cooked.

Remove cake from oven; stand in pan for 5 minutes. Invert the pan onto a wire rack lined with parchment paper. Allow cake to cool completely before dusting with powdered sugar, or topping with icing, and slicing.

1 Preheat oven to 350°F/325°F fan-forced. Grease deep 8-inch square or 9-inch round cake pan; line base and side(s) with parchment paper.

2 Beat butter, extract and sugar in medium bowl with electric mixer until light and fluffy. Beat in eggs, one at a time. Stir in sifted flour and milk, in two batches.

3 Spread mixture into pan; bake about 1 hour. Stand cake 5 minutes; turn, top-side up, onto wire rack to cool.

nutritional count per serving 18.6g total fat (11.6g saturated fat); 364 cal; 43.5g carbohydrate; 5.1g protein; 1.1g fiber

VARIATIONS

orange cake Replace vanilla extract with 1 teaspoon finely grated orange rind and replace ¼ cup of the milk with freshly squeezed orange juice.

chocolate cake Replace ¼ cup of the flour with ¼ cup cocoa powder.

basic butter cookies

Baking from scratch is pure therapy and can give the home cook as much pleasure as it gives those eating the end result. Cookies are especially rewarding. Unlike cake, which can disappear in less time than it takes to make, cookies go a long way. Using very few ingredients, the recipe for these basic cookies is virtually foolproof. But there are some secrets you need to know before you start.

Leave room to spread Place cookies about 1 inch apart on the oven tray. If they are too close together, the cookies won't cook through properly, or they will join together.

[clockwise from top left]
chocolate and hazelnut cookies;
basic butter cookies;
dried cranberry cookies.

Keep cookies fresh If making more than one type of cookie, store each variety in a separate container or they will soften quickly. To re-crisp softened cookies, bake on a non-stick or lined oven tray in a moderate (350°F/325°F fan-forced) oven for about 5 minutes. Transfer to a wire rack to cool.

  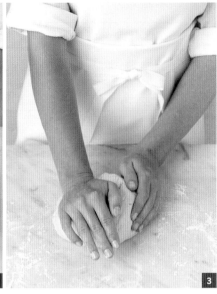

Beat the butter and sifted sugar in a bowl, using an electric mixer, until the mixture changes to a lighter color. Be careful not to overbeat the butter and sugar mixture. Overbeating can produce a very soft mixture, causing the cookies to spread too much in the oven.

Transfer mixture to a large bowl if using a small bowl from an electric mixer with two beaters. Stir in sifted flour, in two batches, to take the effort out of mixing.

Knead dough gently on a lightly floured surface until smooth. Try not to over-handle the dough or the gluten in the flour will develop, producing a tough-textured cookie. The dough must stay cold, too. Run warm hands under cold water, then dry before kneading quickly and lightly.

basic butter cookies

PREP + COOK TIME 30 MINS (+ REFRIGERATION) • MAKES 50

2 sticks butter, softened
1 cup powdered sugar
2½ cups all-purpose flour

TIPS

• Cookies should feel soft in the oven even though they're cooked. Check the cookies a few minutes before the end of baking time—if they feel a little soft, but firm, give one cookie a gentle push with the side of your thumb. It's done if the cookie will slide easily on the tray. The cookies will become crisp on cooling.

• Store cookies in an airtight container for up to 1 week.

• Keep this dough, rolled into a log shape and tightly sealed in plastic wrap, in your fridge for up to 3 days or in your freezer for up to 3 months. Thaw in refrigerator before cutting into slices.

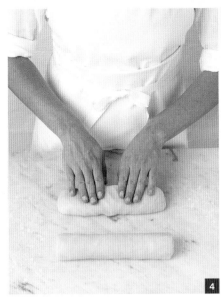

Divide the dough in half and roll each half into a 10-inch log. If you are working in a warm kitchen, refrigerate one dough half to keep it firm. When you are ready to roll it, remove it from the refrigerator.

Cut logs into ½-inch slices, using a sharp knife. Don't press down hard on the log or you will squash it and the cookies will lose their round shape.

Place cookies on parchment-lined oven trays. A flat aluminium tray with little or no sides is best as it allows heat to circulate for even browning. Make sure there is enough space between cookies so they can spread. Bake about 10 minutes or until browned lightly. Rest on trays for a few minutes before cooling on a wire rack.

1 Beat butter and sifted sugar in small bowl with electric mixer until light and fluffy. Transfer mixture to large bowl; stir in flour, in two batches.

2 Knead dough on lightly floured surface until smooth. Divide dough in half; roll each half into a 10-inch log. Wrap in plastic wrap; refrigerate about 1 hour or until firm.

3 Preheat oven to 350°F/325°F fan-forced. Line oven trays with parchment paper.

4 Cut logs into ½-inch slices; place slices on trays about 1 inch apart.

5 Bake cookies about 10 minutes or until browned lightly. Transfer cookies onto wire rack to cool.

nutritional count per cookie 4g total fat (2.6g saturated fat); 75 cal; 8.6g carbohydrate; 0.9g protein; 0.3g fiber

VARIATIONS

chocolate and hazelnut Beat 2 tablespoons sifted cocoa powder into butter and sugar mixture, then stir in ⅓ cup ground hazelnuts and ¼ cup finely chopped milk chocolate bits before adding the flour.

dried cranberry Stir in ⅔ cup finely chopped dried cranberries into butter and sugar mixture.

vanilla Beat 1 teaspoon vanilla extract into butter and sugar mixture.

lemon Beat 1 teaspoon finely grated lemon rind into butter and sugar mixture.

orange Beat 1 teaspoon finely grated orange rind into butter and sugar mixture.

SHOWING OFF

Showing off

We're going to let you in on a little secret: many of the classic dishes that you might order at a restaurant, but wouldn't dare to attempt yourself, are actually simpler than you might expect.

It's natural to feel intimidated by the thought of cooking a glazed baked ham or a beef wellington, and to assume that the time-honored classic recipes are the preserve of master chefs and those with years of cooking experience under their belt. But often, these dishes are classics because they are so simple and dependably delicious. They still require care and attention to get them right, but they are very achievable for beginner and veteran home cooks alike.

It's good to have a repertoire of reliable recipes you can call upon for a dinner party with family or friends. The recipes in this chapter are dinner party classics: they are exquisitely presented, taste extraordinary and, best of all, are hearteningly easy to make. Dazzle your family and friends the next time you invite them over for dinner.

DINNER PARTY RULES

There are a few important, stress-reducing steps you can take to ensure your dinner party is as enjoyable for you as it is for your guests.

MAKE AHEAD OF TIME This is the key to making your dinner party as smooth-running as possible. Cook and prepare what you can ahead of time, either a few hours prior to your guests arriving, or even the day before. You don't want to be madly stirring at the stove when people are walking through your door.

CHOOSE ONE "STAR" COURSE THAT YOU SPEND TIME ON This should preferably be a recipe you've tried before and feel confident cooking again: you don't want to add to your stress by taking on a new, complicated dish with unknown results.

PLAN THE OTHER COURSE, OR COURSES, AROUND YOUR "STAR" COURSE Keep them really simple and, preferably, made ahead. A lemon tart, for example, is easy to make but never fails to attract admiration from everybody. It can be prepared the day before and kept, perfectly poised, in the fridge until required.

REMEMBER TO THINK ABOUT THE DINNER AS A WHOLE If you're planning a rich crème brûlée for dessert, then a light, flavorsome main (such as Thai steamed fish in banana leaves) would be a wonderful prequel. Don't double up on two cream-based courses or two pastry-based courses.

DON'T FEEL PRESSURED TO MAKE EVERYTHING YOURSELF Your guests will already be impressed, so take the pressure off and include some quality store-bought items. For a fantastic antipasto platter, check your local deli for a wide selection of char-grilled vegetables. Pre-made pastry cases are ideal time-savers when teamed with a home-made filling–sweet or savory. And for a quick dessert with maximum impact, fill chocolate dessert cups (often found near meringue shells in supermarkets) with ready-made mousse and top with fresh berries. It'll be our little secret.

IMPRESSIVE CLASSICS

THERE ARE MANY FOODS THAT NON-COOKS (AND COOKS TOO) THINK ARE HARD BECAUSE THEY ARE EXOTIC, OR LEGENDARY, OR BOTH. THE THAI STEAMED FISH RECIPE IN THIS CHAPTER, FOR EXAMPLE, IS STRAIGHTFORWARD ENOUGH, BUT THE AROMATIC HERBS USED AND THE CREATIVE PRESENTATION OF THE DISH HELP TO LIFT THE MEAL INTO ANOTHER DIMENSION. LIKEWISE, THE TERRINE DE CAMPAGNE IS MORE THAN JUST A FANCY NAME FOR MEATLOAF: THIS FLAVOR-PACKED DISH WITH GROUND PORK AND CHICKEN LIVERS IS EASY TO MAKE AND SUPER IMPRESSIVE. IT NEVER FAILS TO DRAW GASPS FROM EVERYONE AT THE TABLE. HERE ARE SOME OTHER SURPRISINGLY SIMPLE RECIPES:

CHICKEN LIVER PATE This silky-smooth pâté is easy and relatively inexpensive to make. The finished pâté can be made ahead and refrigerated, covered with plastic wrap, for up to 1 week.

BEEF WELLINGTON This is another dish you might naturally think you would reserve for ordering at a restaurant but it is very easy to assemble and great for dinner parties. An impressive and hearty dish of succulent beef tenderloin wrapped in golden puff pastry, it looks wonderful sitting center stage on the dinner table and easily cuts into multiple servings. Beef wellington can be prepared and refrigerated ahead of your guests' arrival: it can cook while they have their pre-dinner drinks and snacks.

GLAZED BAKED HAM Synonymous with Christmas entertaining and important occasions, a glazed baked ham is a grand culinary statement but surprisingly quick and easy to prepare.

SOUFFLES These elegant, special-occasion foods are famous for being lighter than air and equally famous for being temperamental. In fact, despite the mystique that surrounds them, soufflés are easy. They key is in the beating and folding of the egg whites, which takes particular care but is not really hard, and the cooking time, which can be easily monitored. Even soufflé mixtures can be made ahead of time, except for the addition of the egg whites. For a soufflé dessert, you can prepare the soufflé mixture (except the egg whites, of course) ahead of time: turn on the oven as you sit down to the main course, then just before dessert, simply whip up the egg whites, fold them into the mixture and pop the soufflés into the oven.

CREME BRULEE This much-loved gourmet dessert is essentially a simple custard. The magic comes when you caramelize the sugar on the top of the cooled custard just before serving. It's the perfect dessert for entertaining because it can be made ahead of time and refrigerated overnight.

prawn and scallop tortellini

Preserved lemons are available from delis and some supermarkets. Bear in mind that only the rind is used in cooking, so discard the flesh from each piece first. Rinse the rind well before chopping finely.

TIPS

• Cover gow gee wrappers with a damp tea towel to stop them from drying out while making the tortellini.

• The tortellini can be made a day ahead; store tortellini in a single layer, covered in plastic wrap, in the refrigerator until ready to cook.

1 pound uncooked medium king prawns, shelled, deveined

8 ounces sea scallops

1 tablespoon olive oil

2 tablespoons finely chopped fresh Vietnamese mint

2 tablespoons finely chopped fresh chervil

2 tablespoons finely chopped preserved lemon rind

7 ounces soft goat's cheese

2 teaspoons sea salt

1 teaspoon cracked black pepper

8½-ounce packet round gow gee dumpling wrappers

lemon dressing

¼ cup lemon juice

½ cup olive oil

1 tablespoon finely chopped fresh chervil

1 tablespoon finely chopped fresh flat-leaf parsley

1 Place ingredients for lemon dressing in screw-top jar; shake well.

2 Coarsely chop prawns and scallops. Heat oil in large frying pan; cook seafood over medium heat until prawns change color. Cool.

3 Combine seafood, herbs, lemon rind, cheese, salt and pepper in medium bowl.

4 To make tortellini, place a gow gee wrapper on work surface; place 1 level tablespoon of the seafood mixture in center, brush edge with water. Fold in half; bring two points together, to make a crescent shape, press gently to seal. Repeat with remaining wrappers and filling.

5 Cook tortellini in large saucepan of boiling water until tortellini floats to the top; drain. Transfer tortellini to large heatproof bowl; drizzle with a little dressing.

6 Serve tortellini drizzled with remaining dressing; sprinkle with extra chervil sprigs.

nutritional count per serving 28.6g total fat (7.1g saturated fat); 323 cal; 1.8g carbohydrate; 15.3g protein; 0.2g fiber

Using your fingers, remove the head, shell, legs and tail. Remove the intestinal vein by slitting down the back with a sharp knife and pulling it out.

Arrange gow gee wrappers on a clean surface. Place a level tablespoon of seafood mixture in the center of each wrapper. Brush edges with a little water.

Fold the wrapper in half and pinch edge together to seal. Repeat process for remaining wrappers and filling.

Bring the ends of the straight edge together to join and form a crescent shape, pressing gently to seal. Cook tortellini in a large saucepan of water.

chicken liver pâté

Pâté can be bought easily nowadays from delis and supermarkets. By making your own, however, you can ensure that ingredients are of a high quality and that the pâté is of the utmost freshness when served.

2 pounds chicken livers
7 ounces ghee (clarified butter)
4 strips bacon, chopped finely
1 small brown onion, chopped finely
¼ cup brandy
½ cup cream
2 teaspoons finely chopped fresh thyme
pinch ground nutmeg

1 Cut any sinew from livers; pull each lobe away from connecting tissue.

2 Heat a quarter of the ghee in large frying pan; cook half the livers, stirring, until browned and barely cooked. Remove from pan. Repeat with another quarter of the ghee and remaining livers.

3 Heat 1 tablespoon of the remaining ghee in the same pan; cook bacon and onion, stirring, until onion softens. Add brandy; bring to a boil.

4 Blend livers, bacon mixture, cream, thyme, nutmeg and 2 tablespoons of the remaining ghee until smooth (you may need to do this in batches).

5 Press pâté into 1-quart dish; melt remaining ghee, pour over pâté in dish. Refrigerate 3 hours or overnight.

nutritional count per teaspoon 1.7g total fat (1g saturated fat); 21 cal; 0.1g carbohydrate; 1.2g protein; 0g fiber

serving ideas serve pâté with lavosh, melba toast or water crackers.

Use a small sharp knife to cut any sinew from the chicken livers, then pull the lobes away from the connecting tissues. The chicken livers need to be as fresh as possible, so it's best to buy them on the day you intend to make the pâté.

Heat a quarter of the ghee in a frying pan and add half the livers, stirring until browned but barely cooked–the livers should be just seared. Remove from pan. Repeat with another quarter of the ghee and remaining livers. Cook bacon and onion, then add brandy and bring to a boil.

Process livers, bacon mixture, cream, thyme, nutmeg and 2 tablespoons of the remaining ghee in a blender, or with a hand blender, to a smooth paste (you may need to do this in batches).

Pour and press the pâté into a 1-quart dish. Melt the remaining ghee and pour over pâté in dish. Refrigerate for 3 hours or overnight to chill.

terrine de campagne

"Country-style terrine" is the literal meaning of this classic dish as it is chunky and rustic.

Juniper berries, the dried fruit from the evergreen tree of the same name, can be found in specialty spice stores and good delicatessens.

12 ounces boneless skinless chicken thighs, chopped coarsely

12 ounces boned pork belly, rind removed, chopped coarsely

10 ounces calves' liver, trimmed, chopped coarsely

3 strips bacon, chopped coarsely

3 cloves garlic, crushed

2 teaspoons finely chopped fresh thyme

10 juniper berries, crushed

2 tablespoons port

¼ cup dry white wine

1 egg, beaten lightly

1 Preheat oven to 300°F/275°F fan-forced. Oil 1½-quart ovenproof terrine dish.

2 Chop or process meats, separately, until coarsely minced; combine in large bowl with remaining ingredients.

3 Press meat mixture into dish; cover with foil. Place terrine dish in baking dish; pour enough boiling water into baking dish to come halfway up sides of terrine dish. Cook 1 hour. Uncover; cook an additional 1 hour.

4 Remove terrine dish from baking dish; cover terrine with parchment. Weight it with another dish filled with heavy cans; cool 10 minutes then refrigerate overnight.

5 Turn terrine onto serving plate. Serve sliced terrine, at room temperature.

nutritional count per serving 28.6g total fat (9.6g saturated fat); 440 cal; 2.5g carbohydrate; 40.4g protein; 0.3g fiber

serving ideas serve terrine with slices of French bread and cornichons.

Chop chicken, pork belly, liver and bacon separately on a clean surface, or process in a food processor, until coarsely minced. Combine meats in a large bowl with the remaining ingredients.

Spoon the meat mixture into a heavy-based 1½-quart terrine dish. Press into the base of the dish using your fingertips to smooth the surface.

Cover terrine dish with foil. Place in a large baking dish and pour enough boiling water into dish to come halfway up the sides of the terrine dish. Cook in a preheated oven for 1 hour. Uncover and cook for an additional 1 hour.

gruyère soufflé

Always ensure the egg yolks and whites are completely separated. The smallest amount of yolk can prevent egg whites from stiffening as they should.

Gruyère is a hard, yellow, swiss cheese (named after the valley of the same name) made from cow's milk. It has a rich nutty flavor and is often used in baking due to its distinctive but not overpowering flavor.

⅓ cup all-purpose flour

1⅔ cups milk

1½ tablespoons butter, chopped

6 eggs, separated

1⅓ cups grated gruyère cheese (or strong cheddar cheese)

4 ounces sliced smoked salmon

1½ teaspoons drained baby capers

1 tablespoon fresh chervil leaves

1 Preheat oven to 400°F/350°F fan-forced. Oil 2-quart ovenproof soufflé dish; place on oven tray.

2 Place flour in small saucepan; gradually whisk in milk until smooth. Cook flour mixture over medium heat, whisking constantly, until mixture boils and thickens. Remove from heat; stir in butter. Whisk in egg yolks and cheese. Transfer mixture to large mixing bowl.

3 Beat egg whites in large bowl with electric mixer until soft peaks form. Fold egg whites into cheese mixture, in two batches. Pour mixture into dish.

4 Bake soufflé about 35 to 40 minutes or until well-risen and browned.

5 Arrange salmon on serving platter, top with capers and chervil; serve with soufflé.

nutritional count per serving 33.8g total fat (18.5g saturated fat); 490 cal; 14.5g carbohydrate; 32.3g protein; 0.5g fiber

Place flour in a saucepan and gradually whisk in the milk until smooth. Keep whisking over medium heat, until mixture boils and thickens. Remove from heat. Stir in the butter, then whisk in egg yolks and cheese. Transfer mixture to a bowl.

Beat egg whites in a separate bowl with electric mixer until soft peaks form.

Carefully fold egg whites into cheese mixture, in two batches. Pour the soufflé mixture into an ovenproof dish.

glazed baked ham

Reserve the rind from the ham after it has been removed. When storing the ham (or the leftovers), re-cover the leg's cut surface with the reserved rind–this will keep it moist.

½ cup honey

½ cup maple syrup

½ cup firmly packed brown sugar

2¼ cups water

14-pound cooked bone-in (leg) ham

1 Preheat oven to 350°F/325°F fan-forced.

2 Combine honey, syrup, sugar and ¼ cup of the water in small saucepan; bring to a boil. Stir over heat until sugar dissolves, bring to a boil; remove from heat, cool 10 minutes.

3 Cut through rind of ham 4 inches from the shank end of the leg. To remove rind, run thumb around edge of rind just under skin. Start pulling rind from widest edge of ham, continue to pull rind carefully away from the fat up to the shank end. Remove rind completely. Score across the fat at about 1¼ -inch intervals, cutting through the surface of the fat (not the meat) in a diamond pattern.

4 Pour the remaining water into large baking dish; place ham on oiled wire rack over dish. Brush ham all over with honey glaze. Roast, uncovered, 1 hour or until browned, brushing frequently with glaze during cooking.

nutritional count per serving 19.4g total fat (7.1g saturated fat); 505 cal; 22.9g carbohydrate; 59g protein; 0g fiber

Use a small sharp knife to cut through the rind about 4 inches from the shank end of the leg. Gently lift rind off in one piece by running your thumb around edge of rind just under the skin. Pull the rind from the widest edge of the ham and up to the shank end until removed.

Score the fat, about ½ inch deep to cut through the surface of the fat, in a diamond pattern, taking care not to cut into the meat. The diagonal scores should be about 1¼ inches apart.

Pour water into a large baking dish to keep the ham moist during cooking. Place ham on an oiled wire rack over the dish and brush all over with glaze. Place in a preheated oven and roast, uncovered, for 1 hour or until browned. Brush frequently with glaze during cooking.

beef wellington

This classic dish was served at countless dinner parties during the 1970s. It has recently crept back onto restaurant menus due to its impressive nature and the ease of preparation.

Beef wellington should always be served with the center slightly pink.

1 tablespoon olive oil
1¾-pound piece beef tenderloin
2 tablespoons butter
1 small brown onion, chopped finely
4 ounces button mushrooms, chopped finely
5 ounces chicken or duck liver pâté
2 sheets puff pastry
1 egg

1 Heat oil in large frying pan; cook beef until browned all over. Wrap in foil; cool.

2 Heat butter in same pan; cook onion and mushrooms, stirring, until tender. Cool.

3 Preheat oven to 475°F/425°F fan-forced. Line oven tray with parchment paper.

4 Stir pâté in medium bowl until soft. Spread over top of beef; top with mushroom mixture, gently pushing onto pâté.

5 Roll out pastry on floured surface into a rectangle large enough to enclose beef; moisten edges with water. Place beef on one end of rectangle, fold pastry over beef; trim excess pastry and press edges to seal. Place beef on tray; brush with egg, then cut small slits in top of pastry.

6 Bake beef for 10 minutes. Reduce temperature to 400°F/350°F fan-forced; bake an additional 20 minutes or until browned lightly. Slice thickly to serve.

nutritional count per serving 52.2g total fat (23g saturated fat); 825 cal; 31.9g carbohydrate; 56.4g protein; 2.7g fiber

serving idea serve with a leafy green salad.

Heat oil in a large frying pan and cook beef, turning occasionally, for about 8 minutes or until browned all over. Wrap in foil and allow to cool.

Spread the softened pâté over the beef. Top with the mushroom mixture, pressing down with your fingers until the mixture sticks to the pâté.

Roll out the puff pastry on a floured surface into a rectangle large enough to enclose the beef. Brush the edges with water to moisten. Place beef on one end of the rectangle, fold pastry over beef, and trim any excess pastry. Press edges to seal.

thai steamed fish in banana leaves

PREP + COOK TIME 40 MINS
(+ REFRIGERATION)
SERVES 4

You will need cotton
string to wrap each
fish leaf.

TIPS

• If bream is unavailable, use
any of your favorite whole
firm-fleshed fish for this recipe.
Cooking times will vary
depending on the fish you use.

• Steaming is best done in a
bamboo steamer because, in a
metal one, condensation on the
lid can drip on to the food and
spoil the appearance. If you
have to use a metal steamer,
cover the fish with parchment
that doesn't touch the steamer.

• Fish leaves can be cooked on
a heated grill for about 15
minutes or until the fish is
cooked as desired.

4 medium whole bream (3½ pounds)
1 large banana leaf
4 fresh small red thai chilies,
　sliced thinly
2 fresh kaffir lime leaves,
　shredded finely
2 green onions, sliced thinly
¼ cup loosely packed fresh
　coriander leaves
¼ cup loosely packed fresh
　thai basil leaves
2 x 4-inch sticks fresh lemon grass

lime and sweet chili dressing
¼ cup sweet chili sauce
2 tablespoons fish sauce
2 tablespoons lime juice
2 tablespoons peanut oil
1 clove garlic, crushed
1 teaspoon grated fresh ginger

1 Make lime and sweet chili dressing.
2 Score fish both sides through thickest part of flesh; place on large tray,
drizzle with half of the dressing. Cover; refrigerate 1 hour.
3 Meanwhile, trim banana leaf into four 12-inch squares. Using tongs, dip one
square at a time into large saucepan of boiling water; remove immediately. Rinse
under cold water; pat dry with absorbent paper. Place leaves on work surface.
4 Combine chili, lime leaves, onion, coriander and basil in medium bowl. Halve
lemon grass sticks lengthwise, then halve crosswise; you will have eight pieces.
5 Place two pieces cut lemon grass on each leaf square; place one fish on each.
Top fish with equal amounts of the herb mixture then fold opposite corners of the
leaf to enclose center part of fish; secure each filled leaf with cotton string.
6 Place filled leaves, in single layer, in large bamboo steamer; steam, covered, in
two batches, over wok of simmering water about 15 minutes or until fish is cooked
through. Serve fish still in leaf, drizzled with remaining dressing.
lime and sweet chili dressing Place ingredients in screw-top jar; shake well.
nutritional count per serving 21.8g total fat (6g saturated fat); 406 cal;
4.1g carbohydrate; 48g protein; 1.3g fiber

Using a sharp knife, score the
flesh of each bream, making
several diagonal cuts on both
sides. Place on tray and drizzle
the prepared dressing over.

Dip banana leaf squares into a
large saucepan of boiling water,
one at a time, to soften. Remove,
then rinse under cold water and
pat dry with absorbent paper.

Lay leaves out on a clean work
surface. Place lemon grass on
each leaf, then fish; top with herb
mixture. Fold opposite corners
to enclose and tie with string.

chocolate soufflé

Egg whites are vital to a soufflé's success. They must be folded very carefully into the mixture. Use a wide-rimmed bowl so folding is easier for you. Use a whisk, spatula or large metal spoon for the folding–the choice is yours. Some cooks like to fold a small amount of the egg white (about a quarter) through the flavored, more solid mixture first to "let the mixture down" a little. Fold in the remaining egg whites in one or two batches depending on the quantity. Experiment a little to determine what works best for you and your soufflés.

⅓ cup superfine sugar

3 tablespoons butter

1 tablespoon all-purpose flour

6½ ounces bittersweet chocolate, melted

2 eggs, separated

2 egg whites

1 tablespoon cocoa powder

1 Preheat oven to 350°F/325°F fan-forced. Grease four ¾-cup soufflé dishes. Sprinkle inside of dishes with a little of the sugar; shake away excess. Place dishes on oven tray.

2 Melt butter in small saucepan, add flour; cook, stirring, about 2 minutes or until mixture thickens and bubbles. Remove from heat; stir in chocolate and egg yolks. Transfer to large bowl.

3 Beat all egg whites in small bowl with electric mixer until soft peaks form. Gradually add remaining sugar, beating until sugar dissolves. Fold egg white mixture into chocolate mixture, in two batches.

4 Divide soufflé mixture among dishes; bake 15 minutes. Serve immediately, dusted with cocoa powder.

nutritional count per serving 27.1g total fat (16.1g saturated fat); 488 cal; 52.3g carbohydrate; 8.1g protein; 0.7g fiber

Grease four soufflé dishes, then sprinkle the insides with sugar, shaking away excess. Place the dishes on an oven tray.

Melt butter in a saucepan, then add flour and cook for 2 minutes. Remove the pan from the heat, add chocolate, stirring, then add egg yolks. Stir mixture well to combine.

Transfer chocolate mixture to a large mixing bowl. Fold in the egg white mixture, in two batches. Stir well to combine and divide between four soufflé dishes. Bake for 15 minutes.

crème brûlée

For many, the best part about crème brûlée is the crisp toffee on top. This is also the hardest part to get right if you don't have a blowtorch (favored by chefs). But we've found topping the custards with powdered sugar makes it easier to caramelize them under the broiler at home.

Make sure you place the crème brûlées as close as possible to the broiler. Surrounding the custards with ice keeps them cool as you heat the top. Of course, you can use a blowtorch if you have one. The adjustable flame melts the sugar quickly, so the filling remains cool.

Professional cooks' blowtorches are available from specialty kitchen shops.

1 vanilla bean
3 cups heavy cream
6 egg yolks
¼ cup superfine sugar
¼ cup powdered sugar

1 Preheat oven to 350°F/325°F fan-forced. Grease six ½-cup ovenproof dishes.
2 Split vanilla bean in half lengthways; scrape seeds into medium heatproof bowl. Place pod in small saucepan with cream; heat without boiling.
3 Add egg yolks and sugar to seeds in bowl; gradually whisk in hot cream mixture. Place bowl over medium saucepan of simmering water; stir over heat about 10 minutes or until custard mixture thickens slightly and coats the back of a spoon. Discard pod.
4 Place dishes in large baking dish; divide custard among dishes. Add enough boiling water to baking dish to come halfway up sides of ovenproof dishes.
5 Bake custards, uncovered, about 20 minutes or until set. Remove custards from dish; cool. Cover; refrigerate overnight.
6 Preheat broiler. Place custards in shallow flameproof dish filled with ice cubes; sprinkle custards evenly with sifted powdered sugar. Using finger, spread sugar over the surface of each custard, pressing in gently; place under broiler until the tops caramelize.

nutritional count per serving 52.1g total fat (32.3g saturated fat); 564 cal; 19.8g carbohydrate; 5.8g protein; 8g fiber

Split the vanilla bean in half lengthways and scrape the seeds out with a knife. Place the seeds in a heatproof bowl. Place the pod in a small saucepan with the thickened cream and heat through, but do not boil.

Combine the egg yolk and sugar with the seeds in the bowl. Slowly whisk in the hot cream mixture. Place the bowl over a saucepan of simmering water. Stir the cream mixture for about 10 minutes or until it coats the back of a spoon.

Remove the chilled custards from the refrigerator and place in a shallow heatproof dish. Fill dish with ice cubes to keep custards cool when broiling the tops. Sprinkle the tops with powdered sugar to help them caramelize under the broiler.

Caramelize the sugar under a preheated hot broiler with the dishes as close as possible to the heat. If you have a blowtorch, use that to brown the sugar. The top should be hard and, when cracked with a spoon, reveal a creamy custard underneath.

lemon tart

Lemon tart appears on almost every restaurant menu, with varying degrees of quality. We guarantee this recipe is as good, if not better, than any lemon tart you've ever tasted. Don't overcook the filling. The custard should feel firm around the outside of the tart, but still a bit wobbly in the middle—it will set as the tart cools.

This tart is best made a day ahead and stored in the refrigerator.

1¼ cups all-purpose flour
⅓ cup powdered sugar
¼ cup ground almonds
1 stick cold butter, chopped
1 egg yolk
2 tablespoons iced water

lemon filling
3 teaspoons finely grated lemon rind
⅓ cup lemon juice
3 eggs
½ cup superfine sugar
⅔ cup light cream

1 Blend or process flour, powdered sugar, ground almonds and butter until crumbly. Add egg yolk and the water; process until combined. Knead dough on floured surface until smooth. Wrap in plastic wrap, refrigerate 30 minutes.

2 Roll pastry between sheets of parchment paper until large enough to line shallow (¾-inch deep) 9½-inch round removable-bottom tart pan. Lift pastry into tin; press into side, trim edge. Cover; refrigerate 30 minutes.

3 Meanwhile, preheat oven to 400°F/350°F fan-forced.

4 Place tart pan on oven tray. Line pastry case with parchment paper, fill with dried beans or rice. Bake, uncovered, 15 minutes. Remove paper and beans; bake about 10 minutes or until browned lightly.

5 Meanwhile, whisk ingredients for lemon filling in medium bowl; stand 5 minutes.

6 Reduce oven to 350°F/325°F fan-forced.

7 Pour lemon filling into pastry case; bake about 30 minutes or until filling has set slightly, cool. Refrigerate until cold.

nutritional count per serving 25.3g total fat (14.3g saturated fat); 410 cal; 38.5g carbohydrate; 6.7g protein; 1.3g fiber

serving idea whipped cream; dust tart with sifted powdered sugar just before serving.

Use a rolling pin to carefully lift the pastry into a removable-bottom tart pan. Press the pastry into the base and side of the pan and trim the edge to fit. Cover and place in the refrigerator to chill.

Line the pastry with parchment paper and fill with dried beans. Bake for 15 minutes, remove the paper and beans, then bake for another 10 minutes or until lightly browned. Remove from the oven and cool slightly. This process of blind baking creates a firm, dry and even crust.

Pour lemon filling into cooled pastry case. Place in a preheated oven and bake for about 30 minutes or until the filling has just set. Allow lemon tart to cool before placing in the refrigerator to chill.

STARTERS

Starters

If you're hosting a dinner party, you'll need to plan ahead and think about the food preparation in terms of your time considerations and the mood of the occasion.

A traditional, three-course, sit-down meal can elevate your dining experience to a special, out-of-the-ordinary occasion, but it can place more pressure on the host's time and preparations. For a more casual and relaxed mood, encourage your guests to mingle and help themselves to finger food before sitting down to the table for the main course.

It's worth putting some thought into the starters you serve—they are the introduction, the greeting, the welcome. They need to be taste-tempting without overwhelming the rest of your meal.
The recipes in this chapter can be used as finger food, while others are more suited to a sit-down first course.

MAKING AN IMPRESSION

REMEMBER, THE FIRST COURSE IS THE INTRODUCTION TO THE MEAL, SO YOU WANT IT TO MAKE AN IMPRESSIVE ENTRANCE. PUT SOME EFFORT INTO MAKING THE FOOD LOOK TEMPTING AND VISUALLY INTERESTING. PAY ATTENTION TO THE RECIPES' PHOTOGRAPHS FOR POINTERS ON PRESENTATION.

FOR PLATTERS OF MIXED APPETIZERS, TRY TO ARRANGE THE FOOD IN COLORS AND SHAPES THAT CREATE AN APPEALING VISUAL EFFECT. PLACE FOODS CLOSE TO EACH OTHER ON THE PLATE, RATHER THAN SPREADING THEM AROUND THE EDGES. USING HERBS OR FRUIT AS A GARNISH CAN LIVEN UP A PLATE.

A WINNING COMBINATION

A versatile and easy way to open a meal is to serve mixed appetizers, arranged either on individual plates or large platters for guests to help themselves. Serving a selection of appetizers is handy if you're short of time because you can mix homemade with good-quality bought items. They're suitable for sit-down or stand-up affairs and they're the perfect way to cater to a range of tastes. The idea of mixed appetizers is not new, of course, and many different cultures around the world have embraced their own versions: the traditional "mezze" is a staple in the Middle East and Greece; the Italians have their antipasto, and the French serve hors d'oeuvres.

The beauty of the mixed platter is that you can bring together any number of flavors into one taste-tempting mix. As a general rule, try to serve at least one fresh salad-derived item with one warm homemade item plus a few good-quality bought items.

THINK OF THE FLAVORS AND TEXTURES

It's good to create a variety of flavors and textures in your meal. You don't want the first course and second course to echo each other. Think about the meal as a whole and once you have decided on one part of it–a roast for the main course perhaps, or a rich velvety chocolate pudding for dessert–then plan the rest of the meal around that choice. If the main course has a rich sauce, you will want to create a light, fresh first course. Or if you're planning to serve a serious pudding for dessert, you might serve a soup first, then a lighter meal as your main course, so that your dinner guests can enjoy the finale. You also have to think of the practicalities of time and space: do you have the time to create complicated individual servings for the first course while the main course is cooking? Can you create the starters ahead of time? Will your first and second courses be competing for counter and oven space at the same time? Make sure you've thought about the cooking times and requirements of each part of the meal and feel confident that your kitchen (and you) will cope before you begin.

HOMEMADE

Perhaps you could make some bruschetta, some mini quiches, or offer some chilled or warm soup (depending on the season) served in demitasse cups containing just a few tantalizing mouthfuls. Combine these homemade provisions with any of the following:

FROM THE SUPERMARKET AND DELI

A variety of dips, such as hummus, baba ganoush and taramasalata.

Pâtés such as chicken liver or smoked salmon.

Salami, smoked pork or beef, ham and other cold meats.

Char-grilled vegetables such as peppers and eggplant.

Marinated mushrooms and artichoke hearts.

Olives, plain or marinated (preferably pitted).

A variety of soft cheeses: brie, camembert, blue cheese.

Marinated chicken wings or kebabs.

Savory breads and crackers from a deli.

Pita bread (cut into small triangles and grilled).

FROM THE GREENGROCER

Salad vegetables perfect for a platter, including: cucumber, radish, celery, carrot, peppers, baby spinach leaves and watercress.

Some cooked vegetables work well as bite-sized appetizers too, such as asparagus and whole baby beans (both served warm with melted butter and lemon) and baby potatoes and carrots (served with melted butter and mint).

FROM THE FISH MARKETS OR LOCAL FRESH SEAFOOD STORE

Prawns, oysters or scallops, served either plain or with simple light sauces.

FROM YOUR LOCAL INDIAN, THAI OR CHINESE RESTAURANT

Purchase a selection of your favorite entrees such as curry puffs, spring rolls, fish cakes, samosas or pakoras.

vietnamese prawn rolls

Soften rice paper in warm water, one at a time, for 15 to 20 seconds. Make sure you don't oversoak them as they will fall apart in your hands.

The rolls can be made at the table by each diner, or ahead of time and stored in the fridge for up to 3 hours. Cover rolls with a damp clean tea towel to keep the rice paper moist.

1½ ounces rice vermicelli noodles, soaked, drained
¼ small Napa cabbage (6 ounces), shredded finely
½ cup loosely packed fresh mint leaves, torn
2 teaspoons brown sugar
2 tablespoons lime juice
1 pound cooked medium king prawns
12 x 8-inch rice paper rounds

hoisin dipping sauce
½ cup hoisin sauce
2 tablespoons rice vinegar

1 Combine chopped vermicelli in medium bowl with cabbage, mint, sugar and juice.
2 Shell and devein prawns; chop meat finely.
3 Meanwhile, make hoisin dipping sauce.
4 Dip one rice paper round into bowl of warm water until soft; place on board covered with tea towel. Top with a little of the prawn meat and noodle filling. Fold and roll to enclose filling. Repeat with remaining rounds, prawn meat and noodle filling.
5 Serve rolls with hoisin dipping sauce.
hoisin dipping sauce Combine ingredients in bowl.
nutritional count per roll 0.9g total fat (0.1g saturated fat); 78 cal; 10.8g carbohydrate; 5.5g protein; 1.7g fiber

Dip one rice paper round in a bowl of warm water for about 15 seconds until soft and pliable. Shake off any excess water and transfer round to a board covered with a clean tea towel.

Place a tablespoon of the prawn meat and noodle mixture at one end of the rice paper round. Make sure you leave a border at both ends to tuck in and avoid overfilling.

Fold the ends of the rice paper round over the filling, then roll up to enclose. Repeat the process for the remaining rice paper rounds and filling.

16 uncooked medium king prawns
(1½ pounds)
1¾ pounds russet potatoes, peeled
grated coarsely
1 teaspoon finely chopped
fresh rosemary
2 cloves garlic, crushed
2 tablespoons olive oil
1 ounce baby arugula leaves

mint aïoli
⅓ cup coarsely chopped fresh mint
1 clove garlic, quartered
1 egg
1 tablespoon dijon mustard
½ cup olive oil

1 Make mint aïoli.

2 Shell and devein prawns, leaving tails intact.

3 To make rösti, squeeze excess moisture from potato; combine in medium bowl with rosemary and garlic. Divide into eight portions.

4 Heat half the oil in large frying pan; cook rösti, in batches, flattening slightly, until browned both sides. Drain.

5 Heat remaining oil in pan; cook prawns until just changed in color.

6 Serve rösti stacked alternately with prawns, mint aïoli and arugula.

mint aïoli Blend or process mint, garlic, egg and mustard until mixture is pureed. With motor running, add oil in a thin, steady stream until aïoli thickens.

nutritional count per serving 39.8g total fat (5.8g saturated fat); 556 cal; 23.6g carbohydrate; 24.9g protein; 3.7g fiber

To make the rösti, use your hands to squeeze out excess liquid from the grated potato. Place in a large bowl, along with the rosemary and garlic. Divide the potato mixture into eight portions.

Heat oil in a large frying pan and add rösti, in batches. Use an egg spatula to flatten each portion slightly. Cook, turning over, until both sides are browned. Transfer to a dish lined with absorbent paper to drain.

bruschetta with tomato, basil and capers

Fantastic served as an entrée, finger food, or a mid-summer snack, this simple and quick-to-prepare recipe is sure to become a family favorite.

6 medium ripe tomatoes, seeded, chopped finely
¼ cup extra virgin olive oil
¼ cup fresh baby basil leaves
2 tablespoons baby capers, rinsed, drained
1-pound loaf wood-fired bread, cut into 12 slices
1 clove garlic, halved

1 Combine tomatoes in medium bowl with 2 tablespoons oil, basil leaves and capers.

2 Toast bread slices both sides on heated grill plate (or grill pan). Rub one side of each slice with the cut side of the garlic; place toast on platter, garlic-side up.

3 Top toasts with tomato mixture; sprinkle with freshly ground black pepper and drizzle with remaining oil.

nutritional count per serving 11.4g total fat (1.6g saturated fat); 296 cal; 39g carbohydrate; 7.7g protein; 3.3g fiber

white bean dip

Many varieties of cooked white beans are available canned, among them cannellini (which is what we used), butter and navy beans—any of these are suitable for this dip.

2 x 14-ounce cans white beans, rinsed, drained
2 cloves garlic, crushed
2 tablespoons lemon juice
⅓ cup olive oil
1 tablespoon fresh basil leaves

1 Blend or process beans, garlic, juice and oil until almost smooth.

2 Sprinkle dip with basil.

nutritional count per tablespoon 3.1g total fat (0.4g saturated fat); 33 cal; 0.6g carbohydrate; 0.5g protein; 0.9g fiber

serving idea wedges of toasted Turkish bread.

[1] bruschetta with tomato, basil and capers
[2] white bean dip
[3] baba ghanoush [page 82]
[4] blue cheese and caramelized onion dip [page 82]

baba ghanoush

For an extra touch of the Middle East, top baba ghanoush with chopped mint, finely chopped pistachios or pomegranate seeds.

This recipe can be refrigerated in an airtight container for up to a week.

2 large eggplants
3 cloves garlic, crushed
2 tablespoons tahini
¼ cup lemon juice
2 tablespoons olive oil
½ teaspoon sweet paprika

1 Preheat broiler. Oil oven tray.
2 Pierce eggplants all over with fork or skewer; place on tray. Broil about 30 minutes or until skin blackens and eggplant is soft, turning occasionally. Stand 15 minutes.
3 Peel eggplants, discard skin; drain eggplants in colander 10 minutes.
4 Blend or process eggplant flesh with remaining ingredients.
nutritional count per ¼ cup 8g total fat (1g saturated fat); 103 cal; 3.6g carbohydrate; 2.5g protein; 3.7g fiber
serving ideas crisp vegetables, pita bread or rice crackers.

blue cheese and caramelized onion dip   PREP + COOK TIME 30 MINS • MAKES 1½ CUPS

2 tablespoons butter
1 large brown onion, chopped finely
2 tablespoons brown sugar
2 tablespoons white wine vinegar
3½ ounces blue cheese, crumbled
¾ cup crème fraîche
¼ cup finely chopped fresh flat-leaf parsley

1 Melt butter in medium saucepan; cook onion, stirring, until onion softens.
2 Add sugar and vinegar; cook, stirring, over low heat, about 10 minutes or until onion is caramelized.
3 Stir in cheese and crème fraîche until smooth. Cool. Cover; refrigerate until cold. Stir in parsley before serving.
nutritional count per teaspoon 1.7g total fat (1.1g saturated fat); 20 cal; 0.7g carbohydrate; 0.4g protein; 0.1g fiber
serving idea wedges of toasted pita bread.

chicken and olive empanadas

Perfect for a party or picnic, these little pastry pockets can be individually wrapped and frozen for up to three months. And they don't require thawing before reheating–pop them straight from the freezer into the oven for a fuss-free snack.

2 cups chicken stock

1 bay leaf

3 boneless skinless chicken thighs

1 tablespoon olive oil

1 small brown onion, chopped finely

2 cloves garlic, crushed

2 teaspoons ground cumin

½ cup raisins

⅓ cup pitted green olives, chopped coarsely

3 sheets store-bought pie crust

1 egg, beaten lightly

1 Place stock and bay leaf in medium frying pan; bring to a boil. Add chicken, reduce heat; poach chicken, covered, about 10 minutes or until cooked through. Cool chicken in liquid 10 minutes; shred chicken finely. Reserve 1 cup of the poaching liquid; discard remainder (or keep for another use).

2 Meanwhile, heat oil in large frying pan; cook onion, stirring, until softened. Add garlic and cumin; cook, stirring, until fragrant. Add raisins and reserved poaching liquid; bring to a boil. Reduce heat; simmer, uncovered, about 15 minutes or until liquid is almost evaporated. Stir in chicken and olives.

3 Preheat oven to 400°F/350°F fan-forced. Grease two oven trays.

4 Using 3½-inch cutter, cut 24 rounds from pastry sheets, re-rolling dough as needed. Place 1 level tablespoon of the filling in center of each round; fold round in half to enclose filling, pinching edges to seal. Using fork, press around edges of empanadas. Place on trays; brush tops with egg.

5 Bake empanadas about 25 minutes. Serve with yogurt.

nutritional count per empanada 12g total fat (5.6g saturated fat); 203 cal; 18.3g carbohydrate; 5.5g protein; 0.9g fiber

serving idea yogurt for dipping.

prawn cocktail

32 cooked medium prawns
⅓ cup mayonnaise
2 tablespoons cream
1 tablespoon tomato sauce
1 teaspoon Worcestershire sauce
½ teaspoon Tabasco sauce
½ teaspoon dijon mustard
2 teaspoons lemon juice
½ head iceberg lettuce, shredded finely

1 Shell and devein prawns.
2 Whisk mayonnaise, cream, sauces, mustard and juice in small bowl.
3 Divide lettuce among serving glasses; top with prawns and sauce.
nutritional count per serving 14.2g total fat (4.2g saturated fat); 300 cal;
7.6g carbohydrate; 34.6g protein; 1.8g fiber
serving idea wedges of lemon.

crab cakes with avocado salsa

PREP + COOK TIME 30 MINS (+ REFRIGERATION) • SERVES 4

Crab meat is available from seafood shops or supermarkets. If you buy it frozen, thaw then drain well before use.

1¼ pounds cooked crab meat
1 cup stale white bread crumbs
1 egg
1 clove garlic, crushed
2 tablespoons mayonnaise
¼ cup finely chopped fresh coriander
½ teaspoon cayenne pepper
1 tablespoon butter
1 tablespoon olive oil

avocado salsa
2 small avocados,
    chopped coarsely
1 medium tomato,
    chopped coarsely
¾ cup loosely packed fresh
    coriander leaves
2 teaspoons Tabasco sauce
1 tablespoon lime juice
1 tablespoon olive oil

1 Combine crab meat, bread crumbs, egg, garlic, mayonnaise, coriander and pepper in medium bowl. Shape mixture into eight patties; place on tray. Cover; refrigerate 1 hour.
2 Meanwhile, make avocado salsa.
3 Heat butter and oil in large frying pan; cook crab cakes, in batches, until browned both sides and heated through. Serve crab cakes topped with salsa.
avocado salsa Combine ingredients in medium bowl.
nutritional count per serving 34.1g total fat (7.8g saturated fat); 481 cal;
17.6g carbohydrate; 25.3g protein; 2.8g fiber

[opposite] prawn cocktail

oysters with three toppings

We used Pacific oysters in this recipe because their full-bodied flavor teams well with these robust dressings.

Serving oysters on a bed of coarse rock salt (or crushed ice) prevents them from sliding around on the plate. Another way to serve them is to take them out of the shells and put them on Chinese porcelain soup spoons, then top with dressings and salsa.

36 oysters, on the half shell
coarse rock salt

ponzu dressing
2 tablespoons light soy sauce
2 teaspoons peanut oil
2 teaspoons mirin
1 tablespoon brown sugar
2 tablespoons lime juice

shallot dressing
⅓ cup white wine vinegar
3 shallots, chopped finely

green mango and cucumber salsa
½ Lebanese cucumber (2 ounces), seeded, chopped finely
1 tablespoon finely shredded green mango
1 tablespoon finely chopped red onion
1 teaspoon finely grated lime rind
1 teaspoon lime juice
1 teaspoon fish sauce
1 tablespoon vegetable oil

1 Make ponzu dressing.
2 Make shallot dressing.
3 Make green mango and cucumber salsa.
4 Serve oysters on bed of rock salt with dressings.

ponzu dressing Stir soy sauce, oil, mirin and sugar in medium saucepan over low heat until sugar dissolves. Stir in lime juice; season. Cool.

shallot dressing Bring vinegar to a boil in small saucepan; remove from heat. Stir in shallots; cool.

green mango and cucumber salsa Combine ingredients in small bowl; season.

nutritional count per serving 6.2g total fat (1.2g saturated fat); 105 cal; 4g carbohydrate; 8.1g protein; 0.3g fiber

scallops with saffron cream

12 scallops in half shell (1 pound)
1 teaspoon olive oil
1 small brown onion, chopped finely
2 teaspoons finely grated lemon rind
pinch saffron threads

⅔ cup cream
1 tablespoon lemon juice
2 teaspoons salmon roe

1 Remove scallops from shells; wash and dry shells. Place shells, in single layer, on serving platter.

2 Rinse scallops under cold water; reserve scallop roe. Gently pat scallops dry with absorbent paper.

3 Heat oil in small saucepan; cook onion, stirring, until softened. Add rind, saffron and cream; bring to a boil. Reduce heat; simmer, uncovered, about 5 minutes or until mixture has reduced to about ½ cup. Remove from heat; stand 30 minutes. Stir in lemon juice; stand 10 minutes. Strain cream mixture into small bowl then back into same cleaned pan; stir over low heat until heated through.

4 Meanwhile, cook scallops, in batches, on heated oiled grill (or grill pan) until browned lightly and cooked as desired.

5 Return scallops to shells; top with cream sauce and roe.

nutritional count per scallop 6.4g total fat (4g saturated fat); 69 cal; 0.8g carbohydrate; 2.3g protein; 0.1g fiber

black olive tapenade

This classic Provençal preparation is used as a dip for raw vegetables, spread on bread and pizza, and served with fish and meats.

2 cups (8 ounces) pitted black olives
1 drained anchovy filet, rinsed
1 tablespoon drained capers, rinsed
2 teaspoons dijon mustard
2 tablespoons olive oil

1 Rinse and drain olives on absorbent paper. Blend or process olives with anchovy, capers and mustard until smooth.

2 With motor running, add oil in a thin steady stream, processing until tapenade is smooth.

nutritional count per tablespoon 3.3g total fat (0.5g saturated fat); 51 cal; 4.6g carbohydrate; 0.6g protein; 0.3g fiber

serving idea wedges of toasted Turkish bread.

money bags

Cut the upper green section of a green onion into four strips using a sharp knife. Repeat process for remaining two onions. Soften in hot water for a few seconds.

Place wrappers on a clean flat surface, topping each one with another to form a star shape.

Add teaspoons of filling to the center of each wrapper and fold up sides to form a pouch. Pinch to enclose, tie with an onion strip, and secure with a toothpick.

1 tablespoon peanut oil
1 small brown onion,
   chopped finely
1 clove garlic, crushed
1 tablespoon grated fresh ginger
4 ounces ground chicken
1 tablespoon finely grated palm sugar
1 tablespoon finely chopped
   roasted unsalted peanuts
2 teaspoons finely chopped
   fresh coriander
3 green onions
24 x 3-inch square wonton wrappers
vegetable oil, for deep-frying

peanut dipping sauce
1 tablespoon peanut oil
2 cloves garlic, crushed
1 small brown onion,
   chopped finely
2 fresh small red chilies,
   chopped coarsely
4-inch stick fresh lemon grass,
   chopped finely
¾ cup coconut milk
2 tablespoons fish sauce
¼ cup dark brown sugar
½ cup crunchy peanut butter
½ teaspoon curry powder
1 tablespoon lime juice

1 Heat oil in wok; stir-fry onion, garlic and ginger until onion softens. Add chicken; stir-fry until chicken changes color. Add sugar; stir-fry about 3 minutes or until sugar dissolves. Stir nuts and coriander into filling mixture.

2 Cut upper green half of each onion into four long slices; discard remaining onion half. Submerge onion strips in hot water for a few seconds to make pliable.

3 Place 12 wrappers on board; cover each wrapper with another, placed on the diagonal to form star shape. Place rounded teaspoons of the filling mixture in center of each star; gather corners to form pouch shape. Tie green onion slice around neck of each pouch to hold closed, secure with toothpick.

4 Make dipping sauce (freeze excess for a future use).

5 Just before serving, heat oil in wok or large saucepan; deep-fry money bags, in batches, until crisp and browned lightly. Drain on absorbent paper; serve with dipping sauce.

peanut dipping sauce Heat oil in small saucepan; cook garlic and onion until softened. Stir in remaining ingredients; bring to a boil. Reduce heat; simmer, stirring, about 2 minutes or until sauce thickens.

nutritional count per money bag 5.1g total fat (0.9g saturated fat); 104 cal; 10.8g carbohydrate; 3.8g protein; 0.6g fiber

nutritional count per tablespoon dipping sauce 4.7g total fat (1.7g saturated fat); 60 cal; 2.5g carbohydrate; 2.2g protein; 0.8g fiber

tuna tartare

Tuna sold as sashimi is the highest quality and has to meet stringent guidelines regarding its handling and treatment after leaving the water. Purchase sashimi-grade tuna from reputable seafood shops; it should be deep red in color, firm to the touch, and have absolutely no odor.

7-ounce piece sashimi tuna, trimmed
1 tablespoon drained capers, rinsed, chopped finely
2 teaspoons prepared horseradish
⅓ cup lime juice
2 small tomatoes (6 ounces), seeded, chopped finely

1 small avocado, chopped finely
1 small red onion, chopped finely
1 baby romaine lettuce, trimmed, leaves separated
1 tablespoon extra virgin olive oil

1 Cut tuna into ¼-inch pieces; combine tuna in medium bowl with capers, horseradish and 1 tablespoon of the juice. Cover; refrigerate 30 minutes.
2 Combine tomato, avocado, onion and remaining juice in medium bowl.
3 Serve lettuce leaves topped with tomato mixture and tuna tartare; drizzle with oil.
nutritional count per serving 10.4g total fat (2.3g saturated fat); 146 cal; 2.4g carbohydrate; 9.8g protein; 1.6g fiber

smoked salmon with capers

10 ounces sliced smoked salmon
1 small red onion, chopped finely
½ cup drained baby capers, rinsed
2 small Belgian endive, leaves separated
1 baby fennel bulb, sliced thinly
2 red radishes, trimmed, sliced thinly

mustard honey dressing
1 teaspoon dijon mustard
2 teaspoons honey
2 tablespoons lemon juice
1 tablespoon finely chopped fresh dill
¼ cup olive oil

1 Make mustard honey dressing.
2 Divide salmon among serving plates; sprinkle with onion and capers. Serve with endive, fennel and radish; drizzle with dressing.
mustard honey dressing Place ingredients in screw-top jar; shake well.
nutritional count per serving 8.8g total fat (1.3g saturated fat); 135 cal; 3.8g carbohydrate; 9.8g protein; 1g fiber

spring rolls

Make sure the oil is very hot before you start deep-frying the spring rolls, and don't overcrowd them in the wok or they won't cook evenly. Use a wok chan or tongs to turn them constantly in the oil for even cooking.

Keep the finished spring rolls warm by placing them on an absorbent-paper-lined oven tray in a very low oven while you finish deep-frying the remainder.

1 ounce rice vermicelli noodles
2 teaspoons peanut oil
4 ounces ground pork
1 clove garlic, crushed
1 fresh small red Thai chili, chopped finely
1 green onion, chopped finely
1 small carrot, grated finely
1 teaspoon fish sauce

1 teaspoon finely chopped coriander root and stem mixture
2 ounces shelled cooked prawns, chopped finely
1 teaspoon corn starch
2 teaspoons water
12 x 5-inch square spring roll wrappers
vegetable oil, for deep-frying

1 Place noodles in medium heatproof bowl; cover with boiling water. Stand until just tender; drain. Using kitchen scissors, cut vermicelli into random lengths.
2 Heat oil in wok; stir-fry pork, garlic and chili until pork changes color. Add onion, carrot, fish sauce, coriander mixture and prawns; stir-fry until vegetables just soften. Place stir-fried mixture in small bowl with noodles; cool.
3 Blend corn starch with the water in small bowl. Place 1 level tablespoon of the filling near one corner of each wrapper. Lightly brush edges of each wrapper with corn starch mixture; roll to enclose filling, folding in ends.
4 Just before serving, heat oil in wok; deep-fry spring rolls, in batches, until golden brown. Drain on absorbent paper.
nutritional count per serving 3.4g total fat (0.6g saturated fat); 61 cal; 4g carbohydrate; 3.3g protein; 0.4g fiber
serving idea sweet chili dipping sauce or any favorite dipping sauce.

beef carpaccio

12-ounce piece beef tenderloin
2 tablespoons olive oil
2 teaspoons finely grated lemon rind
2 tablespoons lemon juice
1 clove garlic, crushed
⅓ cup finely chopped fresh flat-leaf parsley

2 tablespoons finely chopped fresh oregano
⅓ cup finely chopped baby arugula leaves
⅓ cup flaked parmesan cheese

1 Tightly wrap beef filet in plastic wrap; freeze 1 hour or until firm.
2 Unwrap beef; slice as thinly as possible. Arrange slices on serving platter.
3 Combine lemon oil, rind and juice, garlic, parsley, oregano and arugula in small bowl. Serve beef sprinkled with herb mixture and cheese.
nutritional count per serving 7.8g total fat (2.3g saturated fat); 121 cal; 0.3g carbohydrate; 12.3g protein; 0.3g fiber

SALADS

Salads

Sometimes, don't you just crave a salad? After a hectic week at the office or running after the kids, your body just wants to eat fresh, simple, minimally-processed, preferably raw, food.

A well-conceived salad made from fresh and ripe ingredients is a joy to taste and the best way to enjoy those all-important raw ingredients that are recommended for well-being.

A salad can be anything you want it to be. It can be enjoyed on its own as a nourishing light meal or used to add a refreshing balance to another dish. It can be a first course, main course, a picnic companion, a buffet star, casual or elegant, warm or cold, vegetarian or not.

Our approach to salads, like ideas on food in general, has changed over the past 20 years and the modern salad is no longer the all-purpose "mixed salad" of a generation ago, created using iceberg lettuce and a jumble of everything imaginable from the fridge. These days, a good salad consists of one or two key ingredients supported by carefully selected flavors and textures.

Fresh green leaves can stand alone as the perfect green salad or they can provide the background that sets off other salad ingredients. A leafy salad should look fluffy and vibrant, not heavy and settled. To ensure this, dress the salad at the last moment and use only enough dressing to make every leaf glisten, and never enough to run off into a puddle at the bottom of the salad bowl.

BUYING, STORING AND HANDLING SALAD VEGETABLES

LETTUCE AND OTHER LEAVES **Leaf vegetables** should be crisp, brightly colored, and have a sheen. If you're buying iceberg or romaine lettuce or cabbage, choose a size you will use within a week. If you're buying a soft-leaf lettuce or other soft leaves, buy only as much as you can use within a day or two. Endive and radicchio should be used within 2 to 3 days. Except for watercress, leaf vegetables are best stored in a paper bag inside a plastic bag in the refrigerator. For watercress, cut the stems and gather into a bunch, tying loosely with a rubber band; stand in 1 to 2 inches of water in a bowl. Cover with a plastic bag and store in the fridge. Wash salad leaves up to 12 hours ahead and dry in a salad spinner–store as above until needed.

TOMATOES **Ideally, you should buy tomatoes** that have been fully sun-ripened on the vine but these are rarely available in supermarkets. You are more likely to find them at a farmers' market. To improve reasonably ripe tomatoes, place them in a paper bag with a banana (nature's ripening agent) at room temperature for a day or two. Never put tomatoes in the fridge as chilling them damages their cell structure. Store them at room temperature, away from sunlight and preferably, in a single layer. Fully ripened tomatoes should be used within 3 days. To peel tomatoes, cut a tiny cross at the base, place in a bowl, cover with boiling water and stand for 20 seconds. Drain and run cold water over them. Starting at the base, pull off the skin using a small knife.

CUCUMBERS, PEPPERS, CELERY, ZUCCHINI AND MUSHROOMS should be perfectly firm with no soft or discolored spots. Peppers should be glossy and the other vegetables should have a sheen. Buy only as much of these vegetables as you'll use in 4 or 5 days. Store cucumbers and peppers unwrapped in a covered crisper; store the other vegetables in a paper bag inside a plastic bag in the fridge. Vegetables should be washed and cut up as close to serving time as possible. Mushrooms should just be wiped with a damp cloth.

AVOCADOS If you want to eat an avocado the day you buy it, look for one that "yields" all over when gently pressed. If you want an avocado suitable for the next day or so, look for one that is just starting to yield at the neck end and is firm elsewhere. Store them at room temperature and if one is slow to ripen, you can help it along by enclosing it in a paper bag with a ripe apple or banana.

VEGETABLES TO BE COOKED Beans, asparagus, artichokes and snow, sugar or ordinary peas should be firm and crisp with an almost moist-looking sheen. Corn should be brightly colored and glossy. Ideally, these vegetables should be bought only a day or two ahead of use. Store asparagus by standing bunches upright in 1 to 2 inches of water in a jar or other container, drop a plastic bag over the top and store in the fridge. Store the other vegetables in paper bags enclosed in plastic bags in the fridge. Cook them only until they are on the firm side of tender and as close as possible to serving.

CARROTS AND BEETS These and other root vegetables can be bought up to 4 or 5 days ahead and stored in a covered crisper. They are often used raw, finely sliced or grated. If cooked, they are best steamed until just tender and eaten freshly cooked and just warm.

SALAD DRESSINGS

A crisp salad tossed lightly with the perfect amount of dressing can be a match made in heaven. But a salad can be ruined if it is drowned in a strong dressing. The key ingredients in a basic dressing are olive oil and vinegar, and all cooks agree that you should try to use the best quality oil and vinegar you can find. The better the quality, the better your salad will taste. Use a wine vinegar—red, white or perhaps a sherry vinegar. Good wine vinegar has been aged and this should be indicated on the label.

THE TWO GREAT BASIC DRESSINGS ARE FRENCH DRESSING (VINAIGRETTE) AND MAYONNAISE AND TOGETHER THEY FORM THE BASIS FOR MOST SALAD DRESSINGS.

VINAIGRETTE This classic salad dressing is made by mixing together a good wine vinegar or fresh lemon juice, a good olive or nut oil (or a mixture of these two), a dollop of French mustard and a pinch of salt and pepper. This can take on many variations and additions, changing its name along the way to Italian dressing (with garlic, pepper, onion and herbs), roquefort (with crumbled roquefort whisked in) and salsa verde (garlic, herbs and anchovy). You can drizzle a vinaigrette dressing on a whole range of hot or cold salads.

MAYONNAISE This dressing can be as simple as combining egg yolks, vinegar, olive oil, salt and pepper, or it can morph into various other guises with the additions of garlic (aïoli); a dollop of mustard (mustard mayonnaise); gherkins, capers and herbs (tartare sauce); or mustard, gherkins, herbs and anchovy (remoulade). Nothing beats homemade mayonnaise, although many of the expensive ones, sold under chef's names, are also good. Commercial mayonnaise whisked together with your own vinaigrette makes a nice, creamy dressing for lighter-flavored salads.

waldorf salad

¾ cup mayonnaise (see page 118)
¼ cup lemon juice
5 stalks celery, trimmed, sliced thickly
2 medium red apples, sliced thinly
1 small red onion, sliced thinly
1 cup roasted walnuts
1 cup loosely packed fresh flat-leaf parsley leaves

1 Combine mayonnaise and juice in large bowl, add remaining ingredients; toss gently to combine.

nutritional count per serving 35.7g total fat (3.1g saturated fat); 443 cal; 22.4g carbohydrate; 5.8g protein; 6.3g fiber

chicken salad

1 quart boiling water
1 quart chicken stock
1½ pounds chicken breast filets
1 long French bread stick, sliced thinly
2 tablespoons olive oil
½ cup mayonnaise (see page 118)
½ cup sour cream
2 tablespoons lemon juice
4 stalks celery, trimmed, sliced thinly

1 medium white onion, chopped finely
3 large dill pickles, sliced thinly
2 tablespoons finely chopped fresh flat-leaf parsley
1 tablespoon finely chopped fresh tarragon
1 large butter lettuce, leaves separated

1 Bring the water and stock to a boil in large frying pan; poach chicken, covered, about 10 minutes or until cooked through. Cool chicken in liquid 10 minutes; slice thinly. Discard liquid.

2 Meanwhile, preheat broiler. Brush both sides of bread slices with oil; toast under broiler until browned lightly both sides.

3 Whisk mayonnaise, cream and juice in small bowl.

4 Place chicken in large bowl with celery, onion, pickle and herbs; toss gently to combine.

5 Place lettuce leaves on serving platter; top with salad and bread, drizzle with mayonnaise mixture.

nutritional count per serving 41.1g total fat (12.5g saturated fat); 802 cal; 53.3g carbohydrate; 51.9g protein; 6.5g fiber

[opposite] waldorf salad

tuna salad

PREP TIME 15 MINS • SERVES 4

There are many different types of canned tuna available these days. In this salad we prefer to use simple, good-quality tuna in springwater and let the fresh herbs do the talking.

¼ cup olive oil
2 tablespoons white wine vinegar
1 tablespoon lemon juice
2 teaspoons finely chopped fresh basil
2 teaspoons finely chopped
   fresh oregano
1 clove garlic, crushed
1 fresh long red chili, chopped finely
1 medium iceberg lettuce,
   cut into wedges

12-ounce can tuna in springwater,
   drained, flaked
8 ounces cherry tomatoes, halved
1 medium avocado,
   chopped coarsely
1 Lebanese cucumber,
   sliced thinly
1 small red onion,
   sliced thinly

1 Place oil, vinegar, juice, herbs, garlic and chili in screw-top jar; shake well.
2 Place lettuce wedges on serving plate; top with remaining ingredients. Drizzle with dressing.

nutritional count per serving 26.1g total fat (4.9g saturated fat); 357 cal; 4.6g carbohydrate; 24.4g protein; 4.9g fiber

fattoush

PREP + COOK TIME 20 MINS • SERVES 4

This traditional Lebanese salad is made interesting by satisfyingly crunchy pieces of pita bread sprinkled throughout.

Add some freshly chopped iceberg lettuce to any leftover salad to boost its volume and crispness.

2 large pita breads
⅓ cup olive oil
2 tablespoons lemon juice
1 clove garlic, crushed
3 red radishes,
   trimmed, sliced thinly
½ small daikon,
   grated coarsely
2 medium tomatoes,
   chopped coarsely

1 Lebanese cucumber,
   chopped coarsely
1 small red onion,
   sliced thinly
1 small green pepper,
   chopped coarsely
1 cup loosely packed fresh
   mint leaves
1 cup loosely packed fresh
   flat-leaf parsley leaves

1 Preheat broiler to hot.
2 Place bread on oven tray; broil until crisp. Break bread into pieces.
3 Whisk oil, juice and garlic together in large bowl. Mix in half the bread and remaining ingredients.
4 Serve fattoush sprinkled with remaining bread.

nutritional count per serving 19.7g total fat (2.7g saturated fat); 327 cal; 28.1g carbohydrate; 6.8g protein; 5.8g fiber

[opposite] tuna salad

coleslaw

Coleslaw is a nutritious and inexpensive alternative to regular mixed green salad. To ensure your coleslaw remains crisp and fresh for as long as possible, keep everything (including ingredients and equipment) very cold during preparation.

½ small cabbage, shredded finely
1 medium carrot, grated coarsely
4 green onions, sliced thinly
½ cup mayonnaise (see page 118)
1 tablespoon lemon juice

1 Combine ingredients in large bowl.

nutritional count per serving 8.1g total fat (1g saturated fat); 125 cal; 8.8g carbohydrate; 2g protein; 4.5g fiber

tabbouleh

Traditional tabbouleh is made with a great deal of chopped parsley and varying smaller amounts of bulgur, green onion and mint. Go easy on the bulgur: too much and the completed dish will be overly heavy instead of fluffy and light as intended.

¼ cup bulgur
3 medium tomatoes
3 cups coarsely chopped fresh flat-leaf parsley
3 green onions, chopped finely
¼ cup coarsely chopped fresh mint
¼ cup lemon juice
¼ cup olive oil

1 Place bulgur in medium shallow bowl. Halve tomatoes, scoop pulp from tomato over bulgur. Chop tomato flesh finely; spread over bulgur. Cover; refrigerate 1 hour.
2 Place bulgur mixture in large bowl with remaining ingredients; toss gently to combine.

nutritional count per serving 14.1g total fat (2g saturated fat); 189 cal; 9.2g carbohydrate; 3.4g protein; 5.6g fiber

[1] coleslaw
[2] tabbouleh
[3] oak leaf and mixed herb salad [page 102]
[4] thai beef salad [page 102]

oak-leaf and mixed herb salad

1 green oak-leaf lettuce,
   leaves separated
¼ cup coarsely chopped fresh chives
½ cup firmly packed fresh
   flat-leaf parsley leaves
½ cup firmly packed fresh
   chervil leaves

dijon vinaigrette
2 tablespoons olive oil
2 tablespoons white wine vinegar
1 tablespoon dijon mustard
2 teaspoons white sugar

1 Place ingredients for dijon vinaigrette in screw-top jar; shake well.
2 Place salad ingredients in medium bowl with dressing; toss gently to combine.
nutritional count per serving 6.2g total fat (0.9g saturated fat); 69 cal;
2g carbohydrate; 0.7g protein; 1.1g fiber

thai beef salad

In recent years, the Western world has embraced Thai cuisine with great enthusiasm, and this char-grilled salad, found on Thai menus under the name of yum nuah, deliciously explains exactly why.

¼ cup fish sauce
¼ cup lime juice
1 pound beef rump steak
3 Lebanese cucumbers,
   seeded, sliced thinly
4 fresh small red Thai chilies,
   sliced thinly
4 green onions, sliced thinly
8 ounces cherry tomatoes, halved

¼ cup firmly packed fresh
   Vietnamese mint leaves
½ cup firmly packed fresh
   coriander leaves
½ cup firmly packed fresh
   Thai basil leaves
1 tablespoon grated palm sugar
2 teaspoons soy sauce
1 clove garlic, crushed

1 Combine 2 tablespoons of the fish sauce and 1 tablespoon of the juice
in medium bowl with beef; toss beef to coat in marinade. Cover; refrigerate
3 hours or overnight.
2 Drain beef; discard marinade. Cook beef on heated oiled grill pan (or grill or
barbecue) until cooked as desired. Cover beef, stand 5 minutes; slice beef thinly.
3 Meanwhile, combine cucumber, chili, onion, tomato and herbs in large bowl.
4 Place sugar, soy sauce, garlic, remaining fish sauce and remaining juice in
screw-top jar; shake well.
5 Add beef and dressing to salad; toss gently to combine.
nutritional count per serving 8.7g total fat (3.8g saturated fat); 236 cal;
8.2g carbohydrate; 30.6g protein; 3.4g fiber

pasta salad

Pasta salad is another one of those favorites that has as many versions as there are cooks who make it. Because it's eaten cold, it's ideal for picnics or lunch boxes, and as a side salad to grilled chops for a simple midweek meal.

8 ounces orecchiette

2 tablespoons drained sun-dried tomatoes, chopped coarsely

1 small red onion, sliced thinly

1 small green pepper, sliced thinly

½ cup coarsely chopped fresh flat-leaf parsley

sun-dried tomato dressing

1 tablespoon sun-dried tomato pesto

1 tablespoon white wine vinegar

2 tablespoons olive oil

1 Cook pasta in large saucepan of boiling water, uncovered, until just tender; drain. Rinse under cold water; drain.

2 Place ingredients for sun-dried tomato dressing in screw-top jar; shake well.

3 Place pasta in large bowl with remaining ingredients and dressing; toss gently to combine.

nutritional count per serving 12g total fat (1.9g saturated fat); 336 cal; 46g carbohydrate; 8.8g protein; 3.6g fiber

greek salad

This crunchy salad is found on tables all over the world, not just in Greece. The only obligatory ingredients are feta, tomato and onion; use your imagination and add capers, hard-boiled eggs, and red or green peppers—as long as it offers "bite", the sky's the limit.

¼ cup olive oil

1 tablespoon lemon juice

1 tablespoon white wine vinegar

1 tablespoon finely chopped fresh oregano

1 clove garlic, crushed

3 medium tomatoes, cut into wedges

2 Lebanese cucumbers, chopped coarsely

1 small red onion, sliced thinly

1 small red pepper, sliced thinly

½ cup pitted black olives

6 ounces feta cheese, chopped coarsely

1 Whisk oil, juice, vinegar, oregano and garlic in large bowl.

2 Add remaining ingredients to large bowl; toss gently to combine.

nutritional count per serving 25.8g total fat (9.6g saturated fat); 325 cal; 10.8g carbohydrate; 11.5g protein; 3.2g fiber

classic caesar salad

Named after Caesar Cardini, the Italian-American who tossed the first caesar in Mexico during the 1920s, this salad always contains fresh croûtons, crisp romaine lettuce leaves, lightly boiled eggs, lemon juice, olive oil, Worcestershire and parmesan but no one ingredient should dominate.

½ loaf ciabatta
1 clove garlic, crushed
⅓ cup olive oil
2 eggs
3 baby romaine lettuces, trimmed, leaves separated
1 cup flaked parmesan cheese

caesar dressing
1 clove garlic, crushed
1 tablespoon dijon mustard
2 tablespoons lemon juice
2 teaspoons Worcestershire sauce
2 tablespoons olive oil

1 Preheat oven to 350°F/325°F fan-forced.
2 Cut bread into ¾-inch cubes; combine garlic and oil in large bowl with bread. Toast bread on oven tray until croûtons are browned.
3 Place ingredients for caesar dressing in screw-top jar; shake well.
4 Bring water to a boil in small saucepan, add eggs; cover pan tightly, remove from heat. Remove eggs from water after 2 minutes. When cool enough to handle, break eggs into large bowl; add lettuce, mixing gently so egg coats leaves.
5 Add cheese, croûtons and dressing to bowl; toss gently to combine.
nutritional count per serving 39.1g total fat (9.1g saturated fat); 566 cal; 33.1g carbohydrate; 18.4g protein; 5.6g fiber

mixed cabbage coleslaw

Elongated, with pale green, crinkly leaves, Napa cabbage is the most common cabbage used throughout Southeast Asia. It can be shredded or chopped and eaten raw, braised, steamed or stir-fried.

You need about half a small head for this recipe, a quarter of a savoy cabbage and a quarter of a red cabbage.

⅓ cup olive oil
2 tablespoons cider vinegar
2 teaspoons dijon mustard
2 cups finely shredded green cabbage
2 cups finely shredded red cabbage

2 cups Napa cabbage finely shredded
1 medium carrot, grated coarsely
4 green onions, sliced thinly

1 Whisk oil, vinegar and mustard in large bowl, add remaining ingredients; toss gently to combine.
nutritional count per serving 18.4g total fat (2.6g saturated fat); 200 cal; 4.5g carbohydrate; 2.4g protein; 4.7g fiber

[opposite] classic caesar salad

Salad greens

The meaning of salad has expanded considerably over the years, as has the variety of leaves available to us. When crisp, moist and fresh, these lettuces give us the essential ingredients to make a truly great salad that deserves the spotlight. This can be a light, simple dish or a satisfying salade composé.

MIZUNA
A mustard green from Japan where it is traditionally used in soups and other cooked main dishes. It's often found in a mesclun, but its mild, aromatic jagged green leaves can also stand alone. Refrigerate in a plastic bag, unwashed, for up to five days.

WATERCRESS
Sprigs of dark-green watercress look pretty in a bowl and give salads and sandwiches a fresh, peppery tang. Lovely dressed with walnut or hazelnut oil and lemon juice, and a sprinkling of nuts over the top. Both summer and winter varieties are available.

CORAL LETTUCE
A soft baby green with either red or green tightly crinkled leaves. Its leaves have a delicate, sweet flavor, so they're perfect with a mixture of lettuces. You'll often find coral as part of a mesclun salad. Use within two days of purchase and dress lightly.

ROMAINE LETTUCE
Also known as cos, this spear-shaped, crispy lettuce is quite robust in flavor and goes well with rich dressings and substantial companions like egg or bacon. Its coarse outer leaves are often discarded. Baby romaine, a smaller form, has less waste.

LAMB'S LETTUCE (MACHE)
Sometimes called corn lettuce, this salad green has long, spoon-shaped dark leaves that resemble the shape of a lamb's tongue. They have a distinctive, tangy flavor and work best with a light dressing. They can also be cooked. Available in the cooler months.

CURLY ENDIVE
Also known as frisée, curly endive belongs to the chicory family and has its characteristic bitterness played against grassy freshness. Particularly good with beets and also used in mesclun. It will keep in the refrigerator, unwashed, for five days.

Q&A

I love salads and eat them year round as a side dish or as a main meal in the warmer months. I'm constantly told, however, they're just 99 percent water. Is this true or are salad leaves a good source of nutrients?

Most lettuces are about 95 percent water, but some types are very high in nutrients. Watercress, for instance, contains a substance called isothiocyanates, shown to significantly improve the health of smokers' lungs and even prevent cancer. It's packed with vitamins, iron, calcium, phosphorus, potassium, and lutein, as well as mustard oil. All you need to eat is one small bowl a day to get the benefits of this peppery leaf. Arugula, radicchio, romaine and endive are other nutrient-rich lettuces. Generally, dark-colored, bitter-tasting leaves contain more beta-carotene and other antioxidants, as well as the green pigment called chlorophyll, known to purify the blood.

OAK-LEAF LETTUCE
The curly leaves vary from reddish-brown to pale green and resemble the shape of oak leaves. This popular variety of lettuce has a soft texture with a sweet, mild flavor. It is an ideal lettuce to grow because the leaves can be harvested one at a time.

MIGNONETTE LETTUCE
This is a small, soft-leafed lettuce, but crisper and glossier than coral or oak-leaf. It has a good grassy flavor with just a delicate suggestion of bitterness. Its leaves vary from red to green and mix well with romaines, or bland-tasting lettuces such as iceberg.

BELGIAN ENDIVE (CHICORY, WITLOF)
Crisp, tightly furled endive tastes mild and fresh with a touch of bitterness. It is grown in the dark to keep the leaves white and minimize bitterness. It comes in red- and green-tipped varieties, and is good served with vegetables such as beets and asparagus.

ARUGULA
You'll also see this sold as rucola or rocket. It's part of the mustard family, so it's no wonder it has such a strong, peppery, mustard-like flavor. Good with char-grilled vegetables, strong cheeses and balsamic vinegar, and as a pizza topping. Use within a day.

RADICCHIO
A red-leafed Italian chicory with a refreshing bitter taste that's appreciated both raw and grilled. Its antioxidant levels rival those of blueberries. Comes in varieties named after their places of origin, such as round-headed Verona or long-headed Treviso.

MESCLUN
Sold as a pre-mixed pile or bouquet of baby greens, which may include coral, mignonette, oak-leaf or butter lettuce, arugula, spinach, curly endive, mizuna and/or radicchio. If buying loose, grab more than you need and discard the tired-looking leaves.

vietnamese chicken salad

1 pound chicken breast filets

1 large carrot

½ cup rice wine vinegar

2 teaspoons salt

2 tablespoons superfine sugar

1 medium white onion,
  sliced thinly

1½ cups bean sprouts

2 cups finely shredded
  savoy cabbage

¼ cup firmly packed fresh
  Vietnamese mint leaves

½ cup firmly packed fresh
  coriander leaves

1 tablespoon crushed roasted peanuts

2 tablespoons fried shallots

vietnamese dressing

2 tablespoons fish sauce

¼ cup water

2 tablespoons superfine sugar

2 tablespoons lime juice

1 clove garlic, crushed

1 Place chicken in medium saucepan of boiling water; return to a boil. Reduce heat; simmer, uncovered, about 10 minutes or until cooked through. Cool chicken in poaching liquid 10 minutes; discard liquid. Shred chicken coarsely.

2 Meanwhile, cut carrot into matchstick-sized pieces. Combine carrot, vinegar, salt and sugar in large bowl, cover; stand 5 minutes. Add onion, cover; stand 5 minutes. Add sprouts, cover; stand 3 minutes. Drain pickled vegetables; discard liquid.

3 Place ingredients for Vietnamese dressing in screw-top jar; shake well.

4 Place pickled vegetables in large bowl with chicken, cabbage, mint, coriander and dressing; toss gently to combine. Sprinkle with nuts and shallots.

nutritional count per serving 8.9g total fat (2.3g saturated fat); 304 cal; 24.3g carbohydrate; 31g protein; 5.1g fiber

Q&A

I prefer to use skinless breast filets for recipes that call for chicken as it's quick and low in fat. But whether I'm poaching or grilling, I always end up with a tough, dry and stringy filet. What am I doing wrong?

When it comes to chicken filets, you need to be aware that different rules apply for moist-heat cooking (poaching or baking in parchment) and dry-heat cooking (roasting, grilling, frying). When using moist heat, as in poaching, keep the heat low and cook for a longer period of time. Grilled chicken breasts cook in 8-10 minutes, while poached breasts cook in about 20 minutes (this includes the cooling period in the pan). One way to ensure juicy, moist chicken filets is to brine them before cooking as the salt draws moisture into the cells. To brine chicken, place breasts in a solution of salt and water for 1 hour in the refrigerator, then rinse away excess salt.

caprese salad

This simple salad is native to Campania, the largely agricultural region of Italy that's also home to "mozzarella di bufala", the fresh, stretched, buffalo milk cheese that's a key component to this classic salad. Buffalo mozzarella is available locally, but it can be hard to find and expensive, so we used fresh, good-quality bocconcini here with great results.

3 large egg tomatoes, sliced thinly
10 ounces bocconcini cheese, drained, sliced thinly
2 tablespoons olive oil
¼ cup firmly packed fresh basil leaves, torn

1 Overlap slices of tomato and cheese on serving platter.
2 Drizzle with oil; sprinkle with basil.
nutritional count per serving 20.6g total fat (8.8g saturated fat); 246 cal; 1.6g carbohydrate; 13.6g protein; 1.1g fiber

green papaya salad

4-inch stick fresh lemon grass
1 small green papaya
2 cups bean sprouts
1 cup coarsely grated
    fresh coconut
¾ cup loosely packed fresh
    coriander leaves
¾ cup loosely packed fresh
    mint leaves
2 shallots, sliced thinly
½ cup roasted unsalted
    peanuts, chopped coarsely

chili citrus dressing
¼ cup lime juice
¼ cup lemon juice
1 tablespoon grated palm sugar
2 teaspoons fish sauce
1 fresh small red thai chili,
    chopped finely

1 Soak lemon grass in medium heatproof bowl of boiling water about 4 minutes or until tender. Drain; slice lemon grass thinly.
2 Meanwhile, make chili citrus dressing.
3 Peel papaya, quarter lengthways, discard seeds; grate papaya coarsely.
4 Place lemon grass, dressing and papaya in large bowl with sprouts, coconut, herbs and shallots; toss gently to combine. Serve salad sprinkled with nuts.
chili citrus dressing Place ingredients in screw-top jar; shake well.
nutritional count per serving 15.5g total fat (7.3g saturated fat); 251 cal; 16.3g carbohydrate; 7.9g protein; 8.4g fiber

[opposite] caprese salad

salade composé

Literally meaning "composed salad", the ingredients in this dish are layered on top of each other, rather than being tossed together, and the dressing is drizzled over the top.

1 small French bread stick
2 cloves garlic, crushed
¼ cup olive oil
6 strips thick-sliced bacon
5 ounces mesclun
6 medium egg tomatoes,
    sliced thinly
4 hard-boiled eggs,
    halved lengthways

red wine vinaigrette
¼ cup red wine vinegar
1 tablespoon dijon mustard
⅓ cup extra virgin olive oil

1 Preheat broiler.
2 Cut bread into ½-inch slices. Brush both sides with combined garlic and oil; toast under preheated broiler.
3 Cook bacon in large frying pan until crisp; drain on absorbent paper.
4 Meanwhile, place ingredients for red wine vinaigrette in screw-top jar; shake well.
5 Layer bread and bacon in large bowl with mesclun and tomato, top with egg; drizzle with vinaigrette.
nutritional count per serving 51.8g total fat (11.1g saturated fat); 684 cal; 23.4g carbohydrate; 30.5g protein; 3.9g fiber

potato salad

Everyone has a different opinion as to what a potato salad should be– hot or cold, creamy or dressed with vinaigrette, with bacon bits or simply sprinkled with fresh herbs–but you'd be hard-pressed to find one you didn't like. Cover the saucepan while potatoes are cooking, but lift the lid and give them an occasional gentle stir to move them around. Don't overcook them or they will break apart.

4 pounds potatoes, peeled
2 tablespoons cider vinegar
1 cup mayonnaise (see page 118)
4 green onions, sliced thinly
¼ cup finely chopped fresh flat-leaf parsley

1 Cover potatoes with cold water in large saucepan; bring to a boil. Reduce heat; simmer, covered, until tender. Drain; cut into 1-inch pieces. Spread potato on tray, sprinkle with vinegar; refrigerate until cold.
2 Place potato in large bowl with mayonnaise, onion and parsley; toss gently to combine.
nutritional count per serving 30.4g total fat (4.1g saturated fat); 422 cal; 29g carbohydrate; 6.2g protein; 3.7g fiber

[opposite] salade composé

endive, pear and blue cheese salad

Endive, also known as witlof, is a perfect addition to this crunchy salad. Its bitter-yet-creamy flavor goes beautifully with the sharp taste of the blue cheese, and its crisp robust nature makes it a perfect candidate for the rich dressing.

2 red endive, trimmed, leaves separated
2 yellow endive, trimmed, leaves separated
1 medium pear, sliced thinly
¾ cup toasted pecans, coarsely chopped
blue cheese dressing
⅓ cup buttermilk
3 ounces blue cheese, crumbled
1 tablespoon lemon juice

1 Make blue cheese dressing.
2 Place salad ingredients in large bowl; toss gently to combine.
3 Serve salad drizzled with dressing.
blue cheese dressing Whisk ingredients in small bowl until smooth.
nutritional count per serving 24.9g total fat (6.5g saturated fat); 309 cal; 9.9g carbohydrate; 9.5g protein; 5.3g fiber

salade niçoise

The original French salade niçoise was created with the finest local produce from Provence—vine-ripened tomatoes, piquant caperberries, tiny, firm black olives, hand-picked baby beans and fresh tuna caught just off the coast. Our version has adapted a modern approach more suitable to our hectic lifestyle; if you wish, however, instead of using canned tuna, char-grill four 6-ounce tuna steaks briefly and center one of them on each beautiful salad arrangement.

6 ounces baby green beans, trimmed
2 tablespoons olive oil
1 tablespoon lemon juice
2 tablespoons white wine vinegar
4 medium tomatoes,
    cut into wedges
4 hard-boiled eggs, quartered
12-ounce can tuna in springwater,
    drained, flaked
½ cup drained caperberries, rinsed
½ cup pitted small black olives
¼ cup firmly packed fresh
    flat-leaf parsley leaves
14-ounce can drained whole baby
    new potatoes, rinsed, halved

1 Boil, steam or microwave beans until tender; drain. Rinse under cold water; drain.
2 Whisk oil, juice and vinegar in large bowl; add beans and remaining ingredients, toss gently to combine.
nutritional count per serving 16.9g total fat (3.7g saturated fat); 364 cal; 19.5g carbohydrate; 30.9g protein; 5.2g fiber

french dressing

Combine ⅓ cup white wine vinegar, 2 teaspoons dijon mustard and ½ teaspoon sugar in small bowl. Gradually add ⅔ cup olive oil in thin, steady stream, whisking constantly until mixture thickens.

nutritional count per tablespoon 12.2g total fat (1.7g saturated fat); 109 cal; 0.2g carbohydrate; 0g protein; 0g fiber

italian dressing

Place ⅔ cup olive oil, ⅓ cup lemon juice, 1 crushed garlic clove, 2 teaspoons finely chopped fresh oregano, 2 teaspoons finely chopped fresh basil and 2 teaspoons superfine sugar in screw-top jar; shake well.

nutritional count per tablespoon 12.2g total fat (1.7g saturated fat); 112 cal; 0.9g carbohydrate; 0.1g protein; 0.1g fiber

sesame soy dressing

Combine 1 tablespoon toasted sesame seeds, 1 tablespoon sesame oil, 2 finely chopped shallots, 1 tablespoon kecap manis and ¼ cup lime juice in small bowl.

nutritional count per tablespoon 1.4g total fat (0.2g saturated fat); 15 cal; 0.2g carbohydrate; 0.3g protein; 0.1g fiber

ranch dressing

Whisk ½ cup mayonnaise, ¼ cup buttermilk, 1 tablespoon white wine vinegar, 1 finely chopped small brown onion, 1 crushed garlic clove, 1 tablespoon finely chopped fresh chives, 1 tablespoon finely chopped fresh flat-leaf parsley and ¼ teaspoon sweet paprika in small bowl until combined.

nutritional count per tablespoon 4.2g total fat (0.5g saturated fat); 52 cal; 3.2g carbohydrate; 0.5g protein; 0.2g fiber

balsamic and garlic dressing

Whisk 2 tablespoons balsamic vinegar, ¼ cup lemon juice, 1 crushed garlic clove and ¾ cup olive oil in small bowl until combined.

nutritional count per tablespoon 10.9g total fat (1.5g saturated fat); 97 cal; 0.1g carbohydrate; 0g protein; 0g fiber

lemon and macadamia dressing

Whisk ½ cup macadamia oil, ⅓ cup finely chopped roasted macadamia nuts, 2 teaspoons finely grated lemon rind, 2 tablespoons lemon juice and 1 teaspoon superfine sugar in small bowl until combined.

nutritional count per tablespoon 12.4g total fat (1.8g saturated fat); 114 cal; 0.6g carbohydrate; 0.3g protein; 0.2g fiber

red berry vinaigrette

Blend or process ¼ cup red wine vinegar, ½ cup olive oil, 5 ounces fresh raspberries and ¼ cup whole berry cranberry sauce until smooth. Push dressing through fine sieve into small bowl.

nutritional count per tablespoon 9.5g total fat (1.3g saturated fat); 100 cal; 3.4g carbohydrate; 0.2g protein; 0.7g fiber

thousand island dressing

Combine ½ cup mayonnaise, 1½ tablespoons tomato sauce, ½ finely grated small white onion, 8 finely chopped pimiento-stuffed green olives and ½ finely chopped small red pepper in small bowl.

nutritional count per tablespoon 4.3g total fat (0.5g saturated fat); 54 cal; 3.6g carbohydrate; 0.3g protein; 0.4g fiber

green goddess dressing

Combine 1 cup mayonnaise, 2 finely chopped anchovy filets, 2 thinly sliced green onions, 2 teaspoons finely chopped fresh flat-leaf parsley, 2 teaspoons finely chopped fresh chives, 2 teaspoons finely chopped fresh tarragon and 2 teaspoons cider vinegar in small bowl.

nutritional count per tablespoon 24.2g total fat (2.9g saturated fat); 279 cal; 14.6g carbohydrate; 1.2g protein; 0.6g fiber

caesar dressing

Bring water to a boil in small saucepan; using slotted spoon, carefully lower 1 whole egg into water. Cover pan tightly, remove from heat; after 1 minute remove egg from water using slotted spoon. When cool enough to handle, break egg into large bowl; whisk in 2 crushed garlic cloves, ½ teaspoon dijon mustard and 2 finely chopped anchovy filets. Gradually add 1 cup olive oil in thin, steady stream; whisking until mixture thickens slightly. Stir in 2 tablespoons lemon juice.

nutritional count per tablespoon 13g total fat (1.9g saturated fat); 118 cal; 0.1g carbohydrate; 0.5g protein; 0.1g fiber

russian dressing

Boil, steam or microwave 1 large unpeeled red beet until tender; drain, reserving ¼ cup of the cooking liquid. When cool enough to handle, peel then chop beet coarsely. Blend or process beet with 2 tablespoons coarsely chopped pickled onions, 1 tablespoon drained, rinsed capers, ½ cup sour cream and reserved liquid until smooth.

nutritional count per tablespoon 14g total fat (9.2g saturated fat); 163 cal; 7g carbohydrate; 1.8g protein; 1.8g fiber

honey mustard dressing

Whisk ½ cup mayonnaise, ¼ cup cider vinegar, 1 tablespoon honey and 2 teaspoons wholegrain mustard in small bowl until combined.

nutritional count per tablespoon 4.1g total fat (0.5g saturated fat); 55 cal; 4.5g carbohydrate; 0.2g protein; 0.1g fiber

citrus and poppy seed dressing

2 teaspoons finely grated orange rind
¼ cup orange juice
2 tablespoons apple cider vinegar
1 tablespoon poppy seeds
⅓ cup sour cream
2 teaspoons honey mustard
¼ cup water

1 Whisk rind, juice, vinegar, seeds, sour cream and mustard in small bowl. Add water; whisk until combined.

nutritional count per tablespoon 3.1g total fat (1.8g saturated fat); 33 cal; 0.7g carbohydrate; 0.4g protein; 0.2g fiber

serving ideas this dressing goes well with salmon and pasta salad; coleslaw; green leaf salad; and steamed asparagus.

classic mayonnaise

Olive oil, particularly extra virgin, can be too heavy for whipping up into a good, stiff mayonnaise. It does however, offer a beautiful, rich flavor. We use two-thirds extra light olive oil, and one-third regular (or extra virgin if you like) to get the best of both worlds.

Mayonnaise can be stored in the refrigerator for up to 3 days.

2 egg yolks
½ teaspoon salt
1 teaspoon dijon mustard
⅔ cup extra light olive oil
⅓ cup olive oil
1 tablespoon white wine vinegar
1 tablespoon lemon juice

1 Combine egg yolks, salt and mustard in medium bowl. Gradually add oils in a thin, steady stream, whisking constantly until mixture thickens. Stir in vinegar and juice.

nutritional count per tablespoon 19.2g total fat (2.9g saturated fat); 172 cal; 0g carbohydrate; 0.5g protein; 0g fiber

[opposite] classic mayonnaise

SOUPS

Soups

Soup is one of the world's best-loved foods and it's easy to see why: made fresh, using flavorsome ingredients and served, steaming and aromatic in generous bowls, it is both nourishing and satisfying, easy to share, easy to digest and deeply soothing, especially in winter.

There are many types of soup—from cleansing thin broths, to velvety smooth elixirs, to seriously hearty meals in a bowl. Some soups focus on a single ingredient, while others bring together a heady combination of flavors and textures. Traditionally, soup was served as the first of several courses in a meal, but these days we're just as likely to serve it as the main dish rather than a mere opener to a meal. In this chapter, you'll find recipes for some of the world's most popular soups, ranging from the robust variety to the more delicate, lighter ones suitable for serving in the traditional role as the first course.

Making a soup from scratch is not hard, but it can take a little time, which is a precious commodity for most of us, especially during the work week. So try to make your soup on the weekend and reap the benefits during the week.

And don't limit your soup-making to just the winter months. While it is an unbeatable heart-warming food in cold weather, soup can also be a refreshing starter to a summer meal, whether it's in the form of an ice cold gazpacho, cool and elegant vichyssoise or a spicy and restorative tom yum goong.

THE STARTING POINT

A QUALITY STOCK IS AN INDISPENSABLE INGREDIENT THAT GIVES LIFE AND VIGOR TO MANY OF OUR CULINARY STAPLES—SOUPS, CASSEROLES, GRAVIES AND SAUCES. NOT ALL SOUPS ARE MADE WITH STOCK, BUT MANY RELY ON IT AND THE ADDITION OF HOMEMADE STOCK CAN ELEVATE A SOUP FROM DELICIOUS TO SUBLIME.

STOCKS ARE FLAVORSOME LIQUIDS THAT CAN BE MEAT-BASED OR VEGETARIAN. MEAT STOCKS ARE MADE BY SIMMERING MEAT BONES (USUALLY BEEF OR VEAL) AND THEIR TRIMMINGS, WITH AROMATIC VEGETABLES AND HERBS TO EXTRACT THEIR FLAVOR.

CHICKEN AND FISH STOCKS ARE MADE IN THE SAME WAY. VEGETARIAN STOCKS ARE MADE FROM SIMMERING VEGETABLES AND HERBS ALONE.

MAKING YOUR OWN STOCK IS EASY AND ECONOMICAL, AND ONCE MOST COOKS HAVE MADE THEIR FIRST BATCH, THEY FIND THAT KEEPING A SUPPLY OF HOMEMADE STOCK ON HAND QUICKLY BECOMES A KITCHEN MUST-HAVE. THOUGH IT DOES TAKE TIME TO CREATE, IT ISN'T A COMPLICATED PROCESS AND THE RESULTS ARE WORTH IT. MAKE A GENEROUS BATCH SO YOU CAN FREEZE IT IN USER-FRIENDLY PORTIONS.

TO SERVE

While the wafts of steaming soup are usually enough to beckon your guests, the addition of a simple, well-matched garnish makes the bowl look all the more inviting. Keep it simple: a sprinkling of chopped parsley, chives or other fresh herb is all it takes to bring your soup to life. Dill is the perfect complement to borscht, fennel is good for fish soups. Cream soups can be topped with a small swirl of cream plus some chopped chives. A few thin shavings of parmesan cheese are delicious on thick vegetable soups. Potato and pumpkin soups look good with a few crisp croûtons in the center (see below). And for chilled soups, one or two slices of lemon or lime, cut paper-thin, or some finely shredded lettuce or a tiny bouquet of watercress adds a sparkle.

ON THE SIDE

A generous serving of good-quality bread is an ideal partner for most soups. Warm savory muffins or toast topped with grilled cheese are also popular companions and help to turn a bowl of soup into a satisfying meal. If you are serving an elegant soup as a first course, then melba toast is the perfect accompaniment. To make, lightly toast slices of white sandwich bread, cut off the crust, and with a thin, sharp knife, split each slice of toast through the middle. Cut into small triangles and bake in a moderately hot oven until golden, checking often so they don't get too brown. If you're not using them immediately, you can store them in an airtight container and reheat briefly in a moderate oven.

HOW TO MAKE CROUTONS

REMOVE THE CRUST FROM THICKLY SLICED BREAD, THEN CUT INTO SMALL CUBES.

FRY BREAD CUBES IN A MIXTURE OF OIL AND BUTTER UNTIL GOLDEN.

DRAIN CROUTONS ON ABSORBENT PAPER. THEN STORE IN AN AIRTIGHT CONTAINER.

BRIEFLY REHEAT CROUTONS IN A MODERATE OVEN.

STOCK BASICS

Meat and chicken stocks require hours of simmering to extract the gelatin from the bones for a rich base flavor—brown the meat first to help enhance colors and flavors. Fish and vegetable stocks require a short amount of simmering: you won't extract any more flavor if you cook them longer and, in fact, if cooked for too long, they can lose their freshness. Vegetables can also be browned before simmering for a deeper color and flavor.

After simmering, strain out the solids and pour the liquid into a bowl. Refrigerate the liquid until chilled, then scrape the solidified fat layer from the top. Store beef, veal, chicken and vegetable stocks in the fridge for 2 to 3 days, fish stock for 2 days, and all of them can be frozen for months.

A WORD ON COMMERCIAL STOCKS The packaged liquid stocks available in supermarkets are high-quality products and it's worth keeping a supply in the pantry. The same goes for the jars of concentrated stock available from delis, some butchers and gourmet food stores. Be aware that these products are inherently salty so adjust final seasonings accordingly. The advantage of homemade stocks is that they have no added salt, giving you greater control over the saltiness of your final dish.

beef stock

PREP + COOK TIME 5 HOURS 10 MINS (+ COOLING & REFRIGERATION) • MAKES 3½ QUARTS

Before simmering, brown your veggies in the oven with the bones for a richer, more flavorsome stock.

4 pounds meaty beef bones
2 medium brown onions, chopped coarsely
5½ quarts water
2 stalks celery, trimmed, chopped coarsely
2 medium carrots, chopped coarsely
3 bay leaves
2 teaspoons black peppercorns
3 quarts water, extra

1 Preheat oven to 400°F/350°F fan-forced.
2 Roast bones on an oven tray, uncovered, about 1 hour or until browned.
3 Place bones and onion in large saucepan or pot with the water, celery, carrot, bay leaves and peppercorns; bring to a boil. Reduce heat; simmer, uncovered, 3 hours, skimming surface occasionally. Add extra water; simmer, uncovered, 1 hour. Strain stock through muslin-lined sieve or colander into large heatproof bowl; discard solids. Allow stock to cool, cover; refrigerate until cold. Skim and discard surface fat before using.
nutritional count per 1 cup 2g total fat (0.9g saturated fat); 62 cal; 2.3g carbohydrate; 8g protein; 1.1g fiber

chicken stock

PREP + COOK TIME 2 HOURS 10 MINS (+ COOLING & REFRIGERATION) • MAKES 3½ QUARTS

Apart from being the base ingredient for most soups, stock has many a useful purpose in the kitchen. For example, replace water with stock when cooking rice for a delicate infusion of flavors, or add stock to pasta sauce for a more full-bodied result.

4 pounds chicken bones
2 medium onions, chopped coarsely
2 stalks celery, trimmed, chopped coarsely
2 medium carrots, chopped coarsely
3 bay leaves
2 teaspoons black peppercorns
5 quarts water

1 Place ingredients in large saucepan or pot; simmer, uncovered, 2 hours, skimming surface occasionally.
2 Strain stock through muslin-lined sieve or colander into large heatproof bowl; discard solids. Allow stock to cool, cover; refrigerate until cold. Skim and discard surface fat before using.
nutritional count per 1 cup 0.6g total fat (0.2g saturated fat); 25 cal; 2.3g carbohydrate; 1.9g protein; 1.1g fiber

fish stock

Ask your local seafood market or butcher to set aside bones for your stock. Alternatively, use those reserved from previous meals, such as the chicken carcass from a roast. Bones can be frozen for up to 3 months before use, however, as in most recipes, it is best to use fresh ingredients where possible.

3 pounds fish bones

3 quarts water

1 medium onion, chopped coarsely

2 stalks celery, trimmed, chopped coarsely

2 bay leaves

1 teaspoon black peppercorns

1 Combine ingredients in large saucepan; simmer, uncovered, 20 minutes.

2 Strain stock through muslin-lined sieve or colander into large heatproof bowl; discard solids. Allow stock to cool, cover; refrigerate until cold. Skim and discard surface fat before using.

nutritional count per 1 cup 0.2g total fat (0.1g saturated fat); 15 cal; 1.1g carbohydrate; 1.9g protein; 0.6g fiber

vegetable stock

It's a good idea not to go overboard when seasoning your stock–keep the flavors mild and simple at this stage. Add the appropriate amounts of zest or other flavorings to the soup once the stock is added.

2 large carrots, chopped coarsely

2 large parsnips, chopped coarsely

4 medium onions, chopped coarsely

10 stalks celery, trimmed, chopped coarsely

4 bay leaves

2 teaspoons black peppercorns

1½ gallons water

1 Combine ingredients in large saucepan; simmer, uncovered, 1½ hours.

2 Strain stock through muslin-lined sieve or colander into large heatproof bowl; discard solids. Allow stock to cool, cover; refrigerate until cold. Skim and discard surface fat before using.

nutritional count per 1 cup 0.2g total fat (0g saturated fat); 36 cal; 5.7g carbohydrate; 1.4g protein; 2.9g fiber

minestrone

Roast ham hock and onion in a preheated oven for about 30 minutes or until cooked. Roasted hock and onion adds a rich depth of flavor to the broth.

Once the broth has been made, remove the hock and strain the broth through a muslin-lined sieve into a large heatproof bowl. Discard the remaining solids.

Remove the ham from the hock and, using two forks, shred the meat coarsely. Discard the bone, fat and skin. Add the meat to the pan to make the tomato-based broth for the minestrone.

1 ham hock (2 pounds)
1 medium brown onion, quartered
1 stalk celery, trimmed, chopped coarsely
1 teaspoon black peppercorns
1 bay leaf
1 gallon water
1 tablespoon olive oil
1 large carrot, chopped finely
2 stalks celery, trimmed, chopped finely, extra

3 cloves garlic, crushed
¼ cup tomato paste
2 large tomatoes, chopped finely
1 small leek, sliced thinly
1 cup small pasta shells
15-ounce can white beans, rinsed, drained
½ cup coarsely chopped fresh flat-leaf parsley
½ cup coarsely chopped fresh basil
½ cup flaked parmesan cheese

1 Preheat oven to 425°F/400°F fan-forced.

2 Roast ham hock and onion in baking dish, uncovered, 30 minutes.

3 Place hock and onion in large saucepan with celery, peppercorns, bay leaf and the water; bring to a boil. Reduce heat; simmer, uncovered, 2 hours.

4 Remove hock from broth. Strain broth through muslin-lined sieve or colander into large heatproof bowl; discard solids. Allow broth to cool, cover; refrigerate until cold.

5 Remove ham from hock; shred coarsely. Discard bone, fat and skin.

6 Meanwhile, heat oil in large saucepan; cook carrot and extra celery, stirring, 2 minutes. Add ham, garlic, paste and tomato; cook, stirring, 2 minutes.

7 Discard fat from surface of broth. Pour broth into a large measuring cup; add enough water to make 2 quarts. Add broth to pan; bring to a boil. Reduce heat; simmer, covered, 20 minutes.

8 Add leek, pasta and beans to pan; bring to a boil. Reduce heat; simmer, uncovered, until pasta is tender. Remove from heat; stir in herbs. Serve soup sprinkled with cheese.

nutritional count per serving 7.2g total fat (2.4g saturated fat); 207 cal; 19.6g carbohydrate; 12.7g protein; 6.1g fiber

cream of chicken soup

2 quarts water
1 quart chicken stock
4-pound whole chicken
1 medium carrot,
    chopped coarsely
1 stalk celery, trimmed,
    chopped coarsely
1 medium brown onion,
    chopped coarsely

3 tablespoons butter
⅓ cup all-purpose flour
2 tablespoons lemon juice
½ cup cream
¼ cup finely chopped fresh
    flat-leaf parsley

1 Place the water and stock in large saucepan with chicken, carrot, celery and onion; bring to a boil. Reduce heat; simmer, covered, 1½ hours. Remove chicken from pan; simmer broth, covered, 30 minutes.

2 Strain broth through muslin-lined sieve or colander into large heatproof bowl; discard solids.

3 Melt butter in large saucepan, add flour; cook, stirring, until mixture thickens and bubbles. Gradually stir in broth and juice; stir over heat until mixture boils and thickens slightly. Add cream, reduce heat; simmer, uncovered, about 25 minutes, stirring occasionally.

4 Meanwhile, remove and discard skin and bones from chicken; shred meat coarsely. Add chicken to soup; stir over medium heat until hot. Serve soup sprinkled with parsley.

nutritional count per serving 59.2g total fat (26.2g saturated fat); 796 cal; 15.7g carbohydrate; 50.7g protein; 2.5g fiber

serving idea warm slices of crusty bread.

chicken and vegetable soup

3-pound whole chicken
1 small brown onion, halved
2 quarts water
5 black peppercorns
2 bay leaves
1½ tablespoons butter
2 stalks celery, trimmed,
    sliced thinly

2 medium carrots, cut into
    ½-inch pieces
1 large potato, cut into
    ½-inch pieces
5 ounces snow peas, trimmed,
    chopped coarsely
3 green onions, sliced thinly
9-ounce can corn kernels, drained

1 Place chicken, brown onion, the water, peppercorns and bay leaves in large saucepan; bring to a boil. Reduce heat; simmer, covered, 2 hours.

2 Remove chicken from pan. Strain broth through colander into large bowl; discard solids. Allow broth to cool, cover; refrigerate overnight. When chicken is cool enough to handle, remove and discard skin and bones. Shred meat coarsely; cover, refrigerate overnight.

3 Heat butter in same cleaned pan; cook celery, carrot and potato, stirring, until onion softens. Skim and discard fat from surface of broth. Add to pan; bring to a boil. Reduce heat; simmer, covered, 10 minutes or until vegetables are just tender.

4 Add snow peas, green onion, corn and reserved chicken to soup; cook, covered, 5 minutes or until heated through.

nutritional count per serving 9.2g total fat (2.8g saturated fat); 283 cal; 18.8g carbohydrate; 29.1g protein; 4.2g fiber

vietnamese beef pho

PREP + COOK TIME 1 HOUR 40 MINS • SERVES 6

Large bowls of pho (noodle soup) are a breakfast favorite throughout Vietnam, but we like to eat it any time of the day.

Round steak, gravy beef (shin) and skirt steak are all suitable for this recipe.

2 quarts water
1 quart beef stock
2 pounds chuck steak
2 star anise
3-inch piece fresh ginger peeled and grated
⅓ cup Japanese soy sauce
6½ ounces bean thread noodles
¼ cup loosely packed fresh coriander leaves

1½ cups bean sprouts
⅓ cup loosely packed fresh mint leaves
4 green onions, sliced thinly
2 fresh long red chilies, sliced thinly
¼ cup fish sauce
1 medium lemon, cut into six wedges

1 Place the water and stock in large saucepan with beef, star anise, ginger and soy sauce; bring to a boil. Reduce heat; simmer, covered, 30 minutes. Uncover, simmer about 30 minutes or until beef is tender.

2 Meanwhile, place noodles in medium heatproof bowl, cover with boiling water; stand until just tender, drain. Combine coriander, sprouts, mint, onion and chili in medium bowl.

3 Remove beef from pan. Strain broth through muslin-lined sieve or colander into large heatproof bowl; discard solids. When beef is cool enough to handle, remove and discard fat and sinew. Slice beef thinly, return to same cleaned pan with broth; bring to a boil. Stir in fish sauce.

4 Divide noodles among soup bowls; ladle hot beef broth into bowls, sprinkle with sprout mixture, serve with lemon.

nutritional count per serving 8g total fat (3.3g saturated fat); 279 cal; 11.8g carbohydrate; 38.3g protein; 2.4g fiber

scotch broth

9 cups water
2 pounds lamb neck chops
¾ cup pearl barley
1 large brown onion,
   chopped coarsely
2 medium carrots,
   chopped coarsely

1 medium leek, sliced thinly
2 cups finely shredded
   savoy cabbage
½ cup frozen peas
2 tablespoons finely chopped
   fresh flat-leaf parsley

1 Place the water, lamb and barley in large saucepan; bring to a boil. Reduce heat; simmer, covered, 1 hour, skimming fat from surface occasionally. Add onion, carrot and leek; simmer, covered, about 30 minutes or until carrot is tender.
2 Remove lamb from pan. When cool enough to handle, remove and discard bones; shred lamb meat coarsely.
3 Return lamb meat to soup with cabbage and peas; cook, uncovered, about 10 minutes or until peas are tender. Serve soup sprinkled with parsley.
nutritional count per serving 24.4g total fat (10.7g saturated fat); 544 cal; 32.8g carbohydrate; 43.2g protein; 10.7g fiber

vichyssoise

Vichyssoise (pronounced vish-ee-swaz) is a French-style cold soup made with potatoes and leeks. Use only the white part of the leeks in this recipe to preserve the creamy whiteness of the soup.

2 tablespoons butter
1 large brown onion, chopped finely
1 large leek, sliced thickly
4 medium potatoes, chopped coarsely
1½ quarts chicken stock
1¼ cups cream
2 tablespoons finely chopped fresh chives

1 Heat butter in large saucepan; cook onion and leek, stirring, about 10 minutes or until soft. Add potato and stock; bring to a boil. Reduce heat; simmer, covered, 15 minutes.
2 Stand soup 10 minutes then blend or process, in batches, until smooth. Stir cream into soup; cover, refrigerate 3 hours or overnight. Serve soup sprinkled with chives.
nutritional count per serving 40.6g total fat (26.3g saturated fat); 550 cal; 32.8g carbohydrate; 12g protein; 5.6g fiber

[1] scotch broth
[2] vichyssoise
[3] borscht [page 132]
[4] pea and ham soup [page 132]

borscht

Borscht is a thick beet-based soup from Russia, beautifully rich in both color and flavor. It can be refrigerated for up to three days and frozen for about three months. When reheating borscht, do not bring it to a boil or it will lose its wonderful color.

3 tablespoons butter
2 medium brown onions, chopped coarsely
4 pounds red beets, peeled, grated coarsely
2 medium potatoes, chopped coarsely
2 large tomatoes, chopped coarsely
3 bay leaves
2 medium carrots, chopped coarsely
2½ quarts water
⅓ cup red wine vinegar
1-pound piece gravy beef
4 cups shredded savoy cabbage
½ cup sour cream
2 tablespoons coarsely chopped fresh flat-leaf parsley

1 Melt butter in large saucepan, add onion; cook, stirring, until soft. Add beets, potato, tomato, bay leaves, carrot, the water, vinegar and beef. Bring to a boil; reduce heat, simmer, covered, 1 hour.

2 Remove and discard fat from surface of soup. Remove beef from soup; shred meat using two forks. Return meat to soup with cabbage; simmer, uncovered, 20 minutes.

3 Remove and discard bay leaves. Serve soup topped with sour cream and parsley.

nutritional count per serving 19.1g total fat (11.3g saturated fat); 467 cal; 39.8g carbohydrate; 26.9g protein; 14.6g fiber

pea and ham soup

1 medium brown onion, chopped coarsely
2 stalks celery, trimmed, chopped coarsely
2 bay leaves
3 pounds ham hocks
2½ quarts water
1 teaspoon cracked black pepper
2 cups green split peas

1 Place onion, celery, bay leaves, hocks, the water and pepper in large saucepan; bring to a boil. Reduce heat; simmer, covered, about 1½ hours. Add peas; simmer, covered, 30 minutes or until peas are tender.

2 Remove hocks from pan; when cool enough to handle, remove meat from hocks. Shred meat finely. Discard bones, fat and skin; remove and discard bay leaves.

3 Stand soup 10 minutes then blend or process half the soup mixture, in batches, until smooth. Return to pan with remaining soup mixture and ham; stir soup until heated through.

nutritional count per serving 4.9g total fat (1.4g saturated fat); 278 cal; 31g carbohydrate; 23.5g protein; 7.3g fiber

cream of pumpkin soup

Pumpkin soup is one of those simple, comforting classics that everyone loves. It needs nothing more than a thick slice of warm, buttered bread to dunk in and mop up the creamy pumpkin goodness.

You can use any type of pumpkin variety in this soup, but to get that sweet nutty flavor and velvety smooth texture, butternut pumpkin is the best.

3 tablespoons butter

1 large brown onion, chopped coarsely

3 strips bacon, chopped coarsely

3 pounds pumpkin, chopped coarsely

2 large potatoes, chopped coarsely

5 cups chicken stock

½ cup cream

1 Melt butter in large saucepan; cook onion and bacon, stirring, until onion softens. Stir in pumpkin and potato.

2 Stir in stock, bring to a boil; simmer, uncovered, about 20 minutes or until pumpkin is soft.

3 Stand soup 10 minutes then blend or process, in batches, until smooth. Return soup to same cleaned pan, add cream; stir until heated through.

nutritional count per serving 20.9g total fat (12.3g saturated fat); 372 cal; 28g carbohydrate; 16.2g protein; 4.2g fiber

lamb shank and vegetable soup

Mixed dried beans, lentils or potato make a nice addition to this hearty soup.

4 lamb shanks (2 pounds)

2 medium white onions, chopped coarsely

2 cloves garlic, crushed

2 medium potatoes, chopped coarsely

2 medium carrots, chopped coarsely

2 stalks celery, trimmed, chopped coarsely

14-ounce can chopped tomatoes

1½ quarts beef or chicken stock

½ cup tomato paste

2 medium zucchini, chopped coarsely

1 Place shanks, onion, garlic, potato, carrot, celery, undrained tomatoes, stock and paste in large saucepan; bring to a boil. Reduce heat; simmer, covered, 1 hour.

2 Add zucchini; simmer, uncovered, another 30 minutes or until shanks are tender.

3 Remove shanks from soup. When cool enough to handle, remove meat from bones, discard bones. Return meat to soup, stir until heated through.

nutritional count per serving 9.2g total fat (3.9g saturated fat); 362 cal; 29.2g carbohydrate; 39.7g protein; 8.5g fiber

Soup accompaniments

Soups can be a clever way to impress a crowd or soothe yourself on a cold day. For many of us, though, it has become a trusty back-up in the freezer when we need some quick sustenance. What you serve with it can make or break it. Here are some ideas that will help you make a meal out of soup.

PAPRIKA BUTTER
Melt ½ stick butter in a small frying pan; add 2 teaspoons ground hot paprika. Cook, stirring regularly, 2 minutes; remove from the heat. Stir in 2 finely chopped green onions and divide between serving bowls. Serve immediately.

CHILI PARMESAN CRISPS
Combine 1 cup finely grated parmesan cheese and ½ finely chopped long red chili; drop level tablespoons of mixture onto an oven tray lined with parchment paper. Bake crisps in a hot oven about 3 minutes; stand until set before serving with soup.

GREMOLATA
Combine ⅓ cup finely chopped fresh flat-leaf parsley, 1 tablespoon finely grated lemon rind and 2 cloves finely chopped garlic in a small bowl. Keep covered with plastic wrap or in an airtight container in the fridge until ready to use.

TORTILLA CRISPS
Slice soft corn tortillas into thin strips; shallow-fry in vegetable oil, in batches, until browned lightly. Drain on absorbent paper. Serve with tomato soup, or scatter on top of pureed red kidney bean soup along with cubes of avocado or a spoonful of chili con carne.

BACON TOAST
Thinly slice a loaf of ciabatta; toast slices on one side under a preheated broiler. Turn slices and spread with wholegrain mustard. Top with a mixture of coarsely chopped cooked crisp bacon and finely grated parmesan cheese; broil until browned lightly.

CINNAMON CREAM
Lightly whip some thickened cream with an electric mixer until soft peaks form; sprinkle a little ground cinnamon over cream to taste. Top serving cups or soup bowls with a spoonful of cream or place in the refrigerator, covered, until needed.

Q&A

Although store-bought melba toast is convenient, it can be expensive, so I would like to make it at home using a reliable recipe. What is the trick to getting it so thin, crispy and perfect?

Preheat your broiler on high and toast 8 slices of white bread lightly on both sides. Remove the crust from the bread and, carefully, using a sharp knife, split each slice of bread lengthways into 2 slices so you end up with 16 slices that are only toasted on one side. Place the slices you've just made back under the broiler and cook the untoasted side until crisp. The sides of the bread will curl as a result, and this is the effect you are after. You can also make melba toast earlier in the day. Set it aside and warm in an oven preheated to 325°F/300°F fan-forced for a few minutes before serving. For best results use wire trays to allow airflow around both sides of bread.

GRUYERE TOAST
Cut a French bread stick into thick slices; toast slices on one side under a preheated broiler. Turn slices over and sprinkle tops with finely grated gruyère cheese; place under the broiler until the cheese melts. Serve hot gruyère toast alongside soup bowls.

SPICED YOGURT
Dry-fry 1 teaspoon ground coriander, 1 teaspoon ground cumin and ½ teaspoon hot paprika in a non-stick frying pan until fragrant. Combine spices in a small bowl with 1 cup yogurt and ¼ cup finely chopped fresh mint.

PISTOU
Blend or process 2 cups fresh basil leaves, 1 quartered clove garlic, ¼ cup finely grated parmesan cheese and ¼ cup extra virgin olive oil until smooth. Refrigerate, covered. If storing for a few days, omit the cheese when preparing and stir in just before serving.

DILL CREAM
Combine ½ cup sour cream with 1 tablespoon finely chopped fresh dill in a small bowl. Place dollops of dill cream on top of soup or place in the refrigerator, covered, until needed; serve extra chopped dill sprinkled over bowl of dill cream just before serving.

ANCHOVY TOAST
Combine 3 tablespoons soft butter, 6 minced anchovy filets and 2-3 tablespoons finely chopped fresh garlic chives in a bowl. Toast bread slices on one side under a preheated broiler. Spread untoasted side with anchovy butter; broil until browned lightly.

CUCUMBER AND ONION SALSA
Combine ¼ cup sour cream, 1 finely chopped, seeded Lebanese cucumber, 1 finely chopped small red onion and 1 finely chopped small red Thai chili in a small bowl. Place in the refrigerator, covered, until needed or serve on the side with soup.

french onion soup with gruyère croûtons

PREP + COOK TIME
1 HOUR 10 MINS
SERVES 4

3 tablespoons butter
4 large brown onions,
    sliced thinly
¾ cup dry white wine
3 cups water
1 quart beef stock
1 bay leaf
1 tablespoon all-purpose flour
1 teaspoon fresh thyme leaves

gruyère croûtons
1 small French bread,
    cut in ½-inch slices
½ cup coarsely grated
    gruyère cheese

A tablespoon of cognac, stirred into the soup at the last minute, is an excellent addition.

1 Melt butter in large saucepan, add onion; cook, stirring occasionally, about 30 minutes or until caramelized.

2 Meanwhile, bring wine to a boil in large saucepan; boil 1 minute then stir in the water, stock and bay leaf, return to a boil. Remove from heat.

3 Stir flour into onion mixture; cook, stirring, 2 minutes. Gradually add hot broth mixture to onion mixture, stirring, until mixture boils and thickens slightly. Reduce heat; simmer, uncovered, stirring occasionally, 20 minutes. Discard bay leaf; stir in thyme.

4 Meanwhile, make gruyère croûtons.

5 Serve bowls of soup topped with croûtons.

gruyère croûtons Preheat broiler. Toast bread on one side then turn and sprinkle with cheese; broil croûtons until cheese browns lightly.

nutritional count per serving 16.7g total fat (10g saturated fat); 364 cal; 31.1g carbohydrate; 13.4g protein; 3.9g fiber

serving idea sprinkle soup with extra thyme leaves.

Q&A

When the weather turns cold, my family asks for French onion soup but chopping all those onions brings so many tears to my eyes. How do chefs stay dry-eyed? I've never seen a chef shed a tear while chopping onions.

When we chop onions, we break cells that combine with enzymes to emit gases. These gases are dissolved by the water in our eyes. Oxygen in the air converts the dissolved gas into sulfuric acid, so our eyes water to wash away the acid. Many tricks have been tried to overcome this problem, everything from keeping onions cold before cutting, and wearing goggles to chewing gum–it's believed breathing through the mouth keeps fumes away from the eyes. But chefs hold back the tears by cutting onions very fast with a sharp knife. This minimizes the time for the gases to diffuse and get to their eyes. So if all the other methods fail for you, simply learn to chop like a chef.

seafood laksa

To make the laksa paste, soak the dried chilies in a small heatproof bowl of boiling water for about 10 minutes or until softened. Always wear rubber gloves whenever handling chili.

On a clean chopping board, coarsely chop the root and stems of fresh coriander using a sharp knife. You need to chop enough to make 1 tablespoon of root and stem mixture.

Place rice stick noodles in a large heatproof bowl and cover with boiling water. Soak noodles until tender, stirring with a fork to separate.

12 uncooked medium
   king prawns
1 quart chicken stock
3¼ cups coconut milk
4 fresh kaffir lime leaves,
   shredded finely
5 ounces rice stick noodles
10 ounces scallops, roe removed
5 ounces marinated tofu,
   cut into ¾-inch pieces
2 tablespoons lime juice
2 cups bean sprouts
4 green onions, sliced thinly
1 fresh long red chili, sliced thinly
½ cup loosely packed fresh
   coriander leaves

laksa paste
3 dried medium chilies
⅓ cup boiling water
2 teaspoons peanut oil
1 small brown onion,
   chopped coarsely
2 cloves garlic, quartered
¾-inch piece fresh ginger, grated
4-inch stick fresh lemon grass,
   chopped finely
1 tablespoon halved unroasted,
   unsalted macadamias
1 tablespoon coarsely chopped fresh
   coriander root and stem mixture
½ teaspoon ground turmeric
½ teaspoon ground coriander
¼ cup loosely packed fresh
   mint leaves

1 Shell and devein prawns, leaving tails intact.

2 Make laksa paste.

3 Cook paste in large saucepan, stirring, about 5 minutes or until fragrant. Stir in stock, coconut milk and lime leaves; bring to a boil. Reduce heat; simmer, covered, 20 minutes.

4 Meanwhile, place noodles in large heatproof bowl, cover with boiling water; stand until tender, drain.

5 Add prawns to laksa mixture; simmer, uncovered, about 5 minutes or until prawns change color. Add scallops and tofu; simmer, uncovered, about 3 minutes or until scallops change color. Remove from heat; stir in juice.

6 Divide noodles among serving bowls; ladle laksa into bowls, top with sprouts, onion, chili and coriander.

laksa paste Cover chilies with the water in small heatproof bowl, stand 10 minutes; drain. Blend or process chilies with remaining ingredients until smooth.

nutritional count per serving 35.4g total fat (25.9g saturated fat); 528 cal; 25.1g carbohydrate; 25.7g protein; 5g fiber

gazpacho

Gazpacho is a chilled soup originating in the southern province of Andalusia in Spain where long, sunny summers produce an explosion of vegetables. It has a wonderfully refreshing flavor that only gets better when made a day ahead. Refrigerate, covered, overnight to taste it at its best.

3 cups tomato juice

8 medium Roma tomatoes, chopped coarsely

1 medium red onion, chopped coarsely

1 clove garlic

1 Lebanese cucumber, chopped coarsely

1 small green pepper, chopped coarsely

2 slices white bread, crust removed, chopped coarsely

2 teaspoons Tabasco sauce

1 small white onion, chopped finely

½ Lebanese cucumber, seeded, chopped finely, extra

½ small yellow pepper, chopped finely

2 teaspoons olive oil

1 tablespoon vodka

2 tablespoons finely chopped fresh coriander

1 Blend or process juice, tomato, red onion, garlic, coarsely chopped cucumber, green pepper, bread and sauce, in batches, until pureed. Strain through sieve into large bowl, cover; refrigerate 3 hours.

2 Combine white onion, finely chopped cucumber, yellow pepper, oil, vodka and coriander in small bowl.

3 Serve soup topped with vegetable mixture.

nutritional count per serving 2.6g total fat (0.3g saturated fat); 131 cal; 16.9g carbohydrate; 4.8g protein; 4.9g fiber

serving idea slices of crusty bread.

tom yum goong

Tom yums are the most popular soups in Thailand. Translated loosely as broth or stock (tom) and combined spicy sour (yum), this soup is far more than the name would indicate. Sour and tangy, without the sweetness of coconut, tom yum goong's unique taste comes from the combination of spicy ingredients, like chili and curry paste, with sour ones, like lime juice and tamarind.

1¾ pounds uncooked large king prawns

1 tablespoon peanut oil

1½ quarts water

2 tablespoons red curry paste

1 tablespoon tamarind concentrate

4-inch stick fresh lemon grass, chopped finely

2 fresh small red Thai chilies, chopped coarsely

½-inch piece fresh ginger, peeled and grated

1 teaspoon ground turmeric

6 fresh kaffir lime leaves, shredded finely

1 teaspoon grated palm sugar

4 ounces fresh shiitake mushrooms, halved

2 tablespoons fish sauce

2 tablespoons lime juice

¼ cup loosely packed Vietnamese mint leaves

¼ cup loosely packed fresh coriander leaves

1 Shell and devein prawns, leaving tails intact; reserve heads and shells.

2 Heat oil in large saucepan; cook prawn shells and heads, stirring, about 5 minutes or until a deep orange in color.

3 Add 1 cup of the water and curry paste to pan; bring to a boil, stirring. Add remaining water; return to a boil. Reduce heat; simmer, uncovered, 20 minutes. Strain broth through muslin-lined sieve or colander into large heatproof bowl; discard solids.

4 Return broth to same cleaned pan. Add tamarind, lemon grass, chili, ginger, turmeric, lime leaves and sugar; bring to a boil. Boil, stirring, 2 minutes. Add mushrooms, reduce heat; cook, stirring, 3 minutes. Add prawns; simmer, uncovered, about 5 minutes or until prawns are cooked as desired. Remove from heat; stir in sauce and juice.

5 Serve bowls of soup sprinkled with mint and coriander.

nutritional count per serving 9g total fat (1.3g saturated fat); 203 cal; 3.9g carbohydrate; 25.2g protein; 2.3g fiber

fish chowder

PREP + COOK TIME 45 MINS • SERVES 4

Chowder is thought to have originated on the Atlantic seacoast, where fishermen at sea would cook a portion of each day's catch in a flour-thickened stew and eat it with any available bread on board, no matter how stale. Thankfully, the tradition has evolved, and the standard accompaniment has become crushed saltines or a handful of oyster crackers sprinkled into each serving bowl.

3 tablespoons butter
1 large brown onion, chopped coarsely
1 clove garlic, crushed
2 strips bacon, chopped coarsely
2 tablespoons all-purpose flour
3 cups milk

2 cups vegetable stock
2 medium potatoes, chopped coarsely
12 ounces firm white fish filets, chopped coarsely
2 tablespoons finely chopped fresh chives

1 Melt butter in large saucepan; cook onion, garlic and bacon, stirring, until onion softens.

2 Add flour to pan; cook, stirring, 1 minute. Add milk, stock and potato; bring to a boil. Reduce heat; simmer, covered, about 10 minutes or until potato is tender.

3 Add fish; simmer, uncovered, about 4 minutes or until fish is barely cooked. Sprinkle soup with chives.

nutritional count per serving 19.5g total fat (11.6g saturated fat); 433 cal; 28.4g carbohydrate; 34.8g protein; 2.4g fiber

serving idea slices of crusty bread.

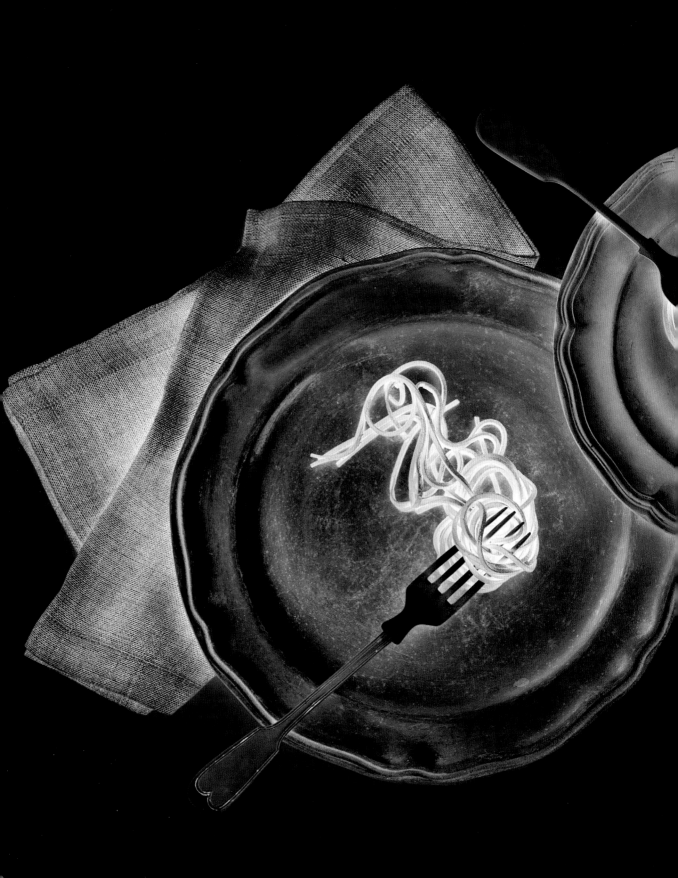

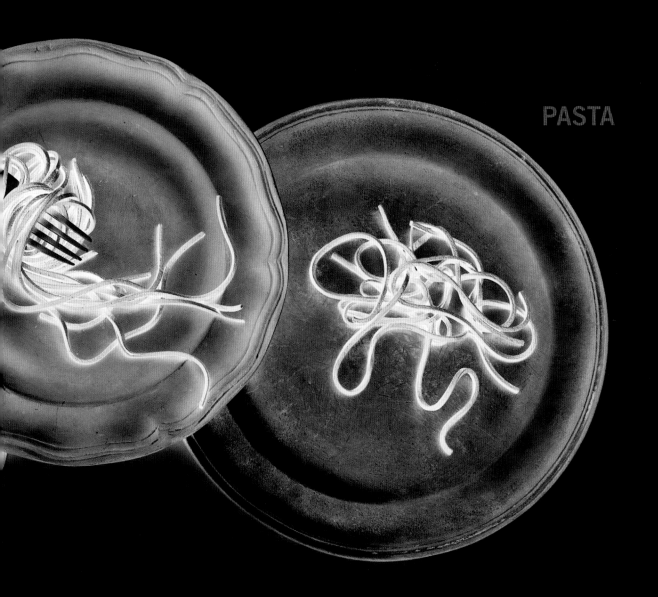

PASTA

Pasta

Thankfully, the Italians took their pasta with them when they began migrating around the globe. Now, their gift to the world is an international staple and most households couldn't imagine living without it. It's quick and easy to cook, can be matched with endless varieties of sauce, and appeals to children and adults alike.

ITALIANS LOVE THEIR PASTA AND EAT IT WITH MUCH LESS SAUCE THAN WE DO: THEY REGARD THE PASTA ITSELF AS THE MAIN ATTRACTION AND THE SAUCE AS A DRESSING. GIVE IT A TRY AND MAKE SURE YOU INVEST IN GOOD-QUALITY PASTA TO REALLY ENJOY ITS AUTHENTIC FLAVOR.

COOKING PASTA

ALL PASTA NEEDS TO BE BOILED, EVEN IF YOU ARE THEN BAKING IT. THE ONLY EXCEPTION TO THIS IS NO-BOIL LASAGNE SHEETS, WHICH CAN BE USED STRAIGHT FROM THE PACKET. FRESH PASTA WILL TAKE LESS TIME TO COOK THAN DRIED PASTA.

THE STARTING POINT FOR PERFECT PASTA IS TO USE A LARGE SAUCEPAN AND PLENTY OF WATER. BRING THE WATER TO A ROLLING BOIL, THEN ADD SALT (THE ITALIANS USE PLENTY OF SALT AT THIS POINT). ADD THE PASTA GRADUALLY SO THE WATER DOES NOT STOP BOILING. FOR LONG PASTA, HOLD THE STRANDS AND FEED THEM GRADUALLY INTO THE SAUCEPAN AS THEY SOFTEN IN THE WATER. KEEP THE WATER BOILING FAST TO KEEP THE PASTA MOVING. TEST THE PASTA BY SCOOPING OUT A PIECE AND BITING IT. FOR PERFECTLY COOKED PASTA, IT NEEDS TO BE AL DENTE–LITERALLY TRANSLATED AS "TO THE TOOTH"– COOKED THROUGH BUT FIRM TO BITE. FRESH PASTA SHOULD ONLY TAKE 2 TO 3 MINUTES; DRIED PASTA WILL TAKE BETWEEN 5 AND 12 MINUTES, DEPENDING ON FRESHNESS AND THICKNESS. DRAIN THE COOKED PASTA IN A COLANDER IN THE SINK, SAVING A LITTLE OF THE STARCHY COOKING WATER TO ADD TO THE SAUCE YOU ARE MAKING. DON'T RINSE THE PASTA: YOU WILL DIMINISH ITS FLAVOR IF YOU WASH AWAY THE STARCH AND SALT.

KINDS OF PASTA

THERE ARE HUNDREDS OF DIFFERENT VARIETIES OF PASTA, BUT THEY ARE ALL GENERALLY MADE OF A SIMPLE DOUGH OF FLOUR AND WATER. AVAILABLE FRESH OR DRY, THEY CAN BE MADE FROM A VARIETY OF DIFFERENT FLOURS, SOME ENRICHED WITH EGG, AND OTHERS ARE COLORED WITH INGREDIENTS SUCH AS SPINACH AND TOMATO.

STORING PASTA

DRIED PASTA WILL KEEP INDEFINITELY, IN A COOL, DRY PLACE, IN ITS UNOPENED PACKAGING OR IN AN AIRTIGHT CONTAINER AFTER OPENING. FRESH PASTA WILL KEEP FOR 3 TO 4 DAYS IN THE REFRIGERATOR; IT WILL STICK TOGETHER IF KEPT ANY LONGER. PASTA CAN BE FROZEN BUT MAY GLUE TOGETHER AS IT THAWS.

DRIED PASTA This is the most widely recognizable type of pasta, available in mass-produced packets and boxes in your local supermarket. Good-quality dried pasta is made with semolina flour milled from durum wheat (in fact, this is enshrined in law in Italy). When you're selecting your pasta, look for "100% durum wheat". You'll find both Italian and American-made products of this quality. Mass-produced does not necessarily mean lesser quality: some of the biggest pasta manufacturers make top-quality pasta.

FRESH PASTA Soft and pliable, fresh pasta is found in the refrigerated section of most supermarkets, delicatessens or gourmet grocery stores. You can also make it at home using a small hand-operated or electric machine with rollers and cutters. Fresh pasta is usually made with plain flour and eggs. It is not superior to dried pasta: both have the same taste and consistency when cooked properly.

EGG PASTA Made with egg and soft wheat flour, egg pasta is available dried or fresh.

WHOLE GRAIN PASTA Part whole grain and part white flour, this variety is light brown in appearance and has a slightly different texture and nuttier flavor. It contains more fiber than refined-wheat pasta.

FLAVORED PASTA These are the colored dried pastas available alongside other pasta. They are lightly flavored with spinach, tomato or basil.

SHAPES OF PASTA

Dried pasta is available in an abundance of shapes, from small tubes to spirals to more elaborate shapes. Some tube pastas have ridges and these, together with the more complex shapes, are designed for grabbing and holding onto the sauce.

LONG STRANDS spaghetti, spaghettoni (thicker), spaghettini (thinner), capellini (very thin) and angel hair (fine, delicate, usually shaped into a nest).

TUBULAR macaroni (short and thick), elbow macaroni (with a bend in the middle), rigatoni (short and wide, with ridged surface) and bucatini (long and thin).

FLAT RIBBONS fettuccine (plain or colored), tagliatelle (wider), tagliolini (narrower) and linguine (narrower still).

LARGE SHEETS lasagne, flat or with ripple edges, plain or verde (green, spinach-flavored).

STUFFED PASTA ravioli (square or round), agnolotti (turnovers), tortellini (turnovers twisted into a ring).

PASTA FOR SOUP tiny shapes such as stelline (stars) and orzo or risoni (rice-grain shapes).

PASTA SHAPES DESIGNED TO "GRAB AND HOLD" CHUNKY SAUCES penne, conchiglie (shells–available in several sizes), fusilli (corkscrews), orecchiette (little ears) and farfalle (butterflies or bow-ties).

Know your pasta

Nobody can argue that when it comes to pasta, the home cook is spoiled with choices. Along with the huge variety of shapes available in both dried and fresh form, there's a profusion of sauces that go with them. Before we can do a good job matching these, we need to know our fusilli from our fettuccine.

PENNE
Italian for "pen", this dried pasta resembles a quill, and has angled ends and ridges to hold chunky sauces. Penne is also available in a smooth variety to complement finer sauces.

CONCHIGLIE
"Shellfish" or "shells" have concave, ridged shapes that hold sauces well. A dried type, this is great in hearty soups like minestrone, or added to a vegetable salad. Available in different sizes: conchigliette (small), conchiglioni (larger).

FARFALLE
"Butterflies" are rectangular pieces of dried pasta that are pinched in the center to resemble bow ties. This pretty shape is thick enough for a host of sauces. Also good in soups and salads.

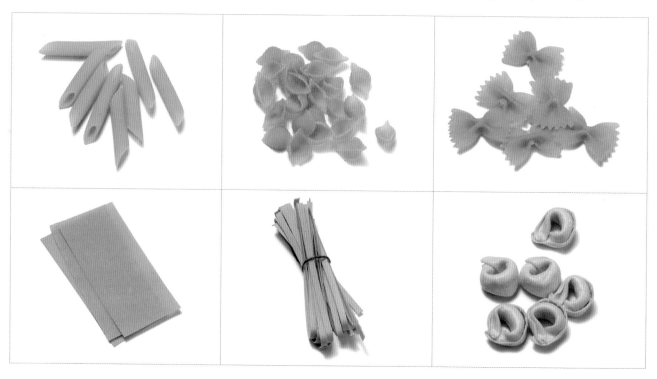

LASAGNE
From the Latin word *lasanum* ("pot"), these sheets are designed to be baked between layers of sauce in the oven. Also comes with rippled edges. Available fresh or dried–fresh is best if you want to assemble and bake the lasagne without par-boiling the sheets.

FETTUCCINE
"Little slices" are ribbon-shaped strands of pasta, traditionally made with egg. It is northern Italy's most famous fresh pasta, though it now comes in a dried version, with or without egg. Suits creamy sauces–as in the rich, buttery alfredo sauce.

TORTELLINI
"Little tarts" are ring-shaped pasta, typically filled with meat, cheese or minced vegetables. Tortellini is commonly served in a broth or a cream-based sauce. Fresh tortellini has more filling inside so it is plumper and cooks faster than dried tortellini.

Q&A

When I order pasta at restaurants, I end up with an oversauced dish, so I can't actually taste or feel the pasta. I'm having some Italian friends over for dinner and want to know the correct way to sauce pasta.

In Italy, just enough sauce is added to lightly cling to the pasta–no extra sauce is seen at the bottom of the bowl. To avoid this problem, don't ladle the sauce over the serving bowls or in a big mixing bowl as the pasta and sauce will not combine well. The best method is to drain the pasta, return it to the drained pan, add only enough sauce to coat the pasta and briefly combine over moderate heat for about 30 seconds. Never run cold water over the drained pasta to keep it from cooking further as this removes much of the flavor. Pasta should be cooked for just enough time so it remains al dente (firm in the center) by the time it arrives on the table.

GNOCCHI
Derived from *nocchio*, "knot in wood", gnocchi are small dumplings made from flour, semolina or potato. They should be fresh and can be boiled, broiled or baked as in *gnocchi alla romana*, where they are oven-baked with butter and parmesan.

RAVIOLI
"Little turnips", squares of pasta stuffed with cheese, vegetables or meat. Usually made from fresh pasta either by hand or in molds. Ravioli are a match for tomato-based sauces, including bolognese, or they can be served with butter, olive oil or cream.

RIGATONI
Italian for "large, ridged", this dried ribbed, tubular pasta is perfect with any sauce, from cream or cheese (especially ricotta) to the chunkiest meat sauces–a tomato and sausage one matches beautifully. Rigatoni is also good for pasta bakes.

FUSILLI
"Little spindles", also known as corkscrews, are a dried spiral pasta. Fusilli can be topped with any sauce, makes a great addition to casseroles or can be turned into a wonderful salad. Also comes in a longer, coil-like shape called *fusilli col buco*.

PAPPARDELLE
From the Italian verb *pappare*, meaning "to gobble up", pappardelle are broad, flat or frilly ribbons of pasta. Goes well with red meat sauces (rabbit is a Tuscan favorite), chunky tomato and mushroom sauces as in *pappardelle boscaiola*, or with cream.

ORECCHIETTE
"Little ears" are named after their shape, resembling tiny human ears. It's a chewy pasta that's traditional in southern Italy's Puglia region, where it is made from semolina. There it is served with oil, sausage and leafy greens. Good with ragu and in salads too.

fresh pasta

Making fresh pasta is a lot simpler than many people think. The few ingredients needed are readily available and inexpensive, and the process can be really satisfying. Once you have mastered the basics, have some fun experimenting with colors and flavors by adding pureed vegetables to the mix.

2 cups all-purpose flour
2 teaspoons salt
3 eggs

1 Sift flour and salt onto counter or into large bowl; make a well in the center.
2 Break eggs into well; using fingers, gradually mix flour into eggs. Press mixture into a ball. Knead dough on floured surface 10 minutes or until smooth and elastic.
3 Cut dough in half; roll each half through pasta machine set on thickest setting. Fold dough in half; roll through machine again. Repeat folding and rolling, adjusting setting on machine to become less thick with each roll, dusting dough with a little extra flour when necessary. Roll until 1$\frac{1}{16}$-inch thick or until desired thickness is reached. Cut pasta sheets into desired pasta shape.

nutritional count per 100g 4.1g total fat (1.2g saturated fat); 274 cal; 46.2g carbohydrate; 11.2g protein; 2.4g fiber

Press the dough into a ball, then roll and stretch it on a floured surface. Using the heel of your hand, push the dough gently along the surface. After about 10 minutes, the dough should be smooth and springy.

Adjust the hand roller to the thickest setting. Cut the dough in half and feed each half through the roller. Fold dough in half and feed the pieces through the roller again. Begin rolling the dough thinner, by turning the dial to the next thinnest setting. Guide the dough through the roller again, dusting it with flour if necessary.

The pasta should be $\frac{1}{16}$-inch thick. You might find it easier to work with a helper, so one person can turn the crank and the other can guide the dough into the roller with one hand and catch it with the other hand. Be careful not to stretch or tear the sheet.

Connect the cutting attachment to the hand roller according to your manual's instructions. Drape the sheet of pasta over one hand as you feed it through the roller.

Q&A

I'd like to start making my own pasta at home because store-bought fresh pasta can be expensive and not always great quality. Should I invest in a motorized machine or stick to a traditional hand-operated model?

If you want to make pasta at home, avoid electric machines and stick to the manual types. The electric ones might make light, fast work of rolling and cutting the dough but they have their drawbacks too. On a machine, the rolling is done by squeezing the dough to thinness (compression), whereas hand rollers combine compression and stretching. This makes the pasta's texture more resilient. Hand rollers create a more mottled surface, which picks up sauces more efficiently, so the pasta tastes even better. You'll also get more satisfaction cutting the pasta yourself and deciding its length. Hand-rolled pasta is easier to manage too, compared with machine-cut pasta.

spaghetti bolognese

PREP + COOK TIME 2 HOURS 35 MINS • SERVES 6

Pasta-lovers the world over have made this dish, originally from Bologna in northern Italy, their own. The biggest secret of a good bolognese is long, slow cooking to concentrate the complex flavor.

2 teaspoons olive oil
6 slices pancetta (3 ounces), chopped finely
1 large white onion, chopped finely
1 medium carrot, chopped finely
2 stalks celery trimmed, chopped finely
1¼ pounds ground beef
5 ounces chicken livers, trimmed, chopped finely

1 cup milk
3 tablespoons butter
1½ cups beef stock
1 cup dry red wine
13-ounce can tomato puree
2 tablespoons tomato paste
¼ cup finely chopped fresh flat-leaf parsley
1½ pounds fresh spaghetti
½ cup shaved parmesan cheese

1 Heat oil in large heavy-based frying pan; cook pancetta, stirring, until crisp. Add onion, carrot and celery; cook, stirring, until vegetables soften.
2 Add beef and liver to pan; cook, stirring, until beef changes color. Stir in milk and butter; cook, stirring occasionally, until liquid reduces to about half.
3 Add stock, wine, puree and paste to pan; simmer, covered, 1 hour. Uncover; simmer 1 hour. Remove from heat; stir in parsley.
4 Meanwhile, cook pasta in large saucepan of boiling water until tender; drain.
5 Serve pasta topped with bolognese sauce and cheese.
nutritional count per serving 26.6g total fat (13g saturated fat); 599 cal; 41g carbohydrate; 39.2g protein; 5.5g fiber

fettuccine alfredo

PREP + COOK TIME 30 MINS • SERVES 4

This sauce is named after the Roman restaurateur Alfredo di Lello who created the dish in the 1920s. Do not reduce the cream mixture too rapidly or by too much as this sauce can burn. Check and stir once or twice and take the pan off the heat when it is reduced correctly.

1 pound fresh fettuccine pasta
6 tablespoons butter
1¼ cups cream
½ cup finely grated parmesan cheese

1 Cook pasta in large saucepan of boiling water until tender; drain. Return to pan.
2 Meanwhile, melt butter in medium frying pan, add cream; bring to a boil. Reduce heat; simmer, uncovered, about 5 minutes or until sauce reduces by half. Stir in cheese, over low heat, about 2 minutes or until cheese melts.
3 Add sauce to pasta; toss gently to coat.
nutritional count per serving 53.4g total fat (34.5g saturated fat); 914 cal; 87.5g carbohydrate; 19.4g protein; 4.1g fiber

[opposite] spaghetti bolognese

fettuccine carbonara

Italian recipes vary from region to region, reflecting the ingredients available there. While "charcoal burners' fettuccine" is made without cream in the south, it includes cream, as our recipe does, in the north of the country.

1 pound fresh fettuccine pasta

4 tablespoons butter

6 strips bacon, sliced thinly

1 clove garlic, crushed

½ teaspoon cracked black pepper

1¼ cups cream

2 eggs, beaten lightly

½ cup finely grated parmesan cheese

½ cup finely grated romano cheese

2 teaspoons coarsely chopped fresh chives

1 Cook pasta in large saucepan of boiling water until tender; drain.

2 Meanwhile, melt butter in medium frying pan; cook bacon, stirring, 5 minutes.

3 Add garlic, pepper and cream to pan; simmer, uncovered, until sauce reduces by half. Remove from heat. Stir in egg and cheeses.

4 Add pasta to sauce; stir to coat. Serve pasta sprinkled with chives.

nutritional count per serving 66.7g total fat (39g saturated fat); 876 cal; 33.6g carbohydrate; 53.7g protein; 2.4g fiber

spaghetti with pesto

Pesto can be made in advance and stored in the refrigerator for up to one week. If doing this, omit the parmesan cheese when blending, and stir it through just before serving.

2 cloves garlic, chopped coarsely

⅓ cup roasted pine nuts

½ cup finely grated parmesan cheese

2 cups firmly packed fresh basil leaves

½ cup olive oil

1 pound spaghetti

½ cup flaked parmesan cheese

1 Blend or process garlic, nuts, grated cheese and basil until almost smooth. Gradually add oil in a thin, steady stream, processing until thick.

2 Cook pasta in large saucepan of boiling water, until just tender; drain, reserving ¼ cup of the cooking liquid.

3 Combine pasta, pesto and reserved cooking liquid in large bowl. Serve with flaked cheese.

nutritional count per serving 45.2g total fat (8.9g saturated fat); 859 cal; 86.2g carbohydrate; 23.6g protein; 5.6g fiber

serving ideas pesto also goes well with both creamy and grilled polenta, barbecued fish, pan-fried lamb and beef.

[1] fettuccine carbonara
[2] spaghetti with pesto
[3] macaroni and cheese [page 154]
[4] spinach and ricotta cannelloni [page 154]

macaroni and cheese

This recipe freezes well; you could double the recipe and freeze one batch for a rainy day.

10 ounces macaroni pasta

4 strips bacon, chopped finely

3 tablespoons butter

⅓ cup all-purpose flour

1 quart milk

1 cup coarsely grated cheddar cheese

½ cup finely grated pecorino cheese

2 tablespoons wholegrain mustard

½ cup stale bread crumbs

2 tablespoons butter, extra

1 Preheat oven to 350°F/325°F fan-forced. Oil deep 2-quart ovenproof dish.

2 Cook pasta in large saucepan of boiling water until tender; drain.

3 Meanwhile, cook bacon in medium saucepan, stirring, until crisp; drain on absorbent paper.

4 Melt butter in same pan, add flour; cook, stirring, 1 minute. Gradually stir in milk; cook, stirring, until sauce boils and thickens. Cool 2 minutes; stir in cheeses and mustard.

5 Combine pasta, sauce and bacon in large bowl; pour mixture into dish. Top with bread crumbs, dot with extra butter. Bake about 30 minutes or until browned.

nutritional count per serving 47.5g total fat (27.8g saturated fat); 922 cal; 78.8g carbohydrate; 43.1g protein; 3.5g fiber

serving idea serve with a baby spinach, grape tomato and celery salad.

spinach and ricotta cannelloni

The cannelloni can be prepared completely up to a day ahead, ready to go into the oven. Keep it covered in the refrigerator overnight.

2 pounds spinach, trimmed, chopped coarsely

1 pound ricotta cheese

2 eggs

1½ cups coarsely grated parmesan cheese

¼ cup finely chopped fresh mint

3 teaspoons finely chopped fresh thyme

2 teaspoons finely chopped fresh rosemary

8 ounces cannelloni tubes

creamy tomato sauce

1 tablespoon olive oil

1 medium brown onion, chopped finely

4 cloves garlic, crushed

4 x 14-ounce cans diced tomatoes

½ cup cream

1 teaspoon sugar

1 Make creamy tomato sauce.

2 Meanwhile, preheat oven to 350°F/325°F fan-forced.

3 Cook washed, drained (not dried) spinach in heated large saucepan, stirring, until wilted. Drain; when cool enough to handle, squeeze out excess moisture.

4 Combine spinach in large bowl with ricotta, eggs, ½ cup of the parmesan cheese and the herbs. Using a large piping bag, fill pasta with spinach mixture.

5 Spread a third of the tomato sauce into shallow 10-inch x 14-inch ovenproof dish; top with pasta, in single layer, then top with remaining sauce. Bake, covered, 20 minutes. Uncover, sprinkle pasta with remaining parmesan; cook another 15 minutes or until pasta is tender and cheese is browned lightly.

creamy tomato sauce Heat oil in large saucepan; cook onion, stirring, until softened. Add garlic; cook, stirring, until fragrant. Add undrained tomatoes; bring to a boil. Reduce heat; simmer, uncovered, stirring occasionally, about 20 minutes or until sauce thickens slightly. Cool 10 minutes; blend or process sauce with cream and sugar until smooth.

nutritional count per serving 31g total fat (17.1g saturated fat); 577 cal; 41.8g carbohydrate; 28.7g protein; 8.3g fiber

spaghetti and meatballs

PREP + COOK TIME 50 MINS • SERVES 4

Anchovies are always a feature in this popular Italo-American pasta dish, however, if you're cooking for someone who doesn't like them, you can omit them. A teaspoon of baby capers can be added to the tomato mixture for an extra-salty sensation.

1 pound ground pork and veal mix
½ cup stale bread crumbs
1 egg
¼ cup finely grated parmesan cheese
1 tablespoon olive oil
1 medium brown onion, chopped coarsely
2 cloves garlic, quartered
1 fresh small red Thai chili

6 anchovy filets
1 cup drained sun-dried tomatoes
¼ cup tomato paste
1 cup chicken stock
12 pimiento-stuffed olives, sliced thinly
12 ounces spaghetti
⅓ cup coarsely chopped fresh flat-leaf parsley

1 Combine meat, bread crumbs, egg and cheese in medium bowl; roll level tablespoons of mixture into balls.

2 Heat oil in medium frying pan; cook meatballs, uncovered, until browned.

3 Blend or process onion, garlic, chili, anchovy, tomatoes and paste until smooth. Combine tomato mixture with stock in medium saucepan; bring to a boil. Add meatballs and olives; simmer, uncovered, 15 minutes.

4 Meanwhile, cook spaghetti in large saucepan of boiling water until tender; drain.

5 Serve spaghetti topped with meatballs and sauce; sprinkle with parsley.

nutritional count per serving 20.6g total fat (6.3g saturated fat); 709 cal; 78.8g carbohydrate; 47.5g protein; 7.9g fiber

vegetarian lasagne

This is traditional lasagne redesigned for vegetarians, but the flavors are so rich that meat-eaters will love it too.

3 medium red peppers

1 medium eggplant, sliced thinly

1 tablespoon coarse cooking salt

3 medium zucchini, sliced thinly

1 medium sweet potato, sliced thinly

cooking-oil spray

2 cups bottled tomato pasta sauce

8 ounces no-boil lasagne sheets

2½ cups coarsely grated mozzarella cheese

⅓ cup coarsely grated parmesan cheese

white sauce

3 tablespoons butter

2 tablespoons all-purpose flour

1¼ cups milk

¼ cup coarsely grated parmesan cheese

1 Quarter peppers; discard seeds and membranes. Roast under broiler or in very hot oven, skin-side up, until pepper skin blisters and blackens. Cover pepper pieces in plastic or paper for 5 minutes; peel away skin.

2 Reduce oven to 400°F/350°F fan-forced. Place eggplant in colander, sprinkle all over with salt; stand 20 minutes. Rinse eggplant under cold water; drain on absorbent paper.

3 Meanwhile, make white sauce.

4 Place eggplant, zucchini and sweet potato, in single layer, on oven trays; spray with oil. Roast about 20 minutes or until browned and tender.

5 Oil deep rectangular 2-quart ovenproof dish. Spread ⅔ cup of the pasta sauce into dish; top with a quarter of the lasagne sheets, ⅓ cup of the pasta sauce, eggplant and a third of the mozzarella. Layer cheese with another quarter of the lasagne sheets, ⅓ cup of the pasta sauce, peppers, and another third of the mozzarella. Layer mozzarella with another quarter of the lasagne sheets, ⅓ cup of the pasta sauce, zucchini, sweet potato, remaining mozzarella, remaining lasagne sheets and remaining pasta sauce. Top with white sauce, sprinkle with parmesan.

6 Bake lasagne, uncovered, about 30 minutes or until browned lightly. Stand 10 minutes before serving.

white sauce Heat butter in small saucepan, add flour; cook, stirring, until mixture thickens and bubbles. Gradually stir in milk; stir until mixture boils and thickens. Remove from heat; stir in cheese.

nutritional count per serving 32.5g total fat (19g saturated fat); 763 cal; 82g carbohydrate; 37.5g protein; 9.9g fiber

penne puttanesca

PREP + COOK TIME 30 MINS • SERVES 4

According to one folk legend, this dish is prepared in the style of prostitutes in Rome; deliberately robust in scent and hearty in flavor so as to attract clients. Another spin on the same legend says that this sauce was a favorite among the ladies because, since it was so quick to prepare, they could cook it from ingredients kept in their cupboards without wasting time between clients.

1 pound penne pasta
⅓ cup extra virgin olive oil
3 cloves garlic, crushed
1 teaspoon chili flakes
5 medium tomatoes, chopped coarsely
6 ounces pitted kalamata olives

8 drained anchovy filets, chopped coarsely
⅓ cup drained capers, rinsed
⅓ cup coarsely chopped fresh flat-leaf parsley
2 tablespoons finely shredded fresh basil

1 Cook pasta in large saucepan of boiling water, uncovered, until just tender; drain.
2 Meanwhile, heat oil in large frying pan; cook garlic, stirring, until fragrant. Add chili and tomato; cook, stirring, 5 minutes. Add remaining ingredients; cook, stirring occasionally, about 5 minutes or until sauce thickens slightly.
3 Add pasta to sauce; toss gently to coat.
nutritional count per serving 21.1g total fat (3.1g saturated fat); 690 cal; 10.2g carbohydrate; 18.6g protein; 7.9g fiber

fettuccine boscaiola

PREP + COOK TIME 30 MINS • SERVES 4

1 pound fresh fettuccine pasta
2 teaspoons olive oil
6 ounces button mushrooms, sliced thickly
2 cloves garlic, crushed
6 ounces shaved ham, chopped coarsely
¼ cup dry white wine
1¼ cups cream
2 tablespoons coarsely chopped fresh chives

1 Cook pasta in large saucepan of boiling water until tender; drain.
2 Meanwhile, heat oil in large saucepan; cook mushrooms, garlic and ham, stirring, until ingredients are browned lightly. Add wine; boil, uncovered, until wine reduces by half.
3 Add cream to mushroom mixture; reduce heat. Simmer, uncovered, until sauce thickens slightly.
4 Add chives and pasta to sauce; toss to combine.
nutritional count per serving 38.1g total fat (22.7g saturated fat); 822 cal; 87.8g carbohydrate; 26.8g protein; 5.7g fiber

chili prawn linguine

PREP + COOK TIME 30 MINS • SERVES 4

1 pound linguine pasta

⅓ cup olive oil

12 ounces uncooked medium king prawns, peeled

3 fresh small red Thai chilies, chopped finely

2 cloves garlic, crushed

½ cup finely chopped fresh flat-leaf parsley

2 teaspoons finely grated lemon rind

1 Cook pasta in large saucepan of boiling water until tender; drain.

2 Meanwhile, heat oil in large frying pan; cook prawns, chili and garlic, stirring, until prawns are just cooked through. Remove from heat; stir in parsley and rind.

3 Combine pasta with prawn mixture in large bowl; toss gently.

nutritional count per serving 20.8g total fat (3g saturated fat); 682 cal; 85.5g carbohydrate; 34.7g protein; 4.8g fiber

chicken and mushroom pasta bake

PREP + COOK TIME 50 MINS • SERVES 4

Rigatoni, a ridged, tube-shaped pasta, is ideal for "pasta al forno" (baked dishes) because it is wide and the hearty fillings cling to the indentations around the edges.

12 ounces rigatoni pasta

4 tablespoons butter

1¼ pounds chicken breast filets, cut into ½-inch pieces

4 ounces button mushrooms, sliced thinly

2 tablespoons all-purpose flour

2 cups milk

½ cup coarsely grated romano cheese

1¼ cups coarsely grated cheddar cheese

6 ounces asparagus, trimmed, chopped coarsely

¼ cup chopped fresh flat-leaf parsley

1 Preheat oven to 400°F/350°F fan-forced.

2 Cook pasta in large saucepan of boiling water, uncovered, until just tender; drain.

3 Meanwhile, heat 2 tablespoons of the butter in large frying pan; cook chicken, in batches, until browned and cooked through. Remove from pan.

4 Heat remaining butter in same pan; cook mushrooms, stirring, until tender. Add flour; cook, stirring, 1 minute. Gradually stir in milk. Stir over medium heat until mixture boils and thickens. Stir in chicken, ¼ cup of the romano cheese, ¾ cup of the cheddar cheese and the asparagus.

5 Combine chicken mixture and drained pasta in 2½-quart ovenproof dish; sprinkle with remaining cheeses. Bake about 15 minutes or until top browns lightly. Serve pasta bake sprinkled with parsley.

nutritional count per serving 37.3g total fat (22.3g saturated fat); 903 cal; 75.2g carbohydrate; 64g protein; 4.8g fiber

beef lasagne

No-boil lasagne sheets are thinner than the dried uncooked version and do not require any pre-boiling. Just layer them in an ovenproof dish (large in area and shallow, rather than high-sided, is best) with a favorite meat, chicken or vegetable sauce, various cheeses and a béchamel sauce or similar. Make sure the filling is saucy enough to provide the pasta with enough moisture to rehydrate it.

1 tablespoon olive oil
1 medium brown onion, chopped finely
1 medium carrot, chopped finely
1 stalk celery, trimmed, chopped finely
2 cloves garlic, crushed
1 pound ground beef
⅓ cup dry red wine
28-ounce can crushed tomatoes
2 tablespoons tomato paste
½ cup water
4 slices prosciutto, chopped finely

1 tablespoon coarsely chopped fresh oregano
2 tablespoons coarsely chopped fresh flat-leaf parsley
18 no-boil lasagne sheets
½ cup grated parmesan cheese
cheese sauce
4 tablespoons butter
⅓ cup all-purpose flour
1 quart milk
¾ cup grated parmesan cheese
pinch ground nutmeg

1 Heat oil in large frying pan; cook onion, carrot, celery and garlic, stirring, until onion is soft. Add beef; cook, stirring, until browned. Add wine; bring to a boil. Stir in undrained tomatoes, paste and the water; reduce heat. Simmer, uncovered, about 1 hour or until mixture is thick. Stir in prosciutto and herbs; cool slightly.

2 Meanwhile, make cheese sauce.

3 Preheat oven to 350°F/325°F fan-forced. Oil shallow 3-quart ovenproof dish.

4 Place six lasagne sheets into dish. Spread with half the meat sauce; drizzle with 1 cup of the cheese sauce. Repeat layering; top with remaining pasta sheets then spread with remaining cheese sauce and sprinkle with cheese.

5 Bake lasagne about 45 minutes or until pasta is tender and cheese is browned lightly.

cheese sauce Melt butter in heated large saucepan, add flour; cook, stirring, until mixture bubbles and thickens. Remove from heat; gradually stir in milk. Cook, stirring, until mixture boils and thickens. Remove from heat; stir in cheese and nutmeg. Cool 10 minutes.

nutritional count per serving 32.5g total fat (17.2g saturated fat); 716 cal; 62g carbohydrate; 38.7g protein; 5.6g fiber

pastitsio

Pastitsio is to the Greek kitchen as lasagne is to an Italian cucina – a rich and comforting layered meat, tomato and pasta bake traditionally smothered with a creamy béchamel sauce. Some recipes do not call for cinnamon in the meat sauce, but it's a classic signature flavor that has made it one of the most well-known of all Greek baked dishes. If you can find bucatini, a long, hollow pasta slightly thicker than spaghetti, use it instead of a shorter macaroni.

8 ounces macaroni pasta
2 eggs, beaten lightly
¾ cup coarsely grated
    parmesan cheese
2 tablespoons stale bread crumbs

meat sauce
1 tablespoon olive oil
2 medium brown onions,
    chopped finely
1½ pounds ground beef
14-ounce can chopped tomatoes
⅓ cup tomato paste
½ cup beef stock
¼ cup dry white wine
½ teaspoon ground cinnamon
1 egg, beaten lightly

cheese topping
6 tablespoons butter
½ cup all-purpose flour
3½ cups milk
1 cup coarsely grated
    parmesan cheese
2 egg yolks

1 Preheat oven to 350°F/325°F fan-forced. Oil shallow 2½-quart ovenproof dish.

2 Make meat sauce. Make cheese topping.

3 Cook pasta in large saucepan of boiling water until tender; drain.

4 Combine warm pasta, egg and cheese in large bowl. Press pasta over base of dish; top with meat sauce, pour cheese topping over, smooth surface then sprinkle with bread crumbs.

5 Bake pastitsio about 1 hour or until browned lightly. Stand 10 minutes before serving.

meat sauce Heat oil in large saucepan; cook onion, stirring, until soft. Add beef; cook, stirring, until well-browned. Stir in undrained tomatoes, paste, stock, wine and cinnamon; simmer, uncovered, until thick. Cool 10 minutes; stir in egg.

cheese topping Melt butter in medium saucepan, add flour; cook, stirring, until mixture thickens and bubbles. Gradually stir in milk; cook, stirring, until sauce boils and thickens. Remove from heat; stir in cheese. Cool 5 minutes; stir in egg yolks.

nutritional count per serving 41.6g total fat (21.8g saturated fat); 822 cal; 54.4g carbohydrate; 54g protein; 3.8g fiber

vegetable gnocchi with cheese sauce

PREP + COOK TIME
2 HOURS 40 MINS
(+ REFRIGERATION)
SERVES 6

2¼ pounds russet potatoes
1 medium sweet potato
9½ ounces spinach,
    trimmed, chopped
3 eggs
½ cup coarsely grated
    parmesan cheese
2 cups all-purpose flour,
    approximately
2 tablespoons olive oil
3½ ounces blue cheese, crumbled
⅓ cup finely grated pecorino cheese

cheese sauce
2 tablespoons butter
2 tablespoons all-purpose flour
2½ cups milk
⅔ cup cream
½ cup finely grated
    gruyère cheese
⅔ cup finely grated
    pecorino cheese

On a lightly floured surface, roll the kneaded parmesan mixture, and potato and spinach mixture into three sausage shapes. Cut each sausage into 1-inch balls.

Roll the front of a fork over each ball, pressing lightly, to create grooves. The grooves on gnocchi are not only for presentation – they help pick up the sauce.

1 Boil or steam unpeeled potatoes until tender; drain. When cool enough to handle, peel potatoes; chop coarsely.

2 Meanwhile, microwave unpeeled sweet potato on HIGH (100%) about 8 minutes or until tender; drain. Peel when cool enough to handle. Boil, steam or microwave spinach until wilted; drain.

3 Using wooden spoon, push potato through fine sieve or food mill into large bowl. Divide potato mash among three medium bowls; stir one egg into each bowl until mixture is combined. Using wooden spoon, stir parmesan cheese into one of the bowls. Push sweet potato through fine sieve into the second bowl; stir to combine. Stir spinach into the third bowl. Stir about ⅓ cup of flour into parmesan-flavored mixture to make a firm dough. Stir about ½ cup of flour into both the sweet potato and spinach mixtures to make a firm dough.

4 Roll each portion of dough on floured surface into 1-inch-thick sausage shape. Cut each sausage shape into 1-inch pieces; roll pieces into balls. Roll each ball along the inside tines of a fork, pressing lightly on top of ball with index finger to form classic gnocchi shape–grooves on one side and a dimple on the other. Place gnocchi, in single layer, on floured trays; cover, refrigerate 1 hour.

5 Cook gnocchi, in batches, in large saucepan of boiling water about 2 minutes or until gnocchi float to surface. Remove from pan with slotted spoon; drain. Gently toss gnocchi in large bowl with oil.

6 Make cheese sauce. Pour sauce over gnocchi; toss gently to coat.

7 Divide gnocchi among six oiled 1½-cup ovenproof dishes; sprinkle with blue cheese then pecorino cheese. Place under hot broiler about 3 minutes or until cheese browns lightly.

cheese sauce Melt butter in medium saucepan, add flour; cook, stirring, until mixture thickens and bubbles. Gradually add milk and cream; stir until mixture boils and thickens. Remove from heat; stir in cheeses.

nutritional count per serving 40.4g total fat (22.4g saturated fat); 786 cal; 74.6g carbohydrate; 27.5g protein; 7.1g fiber

cheese and spinach tortellini with gorgonzola sauce

PREP + COOK TIME 20 MINS
SERVES 4

2 tablespoons butter
2 tablespoons all-purpose flour
1 cup milk
¾ cup cream
4 ounces gorgonzola cheese, chopped coarsely
1½-pound packaged cheese and spinach tortellini
¼ cup loosely packed fresh flat-leaf parsley

This sauce is also delicious served with pumpkin gnocchi or steaks. Or to make a quick starter, place a canned pear half in a ramekin, top with the sauce and some bread crumbs and broil until golden.

1 Melt butter in medium saucepan, add flour; cook, stirring, about 2 minutes or until mixture bubbles and thickens. Gradually stir in milk and cream; bring to a boil. Reduce heat; simmer, uncovered, until sauce boils and thickens. Remove from heat; stir in cheese.

2 Meanwhile, cook pasta in large saucepan of boiling water until pasta floats to the top; drain.

3 Combine pasta with sauce; sprinkle with parsley.

nutritional count per serving 58.5g total fat (37.4g saturated fat); 895 cal; 56.2g carbohydrate; 34g protein; 5.8g fiber

angel hair with arugula and chili

PREP + COOK TIME 20 MINS • SERVES 4

Also known as capelli d'angelo, angel hair is sold as small, circular nests of very fine, delicate pasta strands; its cooking time is minimal because it's extremely thin.

2 tablespoons olive oil
1 teaspoon dried chili flakes
2 cloves garlic, crushed
½ teaspoon cracked black pepper
¼ cup lemon juice
12 ounces angel hair pasta
3 ounces arugula leaves
2 medium tomatoes, seeded, chopped coarsely
⅔ cup firmly packed fresh basil leaves

1 Heat oil in large frying pan; cook chili and garlic, stirring, until fragrant. Add pepper and juice; stir until hot.

2 Meanwhile, cook pasta in large saucepan of boiling water until tender; drain.

3 Combine chili mixture and pasta in large bowl with arugula, tomato and basil.

nutritional count per serving 10.4g total fat (1.5g saturated fat); 420 cal; 66.4g carbohydrate; 12.1g protein; 4.8g fiber

spaghetti alla vongole

This delicate and decorative pasta dish is a specialty of Venice.

3 pounds clams
1 tablespoon coarse cooking salt
¼ cup olive oil
1 medium brown onion, chopped finely
2 cloves garlic, crushed
2 drained anchovy filets, chopped finely
1 fresh red Thai chili, chopped finely
2 teaspoons chopped fresh thyme
3 pounds Roma tomatoes, peeled, seeded, chopped finely
2 tablespoons chopped fresh flat-leaf parsley
1 pound spaghetti

1 Rinse clams under cold water and place in large bowl. Sprinkle with salt, cover with cold water and soak for 2 hours (this purges them of any grit). Discard water, then rinse clams thoroughly; drain.

2 Heat 2 tablespoons of the oil in large saucepan, add clams; cover with tight-fitting lid. Cook over high heat about 8 minutes or until all clams have opened.

3 Strain clam cooking liquid through muslin or clean tea towel. Return liquid to same cleaned pan; cook, uncovered, until liquid is reduced to 1 cup. Reserve clam stock.

4 Heat remaining oil in another saucepan; cook onion, garlic, anchovy, chili and thyme, stirring, until onion is soft. Add tomato and reserved clam stock; cook, uncovered, about 10 minutes or until sauce is thickened. Add clams, stir until heated through. Stir in parsley.

5 Meanwhile, cook pasta in large saucepan of boiling water, uncovered, until just tender; drain.

6 Toss clam sauce through spaghetti.

nutritional count per serving 10.5g total fat (1.5g saturated fat); 428 cal; 60.8g carbohydrate; 19.8g protein; 4.5g fiber

Q&A

The last time I cleaned clams with cold water and salt, it didn't work so well and my guests were left to eat a slightly gritty pasta dish. What did I do wrong and can you recommend another cleaning method?

The cold water method should work as clams filter water as they breathe, pushing salt and sand out of their shells. You need to leave the clams in the water for at least 20 minutes, then pull them up and out of the bowl—do not pour them into a strainer because you will be pouring the expelled sand at the bottom of the bowl back over the clams. If you want to try another method however, add a handful of polenta to the bowl of water. The clams feed on the polenta and this causes them to burp. As they burp, they emit any debris inside the shell. Always make sure the water is cold—warm water will cause the shells to open and spoil the meat.

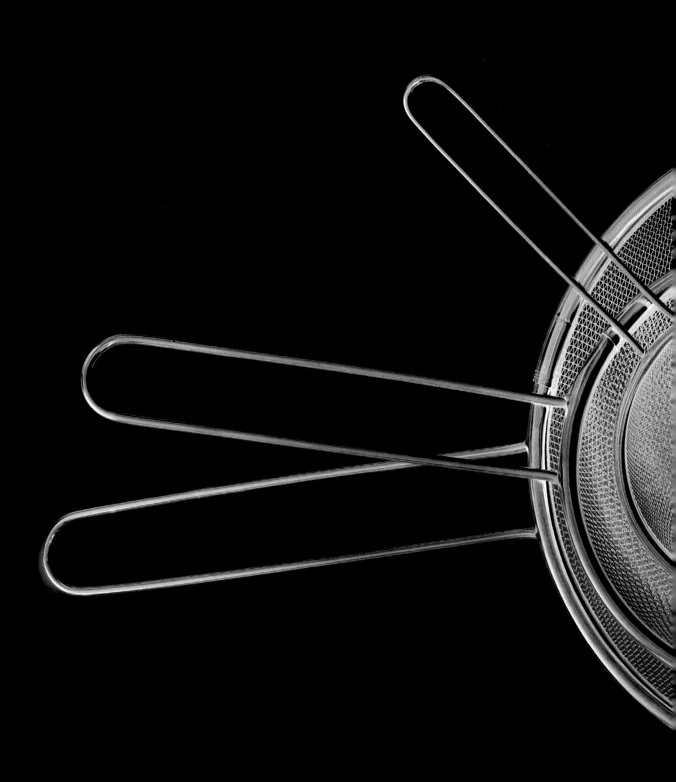

RICE

Rice

It's hard to think of a more versatile ingredient than rice: used by cultures around the globe, it adapts itself to both savory and sweet recipes, appearing in the most exotic Eastern and Asian dishes, all the way through to an old-fashioned rice pudding.

Look at supermarket shelves and the story of our love affair with rice is evident in the different varieties now available. Many of the specialty rices–arborio, basmati, jasmine, sushi rice–were once scarcely available as imports, but are now grown around the world. When it is first harvested, rice has a rough outside layer or hull: under the hull is a bran layer and under the bran is the grain of rice. Most of the rice eaten around the world is white (polished) rice, which has been hulled and had its bran layer removed. It is tender and easily digested. Rice that has been hulled but still has the bran layer intact is brown rice. It has a nutty taste and a chewy texture and takes longer to cook than white. Brown rice is more filling and more nutritious because the bran layer is rich in B vitamins and dietary fiber.

HOW TO COOK RICE

Ideally, you want to cook rice so that the grains are tender but separate rather than stuck together or lumpy. There are two methods for cooking rice:

BOILED RICE This method makes it very easy to keep the grains separate, but you do throw away some of the rice flavor with the cooking water. Bring a large saucepan of lightly salted water to a rolling boil. Slowly sprinkle in the rice, stir once, then cook, uncovered, keeping the water at a brisk boil. Start testing the rice after 10 minutes. The rice should be tender but firm in the center, not mushy. Drain and run hot water through to separate the grains.

ABSORPTION METHODS This method retains all the flavor of the rice and is therefore often preferred. There are two ways to cook rice by absorption. Many cooks recommend rinsing the rice first in a sieve, rubbing it with your fingers, to help dislodge surface starch.

i) In a large saucepan, place double the amount of lightly salted water, by volume, as the amount of rice. Cover and bring to a boil over high heat. Uncover and slowly sprinkle in the rice, keeping the heat high so the water does not stop boiling. Stir once, then cover again with a tight-fitting lid; turn the heat to very low. Cook for 10 minutes without removing the lid. Remove from the heat, stand with the lid on for at least another 10 minutes, then fluff up with a fork.

ii) Place the rice in a large saucepan, add a pinch of salt and cold water to cover. Shake the pan from side to side to level the surface. Place the tip of your index finger on the surface of the rice and add more cold water until it comes up to your first finger joint. This applies regardless of the quantity you are cooking. Bring to a boil and cook until the water evaporates, leaving steam holes in the rice; cover with a tight-fitting lid and turn the heat to very low. Cook for about 10 minutes or until the rice is tender but firm in the center. Don't lift the lid until the last minute or two of cooking, then quickly remove a few grains of rice to test and replace the lid immediately. When cooked, remove the pan from the heat, stand with the lid on for 10 minutes, then fluff up with a fork.

TYPES OF RICE

LONG-GRAIN RICE When cooked, this rice looks light and fluffy and the grains remain separate. Available in both white and brown rice varieties, long grain rice is suitable for most savory dishes and is perfect for pilafs, salads and stuffings and for Indian, Middle Eastern, Italian and Spanish dishes. Long-grain rices include:

• BASMATI A fragrant, long-grain white rice with a nutty aroma, favored for Indian dishes. When cooked, the grains are firm, separate and dry.

• JASMINE A fragrant, long-grain white rice with a delicate floral aroma that is used throughout Southeast Asia. It is softer than basmati and when cooked, its grains are slightly sticky.

• JASMATI A hybrid, aromatic rice that is a cross between basmati and jasmine rice. It is soft textured with a mild flavor.

MEDIUM-GRAIN RICE The grains of this rice are rounded and a little longer than they are fat. When cooked, it is slightly clingy, making it ideal for rice croquettes and molds and also for eating with chopsticks. It's favored in Chinese cooking. Varieties of medium-grain rice include:

• ARBORIO, CARNAROLI AND VIALONE NANO These are rices used specifically for risotto. They have a soft texture and their special quality is that they can absorb liquid and stand up to long cooking and stirring without becoming soft and mushy. At the same time, they release just enough starch to give creaminess. Arborio is the best known and least expensive of these risotto rices. Carnaroli is the aristocrat of risotto rices because of its fine flavor and texture. Vialone nano has a stubbier grain. Risotto rices are also good for paella.

• CALROSE is the brand-name of a medium-grain white rice that has been developed as an all-purpose rice. It gives different results according to how it is cooked--separate and fluffy after short cooking and rinsing, moist and easily compacted after longer cooking without rinsing. Calrose brown rice is also available.

SHORT-GRAIN RICE The round, fat grains of this rice cook to a soft, moist texture and cling together, making it perfect for puddings and a good food for babies before they get teeth. Short-grain rice is favored in Spain for paella and in Japan for sushi. The moist, sticky grains are ideal for eating with chopsticks. In Southeast Asia, sticky short-grain rice (both white and black) is used to make desserts such as black sticky rice pudding. Short-grain rice includes:

• GLUTINOUS Also known as sticky rice, its short, fat grains become sticky and cling together when cooked, allowing it to be easily formed into small balls. It is used mainly for desserts and rice cakes.

• KOSHIHIKARI AND NISHIKI Also called sushi rices, these rices are moist and tender when cooked, but still firm and clingy enough to be picked up with chopsticks.

• BLACK RICE A variety of glutinous rice, black-brown when raw and deep purple when cooked.

• CALASPARRA A short-grain Spanish rice suited to making paella as it can absorb 2½ to 3 times its own volume of liquid.

NOTE Some medium/short-grain varieties are interchangeable. If short-grain is called for, you can use medium. If medium if called for, use long for dishes like croquettes, and short for puddings.

STORING RICE

WHITE RICE WILL KEEP IN AN AIRTIGHT CONTAINER IN A COOL, DRY PLACE FOR UP TO 2 YEARS. THE OIL IN THE BRAN COATING OF BROWN RICE SHORTENS ITS STORAGE LIFE: IT WILL KEEP IN THE SAME CONDITIONS AS WHITE RICE FOR 6 MONTHS.

ONCE COOKED, KEEP RICE IN A COVERED CONTAINER IN THE REFRIGERATOR AND USE WITHIN A WEEK. LEFTOVER LONG-GRAIN RICE IS PERFECT FOR FRIED RICE.

Know your rice

The whole world loves rice. It all started with Asian fried rice. Then the Italians showed us risotto, the Spaniards gave us paella, sushi made its way from Japan, and the Near East introduced us to pilaf. But despite our love for the grain, not all rice is created equal. Each has its virtues and uses.

LONG-GRAIN
Long and slender, the grains stay dry, separate and fluffy after cooking, so it is the right choice for most savory uses. Perfect as a plain accompaniment or a bed for sauces. Great in rice salads, Indian and Middle Eastern pilafs, and Mediterranean soups.

BASMATI
A fragrant long-grain rice, originally from Pakistan. It should be cooked by the absorption method to retain its warm aroma and taste. The grain is prized for its low-GI rating, which means it helps control blood glucose levels and keeps you satisfied for longer.

JASMINE
A long-grain Thai rice that is also aromatic but is softer and a little more clingy than basmati once cooked. Jasmine is the perfect accompaniment for Southeast Asian food. It should be cooked by the absorption method to preserve its aroma and taste.

BROWN
Brown rice retains the high-fiber, nutritious bran coating that's removed from white rice when hulled. It takes longer to cook than white rice and has a chewier texture. Once cooked, the long grains stay separate, while the short grains are soft and stickier.

WILD RICE
Not a member of the rice family at all but the seed of an aquatic grass native to the cold regions of North America. Wild rice has a strong nutty taste and can be expensive, so it is best used combined with brown and white rices in pilafs, stuffings and salads.

WILD RICE BLEND
A packaged blend of white long-grain rice and wild rice. With its dark brown, almost black grains, crunchy, resilient texture and smoky flavor, wild rice contrasts nicely with mild-tasting white rice. Perfect with lentils, fish, in pilafs or added to soups.

Q&A

My family eats lots of rice but we can't agree on variety. I prefer brown long-grain because it is so nutritious, has great flavor and is non-sticky. The drawback is the longer cooking time. My husband and children, however, don't like its strong taste and prefer softer, milder white rices. Can you suggest a compromise?

A good compromise between nutrient-rich brown rice and tender, fast-cooking white rice is parboiled (converted) rice. Although it might sound like a modern product, parboiling was discovered in ancient India, where the process was used to preserve rice and retain the nutrients that are lost during milling. Parboiled rice stores better than brown rice because it has no bran or germ oil, so it won't go rancid. It cooks to a firm, separate grain and doesn't become sticky if overcooked. The rice can be used in most dishes (except desserts) and reheats well.

CALROSE
A medium grain developed in California in the 1950s; the variety is no longer grown, but many brands use "calrose" as a generic name for their medium-grain rice. It's easier to work with than sushi rice as it's not as clingy.

ARBORIO
The best-known of the Italian risotto rices, which partly dissolve when cooked to achieve a clinging, creamy texture but, at the same time, remain firm to the bite (al dente), so the rice won't become mushy. Other risotto rices include carnaroli and vialone nano.

GLUTINOUS
Also known as sticky rice, this variety is a stickier version of short-grain rice. Its plump, distinctively flavored grains cling together when cooked, so they can be easily formed into small balls for dipping into savory dishes and soaking up the sauce.

BLACK
Also known as purple rice, black rice is unmilled, leaving the dark husk in place, which colors the grain when cooked. It has a nutty taste and crunchy texture. There are hundreds of varieties across Asia, from Chinese black rice to Thai black sticky rice.

NISHIKI
A Japanese variety that's often sold as medium-grain rice, but is actually a slightly longer short-grain rice. Like Koshihikari (right), Nishiki cooks to the tender and lightly clinging texture that is right for sushi. This light, fresh-tasting grain is also grown in California.

KOSHIHIKARI
A premium Japanese short-grain rice, distinguished by its aroma, sweet flavor and sticky texture. Its small, round grains cook to a softness with just enough cling to be eaten with chopsticks. Perfect for sushi and rice desserts. Also sold as "sushi rice".

mushroom risotto

Unlike some other rice dishes, risotto does not require you to rinse the rice before you begin to cook. In fact, the starch is essential to the dish. The initial toasting of the rice loosens the starch in each grain. As liquid is added to the rice and stirred in, gently and almost constantly, more starch is released. This process will eventually leave you with a soft, creamy and evenly cooked risotto.

⅓ ounce dried chanterelle mushrooms
⅓ ounce dried porcini mushrooms
1 quart chicken or vegetable stock
2 cups water
3 tablespoons butter
4 ounces cremini mushrooms, trimmed
4 ounces button mushrooms, sliced thickly

2 portobello mushrooms, halved, sliced thickly
4 shallots, chopped finely
2 cloves garlic, crushed
2 cups arborio rice
½ cup dry white wine
½ cup finely grated parmesan cheese
2 tablespoons finely chopped fresh chives

1 Combine chanterelle and porcini mushrooms, stock and the water in medium saucepan; bring to a boil. Reduce heat; simmer, covered.
2 Meanwhile, melt tablespoons of the butter in large saucepan; add remaining mushrooms to pan. Cook, stirring, until mushrooms are tender and liquid evaporates; remove from pan.
3 Melt remaining butter in same pan; cook shallots and garlic, stirring, until shallots soften. Add rice; stir to coat rice in butter mixture. Return mushrooms cooked in butter to pan with wine; bring to a boil. Reduce heat; simmer, uncovered, until liquid has almost evaporated. Add 1 cup simmering stock mixture; cook, stirring, over low heat, until stock is absorbed. Continue adding stock mixture, in 1 cup batches, stirring, until absorbed between additions. Total cooking time should be about 25 minutes or until rice is tender. Stir in cheese and chives.

nutritional count per serving 15.4g total fat (9.4g saturated fat); 572 cal; 82.2g carbohydrate; 17.9g protein; 4.4g fiber

Using a sharp knife, cut both the portobello and button mushrooms into thick slices, and trim the edges of the cremini mushrooms.

Once the vegetables are cooked and softened, stir in the rice. Cook, stirring constantly, to coat the rice with butter.

Add 1 cup of simmering stock mixture and cook, stirring constantly, over a low heat, until stock is absorbed. Continue adding stock, 1 cup at a time, stirring constantly and allowing each addition to be absorbed before adding the next cup.

prawn and asparagus risotto

PREP + COOK TIME 1 HOUR 10 MINS • SERVES 4

1 pound uncooked medium
   king prawns
3 cups chicken stock
3 cups water
1 tablespoon butter
1 tablespoon olive oil
1 small brown onion,
   chopped finely
2 cups arborio rice

½ cup dry sherry
1 tablespoon butter, extra
2 teaspoons olive oil, extra
2 cloves garlic, crushed
1 pound asparagus, chopped coarsely
⅓ cup coarsely grated
   parmesan cheese
⅓ cup coarsely chopped fresh basil

1 Shell and devein prawns; chop prawn meat coarsely.

2 Place stock and the water in large saucepan; bring to a boil. Reduce heat; simmer, covered.

3 Meanwhile, heat butter and oil in large saucepan; cook onion, stirring, until soft. Add rice; stir rice to coat in onion mixture. Add sherry; cook, stirring, until liquid is almost evaporated. Stir in 1 cup simmering stock mixture; cook, stirring, over low heat until liquid is absorbed. Continue adding stock mixture, in 1-cup batches, stirring, until absorbed after each addition. Total cooking time should be about 35 minutes or until rice is tender.

4 Heat extra butter and extra oil in medium frying pan; cook prawn meat and garlic, stirring, until prawn just changes color.

5 Boil, steam or microwave asparagus until just tender; drain. Add asparagus, prawn mixture and cheese to risotto; cook, stirring, until cheese melts. Stir in basil.

nutritional count per serving 14.7g total fat (5.5g saturated fat); 602 cal; 82.8g carbohydrate; 26.3g protein; 2.6g fiber

baked pumpkin and spinach risotto

PREP + COOK TIME 50 MINS • SERVES 4

1 pound pumpkin or butternut
   squash, chopped coarsely
2 tablespoons olive oil
1½ cups chicken stock
5 cups water
1 large brown onion,
   chopped coarsely
2 cloves garlic, crushed

2 cups arborio rice
½ cup dry white wine
1 pound spinach, trimmed,
   chopped coarsely
½ cup pine nuts, roasted
½ cup coarsely grated
   parmesan cheese
½ cup cream

1 Preheat oven to 425°F/400°F fan-forced.

2 Combine pumpkin with half of the oil in baking dish. Bake, uncovered, about 20 minutes or until tender.

3 Meanwhile, combine stock and the water in large saucepan; bring to a boil. Reduce heat; simmer.

4 Heat remaining oil in large saucepan; cook onion and garlic, stirring, until onion is soft. Add rice; stir to coat in mixture. Add wine; stir until almost evaporated. Stir in 1 cup simmering stock mixture; cook, stirring, over low heat until liquid is absorbed. Continue adding stock mixture, in 1-cup batches, stirring, until liquid is absorbed after each addition. Total cooking time should be about 30 minutes or until rice is just tender.

5 Add spinach, pine nuts, cheese and cream; cook, stirring, until spinach wilts. Gently stir in baked pumpkin.

nutritional count per serving 41.6g total fat (13.8g saturated fat); 835 cal; 91.5g carbohydrate; 19.3g protein; 5.7g fiber

jambalaya

PREP + COOK TIME 1 HOUR 30 MINS • SERVES 4

This dish is a real one-pot-wonder. Very similar to the Spanish paella, jambalaya is the American version and, like paella, often contains seafood.

1 tablespoon olive oil
4 dried chorizo sausages
14 ounces chicken breast filets
1 medium red onion, chopped finely
1 medium red pepper, chopped finely
2 cloves garlic, crushed
2 tablespoons finely chopped pickled jalapeño chilies

1 teaspoon dried oregano
¼ teaspoon cayenne pepper
1 bay leaf
2 tablespoons tomato paste
1½ cups white long-grain rice
14-ounce can crushed tomatoes
2 cups chicken stock

1 Heat oil in large saucepan; cook sausages, turning occasionally, until browned. Remove from pan; slice thickly. Add chicken to pan; cook, turning occasionally, until browned. Remove from pan; slice thickly.

2 Cook onion, pepper and garlic in same pan, stirring, until pepper softens. Add chili; cook, stirring, 1 minute. Add spices, bay leaf and paste; cook, stirring, 2 minutes. Add rice; stir to coat in mixture.

3 Add undrained tomatoes and stock, bring to a simmer. Return sausage and chicken to pan; cook, covered, about 45 minutes or until rice is tender and liquid is absorbed.

nutritional count per serving 62.3g total fat (21.2g saturated fat); 1112 cal; 73g carbohydrate; 63.3g protein; 4.5g fiber

khitcherie

Khitcherie, a classic Indian rice and lentil dish, is the forefather to the English breakfast staple, kedgeree, a mixture of curried rice, smoked fish, and boiled eggs that is still enjoyed across England today.

1 cup yellow split peas
2 tablespoons ghee
1 medium brown onion, chopped finely
2 cloves garlic, crushed
2 long green chilies, sliced thinly
1-inch piece fresh ginger, grated
½ teaspoon ground turmeric
1 teaspoon cumin seeds
½ teaspoon garam masala

1 teaspoon ground coriander
1 cinnamon stick
4 fresh curry leaves
1½ cups basmati rice, rinsed, drained
1 cup raisins
1 quart hot water
1 tablespoon lime juice
½ cup roasted unsalted cashews

1 Place split peas in small bowl; cover with cold water, stand 1 hour, drain.

2 Heat ghee in large deep frying pan; cook onion, garlic, chili, ginger, spices and curry leaves, stirring, until onion softens.

3 Add peas, rice, raisins and the hot water to pan; bring to a boil. Reduce heat; simmer, covered, about 15 minutes or until rice is tender.

4 Remove pan from heat, discard cinnamon stick, stir in juice; stand, covered, 5 minutes. Sprinkle khitcherie with nuts before serving.

nutritional count per serving 13.2g total fat (5.1g saturated fat); 496 cal; 76.3g carbohydrate; 14.3g protein; 6.5g fiber

classic pilaf

Pilaf, pulau, pilav or pellao, all are the same cooked grain (usually rice) dish with different spellings in their respective countries of origin. The secret of a perfect pilaf is to rinse the grain thoroughly, to remove excess starch, then soak it briefly. Soaking before cooking softens the grains and results in a fluffier pilaf.

1⅓ cups basmati rice, rinsed, drained
2½ cups chicken stock
pinch saffron threads
3 tablespoons butter
1 medium brown onion, chopped finely

2 cloves garlic, crushed
1 cinnamon stick
6 cardamom pods
1 bay leaf
⅓ cup golden raisins
½ cup roasted unsalted cashews

1 Place rice in medium bowl, cover with cold water; stand 20 minutes, drain.

2 Heat stock and saffron in small saucepan.

3 Meanwhile, melt butter in large saucepan; cook onion and garlic, stirring, until onion softens. Stir in cinnamon, cardamom and bay leaf; cook, stirring, 2 minutes.

4 Add rice; cook, stirring, 2 minutes. Add stock mixture and raisins; simmer, covered, about 10 minutes or until rice is tender and liquid is absorbed.

5 Sprinkle pilaf with nuts just before serving.

nutritional count per serving 20.6g total fat (8.8g saturated fat); 509 cal 68.7g carbohydrate; 10.5g protein; 3g fiber

[1] khitcherie
[2] classic pilaf

steamed jasmine rice

Jasmine rice is a fragrant long-grain white rice with a delicate floral aroma; it is softer than basmati and, when cooked, its grains are slightly sticky. Store leftover cooked rice in a covered container in the refrigerator and use within a week.

2 cups jasmine rice
1 quart cold water

1 Place rice and the water in large saucepan with a tight-fitting lid; bring to a boil, stirring occasionally.

2 Reduce heat as low as possible; cook rice, covered tightly, about 12 minutes or until all water is absorbed and rice is cooked as desired. Do not remove lid or stir rice during cooking time. Remove from heat; stand, covered, 10 minutes before serving.

nutritional count per serving 0.5g total fat (0.1g saturated fat); 354 cal; 79g carbohydrate; 6.6g protein; 0.8g fiber

coconut rice with coriander

Calrose is the brand-name of a medium-grain white rice that has been developed to serve as an all-purpose rice. It gives different results according to how it is cooked– separate and fluffy after short cooking and rinsing, moist and easily compacted after longer cooking without rinsing. Calrose brown rice is also available.

½ cup shredded coconut
2 tablespoons vegetable oil
2 teaspoons chili oil
1 medium brown onion, chopped coarsely
1 medium red pepper, chopped coarsely
1-inch piece fresh ginger, peeled and grated
3 cloves garlic, crushed
1½ cups calrose rice
1½ cups chicken stock
1 cup water
5-ounce can coconut milk
3 green onions, chopped coarsely
¼ cup coarsely chopped fresh coriander
¼ cup lemon juice
¼ cup fresh coriander leaves

1 Heat wok; add coconut, stir constantly until browned lightly. Remove from wok.

2 Heat oils in wok; stir-fry brown onion, pepper, ginger and garlic until onion softens. Add rice; stir-fry 2 minutes. Add stock, the water and coconut milk; simmer, covered, about 20 minutes or until liquid is absorbed and rice is tender.

3 Remove wok from heat; stir in green onion, chopped coriander, juice and half the toasted coconut. Sprinkle with remaining toasted coconut and coriander leaves.

nutritional count per serving 26.2g total fat (13.9g saturated fat); 546 cal; 66.4g carbohydrate; 9g protein; 4.5g fiber

1¾ cups long-grain white rice
1¼ cups water
13½-ounce can coconut cream
½ teaspoon salt
1 teaspoon sugar
½ teaspoon ground turmeric
pinch saffron threads

TIP

• This recipe is easy to cook in a microwave oven. Place ingredients in a large microwave-safe bowl; cover with absorbent paper, and cook on HIGH (100%) for 10 minutes. Pause, stir; cook, covered with absorbent paper, another 2 minutes on HIGH (100%). Pause and mix with a fork; cook uncovered on MEDIUM (50%) for 2 minutes.

1 Soak rice in large bowl of cold water for 30 minutes. Pour rice into strainer; rinse under cold water until water runs clear. Drain.

2 Place rice and remaining ingredients in large heavy-based saucepan; cover, bring to a boil, stirring occasionally. Reduce heat; simmer, covered, about 15 minutes or until rice is tender. Remove from heat; stand, covered, 5 minutes.

nutritional count per serving 21.1g total fat (18.2g saturated fat); 523 cal; 73.9g carbohydrate; 7.7g protein; 2.4g fiber

1½ cups white long-grain rice
14-ounce can red salmon
5 tablespoons butter
⅓ cup coarsely chopped fresh flat-leaf parsley
2 teaspoons lemon juice
3 hard-boiled eggs, chopped coarsely

1 Cook rice in large saucepan of boiling water until tender; drain.

2 Drain salmon; discard skin and bones. Flake flesh.

3 Melt butter in large frying pan, add rice, parsley and juice; cook, stirring, until heated through. Add salmon and eggs; cook, stirring gently, until heated through.

nutritional count per serving 20.5g total fat (9.9g saturated fat); 421 cal; 39.7g carbohydrate; 19.1g protein; 0.6g fiber

serving idea lemon wedges.

paella

Calasparra rice is a short-grain rice available from gourmet food stores and Spanish delicatessens. If you can't find calasparra, any short-grain rice can be substituted.

1 pound clams
1 tablespoon coarse cooking salt
1 pound uncooked medium prawns
1 pound small black mussels
2 tablespoons olive oil
3 cups chicken stock
pinch saffron threads
7 ounces chicken thigh filets,
    chopped coarsely
1 dried chorizo sausage,
    sliced thickly
1 large red onion,
    chopped finely

1 medium red pepper,
    chopped finely
2 cloves garlic, crushed
2 teaspoons smoked paprika
2 medium tomatoes, peeled,
    seeded, chopped finely
1½ cups calasparra rice
1 cup frozen peas
2 tablespoons finely chopped
    fresh flat-leaf parsley

1 Rinse clams under cold water, place in large bowl with salt; cover with cold water, stand 2 hours. Drain then rinse.

2 Shell and devein prawns, leaving tails intact. Reserve shells. Scrub mussels and remove beards.

3 Heat 2 teaspoons of the oil in large saucepan, add prawn shells; cook, stirring, until red. Add stock; bring to a boil. Reduce heat; simmer, uncovered, 20 minutes. Strain through fine sieve into a bowl; add saffron to the liquid. Discard prawn shells.

4 Heat another 2 teaspoons of the oil in 18-inch paella pan or large frying pan, add chicken; cook until browned all over, remove from pan. Add chorizo to pan; cook until browned all over. Remove chorizo from pan; drain on absorbent paper.

5 Heat remaining oil in pan, add onion, pepper, garlic, paprika and tomato; cook, stirring, until soft. Add rice; stir to coat in mixture.

6 Add chicken, chorizo and stock to pan; stir until combined. Bring mixture to a boil; reduce heat, simmer, uncovered, about 15 minutes or until rice is almost tender.

7 Sprinkle peas over rice; place clams, prawns and mussels evenly over surface of paella. Cover pan with a lid or large sheets of foil; simmer about 5 minutes or until prawns are cooked and mussels and clams have opened (discard any that do not). Sprinkle with parsley; serve immediately.

nutritional count per serving 18.9g total fat (5.2g saturated fat); 509 cal; 49.1g carbohydrate; 33.6g protein; 3.7g fiber

brown rice sushi

Spread rice in a non-metallic dish, slicing it with a spatula to break up lumps and separate grains. At the same time, pour in the sushi vinegar gradually.

Place a nori sheet, shiny-side down, across mat 1 inch from the edge closest to you. Dip fingers into bowl of vinegared water, pick up a third of the rice, place across center of nori sheet.

Pick up mat with thumb and index fingers, holding filling in place with remaining fingers, and roll mat away from you. Press gently, wrapping the nori around the rice and filling.

1 cup brown short-grain rice
2 cups water
1 tablespoon rice vinegar
3 sheets toasted nori (yaki-nori)
1 Lebanese cucumber,
   seeded, cut into matchsticks
1 ounce snow pea sprouts, trimmed
2 tablespoons Japanese soy sauce

sushi vinegar
2 tablespoons rice vinegar
2 teaspoons white sugar
¼ teaspoon fine salt

chicken teriyaki
3 ounces chicken breast, sliced thinly
2 tablespoons teriyaki sauce
1 clove garlic, crushed
cooking-oil spray

1 Wash rice several times in large bowl with cold water until water is almost clear. Drain rice in strainer for at least 30 minutes.

2 Meanwhile, make sushi vinegar and chicken teriyaki.

3 Place rice and the water in medium saucepan, cover tightly; bring to a boil. Reduce heat; simmer, covered, about 30 minutes or until water is absorbed. Remove from heat; stand, covered, 10 minutes.

4 Spread rice in a large, non-metallic, flat-bottomed bowl. Using plastic spatula, repeatedly slice through rice at a sharp angle to break up lumps and separate grains, gradually pouring in sushi vinegar at the same time.

5 Continue to slice and turn the rice mixture with one hand; fan the rice with the other hand about 5 minutes or until it is almost cool. Cover rice with damp cloth to keep it from drying out while making sushi.

6 Add rice vinegar to medium bowl of cold water. Place one nori sheet, shiny-side down, lengthways across bamboo mat about 1 inch from edge of mat closest to you. Dip fingers of one hand into bowl of vinegared water, shake off excess; pick up a third of the rice, place across center of nori sheet.

7 Wet fingers again, then, working from left to right, gently rake rice evenly over nori, leaving 1-inch strip on far side of nori uncovered. Build up rice in front of uncovered strip to form a mound to keep filling in place.

8 Place one-third of the cucumber, sprouts and chicken in a row across center of rice, making sure the filling extends to both ends of the rice.

9 Starting with edge closest to you, pick up mat using thumb and index fingers of both hands; use remaining fingers to hold filling in place as you roll mat away from you. Roll forward, pressing gently but tightly, wrapping nori around rice and filling. Working quickly, repeat process to make a total of three rolls. Cut each roll into four pieces. Serve with soy sauce, and wasabi, if you like.

sushi vinegar Combine ingredients in small pitcher.

chicken teriyaki Combine chicken, sauce and garlic in small bowl. Spray heated small frying pan with cooking-spray oil for 1 second. Cook chicken, stirring, until cooked through. Cool.

nutritional count per serving 2.3g total fat (0.5g saturated fat); 253 cal; 43.1g carbohydrate; 12.8g protein; 3.4g fiber

combination fried rice

You will need to cook 1⅓ cups white long-grain rice the day before making this recipe. Spread it in a thin layer on a tray and refrigerate it overnight.

Dried Chinese sausages, also called lap cheong, are usually made from pork and sold, several strung together, in all Asian food stores.

2 teaspoons peanut oil
3 eggs, beaten lightly
1 tablespoon peanut oil, extra
2 cloves garlic, crushed
2 teaspoons grated fresh ginger
6 green onions, sliced thinly
4 cups cooked white long-grain rice
7 ounces cooked shelled small prawns

7 ounces Chinese barbecued pork, sliced thinly
3 dried Chinese sausages, sliced thinly
¾ cup frozen peas, thawed
1 cup bean sprouts
2½ tablespoons light soy sauce

1 Heat half of the oil in wok, add half of the egg; swirl wok so egg forms an omelette over base. Cook omelette until set; remove, cool. Repeat with remaining oil and remaining egg. Roll omelettes, slice thinly.

2 Heat extra oil in wok; stir-fry garlic, ginger and onion until fragrant. Add rice, prawns, pork, sausage, peas, sprouts, sauce and omelette strips; stir-fry until heated through.

nutritional count per serving 24.8g total fat (7.9g saturated fat); 615 cal; 58.7g carbohydrate; 36.1g protein; 5.8g fiber

nasi goreng

Nasi goreng, which translates simply as "fried rice" in Indonesia and Malaysia, was first created to use up yesterday's leftovers. You will need to cook 2 cups white long-grain rice the day before making this recipe. Spread it in a thin layer on a tray and refrigerate it overnight.

1½ pounds cooked medium king prawns
1 tablespoon peanut oil
6 ounces dried Chinese sausages, sliced
1 medium brown onion, sliced thinly
1 medium red pepper, sliced thinly
2 fresh long red chilies, sliced thinly
2 cloves garlic, crushed

1-inch piece fresh ginger, grated
1 teaspoon shrimp paste
4 cups cold cooked white long-grain rice
2 tablespoons kecap manis
1 tablespoon light soy sauce
4 green onions, sliced thinly
1 tablespoon peanut oil, extra
4 eggs

1 Shell and devein prawns.

2 Heat half the oil in wok; stir-fry sausage, in batches, until brown. Remove from wok.

3 Heat remaining oil in wok; stir-fry onion, peppers, chili, garlic, ginger, and paste until vegetables soften. Add prawns and rice; stir-fry 2 minutes. Return sausage to wok with sauces and half the green onion; stir-fry until combined.

4 Heat extra oil in large frying pan; fry eggs, one side only, until just set. Divide nasi goreng among serving plates, top each with an egg; sprinkle with remaining green onion.

nutritional count per serving 25.7g total fat (7.4g saturated fat); 653 cal; 48.5g carbohydrate; 54.7g protein; 3.3g fiber

lamb biryani

An elaborate layered dish inspired by moghul royalty, the regal biryani is still a spectacular Indian curry fit for a king. Perfect for entertaining, our version takes time but is worth every bit of effort.

Masala simply means blended flavors, so it can be whole spices, a paste or a powder, and can include herbs as well as spices and other seasonings. Traditional dishes are usually based on and named after particular masalas. Garam masala, used here, is a North Indian blend of spices containing varying proportions of cloves, cinnamon, cardamom, coriander, fennel and cumin, roasted and ground together. Black pepper and chili can also be added for a hotter version.

2 pounds lamb shoulder, cut into 1¼-inch pieces
1¼-inch piece fresh ginger, grated
2 cloves garlic, crushed
2 fresh small red Thai chilies, chopped finely
2 teaspoons garam masala
1 tablespoon finely chopped fresh coriander
¼ teaspoon ground turmeric
½ cup yogurt
2 tablespoons ghee
½ cup sliced almonds
¼ cup golden raisins
2 medium brown onions, sliced thickly
½ cup water
pinch saffron threads
1 tablespoon hot milk
1½ cups basmati rice
¼ cup firmly packed fresh coriander leaves

1 Combine lamb, ginger, garlic, chili, garam masala, chopped coriander, turmeric and yogurt in medium bowl. Cover; refrigerate overnight.

2 Heat half the ghee in large saucepan; cook nuts and raisins, stirring, until nuts brown lightly. Remove from pan.

3 Heat remaining ghee in same pan; cook onion, covered, 5 minutes. Uncover; cook, stirring occasionally, about 5 minutes or until browned lightly. Reserve half of the onion.

4 Add lamb mixture to pan; cook, stirring, until browned. Add the water; bring to a boil. Reduce heat; simmer, covered, 1 hour. Uncover; simmer about 30 minutes or until lamb is tender and sauce is thickened.

5 Meanwhile, combine saffron and milk in small bowl; stand 15 minutes.

6 Cook rice in medium saucepan of boiling water, uncovered, 5 minutes; drain.

7 Preheat oven to 350°F/325°F fan-forced.

8 Spread half the lamb mixture into oiled deep 2-quart ovenproof dish. Layer with half the rice; top with remaining lamb mixture then remaining rice. Drizzle milk mixture over rice; cover tightly with greased foil and lid.

9 Bake biryani about 30 minutes or until rice is tender. Serve biryani topped with reserved onion, nut and raisin mixture and coriander leaves.

nutritional count per serving 38.6g total fat (17.4g saturated fat); 886 cal; 73.8g carbohydrate; 58.7g protein; 3.4g fiber

NOODLES

Noodles

Noodles are a perfect food for modern times: they're quick and easy to prepare and, when teamed with vegetables and meat, they make a nutritious, balanced and delicious meal. The Chinese have known this for 2000 years and are as passionate about their noodles as the Italians are about their pasta. Like pasta, noodles are made from a simple dough, but they differ from their European counterparts because they're not solely wheat-based: they are also made from rice, buckwheat and vegetable starches such as mung bean. Noodles are incredibly versatile: they can be eaten hot or cold, boiled, deep-fried, stir-fried, or added to a fragrant soup. They play a prominent role in all Asian cooking but the Chinese and Japanese cuisines are particularly devoted to them and have developed a glorious array of varieties. Check out the growing display of noodles at the supermarket—or visit an Asian grocery store—and you'll discover a whole new world of possibilities.

STORING NOODLES

LIKE PASTA, DRIED NOODLES CAN BE STORED INDEFINITELY IN THEIR UNOPENED PACKAGES OR IN AIRTIGHT CONTAINERS. FRESH NOODLES LIKE HOKKIEN SHOULD BE STORED IN THE REFRIGERATOR, WHERE THEY WILL KEEP FOR WEEKS UNOPENED. ONCE OPENED, WRAP THEM IN PLASTIC WRAP, ENCLOSE IN A PLASTIC BAG, AND THEY'LL KEEP UNTIL THE USE-BY DATE.

TYPES OF NOODLES

WHEAT NOODLES

EGG NOODLES Also called yellow noodles or ba mee, these all-purpose noodles are made from wheat flour and eggs. They are available fresh or dried, and range from very fine strands to spaghetti-like lengths. Dried noodles are often sold in nest-like swirls. To prepare, soak in hot water for 10 minutes. Drain, loosening the strands, then cook in a large saucepan of boiling water with a little peanut oil.

FRIED NOODLES Also called crispy noodles, these deep-fried egg noodles are sold often in 3-ounce packs. Add straight to dishes, no cooking required.

HOKKIEN NOODLES These long, fat Chinese noodles are also called stir-fry noodles. They're thick and soft, having been parboiled before packing. The beauty of these noodles is that they don't need cooking, just reheating: cover them in boiling water, gently separating the strands with a fork.

RAMEN This was traditionally the name of a Japanese soup with noodles, but now refers to the instant, wavy-shaped noodles sold with a packet of soup base. These are very popular in Japan.

SOMEN These fine, delicate, white Japanese noodles are cooked in the same way as pasta, only they need to be rinsed after draining.

UDON NOODLES These thick white wheat noodles are sold fresh or dried. To cook, add them to a large saucepan of boiling water, stir, add cold water, boil, then reduce heat and cook until tender (3 minutes for fresh udon; 8-10 minutes for dried). Drain and run under cold water.

RICE NOODLES

FRESH RICE NOODLES These white, flat Chinese noodles are prized for their chewy, satiny texture and mild flavor, which lets stronger flavors shine. They come in various widths or in sheets to be cut as desired. They do not need preliminary boiling, just a short soak in hot water to soften them and remove excess starch.

RICE PAPER SHEETS Used to create the wrappings for summer rolls (a popular Vietnamese snack), these sheets are round and translucent. To use them, soften them briefly in hot water then wrap them around fresh ingredients such as vegetables, shredded chicken, seafood and herbs and serve with a dipping sauce.

RICE STICKS These are available in various widths– thin for soups and wide for stir-fries. Dried white rice noodles need to be soaked and softened in hot water before they are added to dishes to prevent them from sticking together.

RICE VERMICELLI These fine, dried noodles are often used instead of wheat noodles in the popular stir-fry dish, Singapore noodles–a combination of noodles, vegetables, chicken and prawns. They can be prepared in two ways. Vermicelli can be soaked in hot water until softened, boiled briefly, then rinsed with hot water. They can also be cut into shorter lengths and deep-fried until puffed up and crunchy, and then used in Chinese chicken salad, or as a garnish or bed for sauces.

BUCKWHEAT NOODLES

SOBA NOODLES These fresh or dried Japanese noodles are made from pure buckwheat or a combination of buckwheat and wheat flour. Some also contain green tea powder or dried herbs. Soba are not as simple to cook as other noodles (see Q&A, page 193).

MUNG BEAN NOODLES

BEAN THREAD NOODLES Also called cellophane or glass noodles (they become transparent when cooked), these fine, dried noodles are made from ground mung beans. Sold in bundles, they must be soaked in hot water before use. They can also be deep-fried like rice vermicelli.

Know your noodles

Along with the pasta craze came the noodle boom. Asian noodles were soon everywhere. Long, skinny ones, short fat ones, white rice ones and yellow wheat ones. These nutritious ribbons can keep your meals light or can extend them. And when done right, you'll feel like you've brought home a take-out meal.

HOKKIEN
These plump, yellow, fresh wheat noodles are the most popular stir-fry noodles as they soak up sauce so easily. They are good in meat-based soups, too. Hokkien also come in a thin version, which can be used interchangeably with fresh Singapore noodles.

FRIED
Also known as crispy noodles, these wheat flour and egg noodles have been deep-fried until crisp, then dried and packaged. They are often used in the popular Chinese dish sang choy bow and the Thai stir-fry, mee krob. Or add them straight to salads.

BEAN THREAD
Also called fen si, sai fun or cellophane noodles because their long, thin strands resemble clear plastic. They are made from mung bean flour, and have a gelatinous, springy texture that is perfect for soaking up dressings. Also used in Thai desserts.

SOBA
These thin, grey-brown buckwheat noodles can be eaten chilled with a Japanese-style dipping sauce and as a salad with various sea vegetables, blanched vegetables and tofu. Also served cold with a topping of seafood, fish or meat, or add them to hot broths.

SHANGHAI
Fresh thick, round wheat noodles, similar to hokkien but paler in color, and usually sold unoiled. Also available as dried thin white noodles, which need to be boiled for up to 15 minutes, or until soft. Shanghai noodles are often used in stir-fries.

RAMEN
Popular Japanese wheat noodles, sold in dried, fresh, steamed and instant forms. Common toppings are negi (leek), shinachiku (seasoned bamboo shoots), nori (dried seaweed), yakibuta (grilled pork), narutomaki (fish cake) and soft-boiled egg.

Q&A

My diet already includes plenty of wheat and rice, so I'd like to start eating other grains. I know soba noodles are high in protein and fiber, and I've enjoyed them at Japanese restaurants. Are they tricky to prepare?

Soba or buckwheat noodles can be made with 100 percent buckwheat (gluten-free) or a blend of buckwheat and wheat. Those that contain wheat are less "floury" in texture and easier to prepare. Whole soba noodles need a little more attention. Bring a large pan of water to a boil–the pan should be large enough to allow water to circulate around the noodles. Add noodles gradually so the water doesn't stop boiling, then cook until just tender. Drain. Rinse noodles under cold water then drain again.

FRESH RICE
These white, shiny noodles are chewy and slippery in texture. When cut very thin, they are known as mei fun–as in the stir-fry dish with shrimp. The thicker noodles are named hor fun or chow fun, after the Chinese stir-fry containing meat, fish or vegetables.

RICE STICK
These have a little less chew than the fresh versions. The thin noodles are used in soups, while the wide flat ones are added to stir-fries, including the famous Southeast Asian dish, pad thai. They can also be fried until crisp and puffed, and used as a garnish.

RICE VERMICELLI
Made of rice flour and water, vermicelli are often compressed into tablets and dried, and are slightly longer than bean threads. They are used in spring rolls and cold salads, and when deep-fried until crispy can be used in chicken salad or as a garnish.

SOMEN
Extremely thin noodles made from hard wheat–if eggless, they are labelled somen, and tamago if made with egg. These Japanese noodles are traditionally eaten in cold dishes but can be served in warm broth. Avoid overcooking, as they become sticky.

UDON
Broad, creamy-white Japanese wheat noodles with a mild taste and slippery texture. Particularly popular in southern Japan, udon are known as soup noodles, but are also good in stir-fries and hotpots. Available fresh and dried, in round, square or ribbon shapes.

FRESH EGG
Made from wheat flour and eggs, these golden noodles are available fresh or dried. They range in width from fine vermicelli to wide flat ribbons, and are mainly used in Chinese stir-fries and soups. Can also be crispy-fried and used to garnish stir-fries.

singapore noodles

You will need to purchase a large rotisserie chicken weighing about 2 pounds to get the amount of shredded meat needed for this recipe.

Fresh Singapore noodles are pre-cooked wheat noodles best described as a thinner version of hokkien. They are sold packaged in the refrigerated section of the supermarket.

14 ounces fresh Singapore noodles
1 teaspoon peanut oil
1 small brown onion, sliced finely
2 strips bacon, chopped finely
1-inch piece fresh ginger, grated
1 tablespoon mild curry powder
3 cups shredded roasted chicken
6 ounces Chinese barbecued pork, sliced thinly
6 green onions, sliced thinly
½ cup sweet sherry
¼ cup light soy sauce

1 Place noodles in large heatproof bowl, cover with boiling water; separate with fork, drain.
2 Heat oil in wok; stir-fry brown onion, bacon and ginger, about 2 minutes or until onion softens and bacon is crisp. Add curry powder; stir-fry until fragrant.
3 Add noodles and remaining ingredients; stir-fry until hot.
nutritional count per serving 18.6g total fat (5.6g saturated fat); 560 cal; 37.0g carbohydrate; 50.9g protein; 3.3g fiber

Place the barbecued pork on a clean chopping board. Using a very sharp knife, cut the pork into thin slices.

To prepare Singapore noodles, place them in a heatproof bowl, pour boiling water over, and separate strands with a fork.

pad thai

Place soaked tamarind pulp in a fine strainer over a bowl and push as much pulp as possible through the strainer by pressing down with the back of a spoon.

Place preserved turnip, flat-side down, on a clean chopping board and, using a sharp knife, cut into slices. Chop slices into very small pieces.

Place turnip, garlic, dried shrimp and chili in a mortar (bowl), grinding each ingredient with a pestle before adding the next one, to make a paste. Or process the ingredients using a hand blender or food processor.

1½ ounce tamarind pulp

½ cup boiling water

2 tablespoons grated palm sugar

⅓ cup sweet chili sauce

⅓ cup fish sauce

12 ounces rice stick noodles

12 uncooked medium prawns

2 cloves garlic, crushed

2 tablespoons finely chopped preserved turnip

2 tablespoons dried shrimp

1 tablespoon grated fresh ginger

2 fresh small red Thai chilies, seeded, chopped coarsely

1 tablespoon peanut oil

8 ounces ground pork

3 eggs, beaten lightly

2 cups bean sprouts

4 green onions, sliced thinly

⅓ cup coarsely chopped fresh coriander

¼ cup coarsely chopped roasted unsalted peanuts

1 lime, quartered

1 Soak tamarind pulp in the boiling water 30 minutes. Pour tamarind into fine strainer over small bowl; push as much tamarind pulp through strainer as possible, scraping underside of strainer occasionally. Discard any tamarind solids left in strainer; reserve pulp liquid in bowl. Mix sugar and sauces into bowl with pulp liquid.

2 Meanwhile, place noodles in large heatproof bowl; cover with boiling water. Stand until just tender; drain.

3 Shell and devein prawns, leaving tails intact.

4 Blend or process garlic, turnip, shrimp, ginger and chili until mixture forms a paste.

5 Heat oil in wok; stir-fry garlic paste until fragrant. Add pork; stir-fry until just cooked through. Add prawns; stir-fry 1 minute. Add egg; stir-fry until egg just sets. Add noodles, tamarind mixture, sprouts and half of the onion; stir-fry, tossing gently until combined. Remove from heat; add remaining green onion, coriander and nuts, toss gently until combined. Serve with lime wedges.

nutritional count per serving 19.7g total fat (4.5g saturated fat); 624 cal; 65.6g carbohydrate; 42.6g protein; 5.4g fiber

tip Preserved turnip is also called hua chai po or cu cai muoi, or dried radish because of its similarity to daikon. Sold packaged whole or sliced, it is very salty and must be rinsed and dried before use.

vegetarian pad thai

Soaking the rice stick noodles (sen lek) in hot water before stir-frying makes them tender and helps prevent them from sticking together. Sen lek are the traditional noodles used in pad thai, and before soaking, measure about ⅛-inch in width; other thin rice noodles can be substituted.

7 ounces rice stick noodles
2 cloves garlic, quartered
2 tablespoons finely chopped preserved turnip
2 fresh small red Thai chilies, chopped coarsely
¼ cup peanut oil
2 eggs, beaten lightly
1 cup fried shallots

4 ounces fried tofu, cut in small pieces
¼ cup coarsely chopped roasted unsalted peanuts
3 cups bean sprouts
6 green onions, sliced thinly
2 tablespoons soy sauce
1 tablespoon lime juice
2 tablespoons coarsely chopped fresh coriander

1 Place noodles in large heatproof bowl; cover with boiling water, stand until noodles just soften, drain.

2 Meanwhile, using mortar and pestle, crush garlic, turnip and chili until mixture forms a paste.

3 Heat 2 teaspoons of the oil in wok. Pour egg into wok; cook over medium heat, tilting wok, until almost set. Remove omelette from wok; roll tightly, slice thinly.

4 Heat remaining oil in wok; stir-fry garlic paste and fried onion until fragrant. Add tofu; stir-fry 1 minute. Add half of the nuts, half of the sprouts and half of the green onion; stir-fry until sprouts are just wilted. Add noodles, sauce and juice; stir-fry, tossing gently until combined. Remove from heat; toss omelette strips, coriander and remaining nuts, sprouts and green onion through pad thai.

nutritional count per serving 24.3g total fat (4.4g saturated fat); 339 cal; 15.2g carbohydrate; 13.4g protein; 4.3g fiber

mee krob

Thais serve mee krob by dividing the vermicelli among bowls, then presenting the sauce in a separate bowl. Onion, omelette and coriander are also served in separate small bowls, with each diner taking as much as desired of the three to sprinkle over the top of his or her dish.

5 ounces fresh firm silken tofu
vegetable oil, for deep-frying
4 ounces rice vermicelli noodles
2 tablespoons peanut oil
2 eggs, beaten lightly
1 tablespoon water
2 cloves garlic, crushed
2 fresh small red Thai chilies, chopped finely
1 small green Thai chili, chopped finely

2 tablespoons grated palm sugar
2 tablespoons fish sauce
2 tablespoons tomato sauce
1 tablespoon rice wine vinegar
7 ounces ground pork
7 ounces cooked small prawns, shelled, chopped coarsely
6 green onions, sliced thinly
¼ cup firmly packed fresh coriander leaves

Be careful when deep-frying the vermicelli: slide rather than drop them into the oil to help prevent splattering. Add them in small batches so the oil temperature doesn't reduce. Vermicelli puff immediately and must be removed from the oil quickly with a metal slotted spoon or tongs.

1 Pat tofu all over with absorbent paper; cut into slices, then cut each slice into ½-inch-wide matchsticks. Spread tofu, in single layer, on absorbent-paper-lined tray; cover with more absorbent paper, stand at least 20 minutes.

2 Meanwhile, heat vegetable oil in wok; deep-fry noodles quickly, in batches, until puffed. Drain on absorbent paper.

3 Using same heated oil, deep-fry drained tofu, in batches, until browned lightly. Drain on absorbent paper. Discard oil from wok.

4 Heat 2 teaspoons of the peanut oil in cleaned wok. Pour half of the combined egg and water into wok; cook over medium heat, tilting wok, until almost set. Remove omelette from wok; roll tightly, slice thinly. Heat 2 more teaspoons of the peanut oil in wok; repeat with remaining egg mixture.

5 Combine garlic, chilies, sugar, sauces and vinegar in small bowl; pour half of the chili mixture into small jar (or bowl), reserve.

6 Combine pork in bowl with remaining half of the chili mixture. Heat remaining peanut oil in wok; stir-fry pork mixture about 5 minutes or until pork is cooked through. Add prawns; stir-fry 1 minute. Add tofu; stir-fry, tossing gently to combine.

7 Remove wok from heat; add reserved chili mixture and half of the onion, toss to combine. Add noodles; toss gently to combine. Sprinkle with remaining onion, omelette strips and coriander.

nutritional count per serving 20.7g total fat (4.5g saturated fat); 361 cal; 17.6g carbohydrate; 25.6g protein; 1.9g fiber

beef chow mein

PREP + COOK TIME 25 MINS • SERVES 4

1 tablespoon vegetable oil
1 pound ground beef
1 medium brown onion, chopped finely
2 cloves garlic, crushed
1 tablespoon curry powder
1 large carrot, chopped finely
2 stalks celery, trimmed, sliced thinly

5 ounces mushrooms, sliced thinly
1 cup chicken stock
⅓ cup oyster sauce
2 tablespoons dark soy sauce
14 ounces thin fresh egg noodles
½ cup frozen peas
½ small Napa cabbage, shredded coarsely

1 Heat oil in wok; stir-fry beef, onion and garlic until beef is browned. Add curry powder; stir-fry about 1 minute or until fragrant. Add carrot, celery and mushrooms; stir-fry until vegetables soften.

2 Add stock, sauces and noodles; stir-fry 2 minutes. Add peas and cabbage; stir-fry until cabbage just wilts.

nutritional count per serving 15.7g total fat (4.6g saturated fat); 615 cal; 70.6g carbohydrate; 42.3g protein; 8.4g fiber

vietnamese noodle and chicken salad

PREP + COOK TIME 40 MINS • SERVES 6

You can poach, shred and refrigerate the chicken a day ahead. The dressing and salad vegetables can also be prepared a day ahead; store separately in the refrigerator. Simply combine the prepared ingredients with the noodles when you're ready. Or poach and shred the chicken, and use it warm with the salad ingredients and noodles.

2 quarts water
1¾ pounds chicken breast filets
7 ounces vermicelli noodles
4 ounces snow peas, trimmed
8 green onions
2 medium carrots
½ medium Napa cabbage, shredded finely
2 cups bean sprouts
1 cup firmly packed fresh mint leaves
1 cup firmly packed fresh coriander leaves
½ cup roasted unsalted peanuts, chopped coarsely

sweet chili dressing
½ cup lime juice
2 tablespoons fish sauce
3 teaspoons sambal oelek
2 teaspoons sesame oil
1 tablespoon brown sugar
1 clove garlic, crushed

1 Bring the water to a boil in large saucepan; add chicken. Simmer, uncovered, about 10 minutes or until chicken is cooked. Cool chicken in poaching liquid 10 minutes; drain. Using two forks, shred chicken coarsely.

2 Place noodles in large heatproof bowl, cover with boiling water; stand until tender, drain. Rinse under cold water, drain.

3 Meanwhile, make sweet chili dressing.

4 Slice snow peas and onions diagonally into thin strips. Halve carrots crossways; cut into matchsticks. Combine peas, onion, carrot, cabbage, sprouts, herbs and chicken in large bowl with noodles; drizzle with dressing. Serve sprinkled with nuts.

sweet chili dressing Place ingredients in screw-top jar; shake well.

nutritional count per serving 15.1g total fat (3.1g saturated fat); 424 cal; 30.9g carbohydrate; 37.7g protein; 6.4g fiber

Q&A

I've always used plain rice vermicelli for Vietnamese noodle salad but can I use bean thread noodles instead? I have a packet in the pantry but the cooking instructions are not in English. How do I prepare them?

Bean thread or cellophane noodles are even thinner than vermicelli. These crystal-clear dried noodles are made from the flour of the green mung bean. Like vermicelli, you can fry them straight from the packet for a garnish, or soften them until white and slippery. There are two ways to do this–place them in a pan of boiling water for about 30 seconds, remove them from the heat and leave them for 1 to 2 minutes; or simply soak them in warm water until tender. The latter method will preserve their texture better. Whereas vermicelli are good in both hot and cold dishes, bean threads are better suited to cold dishes since their web-like strands are harder to separate.

mee goreng

1 pound fresh wheat noodles

vegetable oil, for deep-frying

1 small white onion, sliced thinly

2 tablespoons raw peanuts

2 tablespoons peanut oil

1 pound pork filets, sliced thinly

5 cloves garlic, crushed

2 tablespoons grated fresh ginger

3 fresh red Thai chilies, chopped finely

10 fresh water chestnuts, peeled and sliced thinly

   or one 8-ounce can water chestnuts, drained

18 snake beans, sliced thickly

2 stalks celery, trimmed, chopped finely

2 baby bok choy, chopped coarsely

2 green onions, chopped coarsely

⅓ cup kecap manis

2 tablespoons sweet chili sauce

1 tablespoon thick tamarind concentrate

⅓ cup vegetable stock

1 teaspoon sesame oil

1 Cook noodles in large saucepan of boiling water, uncovered, until just tender; drain.

2 Heat vegetable oil in small saucepan. Deep-fry white onion until browned; drain on absorbent paper. Deep-fry peanuts until browned lightly; drain on absorbent paper. Blend or process onion and peanuts until chopped finely.

3 Heat half of the peanut oil in heated large wok; stir-fry pork until browned and cooked as desired. Remove pork; cover to keep warm.

4 Heat remaining peanut oil in wok; stir-fry garlic, ginger and chili until fragrant. Add water chestnuts and vegetables; stir-fry 2 minutes.

5 Return pork to pan with noodles, kecap manis, sauce, tamarind, stock and sesame oil; stir-fry until heated through. Serve sprinkled with onion and peanut mixture.

nutritional count per serving 43.3g total fat (14.9g saturated fat); 925 cal; 81.7g carbohydrate; 44.3g protein; 16.2g fiber

fried noodles with chinese sausage

14 ounces wide fresh rice noodles

2 teaspoons peanut oil

9 ounces dried Chinese sausages, sliced thickly

1 medium brown onion, chopped coarsely

2 cloves garlic, crushed

4 ounces shiitake mushrooms, chopped coarsely

1 small Napa cabbage, chopped coarsely

¼ cup chicken stock

¼ cup char siu sauce

2 tablespoons lime juice

½ cup loosely packed fresh coriander leaves

¼ cup loosely packed fresh mint leaves

⅓ cup coarsely chopped roasted unsalted cashews

1 fresh long red chili, sliced thinly

1 Place noodles in large heatproof bowl, cover with boiling water; separate with fork, drain.

2 Heat oil in wok; stir-fry sausage, onion, garlic and mushrooms until sausage is browned and vegetables tender.

3 Add cabbage; stir-fry until cabbage wilts. Add stock, sauce, juice and noodles; stir-fry until hot. Remove from heat; sprinkle with coriander and mint. Serve with nuts and chili.

nutritional count per serving 28.4g total fat (7.8g saturated fat); 517 cal; 43.6g carbohydrate; 17.6g protein; 9.8g fiber

hokkien mee

Hokkien mee is a flavorful fried noodle, vegetable and beef dish that has become synonymous with fried noodles and is eaten all over the world wherever noodle shops are found.

14 ounces hokkien noodles

1 tablespoon peanut oil

1¼ pound piece beef tenderloin, sliced thinly

1 medium brown onion, sliced thinly

2 cloves garlic, crushed

1 medium red pepper, sliced thinly

4 ounces baby corn, halved lengthways

5 ounces snow peas, trimmed, halved diagonally

2 baby bok choy, chopped coarsely

¼ cup char siu sauce

1 tablespoon dark soy sauce

¼ cup chicken stock

1 Place noodles in medium heatproof bowl, cover with boiling water; separate with fork, drain.

2 Heat half the oil in wok; stir-fry beef, in batches, until browned. Remove from wok.

3 Heat remaining oil in wok; stir-fry onion, garlic and pepper until tender.

4 Return beef to wok with noodles, corn, snow peas, bok choy, sauces and stock; stir-fry until vegetables are tender and beef is cooked as desired.

nutritional count per serving 32.3g total fat (13.8g saturated fat); 809 cal; 75.5g carbohydrate; 47.1g protein; 13.3g fiber

char kway teow

Dried Chinese sausages, also called lap cheong, are usually made from pork but can also be made with duck liver or beef. Red-brown in color and sweet-spicy in flavor, the 5-inch dried links are sold, several strung together, in all Asian food stores.

14 ounces wide fresh rice noodles
8 ounces uncooked small prawns
8 ounces squid tubes
⅓ cup peanut oil
8 ounces firm white fish filets, skinned, cut into 1-inch pieces
2 cloves garlic, crushed
2 fresh small red Thai chilies, chopped finely
1½-inch piece fresh ginger, grated
2 eggs, beaten lightly
5 green onions, sliced thinly
2 cups bean sprouts
4 ounces dried Chinese sausage, sliced thinly
2 tablespoons dark soy sauce
1 tablespoon kecap manis
1 tablespoon light soy sauce

1 Place noodles in large heatproof bowl; cover with boiling water, separate with fork, drain.

2 Shell and devein prawns, leaving tails intact. Cut squid down center to open out; score inside in diagonal pattern, then cut into ¾-inch-wide strips.

3 Heat 1 tablespoon of the oil in wok; stir-fry fish and squid, in batches, until browned lightly. Place in large bowl; cover to keep warm.

4 Heat another tablespoon of the oil in wok; stir-fry prawns, garlic, chili and ginger until prawns just change color. Add to bowl with fish and squid; cover to keep warm.

5 Heat remaining oil in wok; stir-fry egg, onion and sprouts until egg is just set. Slide egg mixture onto plate; cover to keep warm.

6 Stir-fry sausage in wok until crisp; drain. Return sausage to wok with seafood, egg mixture, sauces and noodles; stir-fry until hot.

nutritional count per serving 29.9g total fat (6.9g saturated fat); 548 cal; 27g carbohydrate; 41.1g protein; 3.3g fiber

Q&A

I recently became a vegetarian and tried making char kway teow using tofu instead of sausage and seafood. The result was very bland. What other meat substitutes can I use to create more complex flavors? I still eat eggs.

It is possible to make a good dish without meat. In fact, you can find street vendor stalls in Singapore that sell vegetarian versions of char kway teow. Plain tofu is great for soaking up flavor but it won't add any flavor to the dish. Try using smoked tofu or the nutty-like tofu-tempeh–tofu speckled with chunky tempeh (semi-fermented soy beans). You can also use frozen baked taro balls. All these products are sold at health food stores. The chicken eggs can be replaced with richer-tasting duck eggs, and peanuts will add both crunch and flavor to the dish. Vegetarians often use mushrooms (shiitake) and root vegetables (sweet potato) as flavor enhancers, too.

crab and soba salad

Soba are fresh or dried Japanese noodles made from buckwheat and wheat flour, sometimes with egg yolks; called matcha soba when Japanese green tea is added.

Serve cold with a dipping sauce and side dishes of tempura, or in a hot broth, plain or with clams, chicken, mushroom or other meats or vegetables, and various garnishes. They are a popular fast food in Japan.

8 ounces soba noodles

1 Lebanese cucumber, seeded, sliced thinly

1 small red onion, chopped finely

1 medium carrot, cut into matchsticks

2 ounces baby spinach leaves, sliced thinly

12 ounces fresh crab meat

1 tablespoon drained pickled ginger, sliced thinly

ginger miso dressing

2½-inch piece fresh ginger, peeled and chopped coarsely

2 tablespoons drained pickled ginger

2 cloves garlic

⅓ cup yellow miso paste

½ teaspoon wasabi paste

½ cup rice vinegar

½ cup vegetable oil

2 tablespoons water

1 Make ginger miso dressing.

2 Cook noodles in large saucepan of boiling water, uncovered, until just tender; drain. Rinse under cold water; drain.

3 Combine noodles in large bowl with cucumber, onion, carrot, spinach, half the crab and half the dressing. Divide salad among serving plates; top with remaining crab, ginger and remaining dressing.

ginger miso dressing Blend or process ingredients until smooth.

nutritional count per serving 32.4g total fat (4g saturated fat); 671 cal; 55.9g carbohydrate; 35.9g protein; 5.9g fiber

sweet soy fried noodles

Known as "pad sieu" this traditional Thai dish is similar to the famous "pad thai", but uses kecap manis (a thick, sweet soy sauce) to give it its special flavor. Fresh rice noodles can be purchased in various widths or large sheets weighing approximately 1 pound, which are cut into the noodle width desired.

1 pound fresh wide rice noodles

1 tablespoon peanut oil

3 cloves garlic, sliced thinly

2 eggs, beaten lightly

9 ounces gai lan, chopped coarsely

6 ounces snake beans, cut into 2-inch lengths

⅓ cup kecap manis

2 tablespoons light soy sauce

½ teaspoon dried chili flakes

11-ounce packet fried tofu, cut into ¾-inch cubes

4 green onions, sliced thinly

¾ cup loosely packed Thai basil leaves

1 Place noodles in large heatproof bowl, cover with boiling water; separate with fork, drain.

2 Heat oil in wok; stir-fry garlic until fragrant. Add egg; stir-fry until set. Add vegetables, sauces and chili; stir-fry until vegetables are tender. Add noodles, tofu, onion and basil; stir-fry until hot.

nutritional count per serving 18.2g total fat (4g saturated fat); 487 cal; 55.4g carbohydrate; 20.1g protein; 9.8g fiber

udon noodle and prawn broth

PREP + COOK TIME 30 MINS • SERVES 4

Udon noodles are broad, white Japanese wheat noodles. Particularly popular in southern Japan, udon are best known as soup noodles, but are also good in stir-fries and hotpots. Available fresh and dried, in round, square or ribbon shapes.

3 cups fish stock
3 cups water
4-inch stick fresh lemon grass, chopped coarsely
4 fresh kaffir lime leaves, shredded
3-inch piece fresh ginger, peeled, sliced thinly
2 fresh small red Thai chilies, chopped coarsely

1 tablespoon fish sauce
2 pounds uncooked medium king prawns
6 ounces fresh udon noodles
8-ounce can sliced bamboo shoots, rinsed, drained
4 ounces fresh shiitake mushrooms, sliced thickly
2 ounces baby spinach leaves

1 Combine stock, the water, lemon grass, lime leaves, ginger, chili and sauce in large saucepan; bring to a boil. Reduce heat, simmer broth, uncovered, 10 minutes.
2 Meanwhile, shell and devein prawns.
3 Strain broth through sieve into large bowl; discard solids. Return broth to pan with prawns, noodles, bamboo shoots and mushrooms. Simmer, uncovered, about 5 minutes or until prawns change in color and noodles are cooked as desired. Remove from heat; stir in spinach.

nutritional count per serving 1.5g total fat (0.3g saturated fat); 206 cal; 16.2g carbohydrate; 30.3g protein; 2.3g fiber

chilled soba

PREP + COOK TIME 20 MINS (+ CHILLING) • SERVES 4

The Japanese celebrate New Year's Eve by eating soba noodles as the clock strikes midnight. This is known as "Toshi-koshi soba", which literally means "Across the Years Noodles". The noodles symbolize longevity.

8 ounces dried soba noodles
¾ cup dashi
2 tablespoons Japanese soy sauce
2 tablespoons mirin
½ teaspoon sugar

2 green onions, chopped finely
1 teaspoon wasabi
½ toasted seaweed sheet (yaki-nori), sliced thinly

1 Cook noodles in large saucepan of boiling water, uncovered, until just tender; drain. Rinse under cold water; drain.
2 Heat dashi, sauce, mirin and sugar in small saucepan, stirring, until sugar dissolves; cool dipping sauce.
3 Divide dipping sauce, onion and wasabi among individual side dishes.
4 Just before serving, place noodles in a strainer and immerse in iced water to chill. Drain and divide among serving baskets or dishes; top with seaweed strips.
5 Add onion and wasabi to dipping sauce according to taste, then dip noodles in sauce before eating.

nutritional count per serving 0.8g total fat (0.2g saturated fat); 228 cal; 44.1g carbohydrate; 7.7g protein; 2.3g fiber

VEGETABLES

Vegetables

There will always be times in your life when you've eaten an excess of fast or rich food, and all you want is a plate of steamed vegetables for a dose of sheer, unadulterated goodness. And for the rest of the time, you can enjoy vegetables in their multiple guises: trusty accompaniments to the main dish; the star attraction in a fragrant curry; crunchy just-cooked ingredients in a tasty Asian stir-fry; or sliced and char-grilled on the barbecue. The possibilities are endless.

BUYING VEGETABLES

When they are fresh, vegetables should appear healthy-looking and vibrant, and most have a sheen. Greens should be crisp and bright, the cabbage family firm and tightly packed, tomatoes should be gleaming and richly colored, eggplant and peppers should be smooth and glossy, root vegetables such as carrots, potatoes and beets should be well shaped and unmarked (potatoes are actually better-tasting if they still have some dirt on them as the high pressure hoses used to clean them can damage their skins).

When you're selecting potatoes at the market, think about the way you want to cook them because different varieties are better for different uses. For example, high starch, floury varieties that boil well will not bake satisfactorily. Yukon gold or red bliss varieties are best for boiling and mashing while russets or new potatoes are good for baking.

Greens and vegetable flowers and fruits—such as globe artichokes, broccoli, cauliflower, eggplant, peppers and zucchini—are best used within a few days of buying them. Root vegetables should be used within a week or so. Peas and sweetcorn should be eaten the day you buy them because they gradually lose sweetness and tenderness.

STORING AND HANDLING VEGETABLES

Store leaf vegetables, peas, beans, corn, globe artichokes, broccoli, cauliflower, cut pumpkin and beets in paper bags or loosely wrapped in greaseproof paper, enclosed in plastic bags.

Store carrots, eggplant and peppers unwrapped in a covered crisper.

Store onions and potatoes in a cool, dark place on racks or in baskets off the floor.

Canned Asian vegetables can be kept in a container of water in the refrigerator for 2 or 3 days; the water should be changed daily. Fresh water chestnuts can be stored unpeeled and uncut in your refrigerator's crisper for up to 3 days. Fresh bamboo shoots and lotus root should be enclosed in a paper bag, then a plastic one, and refrigerated for up to 3 days.

ASIAN VEGETABLES

THERE IS AN EXTENDED FAMILY OF VEGETABLES TO DISCOVER AT YOUR ASIAN GROCERY STORE, AND FOR AUTHENTICITY IN YOUR ASIAN COOKING, IT'S REWARDING TO EXPLORE THEM. ASIAN VEGETABLES CAN SOMETIMES REQUIRE CONSIDERABLE PREPARATION IN ADVANCE, BUT ONCE PREPARED, THEY ARE COOKED QUICKLY TO PRESERVE THEIR TEXTURES, WHICH ARE AS IMPORTANT AS FLAVORS IN ASIAN COOKING.

THREE POPULAR ASIAN VEGETABLES

BAMBOO SHOOTS are available canned and sometimes fresh in Asian food shops; they are tender mild-flavored shoots (from the base of bamboo plants) used in soups and stir-fries.

LOTUS ROOT is the crisp, delicately flavored root of a water lily, used in salads and stir-fries. It can be bought canned or frozen and sometimes fresh. Fresh lotus root is usually cut crossways into slices, which are decoratively patterned with holes and often used for their visual appeal.

WATER CHESTNUTS are the corms (solid bulbs) of an aquatic plant native to Southeast Asia. Available fresh and canned, they are the size of a walnut and are prepared by peeling off the dark skin to reveal a crunchy white flesh. They are used in a variety of ways: chopped to go in ground meat dishes and wontons, sliced for stir-fries and boiled whole from vending carts.

COOKING VEGETABLES

BOILING There's an old-fashioned rule of thumb when boiling vegetables: those that grow "in the cold and the dark" (root vegetables) should be boiled "in the cold and the dark"–that is, placed in cold salted water and heated to boiling with the lid on. Vegetables that grow above ground "in the heat and the light" should be boiled "in the heat and the light"–that is, placed in boiling water from the start and cooked without a lid. Once cooked, drain the vegetables, return to the saucepan, and shake briefly over low heat to dry.

STEAMING While it takes almost as long as boiling, steaming your vegetables is preferred by most cooks because the vegetables retain all their flavor without leaching out the nutrients into the cooking water. Place the vegetables in a steamer (the water should not touch the steamer nor the vegetables) and cover with a tight-fitting lid.

ROASTING/BAKING For vegetables to accompany a roast, par-boil for 5 minutes, dry as for boiled root vegetables and score the surface with a fork. Place around roast meat for half an hour before the roast is done, spooning with pan juices and turning once. For a crunchier roast potato, roast on an oiled oven tray by themselves.

CHAR-GRILLING OR BARBECUING These cooking methods give vegetables a smoky flavor. Slice vegetables such as eggplant and zucchini, and brush with olive oil. Place on a hot ridged grill or barbecue, press down with tongs, turning, until barely tender and marked with char stripes.

STIR-FRYING Vegetables are usually diced or cut into strips for stir-frying and added to a steaming hot wok in the order of the time they take to par-cook–that is, the longest-cooking vegetables go first, the quickest-cooking last. Stir-fried vegetables should still be crunchy at the end of the cooking.

PAN-FRYING Heat a little oil or butter, or a little of both, over medium heat until the oil gives off a haze or the butter stops sizzling. Fry the vegetables until browned and tender, turning once; remove and drain on absorbent paper.

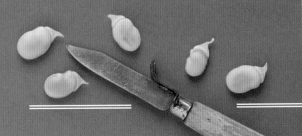

hasselback potatoes

This Swedish version of roasted potatoes produces a wonderfully crisp crust and makes an excellent accompaniment to roast beef or lamb.

4 medium red potatoes, peeled and halved horizontally
2 tablespoons butter, melted
1 tablespoon olive oil
¼ cup packaged bread crumbs
½ cup finely grated cheddar cheese

1 Preheat oven to 350°F/325°F fan-forced.
2 Place one potato half, cut-side down, on chopping board; place a chopstick on board along each side of potato. Slice potato thinly, cutting through to chopsticks to prevent cutting all the way through. Repeat with remaining potato halves.
3 Coat potatoes in combined butter and oil in medium baking dish; place, rounded-side up, in single layer. Roast 1 hour, brushing frequently with oil mixture.
4 Sprinkle combined bread crumbs and cheese over potatoes; roast about 10 minutes or until browned.
nutritional count per serving 14.1g total fat (6.6g saturated fat); 293 cal; 30.4g carbohydrate; 9.5g protein; 3.5g fiber

Place a potato half, cut-side facing down, on a chopping surface. Position a chopstick on either side of potato half.

Using a very sharp knife, slice the potato half thinly – the chopsticks will prevent you from cutting right through to the bottom. Repeat for remaining potato halves.

Roast potatoes, cut-side down, in a preheated oven for 1 hour, brushing regularly with oil and butter mixture. Turn potatoes over and sprinkle bread crumb and cheese mixture on top. Roast for another 10 minutes or until browned.

asparagus hollandaise

2 pounds asparagus, trimmed

hollandaise sauce

2 tablespoons water

2 tablespoons white wine vinegar

¼ teaspoon cracked black pepper

2 egg yolks

1½ sticks unsalted butter, melted

1 Make hollandaise sauce.

2 Boil, steam or microwave asparagus until tender. Serve asparagus on a large platter drizzled with hollandaise sauce.

hollandaise sauce Bring the water, vinegar and pepper to the boil in small saucepan. Reduce heat; simmer, uncovered, until liquid is reduced to 1 tablespoon. Strain mixture through fine sieve into medium heatproof bowl; cool 10 minutes. Whisk egg yolks into vinegar mixture. Set bowl over medium saucepan of simmering water; do not allow water to touch base of bowl. Whisk mixture over heat until thickened. Remove bowl from heat; gradually whisk in melted butter in a thin, steady stream, whisking constantly until sauce is thick and creamy.

nutritional count per serving 44g total fat (26.9g saturated fat); 430 cal; 2.8g carbohydrate; 6.1g protein; 2.6g fiber

serving ideas add a poached egg and some fresh dill for a gourmet breakfast. Spoon hollandaise sauce over globe artichokes, and steamed or poached fish.

roasted peppers

4 large red peppers

1 sprig rosemary

2 cloves garlic, sliced thinly

1 cup olive oil, approximately

TIP

• When using roasted peppers, remove from oil and drain on absorbent paper to remove as much oil as possible.

1 Preheat oven to 475°F/450°F fan-forced.

2 Quarter peppers; discard seeds and membranes. Place in large baking dish. Roast, skin-side up, until skin blisters and blackens. Remove from oven.

3 Cover pepper pieces with plastic or paper for 5 minutes; peel away skin. Place pepper quarters in large sterilized jar; add rosemary and garlic. Pour in enough oil to cover peppers. Store in refrigerator for up to 2 months.

nutritional count per serving 28.7g total fat (4g saturated fat); 291 cal; 6g carbohydrate; 2.4g protein; 1.8g fiber

[opposite] asparagus hollandaise

Know your vegetables

Today's vegetables bear little resemblance to the limp, gray-green culinary selections on our plates only two decades ago. They have now become a source of pleasure appreciated for their bright colors, crisp or tender textures and distinctive flavors. Some greens are still seasonal delicacies.

GLOBE ARTICHOKE
Part of the thistle family and not to be confused with Jerusalem artichokes (the tubers). Globes have round or conical-shaped heads made up of leathery-like petals. You can eat the tender heart and juicy base of the petals. Best from late winter to spring.

GREEN BEANS
There are a few varieties of green or french beans. Most have been bred to be stringless–to check, nip off an end with a thumbnail and test if you can pull down a string. Tender baby greens are simply green beans picked young. Available year-round.

SNAKE BEANS
Sometimes known as yard-long beans, this variety is stronger flavored than the common green bean, but can be used interchangeably in recipes. You'll find them in Asian shops, if not in ordinary greengrocers. They peak in the summer and autumn months.

BROAD BEANS
Broad or fava beans have bright green, slightly furry pods. When young, the beans inside can be eaten raw with their skin intact. The skin on the large, mature beans becomes tough and bitter, and must be removed. Mostly available from winter to spring.

BORLOTTI BEANS
Distinguished by their reddish-brown streaked pods and seeds. Only the seeds are cooked, and these lose their streaks once cooked. Their mealy texture makes them perfect for minestrone or stews. Fresh borlotti are available in autumn. Also sold dried.

BEETS
The rich maroon flesh of this root vegetable is sweet and nutritious. It can be baked or boiled and added to salads, or served with other roasted vegetables. It has an earthier flavor when eaten raw, grated in salads. Peaks mid-winter to early summer.

Q&A

Each time celeriac comes into season–from autumn to early spring–I'm tempted to buy it. Friends have served it up as a zesty salad bed for squid and a prawn remoulade, and it has the most amazing taste. Its hairy, gnarly roots and tough knotted skin have always put me off, though. How difficult is it to remove?

It's not too hard, once you know how, and it's well worth the effort. Wash the roots to remove as much dirt as possible. Then use a sharp knife to trim away the roots and skin. Slice the celeriac and immediately toss it into a bowl of water acidulated with lemon juice or the flesh will turn brown. Because the roots and dirt-filled crevices have to be trimmed away, you'll lose about a quarter of the celeriac during peeling. A 1-pound celeriac will yield about 2 cups once peeled and sliced. Pat dry and use a processor or hand grater to shred the celeriac.

BROCCOLI
Part of the cabbage family, along with cauliflower, broccoli is high in beneficial antioxidants and vitamins C and A. Cook, uncovered, to preserve its vibrant green color, and until it is tender but still firm. Best from midwinter to spring.

BROCCOLINI
A Japanese cross-breed of gai lan and broccoli, but sweeter and more tender than the latter. Can be substituted for broccoli, although the whole vegetable is used–trim by cutting off the very ends of the stalks and washing well, just before cooking.

CAULIFLOWER
The most delicately flavored member of the cabbage family, cauliflower is good boiled or steamed and served with white or cheese sauces, broken into florets and stir-fried, or made into fritters or a creamy soup. Available year-round but peaks in winter.

SWISS CHARD
Closely related to and often mistaken for spinach, swiss chard, sometimes called silver beet, has an earthier, slightly bitter taste. Its ribbed leaves can be sliced and added to salads, soups, meat stews, rice, pasta, stir-fries or cheese pies. Available year-round.

CELERIAC
Also called celery root, celeriac is the bulb of a type of celery. Under the brown knobby skin is an ivory-colored flesh with a faint celery flavor. Peel, grate and use in a remoulade, a citrus-dressed salad, or add to soup or mash. Its season is autumn to spring.

CHAYOTE
Choko or christophine are the other names for this South American tuber. Some describe its taste as bland, others say it is subtle. It can be used like a potato in recipes, but the skin has a tacky sap, so wear gloves when peeling it. Available early winter.

Know your vegetables

Vegetables are a welcome addition to any meal, often becoming the central focus, especially as their nutritional value is now better understood. From elaborate salads to soufflés and casseroles to pasta dishes, using plant-based sauces, vegetables have become a daily source of discovery.

FENNEL
A vegetable and herb in one with a licorice-like taste. The bulb can be eaten raw or cooked, the fronds can be used to flavor salmon or salads, while the seeds can be added to sauces, vegetables and breads. Winter is its season; baby fennel is picked in spring.

JERUSALEM ARTICHOKE
This knobbly tuber is actually native to the Americas and belongs to the sunflower family. Its flavor is delicately earthy, nutty and sweet, and it is tender when cooked. Great in soups, or baked like a potato, or pureed for a side dish. Available autumn to spring.

KALE
This strong-flavored member of the cabbage family is very high in antioxidants. Called cavolo nero by the Italians, it can be sauteed, boiled, braised, added to stews, or used like cabbage. Kale is best during winter. The summer variety is paler and thinner.

KOHLRABI
This round purple or green globe is a member of the cabbage family and develops a bulbous stem above ground. The bulb has a delicate cauliflower/turnip flavor and can be added to soups and casseroles, or used like potatoes. It comes into season in winter.

OKRA
This is used in the cuisine of India, East Asia, the Middle East, as well as the Mississippi region of the U.S. It tastes like eggplant but is part of the mallow family, which explains its gummy texture. Add to rice, stews and curries. In season summer and autumn.

PARSNIP
Their nutty sweetness is especially good when steamed and dressed with a garlic and cream sauce or in a curried parsnip soup, or simply baked. Can be substituted for potatoes. Available all year but the cold develops their sweet/savory flavor in winter.

Q&A

When I shop at the greengrocers, I usually have a rough idea of what I'll be cooking for the week and select my fruit and vegetables accordingly. Is this a bad way to shop? Should I be thinking more about seasonality?

Determining your grocery list from a weekly menu is a smart way to shop–but only if you are buying in season. When vegetables come into season, supply is high, so the prices drop. Over a year, you can save quite a bit of money. Vegetables that have been grown and harvested during peak condition will also be fresher, taste better as a result and last longer. Most greengrocers have in-store flyers on what's in season, so pick one up next time you are there. You can refer to it when you think about your weekly menu and compile your shopping list. And don't forget that buying locally grown seasonal produce will reduce your carbon footprint, too.

GREEN PEAS
The pods of this variety of pea are not eaten. Select carefully and use promptly as peas deteriorate soon after being picked. Serve boiled with any meat or fish, or pureed with potato. Good in soups, pastas and risottos, too. Best in spring and summer.

SNOW PEAS
Flat edible pods enclosing tiny peas that do not mature. Eaten whole or sliced, snow peas can be blanched and served with meat or fish, or used raw in salads, stir-fries or noodle dishes. Can also be added to soups at the end. Available year-round.

SUGAR SNAP PEAS
Not to be mistaken for green peas, snap or sugar snap peas have an edible crisp, sweet pod. They can be briefly boiled, used raw in salads, or added raw to stir-fries and noodle dishes. Small ones can be used in risottos and pasta sauces. Available all year.

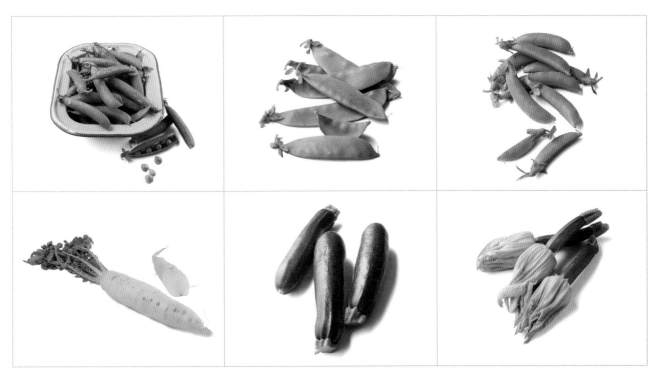

DAIKON
A very large Asian radish, daikon can be served raw in salads, pickled, grated as a garnish, simmered in soups or added to stir-fries. The Japanese cook it in the water in which rice has been washed to keep it white and reduce any bitterness. Best in winter.

ZUCCHINI
Grown virtually everywhere, zucchini has a subtle, sweet flavor when steamed, grilled, fried and baked– they should never be boiled for too long. Best in winter to spring, available in green and yellow, and as the yellow round variety called patty pan squash.

ZUCCHINI FLOWERS
The flowers of zucchini are harvested before they are fully grown and still young enough to have tender edible seeds. A summer treat to dip into batter and deep-fry or stuff with a savory cheese mixture, coat with egg and bread crumbs, and pan-fry.

artichoke hearts vinaigrette

The classic artichoke season runs from the end of winter to early summer, peaking in early to mid-spring, though some varieties introduced in recent years may appear as early as autumn. Size does not indicate quality. The important thing is that the leaves are tightly closed around the head, the stem firm and rigid, and the artichoke plump and heavy for its size. Tiny artichokes may have looser leaves, but they should be firm and springy and when pulled back, make a definite snap.

1 medium lemon, chopped coarsely
20 small globe artichokes (4 pounds)
2 cups dry white wine
¼ cup loosely packed fresh thyme leaves
5 cloves garlic, unpeeled
½ cup lemon juice
2 teaspoons sea salt flakes
1 cup white wine vinegar
2 cups water
1 tablespoon extra virgin olive oil

1 Place lemon in large bowl half-filled with water. Discard outer leaves from artichokes; cut tips from remaining leaves. Trim, then peel stalks; place artichokes in lemon water.

2 Cut a piece of parchment into a round shape to fit inside a large saucepan.

3 Place wine, thyme, garlic, juice, salt, vinegar, the water and drained artichokes in large saucepan; cover with parchment-paper round. Bring to a boil then simmer, covered, about 25 minutes or until artichokes are tender. Cool in poaching liquid about 30 minutes.

4 Whisk ½ cup of the poaching liquid in small bowl with oil (discard remaining liquid).

5 Halve artichokes lengthways; using small knife, remove chokes. Divide artichokes among serving bowls; drizzle with poaching mixture. If you like, sprinkle with extra thyme leaves and serve with crusty bread.

nutritional count per serving 5.5g total fat (0.7g saturated fat); 207 cal; 6.7g carbohydrate; 10.4g protein; 4.4g fiber

To prepare an artichoke, remove any tough outer leaves by pulling them off with your fingers.

Using a sharp knife, trim the stalk and the top. Trim tips of remaining leaves. Place peeled artichokes in a bowl of water with some chopped lemons to stop artichoke from discoloring.

Place artichokes in a large pan, along with poaching ingredients. Cover pan with a round of parchment paper to fit pan. Cook artichokes until tender, then cool in pan.

Using a small, sharp knife, cut artichokes in half, lengthways. Carefully remove the choke in the center and divide artichokes among serving bowls.

caramelized red onion

This recipe makes enough to go with six servings of grilled steak, but it is worth making double the quantity or more because it is so useful to have on hand.

You can also use brown onions in this recipe.

Caramelized onion will keep for weeks in a lidded container in the refrigerator.

3 tablespoons butter
4 medium red onions, sliced thinly
1 tablespoon brown sugar
⅓ cup dry red wine
¼ cup beef stock
1 tablespoon balsamic vinegar

1 Melt butter in large frying pan; cook onion over low heat, stirring occasionally, about 30 minutes.

2 Add sugar; cook, stirring, about 5 minutes or until onion has caramelized. Add wine, stock and vinegar; bring to a boil then remove from heat.

nutritional count per tablespoon 2.3g total fat (1.5g saturated fat); 38 cal; 2.8g carbohydrate; 0.6g protein; 0.5g fiber

serving ideas this goes well with chicken, burgers, for a pizza topping, a quiche, omelette or sandwich filling, or a garnish for barbecued swordfish.

caramelized fennel tarts

These tarts are easy but impressive. They can be served alone or as part of a vegetarian table, or with delicate filets of sole or trout. The caramelized fennel can be prepared ahead but place it on the pastry bases only when they are ready to go in the oven.

3 tablespoons butter
4 baby fennel bulbs, trimmed, halved lengthways
1 teaspoon finely grated orange rind
½ cup orange juice
1 sheet puff pastry
2 teaspoons finely chopped fresh thyme

1 Preheat oven to 425°F/400°F fan-forced. Oil and line two oven trays.

2 Melt butter in large frying pan; cook fennel until browned lightly. Add rind and juice; bring to a boil. Reduce heat; simmer, uncovered, about 5 minutes or until fennel is caramelized and tender.

3 Cut pastry sheet into four squares; place on oven trays. Remove fennel from pan, leaving behind the pan juices; divide among pastry squares. Bake about 20 minutes or until pastry is browned.

4 Meanwhile, return pan juices to a boil. Reduce heat; simmer, uncovered, until sauce thickens slightly.

5 Serve tarts drizzled with sauce and sprinkled with thyme.

nutritional count per serving 19.8g total fat (11.9g saturated fat); 274 cal; 19.9g carbohydrate; 3.3g protein; 2.7g fiber

caramelized onion and beet tart

PREP + COOK TIME 1 HOUR
10 MINS (+ FREEZING)
SERVES 6

3 tablespoons butter
4 medium red onions,
    halved, sliced thinly
1 tablespoon red wine vinegar
1 teaspoon fresh thyme leaves
3 medium red beets
    (1 pound), trimmed
1 sheet puff pastry
cooking-oil spray

4 ounces baby arugula leaves
chive oil
½ cup coarsely chopped fresh chives
¾ cup olive oil
1 ice cube
horseradish cream
¾ cup cream
1 tablespoon horseradish cream

1 Melt butter in medium frying pan; cook onion, stirring occasionally, over medium heat about 30 minutes or until caramelized. Stir in vinegar and thyme.

2 Meanwhile, boil, steam or microwave unpeeled beets until just tender; drain. When cool enough to handle, peel then slice beet thinly.

3 Preheat oven to 500°F/475°F fan-forced.

4 Place pastry sheet on flat surface; cut a 9½-inch circle out of pastry. Place on oiled oven tray, prick all over with fork; freeze 10 minutes. Bake pastry about 5 minutes or until browned lightly.

5 Make chive oil. Make horseradish cream.

6 Spread onion mixture over pastry; top with slightly overlapping beet slices. Spray tart lightly with oil; bake 10 minutes.

7 Meanwhile, combine arugula in medium bowl with half of the chive oil; divide among serving plates.

8 Cut tart into six wedges. Place each wedge on arugula, drizzle with remaining chive oil; serve with horseradish cream.

chive oil Blend or process ingredients until smooth.

horseradish cream Beat cream in small bowl with electric mixer until soft peaks form; fold in horseradish cream.

nutritional count per serving 54.5g total fat (20.6g saturated fat); 612 cal; 24.2g carbohydrate; 5.8g protein; 4.6g fiber

Q&A

For years, I've made do with canned or bottled beets. Until I tasted tarts and salads at cafés using fresh beets, I didn't realize what I was missing out on. Now I can't go back to packaged sweetened beets and want to start cooking the fresh variety. Any tips on how to do this, without a mess?

You need to boil, bake or steam beets without peeling them first to retain their nutrients and keep the color from running or "bleeding". Trim the root before cooking, but make sure you don't cut it too close to the beet itself or it will "bleed". Once cooked, the skin will easily rub off, either under cold running water or simply by peeling with your hands after it has cooled slightly. Always wear rubber gloves so you don't stain your skin. An easy way to bake them is to wrap each beet in foil, roast on a tray, then unwrap and peel.

broad beans and thyme

The flavor of these beans is musky and fresh, and they combine beautifully with mint and feta in a salad, or slip easily into a spring vegetable soup. Early in the season they are sweet; later in the season, when they become mealy, they should be pureed.

1½ pounds frozen or fresh broad (fava) beans, thawed
1 tablespoon butter
2 shallots, chopped finely
4 ounces speck, chopped finely
1 tablespoon fresh thyme leaves
1 tablespoon lemon juice

1 Drop beans into medium saucepan of boiling water, return to a boil; drain. When beans are cool enough to handle, peel away gray-colored outer shells.
2 Heat butter in large frying pan; cook shallot and speck, stirring, until speck is browned lightly. Add beans and thyme; cook, stirring, until beans are heated through. Stir in juice.
nutritional count per serving 7.7g total fat (3.5g saturated fat); 141 cal; 2g carbohydrate; 13.9g protein; 4.8g fiber

roasted caramelized parsnips

Caramelizing deepens a parsnip's natural sweetness but doesn't make it oversweet because the more sugar is cooked, the more its sweetness is transformed into deep, roasted flavors.

2 pounds parsnips, halved lengthways
2 tablespoons olive oil
¼ cup brown sugar
1 teaspoon ground nutmeg
1 tablespoon finely chopped fresh flat-leaf parsley

1 Preheat oven to 425°F/400°F fan-forced.
2 Combine parsnip, oil, sugar and nutmeg in large baking dish; roast about 1 hour or until parsnip is browned and tender.
3 Serve parsnip sprinkled with parsley.
nutritional count per serving 9.6g total fat (1.3g saturated fat); 257 cal; 35.8g carbohydrate; 4.1g protein; 5.7g fiber

[1] broad beans and thyme
[2] roasted caramelized parsnips
[3] glazed carrots with hazelnuts [page 226]
[4] braised baby leeks [page 226]

glazed carrots with hazelnuts

A most elegant side dish to grace roast duck, pork or game birds such as quail or guinea fowl.

2 tablespoons butter

1¾ pounds baby carrots, trimmed, peeled

2 teaspoons finely grated orange rind

¼ cup orange juice

2 tablespoons dry white wine

2 tablespoons maple syrup

½ cup coarsely chopped roasted hazelnuts

1 Melt butter in large frying pan; cook carrots, turning occasionally, until almost tender.

2 Add rind, juice, wine and syrup; bring to a boil. Reduce heat; simmer, uncovered, until liquid has almost evaporated and carrots are tender and caramelized.

3 Serve carrots sprinkled with nuts.

nutritional count per serving 17.2g total fat (4.5g saturated fat); 274 cal; 20.8g carbohydrate; 4.1g protein; 7.7g fiber

braised baby leeks

You could serve these leeks on their own as a first course, or as an impressive side to veal or fish. Be sure to supply diners with sharp knives, as even baby leeks can be hard to cut with blunt ones.

16 baby pencil leeks (2½ pounds)

2 tablespoons butter

⅔ cup chicken stock

2 tablespoons dry white wine

1 teaspoon finely grated lemon rind

2 tablespoons lemon juice

¼ cup flaked parmesan cheese

¼ cup coarsely chopped fresh flat-leaf parsley

1 Carefully trim root end from leeks, leaving each leek in one piece. Trim leeks into 6-inch lengths; halve lengthwise. Rinse under cold water; drain.

2 Melt butter in large frying pan; cook leeks, 1 minute. Add stock, wine, rind and juice; bring to a boil. Reduce heat; simmer, covered, 15 minutes or until leeks are tender. Uncover; simmer about 5 minutes or until liquid has reduced by half.

3 Serve leeks drizzled with cooking liquid then sprinkled with cheese and parsley.

nutritional count per serving 8.7g total fat (5.2g saturated fat); 154 cal; 8.3g carbohydrate; 6.5g protein; 6g fiber

creamed spinach

1½ tablespoons butter
1¼ pounds spinach, trimmed
½ cup cream

1 Melt butter in large frying pan; cook spinach, stirring, until wilted.
2 Add cream; bring to a boil. Reduce heat; simmer, uncovered, until liquid reduces by half.
nutritional count per serving 38.7g total fat (25.4g saturated fat); 372 cal; 2.8g carbohydrate; 3.5g protein; 2.1g fiber

brussels sprouts with cream and almonds

PREP + COOK TIME 10 MINS • SERVES 4

Brussels sprouts look just like mini cabbages. Possibly the least-liked vegetable, they are in fact little mouthfuls of nutritional goodness. Avoid overcooking and you will be surprised at how delicious they can be. Usually served as a side dish, their sweet cabbage flavor goes well with nuts, bacon, butter and herbs.

3 tablespoons butter
⅓ cup sliced almonds
2 pounds brussels sprouts, trimmed, halved
2 cloves garlic, crushed
1½ cups cream

1 Melt 1 tablespoon of the butter in large frying pan; cook nuts, stirring, until browned lightly; remove from pan.
2 Melt remaining butter in same pan; cook sprouts and garlic, stirring, until sprouts are browned lightly. Add cream; bring to a boil. Reduce heat; simmer, uncovered, until sprouts are tender and sauce thickens slightly. Serve sprinkled with nuts.
nutritional count per serving 46.7g total fat (28.4g saturated fat); 493 cal; 6.6g carbohydrate; 9.5g protein; 7.3g fiber

chili and herb swede crush

PREP + COOK TIME 30 MINS • SERVES 4

The rutabaga is thought to be a hybrid (cross) of the cabbage and the turnip. It is a relatively "modern" vegetable, known only since the 17th century, unlike its parents which have both been cultivated for thousands of years.

2 pounds rutabagas, peeled and chopped coarsely
3 tablespoons butter
¼ cup cream
1 fresh long red chili, chopped finely
1 tablespoon finely chopped fresh flat-leaf parsley
2 teaspoons finely grated lemon rind

1 Boil, steam or microwave rutabaga until tender; drain.
2 Crush rutabagas with butter and cream in medium bowl; stir in other ingredients.
nutritional count per serving 14.7g total fat (9.7g saturated fat); 185 cal; 8.6g carbohydrate; 2.3g protein; 5.8g fiber

Know your herbs

Dried herbs certainly have their place in the kitchen, especially when the home cook is caught off guard. However, once you start using fresh herbs, you'll never want go back to using just the dried varieties again. One of nature's little surprise packages, fresh herbs pack a big flavor punch.

CHERVIL
A herb belonging to the parsley family, chervil has a faint fennel flavor. It is elegant enough to use in salads, or added to fish, poultry and vegetable dishes. Chervil is one of the classic French fines herbes (along with parsley, chives and tarragon).

DILL
The dark-green feathery, anise-flavored fronds of the dill plant look decorative and are often used as a garnish. Tastes wonderful with fresh, smoked and cured fish, shellfish, cucumber, beets, potatoes and rice, and in a vinaigrette or mayonnaise.

VIETNAMESE MINT
Not really a mint, but a smooth-leafed herb with a flavor that resembles peppery coriander. It is used widely throughout Southeast Asia in laksas, salads, stir-fries and curries. The pretty leaf is also shredded and used as a garnish for many dishes.

CORIANDER
Coriander, also known as cilantro, is essential to Southeast Asian, South American and Middle Eastern cooking. Every part of the plant has its distinctive lemon/anise/sage flavor, and all parts are used–leaves, stems and roots.

OREGANO
The big savory taste and scent of oregano speak of Mediterranean cooking, from Greek moussaka and zucchini or eggplant dishes to Italian pizza and pasta sauces. Unlike most other herbs, it has the best taste and greatest pungency when dried.

GARLIC CHIVES
Their flat, dark-green leaves are a great Asian ingredient, used in soups, stir-fries, egg dishes and noodle dishes. Also good for snipping over salads and into mayonnaise and cream cheese.

Q&A

I always prefer to use fresh herbs over dried ones, but there are times when I simply can't make it to the greengrocer's in time, or the potted herbs on my balcony aren't doing so well. I then reach for the spice pantry but never know how much dried herb to use as a substitute. Are there any rules here?

Generally, a ratio of one part dried herbs to three parts fresh herbs works because most dried herbs have a more intense, concentrated flavor than the fresh ones. For example, when a recipe calls for 1 tablespoon of fresh herbs, 1 teaspoon of dried herbs can be substituted. Of course if your jar of dried herbs has been sitting on the shelf for three years and it has lost its potency, it may take a little more than this. It's also a good idea to add the dried herbs near the beginning of food preparation, unlike fresh herbs, which are added near the end.

THAI BASIL
Very different from common or sweet basil, its green leaves are smaller with a serrated edge and the stem is purplish. Thai basil leaves have a strong aniseed flavor, and are an essential ingredient in many Thai curries, soups and stir-fries. Also used as garnish.

TARRAGON
French tarragon, with its subtle aniseed flavor, complements chicken, eggs and veal, and is essential in a béarnaise sauce. It is also one of the herbs that make up the French fines herbs. Russian and Mexican tarragons are slightly coarser in taste.

BASIL
One of the most valuable culinary herbs, basil features in Mediterranean dishes. Its clove-and-anise perfume works magically with tomatoes and in pesto sauce. Although it is a summer annual, basil can be processed with olive oil and stored in the freezer.

SAGE
The pungent, balsamic taste and scent of sage are classic in stuffings for duck and pork, or with veal and prosciutto for the Italian saltimbocca dish. Deep-fried sage leaves are a delicious garnish for veal and liver and pumpkin ravioli in a butter sauce.

PARSLEY
The trusty workhorse of herbs, parsley works just as well as a garnish as it does in scrambled eggs, a potato salad or in a sauce for corned beef. Flat-leaf (also called continental) parsley has a stronger taste than the curly variety.

MARJORAM
Closely related to and similar in flavor to oregano, but milder and sweeter. Delicious in herb mixtures for omelettes, stuffings, herb scones and herb and cream cheese sandwiches. As with oregano, many chefs prefer dried marjoram to fresh.

scalloped potatoes

This scrumptious layered dish of potato, ham, cream and cheese is certain to become a family favorite.

You could also use Yukon gold potatoes for this recipe.

1¼ pounds medium red potatoes, peeled
4 ounces ham, chopped finely
1¼ cups cream
¾ cup milk
¾ cup coarsely grated cheddar cheese

1 Preheat oven to 350°F/325°F fan-forced; oil 1½-quart baking dish.
2 Using sharp knife, mandolin or V-slicer, cut potatoes into very thin slices; pat dry with absorbent paper. Layer a quarter of the potato in prepared dish; top with a third of the ham. Continue layering remaining potato and ham, finishing with potato.
3 Heat cream and milk in small saucepan until almost boiling; pour over potato mixture. Cover with foil; bake 30 minutes. Remove foil; bake 20 minutes. Top with cheese; bake, uncovered, about 20 minutes or until potato is tender. Stand 10 minutes before serving.
nutritional count per serving 28.9g total fat (18.6g saturated fat); 422 cal; 25.2g carbohydrate; 14.6g protein; 2.7g fiber

the perfect rösti

2 pounds russet potatoes, peeled
1 teaspoon salt
6 tablespoons unsalted butter
2 tablespoons vegetable oil

TIPS

• The perfect rösti have a thick crunchy crust and are moist and buttery inside.

• Rösti are best served immediately but can be kept, loosely covered with foil, in a low oven for up to an hour.

• Do not grate the potato until ready to cook the rösti to avoid discoloring.

• Use the largest holes of a four-sided grater to grate the potatoes coarsely.

1 Grate potatoes coarsely into large bowl; stir in salt, squeeze excess moisture from potatoes. Divide potato mixture into eight portions.
2 Heat 2 tablespoons of the butter and 1 teaspoon of the oil in medium non-stick frying pan; spread one portion of the potato mixture over base of pan, flatten with spatula to form a firm pancake. Cook, uncovered, over medium heat, until golden brown on underside; shake pan to loosen rösti, then invert onto large plate. Gently slide rösti back into pan; cook, uncovered, until other side is golden brown and potato center is tender. Drain on absorbent paper; cover to keep warm. Repeat with the same amounts of remaining butter, oil and potato mixture.
nutritional count per rösti 12.9g total fat (6g saturated fat); 197 cal; 16.4g carbohydrate; 3.1g protein; 2g fiber

potato wedges

You could also use medium white-skinned potatoes for this recipe.

2 pounds fingerling potatoes, unpeeled
2 tablespoons olive oil

1 Preheat oven to 425°F/400°F fan-forced. Lightly oil two oven trays.
2 Cut each potato into wedges; toss wedges and oil in large bowl. Place wedges, in single layer, on trays; roast, uncovered, turning occasionally, about 40 minutes or until crisp and cooked through.
nutritional count per serving 9.4g total fat (1.3g saturated fat); 249 cal; 32.8g carbohydrate; 6g protein; 5g fiber

VARIATIONS These spice combinations can be tossed with the oil and potato wedges before roasting:
lemon pepper Combine 1 tablespoon finely grated lemon rind, 1 tablespoon lemon juice and ½ teaspoon freshly ground black pepper in small bowl.
cajun Combine ½ teaspoon ground oregano, 2 teaspoons ground cumin, 1 teaspoon hot paprika, ½ teaspoon ground black pepper, 1 teaspoon ground turmeric, 1 teaspoon ground coriander and ¼ teaspoon chili powder in small bowl.

the perfect french fry

TIP

• After the first cooking, the fries can stand for several hours before the final deep-frying.

• Corn oil or vegetable oil can also be used.

• Use a cooking thermometer and monitor the oil temperature. Ideal frying temperature is 360°-375° F.

2 pounds russet potatoes, peeled
peanut oil, for deep-frying

1 Cut potatoes lengthwise into ⅓-inch slices; cut each slice lengthwise into ⅓-inch-wide pieces. Stand potato pieces in large bowl of cold water for 30 minutes to avoid discoloration. Drain; pat dry with absorbent paper.
2 Heat oil in deep-fryer, wok or large saucepan; cook fries, in three batches, about 4 minutes each batch or until just tender but not browned. Drain on absorbent paper; stand 10 minutes.
3 Reheat oil; cook fries again, in three batches, separating any that stick together by shaking deep-fryer basket or with a slotted spoon, until crisp and golden brown. Drain on absorbent paper.
nutritional count per serving 12.8g total fat (2.3g saturated fat); 278 cal; 32.8g carbohydrate; 6g protein; 4g fiber

perfect mashed potato

This recipe makes the most smooth, fluffy, irresistible mashed potatoes. Use potatoes high in starch and do not overcook them. Push the potato through a sieve or through a potato ricer or food mill (mouli). You can also use red bliss or Yukon gold potatoes for this recipe.

2 pounds white potatoes, peeled, chopped coarsely

3 tablespoons butter

¾ cup hot milk

1 Boil, steam or microwave potatoes until tender; drain.

2 Using the back of a wooden spoon; push potato through fine sieve into large bowl. Stir in butter and milk.

nutritional count per serving 10.2g total fat (6.6g saturated fat); 246 cal; 30.1g carbohydrate; 6.7g protein; 3.4g fiber

celeriac puree

For celeriac mash to serve with meats, make this recipe with 1 pound of celeriac and use a wooden spoon to beat it into 1 pound of boiled, mashed potatoes–don't use a food processor as it will turn the potato to glue.

2 cups chicken stock

2 pounds celeriac, trimmed, peeled, chopped coarsely

½ cup light cream

1 tablespoon finely chopped fresh chives

1 Bring stock to a boil in medium saucepan; add celeriac, return to a boil. Reduce heat; simmer, covered, about 30 minutes or until celeriac is tender. Drain.

2 Blend or process celeriac in batches with cream until smooth.

3 Serve sprinkled with chives.

nutritional count per serving 14.4g total fat (9.2g saturated fat); 195 cal; 7.4g carbohydrate; 5.2g protein; 8.8g fiber

serving ideas seafood, poultry or game birds such as quail or squab pigeon.

peas with mint butter

You need approximately 2 pounds of fresh pea pods to get the required amount of shelled peas for this recipe.

2¼ cups (12 ounces) fresh shelled peas

3 tablespoons butter, softened

1 tablespoon finely chopped fresh mint

1 teaspoon finely grated lemon rind

1 Boil, steam or microwave peas until tender; drain.

2 Meanwhile, combine remaining ingredients in small bowl.

3 Serve peas topped with butter mixture.

nutritional count per serving 8.6g total fat (5.4g saturated fat); 141 cal; 8.6g carbohydrate; 5.2g protein; 5g fiber

eggplant parmigiana

This is Italian cooking at its rich and gorgeous best. And it's worth every calorie.

2 large eggplants (2 pounds)
olive oil, for shallow-frying
½ cup all-purpose flour
4 eggs, beaten lightly
2 cups packaged bread crumbs
25 ounces bottled tomato pasta sauce

1 cup coarsely grated
  mozzarella cheese
¼ cup finely grated
  parmesan cheese
⅓ cup loosely packed fresh
  oregano leaves

1 Using vegetable peeler, peel random strips of skin from eggplants; discard skins. Slice eggplants thinly.

2 Heat oil in large frying pan.

3 Coat eggplant in flour; shake off excess. Dip in egg, then in bread crumbs. Shallow-fry eggplant, in batches, until browned lightly. Drain on absorbent paper.

4 Preheat oven to 400°F/350°F fan-forced.

5 Spread about one-third of the pasta sauce over base of greased 2½-quart ovenproof dish. Top with about one-third of the eggplant, one-third of the cheeses and one-third of the oregano. Repeat layering.

6 Bake eggplant, covered, 20 minutes. Uncover; bake about 10 minutes or until browned lightly.

nutritional count per serving 27.5g total fat (6.8g saturated fat); 540 cal; 49.4g carbohydrate; 19.9g protein; 8.3g fiber

Using a vegetable peeler, peel off random strips of skin from the eggplant. Slice eggplant thinly with a sharp knife. Repeat steps for the remaining eggplant.

Dip eggplant slices in flour to coat all over and shake off excess. Dip into beaten egg, then coat with bread crumbs.

Arrange one-third of the fried eggplant slices over pasta sauce in an ovenproof dish. Top with one-third of the cheese mixture and one-third of the oregano. Repeat layering until ingredients have been used up.

corn fritters

These corn fritters are perfect for a light meal or afternoon snack that kids will love. Add bacon, sweet chili sauce or an assortment of fresh herbs for variation.

1 cup self-rising flour

½ teaspoon baking soda

1 teaspoon ground cumin

¾ cup milk

2 eggs, separated

2 cups fresh corn kernels

2 green onions, sliced finely

2 tablespoons finely chopped fresh coriander

1 Sift flour, soda and cumin into medium bowl. Gradually whisk in milk and egg yolks until batter is smooth.

2 Beat egg whites in small bowl with electric mixer until soft peaks form.

3 Stir corn, onion and coriander into batter; fold in egg whites.

4 Pour 2 tablespoons of the batter for each fritter into heated oiled large frying pan; spread batter into round shape. Cook fritters about 2 minutes each side. Remove from pan; cover to keep warm.

5 Repeat step 4 to make a total of 18 fritters. Fritters can be served with tomato chutney or salsa and fresh coriander leaves.

nutritional count per fritter 1.3g total fat (0.5g saturated fat); 63 cal; 9.9g carbohydrate; 2.7g protein; 1.2g fiber

TIP

• You can use canned corn kernels, rinsed and drained, instead of the fresh corn kernels, if you like.

roasted balsamic onions

These onions can be made ahead and served hot with steak, pan-fried veal, liver and bacon or roast beef, or cold with any cold meat or poultry.

2 medium red onions, quartered

2 medium brown onions, quartered

2 bulbs garlic, halved horizontally

2 tablespoons olive oil

1 tablespoon balsamic vinegar

1 tablespoon brown sugar

1 Preheat oven to 425°F/400°F fan-forced.

2 Combine ingredients in medium baking dish.

3 Roast, brushing occasionally with pan juices, about 40 minutes or until onions and garlic are tender and caramelized.

nutritional count per serving 9.8g total fat (1.4g saturated fat); 168 cal; 13.9g carbohydrate; 3.5g protein; 5.6g fiber

[opposite] corn fritters

sautéed mushrooms

Peeling mushrooms is time-consuming and unnecessary; many nutrients and much of the flavor is found in the skin. The best way to prepare mushrooms is to wipe them off using damp absorbent paper. This removes grit and prevents them from becoming soggy. They become waterlogged if washed, making them difficult to sauté (they tend to steam in the pan and lose their beautiful flavor).

3 tablespoons butter, chopped
1 small brown onion, chopped finely
1 pound button mushrooms, halved
1 tablespoon malt vinegar
⅓ cup coarsely chopped fresh chives

1 Melt butter in large frying pan; cook onion, stirring, until soft.
2 Add mushrooms; cook, stirring occasionally, 10 minutes or until mushrooms are tender. Add vinegar; bring to a boil. Remove from heat; stir in chives.
3 Serve mushrooms on thick toast, if desired.
nutritional count per serving 10.7g total fat (6.8g saturated fat); 127 cal; 1.7g carbohydrate; 4.9g protein; 3.5g fiber

steamed asian greens with char siu sauce

Almost every vegetable can be steamed, and this is an excellent way to cook them because they retain their shape, flavor, color and goodness. Trim and prepare the vegetables as you would normally, then layer them evenly in the steamer basket. Food can still be overcooked in a steamer, especially green vegetables, which will lose their bright color and look dull and dry, so keep an eye on them.

1 fresh long red chili, sliced thinly
12 ounces broccolini, trimmed
5 ounces snow peas, trimmed
2 baby bok choy, halved
2 tablespoons char siu sauce
2 teaspoons sesame oil
1 tablespoon peanut oil
1 tablespoon toasted sesame seeds

1 Layer chili, broccolini, snow peas and bok choy in parchment-paper-lined bamboo steamer. Steam, covered, over wok of simmering water about 5 minutes or until vegetables are just tender.
2 Combine vegetables, sauce and sesame oil in large bowl.
3 Heat peanut oil in small saucepan until hot; pour oil over vegetable mixture then toss to combine. Serve sprinkled with seeds.
nutritional count per serving 9.5g total fat (1.4g saturated fat); 152 cal; 7g carbohydrate; 6.6g protein; 6.6g fiber

lemon and ricotta-filled zucchini flowers

8 ounces ricotta cheese

2 tablespoons finely grated parmesan cheese

1 teaspoon finely grated lemon rind

1 tablespoon lemon juice

1 tablespoon finely chopped fresh mint

2 tablespoons roasted pine nuts

12 zucchini flowers with stems attached

1 Combine cheeses, rind, juice, mint and nuts in small bowl.

2 Discard stamens from inside zucchini flowers; fill flowers with cheese mixture, twist petal tops to enclose filling.

3 Place zucchini flowers, in single layer, in large bamboo steamer, over large saucepan of boiling water. Steam, covered, about 20 minutes or until zucchini are tender.

nutritional count per serving 13.4g total fat (5.5g saturated fat); 170 cal; 2.2g carbohydrate; 9.6g protein; 1.4g fiber

cauliflower gratin

This is a delicious way to enjoy nutritious cauliflower and fantastic for introducing the unusual tasting veggie to the kids. Serve as a side dish to a roast or on its own as a healthy alternative to macaroni and cheese.

Of course you can use 1½ pounds of regular-sized cauliflower, cut into florets, in place of the babies.

6 baby cauliflowers (1½ pounds), trimmed

3 tablespoons butter

¼ cup all-purpose flour

1½ cups hot milk

½ cup coarsely grated cheddar cheese

¼ cup finely grated parmesan cheese

1 tablespoon packaged bread crumbs

1 Preheat oven to 425°F/400°F fan-forced.

2 Boil, steam or microwave cauliflowers until tender; drain. Place in medium shallow ovenproof dish.

3 Meanwhile, melt butter in medium saucepan, add flour; cook, stirring, until mixture bubbles and thickens. Gradually stir in milk until smooth; cook, stirring, until mixture boils and thickens. Remove from heat, stir in cheeses.

4 Pour cheese sauce over cauliflower in dish; sprinkle with bread crumbs. Bake about 15 minutes or until browned lightly.

nutritional count per serving 14.1g total fat (9g saturated fat); 207 cal; 10.2g carbohydrate; 9.1g protein; 2.2g fiber

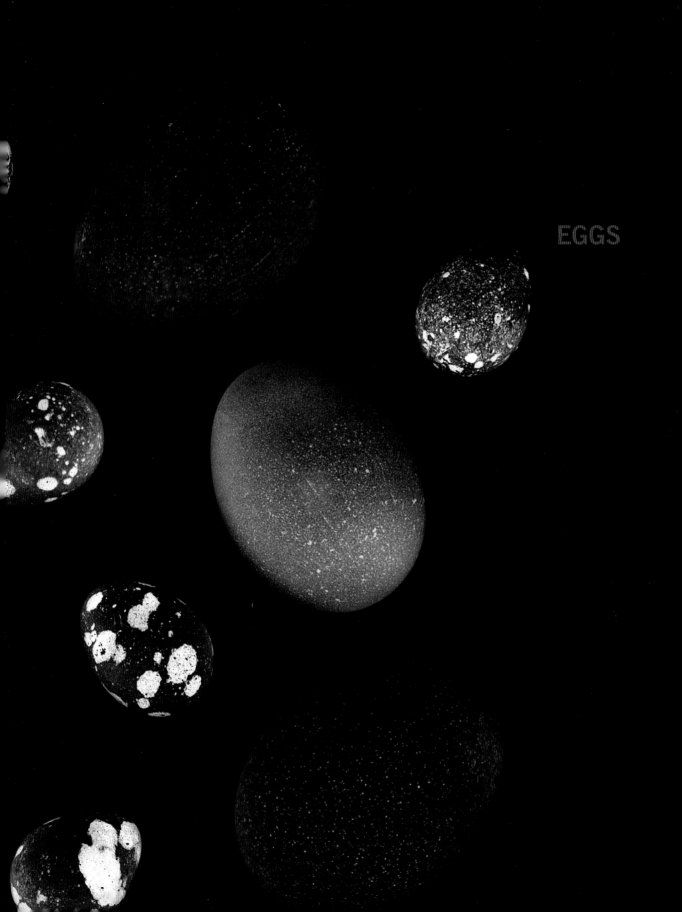

EGGS

Eggs

Late Saturday breakfasts just wouldn't be the same without the scrumptious promise of scrambled eggs with toast. And isn't it always comforting to have the convenience of hard-boiled eggs for an easy afternoon snack or toddler's dinner? Eggs provide us with so many simple pleasures. And delicious ones, too: where would we be without soothing custards, melt-in-the-mouth quiches, sublime hollandaise, dreamy soufflés and meringues, perfectly rich cakes and creamy sauces made silky by the inclusion of our beloved egg?

EGG VARIETIES AND SIZES

HEN EGGS These are the eggs most commonly used in everyday cooking and they are available in medium, large, and extra large sizes. Most recipes call for large eggs; for cakes, use large eggs, too, unless the recipe specifies otherwise.

DUCK EGGS Larger and richer-tasting than hen eggs, these have an average size of 3 ounces. They're harder to find than hen eggs, and you'll need to do research to find a local supplier. They can be used in the same way as hen eggs but are common for baking and making custards: duck egg whites do not whisk up well.

QUAIL EGGS Regarded more as a gourmet ingredient, quail eggs are available from specialized suppliers. These little eggs taste like hen eggs and are prized for their miniature charm.

BUYING AND STORING

You can taste and see the difference in eggs gathered fresh from the chicken coop. Free-range eggs come from happier hens and do taste much better. But the "free-range" label you see in big supermarkets is not always all you'd imagine. If you're buying free-range eggs because you're concerned about animal welfare, look for eggs that are certified organic (check the labels) or go to a farmers' market to find eggs with independent free-range certification.

Eggs are perishable and need to be stored in their carton in the refrigerator to protect them from odors that might penetrate their porous shells. Always check eggs for cracks and leaks before placing the carton in your shopping basket or cart. If you find cracks or leaks once you're back home, make sure to throw the egg away.

Fresh eggs, stored in their carton, should keep for 3 to 4 weeks. Hard-boiled eggs will keep for a week and leftover egg dishes need to be consumed within 3 to 4 days. To check the freshness of a raw egg, place it in a bowl of water: fresh eggs will sink to the bottom while stale eggs will float with the big end upward.

HOW DO YOU LIKE YOUR EGGS?

POACHED The chefs' method of gently lowering eggs, one at a time, into a deep, large saucepan of simmering water works well, but it takes practice to perfect. Here's how you can do it at home: half-fill a lidded saucepan with water, add a dash of white vinegar and bring to a boil. Break each egg into a cup. When the water boils, add the eggs; allow the water to return to a boil, then immediately move the pan off the heat, put the lid on and stand for 4 minutes or until a light film of egg white has set over the yolks. Use a slotted spoon to lift out each egg, place it for a moment (still on the spoon) on absorbent paper and serve immediately. Poach no more than three or four eggs at a time.

FRIED Over medium heat, melt enough butter, bacon fat or oil in a frying pan to cover the bottom. Break each egg into a cup. When the butter begins to bubble, slide the eggs into the pan–the butter should sizzle gently; if not, adjust the heat. Spoon butter over the yolks to set the "veil" of white. When the whites are set but the yolks still wobble, use a spatula to remove eggs. Serve at once.

BOILED There are two methods for boiled eggs:
1. Place eggs in salted boiling water, boil gently for 3 minutes for soft yolks and firm whites, or 7 minutes for hard-boiled eggs. Drain and place immediately into cold water. Tap eggs all over to crack the shell then stand in water a few minutes before peeling.
2. Place eggs snugly in a saucepan, barely cover with cold water, cover with a lid and bring to a boil. As soon as the water boils, remove lid and boil gently 2½ minutes for soft or 7 minutes for hard-boiled.

SCRAMBLED For this breakfast favorite, whisk two to three eggs per person with salt, pepper and a tablespoon of milk or cream per egg. Have ready any additional ingredients such as herbs or smoked fish. Over low heat, melt enough butter in a frying pan to cover the bottom generously. When the butter foams slightly, add the eggs and stir with a wooden spoon, reaching right to the edges. When the eggs are a little softer than you want them, add the herbs etc., stir once more, remove from heat and serve immediately.

SEPARATING EGGS

Have ready two non-plastic bowls and a cup–dry and grease-free. Crack an egg open and, holding your hand over the cup, tip the contents of the egg onto your hand, allowing the white to run through your fingers into the cup, and gently cradling the yolk. Carefully drop the yolk into a bowl. Check the white is free of shell and yolk, then tip it into the other bowl. Scoop out tiny bits of shell in the white with a larger piece of shell. If any yolk spills into the white, it will prevent it from beating up properly, so it must be discarded.

BEATING EGG WHITES

Place the egg whites in clean, dry bowl. A copper bowl is ideal (copper reacts with whites to form a very stable foam), though glass, stainless steel or china bowls are also fine. A standing electric mixer is recommended for beating egg whites, though a whisk or hand-held electric beater also work well. All utensils must be dry and grease-free. Whisk plain whites until they form foamy, drooping peaks. For meringue, start adding sugar gradually at the soft-foam stage and continue whisking until the mixture forms soft upright peaks.

poached eggs

Fresh eggs are essential for perfect poaching. Most store-bought eggs will have a "best-before" date, however, if in doubt, place the egg in a bowl of water. A fresh egg will sink to the bottom while a stale egg will float, wide end up.

2 teaspoons white vinegar

4 eggs

1 Half-fill a large shallow saucepan with at least 2 inches of water; add vinegar. Bring to a boil.

2 Break 1 egg into a small bowl or cup. Swirl the boiling water with a spoon, then slide egg into pan. Repeat with three more eggs. When all eggs are in pan, allow water to return to the boil.

3 Cover pan, turn off heat; stand about 4 minutes or until a light film of egg white sets over yolks.

4 Remove the egg with a slotted spoon and drain on absorbent paper.

nutritional count per egg 5.3g total fat (1.6g saturated fat); 74 cal; 0.2g carbohydrate; 6.7g protein; 0g fiber

Make a whirlpool in the pan of boiling water using a wooden spoon. Putting the eggs into the whirlpool will help keep the whites intact.

Break one egg into a small bowl or cup and gently slide it into the whirlpool. Continue with remaining eggs. Return the water to a boil.

Use a slotted spoon to remove the eggs and drain them on absorbent paper. At this stage you can trim the whites if they look ragged.

Q&A

My poached eggs always look messy; they never look like the eggs I get in cafés.

Most poached eggs come out of the pan with ragged edges. Once you've drained them, place them on a cutting board and quickly trim the edges of the whites with a small sharp knife–it's what chefs do.

poached eggs and smoked salmon on blini

This luxurious café-style breakfast is just as good for a casual lunch or Sunday supper.

8 eggs

7 ounces sliced smoked salmon

2 tablespoons sour cream

1 tablespoon coarsely chopped
   fresh chives

blini

⅓ cup buckwheat flour

2 tablespoons all-purpose flour

1 teaspoon baking powder

1 egg

½ cup buttermilk, room temperature

2 tablespoons butter, melted

1 Make blini.

2 To poach eggs, half-fill a large shallow saucepan with water; bring to a boil. Break 1 egg into a small bowl or cup then slide into pan. Working quickly, repeat process with three more eggs. When all 4 eggs are in pan, return water to a boil. Cover pan, turn off heat; stand about 4 minutes or until a light film of white sets over each yolk. Remove each egg with a slotted spoon and drain on absorbent paper; cover to keep warm. Repeat with remaining eggs.

3 Serve blini topped with eggs, salmon, sour cream and chives.

blini Sift flours and baking powder into medium bowl; gradually whisk in combined egg and buttermilk until mixture is smooth. Stir in butter. Cook blini, in batches, by dropping 1 tablespoon of the batter into heated oiled large frying pan. Cook blini until browned both sides; you will have 12 blini. Cover to keep warm.

nutritional count per serving 25.9g total fat (11.3g saturated fat); 414 cal; 14.1g carbohydrate; 31.5g protein; 1.6g fiber

boiled eggs

To peel boiled eggs, crack the shells gently and leave immersed in cold water at least 5 minutes or until cold. Remove shells, starting from broad end. Wash the eggs, then pat dry using absorbent paper.

4 eggs

1 Place eggs in medium saucepan; add enough cold water to cover eggs. Stir constantly using wooden spoon over high heat until water boils; this will centralize each yolk.

2 Boil, uncovered, until yolks are as soft or as firm as you like. As a guide, 3 minutes will give you set egg white and soft yolk. After 5 minutes, the yolk will be set.

3 Place saucepan of eggs under cold running water about 1 minute or until eggs are cool. This will stop a dark ring from forming around the yolk.

nutritional count per egg 5.3g total fat (1.6g saturated fat); 74 cal; 0.2g carbohydrate; 6.7g protein; 0g fiber

[opposite] poached eggs and smoked salmon on blini

eggs benedict

8 eggs

4 english muffins

7 ounces shaved ham

¼ cup finely chopped fresh chives

hollandaise sauce

1½ tablespoons white wine vinegar

1 tablespoon lemon juice

½ teaspoon black peppercorns

2 egg yolks

4 ounces unsalted butter, melted

1 Make hollandaise sauce.

2 To poach eggs, half-fill a large shallow saucepan with water; bring to a boil. Break 1 egg into a cup then slide into pan. Working quickly, repeat process with three more eggs. When all 4 eggs are in the pan, return water to a boil. Cover pan, turn off heat; stand about 4 minutes or until a light film of white sets over each yolk. Remove each egg with a slotted spoon and drain on absorbent paper; cover to keep warm. Repeat with remaining eggs.

3 Meanwhile, split muffins in half and toast. Serve muffins topped with ham, poached eggs, sauce and chives.

hollandaise sauce Bring vinegar, juice and peppercorns to a boil in small saucepan. Reduce heat; simmer, uncovered, until liquid is reduced by half. Strain through a fine sieve into small heatproof bowl; cool 10 minutes. Whisk egg yolks into vinegar mixture. Set bowl over small saucepan of simmering water; do not allow water to touch base of bowl. Whisk mixture over heat until thickened. Remove bowl from heat; gradually whisk in melted butter in a thin steady stream, whisking constantly until sauce is thick and creamy.

nutritional count per serving 40.6g total fat (21.2g saturated fat); 586 cal; 24.2g carbohydrate; 30.8g protein; 2g fiber

Q&A

Can hollandaise sauce be made in advance and warmed up just before serving? I'd love to make eggs benedict when I'm having friends over for breakfast, but I'm not confident that I can make the hollandaise when I'm short of time.

Hollandaise can be kept warm for about an hour (place the bowl of hollandaise in a larger bowl of warm water) but it really is a sauce that has to be eaten fresh. We suggest you make eggs benedict for a late (rather than early) breakfast to allow yourself time to make the sauce.

creamy scrambled eggs

For light, fluffy scrambled eggs, cook them over medium heat and stir gently-yet-consistently. Once cooked, be sure to remove the mixture from the pan immediately so it does not continue to cook and become dry.

8 eggs
½ cup light cream
2 tablespoons finely chopped fresh chives
2 tablespoons butter

1 Place eggs, cream and chives in medium bowl; beat lightly with fork.

2 Heat butter in large frying pan over low heat. Add egg mixture, wait a few seconds, then use a wide spatula to gently scrape the set egg mixture along the base of the pan; cook until creamy and barely set.

3 Serve eggs immediately, with toast, if you like.

nutritional count per serving 30.2g total fat (16.2g saturated fat); 329 cal; 1.3g carbohydrate; 14g protein; 0g fiber

Whisk the eggs, cream and chives together lightly with a fork.

Melt the butter and add the egg mixture. The heat should not be too high otherwise the eggs will become dry instead of creamy.

Fold the egg mixture from the edge of the pan to the center. Remove from heat when eggs are still creamy and barely set.

Q&A

My scrambled eggs break into big pieces and are always a bit dry. I make them with low-fat milk and butter. Is there any way I can make them soft and creamy without using cream?

The softest, creamiest and most luxurious scrambled eggs are made with cream, but that does make them high in fat. You'll never get really creamy scrambled eggs using low-fat milk, but they'll still be good if you cook them slowly. Don't think of scrambled eggs as a quick dish. Instead, cook them over a very low heat, stirring all the time, until they are set–this will take about 10 minutes.

asian crab and rice omelette

Water is added to the eggs because, when heated, the water turns to steam giving the omelette a light texture.

If you prefer the filling to be more evenly distributed throughout the omelette, add the rice mixture to the whisked eggs before adding them to the pan.

¼ cup peanut oil

4 green onions, chopped finely

2 fresh small red Thai chilies, chopped finely

1 tablespoon red curry paste

2 cups cold cooked jasmine rice

8 ounces fresh crab meat, shredded

2 tablespoons lime juice

2 tablespoons fish sauce

8 eggs

2 tablespoons water

1 Heat 1 tablespoon of the oil in wok; stir-fry onion and chili until onion softens. Add curry paste; stir-fry until fragrant.

2 Add rice; stir-fry until heated through. Place fried rice in large bowl; add crab, juice and sauce, toss to combine.

3 Whisk eggs with the water in medium bowl. Heat about a quarter of remaining oil in same cleaned wok. Pour a quarter of the egg mixture into wok; cook over medium heat, tilting pan, until almost set.

4 Spoon a quarter of the rice mixture into center of omelette; using spatula, fold four sides of omelette over to enclose filling. Press omelette firmly with spatula; turn carefully to brown other side. Remove omelette from wok; cover to keep warm. Repeat with remaining oil, egg and crab fried rice three more times.

nutritional count per serving 26.6g total fat (5.9g saturated fat); 461 cal; 29.4g carbohydrate; 24.9g protein; 2g fiber

serving idea serve with a mixed green salad.

Add the cold cooked rice in batches to the onion mixture in the wok and stir in before adding the next batch. This prevents the rice from clumping together as it fries.

When the omelette is almost set, place a quarter of the rice mixture in the center.

Use a spatula (or your hands, carefully) to fold the four sides of the omelette over the filling to form a packet. Remove from pan and cover to keep warm.

spinach scrambled eggs

2 tablespoons butter

3 ounces spinach leaves

8 slices pancetta

8 eggs

½ cup light cream

4 slices crusty bread

1 Heat half of the butter in large frying pan, add spinach; cook until spinach just wilts. Drain on absorbent paper; cover to keep warm.

2 Preheat broiler. Place pancetta under broiler until crisp; cover to keep warm.

3 Whisk eggs and cream in medium bowl until combined.

4 Heat remaining butter in same cleaned pan over medium heat. Add egg mixture; wait a few seconds, then using a wide spatula, gently scrape the set egg mixture along the base of the pan; cook until creamy and just set.

5 Meanwhile, toast bread. Top toast with pancetta, scrambled eggs and spinach.

nutritional count per serving 25.7g total fat (11.7g saturated fat); 373 cal; 14.4g carbohydrate; 21.7g protein; 1.1g fiber

fried eggs and bacon

For a good fried egg, place a non-stick frying pan over medium heat, melt enough butter, bacon fat or oil to cover the bottom. Break each egg into a small bowl or cup. When the butter begins to bubble, slide the eggs into the pan– the butter should sizzle gently; if not, adjust the heat. Spoon butter over the yolks to set the "veil" of white. When the whites are set but the yolks still wobble, use a spatula to lift the eggs out and serve at once.

4 strips bacon

1 tablespoon vegetable oil

4 eggs

1 medium tomato, halved

1 Cook bacon in oiled medium frying pan until browned and cooked as desired. Remove from pan; cover to keep warm.

2 Add oil to same pan; break eggs into pan or into greased egg rings in pan. Cook, uncovered, until egg white has set and yolk is cooked as desired.

3 Meanwhile, preheat broiler. Place tomato, cut-side up, onto baking tray; season to taste. Place tomato under broiler until browned lightly and just tender.

4 Divide eggs, bacon and tomato among serving plates.

nutritional count per serving 26.3g total fat (6.8g saturated fat); 364 cal; 2.4g carbohydrate; 29.4g protein; 1.1g fiber

serving ideas slices of toast.

[opposite] spinach scrambled eggs

denver omelette

This omelette is called a "western" in most states east of the Mississippi River and a "Denver" in the western half of the country. Its origins are based more on folklore than fact, but it's believed to have been an Americanization of the classic egg foo yung served by Chinese cooks to the work gangs building the east-to-west-coast railway link in the 1840s. Today, the Denver is often cooked, cooled, doused in tomato sauce, and then eaten between slices of white bread.

10 eggs
⅓ cup sour cream
2 fresh small red Thai chilies, chopped finely
2 teaspoons vegetable oil
3 green onions, sliced thinly
1 medium green pepper, chopped finely
3 ounces ham, chopped finely
2 small tomatoes, seeded, chopped finely
½ cup coarsely grated cheddar cheese

1 Break eggs in large bowl, whisk lightly; whisk in sour cream and chili.
2 Heat oil in large non-stick frying pan; cook onion and pepper, stirring, until onion softens. Place onion mixture in medium bowl with ham, tomato and cheese; toss to combine.
3 Pour ½ cup of the egg mixture into same lightly oiled frying pan; cook, tilting pan, over low heat until almost set. Sprinkle about ⅓ cup of the filling over half of the omelette; using spatula, fold omelette over to completely cover the filling.
4 Pour ¼ cup of the egg mixture into empty half of pan; cook over low heat until almost set. Sprinkle about ⅓ cup of the filling over folded omelette, fold omelette over top of first omelette to cover filling. Repeat twice more, using ¼ cup of the egg mixture each time, to form one large layered omelette. Carefully slide omelette onto plate; cover to keep warm.
5 Repeat steps 3 and 4 to make second omelette, using remaining egg and filling. Cut each Denver omelette in half.
nutritional count per serving 30.2g total fat (13.4g saturated fat); 392 cal; 3.5g carbohydrate; 26.7g protein; 1.3g fiber

zucchini and mushroom omelette

1 tablespoon butter
1 clove garlic, crushed
1 ounce button mushrooms, sliced thinly
¼ cup coarsely grated zucchini
1 green onion, chopped finely
2 eggs
1 tablespoon water
¼ cup coarsely grated cheddar cheese

Drain the zucchini well before stirring into the pan by either squeezing it in your hands or in absorbent paper. This is a single serving omelette but you can increase the ingredients proportionately with no problem. If doubling it, the omelette can be cooked all at once but if you want the finished product to serve four, make two omelettes.

1 Heat half of the butter in small frying pan; cook garlic and mushroom, stirring, over medium heat about 2 minutes or until mushroom is lightly browned. Add zucchini and onion; cook, stirring, about 1 minute or until zucchini begins to soften. Remove vegetable mixture from pan; cover to keep warm.

2 Beat eggs and the water in small bowl. Add cheese; whisk until combined.

3 Heat remaining butter in same pan; swirl pan so butter covers base. Pour egg mixture into pan; cook, tilting pan, over medium heat until almost set.

4 Place vegetable mixture evenly over half of the omelette; using spatula, flip other half over vegetable mixture. Using spatula, slide omelette gently onto serving plate.

nutritional count per serving 11.7g total fat (6.1g saturated fat); 145 cal; 0.8g carbohydrate; 8.9g protein; 0.9g fiber

egg-white omelette

PREP + COOK TIME 45 MINS • SERVES 4

It's criminal to waste the 12 egg yolks here, especially when you can freeze them for another day. Drop a single yolk into each section of an ice cube tray then cover the tray and freeze, popping out the yolks as your needs dictate.

Some recipes that call for lots of egg yolks are hollandaise, aïoli, custard, lemon curd, crème brûlée, pots de crème, crème anglaise and zabaglione.

12 egg whites
4 green onions, chopped finely
¼ cup finely chopped fresh chives
¼ cup finely chopped fresh chervil
½ cup finely chopped fresh flat-leaf parsley
½ cup coarsely grated cheddar cheese
½ cup coarsely grated mozzarella cheese

1 Preheat broiler.

2 Beat a quarter of the egg white in small bowl with electric mixer until soft peaks form; fold in a quarter of the combined onion and herbs.

3 Pour mixture into heated oiled 8-inch non-stick frying pan; cook over low heat until omelette is just browned lightly on the bottom.

4 Sprinkle a quarter of the combined cheeses on half of the omelette. Place pan under broiler until cheese begins to melt and omelette sets; fold omelette over to completely cover cheese. Carefully slide onto serving plate; cover to keep warm.

5 Repeat process three times with remaining egg white, onion and herb mixture, and cheeses.

nutritional count per serving 7.9g total fat (5g saturated fat); 148 cal; 1.1g carbohydrate; 18.2g protein; 0.7g fiber

baked eggs

This is the perfect brunch dish for entertaining since you don't have to stand over it while it cooks. Sprinkle chopped fresh parsley over the top of the baked eggs to add gorgeous color and flavor.

1 tablespoon olive oil
3 ounces prosciutto, chopped finely
3 ounces button mushrooms, chopped finely
4 green onions, chopped finely
3 ounces slightly underripe brie cheese, chopped coarsely
8 eggs

1 Preheat oven to 400°F/ 350°F fan-forced. Grease four ¾-cup shallow ovenproof dishes.
2 Heat oil in medium frying pan; cook prosciutto and mushrooms, stirring, until onion softens. Remove pan from heat; stir in half of the cheese. Divide prosciutto mixture among dishes; break two eggs into each dish.
3 Bake, uncovered, 5 minutes. Increase oven to 425°F/400°F fan-forced.
4 Sprinkle remaining cheese over eggs; bake, uncovered, about 5 minutes or until eggs set and cheese melts.
nutritional count per serving 25.3g total fat (9.5g saturated fat); 332 cal; 1.3g carbohydrate; 25.6g protein; 0.9g fiber

mini pea and pancetta frittatas

Use fresh peas when you can in this recipe for a burst of flavor.

1 teaspoon olive oil
4 slices pancetta, chopped finely
1 clove garlic, crushed
6 eggs
⅔ cup light cream
½ cup frozen peas
⅓ cup finely grated parmesan cheese
1 tablespoon finely chopped fresh mint
1 teaspoon finely grated lemon rind
2 tablespoons crème fraîche
36 small fresh mint leaves

1 Preheat oven to 400°F/350°F fan-forced. Grease three 12-hole mini muffin pans.
2 Heat oil in small frying pan; cook pancetta and garlic, stirring, until pancetta is crisp. Cool.
3 Whisk eggs and cream in large pitcher; stir in pancetta mixture, peas, cheese, mint and rind. Pour egg mixture into pan holes.
4 Bake frittatas about 12 minutes or until set. Stand in pan 5 minutes before removing. Serve topped with crème fraîche and mint leaves.
nutritional count per frittata 3.8g total fat (2.1g saturated fat); 43 cal; 0.4g carbohydrate; 1.9g protein; 0.1g fiber

[1] baked eggs
[2] mini pea and pancetta frittatas
[3] goat's cheese soufflé [page 260]
[4] spanish tortilla [page 260]

goat's cheese soufflé

cooking-oil spray
¼ cup packaged bread crumbs
2 tablespoons butter
2 tablespoons all-purpose flour
1 cup milk
4 eggs, separated
¼ teaspoon cayenne pepper
5 ounces firm goat's cheese, crumbled

creamed spinach sauce
6 ounces baby spinach leaves
⅔ cup light cream, warmed

1 Preheat oven to 400°F/ 350°F fan-forced. Spray six 1-cup soufflé dishes with cooking-oil spray, sprinkle with bread crumbs; place on oven tray.

2 Melt butter in small saucepan, add flour; cook, stirring, until mixture bubbles and thickens. Gradually add milk; stir until mixture boils and thickens. Transfer to large bowl; stir in egg yolks, pepper and cheese. Cool 5 minutes.

3 Beat egg whites in small bowl with electric mixer until soft peaks form; gently fold whites, in two batches, into cheese mixture. Divide mixture among dishes.

4 Bake soufflés about 15 minutes or until puffed and browned lightly.

5 Meanwhile, make creamed spinach sauce.

6 Serve soufflés with sauce.

creamed spinach sauce Boil, steam or microwave spinach until just wilted; drain. Using hand, squeeze out excess liquid. Blend or process spinach until almost smooth. With motor running, gradually add cream; process until smooth.

nutritional count per serving 26g total fat (15.2g saturated fat); 314 cal; 8.8g carbohydrate; 11.4g protein; 1.1g fiber

spanish tortilla

1¾ pounds russet potatoes, peeled, sliced thinly
1 tablespoon olive oil
1 large brown onion, sliced thinly
7 ounces dried chorizo sausage, sliced thinly
6 eggs, beaten lightly
1¼ cups light cream
4 green onions, sliced thickly
¼ cup coarsely grated mozzarella cheese
¼ cup coarsely grated cheddar cheese

A Spanish tortilla is an omelette made predominantly with potato. It tastes great served warm or at room temperature, and makes an excellent breakfast, lunch, dinner or appetizer with drinks.

1 Boil, steam or microwave potato until just tender; drain.

2 Meanwhile, heat oil in medium frying pan; cook brown onion, stirring, until softened. Add chorizo; cook, stirring, until crisp. Remove from pan; drain on absorbent paper.

3 Whisk eggs in large bowl with cream, green onion and cheeses; stir in potatoes and chorizo mixture.

4 Pour mixture into heated oiled medium non-stick frying pan; cook, covered, over low heat about 10 minutes or until tortilla is just set. Carefully invert tortilla onto plate, then slide back into pan; cook, uncovered, about 5 minutes or until cooked through.

nutritional count per serving 64.1g total fat (32.5g saturated fat); 811 cal; 29.1g carbohydrate; 30g protein; 3.8g fiber

potato frittata with smoked salmon

PREP + COOK TIME 45 MINS • SERVES 4

You will need a medium ovenproof frying pan with a 7-inch base for this recipe.

2 tablespoons butter
1 tablespoon olive oil
2 medium potatoes,
    cut into ½-inch pieces
1 green onion, chopped finely
8 eggs

¼ cup light cream
⅓ cup finely grated
    parmesan cheese
1 tablespoon finely chopped fresh dill
7 ounces smoked salmon
2 tablespoons sour cream

1 Preheat oven to 425°F/400°F fan-forced.

2 Heat butter and oil in medium frying pan; cook potato, stirring occasionally, until browned and tender. Add onion; cook, stirring gently, 1 minute.

3 Meanwhile, whisk eggs, cream, cheese and dill in medium bowl. Pour into pan; stir gently. Cook frittata over medium heat, about 2 minutes or until bottom sets. Place pan in oven; cook, uncovered, about 10 minutes or until frittata sets.

4 Slide frittata onto serving plate; serve topped with salmon, sour cream and some extra dill, if you like.

nutritional count per serving 34.1g total fat (15.2g saturated fat); 486 cal; 14.3g carbohydrate; 30.2g protein; 2.1g fiber

SAUCES

Sauces

A great sauce can add the perfect finishing touch to a dish, lifting it from merely pleasant to memorable. Having a few classic sauce recipes up your sleeve is a valuable asset: it can help you to whip up a tasty snack, liven up a meal or create something exciting out of leftovers in the fridge.

SOME OF THE SAUCES IN THIS CHAPTER HAVE BEEN FAMILIAR TREASURES FOR GENERATIONS; OTHERS ARE FAIRLY NEW TO WESTERN COOKERY ALTHOUGH THEY HAVE A LONG HISTORY IN OTHER PARTS OF THE WORLD. ALL OF THEM CONTAIN THE PROMISE TO TRANSFORM YOUR BASIC DISHES INTO FOOD THAT SINGS. LEARNING TO MAKE YOUR OWN SAUCES IS NOT HARD AND ONCE YOU HAVE A REPERTOIRE OF CLASSICS, YOU WILL NEVER GO BACK TO THE COMMERCIAL PRODUCTS.

EGG AND BUTTER SAUCES

Hollandaise sauce is famous for its rich, velvety texture, which is derived from a combination of egg yolks and butter. Most commonly seen drizzled over eggs benedict in cafès, it is also the perfect partner for asparagus spears and artichoke hearts.

Hollandaise sauce is also the basis of béarnaise sauce, which contains the addition of tarragon–it is the classic accompaniment to a filet of beef.

Both of these sauces [see pages 266 and 269] can be made by hand or in a blender or food processor. When making by hand, it's important to whisk the egg yolk mixture until it thickens enough to cling to the whisk when it is raised, and that you incorporate the butter completely before adding more. It is crucial to keep the heat low and steady.

Many cooks prefer to make these sauces in a glass bowl over a saucepan rather than in a double boiler because it provides a gentler heat for the delicate ingredients. If the sauces are too thick, or separate, whisk in a tablespoon or two of hot water until the mixture becomes smooth and creamy.

SALSAS

It is no coincidence that these sauces share the name of a South American dance because they are similarly lively and spirited–and can make you break out in a sweat.

While we have only recently embraced the concept of salsas as spicy accompaniments to traditional main courses, they have been relished by generations of Latin Americans and equally enthusiastically incorporated into cuisines around the world–such as the Mediterranean's pesto, salsa verde and skordalia, and South Asia's raita, sambal and satay sauce. While these accompaniments are all very different from each other and made from culturally-specific ingredients, they all share the same reason for being: they are all condiments designed to bring excitement to the food they're served with, to enliven the flavors and give them a kick.

Salsas are a wonderful complement to barbecued meats and fish.

THE CLASSICS

THERE ARE WHITE SAUCES, BROWN SAUCES AND BUTTER SAUCES, AND EACH OF THESE CAN HAVE ANY NUMBER OF VARIATIONS.

White and brown sauces are based on a "roux"–a paste made from equal parts of melted butter and flour–to which a hot liquid is added. White sauce is based on a blond roux (in which the flour is not browned), and brown sauce is based on a brown roux (where the flour is deliberately browned to a nutty color), and the sauces they create are determined by the type of hot liquid added to the roux. It's important to stir the sauces continually while you're making them so they don't get too thick. All sauces intended for spooning over food should run freely off the spoon.

GOOD, CLASSIC SAUCES FOR YOUR REPERTOIRE INCLUDE

BECHAMEL The addition of hot milk to a blond roux produces a basic béchamel or the kind of white sauce we're accustomed to seeing drizzled over cauliflower or used in lasagne. Grated cheese is a popular addition to this sauce. Other variations include onion sauce for corned beef, and mushroom sauce for chicken and steak. The key thing to watch with these white sauces is that they do not get too thick.

VELOUTE This is a pale golden sauce produced when hot stock is added to a blond roux. It's a wonderful sauce on chicken, fish or veal.

ESPAGNOLE This lovely rich and silky brown sauce is created when veal stock is added to a brown roux. Good restaurants create espagnole made with meat stock and pan drippings.

GRAVY While it might not sound as aristocratic as espagnole, gravy is still a distant cousin of the classic brown sauces. Deglazing is the term used when you add liquid (water, wine or stock) to a hot frying pan or baking dish after the meat (or whatever you have been roasting) has been removed. This liquid is stirred over medium-high heat to blend the cooking juices into the liquid, creating a sauce.

DEGLAZING

THE PROCESS OF DEGLAZING IS AT THE HEART OF MAKING A FLAVORFUL GRAVY. YOU CAN MAKE A THIN GRAVY (THE FRENCH TERM IS JUS) BY POURING OFF ALL THE FAT FROM THE BAKING DISH AND DEGLAZING THE PAN WITH STOCK PLUS A LITTLE WINE IF YOU WISH. SCRAPE AND STIR THE COAGULATED PAN JUICES INTO THE LIQUID AS IT HEATS. START WITH TWICE AS MUCH LIQUID AS YOU WANT TO END UP WITH; WHEN IT HAS REDUCED BY HALF, STRAIN THE LIQUID INTO A SAUCEPAN, SEASON LIGHTLY WITH SALT AND PEPPER, AND BRING BACK TO SIMMERING POINT AND ADD BITS OF BUTTER, SWIRLING OR WHISKING THEM IN TO GIVE THE GRAVY A BIT OF BODY.

hollandaise sauce

This recipe makes enough for six servings of eggs benedict (see recipe page 248), a breakfast or brunch specialty consisting of toasted english muffin halves topped with ham, poached egg and hollandaise sauce.

TIP

• If the sauce is too thick or separates, whisk in up to 2 tablespoons of hot water until mixture is smooth and creamy.

2 tablespoons water
2 tablespoons white vinegar
¼ teaspoon cracked black pepper
2 egg yolks
1¾ sticks unsalted butter, melted

1 Bring the water, vinegar and pepper to a boil in small saucepan. Reduce heat; simmer, uncovered, until liquid reduces to 1 tablespoon. Strain through fine sieve into medium heatproof bowl; cool 10 minutes.

2 Whisk egg yolks into vinegar mixture until combined. Set bowl over medium saucepan of simmering water; do not allow water to touch base of bowl. Whisk mixture over heat until thickened.

3 Remove bowl from heat; gradually add melted butter in thin, steady stream, whisking constantly until sauce has thickened.

nutritional count per tablespoon 14.5g total fat (9.2g saturated fat); 131 cal; 0.1g carbohydrate; 0.5g protein; 0g fiber

serving ideas goes well with steamed asparagus and grilled fish.

Whisk the yolk mixture over a pan of simmering water. This is when the sauce could curdle so make sure the water doesn't touch the bottom of the bowl.

Gradually add melted butter in a steady stream, whisking all the time until the sauce is smooth and thick.

Q&A

What's the difference between hollandaise and béarnaise sauce and how do you use each of them?

Béarnaise is started with a reduction of vinegar, shallots, tarragon and pepper–this gives it a stronger flavor than hollandaise, which begins with a reduction of vinegar and pepper. After this initial reduction, the two sauces are made in the same way. Béarnaise goes best with beef–it's the perfect complement. Hollandaise, milder in flavor, goes well with asparagus, eggs and fish.

béarnaise sauce

2 tablespoons white vinegar

2 tablespoons water

1 shallot, chopped finely

2 teaspoons coarsely chopped fresh tarragon

½ teaspoon black peppercorns

3 egg yolks

1¾ sticks unsalted butter, melted

1 tablespoon finely chopped fresh tarragon

TIP

• If sauce separates, whisk in about 1 tablespoon boiling water until mixture is smooth.

1 Bring vinegar, the water, shallot, coarsely chopped tarragon and peppercorns to a boil in small saucepan. Reduce heat; simmer, uncovered, about 2 minutes or until liquid reduces by half. Strain over medium heatproof bowl; discard solids. Cool 10 minutes.

2 Whisk egg yolks into vinegar mixture until combined. Set bowl over medium saucepan of simmering water; do not allow water to touch base of bowl. Whisk mixture over heat until thickened. Remove bowl from heat; gradually whisk in melted butter in thin, steady stream until béarnaise thickens slightly. Stir finely chopped tarragon into sauce.

nutritional count per tablespoon 15.1g total fat (9.5g saturated fat); 138 cal; 0.2g carbohydrate; 0.8g protein; 0g fiber

serving ideas goes well with grilled beef steaks, pan-fried chicken breast filets, white fish filets and steamed or boiled vegetables.

mint sauce

This sauce makes enough for a 4 pound roast leg of lamb.

2 cups firmly packed fresh mint leaves

¼ cup water

¾ cup white wine vinegar

2 tablespoons superfine sugar

1 Chop half of the mint coarsely; place in small heatproof bowl.

2 Combine the water, vinegar and sugar in small saucepan; stir over heat, without boiling, until sugar dissolves. Pour liquid over chopped mint in bowl, cover; stand 3 hours.

3 Strain liquid into bowl; discard mint. Chop remaining mint coarsely; stir into liquid. Blend or process until chopped finely.

nutritional count per tablespoon 0.3g total fat (0.1g saturated fat); 56 cal; 10.1g carbohydrate; 0.9g protein; 1.9g fiber

serving ideas goes well with falafel, mixed bean salad or rice salad.

[opposite] béarnaise sauce

roast beef with espagnole sauce

PREP + COOK TIME
1 HOUR 25 MINS
SERVES 4
(MAKES 1 CUP SAUCE)

2 teaspoons olive oil

1½-pound piece beef sirloin

2 medium carrots, chopped coarsely

4 shallots, quartered

2 stalks celery, trimmed, chopped coarsely

2 teaspoons all-purpose flour

1 tablespoon tomato paste

2 cups beef stock

1 cup water

1 Preheat oven to 400°F/350°F fan-forced.

2 Heat oil in large flameproof dish; cook beef, uncovered, over high heat until browned. Place pan in oven; roast, uncovered, about 45 minutes or until beef is cooked as desired.

3 Remove beef from pan; cover to keep warm. Place pan with juices over high heat, add carrot, shallot and celery; cook, uncovered, stirring occasionally, about 10 minutes or until vegetables are well-browned. Add flour; cook, stirring, about 4 minutes or until mixture is dark brown. Add paste, stock and the water; bring to a boil. Boil, uncovered, about 10 minutes or until sauce thickens.

4 Strain sauce, discard vegetables. Slice beef; serve with espagnole.

nutritional count per serving 23.2g total fat (9.7g saturated fat); 438 cal; 6.4g carbohydrate; 49.7g protein; 2.9g fiber

serving ideas serve this recipe with roasted potatoes and shallots. This sauce also goes well with roast venison.

Cook the piece of sirloin over high heat in a heavy pan until it is brown all over. Roast the beef in the same pan until cooked to your liking.

Keep the beef warm while you make the sauce. Heat the juices in the pan and add carrots, shallots and celery.

Add flour and cook until the mixture browns–this gives the espagnole its depth of flavor. Pour in the stock.

Stir for about 10 minutes over high heat while the sauce reduces and thickens. Strain the sauce and serve it with the beef.

béchamel sauce

Béchamel is one of the "mother" or base sauces of classic French cooking and probably the one sauce that most people learn to cook before leaving home, often with the addition of cheese.

2 tablespoons butter
2 tablespoons all-purpose flour
1¼ cups hot milk
pinch nutmeg

1 Melt butter in medium saucepan, add flour; cook, stirring, until mixture bubbles and thickens.
2 Gradually add milk, stirring, until mixture boils and thickens. Stir in nutmeg.
nutritional count per tablespoon 3.1g total fat (2.1g saturated fat); 42 cal; 2.6g carbohydrate; 1.1g protein; 0.1g fiber
serving ideas goes well with pasta dishes, like lasagne, and grilled fish filets.

sweet chili sauce

6 fresh long red chilies, chopped finely
1 cup white vinegar
1 cup superfine sugar
2 cloves garlic, crushed

1 Combine chili, vinegar and sugar in small saucepan; stir over heat, without boiling, until sugar dissolves. Simmer, uncovered, 15 minutes.
2 Add garlic; simmer, uncovered, about 15 minutes or until mixture reduces by half. Cool.
nutritional count per tablespoon 0.1g total fat (0g saturated fat); 74 cal; 18.4g carbohydrate; 0.1g protein; 0.1g fiber
serving ideas goes well with spring rolls, salt and pepper squid, and thai fish cakes.

satay sauce

This sauce is very versatile: it can be used as a marinade, a dipping sauce or a salad dressing.

Any leftover sauce can be frozen for up to 3 months.

⅓ cup crunchy peanut butter
1 fresh long red chili, chopped finely
5-ounce can coconut milk
2 teaspoons fish sauce
2 teaspoons kecap manis
1 tablespoon lime juice

1 Cook ingredients, stirring, in small saucepan, over low heat until heated through.
nutritional count per tablespoon 6.4g total fat (2.8g saturated fat); 74 cal; 1.3g carbohydrate; 2.5g protein; 1.1g fiber
serving ideas goes well with chicken skewers, steamed vegetables or crisp-fried tofu.

[opposite] béchamel sauce

beurre blanc

Translated as "white butter", this classic French emulsified sauce is composed of a white wine and lemon juice reduction into which chunks of cold butter are whisked until the sauce is thick and smooth.

¼ cup dry white wine
1 tablespoon lemon juice
¼ cup cream
1 stick cold butter, chopped

1 Bring wine and juice to a boil in small saucepan. Boil, without stirring, until reduced by two-thirds.
2 Add cream; return to a boil then reduce heat. Whisk in cold butter, piece by piece, whisking between additions, until sauce is smooth and thickened slightly.
nutritional count per tablespoon 10.4g total fat (6.8g saturated fat); 97 cal; 0.3g carbohydrate; 0.2g protein; 0g fiber
serving ideas goes well with steamed or grilled salmon and steamed vegetables.

salsa verde

This Italian "green sauce" is sublime with grilled or poached fish. Spread onto bread as a sauce for a tuna sandwich, stir into mayonnaise for a great potato salad or spoon onto fish cakes.

½ cup finely chopped fresh flat-leaf parsley
¼ cup finely chopped fresh dill
¼ cup finely chopped fresh chives
1 tablespoon wholegrain mustard
2 tablespoons lemon juice
2 tablespoons drained, rinsed baby capers, chopped finely
1 clove garlic, crushed
⅓ cup olive oil

1 Combine ingredients in small bowl.
nutritional count per tablespoon 6.1g total fat (0.9g saturated fat); 58 cal; 0.4g carbohydrate; 0.2g protein; 0.3g fiber
serving ideas goes well with barbecued steak, chicken and grilled lamb cutlets.

white wine sauce

1½ tablespoons butter
2 shallots, chopped finely
1 teaspoon mustard powder
¾ cup dry white wine
¾ cup fish stock
1¼ cups light cream

1 Melt butter in medium frying pan; cook shallot and mustard powder, stirring, about 3 minutes or until shallot softens. Add wine; cook, uncovered, until wine reduces by two-thirds. Add stock; bring to a boil. Boil, uncovered, about 7 minutes or until reduced by half.

2 Add cream to pan; bring to a boil, then reduce heat. Simmer, uncovered, about 15 minutes or until sauce thickens slightly.

nutritional count per tablespoon 12.4g total fat (8.1g saturated fat); 127 cal; 1g carbohydrate; 0.9g protein, 0g fiber

serving ideas goes well with grilled or barbecued prawns and grilled lobster.

seafood sauce

PREP + COOK TIME 25 MINS • MAKES 2 CUPS

1 cup dry white wine
1 cup béchamel sauce (see page 273)
¾ cup cream
5 ounces mixed shelled seafood (clams, calamari, shrimp, mussels)
2 tablespoons finely chopped fresh dill
1 tablespoon lemon juice

1 Bring wine to a boil in medium frying pan then reduce heat. Simmer, uncovered, until reduced by half.

2 Add béchamel, cream and seafood mix to pan; bring to a boil then reduce heat. Simmer, uncovered, about 5 minutes or until seafood is cooked through. Stir in dill and juice.

nutritional count per tablespoon 5g total fat (3.2g saturated fat); 70 cal; 2.1g carbohydrate; 2.7g protein; 0.1g fiber

serving ideas goes well with grilled fish filets, pasta and grilled beef filets.

mornay

PREP + COOK TIME 10 MINS • MAKES 2 CUPS

1 cup béchamel sauce (see page 273)
¼ cup cream
1 egg yolk
1 cup coarsely grated emmentaler cheese

1 Bring béchamel to a boil in medium saucepan; add cream and egg yolk, whisk 1 minute.

2 Remove sauce from heat; add cheese, stir until cheese melts.

nutritional count per tablespoon 4.4g total fat (2.8g saturated fat); 53 cal; 1.4g carbohydrate; 2.2g protein; 0g fiber

serving ideas goes well with oysters, lobster and grilled fish filets.

chicken and mushroom velouté

PREP + COOK TIME 35 MINS • MAKES 2½ CUPS

Velouté, which translates from the French as "the texture of velvet", is similar to a béchamel except for the fact that a light stock is added to the roux instead of milk. If you're serving this sauce with fish, replace the chicken stock with fish stock; for a vegetarian version, use vegetable stock. Velouté should be served as soon as it is made.

2¼ cups chicken stock
4 tablespoons butter
2 tablespoons all-purpose flour
1 small brown onion, chopped finely
5 ounces button mushrooms, sliced thinly
¼ cup dry white wine
¼ cup pouring cream

1 Place stock in small saucepan; bring to a boil then remove from heat.

2 Melt 3 tablespoons of the butter in medium saucepan, add flour; cook, stirring, about 2 minutes or until mixture bubbles and thickens. Stir in hot stock gradually; bring to a boil. Cook, stirring, until sauce boils and thickens.

3 Reduce heat; simmer, uncovered, about 20 minutes or until reduced by half. Strain sauce into small bowl.

4 Melt remaining butter in medium saucepan; cook onion, stirring, until softened. Add mushrooms; cook, stirring, about 5 minutes or until softened.

5 Add wine to pan; cook, stirring, until almost all liquid evaporates. Add velouté; bring to a boil. Add cream; reduce heat, stir until sauce is heated through.

nutritional count per tablespoon 2.6g total fat (1.7g saturated fat); 31 cal; 0.9g carbohydrate; 0.6g protein; 0.2g fiber

serving ideas goes well with pasta and as a chicken pot pie filling.

tomato ketchup

PREP + COOK TIME 50 MINS (+ COOLING) • MAKES 3½ CUPS

This thick, spicy sauce is a traditional accompaniment to french fries, scrambled eggs, hamburgers and hot dogs.

If tomatoes are in season, coarsely chop 3½ pounds and substitute for the canned variety.

This sauce can be kept, covered, in the refrigerator for up to one month; it's also suitable to freeze.

1 tablespoon olive oil
1 large brown onion, chopped coarsely
2 tablespoons brown sugar
3 x 14-ounce cans diced tomatoes
¼ teaspoon ground allspice
½ teaspoon celery salt
2 tablespoons tomato paste
⅓ cup white vinegar

1 Heat oil in large saucepan; cook onion, stirring, until soft. Add sugar, undrained tomatoes, allspice and celery salt; bring to a boil then reduce heat. Simmer, uncovered, stirring occasionally, about 30 minutes or until mixture thickens. Stir in paste and vinegar; cook, uncovered, 5 minutes.

2 Blend or process sauce until smooth; push through fine sieve into medium bowl. Discard solids. Serve sauce cold.

nutritional count per tablespoon 0.5g total fat (0.1g saturated fat); 15 cal; 1.9g carbohydrate; 0.3g protein; 0.5g fiber

serving ideas goes well with grilled white fish filets, sirloin steak, pork sausages, meat pies and sausage rolls.

[opposite] chicken and mushroom velouté

napoletana sauce

Makes enough sauce for 1 pound pasta, to serve four people.

An equal quantity of canned diced tomatoes can be used instead of fresh tomatoes.

This sauce will keep, covered, in the fridge for up to three days. Freeze in sealed containers for up to three months.

⅓ cup olive oil

1 medium brown onion, chopped finely

3 cloves garlic, crushed

¼ cup loosely packed fresh basil leaves

1 teaspoon sea salt

2 tablespoons tomato paste

3 pounds ripe tomatoes, chopped coarsely

1 Heat half of the oil in large saucepan; cook onion, garlic, basil and salt, stirring, until onion softens. Add paste; cook, stirring, 1 minute.

2 Add tomato; bring to a boil then reduce heat. Simmer, uncovered, stirring occasionally, about 45 minutes or until sauce thickens. Stir in remaining oil; simmer, uncovered, 5 minutes.

nutritional count per tablespoon 1.6g total fat (0.2g saturated fat); 20 cal; 0.9g carbohydrate; 0.4g protein; 0.5g fiber

arrabbiata sauce

Makes enough sauce for 1 pound pasta, to serve four people.

Arrabbiata sauce is traditionally served with penne–combining to make the well-known Italian dish Penne all'Arrabbiata, literally meaning "angry pasta". Its name is derived from the fuming spicy flavor that the chilies provide. If you can't take the heat, remove some of the chili seeds for a milder dish.

¼ cup olive oil

2 fresh small red Thai chilies, chopped finely

1 quart napoletana sauce (see recipe above)

½ cup coarsely chopped fresh flat-leaf parsley

1 Heat half of the oil in large saucepan; cook chili, stirring, 2 minutes.

2 Add sauce; bring to a boil. Stir in remaining oil and parsley.

nutritional count per tablespoon 2.2g total fat (0.3g saturated fat); 24 cal; 0.7g carbohydrate; 0.3g protein; 0.4g fiber

[opposite] napoletana sauce

aïoli

This garlic-flavored mayonnaise originated in the Provence region of southern France, where for centuries it has been a traditional accompaniment to bouillabaisse. These days, it is often enjoyed with fries and seafood as an alternative to traditional mayonnaise or tartare sauce.

4 cloves garlic, quartered

1 teaspoon sea salt

2 teaspoons lemon juice

1 cup mayonnaise (see page 118)

1 Using mortar and pestle, crush garlic and salt to a smooth paste.

2 Combine garlic mixture and remaining ingredients in small bowl.

nutritional count per tablespoon 19.1g total fat (2.8g saturated fat); 172 cal; 0.2g carbohydrate; 0.6g protein; 0.2g fiber

serving ideas goes well with grilled fish filets, crudités, and fried or boiled potatoes.

tartare sauce

1 cup mayonnaise (see page 118)

2 tablespoons finely chopped cornichons

1 tablespoon drained, rinsed baby capers, chopped finely

1 tablespoon finely chopped fresh flat-leaf parsley

2 teaspoons finely chopped fresh dill

2 teaspoons lemon juice

1 Combine ingredients in small bowl.

nutritional count per tablespoon 9.5g total fat (1.4g saturated fat); 87 cal; 0.3g carbohydrate; 0.3g protein; 0g fiber

serving ideas goes well with grilled chicken breast filets, and smoked or fried fish.

skordalia

This recipe makes enough for four servings of lamb kebabs.

If skordalia becomes too thick, add small amounts of hot water until the desired consistency is reached.

[1] aïoli
[2] tartare sauce
[3] skordalia
[4] tangy barbecue sauce [page 282]

1 medium potato, quartered

3 cloves garlic, quartered

2 tablespoons cold water

1 tablespoon lemon juice

1 tablespoon white wine vinegar

⅓ cup olive oil

1 Boil, steam or microwave potato until tender; drain. Cool 10 minutes.

2 Blend or process potato, garlic, the water, juice and vinegar until mixture is pureed. With motor running, gradually add oil in thin, steady stream, processing until mixture thickens.

nutritional count per tablespoon 6.1g total fat (0.9g saturated fat); 67 cal; 2.3g carbohydrate; 0.5g protein; 0.4g fiber

serving ideas goes well with lamb kebabs, fried zucchini or eggplant, and battered fish.

tangy barbecue sauce

This sauce is best made a day ahead. Keep, refrigerated, for up to three days in a screw-top jar.

This recipe makes enough for six beef burgers or 4 pounds of braised short ribs.

1 cup tomato sauce

½ cup apple cider vinegar

¼ cup Worcestershire sauce

⅔ cup firmly packed brown sugar

2 tablespoons yellow mustard

1 fresh small red Thai chili, chopped finely

1 clove garlic, crushed

1 tablespoon lemon juice

1 Combine ingredients in medium saucepan; bring to a boil then reduce heat. Simmer, uncovered, stirring occasionally, 20 minutes.

nutritional count per tablespoon 0.1g total fat (0g saturated fat); 39 cal; 9.3g carbohydrate; 0.3g protein; 0.3g fiber

serving ideas goes well with roasted potato wedges or as a sauce for homemade baked beans.

pork cutlets with charcuterie sauce

PREP + COOK TIME 35 MINS
SERVES 4
(MAKES 1 CUP SAUCE)

1 tablespoon olive oil

4 pork cutlets

1 small brown onion, chopped finely

2 strips bacon

⅔ cup dry white wine

⅔ cup chicken stock

⅓ cup cornichons, sliced thinly lengthways

⅓ cup pitted green olives, sliced thinly

2 teaspoons dijon mustard

2 tablespoons finely chopped fresh flat-leaf parsley

1 Heat oil in large frying pan; cook pork, in batches, until browned both sides and cooked as desired. Cover to keep warm.

2 Add onion and bacon to pan; cook, stirring, until onion softens.

3 Deglaze pan with wine, stirring until mixture reduces by half.

4 Stir in remaining ingredients; bring to a boil. Boil, uncovered, about 1 minute or until sauce thickens slightly.

nutritional count per serving 24.1g total fat (7.4g saturated fat); 406 cal; 7.7g carbohydrate; 33g protein; 0.9g fiber

serving ideas charcuterie sauce also goes well with grilled pork sausages, barbecued veal steaks and pan-fried chicken breast filets.

strawberry coulis

For a delicious dessert, fold ½ cup coulis, the pulp of 2 passionfruit, ½ cup lightly crushed biscotti, 1 cup yogurt and 1 cup vanilla pudding together until just combined. Serve in four glass tumblers.

10 ounces frozen strawberries, thawed
1 tablespoon powdered sugar

1 Push berries through fine sieve into small bowl; discard seeds.
2 Stir sifted powdered sugar into sauce.
nutritional count per tablespoon 0.3g total fat (0g saturated fat); 10 cal; 1.6g carbohydrate; 0.4g protein; 0.6g fiber
serving ideas goes well with puddings, cake and poached fruits.

crème anglaise

Low heat and constant whisking are the key elements to a successful crème anglaise.

Try flavoring the custard with liqueurs, finely grated citrus rind, chocolate, spices or coffee.

1 vanilla bean
1½ cups milk

⅓ cup superfine sugar
4 egg yolks

1 Split vanilla bean in half lengthwise; scrape seeds into medium saucepan, add pod, milk and one tablespoon of the sugar. Bring to a boil then strain into large pitcher. Discard pod.
2 Meanwhile, combine egg yolks and remaining sugar in medium heatproof bowl set over medium saucepan of simmering water; do not allow water to touch base of bowl. Whisk until thick and creamy; gradually whisk in hot milk mixture.
3 Return custard mixture to pan; stir, over low heat, until mixture is just thick enough to coat the back of a spoon.
4 Return custard to bowl; refrigerate about 1 hour or until cold.
nutritional count per tablespoon 2.1g total fat (0.9g saturated fat); 44 cal; 5.2g carbohydrate; 1.4g protein; 0g fiber
serving ideas goes well with fresh figs, chocolate cake and apple pie.

chocolate fudge sauce

This sauce will keep under refrigeration, covered, for up to three days. To serve, reheat sauce briefly in microwave oven on HIGH (100%) or over low heat in small saucepan until it reaches the desired consistency.

7 ounces bittersweet chocolate
1½ tablespoons butter
¼ teaspoon vanilla extract
½ cup cream

1 Place chocolate and butter in small heatproof bowl set over small saucepan of simmering water; do not allow water to touch base of bowl. Stir until chocolate is melted. Add extract and cream; stir until combined. Serve sauce warm.
nutritional count per tablespoon 10.6g total fat (6.7g saturated fat); 140 cal; 10.7g carbohydrate; 1.1g protein; 0.2g fiber
serving ideas goes well with ice cream, puddings, mousses and poached fruit.

sabayon

Sabayon is a light, frothy custard sauce. Be sure to whisk the mixture vigorously to incorporate as much air as possible or your sabayon will be flat. Cooking the mixture too quickly, though, will make it too thick—prevent this by keeping the water in the saucepan at a low simmer.

3 egg yolks
¼ cup superfine sugar
¼ cup dry white wine

1 Place ingredients in medium bowl set over medium saucepan of simmering water; do not allow water to touch base of bowl. Whisk vigorously and continually about 5 minutes or until sauce is thick and creamy.

nutritional count per tablespoon 0.6g total fat (0.2g saturated fat); 17 cal; 2.3g carbohydrate; 0.3g protein; 0g fiber

serving ideas goes well with poached pears, grilled peaches or nectarines, and fresh mango slices.

orange butterscotch sauce

For a lavish touch, add ¼ cup raisins and 1 tablespoon rum or brandy. Serve over ice cream or baked apples.

½ cup heavy cream
½ cup firmly packed brown sugar
½ stick cold butter, chopped
1 teaspoon finely grated orange rind

1 Stir ingredients in small saucepan over low heat, without boiling, until sugar dissolves. Bring to a boil, then reduce heat; simmer, uncovered, 3 minutes.

nutritional count per tablespoon 8g total fat (5.2g saturated fat); 109 cal; 9.3g carbohydrate; 0.3g protein; 0g fiber

serving ideas goes well with pancakes, waffles, sweet crêpes and poached oranges.

Q&A

I've heard of people melting Mars bars in cream to make a sauce for ice cream. Is that really possible and if so, how do I do it?

It is indeed possible and it makes a super-quick and easy sauce for ice cream. All you do is gently heat a chopped up Mars bar in ½ cup of cream. Stir all the time until the chocolate melts and don't allow it to boil. You could also use coarsely chopped after-dinner mints.

[opposite] sabayon

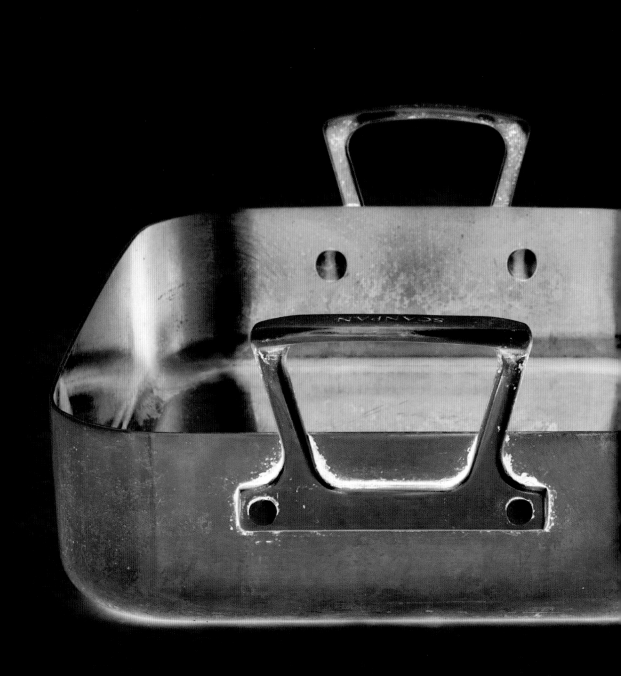

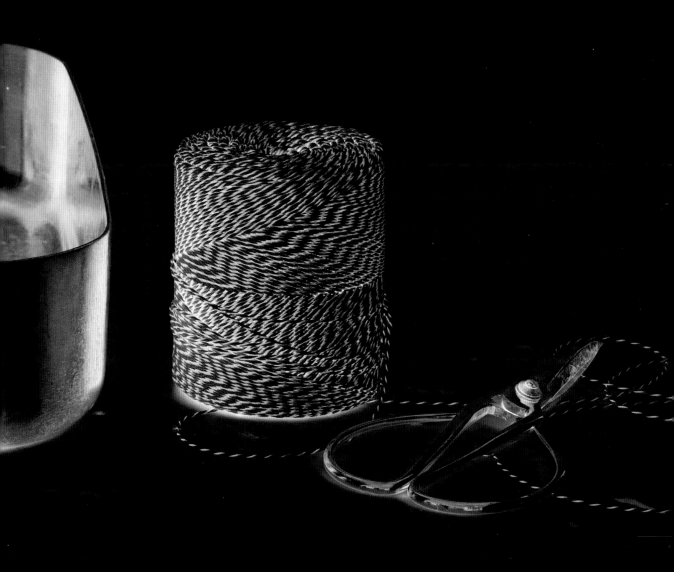

The perfect roast

Many of us have fond memories of weekly roast dinners as we were growing up. They were often a favorite ritual on Sundays at our parents' or grandparents' homes and they were all about bringing family together as much as nourishing our bodies.

And for many of us, that's where they have stayed—a cherished memory from our past, only occasionally reprised for special occasions. Many of us have gotten out of the habit of making what our mothers called a "baked dinner" because we think it takes too long (and it does take time, but you don't have to hang around the kitchen while the roast is in the oven—you can continue typing away at the computer or read a book) or because it's too formal or traditional. But ask your family and friends what their idea of a perfect meal is and many of them will vouch for the nostalgic baked dinner.

The only upside about not having roasts as often as we used to is that, when they do appear, they are memorable. Serve up a roast chicken or a leg of lamb with gravy and melt-in-the-mouth baked vegetables for friends and family and watch their delight. And if you don't want to cook a traditional-size roast, there are mini roasts available in all the major supermarkets. So now there's no excuse: a roast dinner need not be reserved only for ceremonial occasions. It's a sumptuous meal you can revisit at any time—and you get the added benefit of delicious leftovers to enjoy.

COOKING TIPS

CHICKEN Roast chicken requires a preheated hot oven for the first 15 to 20 minutes then reduced heat for another 60 minutes or so. You need to baste occasionally to ensure that the meat remains moist. Roast chicken should be cooked through, but not overdone (see When Is Your Roast Done?, opposite).

BEEF Allow 4 to 5 ounces of meat per person of boneless beef and 5 to 6 ounces for a bone-in roast. The exact cooking times, and frequency of basting, will depend on the cut. To judge when beef is cooked to your taste, insert a fine skewer into the center and check the juices (see When Is Your Roast Done?, opposite).

LAMB Today, most people enjoy roast lamb best when it is browned outside but still pink and juicy inside. When it is medium-well, it will be fairly firm and blush-pink with clear or slightly pinkish juice; when medium-rare, the interior will be soft and reddish pink and the juices "bloody".

ROAST LAMB requires a preheated hot oven. Roast for 20 minutes, then reduce to moderate for the remaining cooking time. Baste with pan juices every 20 minutes. Trimmed roasts, being lean, need to be brushed with oil before cooking and basted every 10 minutes. Allow 10 to 15 minutes per pound, depending on whether you want rare or firm but pink lamb; 20 minutes per pound will give well-done lamb that is just pink in the middle. Start checking for doneness towards the end of cooking time.

CHOOSING YOUR ROAST

CHICKEN Try to find a fresh, free-range, organic chicken. Second-best is fresh, but not free-range, chicken. If cooking a frozen chicken, give it time to thaw out in the refrigerator first. It will lose some of its juices as it thaws, but it will lose less this way. Thaw, uncovered, on several thicknesses of absorbent paper on a plate in the fridge. Never cook a partially frozen bird: it may appear to be cooked through, but unless the internal temperature reached 165°F or higher during cooking, dangerous micro-organisms such as salmonella may have survived. The same considerations apply for other poultry–duck, quail and turkey.

BEEF The best cuts for roasting are filet, rib-eye, rump, sirloin and rib, either on the bone (a "standing" roast) or boned and rolled. Filet is the most tender cut of all and is fatless, so it is perfect for serving with a rich sauce, but rump, sirloin or rib will give more flavor in their own right. You may see cheaper cuts marked "roasting" but these are often tough.

LAMB The best roasting cuts are the leg, which may be bone-in or partly boned (called easy-carve); trimmed roasts, which are usually individual leg muscles seamed out for small, fatless roasts; loin on the bone or boned and rolled; saddle, which is two loins still joined; chump, a choice, small, compact roast with some bone; a rack (ribs), which consists of 8 cutlets still joined or can be ordered by the number of cutlets required (usually 3 or 4 per person, depending on size); the rump; the shoulder, either on the bone, which is tricky to carve, or boned and rolled; the forequarter, which consists of forequarter chops still joined but is usually sold boned and rolled; and for slow-roasting only, a rolled breast, which is a fatty cut.

PORK Roasting cuts are the loin, bone-in or boned and sometimes rolled, which serves 8–10 and is often cut into two smaller roasts; the leg, also very large and often divided into the filet end and the shank end, which is often boned and rolled; rump; filet; individual leg muscles seamed out for small, boneless roasts; shoulder, either on the bone or boned and rolled; and rack or rib on the bone, consisting of 6–8 cutlets in one piece. You may see cheaper cuts than these marked "roasting", but they are often tough.

Suckling pig is the supreme roast pork for a special celebration. A 12–14 pound one will serve 12 to 15 people. It must be ordered well ahead–be sure to measure your oven before ordering to make sure the pig will fit.

WHEN IS YOUR ROAST DONE?

CHICKEN, DUCK AND TURKEY should be cooked through but not overdone. Check by inserting a fine skewer into the thickest part of the thigh near the body; juices should run clear with no tinge of pink. Pink juice means it is underdone.

MEAT To judge when your roasted meat is done to your taste, use a meat thermometer or run a fine skewer into the thickest part of the meat and check the juice that comes out. Red juice means it is rare, pink juice is medium and clear juice is well done.

PORK Don't overcook pork. A hint of pink is fine. Allow 30 minutes per pound if it is over 6 pounds and 40 minutes per 2 pounds if under. Use a meat thermometer or check by inserting a fine skewer into the center towards the end of cooking time. It is done if the skewer goes in easily and juices run clear.

ALL ROASTS SHOULD BE RESTED in a warm place, loosely covered with foil, 15 minutes before serving, to allow the juices to settle and the meat to become more succulent.

roast beef with yorkshire puddings

Roast beef with Yorkshire puddings is the most traditional British meal, but it is every bit as popular here in the United States. While the roast beef is resting, make the gravy and Yorkshire puddings, and serve the roast with crispy baked potatoes, boiled baby carrots and steamed green vegetables.

Checking for doneness To judge when a roast is done to your taste, use a meat thermometer or run a fine skewer into the center and check the juice that comes out. Red juice means rare, pink means medium and clear means well done.

Timing Many people think a roast is one of the simplest meals to put together. And it is–as long as you've got the timing right. Cold plates, cold vegetables, gravy that has sat for too long–all of these things will spoil what is a favorite Sunday or holiday dinner.

The beef We've used a corner piece of beef topside, but you can use rump, sirloin or rib-eye if you prefer. Filet of beef is not usually used in roast beef with Yorkshire pudding because while tender, it doesn't have as much flavor as the other cuts.

Crispy roast potatoes Boil or microwave the potatoes until just cooked. Run the tines of a fork over the surface to rough it up, then place the potatoes in a roasting pan covered with a thin layer of very hot olive oil. Roast in a hot oven for approximately 40 minutes or until crisp.

Hot vegetables Boil, steam or microwave your other vegetables last. Boiled vegetables get cold very quickly so they should be brought to the table and passed around at the last minute.

Marinate the beef in the wine and herb mixture for 3 hours or overnight, covered, in the refrigerator.

Drain the beef and discard the herb mixture. Reserve 1 cup of the marinade to use in the gravy. Place the beef on a bed of vegetables and roast for about 1½ hours.

Pour the pan juices into a pitcher–the oil will rise to the surface. Remove 1½ tablespoons of this oil for cooking the Yorkshire puddings. Discard the remaining oil.

roast beef with yorkshire puddings

PREP + COOK TIME
2 HOURS 35 MINS
(+ REFRIGERATION &
STANDING) • SERVES 8

4-pound corner piece beef
   topside roast
2 cups dry red wine
2 bay leaves
6 black peppercorns
¼ cup wholegrain mustard
4 cloves garlic, sliced
4 sprigs fresh thyme
1 medium brown onion,
   chopped coarsely
2 medium carrots,
   chopped coarsely
1 large leek, chopped coarsely
2 stalks celery, trimmed,
   chopped coarsely
2 tablespoons olive oil

Yorkshire puddings
1 cup all-purpose flour
2 eggs
½ cup milk
½ cup water
gravy
2 tablespoons all-purpose flour
1½ cups beef stock

While the roast is cooking, mix the batter for the Yorkshire puddings and leave to stand for 30 minutes.

Heat the reserved oil in muffin pan until quite hot, then pour in the Yorkshire pudding batter. Return the pan to the hot oven quickly so the puddings will start to cook right away.

To make the gravy, add flour to the reserved pan juices and gradually add combined stock and reserved marinade, stirring constantly until mixture is thick and smooth.

Try adding 1 tablespoon horseradish cream or 1 teaspoon english dry mustard or dried thyme to the Yorkshire pudding mixture. You can also add ale or beef stock instead of the water.

For light fluffy Yorkshire puddings, it is essential that the batter is well-rested and cold, and that the oven and reserved oil are both very hot.

1 Combine beef, wine, bay leaves, peppercorns, mustard, garlic, thyme and onion in large shallow dish. Cover; refrigerate 3 hours or overnight.

2 Preheat oven to 350°F/325°F fan-forced.

3 Drain beef over medium bowl; reserve 1 cup of marinade. Combine carrot, leek and celery in large roasting pan, top with beef; brush beef with oil.

4 Roast beef, uncovered, about 1½ hours. Remove beef from pan, wrap in foil; stand 20 minutes before serving. Increase oven to 425°F/400°F fan-forced.

5 Remove vegetables with slotted spoon; discard vegetables. Pour pan juices into pitcher; stand 2 minutes. Reserve 1½ tablespoons oil from the surface for Yorkshire puddings, discard remaining oil; reserve 2 tablespoons of the pan juices for gravy.

6 Make Yorkshire puddings and gravy. Serve beef with puddings and gravy.

Yorkshire puddings Sift flour into medium bowl; whisk in combined eggs, milk and water all at once until smooth. Stand batter 30 minutes. Spoon reserved oil into eight holes of 12-hole (⅓-cup) muffin pan; heat in oven 2 minutes. Divide batter into pan holes. Bake about 20 minutes or until puffed and golden.

gravy Heat reserved juices in same roasting pan, add flour; cook, stirring, until browned. Gradually add stock and reserved marinade; cook, stirring, until mixture boils and thickens. Strain gravy into heatproof gravy boat.

nutritional count per serving 15.4g total fat (4.8g saturated fat); 519 cal; 21.1g carbohydrate; 61.2g protein; 4g fiber

standing rib roast with roast vegetables

Cooking a rib roast is at once simple and confusing. The meat itself is so flavorful, it doesn't need much seasoning–just a little salt and pepper, and its own natural juices. This much is simple. The hard part is getting the oven temperature and timing right.

Adjusting to size If using a very large roast (more than five ribs), check the temperature when the cooking time is nearly up. Take the roast out of the oven just short of the goal, because larger roasts, and the bone in them, continue to cook and rise in temperature as they rest.

Slicing it You'll be surprised at the difference between the chew of a thickly cut piece of rib roast and a thin slice. For a truly good chew, cut the slices 1-1½ inches thick. Also, as you cut the roast away from the bones, leave some meat on them so you can gnaw on the bones.

Standing rib roast Gets its name from the fact that the bones are included in the roast, so the roast can stand by itself. The bones give the meat great flavor. A rib roast comprises seven ribs, from the shoulder down the back to the loin. We used a 2½ pound (three-rib) roast.

Probing for doneness The best way to judge a standing rib roast's degree of doneness is with a meat thermometer. The internal temperature should be: 135-140°F for rare; 145-150°F for medium-rare; 150-160°F for medium; 160-165°F for medium-well; and 170°F for well-done.

The tong test If you don't have a meat thermometer handy, you can use tongs to test the roast's doneness. Gently prod or squeeze the roast–rare is very soft; medium-rare is soft; medium is springy but soft; medium-well is firm; and well-done is very firm.

Adding flavor When the roast is done, remove it from the oven, set aside, and let it rest so it can redistribute its juices for at least 20 minutes. This is the time to make the sauce.

Using a simple knot, tie kitchen string between each rib bone to ensure the outer layers of meat do not pull away from the rib-eye during roasting.

Brush oil all over the roast and season with pepper. Heat oil in a large flameproof roasting pan and add the roast, fat-side down, and brown. Turn the roast and cook until browned all over.

Heat oil in a separate flameproof roasting pan, add potatoes and cook, stirring, until browned. Add the pumpkin and sweet potato. Place the dish in oven, with the beef, and roast uncovered until cooked.

standing rib roast with roast vegetables   PREP + COOK TIME 1 HOUR 50 MINS • SERVES 4

2½-pound beef standing rib roast

¼ cup olive oil

2 teaspoons cracked black pepper

1 pound potatoes, chopped coarsely

1 pound pumpkin, chopped coarsely

1 pound sweet potato, chopped coarsely

½ cup brandy

1½ cups beef stock

1 tablespoon corn starch

¼ cup water

1 tablespoon finely chopped fresh chives

Transfer the beef juices left in the baking dish to a small saucepan. Add brandy and bring to a boil.

Once you have added the stock, pour in the blended corn starch and water, and continue cooking until the mixture comes to a boil and starts to thicken.

Hold an end rib with one hand to keep the roast steady. Using a very sharp knife, with the other hand, cut between the rib bones to release the slice.

A standing rib roast is also known as a bone-in rib roast.

1 Preheat oven to 400°F/350°F fan-forced.

2 Brush beef with 1 tablespoon of the oil; sprinkle with pepper. Heat 1 tablespoon of the oil in large shallow flameproof roasting pan; cook beef, uncovered, over high heat until browned all over. Roast, uncovered, in oven about 45 minutes or until cooked as desired.

3 Meanwhile, heat remaining oil in another large flameproof roasting pan; cook potatoes, stirring, over high heat until browned lightly. Add pumpkin and sweet potato, place pan in oven with beef; roast, uncovered, about 35 minutes or until vegetables are browned.

4 Place beef on vegetables, cover; return to oven to keep warm. Drain juices from beef pan into medium saucepan, add brandy; bring to a boil. Add stock and blended corn starch and water; cook, stirring, until sauce boils and thickens slightly. Stir in chives; pour into medium heatproof pitcher.

5 Serve beef and vegetables with sauce.

nutritional count per serving 29.2g total fat (8.5g saturated fat); 745 cal; 41.1g carbohydrate; 60.4g protein; 5.4g fiber

lemon and thyme baked chicken

If you only ever learn to cook one great dish in life, make sure it's a roast chicken. Easy, impressive and utterly delicious, this recipe will see you through many dinner parties and family meals.

Thawing poultry Always thaw frozen chicken in the fridge overnight–never on the kitchen counter or in the sink. Place the chicken in a large dish to catch any juices. Once thawed, use within 24 hours.

Keeping meat moist Avoid overcooking the chicken or it will dry out. As a guide, a 3-pound whole stuffed chicken takes about 30 minutes per pound to cook in a 350°F/ 325°F fan-forced oven.

Chicken When buying poultry, keep in mind that birds free to roam outside and fed a natural diet without additives usually taste better. Their proportion of meat to fat is higher compared with commercially raised chickens. Check the label for free-range or organic logos.

Leftovers This chicken is great cold the next day. If using the breast, shred it with clean hands or, using a sharp knife, cut it into slices. Add it to a baguette or sandwich bread, and top it with lettuce and mayonnaise, or put it in a wrap. Also delicious scattered in an avocado salad.

Matching wine A fresh, lemony semillon pairs beautifully with this roast chicken, as does a dry sparkling white or even a fresh riesling. Although light reds such as pinot noir usually go with chicken, the roast's citrus flavorings may interfere with the pinot's delicate notes.

Hold the gravy This recipe is better without any gravy as it will only detract from the thyme and lemon flavored juices coming from the chicken. Roasted or steamed vegetables and crusty bread is all that's needed.

Once you have rinsed the chicken, pat it dry with absorbent paper. This will help the skin to brown more evenly during the roasting process.

Rub oil all over the chicken with clean hands before rubbing with the salt, pepper and thyme mixture.

Push the garlic, fresh thyme sprigs and lemon quarters into the cavity of the chicken.

lemon and thyme baked chicken PREP + COOK TIME 1 HOUR 45 MINS (+ STANDING) • SERVES 4

3-pound whole chicken
1 tablespoon olive oil
1 tablespoon fine salt
2 teaspoons finely cracked black pepper
2 tablespoons fresh thyme leaves
1 bulb garlic, halved crossways
1 medium lemon, cut into wedges
½ bunch fresh thyme sprigs
3 tablespoons butter, softened

Separate the skin from the chicken breast with your fingers, taking care not to tear the skin. Spread the butter and thyme mixture over the entire breast, under the skin.

Once you have secured the skin over the cavity with thin skewers or toothpicks, place the chicken on an oiled wire rack in a roasting pan. Roast, uncovered, for 1 hour 20 minutes or until cooked.

To test chicken for doneness, insert a skewer into the thickest part of the leg, then pull it out and wait for the juices to bubble up to the surface. If the juices are clear, the chicken is done.

Be sure to dry the chicken completely after rinsing–if there is moisture present when you put it in the oven, it will turn to steam, which can prevent the skin from turning a lovely golden brown.

1 Preheat oven to 400°F/350°F fan-forced.

2 Wash chicken under cold water; pat dry inside and out with absorbent paper. Rub chicken with oil. Combine salt, pepper and half the thyme in small bowl; rub onto skin and inside cavity. Place garlic, lemon and thyme sprigs inside cavity.

3 Combine butter and remaining thyme in small bowl. Carefully separate skin from chicken breast with your fingers; spread butter under skin covering breast. Secure skin over cavity with thin skewers or toothpicks.

4 Place chicken on oiled wire rack in shallow roasting pan; roast, uncovered, 1 hour 20 minutes or until chicken is cooked through. Remove chicken from oven, cover loosely with foil; stand 10 minutes.

nutritional count per serving 39.2g total fat (15.1g saturated fat); 513 cal 1g carbohydrate; 39.4g protein; 1.4g fiber

slow-roasted duck legs

Most cooks put roasted duck into the "leave it to the chefs" basket, but it's really not that different from roasting a chicken. Once you give it a try, crispy, tender roast duck will become a new favorite.

Buying duck fresh It wasn't long ago when the only duck you could find was frozen whole duck. Today you can buy whole duck or pieces from butchers and good poultry shops. If planning for a dinner party, it's a good idea to place an order with the butcher in advance.

Reheating duck Duck reheats really well. Simply place in an ovenproof dish in a hot oven or even under a hot broiler and heat through. If you want the skin to be crispier, dab the skin with absorbent paper before placing in the oven or under the broiler.

A red or white meat? Many people think duck, like chicken. must be well done. However, this rule doesn't apply to duck breast, which should be treated more like a steak. Cook it past medium-rare, and you'll lose flavor and compromise texture.

Testing for doneness The duck is done to medium-rare if the juices from the fattest part of the thigh or drumstick run faintly rosy when the duck is pricked with a skewer. For well done, cook until the juices run clear.

The good fat Duck has always been considered the richest of all poultry meats. However, duck meat comprises only about 2 percent fat—most of the fat is found in the skin. Duck fat is also more like olive oil than butter or beef fat. Whereas chicken and turkey both contain high levels of polyunsaturated fats, duck has more monosaturated fat, which is high in linoleic acid—one of the healthy fats found in heart-friendly olive oil.

Place bottled morello cherries in a metal sieve over a large bowl to strain.

Pour chicken stock into combined cherry juice, port, cinnamon, cloves and garlic in a large baking dish.

Arrange the duck legs on a metal rack placed in the baking dish with the cherry juice mixture.

slow-roasted duck legs

PREP + COOK TIME 2 HOURS 20 MINS • SERVES 4

24-ounce jar morello cherries
½ cup port
1 cinnamon stick
3 whole cloves
1 clove garlic, sliced thinly
½ cup chicken stock
4 duck legs (2½ pounds leg and
    thigh portion), excess fat removed

Pour the pan liquid into a medium bowl through a metal sieve to strain.

Using a large metal spoon, skim the fat from the top of the pan juices.

Transfer the skimmed pan juices to a frying pan, add the cherries and bring the mixture to a boil. Reduce heat and allow the mixture to simmer, uncovered, for 5 minutes or until the sauce thickens slightly.

1 Preheat oven to 325°F/300°F fan-forced.

2 Strain cherries over small bowl. Combine cherry juice with port, cinnamon, cloves, garlic and stock in large baking dish. Place duck on metal rack in baking dish; cover tightly with oiled foil. Roast, covered, in oven about 2 hours or until duck meat is tender.

3 Strain pan liquid into medium bowl; skim away fat. Transfer mixture to medium frying pan. Add cherries; bring to a boil. Reduce heat; simmer, uncovered, 5 minutes or until sauce thickens slightly.

4 Serve duck with cherry sauce.

nutritional count per serving 47.3g total fat (12.4g saturated fat); 755 cal; 39.5g carbohydrate; 47.3g protein; 2g fiber

serving idea serve with an apple, toasted walnut and parsley salad.

chicken pot roast
with mustard cream sauce

This is warming comfort food at its best. Don't let the long cooking time discourage you. You'll spend very little time at the stove before the pan goes in the oven.

Browning the meat The initial cooking on the stove top, until the chicken is lightly browned, is an important step in pot roasts. Some recipes skip the step altogether. This browning process intensifies the flavors as the dish cooks and provides it with wonderful color, too.

Use whole chicken There are a few reasons why it is better to buy a whole chicken, and not pieces, for this recipe. Chickens cost less per pound when bought whole. Pre-cut meat is sometimes poorly trimmed, too, and you end up getting less meat per pound.

Cast-iron cookware A heavy ovenproof casserole dish is a must for today's cooks. These stove-to-oven pans come in raw cast-iron (Dutch ovens) and enameled cast-iron (French ovens). Enameled surfaces don't need to be seasoned and provide a non-stick surface.

Time is the essence Pot roasts are a convenience food in that everything happens in one pan, but they're not a quick-fix. Pot roasts only work with long, slow cooking so you can't take a shortcut and turn up the oven heat, hoping it will work its magic in just 45 minutes.

| 1 | 2 | 3 |

Using a sharp knife, peel the shallots. Then, on a clean chopping board, cut each shallot in half.

Place a flameproof casserole dish over a high heat, add the oil and, when hot, add the chicken and cook, turning occasionally, until brown all over. Remove chicken and set aside.

Add the shallots, carrots and parsnips to the same dish and stir to combine. Cook for about 5 minutes, stirring, until the vegetables are browned lightly.

chicken pot roast
with mustard cream sauce

PREP + COOK TIME 2 HOURS 15 MINS • SERVES 4

3-pound whole chicken

1 tablespoon olive oil

12 shallots, halved

20 baby carrots, trimmed

3 small parsnips, chopped coarsely

1 cup dry white wine

2 cups chicken stock

2 dried bay leaves

7 ounces cremini mushrooms

2 tablespoons light cream

2 tablespoons wholegrain mustard

Return chicken to the casserole dish with wine, stock and bay leaves. Bring to a boil, then cover and place in the oven for the first 30 minutes.

To serve, place chicken on a board, breast side up. Pull one leg away from the body so joint is exposed. Carve through socket with a sharp knife to separate leg and thigh from the body. Repeat for the other leg. To remove the wings, tug them from the carcass.

To carve the breast, feel for the breastbone on the top of the chicken. Carve along the breastbone on one side with your knife. Repeat on the other side of the breastbone.

Cremini mushrooms, also known as Roman or Swiss brown, are light-to-dark brown in color with a full bodied flavor. Store on a tray in a single layer, covered with damp, absorbent paper and keep where cool air can circulate around them.

1 Preheat oven to 400°F/350°F fan-forced.

2 Wash chicken under cold water; pat dry inside and out with absorbent paper.

3 Heat oil in large flameproof casserole dish; cook chicken until browned all over. Remove chicken. Cook shallots, carrots and parsnips in same dish, stirring, about 5 minutes or until vegetables are browned lightly.

4 Return chicken to pan with wine, stock and bay leaves; bring to a boil. Cook, covered, in oven 30 minutes. Uncover; cook about 30 minutes or until chicken is cooked through. Add mushrooms; cook, uncovered, about 10 minutes or until mushrooms are tender.

5 Remove chicken and vegetables from pan; cover to keep warm. Add cream and mustard to dish; bring to a boil. Boil, uncovered, about 5 minutes or until sauce thickens slightly.

6 Serve chicken, cut into pieces, with vegetables and mustard cream sauce.

nutritional count per serving 42.2g total fat (13.8g saturated fat); 684 cal; 16.9g carbohydrate; 46.7g protein; 6.6g fiber

roast turkey with forcemeat stuffing

Roasting a whole turkey with the stuffing is an annual tradition for most households. But, every year, when it comes to the table dry and stringy, we complain. For too long we've blamed the bird but the problem is in the cooking. White meat, when prepared properly, can be juicy, tender and delicious.

Food safety tips Thaw frozen turkeys in the fridge—never on the kitchen counter. A large turkey can take more than three days to thaw. Once thawed, leave it in the fridge until it is ready to cook. Stuff the turkey just before cooking.

Stuffing the turkey Stuffing a turkey helps it to cook evenly and provides the bonus of a tasty side dish. Of course, it means you need to allow more time for the turkey to cook (see Cooking guide below) but the wait is well worth it. If, however, you get to the point where the stuffing is not near done but the turkey is, scoop out the stuffing and finish in a dish in the oven.

Cooking guide A 5-pound turkey serves 4-6, takes 2-2½ days to thaw, and 1½-2 hours to cook. A 10-pound serves 8-10, takes 3 days to thaw and 3-3½ hours to cook. A 15-pound serves 10-12, takes 3-3½ days to thaw and 4½-5 hours to cook. A 20-pound serves 15-20, takes 3½ days to thaw and 6-6½ hours to cook.

Storing leftovers Remove the meat from the carcass and store in an airtight container in the refrigerator for up to one week. You can also use the carcass to make stock. To freeze leftover meat, wrap in plastic wrap and place in an airtight container. Freeze for up to a month. Thaw in the fridge overnight.

Creating oven space The sheer size of a turkey means it can take up the whole oven, leaving no room for the vegetables. Cook the vegetables first, cover with foil, and set aside while the turkey cooks. When the turkey is resting, return vegetables to the oven and reheat, uncovered.

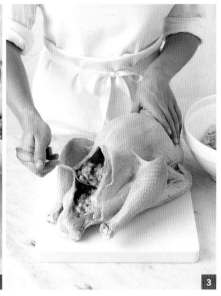

To make the forcemeat stuffing, combine the cooked and cooled onion and bacon mixture in a bowl with the bread crumbs, parsley and ground meat.

Pull open the neck cavity with your fingers and, using a large metal spoon, fill it loosely with the forcemeat stuffing.

Fill the large cavity until it is loosely stuffed. Make sure you do not over-stuff the cavity as the stuffing needs room to expand during cooking.

roast turkey with forcemeat stuffing

**PREP + COOK TIME
3 HOURS 45 MINS
(+ COOLING & STANDING)
SERVES 8**

10-pound turkey

1 cup water

6 tablespoons butter, melted

¼ cup all-purpose flour

3 cups chicken stock

½ cup dry white wine

forcemeat stuffing

3 tablespoons butter

3 medium brown onions, chopped finely

2 strips bacon, chopped coarsely

1 cup stale bread crumbs

½ cup coarsely chopped fresh flat-leaf parsley

8 ounces ground pork

8 ounces ground chicken

Pull the skin over the stuffing and secure with skewers. Tie the legs together with kitchen string.

After the turkey has been cooking for 2 hours, remove it from the oven, uncover and baste with the remaining melted butter. Return to the oven, uncovered, and cook until done.

Hold the turkey below the breast with a carving fork. Using a sharp knife, slice straight down one side of the breastbone with an even stroke. The slices will fall away as they are cut. Continue carving the breast until enough meat has been carved for first servings.

To test if the turkey is cooked, insert a skewer sideways into the thickest part of the thigh, then remove and press flesh to release the juices. If the juice runs clear, the turkey is cooked. Alternatively, insert a meat thermometer into the thickest part of the thigh, without touching the bone; the turkey is cooked when the thermometer reaches 180°F.

1 Preheat oven to 350°F/325°F fan-forced. Make forcemeat stuffing.

2 Discard neck from turkey. Rinse turkey under cold water; pat dry inside and out with absorbent paper. Fill neck cavity loosely with stuffing; secure skin over opening with small skewers. Fill large cavity loosely with stuffing; tie legs together with kitchen string.

3 Place turkey on oiled wire rack in large shallow roasting pan; pour the water into dish. Brush turkey all over with half the butter; cover turkey tightly with two layers of greased foil. Roast 2 hours. Uncover turkey; brush with remaining butter. Roast, uncovered, about 1 hour or until cooked through. Remove turkey from pan, cover loosely with foil; stand 20 minutes.

4 Pour juice from pan into large pitcher; skim 1 tablespoon of fat from juice, return fat to same pan. Skim and discard fat from remaining juice; reserve juice. Add flour to pan; cook, stirring, until mixture bubbles and is well-browned. Gradually stir in stock, wine and reserved juice; cook, stirring, until gravy boils and thickens. Strain gravy into pitcher; serve with turkey.

forcemeat stuffing Melt butter in medium frying pan; cook onion and bacon, stirring, over low heat until onion is soft. Cool. Combine onion mixture and remaining ingredients in large bowl; season to taste.

nutritional count per serving 54.7g total fat (21g saturated fat); 871 cal; 12.8g carbohydrate; 79.6g protein; 1.4g fiber

herbed rack of lamb with potato smash

A fresh herb crust for lamb takes an already-succulent meat to the next level. This coating leaves out the bread crumbs, so when you slice it, the coating won't crumble off, and you can savor every mouthful. All it needs is a simple side of smashed potatoes.

Flavoring potatoes Smashed roasted potatoes are delicious on their own, so if you want to dress them up, go easy. After smashing the potatoes, you can toss them lightly with olive oil and lemon rind, and season with sea salt and black pepper.

Serving sizes We've used a rack with three ribs for each diner. Vary the size depending on the appetite of your guests.

Leaner cuts This recipe uses a french-trimmed lamb cutlet rack. This means the meat and fat from the ends of the bones have been trimmed. The result is a leaner cut of meat and a more elegant presentation.

Salt to serve For those who like extra salt on their food, place a small serving dish of "gourmet" salt on the table. Sea salt flakes deliver the best crunch–don't use table salt for this purpose, as small, solid crystals taste sharp and acrid when sprinkled over cooked food.

Herb variations Anchovies have a very distinct briny flavor so they won't complement all herbs and spices. If you want to vary the flavors in the crust of this recipe, a good blend is fresh rosemary, marjoram, garlic and peppercorns. Process with oil to make a paste and coat lamb.

To make the herb crust, place the herbs, anchovy, garlic and oil in the bowl of a small food processor and process until a paste forms.

Using your hands, press herb mixture evenly over the flesh side of each lamb rack to cover.

Use a potato masher to lightly crush the cooked potatoes, just enough to break the skin and flatten them slightly.

herbed rack of lamb with potato smash

PREP + COOK TIME 1 HOUR • SERVES 6

½ cup firmly packed fresh flat-leaf parsley leaves

½ cup firmly packed fresh mint leaves

¼ cup loosely packed fresh oregano leaves

6 drained anchovy filets, chopped coarsely

4 cloves garlic, chopped coarsely

⅓ cup olive oil

6 x 3 french-trimmed lamb cutlet racks (1¾ pounds)

2 pounds baby new potatoes

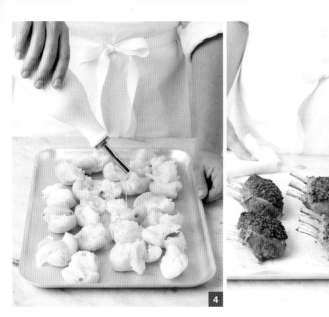

Transfer the smashed potatoes to an oiled oven tray and drizzle the remaining olive oil over the top.

To test if the lamb is done, press the flesh with clean fingers or a pair of tongs. Rare is soft; medium feels springy; and well done is very firm.

Once the lamb has been allowed to rest for about 10 minutes, loosely covered with foil, carve into single cutlets. Using a sharp knife, cut through the meat between each rib.

The herb mixture can be made up to 8 hours ahead; cover the surface with plastic wrap and refrigerate until needed. Prepare the rest of the meal on the day of serving.

1 Preheat oven to 400°F/350°F fan-forced.

2 Blend or process herbs, anchovy, garlic and half the oil until smooth. Place lamb in large, shallow baking dish; press herb mixture onto each rack.

3 Meanwhile, boil, steam or microwave potatoes until just tender; drain. Using potato masher, smash potato roughly; spread potatoes on an oiled oven tray, drizzle with remaining oil.

4 Roast lamb and potatoes, uncovered, about 20 minutes or until lamb is cooked as desired. Remove lamb from oven, cover; stand 10 minutes.

5 Increase oven to 425°F/400°F fan-forced; roast potatoes, uncovered, further 10 minutes or until browned lightly.

6 Serve lamb with potatoes.

nutritional count per serving 25.4g total fat (7.7g saturated fat); 406 cal; 22.2g carbohydrate; 20.5g protein; 4.2g fiber

roast lamb

The baked dinner is as popular today as it has been for generations, though there are a few things we do differently from our grandmothers. For starters, we cook lamb a little less, so it remains juicy and pink.

Best roasting cut Leg of lamb is the favorite when it comes to roasting. A whole leg serves large numbers, and yields plenty of lean, tender meat. It can be divided into two joints–and the filet end has the best flavor.

Buying guide Recognizing quality in lamb is as important as deciding on the right cut. Choose the leanest lamb with firm, creamy-white fat. Avoid meat with excessive fat or with fat that looks crumbly, brittle and yellowish, which indicates it is not a fresh piece of meat.

Setting the temperature Some cuts of lamb are best cooked at a high oven temperature–others are better if they are roasted at low temperatures. Leg of lamb is best roasted at low to moderate temperatures. This results in less shrinkage, better serving yields and juicier meat.

Meat thermometer Checking the degree of doneness in a leg of lamb can be trickier than other cuts. Using a thermometer is by far the safest and most accurate way to check. Avoid piercing the meat more than twice or too much juice will be lost, drying out the meat.

When to salt lamb Although lamb can be seasoned with herbs and spices up to a day before it is baked, never salt it until just before cooking. Adding salt at this stage will draw moisture out of the meat, resulting in a tough, dry roast.

Removing the fat You should avoid removing all the fat from a lamb leg as it helps to flavor and baste the meat as it cooks. If you roast it properly, most of the fat will disappear in the cooking, leaving a nice crispy outside on the roast.

Roast your vegetables Steamed greens have their place on the table but roast lamb needs roasted vegetables to support it. We used potato, pumpkin and onion for winter, but you can use just about any seasonal combination: try Jerusalem artichokes and carrots in spring, peppers and eggplant in summer, celeriac and zucchini in autumn, and so on.

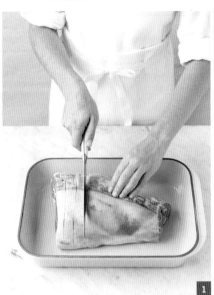

Using a sharp knife, make incisions in the surface of the meat at about ¾-inch intervals.

Liberally sprinkle the combined rosemary and ground sweet paprika all over the lamb. You can rub some of the mixture into the slits, if you like.

To check whether the lamb is done to your liking, insert a meat thermometer into the center of the thickest part of the meat, away from bone and fat.

roast lamb

PREP + COOK TIME 1 HOUR 30 MINS • SERVES 6

4-pound leg of lamb

3 sprigs fresh rosemary, chopped coarsely

½ teaspoon sweet paprika

2 pounds potatoes, chopped coarsely

1-pound piece pumpkin, chopped coarsely

3 small brown onions, halved

2 tablespoons olive oil

2 tablespoons all-purpose flour

1 cup chicken stock

¼ cup dry red wine

Pour some of the strained lamb pan juices back into the same roasting pan and, with a wooden spoon or spatula, stir in flour over heat.

Stir the juice and flour mixture for about 5 minutes or until the mixture begins to bubble and brown.

Slowly add the stock and wine, and stir over a high heat until the gravy starts to boil and becomes thick in consistency. Strain the gravy into a gravy boat.

A leg roast should be rested before serving to allow the meat to relax. The heat of the oven causes the meat fibers to tighten, so as meat rests, the fibers will relax, allowing the meat juices to redistribute themselves throughout the joint. Try to carve the leg across the grain so that each slice has short fibers that feel tender to eat.

1 Preheat oven to 400°F/350°F fan-forced.

2 Place lamb in oiled large roasting pan; using sharp knife, score skin at ¾-inch intervals, sprinkle with rosemary and paprika. Roast lamb 15 minutes.

3 Reduce oven to 350°F/325°F fan-forced; roast lamb about 45 minutes or until cooked as desired.

4 Meanwhile, place potatoes, pumpkin and onions in single layer in large shallow baking dish; drizzle with oil. Roast for last 45 minutes of lamb cooking time.

5 Remove lamb and vegetables from oven; strain pan juices from lamb into medium pitcher. Cover lamb and vegetables to keep warm. Return ¼ cup of the pan juices to roasting pan, stir in flour; stir over heat about 5 minutes or until mixture bubbles and browns. Gradually add stock and wine; stir over high heat until gravy boils and thickens. Strain gravy into a gravy boat.

6 Slice lamb; serve with roasted vegetables and gravy.

nutritional count per serving 17.9g total fat (6.6g saturated fat); 499 cal; 32.3g carbohydrate; 47.7g protein; 5g fiber

greek roast lamb
with skordalia and potatoes

There's more than one tradition when it comes to roast lamb. The Greeks cook theirs slowly until it is well done and mouth-wateringly tender. And the accompaniment? Forget subtlety, only a robust garlic spread and lemony potatoes will do.

When is lamb lamb? Every country uses a different system to classify lamb. Generally, the term indicates sheep under 12 months old. The best way to know what you're really buying is to look at the meat itself. True lamb is light pink in color with white fat and marbling. It also feels "springy" to the touch.

Mutton If the meat is a darker shade of pink going on red, it may still be good to eat, but check the price. You may well find you are buying mutton (at least 2 years old) instead of lamb, and paying a premium price for it.

Adjusting the garlic Skordalia is a matter of taste. Some prefer a mild garlic taste, while others love a little extra garlic. If the taste is too strong, adjust the quantities of potatoes or bread. If the taste is not strong enough, increase the amount of garlic.

Add some nuts In some regions of Greece, walnuts or almonds are added to the skordalia. If you like, add a cup of chopped walnuts or almonds to the food processor at the beginning, with the potatoes, and add the lemon juice to the liquids. The texture will be thick and granular.

Make ahead Skordalia can be prepared up to 1 day ahead. Store in an airtight container and refrigerate. Remove from the refrigerator 3 hours ahead. Just before serving, transfer to a serving bowl and sprinkle with extra lemon thyme, if you like.

Cube the potatoes Lamb roast done the Greek way calls for crunchy potato cubes. The key to this side dish is the lemony cooking liquid, which actually dries out during roasting. Add a little more liquid towards the end of cooking, if needed, to prevent the potatoes from sticking.

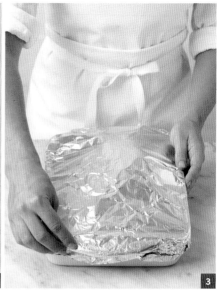

Place a leg of lamb in a large shallow dish and combine with garlic, lemon juice, olive oil, thyme and oregano. Refrigerate for 3 hours or overnight to allow the marinade to flavor the meat.

Transfer lamb to a large roasting pan and place in a preheated oven. Cook, uncovered, for 4 hours.

Remove lamb from oven, cover loosely with foil to keep warm and set aside to rest.

greek roast lamb with skordalia and potatoes

**PREP + COOK TIME
4 HOURS 50 MINS
(+ REFRIGERATION)
SERVES 4**

4-pound leg of lamb
2 cloves garlic, crushed
½ cup lemon juice
2 tablespoons olive oil
1 tablespoon fresh oregano leaves
1 teaspoon fresh lemon thyme leaves
5 large potatoes, cut into
   1-inch cubes
1 tablespoon finely grated lemon rind
2 tablespoons lemon juice, extra
2 tablespoons olive oil, extra
1 teaspoon fresh lemon thyme
   leaves, extra

skordalia

1 medium potato, quartered
3 cloves garlic, crushed
1 tablespoon lemon juice
1 tablespoon white wine vinegar
2 tablespoons water
⅓ cup olive oil

To make the skordalia, push the cooked potatoes through a food mill or fine sieve over a medium bowl. Set aside and allow potatoes to cool for 10 minutes.

Combine garlic, lemon juice, vinegar and the water in a separate bowl with a balloon whisk. Pour the lemon juice mixture into mashed potato, whisking until ingredients are incorporated.

Gradually pour the olive oil, in a slow and steady stream, into the potato mixture, continually whisking until the mixture thickens. If skordalia becomes too thick, add a tablespoon of warm water to thin it out.

Skordalia is a pungent Greek sauce or dip made with bread (or, like we have here, with potato), garlic, lemon juice and olive oil. It can be served with almost any kind of dish, from grilled meats and poultry to fish and raw vegetables.

1 Combine lamb with garlic, juice, oil, oregano and thyme in large shallow dish. Cover; refrigerate 3 hours or overnight.

2 Preheat oven to 325°F/300°F fan-forced.

3 Place lamb in large roasting pan; roast, uncovered, 4 hours.

4 Meanwhile, make skordalia.

5 Combine potatoes in large bowl with rind and extra juice, oil and thyme. Place potatoes, in single layer, on oven tray. Roast potatoes for last 30 minutes of lamb cooking time.

6 Remove lamb from oven; cover to keep warm.

7 Increase oven to 425°F/400°F fan-forced; roast potatoes a further 20 minutes or until browned lightly and cooked through. Serve potatoes and lamb with skordalia.

skordalia Boil, steam or microwave potato until tender; drain. Push potato through food mill or fine sieve into medium bowl; cool 10 minutes. Whisk combined garlic, juice, vinegar and the water into potato. Gradually whisk in oil in a thin, steady stream; continue whisking until skordalia thickens. Stir in about a tablespoon of warm water if skordalia is too thick. Serve sprinkled with extra lemon thyme leaves, if you like.

nutritional count per serving 57g total fat (14g saturated fat); 1090 cal; 51.5g carbohydrate; 91.2g protein; 6.7g fiber

roast leg of pork with apple sauce

Roast pork with crackling tastes too good to be eaten only on special occasions. With a little know-how, you can cook succulent, tender meat and crispy rind at any time of year. And forget those too-sweet store-bought apple sauces—making one yourself is too easy.

Make-ahead sauce Apple sauce can be made one day ahead. Simply store in an airtight container or glass jar and place in the refrigerator until needed. Reheat sauce before serving.

Sauce variations You can add a handful of cranberries to the apples and increase the sugar to reduce any tartness. For a brandied apple sauce, add raisins, chopped roasted hazelnuts and a little brandy.

Storing pork As soon as you get home, store pork in the coldest part of the refrigerator. If you're not cooking it within two days, you can freeze pork for up to six months. Place the pork in an airtight container or sealable plastic bag. To thaw, place the frozen pork in the fridge for 24 to 48 hours, depending on the size, or until thawed.

The right cut A pork roast with crackling requires a different cut of meat from one without crackling. Look for a pork cut with good coverage of fat and rind. This recipe uses pork leg, but other suitable cuts include rack, rolled loin and rolled shoulder.

Make it medium To enjoy roast pork at its juicy best, cook it to medium so there is still a hint of pink in the center Contrary to popular belief, pork doesn't have to be cooked all the way through. Overcooking pork makes the meat tough and dry.

Perfect crackling The three magic ingredients for crispy savory crackling are oil, salt and heat. Make sure the rind is dry and rubbed well with oil and salt. The pork must be placed in a very hot oven for the skin to start bubbling and browning up.

Tying the pork leg Roasts are tied for two reasons—to keep the roast in an attractive round shape and to hold any stuffing or seasoning inside of the roast. It's important to tie the knots properly—if they are too loose, the muscle in the meat will relax and gravity will cause the roast to form into an oval shape. If the knot is too tight, too much juice will seep out of the meat.

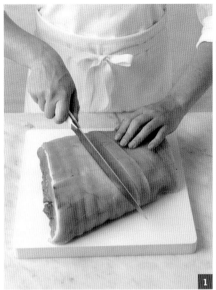

Place pork on a clean chopping board and score the rind at regular intervals, using a sharp knife. This allows moisture and fat to run out of the rind, which makes it crisp.

Tie the pork at 2-inch intervals with kitchen string to secure. Avoid slipping the string into the slits.

Place pork in a shallow roasting pan and, using your fingers, rub the oil all over the skin. Rub the salt over the skin, working it into the slits. This helps to draw any moisture out of the rind and makes it crackle.

roast leg of pork with apple sauce

**PREP + COOK TIME
2 HOURS 40 MINS
(+ STANDING)
SERVES 8**

5-pound boneless pork leg roast, rind on

2 tablespoons olive oil

1 tablespoon sea salt flakes

6 medium potatoes, quartered

2 tablespoons olive oil, extra

2 tablespoons fresh sage leaves

2 tablespoons fresh rosemary leaves

apple sauce

3 large green apples

½ cup water

1 teaspoon sugar

pinch ground cinnamon

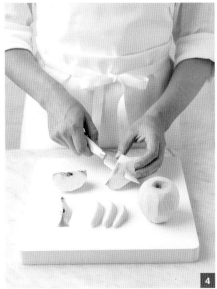

Peel and core the apples. On a clean surface, cut the apples into quarters, then into thick slices.

Place the apples in a medium saucepan on the stove top and add ½ cup of water.

Bring the water to a simmer and cook the apples, uncovered, for about 10 minutes, or until the apple is soft enough to crush with a spoon.

The ancient pairing of pork and apple dates way back to the classical cookery book *Apicius*, a surviving text of the Roman Empire, in which a recipe for diced pork with apple was offered. The combination remains a favorite today, as the sweet crisp flavor of the apple counteracts the creamy fatty texture of the pork beautifully.

1 Preheat oven to 425°F/400°F fan-forced.

2 Score pork rind with sharp knife; tie pork at 2-inch intervals with kitchen string. Place pork in large shallow roasting pan; rub with oil, then salt. Roast, uncovered, 20 minutes.

3 Reduce oven to 350°F/325°F fan-forced; roast pork, uncovered, 2 more hours.

4 Meanwhile, combine potato with extra oil and herbs in large bowl. Place in single layer on oven tray. Roast, uncovered, about 35 minutes.

5 Make apple sauce.

6 Stand pork, covered loosely with foil, 10 minutes before slicing. Serve pork and potatoes with apple sauce.

apple sauce Peel and core apples; slice thickly. Place apples and the water in medium saucepan; simmer, uncovered, about 10 minutes or until apple is soft. Remove pan from heat; stir in sugar and cinnamon.

nutritional count per serving 34g total fat (9.7g saturated fat); 712 cal; 27.4g carbohydrate; 71.9g protein; 4.1g fiber

roast loin of pork

Give the modern generation of leaner, milder-tasting pork an old-fashioned roasting to put the rich, juicy chew back into the meat. In keeping with the traditional theme, this dish begs for a sweet, tangy apple sauce you can make in no time.

Quick apple sauce You can take a shortcut using the microwave oven. Place apple, water, sugar and cinnamon in a heatproof, microwave-safe bowl. Cover with a lid and cook on HIGH/800watts/100% for 3 minutes. Remove cover and cook on HIGH/800watts/100%, stirring every 4 minutes, for 8 minutes or until apples are soft.

Vegetables on the side This pork recipe avoids overpowering flavors, so you can accompany it with just about any vegetable. Try yellow and green squash, baked alongside the pork, to offset the sweetness of the apple sauce. Baked carrots, potatoes and mushrooms work well too.

Salad to serve For a light side dish, toss together a raw vegetable salad. Try shredded spinach, red cabbage and carrot, sprinkled with sliced almonds and raisins, and dressed with apple cider vinegar and oil. Just add a sliced french baguette for a complete meal.

Herb flavorings The simple Mediterranean essence of rosemary and olive oil does extraordinary things to a juicy pork loin roast. Fresh rosemary is always better than dried, but if you're caught without it, substitute a teaspoon dried rosemary for a tablespoon fresh. Other good fresh substitutes for rosemary are sage and thyme.

Preparing the rind Make sure the pork is well chilled, as cold rind and fat is firm and easier to cut. Pork loin has just one rectangular piece of skin to score, which makes the job much easier. You need a very sharp knife to do the job with precision, cutting right through into the fat but not the meat.

Pork rolls Leftover roast pork makes a great filling for Vietnamese pork rolls. Spread combined pâté and mayonnaise inside a warm bread roll, then fill with pork slices and top with grated carrot, green onion and chili. Top with sweet chili sauce, soy sauce, and coriander.

Storing leftovers Allow any leftover pork to cool to room temperature, then store in an airtight container and place in the refrigerator. The pork should be consumed within 2 days.

Place pork loin on a cutting board and score the rind at ⅓-inch intervals, using a sharp knife.

Tie the pork at ¾-inch intervals with kitchen string to secure. Avoid slipping the string into the slits.

Slide a few sprigs of fresh rosemary under the string that holds the pork so that they are well secured.

roast loin of pork with apple sauce

PREP + COOK TIME 2 HOURS • SERVES 8

5-pound boneless loin of pork, rind on

2 sprigs rosemary

1 tablespoon olive oil

1 tablespoon coarse cooking salt

apple sauce

3 large apples

½ cup water

1 teaspoon white sugar

pinch ground cinnamon

TIP

• Ask your butcher to roll and tie the pork at ¾-inch intervals for you, and to score the rind, if it isn't already done.

Place pork in a shallow roasting pan and, using your fingers, rub the oil all over the skin. Rub the salt over the skin, working it into the slits.

When pork is cooked, remove from the oven and cover loosely with foil. Allow the pork to rest for about 15 minutes before cutting into slices.

Transfer the pork to a clean chopping board and, using a sharp knife, cut into slices to serve.

As always when buying meat, your best bet is a supplier you can trust. In general, pork should have fine-grained, pale pink flesh, white fat and thin, smooth skin. Avoid any that has waxy fat or is wet, meaning it has been badly handled and may be from an animal in poor condition.

1 Preheat oven to 500°F/450°F fan-forced.
2 Score pork rind with sharp knife. Tie pork at ¾-inch intervals with kitchen string; tuck rosemary under string. Place pork in large roasting pan; rub with oil, then salt. Roast about 40 minutes or until rind blisters. Drain excess fat from pan.
3 Reduce oven to 350°F/325°F fan-forced. Roast pork about 1 hour. Transfer pork to plate; cover loosely with foil, stand 15 minutes before carving.
4 Meanwhile, make apple sauce.
5 Serve pork with apple sauce.
apple sauce Peel and core apples; slice thickly. Place apples and the water in medium saucepan; simmer, uncovered, about 10 minutes or until apple is soft. Remove pan from heat; stir in sugar and cinnamon. Blend or process mixture until almost smooth.
nutritional count per serving 72g total fat (24.1g saturated fat); 900 cal; 7.7g carbohydrate; 56.7g protein; 1.1g fiber

STIR-FRIES

Stir-fries

The art of stir-frying is one of Asia's many gifts to the world, and the perfect answer to modern living's call for quick, healthy meals any night of the week.

Using a wok over a high heat, the technique of stir-frying evolved in China where traditionally firewood was a precious commodity–and cooking over a fire had to be quick and efficient. Stir-frying emerged, along with the wok itself, as the best way to cook over a very high heat in a very short time.

Stir-frying is fast and fun, and you can have a fragrant bowl of perfectly seared meat, crisp vegetables and noodles ready within minutes. But the key is in the preparation: make sure you have all your ingredients chopped in advance, and all the necessary spices and sauces on hand before you turn on the wok. Then you simply turn up the heat, splash your wok with oil, and begin cooking. Stir-fries make great main courses or you can toss your favorite vegetables together for a healthy side dish.

It's a dynamic way to cook: it's possible to feel the hassles of your day lift from your shoulders as you toss and stir your sizzling, aromatic ingredients into a casual masterpiece.

THE WOK

The uniquely-shaped, round-bottomed wok is the tool of trade for stir-fries. The best ones are those found in Chinese food stores (you'll find loads of these in any Chinatown district, in any major city). Designer woks are usually too heavy and often too shallow, and electric woks just don't get hot enough. Some woks have flat bottoms, which do make the wok stand straight on an electric or ceramic burner without support, but this defeats the purpose of the classic design, which is to concentrate intense heat at the center.

Stir-frying works better on gas burners than an electric stove top because the gas flames surround the wok with the intense heat needed. For cooking on gas, choose a wok made from carbon steel. For an electric stove top, use a cast-iron wok because it holds the heat better than carbon steel.

To clean a wok, wash with hot water only, removing any stuck-on food with a non-metal brush. Dry with a cloth, then place over low heat to dry thoroughly. With repeated use, the wok will acquire a dark, slightly slick surface or patina making it increasingly non-stick.

THE TECHNIQUE

The key to a successful stir-fry is in the preparation: all the needed ingredients should be chopped, diced, measured and immediately at hand. Remember to cut all the food into small, bite-sized pieces.

Heat the wok until it is very hot before adding the oil, then heat the oil until it just starts to smoke before adding any food. Before adding food, use the chan or spatula to swirl the oil around the sides of the wok as well as the base.

KEEP THE HEAT HIGH THROUGHOUT THE COOKING.

Meat should go in first, ahead of vegetables. Stir constantly, and once all pieces of the meat are seared (this should only take a minute), add the vegetables. You might add some liquid at this point, and cover the wok with a lid for the briefest moment to help steam the vegetables. Green vegetables (bok choy, snow peas, etc.) only require a brief toss in the wok at the end of cooking. Remember, you want the vegetables to come out of the wok just-cooked and still crisp and glistening.

Get physical in the kitchen. Stir-frying requires active participation and focus. Keep tossing and stirring constantly so that different pieces of the food are being seared on the bottom of the wok at any one time. Keep one hand on the wok handle while the other hand briskly moves the chan or spatula. Feel free to tilt and move the wok as you need to, to help toss the ingredients.

THE ACCESSORIES

MANY GAS STOVE TOPS THESE DAYS ARE FITTED WITH WOK BURNERS (OR EVEN TWO–SUCH IS THE IMPORTANCE OF WOK COOKING IN OUR KITCHENS TODAY) THAT ARE SPECIFICALLY DESIGNED TO HOLD A WOK AND EMIT AN ESPECIALLY ROBUST FLAME. BUT IF YOU DON'T HAVE A SPECIALIZED BURNER, YOU'LL NEED A WOK STAND TO STOP THE WOK FROM TIPPING OVER.

FOR ELECTRIC OR CERAMIC STOVE TOPS, GET A STAND THAT IS A SOLID METAL RING PUNCHED WITH ABOUT SIX VENTILATION HOLES. FOR A GAS STOVE TOP, GET ONE THAT IS A CIRCULAR WIRE FRAME, AS THE GAS FLAME MIGHT NOT GET ENOUGH AIR TO FUNCTION INSIDE THE MORE SOLID STAND.

FROM THE MOMENT YOUR INGREDIENTS ENTER THE WOK, YOU'LL NEED TO KEEP TOSSING THEM. THE AUTHENTIC TOOL FOR DOING THIS IS CALLED A "CHAN", AVAILABLE FROM ASIAN FOOD STORES. YOU CAN USE A WOODEN SPATULA OR LARGE SPOON, BUT A CHAN IS INEXPENSIVE AND WORKS BETTER BECAUSE ITS BLADE IS THE RIGHT SIZE AND ITS CURVE IS DESIGNED TO FIT THE CURVE OF THE WOK.

singapore chili crab

Notoriously difficult to eat, but irresistibly delicious. Have finger bowls filled with warm water and lemon slices–and plenty of large napkins–with this dish. And don't wear a white shirt or eat this on a first date.

4 x 12-ounce uncooked blue swimmer crabs
2 tablespoons peanut oil
3 cloves garlic, chopped finely
1½-inch piece fresh ginger, peeled, grated
1 fresh small red Thai chili, sliced thinly
⅓ cup bottled tomato pasta sauce

2 tablespoons chili sauce
2 tablespoons japanese soy sauce
⅓ cup water
2 teaspoons white sugar
½ cup firmly packed fresh coriander leaves

1 Lift flap under body of each crab; turn crab over, hold body with one hand while pulling off top part of shell with the other. Discard shell and gills on either side of body. Rinse crab under cold water; chop body into quarters.

2 Heat oil in wok; stir-fry garlic, ginger and chili; stir-fry until fragrant. Add sauces, the water and sugar; stir-fry 2 minutes.

3 Add crab; cook, covered, over medium heat, about 10 minutes or until crab has changed color. Serve sprinkled with coriander.

nutritional count per serving 10.1g total fat (1.8g saturated fat); 173 cal; 8.2g carbohydrate; 11.6g protein; 1.6g fiber

Lift the tail flap then, with a peeling motion, pull off the top shell.

Remove and discard the whitish gills (these are known as dead men's fingers), plus the liver and brain matter.

Rinse the crab well then chop into quarters.

crispy shredded beef

Corned bottom round is beef that is first pickled in brine then cooked submerged in water with spices, herbs, etc. Here we poach the meat in milk to draw out as much salt as possible.

1½-pound piece corned bottom round

1 quart milk, approximately

1 fresh long red chili, chopped coarsely

2 kaffir lime leaves, torn

1-inch piece fresh ginger, chopped coarsely

2 cloves garlic, quartered

15 ounces wide fresh rice noodles

¼ cup peanut oil

1 fresh small red Thai chili, sliced thinly

3 cloves garlic, crushed

1-inch piece fresh ginger, peeled, grated

1 medium red pepper, sliced thinly

5 ounces sugar snap peas, trimmed

1 tablespoon fish sauce

2 tablespoons kecap manis

½ cup loosely packed fresh coriander leaves

1 Place beef with as much milk as needed to cover in large saucepan; bring to a boil. Reduce heat; simmer, uncovered, 10 minutes. Drain beef; discard milk.

2 Place beef, chopped chili, lime leaves, chopped ginger and quartered garlic in same cleaned pan. Cover with cold water; simmer, covered, 1½ hours. Remove beef from pan; discard pan ingredients. Drain beef on wire rack over tray 15 minutes.

3 Meanwhile, place noodles in large heatproof bowl, cover with boiling water; separate with fork, drain.

4 Trim excess fat from beef. Using two forks, shred beef finely. Heat oil in wok; stir-fry beef, in batches, until browned and crisp. Drain.

5 Stir-fry sliced chili, crushed garlic, grated ginger, peppers and peas in wok until vegetables soften. Add sauces; stir-fry 1 minute.

6 Return beef to wok with noodles; stir-fry until hot. Remove from heat; sprinkle with coriander.

nutritional count per serving 29.4g total fat (11.2g saturated fat); 615 cal; 41g carbohydrate; 45.8g protein; 2.8g fiber

Place the beef in a pan with chili, lime, ginger and garlic, cover with water and simmer until tender.

Drain the beef on a wire rack for about 15 minutes to allow it to dry completely.

Slice the beef and using two forks, shred it finely.

Stir-fry beef in batches in hot oil until it is brown and crisp.

char siu lamb and noodle stir-fry

Char siu sauce, salty and flavored with chinese five-spice, has a dominant anise flavor. It turns the surface of meat red.

2 cloves garlic, crushed
¾-inch piece fresh ginger, peeled, grated
1 tablespoon finely grated orange rind
1 teaspoon sesame oil
1½ pounds lamb strips
15 ounces hokkien noodles

2 tablespoons peanut oil
7 ounces sugar snap peas
4 ounces baby corn, halved lengthwise
2 fresh long red chilies, sliced thinly
⅓ cup char siu sauce
2 tablespoons water
1 tablespoon rice wine vinegar

1 Combine garlic, ginger, rind, sesame oil and lamb in medium bowl.
2 Place noodles in large heatproof bowl, cover with boiling water; separate with fork, drain.
3 Heat half the peanut oil in wok; stir-fry peas and corn until just tender. Remove from wok.
4 Heat remaining peanut oil in wok; stir-fry lamb, in batches, until browned all over and cooked as desired. Remove from wok. Return peas, corn and lamb to wok with noodles, chili and combined sauce, water and vinegar; stir-fry until heated through.
nutritional count per serving 29.2g total fat (9.6g saturated fat); 652 cal; 46.6g carbohydrate; 47.1g protein; 8g fiber

beef in satay sauce

1 tablespoon peanut oil
1½ pounds beef strips
1 fresh long red chili, sliced thinly
1 medium brown onion, sliced thinly
1 medium red pepper, sliced thinly
½ cup peanut butter
½ cup coconut cream
¼ cup sweet chili sauce
1 tablespoon japanese soy sauce

1 Heat half the oil in wok; stir-fry beef, in batches, until cooked. Remove beef from wok.
2 Heat remaining oil in wok; stir-fry chili, onion and pepper until soft; remove from wok.
3 Combine peanut butter, coconut cream and sauces in wok; bring to a boil. Return beef and onion mixture to wok; stir-fry until hot.
nutritional count per serving 42.2g total fat (15g saturated fat); 629 cal; 10.6g carbohydrate; 49.8g protein; 6.1g fiber

[1] char siu lamb and noodle stir-fry
[2] beef in satay sauce
[3] chiang mai pork and eggplant [page 344]
[4] cantonese lamb [page 344]

chiang mai pork and eggplant

You can also use a mortar and pestle to make the garlic paste. The theory when using a mortar and pestle is that, by adding and processing the ingredients one at a time, each builds on the next to form a well-integrated mixture. The grinding motion releases the essential oils and flavor of each of the ingredients.

3 fresh small red Thai chilies, halved
6 cloves garlic, quartered
1 medium brown onion, chopped coarsely
1 pound baby eggplants
¼ cup peanut oil
1½ pounds pork leg steaks, sliced thinly
1 tablespoon fish sauce
1 tablespoon dark soy sauce
1 tablespoon grated palm sugar
4 purple Thai regular shallots, sliced thinly
5 ounces snake beans, cut into 2-inch lengths
1 cup loosely packed Thai basil leaves

1 Blend or process chili, garlic and onion until mixture forms a paste.
2 Quarter eggplants lengthwise; slice each piece into 2-inch lengths. Cook eggplant in large saucepan of boiling water until just tender; drain, pat dry.
3 Heat half the oil in wok; stir-fry eggplant, in batches, until browned lightly. Drain.
4 Heat remaining oil in wok; stir-fry pork, in batches, until cooked. Remove from wok.
5 Stir-fry garlic paste in wok about 3 minutes or until fragrant and browned lightly. Add sauces and sugar; stir-fry until sugar dissolves.
6 Add shallot and beans; stir-fry until beans are tender. Return eggplant and pork to wok; stir-fry until hot. Remove from heat; sprinkle with basil.
nutritional count per serving 19.3g total fat (4.1g saturated fat); 400 cal; 10.1g carbohydrate; 43.6g protein; 5.8g fiber

cantonese lamb

Char siu sauce can also be labeled Chinese barbecue sauce. You can use lamb loin for this recipe, if you prefer, slicing it thinly before use.

1 tablespoon peanut oil
1½ pounds lamb strips
1 medium brown onion, sliced thinly
1 clove garlic, crushed
5 ounces snow peas, trimmed
5 ounces sugar snap peas, trimmed
⅔ cup frozen peas
4 ounces baby corn, halved lengthways
1 tablespoon dark soy sauce
1 tablespoon char siu sauce
¼ cup chicken stock
1 tablespoon corn starch
2 tablespoons lime juice

1 Heat half the oil in wok; stir-fry lamb, in batches, until browned.
2 Heat remaining oil in wok; stir-fry onion and garlic until onion softens. Add peas and corn; stir-fry until corn is almost tender.
3 Return lamb to wok with sauces and stock; stir-fry 2 minutes or until lamb is cooked. Stir in blended corn starch and juice; stir-fry until sauce boils and thickens.
nutritional count per serving 23.2g total fat (8.9g saturated fat); 473 cal 16g carbohydrate; 47.6g protein; 5.4g fiber

teriyaki beef

Mirin is a Japanese sweet rice wine used only for cooking. Sake is also a rice wine but is made for drinking, used as an ingredient only in certain dishes. If mirin is unavailable, dry sherry, vermouth or brandy can be used as a substitute.

⅓ cup teriyaki sauce
½ cup hoisin sauce
2 tablespoons mirin
1 tablespoon peanut oil
1½ pounds beef strips
8 ounces broccoli, cut into florets
8 ounces sugar snap peas, trimmed
4 ounces fresh baby corn, halved lengthways
1½-inch piece fresh ginger, peeled, grated
1½ cups bean sprouts

1 Combine sauces and mirin in small bowl.
2 Heat half the oil in wok; stir-fry beef, in batches, until browned.
3 Heat remaining oil in wok; stir-fry broccoli until almost tender.
4 Return beef to wok with sauce mixture, peas, corn and ginger. Stir-fry until vegetables and beef are cooked. Remove from heat; sprinkle with sprouts.

nutritional count per serving 20.7g total fat (7.2g saturated fat); 496 cal; 23.2g carbohydrate; 48g protein; 10.5g fiber

sang choy bow

Sang choy bow is eaten with your fingers–the lettuce wrapped around the savory meat filling. You can use ground chicken or a pork and veal mix instead; you can also serve the pork mixture in small endive or betel leaves as cocktail food.

2 teaspoons sesame oil
1 small brown onion, chopped finely
2 cloves garlic, crushed
¾-inch piece fresh ginger, peeled, grated
1 pound lean ground pork
3 ounces shiitake mushrooms, chopped finely

2 tablespoons water
2 tablespoons light soy sauce
2 tablespoons oyster sauce
1 tablespoon lime juice
2 cups bean sprouts
4 green onions, sliced thinly
¼ cup coarsely chopped fresh coriander
12 large butter lettuce leaves

1 Heat oil in wok; stir-fry brown onion, garlic and ginger until onion softens. Add pork; stir-fry until changed in color.
2 Add the mushrooms, water, sauces and juice; stir-fry until mushrooms are tender. Remove from heat. Add sprouts, green onion and coriander; toss to combine.
3 Spoon sang choy bow into lettuce leaves to serve.

nutritional count per serving 11.5g total fat (3.6g saturated fat); 266 cal; 8.9g carbohydrate; 29.3g protein; 4.1g fiber

beef sukiyaki

In Japan, sukiyaki is traditionally shared at the table from the pan in which it was cooked, making it a great dish for a fun dinner party. Diners use their chopsticks to dip the piping hot ingredients into their individual bowls of egg.

14 ounces fresh udon noodles
10 ounces fresh firm silken tofu
4 eggs
¼ cup vegetable oil
1¼ pounds beef rump steak, trimmed, sliced thinly
8 oyster mushrooms
4 green onions, sliced thinly
10 ounces spinach, trimmed, chopped coarsely
2 cups bean sprouts

broth
1 cup Japanese soy sauce
½ cup sake
½ cup mirin
½ cup water
½ cup white sugar
2 cloves garlic, crushed

1 Combine ingredients for broth in medium saucepan; cook over medium heat, stirring, until sugar dissolves. Remove from heat; cover to keep warm.
2 Place noodles in heatproof bowl, cover with boiling water; separate with fork, drain. Cut into random lengths.
3 Cut tofu into ¾-inch cubes; spread, in single layer, on absorbent-paper-lined-tray. Cover tofu with more absorbent paper, stand 10 minutes.
4 Break eggs into individual serving bowls; beat lightly.
5 Heat half the oil in wok; stir-fry beef, in batches, until browned.
6 Heat half the remaining oil in wok; stir-fry tofu, in batches, until browned.
7 Add remaining oil to wok; stir-fry mushrooms, onion, spinach and sprouts until vegetables are just tender.
8 Return beef and tofu to wok with noodles and broth; stir-fry until hot.
Serve sukiyaki from wok, with each diner using chopsticks to pick up sukiyaki ingredients and dip in their individual bowl of egg and eat.
nutritional count per serving 52g total fat (17.2g saturated fat); 1151 cal; 87.4g carbohydrate; 65.7g protein; 13.6g fiber

Q&A

Do I have to dip the sukiyaki in raw egg? I worry about the health risks of eating raw egg.

It's true that there are some people in the community who should avoid eating raw eggs: pregnant women, the elderly and those with immune deficiencies. However, if you don't like the idea of eating raw egg, then simply eat the sukiyaki just as it is.

Asian vegetables

Asian greens, herbs, mushrooms and other vegetables are becoming more and more common in our supermarkets and greengrocers. And it's a good thing, because nothing can satisfactorily replace them in Asian recipes.

TAT SOI
A mild-flavored cabbage also known as rosette, flat or spoon cabbage because of its spoon-shaped leaves and the way it grows. Eaten raw in salads.

BOK CHOY
Usually sold in bundles of three or four plants, bok choy has crisp white stems and tender, mildly cabbage-flavored leaves with an acid tang. Often used in stir-fries or cooked alone and dressed with Chinese sauces.

CHOY SUM
Also called flowering bok choy or bok choy sum, this has small yellow flowers, which are eaten with the leaves and stems. It has a mild mustard sort of flavor; can be steamed or stir-fried.

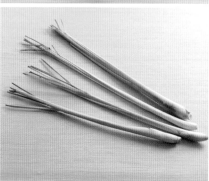

LEMON GRASS
A very fibrous plant so only the inner stem is used. Cut the stalks short and peel away the tough outer layers until you come to the more tender white part at the base.

OYSTER MUSHROOMS
These mushrooms are delicate in flavor and texture so they should not be used with strong-flavored ingredients likely to overwhelm them. Use them raw or cook briefly–they become unpleasantly slippery if cooked for too long.

GREEN PAPAYA
This is simply underripe papaya. It varies in length and shape, and is mostly used, raw or cooked, in Thai recipes. Grated green papaya features in many Thai salads.

Q&A

Is there a general rule for cooking Asian greens? I'd really like to cook them the way they do in my local Asian restaurants.

The trick is brief cooking–whether steaming or stir-frying. Gai Lan is the vegetable you most often find at dim sum shops–it's steamed just until wilted, the stalks remain crisp and then it's drizzled with oyster sauce.

NAPA CABBAGE
This crunchy cabbage, also called wombok, is delicious raw, stir-fried, steamed or braised for Asian dishes. It can be used in place of white cabbage in hearty stews, casseroles, or stuffed with meat filling.

KAFFIR LIME LEAVES
Quite different in scent and flavor from ordinary lime leaves, these give a heady citrus freshness to soups, curries, fish and poultry dishes. They are somewhat tough, so shred finely or, if used whole, remove them before serving.

SHIITAKE MUSHROOMS
The earthy fragrance and flavor of shiitake are very different from those of any other mushroom. Available fresh or dried; soak dried caps in warm water and discard the tough stems.

GAI LAN
Also known as Chinese broccoli, this vegetable is prized for its crunchy texture and flavor, resembling that of European broccoli. The white flowers, stems and leaves are eaten. Often cooked with oyster sauce; it can be steamed, boiled or stir-fried.

KANG KONG
Also known as water spinach, this delicate green vegetable has long, hollow stems and thin leaves. Use the leaves and top half of the stems, cut into 2-inch lengths. Stir-fry, dip in batter and deep-fry, or serve steamed with kecap manis or a savory sauce.

BETEL LEAVES
Sold in bunches, often under their Vietnamese name, lá lốp; these leaves are used as a wrapping for rice, ground meats, etc. The betel used for chewing is related but a different plant.

thai basil chicken and snake bean stir-fry

PREP + COOK TIME 40 MINS
(+ REFRIGERATION)
SERVES 4

1¾ pounds chicken thigh filets,
   sliced thinly
¼ cup fish sauce
1 tablespoon grated palm sugar
¼ teaspoon ground white pepper
1 tablespoon peanut oil
3 cloves garlic, sliced thinly
¾-inch piece fresh ginger, peeled,
   sliced thinly
½ teaspoon dried chili flakes

8 ounces snake beans, cut into
   2-inch lengths
2 medium yellow peppers,
   sliced thinly
⅓ cup Chinese cooking wine
⅓ cup lemon juice
1 tablespoon dark soy sauce
½ cup loosely packed Thai
   basil leaves

There are more than two dozen varieties of basil, and the one used here is Thai basil, also known as horapa. It has very small leaves and purplish stems, with a slight licorice or aniseed taste. It's one of the basic flavors of Thai cuisine.

1 Combine chicken, fish sauce, sugar and pepper in large bowl. Cover; refrigerate 1 hour.
2 Heat oil in wok; stir-fry chicken mixture 10 minutes or until almost cooked. Add garlic, ginger, chili, beans and peppers; stir-fry until beans are tender.
3 Add wine, juice and soy sauce; bring to a boil. Reduce heat; simmer, uncovered, 2 minutes. Remove from heat; stir in basil.
nutritional count per serving 19.4g total fat (5.2g saturated fat); 388 cal; 8.6g carbohydrate; 42.4g protein; 3.3g fiber

Use a clean board and a sharp knife to thinly slice the chicken thigh filets.

Use a fine grater to grate the palm sugar (you can use brown sugar if you can't find palm sugar, but palm sugar gives the authentic Thai taste).

Peel the ginger and slice it thinly using a small, very sharp knife.

Pour in the Chinese cooking wine, lemon juice and soy sauce and bring to a boil.

peking duck

This famous Chinese dish is prized for the crunchy duck skin. Chinese restaurants serve two dishes using Peking duck: pancakes, which are served with skin and little meat, while the remaining duck meat is often served in a noodle or stir-fry dish.

You can buy pancakes in several sizes at Asian grocery stores. The small pancakes make great canapé bases.

2-pound Chinese barbecued duck
24 Peking duck pancakes
4 green onions, cut into thin strips
⅔ cup hoisin sauce
2 cups bean sprouts
2 Lebanese cucumbers, halved lengthways,
    seeded, cut into thin strips

1 Remove meat and skin from duck; discard bones. Chop meat and skin coarsely.
2 Heat pancakes by folding each into quarters, place in steamer set over large pan of simmering water; steam until warm and pliable.
3 Heat wok; stir-fry duck and onion until onion just softens. Add half the sauce; stir-fry until hot. Remove from heat; stir in sprouts.
4 Serve duck mixture with pancakes, cucumber and remaining sauce.
nutritional count per serving 40.6g total fat (11.6g saturated fat); 649 cal; 35.1g carbohydrate; 33.5g protein; 7.3g fiber

mongolian garlic lamb

This popular Chinese restaurant dish has its origins in the campfire-braised meats, packed with masses of garlic, eaten by Mongol herders in the vast expanses of the Euro-Asian plains.

3 cloves garlic, crushed
1 tablespoon corn starch
¼ cup dark soy sauce
⅓ cup sweet sherry
1½ pounds lamb loin, sliced thinly
2 tablespoons peanut oil
1 tablespoon brown sugar
1 teaspoon sesame oil
8 green onions, sliced thinly

1 Combine garlic, corn starch, half the sauce and half the sherry in large bowl; add lamb, mix well.
2 Heat peanut oil in wok; stir-fry lamb mixture, in batches, until browned.
3 Return lamb to wok with sugar, sesame oil and remaining sauce and sherry; stir-fry until sauce thickens slightly. Remove from heat; serve stir-fry sprinkled with onion.
nutritional count per serving 28g total fat (9.8g saturated fat); 492 cal; 12.4g carbohydrate; 43.1g protein; 0.8g fiber

sweet chili plum chicken with noodles

PREP + COOK TIME 25 MINS
(+ REFRIGERATION)
SERVES 4

Water chestnuts are the corms (solid bulbs) of an aquatic plant native to Southeast Asia. They are about the size of a walnut and have been eaten in China for centuries, especially in the south where they are sometimes grown in paddies between rice plants. Peel off the dark outer skin to reveal crunchy white flesh. Sometimes available fresh, they are more commonly sold canned.

¼ cup sweet chili sauce
2 tablespoons plum sauce
1½ pounds chicken thigh filets, sliced thinly
15 ounces hokkien noodles
8-ounce can water chestnuts, rinsed, halved

8 green onions, sliced thickly
1 fresh long red chili, sliced thinly
2 cloves garlic, crushed
10 ounces bok choy, trimmed, chopped coarsely

1 Combine sauces with chicken in large bowl. Cover; refrigerate 1 hour.
2 Heat oiled wok; stir-fry chicken mixture, in batches, until browned. Remove from wok.
3 Meanwhile, place noodles in medium heatproof bowl; cover with boiling water, separate with fork, drain.
4 Stir-fry chestnuts, onion, chili and garlic in wok 2 minutes. Return chicken to wok with bok choy; stir-fry until chicken is cooked. Serve with noodles.

nutritional count per serving 14.9g total fat (4.2g saturated fat); 481 cal; 43.1g carbohydrate; 41g protein; 5.4g fiber

---

pork larb with broccolini

PREP + COOK TIME 25 MINS • SERVES 4

Larb is the national dish of Laos and is also a staple of Thai cuisine.

Palm sugar is an unrefined sugar used in Asian and Indian cooking. If you can't find it, you can use brown sugar instead.

1 tablespoon peanut oil
2 cloves garlic, crushed
1¼ pounds ground pork
⅓ cup grated palm sugar
2 tablespoons fish sauce
4 kaffir lime leaves, sliced finely
½ cup fried shallots
⅓ cup roasted unsalted peanuts

12 ounces broccolini, trimmed, halved lengthways
1 tablespoon lime juice
1 cup loosely packed fresh coriander leaves
1 fresh long red chili, sliced thinly
2 tablespoons coarsely chopped roasted unsalted peanuts

1 Heat oil in wok; stir-fry garlic and pork until pork is browned through. Remove from wok with slotted spoon.
2 Add sugar, sauce, lime leaves, shallots and nuts to wok; bring to a boil. Reduce heat; simmer, uncovered, 1 minute. Return pork to wok; cook, uncovered, about 2 minutes or until larb mixture is slightly dry and sticky.
3 Meanwhile, boil, steam or microwave broccolini; drain.
4 Stir juice and three-quarters of the coriander into larb off the heat; serve tossed with broccolini and sprinkled with remaining coriander, chili and coarsely chopped nuts.

nutritional count per serving 23.9g total fat (6g saturated fat); 480 cal; 25g carbohydrate; 39.5g protein; 5.5g fiber

salt and pepper tofu

It is important that the tofu is as well drained as possible before it is deep-fried. If you have the time, a few hours before you want to make the dish, pat the whole piece of tofu with absorbent paper, then place it in a strainer or colander lined with absorbent paper set over a large bowl. Weight the tofu piece with a saucer topped with a heavy can; allow to drain for up to 3 hours. Chop the tofu just before deep-frying.

2 x 10-ounce packets fresh firm tofu
1 small red pepper, sliced thinly
1 small yellow pepper, sliced thinly
3 ounces snow peas, sliced thinly
1 small carrot, sliced thinly
1 cup bean sprouts
½ cup loosely packed fresh
    coriander leaves
1 teaspoon coarsely ground
    black pepper
1 tablespoon sea salt
¼ teaspoon five-spice powder
⅓ cup all-purpose flour
peanut oil, for deep-frying

chili lime dressing
2 tablespoons peanut oil
¼ cup lime juice
2 tablespoons sweet chili sauce

1 Dry tofu with absorbent paper. Cut each piece in half horizontally; cut each half into quarters (you will have 16 pieces). Place tofu pieces, in single layer, on absorbent paper. Cover with more absorbent paper; stand 15 minutes.

2 Meanwhile, combine peppers, snow peas, carrot, sprouts and coriander in large bowl.

3 Make chili lime dressing by whisking ingredients together in small bowl.

4 Combine pepper, salt, five-spice and flour in medium bowl; coat tofu in mixture, shake away excess. Heat oil in wok; deep-fry tofu, in batches, until browned lightly. Drain on absorbent paper.

5 Serve salad topped with tofu; drizzle with dressing.

nutritional count per serving 28.2g total fat (4.7g saturated fat); 424 cal; 17.8g carbohydrate; 22g protein; 6.1g fiber

Q&A

Can you tell me the difference between various tofus? I know there's silken tofu and firm tofu, but I don't know when to use each type.

This recipe for salt and pepper tofu uses firm tofu because it's dry and, when floured, it will fry to a crispy finish. Silken tofu on the other hand, is soft and moist and is usually used instead of cream or soft cheese by people who want to avoid dairy products.

sweet and sour pork

Sweet and sour sauce is often described as the "yin yang" of Chinese cooking. The Chinese consider the two flavors essential to a well-balanced meal.

1½ pounds pork filet, sliced thinly
1 tablespoon sweet sherry
½ cup light soy sauce
¾ cup all-purpose flour
vegetable oil, for deep-frying
1 tablespoon vegetable oil, extra
1 medium red onion,
    chopped coarsely
2 cloves garlic, crushed
1 medium red pepper,
    chopped coarsely
1 medium green pepper,
    chopped coarsely

1 medium carrot,
    sliced thinly
1 pound fresh pineapple,
    chopped coarsely
5 ounces sugar snap peas,
    trimmed
⅓ cup chicken stock
¼ cup tomato sauce
¼ cup white vinegar
¼ cup sugar
½ cup loosely packed fresh
    coriander leaves

1 Combine pork with sherry and 2 tablespoons of the soy sauce in medium bowl; coat pork in flour, shake off excess.

2 Heat oil in wok; deep-fry pork, in batches, until browned and crisp. Drain on absorbent paper. (Strain oil, save for another use.)

3 Heat extra oil in wok; stir-fry onion and garlic until onion softens. Add peppers and carrot; stir-fry until vegetables are tender. Return pork to wok with pineapple, peas, remaining soy sauce, stock, tomato sauce, vinegar and sugar; stir-fry until hot. Remove from heat; stir in coriander.

nutritional count per serving 20.2g total fat (3.6g saturated fat); 650 cal; 57.7g carbohydrate; 53.7g protein; 7.5g fiber

Q&A

What's the difference between dark soy sauce, light soy sauce and tamari? And when should you use each of them?

Dark soy sauce is used as a table condiment in Asia in much the same way as we use salt, and also in dipping sauces. Light soy sauce has a lighter color and flavor but is saltier–it's good in stir-fries. Tamari is a thick japanese soy sauce used as a dipping sauce and for basting.

burmese clam and mussel stir-fry

PREP + COOK TIME 35 MINS (+ STANDING) • SERVES 4

It is important to check that fresh mussels are alive when you buy them; it is equally important to be sure that they were still alive when cooked, this time by discarding any that have not opened, as live ones open when heated.

1 pound large black mussels
1 pound clams
2 teaspoons shrimp paste
1 small red onion, quartered
2 x 4-inch sticks fresh lemon grass, chopped finely
4 fresh kaffir lime leaves
¾-inch piece fresh galangal, peeled, sliced thinly

2 tablespoons sambal oelek
1 tablespoon grated palm sugar
2 tablespoons peanut oil
¼ cup lime juice
1 tablespoon corn starch
¼ cup water
2 green onions, sliced thickly
1 fresh long red chili, sliced thinly

1 Scrub mussels; remove beards.

2 Rinse clams under cold water; place in large bowl, sprinkle with salt, cover with water. Soak 1½ hours; rinse, drain.

3 Meanwhile, wrap shrimp paste securely in small piece of foil. Heat wok; stir-fry shrimp paste packet until fragrant. Discard foil; blend or process shrimp paste with red onion, lemon grass, lime leaves, galangal, sambal and sugar until mixture forms a smooth paste.

4 Heat oil in wok; stir-fry paste 5 minutes. Add mussels, clams and juice; stir-fry 2 minutes. Cover wok; cook about 5 minutes or until mussels and clams open (discard any that do not).

5 Uncover wok, stir in blended corn starch and the water; stir-fry until sauce boils and thickens. Sprinkle with green onion and chili.

nutritional count per serving 10.5g total fat (1.8g saturated); 173 cal; 12.2g carbohydrate; 6.9g protein; 0.9g fiber

garlic and chili seafood stir-fry

PREP + COOK TIME 45 MINS • SERVES 4

1½ pounds uncooked medium king prawns
2 cleaned squid tubes (10 ounces)
20-ounce baby octopus, quartered
¼ cup peanut oil
6 cloves garlic, sliced thinly
¾-inch piece fresh ginger, peeled sliced thinly
2 fresh long red chilies, sliced thinly
2 tablespoons chinese cooking wine
1 teaspoon superfine sugar

4 green onions, cut in 1½-inch pieces
chili fried shallots
1 tablespoon fried shallots
1 teaspoon sea salt flakes
½ teaspoon dried chili flakes

1 Shell and devein prawns, leaving tails intact. Cut squid down center to open out; score inside in diagonal pattern then cut into thick strips. Quarter octopus lengthwise.

2 Combine ingredients for chili fried shallots in small bowl.

3 Heat 1 tablespoon of the oil in wok; stir-fry prawns until they change color, remove from wok. Heat another tablespoon of the oil in wok; stir-fry squid until cooked through, remove from wok. Heat remaining oil in wok; stir-fry octopus until tender.

4 Stir-fry garlic, ginger and chili in wok until fragrant. Return seafood to wok with remaining ingredients; stir-fry until hot.

5 Serve stir-fry sprinkled with chili shallots.

nutritional count per serving 4.7g total fat (0.8g saturated fat); 110 cal; 0.8g carbohydrate; 15.5g protein; 0.3g fiber

thai vegetable stir-fry

PREP + COOK TIME 30 MINS (+ STANDING) • SERVES 4

Pour juice and sauce down the side of the wok rather than directly into the center of the food, so that it is already sizzling by the time it touches the food and therefore won't lower the temperature.

1 large eggplant
10 ounces fresh firm silken tofu
1 medium brown onion
2 tablespoons peanut oil
1 clove garlic, crushed
2 fresh small red Thai chilies, sliced thinly
1 tablespoon grated palm sugar
1½ pounds gai lan, chopped coarsely
2 tablespoons lime juice
⅓ cup soy sauce
⅓ cup coarsely chopped fresh Thai basil

1 Cut unpeeled eggplant in half lengthways; cut each half into thin slices. Place eggplant in colander, sprinkle with salt; stand 30 minutes.

2 Meanwhile, pat tofu all over with absorbent paper; cut into ¾-inch squares. Spread tofu, in single layer, on absorbent-paper-lined tray; cover tofu with more absorbent paper, stand at least 10 minutes.

3 Cut onion in half, then cut each half into thin even-sized wedges. Rinse eggplant under cold water; pat dry with absorbent paper.

4 Heat oil in wok; stir-fry onion, garlic and chili until onion softens. Add sugar; stir-fry until dissolved. Add eggplant; stir-fry, 1 minute. Add gai lan; stir-fry until just wilted. Add tofu, juice and sauce; stir-fry, tossing gently until combined. Remove from heat; toss basil through stir-fry.

nutritional count per serving 14.8g total fat (2.4g saturated fat); 275 cal; 13g carbohydrate; 17g protein; 12.3g fiber

Braises & stews

Some of the best things in life take time. Casseroles and other slow-cooked foods are among them, providing us with replenishing, heavenly meals infused with flavor and melt-in-your-mouth tenderness. Many of the world's best-loved dishes are slow-cooked meals: the classic French offerings of beef bourguignon and coq au vin, Hungarian goulash, Irish stew, chili con carne, and even humble curried sausages, which taste extraordinary when cooked with extra time.

WHETHER IT'S A CASSEROLE, BRAISE, POT ROAST OR STEW, SLOW-COOKED FOODS ARE LUXURIOUS, FLAVORFUL AND HEART-WARMING–AND RELISHED EQUALLY AT DINNER PARTIES OR AS FAMILY FAVORITES. CASSEROLES ALSO FREEZE BEAUTIFULLY, GIVING YOU A WONDERFUL COMFORTING MEAL AT YOUR CONVENIENCE WHEN YOU CRAVE IT.

SLOW-COOKED STYLES

The guiding principle of slow cooking is that the ingredients are cooked slowly with liquid so they become tender and their flavors blend. We tend to call all these dishes casseroles but there are, in fact, a few subtle variations on the theme, with slight differences in technique and liquid/meat ratios:

CASSEROLE "Casserole" is the generic term for all food cooked slowly with liquid in a covered vessel in the oven.

BRAISE A type of casserole, this particular method begins with browning the meat on the stove top first before adding the liquid and then transferring it to the oven. The liquid usually consists of water, stock or wine (or a combination of these), and it is added until the food is half-submerged (a braise uses a small amount of liquid in relation to the quantity of meat). As the dish begins to cook, steam releases from the liquid and works to flavor and tenderize the food. Additional liquid is sometimes added during cooking to ensure adequate moisture. Braises generally use smaller pieces of meat or small cuts with bone-in such as lamb shanks.

POT-ROASTING This is another kind of braise, which uses the same technique described above, the difference is that the meat is in one large piece, such as a whole chicken or a joint of beef, lamb or pork. Braising can be carried out entirely on the stove top, but most cooks find they get better results by transferring the ingredients to the oven once liquid is added.

STEW Generally, a stew uses more liquid and takes less time to cook as the meat is completely submerged. The key difference is that it is cooked on the stove top and served directly in its cooking liquid.

CHOOSING A CASSEROLE DISH

When you're choosing a casserole dish, you should consider getting a flameproof one: this means a dish that is not only ovenproof but has the versatility of going directly onto the stove top in the same way as a saucepan or frying pan. Many casserole dishes call for browning recipes on the stove top first before adding the liquid and cooking in the oven (braising). A flameproof casserole dish allows you to do all this in one vessel. But it needs to have a thick, cast base, like a good frying pan, so that it will distribute the heat and brown the meat evenly.

If you buy an ovenproof, but not a flameproof, casserole dish, you will need to do the browning in a frying pan and then transfer the food to the dish before continuing with the recipe.

Buy a casserole dish big enough to hold a whole chicken comfortably: if that is sometimes too large for your recipe, make more and freeze the rest (see Freezing, opposite).

BRAISING TECHNIQUES

Many beef and chicken dishes we know and love are braises. For browning on the stove top, use a flameproof casserole dish and heat half of the butter or oil; brown the meat in small batches, and give the meat plenty of room. Add the rest of the butter as needed. Steam will not escape as readily as it would from a frying pan since a casserole dish is deeper, so keep the heat high and allow more space for the steam to escape or the meat will stew and not brown. If the butter becomes very dark, remove and use a fresh pat for the vegetables if they also require browning.

Some recipes coat the meat in flour before browning–the flour thickens the pan juices slightly, creating a lovely gravy.

REDUCED-FAT BRAISING

If you find your braises are too fatty, don't reduce the butter or oil in the recipe as this helps produce flavor; instead, make the casserole at least a few hours ahead. When cooked, pour off the liquid into a bowl; refrigerate the liquid until the fat solidifies on the surface. Remove the fat, return the juices to the casserole, then reheat.

FREEZING

Casseroles and stews–and all of these slow-cooked meals–freeze beautifully. The only ingredient that tends not to freeze so well is potato, which turns mushy when thawing, so if you know ahead of time that you're freezing, leave out the potato and add freshly-cooked pieces when it's time to eat it.

SLOW COOKERS

These are electrical appliances that are specially designed to slowly simmer food. They are equipped with low cooking settings that allow the food to gently simmer for a long time– all day if you choose–or you can reduce the cooking time by about half if using the high setting. These appliances are available in various shapes and sizes, and with a host of different features. The 4½-quart size cookers are the most popular size. If you're in the market for a slow cooker, research the subject fully: check out the cookers and their features carefully to make sure the appliance suits your needs.

Most soup, stew, casserole, tagine and curry recipes are perfect to use in the slow cooker. The trick is to make sure there is enough liquid in the cooker for the long, slow, cooking time. Once you get to know the cooker, you'll be able to adapt a lot of your favorite recipes. Some roasts work well in the slow cooker, too. Use recipes that would normally slow cook, well-covered in an oven set at a low temperature.

Getting the best from your slow cooker

There's something wonderful about the aroma, flavor and texture of a slow-cooked meal. Slow cookers are perfect for this way of cooking. First, read the manufacturer's instruction manual carefully, it will advise you never to leave the appliance operating unattended at any time; this, of course, is a safety measure.

These appliances are available in various shapes and sizes, and with a host of different features. For example, some have timers that cut off after the cooking time is over, some don't; some have timers that reduce the temperature and keep the food warm until you decide to eat. If you're in the market for a slow cooker, research the subject fully: check out the cookers and their features carefully to make sure the appliance suits your needs. They are all "safe" in terms of making sure the food reaches the correct temperatures to destroy any harmful bacteria during the long slow cooking times.

We used a 4½-quart slow cooker for the slow-cooker recipes in this chapter as it's the most popular size. If you have a smaller or larger slow cooker than the one we used, you will have to decrease or increase the quantity of food, and almost certainly the liquid content, in the recipes.

HANDY HINTS

MOST RECIPES USING RED MEAT RECOMMEND that the meat is browned first, as if you were making a casserole. Do this in a heated oiled large frying pan, adding the meat in batches, and turning the meat so it browns all over. Overcrowding the pan will result in stewed, not browned, meat. If you're pressed for time, the meat and/or vegetables can be browned the night before. Once everything is browned, put it into a sealable container, along with any juices, and refrigerate until the next day.

SOME RECIPES SUGGEST TOSSING THE MEAT IN FLOUR before browning, some don't. Usually when the meat is floured, the finished sauce will be thick enough to make a light coating of gravy. If the meat is not floured, it might be necessary to thicken the sauce. Usually plain flour or corn starch are used for thickening; corn starch results in a less-cloudy sauce than using flour. The flour or corn starch needs to be blended with butter or a cold liquid such as water or some of the cooled sauce from the slow cooker. Stir the flour mixture into the sauce at the end of the cooking time, while the slow cooker is on the highest setting, then put the lid back on and leave the sauce to thicken–this will take 10 to 20 minutes.

AS A GENERAL RULE for casserole, stew, curry and tagine recipes, place the vegetables into the cooker, put the meat on top of the vegetables, then add the liquid. Soups are easy, just make sure the cooker is at least half-full. Roasts, using whole pieces of meat or poultry, and pot roasts are sometimes cooked with hardly any liquid–especially if the meat is cooking on a bed of vegetables–sometimes a little liquid is added simply to make a sauce or gravy. Corned meats are usually cooked in enough liquid to barely cover them.

SOME MEATS PRODUCE A LOT OF FAT IF COOKED OVER A LONG PERIOD OF TIME There are a couple of gadgets available in kitchen/cookware shops for removing fat: one is a type of brush that sweeps away the fat; the other is a type of pitcher that separates the fat from the liquid. However, one of the easiest ways to remove fat is to soak it up using sheets of absorbent kitchen paper on the surface. The best way of all is to refrigerate the food, the fat will set on top of the liquid, then it can simply be lifted off and discarded.

WHAT SETTING DO I USE?

Use the low setting for long, all-day cooking, or reduce the cooking time by about half if using the high setting. The food will reach simmering point on either setting. If your slow cooker has a warm setting, this is not used for cooking; it's used to keep the cooked food warm until you're ready to serve. If you need to add ingredients or thicken the sauce after cooking time, turn the covered slow cooker to high. Remove the lid and add the ingredients or thickening, replace the lid and leave the cooker to heat the added ingredients or to thicken the sauce, between 10 and 20 minutes.

WHAT CUTS OF MEAT SHOULD I USE?

Use secondary, cheaper, tougher cuts of red meat. The long, slow, cooking time will tenderize the cuts, and the flavors will be excellent; it's a waste to use expensive primary cuts. Other types of meat (secondary/stewing cuts) such as venison, goat, rabbit, lamb, etc., are suitable to use in the slow cooker.
All kinds of poultry cook well in a slow cooker but be careful not to overcook it as it will become stringy. If you can access mature birds, such as boiling fowls or wild duck etc., the long, slow, cooking times will tenderize the flesh, making it very flavorsome.
Seafood is generally not suitable to use in a slow cooker as it toughens quickly. However, there are many sauces that go well with seafood and can be cooked in the slow cooker; add the seafood just before you're ready to serve. Large octopus will cook and become tender in a slow cooker.

CAN I USE MY FAVORITE RECIPES?

Most soup, stew, casserole, tagine and curry recipes are perfect to use in the slow cooker. The trick is to make sure there is enough liquid in the cooker for the long, slow, cooking time. Once you get to know the cooker, you'll be able to adapt a lot of your favorite recipes. Some roasts work well in the slow cooker, too. Use recipes that you would normally slow cook, well-covered in an oven set at a low temperature. Also, some conventionally slow-cooked desserts and steamed pudding recipes can be used.

A NOTE ON DRIED BEANS

We use canned beans, but should you want to use dried beans instead, there are few things you must do to prevent food poisoning.
All kidney-shaped beans of all colors and sizes are related to each other and must be washed, drained, then boiled in fresh water until tender– there's no need for overnight soaking; the time depends on the type of bean. Then, like canned beans, add them to the food in the slow cooker. Soy beans and chickpeas are fine to use raw in the slow cooker, just rinse them well first; there's no need for overnight soaking.

FREEZING LEFTOVERS

The slow cooker's capacity allows you to cook quite a bit of food at once, so if there's any left over, it's smart to freeze some for another time. There is always a lot of liquid to contend with in the slow cooker so remove the meat and vegetables to appropriate-sized freezer-friendly containers, pour in enough of the liquid to barely cover the meat, etc., seal the container, and freeze–while it's hot is fine–for up to three months. Any leftover liquid can be frozen separately and used as a base for another recipe, such as soup or a sauce.

IMPORTANT SAFETY TIPS

• Read the instruction manual carefully.
• Make sure the cooker sits flat on the counter away from water, any heat source (gas flames, stove tops, ovens), curtains, walls, children and pets.
• Make sure the electrical cord is away from any water or heat source, and not dangling on the floor.
• Do not touch any metal part of the cooker while it's in use, as they get very hot.

GENERAL CLEANING

Most slow cooker inserts can be washed in hot soapy water. To remove cooked-on food, soak in warm water, then scrub lightly with a plastic or nylon brush. Never put a hot insert under cold water, as this can cause the insert to break. The outer metal container should never be placed in water; wipe the outside with a damp cloth and dry.

boeuf bourguignon

A French classic, this was a favorite dinner-party dish 20 or 30 years ago. Thanks to the resurgence in popularity of rich and rustic comfort food, it has now reappeared on restaurant menus and in the repertoire of many home cooks.

10 ounces baby brown onions
2 tablespoons olive oil
4 pounds boneless beef shin or
    chuck, trimmed, chopped coarsely
3 tablespoons butter
4 strips bacon, chopped coarsely
14 ounces button mushrooms, halved
2 cloves garlic, crushed
¼ cup all-purpose flour

1¼ cups beef stock
2½ cups dry red wine
2 bay leaves
2 sprigs fresh thyme
½ cup coarsely chopped fresh
    flat-leaf parsley

1 Peel onions, leaving root end intact so onion remains whole during cooking.

2 Heat oil in large flameproof dish; cook beef, in batches, until browned.

3 Add butter to dish; cook onions, bacon, mushrooms and garlic, stirring, until onions are browned lightly.

4 Sprinkle flour over onion mixture; cook, stirring, until flour mixture thickens and bubbles. Gradually add stock and wine; stir over heat until mixture boils and thickens. Return beef and any juices to dish, add bay leaves and thyme; bring to a boil. Reduce heat; simmer, covered, about 2 hours or until beef is tender, stirring every 30 minutes.

5 Remove from heat; discard bay leaves. Stir in parsley.

nutritional count per serving 31.4g total fat (12.1g saturated fat); 636 cal; 6.6g carbohydrate; 80.3g protein; 2.8g fiber

Peel the baby brown onions but leave the root intact. It's important to this dish that the onions remain whole during the long cooking.

Cook the beef chunks in batches in a flameproof dish until they're browned. If you cook too many pieces at a time they'll stew rather than brown.

Sprinkle the flour over the softened onion-bacon mixture and stir until the flour mixture bubbles and thickens.

Gradually add stock and wine, stirring all the time, until the mixture comes to a boil and starts to thicken.

beef stroganoff

A classic Russian recipe known for at least two centuries, "Stroganov" was first brought to Europe by those fleeing the country after the fall of Imperial Russia. It became a popular dinner party dish, cooked at the table in a chafing dish. It remains a favorite in many families' weeknight repertoires because it's so quick to make.

2 tablespoons vegetable oil
1¼ pounds beef rump steak,
    sliced thinly
1 medium brown onion,
    sliced thinly
2 cloves garlic, crushed
14 ounces button mushrooms,
    sliced thickly

1 teaspoon sweet paprika
2 tablespoons dry red wine
1 tablespoon lemon juice
2 tablespoons tomato paste
1¼ cups sour cream
1 tablespoon coarsely chopped
    fresh dill

1 Heat half the oil in large frying pan; cook beef, in batches, until browned lightly.
2 Heat remaining oil in same pan; cook onion and garlic, stirring, until onion softens. Add mushrooms and paprika; cook, stirring, until mushrooms are tender.
3 Return beef to pan with wine and juice; bring to a boil. Reduce heat; simmer, covered, about 5 minutes or until beef is tender. Add paste, sour cream and dill; cook, stirring, until heated through.

nutritional count per serving 43.3g total fat (22.4g saturated fat); 589 cal; 5.9g carbohydrate; 41.4g protein; 3.7g fiber

serving ideas steamed rice, mashed potato or fettuccine.

hungarian veal goulash

TIP

• To cook goulash on the stove top, follow the method using a large saucepan. Simmer the goulash, covered, over low heat, excluding potato and carrot, for 40 minutes. Add potato and carrot; simmer for 30 minutes or until veal and vegetables are tender.

2-pound boned veal shoulder,
    chopped coarsely
¼ cup all-purpose flour
1 tablespoon sweet paprika
2 teaspoons caraway seeds
½ teaspoon cayenne pepper
2 tablespoons olive oil
1 tablespoon butter
1 large brown onion,
    chopped coarsely

2 cloves garlic, crushed
2 tablespoons tomato paste
1½ cups beef stock
14-ounce can crushed tomatoes
3 small potatoes, quartered
2 medium carrots, chopped coarsely
½ cup coarsely chopped fresh
    flat-leaf parsley

1 Toss veal in combined flour and spices to coat; shake away excess flour. Heat half the oil and half the butter in large frying pan; cook veal, in batches, until browned all over. Transfer to 4½-quart (18-cup) slow cooker.
2 Heat remaining oil and butter in same pan; cook onion and garlic, stirring, until onion is soft. Stir in paste and stock; bring to a boil. Stir into cooker with undrained tomatoes, potato and carrot; cook, covered, on low, 8 hours.
3 Season to taste. Serve goulash sprinkled with parsley.

nutritional count per serving 12.6g total fat (3.5g saturated fat); 360 cal; 19g carbohydrate; 40.2g protein; 4.1g fiber

[1] beef stroganoff
[2] hungarian veal goulash
[3] chili con carne [page 370]
[4] lamb with sweet potato and raisins [page 370]

chili con carne

Use leftover chili con carne (a Mexican dish that means meat stew with chili bean sauce) as a topping for nachos, a filling for tacos or even served solo on a piece of toasted Turkish bread topped with coleslaw for an easy dinner.

1 cup dried kidney beans
3 pounds beef chuck steak
2 quarts water
1 tablespoon olive oil
2 medium brown onions, chopped coarsely
2 cloves garlic, crushed
2 teaspoons ground cumin
2 teaspoons ground coriander

½ teaspoon cayenne pepper
2 teaspoons sweet paprika
2 x 14-ounce cans crushed tomatoes
1 tablespoon tomato paste
4 green onions, chopped coarsely
2 tablespoons coarsely chopped fresh coriander
⅓ cup finely chopped pickled jalapeño chilies

1 Place beans in medium bowl, cover with water; stand overnight, drain.

2 Combine beef with the water in large saucepan; bring to a boil. Reduce heat, simmer, covered, 1½ hours.

3 Drain beef in large muslin-lined strainer over bowl; reserve 3½ cups of the cooking liquid. Using two forks, shred beef.

4 Heat oil in same pan; cook brown onion and garlic, stirring, until onion is soft. Add spices; cook, stirring, until fragrant. Add beans, undrained tomatoes, paste and 2 cups of the reserved liquid; bring to a boil. Reduce heat, simmer, covered, 1 hour.

5 Add beef and remaining reserved liquid to pan; simmer, covered, 30 minutes or until beans are tender. Remove from heat; stir in green onions, coriander and chili.

nutritional count per serving 11.4g total fat (3.9g saturated fat); 358 cal; 14.7g carbohydrate; 45.1g protein; 7.6g fiber

serving idea steamed rice.

lamb with sweet potato and raisins

Ras el hanout is a blend of Moroccan spices, it's available in delis and specialty food stores. If you can't find it, use a Moroccan seasoning available in supermarkets.

2 tablespoons olive oil
2½ pounds boned lamb shoulder, chopped coarsely
1 large brown onion, sliced thickly
4 cloves garlic, crushed
2 tablespoons ras el hanout
2 cups chicken stock
½ cup water
1 tablespoon honey
2 medium sweet potatoes, peeled, chopped coarsely

14-ounce can chickpeas, rinsed, drained
1 cinnamon stick
3 cardamom pods, bruised
⅓ cup raisins, halved
⅓ cup coarsely chopped blanched almonds, toasted
½ cup loosely packed fresh coriander leaves

TIP

• To cook casserole on stove top, follow method using a large saucepan. Simmer casserole, covered, over low heat, excluding sweet potato and chickpeas, for 50 minutes. Add sweet potato and chickpeas; simmer 30 minutes or until lamb and sweet potatoes are tender.

1 Heat half the oil in large frying pan; cook lamb, in batches, until browned all over. Remove lamb from pan.

2 Heat remaining oil in same pan; cook onion and garlic, stirring, until onion is soft. Add ras el hanout; cook, stirring, until fragrant. Remove from heat; stir in stock, the water and honey.

3 Place potatoes in 4½-quart slow cooker; mix in chickpeas, cinnamon, cardamom, lamb and onion mixture. Cook, covered, on low, 4 hours. Season.

4 Stir in raisins; serve sprinkled with nuts and coriander.

nutritional count per serving 24.1g total fat (6.9g saturated fat); 564 cal; 35g carbohydrate; 48.6g protein; 6.2g fiber

lamb shank stew

PREP + COOK TIME 3 HOURS 10 MINS • SERVES 8

The term "to french" in cooking means "cut in the French manner". Shanks, racks, crown roasts and cutlets are sold "frenched". French-trimmed shanks have had the upper ends of the bones trimmed slightly short and scraped (the point is to expose the cleaned bone), while the shank meat itself has been trimmed of excess fat, membrane and sinew. Shanks require long cooking to bring out their best taste and texture, and frenching them makes the end result more tender, less fatty and totally delicious.

8 french-trimmed lamb shanks
8 cloves garlic, halved
2 medium lemons
2 tablespoons olive oil
3 large brown onions, chopped coarsely
2 cups dry red wine
3 medium carrots, quartered lengthwise

3 stalks celery, trimmed, chopped coarsely
4 bay leaves
8 sprigs fresh thyme
7 cups chicken stock
½ cup finely chopped fresh flat-leaf parsley
¼ cup finely chopped fresh mint leaves

1 Pierce meatiest part of each shank in two places with sharp knife; press garlic into cuts.

2 Grate rind of both lemons finely; reserve. Halve lemons; rub cut sides all over shanks.

3 Preheat oven to 350°F/325°F fan-forced.

4 Heat oil in large flameproof dish; cook shanks, in batches, over heat until browned. Cook onion, stirring, in same dish until softened. Add wine; bring to a boil, then remove dish from heat.

5 Place carrot, celery and shanks, in alternate layers, on onion mixture in dish. Top with bay leaves and thyme; carefully pour stock over the top. Cover dish tightly with lid or foil; cook in oven about 3 hours or until meat is tender.

6 Combine reserved grated rind and herbs in bowl.

7 Transfer shanks to platter; cover to keep warm. Strain pan juices through muslin-lined sieve into medium saucepan; discard solids. Boil pan juices, uncovered, stirring occasionally, until reduced by half.

8 Serve shanks sprinkled with rind-herb mixture, drizzle with pan juices.

nutritional count per serving 15.5g total fat (5.6g saturated fat); 329 cal; 8.8g carbohydrate; 26.8g protein; 3.8g fiber

corned beef with parsley sauce

PREP + COOK TIME
2 HOURS (+ STANDING &
COOLING) • SERVES 4

3-pound whole piece corned beef
  (bottom round)
2 bay leaves
6 black peppercorns
1 large brown onion,quartered
1 large carrot, chopped coarsely
1 tablespoon brown malt vinegar
¼ cup firmly packed brown sugar

parsley sauce
3 tablespoons butter
¼ cup all-purpose flour
2½ cups milk
⅓ cup grated cheddar cheese
⅓ cup finely chopped fresh
  flat-leaf parsley
1 tablespoon mild mustard

The "corn" in corned
beef actually refers
to the large grains
(or, in old-English,
"corns") of salt that
were originally used
to preserve the beef
without refrigeration.
We still corn beef
today because of the
delicious flavor and
texture that comes
from the extended
brining of the meat.

1 Place beef, bay leaves, peppercorns, onion, carrot, vinegar and half of the
sugar in large saucepan. Add enough water to just cover beef; simmer, covered,
about 1½ hours or until beef is tender. Cool beef 1 hour in liquid in pan.

2 Remove beef from pan; discard liquid. Sprinkle sheet of foil with remaining
sugar, wrap beef in foil; stand 20 minutes before serving.

3 Make parsley sauce.

4 Serve sliced corned beef with parsley sauce.

parsley sauce Melt butter in small saucepan, add flour; cook, stirring, until
bubbling. Gradually stir in milk; cook, stirring, until sauce boils and thickens.
Remove from heat; stir in cheese, parsley and mustard.

nutritional count per serving 35.8g total fat (19.3g saturated fat); 842 cal;
31g carbohydrate; 97g protein; 2.5g fiber

Q&A

I see corned beef hash on diner menus all the time, and order it frequently when I'm out for breakfast.
I'd like to make it at home. Is it difficult to prepare?

Many people cook corned beef just so they can make corned beef hash. Store-bought corned beef just
doesn't make the grade. Corned beef hash is a mixture of cold boiled potato, chopped finely, cooked corned
beef, chopped finely or shredded, and a few finely chopped green onions. Mix it all together and make one
big flat patty or several smaller patties, cook in hot olive oil until brown and crisp on both sides, and serve
with a poached egg on top, drizzled with some sweet chili sauce.

braised sweet ginger duck

Star anise is the dried, star-shaped seed pod of a small evergreen tree grown from Southwest China through Southeast Asia to Japan. Each fruit's pod has, as a rule, eight points with a total span of about ¾ inches, and each point contains a seed. The star-shaped pod can be used whole as a flavoring or the seeds alone as a spice; both can be used ground.

4-pound whole duck
3 cups water
½ cup Chinese cooking wine
⅓ cup soy sauce
¼ cup firmly packed brown sugar
1 whole star anise
3 green onions, halved

3 cloves garlic, quartered
4-inch piece fresh ginger, unpeeled, chopped coarsely
2 teaspoons sea salt
1 teaspoon five-spice powder
1½ pounds baby bok choy, halved

1 Preheat oven to 350ºF/325ºF fan-forced.

2 Discard neck from duck, wash duck; pat dry with absorbent paper. Score duck in thickest parts of skin; cut duck in half through breastbone and along both sides of backbone, discard backbone. Tuck wings under duck.

3 Place duck, skin-side down, in medium shallow roasting pan; add combined water, wine, soy, sugar, star anise, onion, garlic and ginger. Cover; roast about 1 hour or until duck is cooked as desired.

4 Increase oven temperature to 425ºF/400ºF fan-forced. Remove duck from braising liquid; strain liquid through muslin-lined sieve into large saucepan. Place duck, skin-side up, on wire rack in same pan. Rub combined salt and five-spice all over duck; roast duck, uncovered, about 30 minutes or until skin is crisp.

5 Skim fat from surface of braising liquid; bring to a boil. Reduce heat; simmer, uncovered, 10 minutes. Add bok choy; simmer, covered, about 5 minutes or until bok choy is just tender.

6 Cut duck halves into two pieces; divide bok choy, braising liquid and duck among plates.

nutritional count per serving 105.7g total fat (31.7g saturated fat); 1190 cal; 17.9g carbohydrate; 40.8g protein; 3.5g fiber

serving idea steamed jasmine rice.

Score the duck through the skin and fat. There are two reasons for this: it helps the flavors to be absorbed more easily into the flesh, and it aids in crisping up the skin.

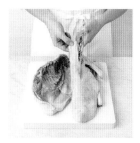

Cut along both sides of the backbone using poultry shears. Discard the backbone. You now have two duck halves.

Once the duck has been braised and is cooked through, place the halves, skin-side up, on a wire rack and rub in the five-spice and salt mixture.

cassoulet

Our version of this classic takes its lead from the traditional versions of Languedoc and Castelnaudary, but we've given it an update to make it a simpler, quicker and healthier dish. Haricot, great northern, cannellini or navy beans can be used in this recipe.

1½ cups dried white beans
10-ounce boned pork belly, rind removed, sliced thinly
5-ounce piece slab bacon, rind removed, diced into ⅓-inch pieces
1½ pound piece boned lamb shoulder, diced into 1-inch pieces
1 large brown onion, chopped finely
1 small leek, sliced thinly
2 cloves garlic, crushed

3 sprigs fresh thyme
14-ounce can crushed tomatoes
2 bay leaves
1 cup water
1 cup chicken stock
2 cups stale bread crumbs
⅓ cup coarsely chopped fresh flat-leaf parsley

1 Place beans in medium bowl, cover with water; soak overnight, drain. Rinse under cold water; drain. Place beans in medium saucepan of boiling water; bring to a boil. Reduce heat; simmer, covered, about 15 minutes or until beans are just tender. Drain.

2 Preheat oven to 300°F/275°F fan-forced.

3 Cook pork in large flameproof casserole dish over heat, pressing down with back of spoon on pork until browned all over; remove from dish. Cook bacon in same pan, stirring, until crisp; remove from dish. Cook lamb, in batches, in same pan, until browned all over.

4 Cook onion, leek and garlic in same dish, stirring, until onion softens. Add thyme, undrained tomatoes, bay leaves, the water, stock, beans and meat; bring to a boil. Cover; cook in oven 45 minutes. Remove from oven; sprinkle with combined bread crumbs and parsley. Return to oven; cook, uncovered, about 45 minutes or until liquid is nearly absorbed and beans are tender.

nutritional count per serving 28g total fat (10.7g saturated fat); 654 cal; 39.5g carbohydrate; 54.9g protein; 12.1g fiber

braised pork with pears and cider

2 tablespoons olive oil
2-pound piece pork neck
1-inch piece fresh ginger, peeled sliced thinly
2 cloves garlic, sliced thinly
½ teaspoon ground fennel

3 cups sweet cider
2 cups chicken stock
2 large pears, peeled, cored cut into thick wedges
½ cup coarsely chopped fresh flat-leaf parsley

1 Preheat oven to 325°F/300°F fan-forced.

2 Heat oil in large flameproof dish; cook pork until browned all over. Remove from dish.

3 Cook ginger and garlic in same pan, stirring, until fragrant. Add fennel; cook, stirring, 1 minute. Add cider and stock; bring to a boil. Return pork to pan, cover; cook in oven 1 hour. Uncover; cook in oven 30 minutes. Add pear; cook, uncovered, about 30 minutes or until pear is tender. Remove pork, cover, stand 5 minutes before slicing thickly. Stir parsley into braising liquid.

4 Serve pork with drizzled braising liquid.

nutritional count per serving 29.8g total fat (8.3g saturated fat); 671 cal; 34.7g carbohydrate; 55.1g protein; 3.5g fiber

beef stew with parsley dumplings

PREP + COOK TIME 2 HOURS 50 MINS • SERVES 4

This recipe can be made, up to step 4, in a slow cooker or a pressure cooker if you have one; make sure you follow the instructions stated in the cooker's manual.

2-pound beef chuck steak, diced into 2-inch pieces
2 tablespoons all-purpose flour
2 tablespoons olive oil
2 tablespoons butter
2 medium brown onions, chopped coarsely
2 cloves garlic, crushed
2 medium carrots, chopped
1 cup dry red wine
2 tablespoons tomato paste
2 cups beef stock
4 sprigs fresh thyme

parsley dumplings
1 cup self-rising flour
3 tablespoons butter
1 egg, beaten lightly
¼ cup coarsely grated parmesan cheese
¼ cup finely chopped fresh flat-leaf parsley
⅓ cup drained sun-dried tomatoes, chopped finely
¼ cup milk

1 Preheat oven to 350°F/325°F fan-forced.

2 Coat beef in flour; shake off excess. Heat oil in large flameproof casserole dish; cook beef, in batches, until browned all over.

3 Melt butter in same pan; cook onion, garlic and carrot, stirring, until vegetables soften. Add wine; cook, stirring, until liquid reduces to ¼ cup. Return beef to pan with paste, stock and thyme; bring to a boil. Cover; cook in oven 1¾ hours.

4 Meanwhile, make parsley dumpling mixture.

5 Remove dish from oven; uncover. Drop level tablespoons of the dumpling mixture, about 1 inch apart, onto top of stew. Cook, uncovered, in oven another 20 minutes or until dumplings are browned lightly and cooked through.

parsley dumplings Place flour in medium bowl; rub in butter. Stir in egg, cheese, parsley, tomato and enough milk to make a soft, sticky dough.

nutritional count per serving 39.7g total fat (17.4g saturated fat); 827 cal; 43g carbohydrate; 63.9g protein; 6.7g fiber

irish stew

This is a classic peasant dish from Ireland that traditionally uses mutton and the cheapest local ingredients available, which are root vegetables and barley.

1½ pounds lamb neck chops
2 large brown onions, chopped coarsely
1 large carrot, chopped coarsely
1 large parsnip, chopped coarsely
2 pounds potatoes, chopped coarsely
3½ cups beef stock
2 tablespoons tomato paste

1 tablespoon Worcestershire sauce
2 sprigs thyme
¼ cup coarsely chopped fresh flat-leaf parsley

1 Preheat oven to 325°F/300°F fan-forced.

2 Layer chops and vegetables in large ovenproof dish; pour over combined stock, paste and sauce. Add thyme. Cook, covered, 2 hours. Uncover; cook 30 minutes or until lamb and vegetables are tender.

3 Serve stew sprinkled with parsley.

nutritional count per serving 19.3g total fat (8.6g saturated fat); 538 cal; 46.8g carbohydrate; 39.7g protein; 8.5g fiber

chicken cacciatore

Anchovies are a "secret" ingredient in many savory dishes, merging into the flavors of the other ingredients to add depth and richness. Soaking them first in milk removes their fishy taste and some of their saltiness.

2 tablespoons olive oil
3 pounds chicken thigh cutlets, skin on
1 medium brown onion, chopped finely
1 clove garlic, crushed
½ cup dry white wine
2 tablespoons white wine vinegar
½ cup chicken stock

14-ounce can crushed tomatoes
¼ cup tomato paste
2 drained anchovy filets, chopped finely
½ cup pitted black olives, chopped coarsely
½ cup coarsely chopped fresh flat-leaf parsley

1 Heat half the oil in large saucepan; cook chicken, in batches, until browned all over. Remove chicken from pan.

2 Heat remaining oil in same pan; cook onion and garlic, stirring, until onion softens. Stir in wine, vinegar, stock, undrained tomatoes, paste and anchovies.

3 Return chicken to pan, fitting pieces tightly together in a single layer; bring to a boil. Reduce heat; simmer, covered, 20 minutes. Uncover; simmer about 30 minutes or until chicken is tender and sauce is reduced. Skim fat from surface; stir in olives and parsley.

nutritional count per serving 39.9g total fat (10.8g saturated fat); 587 cal; 10.8g carbohydrate; 40.5g protein; 3.1g fiber

[1] irish stew
[2] chicken cacciatore
[3] coq au vin [page 380]
[4] osso buco [page 380]

coq au vin

PREP + COOK TIME 1 HOUR 30 MINS • SERVES 4

1½ pounds spring onions
¼ cup olive oil
6 strips bacon, chopped coarsely
10 ounces button mushrooms
2 cloves garlic, crushed
8 chicken thigh filets
¼ cup all-purpose flour
2 cups dry red wine
1½ cups chicken stock
2 tablespoons tomato paste
3 bay leaves
4 sprigs fresh thyme
2 sprigs fresh rosemary

1 Trim green ends from onions, leaving about 1½ inches of stem attached; trim roots. Heat 1 tablespoon of the oil in large frying pan; cook onions, stirring, until browned all over. Remove onions from pan.
2 Add bacon, mushrooms and garlic to pan; cook, stirring, until bacon is crisp, remove from pan.
3 Coat chicken in flour; shake off excess. Heat remaining oil in same pan. Cook chicken, in batches, until browned all over; drain on absorbent paper.
4 Return chicken to pan with wine, stock, paste, bay leaves, herbs, onions and bacon mixture. Bring to a boil; reduce heat, simmer, uncovered, about 35 minutes or until chicken is tender and sauce has thickened slightly.
nutritional count per serving 43.6g total fat (11.8g saturated fat); 820 cal; 16.3g carbohydrate; 67.8g protein; 6.4g fiber

osso buco

PREP + COOK TIME 2 HOURS 45 MINS • SERVES 6

As it has become more fashionable, gremolata has morphed into many guises well removed from its original form. Originally, as we've shown here, it was the garnish strewn over steaming osso buco so the scent of its combined ingredients would excite the palate once they hit the heat. Now, it's made from any number of aromatic ingredients and sprinkled over many different dishes, from soups to steamed vegetables.

12 pieces veal osso buco (7 pounds)
¼ cup all-purpose flour
¼ cup olive oil
3 tablespoons butter
1 medium brown onion, chopped coarsely
2 cloves garlic, crushed
3 stalks celery, trimmed, chopped coarsely
2 large carrots, chopped coarsely
4 medium tomatoes, chopped coarsely
2 tablespoons tomato paste
1 cup dry white wine
1 cup beef stock
14-ounce can crushed tomatoes
3 sprigs fresh thyme
¼ cup coarsely chopped fresh flat-leaf parsley

gremolata
1 tablespoon finely grated lemon rind
⅓ cup finely chopped fresh flat-leaf parsley
2 cloves garlic, chopped finely

1 Coat veal in flour, shake off excess.

2 Heat oil in large flameproof dish; cook veal, in batches, until browned all over.

3 Melt butter in same flameproof dish; cook onion, garlic, celery and carrot, stirring, until vegetables soften. Stir in remaining ingredients.

4 Return veal to dish, fitting pieces upright and tightly together in a single layer; bring to a boil. Cover, reduce heat; simmer 1¾ hours. Uncover; cook 30 minutes.

5 Meanwhile, make gremolata.

6 Remove veal from dish; cover to keep warm. Bring sauce to a boil; boil, uncovered, about 10 minutes or until sauce thickens slightly.

7 Divide veal among serving plates; top with sauce, sprinkle with gremolata. Osso buco can be served with mashed potatoes or soft polenta, if you like.

gremolata Combine ingredients in small bowl.

nutritional count per serving 16.3g total fat (5.2g saturated fat); 492 cal; 14g carbohydrate; 63.2g protein; 6g fiber

octopus braised in red wine

PREP + COOK TIME 2 HOURS • SERVES 8

Octopus belongs to the same family as squid, and can be cooked in the same way. Baby octopus is tender but larger ones are tough and must be tenderized by pounding–this will usually have been done at the seafood counter.

1 tablespoon olive oil

1 medium brown onion, chopped finely

2 cloves garlic, crushed

2 baby fennel bulbs, trimmed, chopped coarsely

5 medium vine-ripened tomatoes, chopped coarsely

3 bay leaves

1 teaspoon dried chili flakes

1¼-pound baby whole octopus

⅔ cup dry red wine

2 tablespoons finely chopped fresh flat-leaf parsley

1 Preheat oven to 400°F/350°F fan-forced.

2 Heat oil in large frying pan; cook onion and garlic, stirring, until onion softens. Add fennel; cook, stirring, 5 minutes. Add tomato, bay leaves and chili; cook, stirring occasionally, about 10 minutes or until mixture thickens and fennel softens.

3 Combine fennel mixture, octopus and wine in medium baking dish; bake, covered, about 45 minutes. Uncover; bake about 40 minutes or until octopus is tender and browned lightly.

4 Cut octopus into bite-sized pieces. Stir in parsley. Serve with crusty bread.

nutritional count per serving 3g total fat (0.3g saturated fat); 118 cal; 3.1g carbohydrate; 15.2g protein; 1.8g fiber

18 large cabbage leaves
½ cup uncooked white
   long-grain rice
8 ounces ground pork
1 medium brown onion,
   chopped finely
¼ cup finely chopped fresh dill
1 clove garlic, crushed
1 tablespoon tomato paste

2 teaspoons ground cumin
1 teaspoon ground coriander
1 teaspoon ground allspice
4 cloves garlic, quartered
2 medium tomatoes,
   chopped coarsely
2 x 14-ounce cans crushed tomatoes
¼ cup lemon juice

1 Discard thick stems from 12 cabbage leaves; reserve remaining leaves.
Boil, steam or microwave trimmed leaves until just pliable; drain. Rinse under
cold water; drain. Pat dry with absorbent paper.
2 Combine rice, pork, onion, dill, crushed garlic, paste and spices in medium bowl.
3 Place one trimmed leaf, vein-side up, on board; cut leaf in half lengthways.
Place a level tablespoon of the pork mixture at stem end of each half; roll each
half firmly to enclose filling. Repeat with remaining trimmed leaves.
4 Place reserved leaves in base of wide saucepan. Place only enough rolls,
seam-side down, in single layer, to completely cover leaves in base of saucepan.
Top with quartered garlic, chopped fresh tomato then remaining rolls.
5 Pour undrained tomatoes and juice over cabbage rolls; bring to a boil.
Reduce heat; simmer, covered, 1 hour. Uncover; simmer about 30 minutes or
until cabbage rolls are cooked through.
6 Divide cabbage rolls and sauce among serving plates.
nutritional count per serving 3.6g total fat (1.1g saturated fat); 192 cal;
24.7g carbohydrate; 14.3g protein; 9.7g fiber
serving idea serve rolls with thick Greek-style yogurt flavored with a little finely
chopped preserved lemon rind.

Cut off and discard the thick
stems from 12 cabbage leaves.
The filling will be rolled in these
leaves so make sure there are
no tears in them.

Place level tablespoons of the
filling mixture at one end of
the softened leaves and roll
up neatly, folding in the sides,
to enclose the filling.

Place cabbage rolls, seam-side
down in one layer in pan. Add
garlic and tomato and then put
remaining rolls on top. Pour the
tomato mixture over.

seafood stew with chermoulla

Chermoulla is a Moroccan blend of fresh herbs, spices and condiments traditionally used for preserving or seasoning meat and fish. We used our chermoulla blend here as a quick flavoring for the stew, but you can also use it as a sauce or marinade. You can keep freshly made chermoulla in the refrigerator, covered with a thin layer of olive oil to preserve it, for up to a month.

1 pound black mussels
1½ pounds uncooked medium
   king prawns
10 ounces kingfish or tuna filet,
   skinned
1 squid tube
1 tablespoon olive oil
1 large brown onion, chopped finely
3 cloves garlic, crushed
1 medium red pepper, chopped finely
½ cup dry white wine
1 cup fish stock
14-ounce can diced tomatoes

chermoulla
½ cup finely chopped fresh coriander
½ cup finely chopped fresh
   flat-leaf parsley
1 clove garlic, crushed
2 tablespoons white wine vinegar
2 tablespoons lemon juice
½ teaspoon ground cumin
2 tablespoons olive oil

1 Scrub mussels; remove beards. Shell and devein prawns, leaving tails intact. Dice fish into 1-inch pieces. Cut squid down center to open out; score inside in diagonal pattern then cut into thick strips.

2 Heat oil in large saucepan; cook onion, garlic and peppers, stirring, until onion softens. Stir in wine; cook, uncovered, until wine is almost evaporated. Add stock and undrained tomatoes; bring to a boil. Add seafood, reduce heat; simmer, covered, about 5 minutes or until squid is tender and mussels open (discard any that do not).

3 Meanwhile, combine ingredients for chermoulla in small bowl.

4 Stir half of the chermoulla into stew. Divide stew among bowls; divide remaining chermoulla over the top of each bowl. Serve with a warmed baguette, if desired.

nutritional count per serving 17.5g total fat (3g saturated fat); 410 cal; 8.7g carbohydrate; 48.6g protein; 3.5g fiber

curried sausages

1½ pounds thick beef sausages
2 tablespoons butter
1 medium brown onion,
   chopped coarsely
1 tablespoon curry powder
2 teaspoons all-purpose flour
2 large carrots,
   chopped coarsely

2 stalks celery, trimmed,
   chopped coarsely
1 pound baby new potatoes, halved
2 cups beef stock
1 cup loosely packed fresh
   flat-leaf parsley leaves

1 Cook sausages, in batches, in heated deep large frying pan until cooked through. Cut each sausage into thirds.

2 Melt butter in same cleaned pan; cook onion, stirring, until soft. Add curry powder and flour; cook, stirring, 2 minutes.

3 Add vegetables and stock; bring to a boil. Reduce heat; simmer, covered, about 15 minutes or until vegetables are tender. Add sausages; simmer, uncovered, until sauce thickens slightly. Stir in parsley.

nutritional count per serving 55.8g total fat (27.3g saturated fat); 760 cal; 29.8g carbohydrate; 30.1g protein; 12.8g fiber

chicken, olive and preserved lemon tagine

PREP + COOK TIME
2 HOURS 15 MINS
(+ STANDING)
SERVES 8

1 cup dried chickpeas
2 tablespoons all-purpose flour
2 teaspoons hot paprika
8 chicken drumsticks
8 chicken thigh cutlets
3 tablespoons butter
2 medium red onions,
　sliced thickly
3 cloves garlic, crushed
1 teaspoon cumin seeds
½ teaspoon ground turmeric

½ teaspoon ground coriander
¼ teaspoon saffron threads
1 teaspoon dried chili flakes
1 teaspoon ground ginger
3 cups chicken stock
2 tablespoons finely sliced
　preserved lemon rind
⅓ cup pitted green olives
2 tablespoons finely chopped
　fresh coriander

For a traditional accompaniment bring 1½ cups chicken stock to a boil in a small saucepan; remove from the heat. Stir in 1½ cups couscous; rest about 5 minutes, fluffing with a fork. Stir in 2 tablespoons lemon juice and ½ cup chopped fresh coriander.

1 Place chickpeas in medium bowl, cover with water; stand overnight, drain. Rinse under cold water; drain. Place chickpeas in medium saucepan of boiling water; return to a boil. Reduce heat; simmer, uncovered, about 40 minutes or until chickpeas are tender.

2 Preheat oven to 325ºF/300ºF fan-forced.

3 Place flour and paprika in paper or plastic bag, add chicken pieces, in batches; shake gently to coat chicken in flour mixture.

4 Melt butter in large flameproof casserole dish; cook chicken pieces, in batches, until browned. Cook onion in same dish, stirring, until softened. Add garlic, cumin, turmeric, ground coriander, saffron, chili and ginger; cook, stirring, until fragrant. Return chicken with stock to dish; bring to a boil, then cook, covered, in oven 30 minutes. Add drained chickpeas; cook tagine, covered, 1 hour.

5 Remove tagine from oven. Stir in lemon rind, olives and fresh coriander just before serving.

nutritional count per serving 32g total fat (11.5g saturated fat); 492 cal; 16.4g carbohydrate; 39.8g protein; 2.6g fiber

Stew accompaniments

Stews are only half-finished without an accompaniment.

SOFT POLENTA

Combine 3 cups water and 2 cups vegetable stock in large saucepan; bring to a boil. Gradually stir in 2 cups polenta. Reduce heat; simmer, stirring, about 10 minutes or until polenta thickens. Add 1 cup milk, 3 tablespoons butter and ¼ cup finely grated parmesan cheese; stir until cheese melts.

PARSNIP MASH

Boil, steam or microwave 2 pounds coarsely chopped, peeled parsnip until tender; drain. Mash parsnip in medium bowl with ¾ cup hot milk until smooth; stir in 2 crushed garlic cloves and 3 tablespoons soft butter. The same amount of celeriac, sweet potato or pumpkin can be used instead of parsnip.

ROAST POTATOES

Preheat oven to 400°F/350°F fan-forced. Lightly oil oven tray. Boil, steam or microwave 6 halved medium potatoes 5 minutes; drain. Pat dry with absorbent paper; cool 10 minutes. Gently rake rounded sides of potatoes with tines of fork; place potato in single layer, cut-side down, on oven tray. Brush with 2 tablespoons olive oil; roast, uncovered, in oven about 50 minutes or until potatoes are browned lightly and crisp.

COUSCOUS

Combine 1½ cups couscous with 1½ cups boiling water in large heatproof bowl, cover; stand about 5 minutes or until water is absorbed, fluffing with fork occasionally. Stir in 2 ounces finely shredded baby spinach leaves or some coarsely chopped fresh herbs of your choice, or 2 finely chopped green onions.

CREAMY MASHED POTATOES
Boil, steam or microwave 1½ pounds coarsely chopped potatoes until tender; drain. Mash potato with 4 tablespoons soft butter and ½ cup hot light cream in medium bowl until smooth.

STEAMED GAI LAN IN OYSTER SAUCE
Boil, steam or microwave 2 pounds halved gai lan until tender; drain. Heat 1 tablespoon peanut oil in wok; stir-fry gai lan, 2 tablespoons oyster sauce and 1 tablespoon light soy sauce about 2 minutes or until gai lan is tender.

PILAF
Melt 3 tablespoons butter in medium saucepan; cook 1 crushed garlic clove, stirring, until fragrant. Add 1 cup basmati rice; cook, stirring, 1 minute. Add 1 cup chicken stock and 1 cup water; bring to a boil. Reduce heat; simmer, covered, about 20 minutes or until rice is tender. Remove from heat; fluff rice with fork. Stir in ¼ cup coarsely chopped fresh flat-leaf parsley and ¼ cup roasted sliced almonds.

TOMATO AND HERB SALAD
Place 5 coarsely chopped medium tomatoes, 2 tablespoons chopped fresh mint, ¼ cup chopped fresh flat-leaf parsley and 2 tablespoons chopped fresh dill in medium bowl. Place 2 cloves crushed garlic, 2 tablespoons lemon juice, 1 tablespoon olive oil and 2 teaspoons white vinegar in screw-top jar; shake well. Drizzle dressing over salad; toss to combine.

PIES

Pies

Nothing says good, honest food like a pie. The sight of one, with its golden pastry lid bulging with goodness, is a sure way to make everyone smile on a cold day. Pie fillings can be made from a huge variety of vegetables and meats, and they are a great way of giving new life to leftovers. Pies can also be made in smaller, single-serving sizes, which are perfect for picnics and casual meals on cozy nights.

WHEN IS A PIE A PIE?

THE USUAL DEFINITION OF A PIE, AS OPPOSED TO A TART, IS THAT A PIE HAS A TOP CRUST, ALTHOUGH THERE ARE EXCEPTIONS–THE MAIN EXAMPLE IS THE QUICHE, WHICH CONSISTS OF A SAVORY CUSTARD IN AN OPEN PASTRY CASE.

A PIE MAY ALSO HAVE A BOTTOM CRUST AS WELL. PIES WITH A TOP CRUST, OR LID, BUT NO BASE ARE CALLED ONE-CRUST PIES. PIES WITH A LID AND A BOTTOM CRUST ARE CALLED TWO-CRUST OR DOUBLE-CRUST PIES. PIE CRUST CAN ALSO BE FOLDED AROUND SWEET OR SAVORY FILLINGS AND SEALED, CALLED TURNOVERS OR HANDPIES.

THE PIE DISH

YOU CAN MAKE A PIE IN JUST ABOUT ANY OVENPROOF CASSEROLE OR BAKING DISH, ALTHOUGH THE TRADITIONAL PIE DISH IS ROUND AND HAS SLIGHTLY SLOPING SIDES WITH A RIM TO ANCHOR THE PASTRY BASE TO THE LID–WITH THE PASTRY FLUTED OR DECORATIVELY MARKED IN SOME WAY TO MAKE THE PIE LOOK HANDSOME AND IMPRESSIVE. BUT YOU DON'T NEED A SPECIAL PIE DISH: RAMEKINS, A PUDDING MOLD, A CAKE PAN OR EVEN A BAKING DISH CAN BE USED TO COOK A PIE.

METAL PIE DISHES ARE CONSIDERED BETTER FOR BROWNING BOTTOM-CRUST PIES. CERAMIC PERFORMS WELL FOR ONE-CRUST PIES BECAUSE IT TAKES UP HEAT SLOWLY, WHICH HEATS THE FILLING GENTLY AND EVENLY. CERAMIC DISHES ALSO WORK WELL FOR TWO-CRUST PIES WITH A LONG COOKING PERIOD.

PASTRY

RESTING IT ONCE YOU'VE MADE THE PASTRY, WRAP IT IN PLASTIC WRAP AND REFRIGERATE IT FOR 30 MINUTES (OR AS DIRECTED) SO ITS MOISTURE CONTENT WILL EVEN OUT AND THE GLUTEN WILL HAVE TIME TO RELAX. THIS MINIMIZES THE PASTRY SHRINKING DURING BAKING.

ROLLING IT AFTER RESTING, PASTRY IS BEST ROLLED ON A COOL SURFACE (MARBLE IS IDEAL). ROLL ON A FLOURED SURFACE OR BETWEEN TWO SHEETS OF PARCHMENT PAPER, WAX PAPER OR PLASTIC WRAP. IF ROLLING DIRECTLY ON THE WORK SURFACE, KEEP TURNING THE PASTRY TO ENSURE THAT IT IS NOT STICKING. USE SHORT, LIGHT STROKES, STARTING FROM THE CENTER EACH TIME, TO ROLL THE PASTRY TOWARDS YOU OR AWAY FROM YOU. ROLL TO THE EDGE OF THE PASTRY, NOT OVER THE EDGE.

REST AGAIN REST THE PASTRY AGAIN ONCE IT IS ROLLED OUT AND ASSEMBLED IN THE PIE DISH, BEFORE BAKING. THIS WILL ALLOW THE GLUTEN TO RELAX AND MINIMIZE PASTRY SHRINKAGE.

STORING PASTRY

COOL COOKED PASTRIES COMPLETELY BEFORE STORING. THEY KEEP WELL IN AIRTIGHT CONTAINERS, BUT AFTER A WEEK OR SO THEY SLOWLY BECOME "TIRED"–IT IS BEST TO FREEZE THEM IF YOU WANT TO KEEP THEM LONGER.

PIE CRUSTS

For pies with only a bottom crust (called pies because they're too deep to be a tart) the bottom crust may be shortcrust, puff or even filo pastry. A top crust may be shortcrust or puff pastry.

TWO-CRUST PIES Roll out two-thirds of the pastry, allowing a ¾-inch overhang on the dish. Drape the pastry over the rolling pin and gently transfer it to the dish, without stretching (if the pastry breaks, patch it up with a pastry scrap). Press the pastry evenly over base and side of the dish, pushing out any air pockets. Fill with prepared cooled filling. Roll out the remaining pastry about ¾ inch larger than the pie dish, moisten the outer edge of the base pastry, then drape the lid over the filling. Press the edges together firmly to seal. Trim off the overhanging pastry, angling the knife slightly under the rim as you turn the dish. Mark the pastry along the rim with a fork. Brush the top with an egg wash to glaze and help brown the pastry.

ONE-CRUST PIES If the filling of a lidded pie is not firm enough to mound in the center to support the top crust, place a greased pie funnel or an upside-down egg cup in the center of the pie. Roll out the pastry to about 1½ inches larger than the top of the dish; cut a ⅓-inch strip from around the edge of the rolled-out pastry, as wide as the rim of the pie dish, to make a collar for the rim. Moisten the rim of the dish with water and press the pastry collar onto it. Moisten the pastry collar and, using the rolling pin, lay the pastry lid over the pie filling, pressing together the pastry strip and lid, without stretching the pastry (over-stretching the pastry will make it shrink during baking). Trim away any excess using the method described for two-crust pies. A pie funnel–also called a pastry bird–will also help to vent the pie. Alternatively, cut a few slashes in the pastry to allow the steam to escape.

quiche lorraine

Named after the region straddling the French-German border, the classic quiche lorraine is thought to be the original quiche. The pastry used for the first quiches is thought to have been a bread dough, which morphed over the centuries to the crisp shortcrust identified with the open tart today. With its creamy custardy filling and buttery shell, it's still practically everyone's favorite.

1 medium brown onion,
   chopped finely
3 strips bacon, chopped finely
3 eggs
1¼ cups cream
½ cup milk
¾ cup coarsely grated
   gruyère cheese

pastry
1¾ cups all-purpose flour
10 tablespoons cold butter,
   chopped coarsely
1 egg yolk
2 teaspoons lemon juice
⅓ cup iced water, approximately

1 Make pastry.

2 Preheat oven to 400°F/350°F fan-forced.

3 Roll pastry between sheets of parchment paper large enough to line a deep 9-inch removable-bottom tart pan. Lift pastry into pan; gently press pastry around side. Trim edge, place pan on oven tray. Cover pastry with parchment paper; fill with dried beans or rice. Bake 10 minutes; remove paper and beans. Bake pastry another 10 minutes or until golden brown; cool.

4 Reduce oven to 350°F/325°F fan-forced.

5 Cook onion and bacon in heated oiled small frying pan until onion is soft; drain on absorbent paper, cool. Sprinkle bacon mixture over pastry case.

6 Whisk eggs in medium bowl; whisk in cream, milk and cheese.

7 Pour egg mixture into pastry case. Bake about 35 minutes or until filling is set. Stand 5 minutes before removing from pan.

pastry Sift flour into bowl; rub in butter. Add egg yolk, juice and enough water to make ingredients cling together. Knead gently on lightly floured surface until smooth; cover, refrigerate 30 minutes.

nutritional count per serving 51.8g total fat (35.4g saturated fat); 751 cal; 35.4g carbohydrate; 22.1g protein; 2g fiber

Use the rolling pin to gently lift the pastry dough into the pan. Press the pastry into the sides of the pan and trim the edges.

Place a sheet of baking paper in the pan and sprinkle in some dried beans to weigh it down and keep the pastry from rising.

Once the pastry case is cooked and cooled, sprinkle cooled bacon mixture over it and pour over the custard mix.

curried chicken pies

The filling for this recipe has only a mild curry flavor. If you want to make it hotter, either use a hot curry powder or increase the amount of chili powder.

3½-pound chicken
6 tablespoons butter
1 small leek, chopped finely
1 medium white onion,
    chopped finely
1 medium red pepper,
    chopped finely
2 stalks celery, trimmed,
    chopped finely

3 teaspoons curry powder
¼ teaspoon chili powder
¼ cup all-purpose flour
⅓ cup sour cream
½ cup finely chopped fresh
    flat-leaf parsley
2 sheets puff pastry
1 egg, beaten lightly

1 Place chicken in large saucepan, add enough water to just cover chicken; bring to a boil. Reduce heat; simmer, uncovered, 1 hour. Remove pan from heat; when cool enough to handle, remove chicken from stock. Reserve 1¾ cups of the stock for this recipe.

2 Preheat oven to 400°F/350°F fan-forced.

3 Remove skin and bones from chicken; chop chicken flesh roughly.

4 Heat butter in large frying pan, add leek, onion, pepper and celery; cook, stirring, until vegetables are soft.

5 Add curry powder and chili powder; cook, stirring, until fragrant. Stir in flour. Add reserved stock, stir over heat until mixture boils and thickens; reduce heat, simmer 1 minute, remove from heat. Stir in sour cream, chicken and parsley. Spoon mixture into six 1¼-cup ovenproof dishes.

6 Cut pastry into six rounds large enough to cover top of each dish. Lightly brush pastry with egg. Place pies on oven tray.

7 Bake pies 10 minutes. Reduce oven to 350°F/325°F fan-forced; bake further 15 minutes or until pastry is golden brown.

nutritional count per serving 52.8g total fat (25.4g saturated fat); 718 cal; 28.5g carbohydrate; 33.3g protein; 3g fiber

chicken and leek pie

2 cups chicken stock
1¼ pounds chicken breast filets
1 tablespoon olive oil
3 tablespoons butter
1 large leek, sliced thinly
2 stalks celery, trimmed,
    chopped finely
2 tablespoons all-purpose flour

2 teaspoons fresh thyme leaves
½ cup milk
1 cup cream
2 teaspoons wholegrain mustard
2 sheets refrigerated pie crust
1 sheet puff pastry
1 egg yolk

The part of the leek that is eaten is the thick white stem and the first, pale part of the green top. Because leeks are planted deep to keep them white, they harbor soil between the leaves and have to be washed thoroughly to remove it.

1 Bring stock to a boil in medium saucepan. Add chicken; return to a boil. Reduce heat; simmer, covered, about 10 minutes or until chicken is cooked. Remove from heat; stand chicken in poaching liquid 10 minutes. Remove chicken; chop coarsely. Reserve ⅓ cup of the poaching liquid; keep remainder for another use or discard.

2 Heat oil and butter in medium saucepan; cook leek and celery, stirring, until leek softens. Add flour and thyme; cook, stirring, 1 minute. Gradually stir in reserved poaching liquid, milk and cream; cook, stirring, until mixture boils and thickens. Stir in chicken and mustard. Cool 10 minutes.

3 Preheat oven to 400°F/350°F fan-forced. Oil 6-cup ovenproof dish.

4 Line base and side of dish with pie crust pastry, trim to fit; prick well all over with fork. Bake 10 minutes; cool 5 minutes.

5 Spoon chicken mixture into pastry case; place puff pastry over filling, trim to fit dish. Brush pastry with egg yolk; cut two small slits in top of pastry. Bake about 20 minutes or until browned lightly.

nutritional count per serving 56g total fat (30.1g saturated fat); 800 cal; 42.5g carbohydrate; 31.1g protein; 3.6g fiber

farmhouse chicken pie

PREP + COOK TIME 1 HOUR 15 MINS • SERVES 6

4 tablespoons butter
1 medium leek, sliced thickly
⅓ cup all-purpose flour
¾ cup milk
1 cup chicken stock
3 cups coarsely chopped
   cooked chicken
1 cup chopped broccoli

1 small red pepper, chopped finely
10-ounce can corn kernels, drained
¼ cup coarsely chopped fresh
   flat-leaf parsley
2 sheets puff pastry
1 egg

1 Melt butter in medium saucepan; cook leek, stirring, about 1 minute or until leek is soft. Add flour; cook, stirring, until mixture bubbles. Remove from heat, gradually stir in milk and stock; cook, stirring, over heat until mixture boils and thickens. Remove from heat; stir in chicken, broccoli, pepper, corn and parsley.

2 Preheat oven to 400°F/350°F fan-forced.

3 Spoon filling into 9-inch pie dish. Cut 1-inch wide strips from one sheet of pastry and place them around the lip of dish. Brush strips lightly with egg. Place second sheet of pastry over filling and lip to cover dish. Trim edge, scallop edge firmly to seal, decorate with pastry scraps, if desired. Brush top of pastry with egg.

4 Bake pie about 10 minutes; reduce oven to 350°F/325°F fan-forced, bake another 20 minutes or until pastry is brown.

nutritional count per serving 29.4g total fat (9.1g saturated fat); 548 cal; 37.3g carbohydrate; 29.3g protein; 4.2g fiber

chunky beef and vegetable pie

PREP + COOK TIME 2 HOURS 40 MINS • SERVES 8

You may choose not to buy a special pie dish or dishes, but to use ramekins, an ovenproof dish, a pudding mold, a soufflé dish, a cake pan or even a baking dish for your pies. The purpose of the wide rim on a classic pie dish is to hold an extended double crust, fluted or decoratively marked in some way to make the pie look handsome and impressive.

1 tablespoon olive oil
3 pounds beef chuck, cut into
   1-inch pieces
4 tablespoons butter
1 medium brown onion, chopped
   finely
1 clove garlic, crushed
¼ cup all-purpose flour
1 cup dry white wine
3 cups hot beef stock
2 tablespoons tomato paste
2 stalks celery, trimmed,
   cut into 1-inch pieces

2 medium potatoes,
   cut into 1-inch pieces
1 large carrot,
   cut into 1-inch pieces
1 large zucchini,
   cut into 1-inch pieces
5 ounces mushrooms, quartered
1 cup frozen peas
½ cup finely chopped fresh
   flat-leaf parsley
2 sheets puff pastry
1 egg, beaten lightly

1 Heat oil in large saucepan; cook beef, in batches, until browned all over. Remove from pan.

2 Melt butter in same pan; cook onion and garlic, stirring, until onion softens. Add flour; cook, stirring, until mixture thickens and bubbles. Gradually stir in wine and stock; stir until mixture boils and thickens slightly.

3 Return beef to pan with paste, celery, potato and carrot; bring to a boil. Reduce heat; simmer, covered, 1 hour.

4 Add zucchini and mushrooms; simmer, uncovered, about 30 minutes or until beef is tender. Add peas; stir until heated through. Remove from heat; stir in parsley.

5 Preheat oven to 425°F/400°F fan-forced.

6 Divide warm beef mixture between two deep 10-inch pie dishes; brush outside edge of dishes with a little egg. Top each pie with a pastry sheet, pressing edges to seal. Trim pastry; brush pastry with egg.

7 Bake pies about 20 minutes or until browned.

nutritional count per serving 27.6g total fat (13.3g saturated fat); 577 cal; 28.6g carbohydrate; 46.4g protein; 4.9g fiber

Q&A

Sometimes when I make a pie, especially a large one, it sags in the middle. How can I prevent this?

The best way is by mounding the filling in the center of the pie dish–if the filling is not firm enough to mound (or too chunky), use a funnel, pie bird or upturned eggcup in the center of the dish and ease the pastry over that. A china pie bird looks the best, with its little head and open beak poking through a slit in the pastry, but they're not used often anymore and are hard to come by–look for them in antique shops and thrift stores.

crab, fennel and herb quiche

When you trim the fennel for slicing, put the leaves aside to be chopped later. We used lump crab meat from the fish market, but well-drained canned crab meat will work very well.

3 sheets refrigerated pie crust
1 tablespoon olive oil
1 medium fennel bulb, sliced
8 ounces crab meat
2 tablespoons finely chopped
    fennel fronds
2 tablespoons finely chopped
    fresh flat-leaf parsley

½ cup coarsely grated
    cheddar cheese
quiche filling
1¼ cups cream
¼ cup milk
3 eggs

1 Preheat oven to 400°F/350°F fan-forced. Oil 12-hole (⅓-cup) muffin pan.

2 Cut twelve 3½-inch rounds from pastry; press into pan holes.

3 Heat oil in large frying pan; cook fennel, stirring, about 5 minutes or until fennel softens and browns slightly. Divide fennel among pastry cases; top with combined crab, fronds, parsley and cheese.

4 Make quiche filling; pour into pastry cases.

5 Bake quiches about 25 minutes. Stand in pan 5 minutes before serving.

quiche filling Whisk ingredients in large pitcher.

nutritional count per quiche 27.1g total fat (15g saturated fat); 361 cal; 20.3g carbohydrate; 9g protein; 1.3g fiber

steak and kidney pie

The French name for puff pastry is mille-feuille, meaning a thousand leaves. It consists of hundreds of tissue-paper-thin layers of crisp pastry, which, when baked, separate and puff up to make a crisp, fragile pastry.

10 ounces beef kidneys
3 pounds beef chuck steak,
    chopped coarsely
2 medium brown onions,
    sliced thinly
1 cup beef stock

1 tablespoon soy sauce
¼ cup all-purpose flour
½ cup water
2 sheets puff pastry
1 egg, beaten lightly

1 Remove fat from kidneys; chop kidneys finely. Place kidneys, steak, onion, stock and sauce in large saucepan; simmer, covered, about 1 hour or until steak is tender.

2 Preheat oven to 400°F/350°F fan-forced.

3 Stir blended flour and water into beef mixture; stir until mixture boils and thickens. Transfer to 1½-quart ovenproof dish.

4 Cut pastry into 2½-inch rounds. Overlap rounds on beef mixture; brush with egg. Bake pie about 30 minutes or until browned.

nutritional count per serving 25.8g total fat (12.2g saturated fat); 609 cal; 27.2g carbohydrate; 65.9g protein; 1.6g fiber

[1] crab, fennel and herb quiche
[2] steak and kidney pie
[3] shepherd's pie [page 400]
[4] roasted vegetable tart
[page 400]

shepherd's pie

Shepherd's pie is traditionally made from cooked lamb (and any of the vegetables, too, leftover with the Sunday roast). A similar potato-topped pie, usually made with ground beef, is called cottage pie.

3 tablespoons butter

1 medium brown onion, chopped finely

1 medium carrot, chopped finely

½ teaspoon dried mixed herbs

4 cups finely chopped cooked lamb

¼ cup tomato paste

¼ cup tomato sauce

2 tablespoons Worcestershire sauce

2 cups beef stock

2 tablespoons all-purpose flour

⅓ cup water

potato topping

5 medium potatoes, chopped coarsely

4 tablespoons butter

¼ cup milk

1 Preheat oven to 400°F/350°F fan-forced. Oil shallow 2½-quart (10-cup) ovenproof dish.

2 Make potato topping.

3 Meanwhile, heat butter in large saucepan; cook onion and carrot, stirring, until tender. Add mixed herbs and lamb; cook, stirring, 2 minutes. Stir in paste, sauces and stock, then blended flour and water; stir over heat until mixture boils and thickens. Pour mixture into dish.

4 Drop heaped tablespoons of potato topping onto lamb mixture. Bake in oven about 20 minutes or until browned and heated through.

potato topping Boil, steam or microwave potato until tender; drain. Mash with butter and milk until smooth.

nutritional count per serving 36.2g total fat (20.2g saturated fat); 712 cal; 44.7g carbohydrate; 48.8g protein; 6g fiber

roasted vegetable tart

Garlic is easy to roast and has a more mellow taste than it does raw or fried. Make it and freeze it by the tablespoon wrapped tightly in plastic wrap. Roasted garlic beaten with softened butter adds a whole new dimension of flavor to mashed potato or steamed corn cobs.

6 tablespoons cold butter, chopped

1¼ cups all-purpose flour

½ cup grated parmesan cheese

1 egg yolk

1 tablespoon chopped fresh chives

3 teaspoons iced water

½ large butternut squash (1¼ pounds), chopped coarsely

10 baby red beets, trimmed

10 shallots, peeled

8 cloves garlic

2 tablespoons olive oil

roast garlic cream

1 tablespoon finely chopped fresh dill

¾ cup sour cream

2 tablespoons milk

1 Process butter, flour and cheese until butter is combined. Add egg yolk, chives and water, process until mixture just clings together. Wrap in plastic; refrigerate for 30 minutes.

2 Preheat oven to 400°F/350°F fan-forced. Combine squash, beets, shallots and garlic with oil in large baking dish; bake about 45 minutes or until tender.

3 Meanwhile, roll dough between parchment sheets until large enough to fit the base and sides of 4-inch x 13-inch rectangular tart pan. Lift pastry into pan, press into sides; trim edges. Place pan on oven tray; refrigerate 30 minutes.

4 Peel beets, wearing disposable gloves. Squeeze flesh from garlic skins; reserve garlic for roast garlic cream. Cover vegetables to keep warm.

5 Reduce oven to 350°F/325°F fan-forced. Line pastry with parchment paper; fill with dried beans or rice. Bake 15 minutes. Remove paper and beans; bake further 10 minutes or until browned and crisp.

6 Combine reserved garlic with all ingredients for roast garlic cream in small bowl.

7 Fill tart shell with roasted vegetables; serve warm with roast garlic cream.

nutritional count per serving 12.9g total fat (7.1g saturated fat); 186 cal; 12.9g carbohydrate; 4g protein; 1.7g fiber

fish mornay pies

PREP + COOK TIME 55 MINS • SERVES 4

Make these pies in advance for a dinner party, but do not broil. When your guests arrive, place the pies in a moderate oven for 20 to 25 minutes until heated through and lightly browned.

2½ cups milk
½ small brown onion
1 bay leaf
6 black peppercorns
4 x 6-ounce sea bass filets, skinned
3 large potatoes, chopped coarsely
1¼ pounds celeriac, chopped coarsely

1 egg yolk
½ cup finely grated parmesan cheese
¾ cup light cream
4 tablespoons butter
¼ cup all-purpose flour
2 tablespoons coarsely chopped fresh flat-leaf parsley

1 Place milk, onion, bay leaf and peppercorns in large saucepan; bring to a boil. Add fish, reduce heat; simmer, covered, about 5 minutes or until cooked through. Remove fish from pan; divide fish among four 1½-cup ovenproof dishes. Strain milk through sieve into medium pitcher. Discard solids; reserve milk.

2 Boil, steam or microwave potato and celeriac, separately, until tender; drain. Push potato and celeriac through sieve into large bowl; stir in yolk, cheese, ¼ cup of the cream and half of the butter until smooth. Cover to keep warm.

3 Meanwhile, melt remaining butter in medium saucepan; add flour, cook, stirring, about 3 minutes or until mixture bubbles and thickens slightly. Gradually stir in reserved milk and remaining cream; cook, stirring, until mixture boils and thickens. Stir in parsley.

4 Divide mornay mixture among dishes; cover each with potato mixture. Place pies on oven tray; place under hot grill until browned lightly.

nutritional count per serving 47.8g total fat (28.9g saturated fat); 832 cal; 42.8g carbohydrate; 53.9g protein; 8.7g fiber

Meat pies have variations in virtually every cuisine around the world, from Latin or South American empanadas, often filled with spicy chorizo sausage or seafood, to Jamaican beef patties stuffed with spicy ground beef, to Irish meat pies, richly filled with Stout beer, onions and bacon. They are a handy, quick, portable meal or snack; make extra, freeze them, and bake them individually as needed.

1½ cups all-purpose flour

1 stick cold butter, chopped coarsely

1 egg

1 tablespoon iced water, approximately

2 sheets puff pastry

1 egg, extra

beef filling

1 tablespoon vegetable oil

1 small brown onion, chopped finely

1¼ pounds ground beef

15-ounce can crushed tomatoes

2 tablespoons tomato paste

2 tablespoons Worcestershire sauce

¾ cup beef stock

1 Process flour and butter until crumbly. Add egg and enough of the water to make ingredients cling together. Knead pastry on floured surface until smooth. Cover; refrigerate 30 minutes.

2 Meanwhile, make beef filling.

3 Oil six ⅔-cup mini pie tins. Divide pastry into six portions; roll each between sheets of parchment paper until large enough to line tins. Lift pastry into tins, gently press over base and sides; trim edges. Refrigerate 30 minutes.

4 Cut six 4½-inch rounds from puff pastry; refrigerate until required.

5 Preheat oven to 400°F/350°F fan-forced.

6 Place pastry cases on oven tray; line pastry with parchment paper then fill with dried beans or rice. Bake 10 minutes. Remove paper and beans; bake an additional 5 minutes. Cool.

7 Fill pastry cases with beef filling; brush edges of pastry with extra egg. Top with puff pastry rounds; press edges to seal. Brush tops with egg. Cut steam holes in top of pies. Bake about 20 minutes or until pastry is golden. Serve pies with tomato sauce, if you like.

beef filling Heat oil in large saucepan; cook onion and beef, stirring, until beef is well browned. Stir in undrained tomatoes, paste, sauce and stock; bring to a boil. Reduce heat; simmer, uncovered, about 20 minutes or until thick. Cool.

nutritional count per pie 38.7g total fat (13.8g saturated fat); 688 cal; 52.4g carbohydrate; 31.2g protein; 3.5g fiber

Q&A

What's the best way to reheat a pie?

Pies are best reheated in a low oven. If you reheat them on too high a temperature, the pastry will burn before the filling heats. It's always best to thaw a frozen pie before reheating. The microwave oven does not reheat pies successfully–it makes the pastry become soggy. However, you can defrost a frozen pie in the microwave and then gently reheat it in the oven.

gruyère, leek and bacon tart

A firm, pale yellow, cow-milk cheese from the Fribourg state in Switzerland, gruyère is also produced in many regions of France. It has a sweet, nutty taste and is delicious eaten as is or used in cooking–try making macaroni and cheese with gruyère for a flavor sensation.

3 tablespoons butter
2 medium leeks, sliced thinly
2 strips bacon, chopped finely
2 sheets puff pastry
2 eggs

½ cup cream
1 teaspoon fresh thyme leaves
½ cup finely grated
   gruyère cheese

1 Preheat oven to 425°F/400°F fan-forced. Oil 9½-inch removable bottom tart pan; place pan on oven tray.

2 Melt butter in medium frying pan; cook leek, stirring occasionally, 15 minutes or until soft. Remove from pan. Cook bacon in same pan, stirring, until crisp; drain on absorbent paper.

3 Meanwhile, place one pastry sheet in tart pan; overlap with second sheet to form cross shape, trim away overlapping pastry. Prick pastry base with fork, line with parchment paper; fill with dried beans or rice. Bake 20 minutes. Remove paper and beans; cool pastry case. Reduce oven to 400°F/350°F fan-forced.

4 Whisk eggs, cream and thyme in small bowl.

5 Spread leek into pastry case; top with bacon. Pour in egg mixture; sprinkle with cheese. Bake tart about 20 minutes or until filling sets. Cool 10 minutes before serving.

nutritional count per serving 34.8g total fat (20.2g saturated fat); 466 cal; 24.5g carbohydrate; 14.4g protein; 2.8g fiber

spanakopita

Filo pastry consists of paper-thin sheets of raw pastry, which are used by brushing with oil or melted butter and stacking one on another, then cutting or folding as the recipe directs. It makes a distinctly layered, crackling-crisp, airy crust or wrapping for small pastries such as spanakopita.

3 pounds Swiss chard, trimmed
1 tablespoon olive oil
1 medium brown onion,
   chopped finely
2 cloves garlic, crushed
1 teaspoon ground nutmeg
7 ounces feta cheese, crumbled
1 tablespoon finely grated lemon rind
¼ cup chopped fresh mint leaves

¼ cup chopped fresh flat-leaf parsley
¼ cup chopped fresh dill
4 green onions, chopped finely
16 sheets filo pastry
1 stick butter, melted
2 teaspoons sesame seeds

1 Boil, steam or microwave Swiss chard until just wilted; drain. Squeeze out excess moisture; drain on absorbent paper. Chop coarsely; spread out on absorbent paper.

2 Heat oil in small frying pan; cook onion and garlic, stirring, until onion is soft. Add nutmeg; cook, stirring, until fragrant. Combine onion mixture and chard in large bowl with feta, rind, herbs and green onion.

3 Preheat oven to 350°F/325°F fan-forced.

4 Brush one sheet of filo with butter; fold lengthwise into thirds, brushing with butter between each fold. Place rounded tablespoon of chard mixture at the bottom of one narrow edge of folded filo sheet, leaving a border. Fold opposite corner of filo diagonally across the filling to form large triangle; continue folding to end of filo sheet, retaining triangular shape. Place on oiled oven tray, seam-side down; repeat with remaining ingredients.

5 Brush spanakopita with remaining butter; sprinkle with sesame seeds. Bake about 15 minutes or until browned lightly.

nutritional count per spanakopita 11.1g total fat (6.4g saturated fat); 165 cal; 11g carbohydrate; 4.7g protein; 1.5g fiber

beef pasties

PREP + COOK TIME 1 HOUR 15 MINS • MAKES 16

1 pound white potatoes, peeled, chopped coarsely
1 tablespoon olive oil
1 small brown onion, chopped finely
2 cloves garlic, crushed
1 medium carrot, chopped finely
1 stalk celery, trimmed, chopped finely

12 ounces ground beef
⅓ cup dry red wine
1 cup beef stock
¼ cup tomato paste
½ cup frozen peas
8 sheets puff pastry, thawed
1 egg, beaten lightly

1 Boil, steam or microwave potato until tender; drain. Mash in medium bowl.

2 Meanwhile, heat oil in medium saucepan; cook onion and garlic, stirring, until onion softens. Add carrot and celery; cook, stirring, until vegetables are tender. Add beef; cook, stirring, until it changes color.

3 Stir in wine, stock, paste and peas; cook, uncovered, about 5 minutes or until mixture thickens slightly. Stir potato into beef mixture; cool 10 minutes.

4 Preheat oven to 350°F/325°F fan-forced. Oil two oven trays.

5 Cut two 5½-inch rounds from each pastry sheet. Spoon filling evenly in center of each round. Brush edge of pastry with egg; fold over to enclose filling, pressing around edge with fork to seal. Place pasties on oven trays.

6 Bake pasties about 30 minutes or until browned lightly.

nutritional count per pasty 22g total fat (11.1g saturated fat); 389 cal; 34.9g carbohydrate; 10.9g protein; 2.3g fiber

Diced lamb can be bought from supermarkets and butchers. If you prefer to dice the lamb yourself, shoulder meat is very good. Ask the butcher to bone the shoulder for you, and discard as much fat as possible.

2 tablespoons olive oil
14 ounces diced lamb
4 baby onions, quartered
1 tablespoon all-purpose flour
¼ cup dry red wine
¾ cup beef stock
1 tablespoon tomato paste
1 tablespoon fresh rosemary leaves

2 sheets puff pastry
1 egg, beaten lightly
4 fresh rosemary sprigs
2 tablespoons butter
2½ cups frozen peas
1 tablespoon lemon juice
½ cup water

1 Heat half of the oil in large saucepan; cook lamb, in batches, uncovered, until browned all over. Heat remaining oil in same pan; cook onion, stirring, until soft. Add flour; cook, stirring, until mixture bubbles and thickens. Gradually add wine, stock, paste and rosemary leaves; stir until mixture boils and thickens. Stir in lamb; cool 10 minutes.

2 Preheat oven to 400°F/350°F fan-forced. Oil four holes of 6-hole (¾-cup) jumbo muffin pan.

3 Cut two 5-inch rounds from opposite corners of each pastry sheet; cut two 3½-inch rounds from remaining corners of each sheet. Place larger rounds in prepared holes to cover bases and sides; trim any excess pastry, prick bases with fork.

4 Spoon lamb mixture into pastry cases; brush around edges with a little egg. Top pies with smaller rounds; gently press around edges to seal. Brush pies with remaining egg; press one rosemary sprig into top of each pie.

5 Bake pies about 15 minutes or until browned lightly. Stand 5 minutes in pan before serving.

6 Meanwhile, heat butter in medium saucepan; cook peas, juice and the water, uncovered, stirring occasionally, about 5 minutes or until peas are just tender.

nutritional count per serving 42.7g total fat (18.6g saturated fat); 686 cal; 40.4g carbohydrate; 33.1g protein; 6.1g fiber

Q&A

Which pies do you suggest I take on a picnic?

The obvious picnic pies are quiches–keep them in the dish they were cooked in and wrap them loosely in foil. That way they'll travel well and stay warm. Individual meat, fish or vegetable pies are also great for picnics and apple turnovers, cooked the day before, heated in the oven in the morning and wrapped in foil make the perfect road trip breakfast with a thermos of coffee.

CURRIES

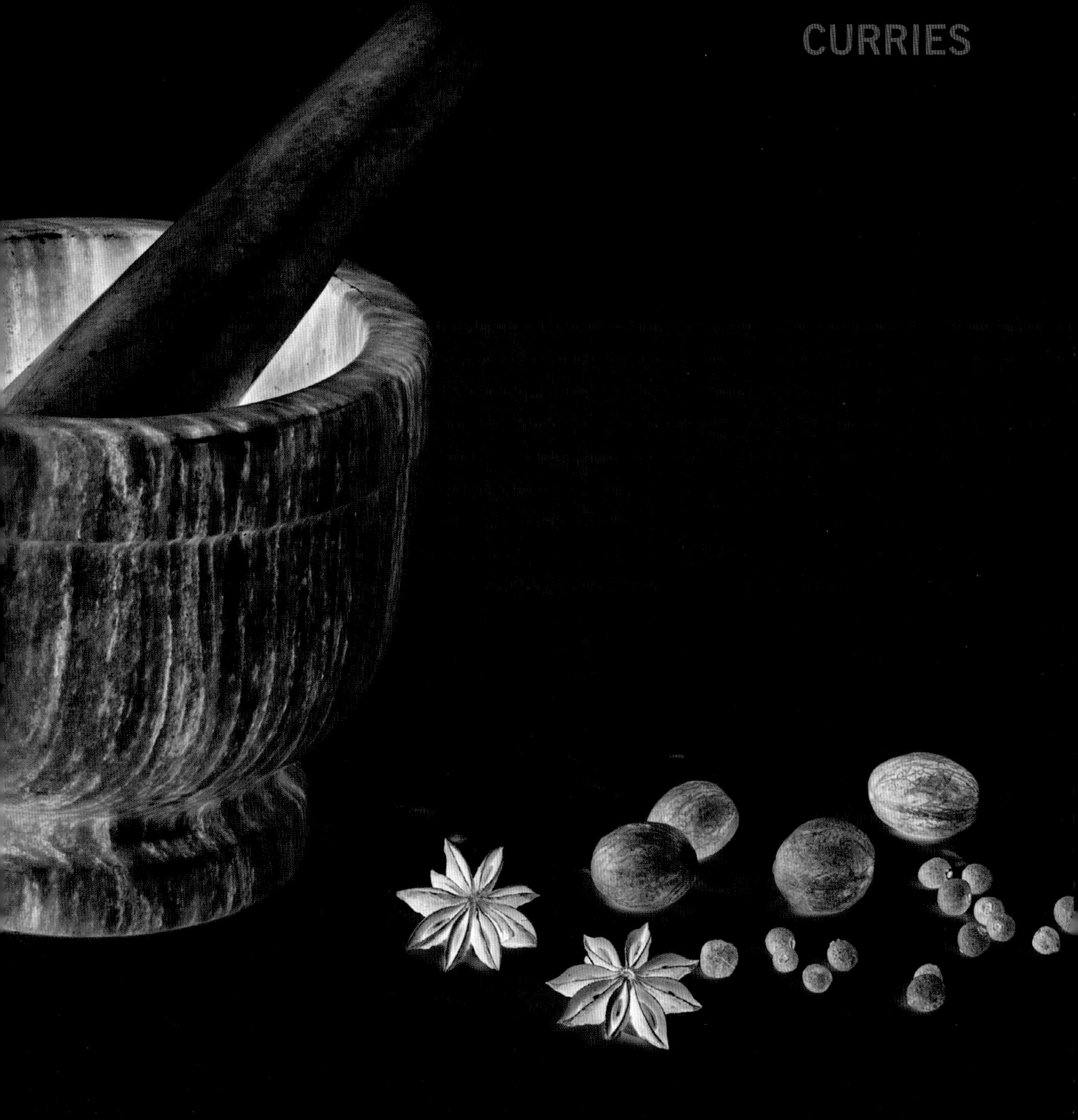

Curries

Yes, curry recipes usually involve a long list of exotic ingredients. But that doesn't mean they are hard to make—they're just more of an adventure. And once you've stocked your pantry with all those fragrant, earthy-toned spices, you'll want to use them again and again.

The word curry is derived from a Tamil (southern Indian) word literally meaning "gravy", and is used to describe a large variety of savory, stew-like dishes flavored with herbs and/or spices. While Indian and Thai curries are the most familiar to us, curries also feature strongly in the cuisines of Pakistan, Sri Lanka, Africa, Southeast Asia (Vietnam, Malaysia, Indonesia, Cambodia, Burma) and the Pacific Islands.

While all curries are based on curry pastes—aromatic mixtures of fresh or dried herbs and spices—the content of those pastes is very different on the Indian subcontinent from those made in Southeast Asia. Indian curry pastes are generally very powdery, made from ground dried spices and few, if any, herbs.

Thai curry pastes on the other hand—and those of Indonesia, Malaysia, Cambodia and Vietnam—are moist blends of mainly fresh herbs and spices. The dry, aromatic spices that feature so prominently in Indian curries are used much more sparingly in Thai cooking.

Indian curries are generally cooked for longer than their Thai counterparts and tend to be thicker and more stew-like while Thai curries are more soup-like. Indian curries generally have deeper, smokier flavors while Thai curries are often sweeter. All of them are delicious and there are literally hundreds of different curry recipes to choose from, featuring meat, poultry, seafood and vegetables. Explore them all.

GRINDING SPICES

Many Asian chefs and home cooks insist that, for the very best results, you need to grind your own spices from whole seeds just before using them. And certainly, if you have the time, grinding your spices in a mortar and pestle is one of those rewarding, back-to-basics activities that brings you closer to the food you're making—and it's stimulating for the olfactory nerves, too, as the aromas of all the spices and herbs are released.

But this is not always possible, so if you need to purchase your curry powders and spices then try to source them from an Asian grocery store (preferably one where the stock is continually renewed) or failing that, from the spice section at your supermarket. Your ground spices and curry powders must be kept fresh in airtight containers. Older stale spices lose their taste, will add nothing to your dish, and will leave you feeling disappointed with the result.

THAI CURRIES	INDIAN CURRIES

THAI CURRIES

IN THAILAND, CURRY IS CALLED "GAENG PHET" (LITERALLY, "HOT LIQUID") AND REFERS TO SOUPS AND CURRIES. THAI CURRIES USUALLY CONSIST OF CURRY PASTE, COCONUT MILK OR WATER, AND MEAT AND VEGETABLES. THERE ARE DOZENS OF VARIATIONS DEPENDING ON THE TYPE OF CURRY PASTE, LIQUID AND COMBINATION OF MEATS, HERBS, VEGETABLES AND FRUITS USED.

The key ingredients in most Thai curry pastes are "wet" (produced from fresh herbs) and fragrant: fresh chilies, lemon grass, galangal, garlic, shallot, kaffir lime, coriander and shrimp paste.

Thai curries use more fresh herbs and garlic and fewer dry spices than Indian curries. In fact, there are only two curry dishes in Thailand that are based mainly on dried herbs and spices, rather then fresh ones: the popular Massaman and Panang curries. When spices are used, they are most likely to be hot chili peppers, cumin seeds, coriander seeds and/or turmeric.

Thai curries are most commonly categorized by their color–red, green and yellow– which is determined by the curry paste.
GREEN CURRY Usually considered the hottest (spiciest) of Thai curries, green curry is based on a curry paste made from fresh green chilies, shallots, lemon grass, white pepper, coriander root, garlic, kaffir lime rind and shrimp paste with sweet basil leaves, round green eggplant and kaffir lime leaves adding to the attractive green color of the final curry dish.
RED CURRY While it looks more fiery than green curry, red curry is usually milder and made with dried long red chilies, garlic, fresh lemon grass, fresh turmeric and shrimp paste and any of the following: coriander, cumin, shallots, kaffir lime rind and galangal.
YELLOW CURRY Yellow curry paste is a more mellow sweet-spicy blend based on turmeric and curry powder with coriander, cumin, lemon grass, galangal, shrimp paste and dry red chilies to create a curry that is a lovely rich golden color.

INDIAN CURRIES

SPICES ARE THE HEART AND SOUL OF ALL INDIAN CURRY RECIPES. A BASIC CURRY BEGINS WITH MAKING A FRAGRANT MIXTURE OF ONIONS, GARLIC AND SPICES IN A BIG POT, TO WHICH YOU ADD WATER, STOCK OR COCONUT MILK (OR A COMBINATION OF THESE) AND THEN THE CHICKEN, MEAT AND/ OR VEGETABLES.

A huge variety of spices can be used, but a few crucial star performers in Indian curries are: cumin seeds, coriander seeds, fenugreek, turmeric, and cardamom. These usually form the basic ingredients for an Indian curry.

Other aromatic ingredients such as asafoetida, allspice, garam masala (a mixed blend), clove, cinnamon, nutmeg, green or red chili, aniseed and black pepper are also prominent in Indian recipes and might be included for specific types of curry powder. Onion, ginger and garlic are essential ingredients in any curry, but Indian dishes typically make very little use of herbs. The most frequent is coriander leaf, and this is always used fresh, never dried. In fact, coriander leaves are usually added towards the end of cooking and most often only as a garnish.

To thicken a curry sauce, Indian cooking often includes pureed vegetables, yogurt, cream, coconut milk or ground nuts such as almonds and pistachios to give it body.

There is a huge range of Indian curries: every region of India has its own dishes with their own distinct flavors and spice combinations.

Indian curries don't have to be hot: they range from the very mild to only-for-the-brave (the famous Vindaloo, for example). If you are a beginner curry eater, start with the mild options and work your way up from there.

green curry paste

These four curry paste recipes make 1 cup. Use the amount of paste required in each curry recipe, then freeze the rest, in one tablespoon batches, for up to 3 months.

2 teaspoons ground coriander

2 teaspoons ground cumin

10 long green chilies, chopped coarsely

10 small green chilies, chopped coarsely

1 teaspoon shrimp paste

1 clove garlic, quartered

4 green onions, chopped coarsely

4-inch stick fresh lemon grass, chopped finely

½-inch piece fresh galangal, peeled, chopped finely

¼ cup coarsely chopped fresh coriander root and stem mixture

1 tablespoon peanut oil

1 Dry-fry ground coriander and cumin in small frying pan over medium heat, stirring until fragrant.

2 Blend or process spices with chilies, paste, garlic, onion, lemon grass, galangal and coriander mixture until mixture forms a paste.

3 Add oil to paste; continue to blend until smooth.

nutritional count per tablespoon 1.6g total fat (0.3g saturated fat); 16 cal; 0.3g carbohydrate; 0.2g protein; 0.2g fiber

red curry paste

Commercial curry pastes can't compare to the amazing blend of flavors created by homemade ones; however, they do save time. Jars of Thai and Indian curry pastes are available in most supermarkets, but you may have to adjust the amounts used to those called for in our recipes.

20 dried long red chilies

1 teaspoon ground coriander

2 teaspoons ground cumin

1 teaspoon hot paprika

2 teaspoons finely chopped peeled fresh ginger

3 large cloves garlic, quartered

1 medium red onion, chopped coarsely

2 x 4-inch sticks fresh lemon grass, sliced thinly

1 fresh kaffir lime leaf, sliced thinly

2 tablespoons coarsely chopped fresh coriander root and stem mixture

2 teaspoons shrimp paste

1 tablespoon peanut oil

1 Place whole chilies in small heatproof bowl, cover with boiling water; stand 15 minutes, drain.

2 Meanwhile, dry-fry ground coriander, cumin and paprika in small frying pan over medium heat until fragrant.

3 Blend or process chilies and spices with ginger, garlic, onion, lemon grass, lime leaf, coriander mixture and paste until mixture forms a paste.

4 Add oil to paste; continue to blend until smooth.

nutritional count per tablespoon 1.6g total fat (0.3g saturated fat); 22 cal; 1.2g carbohydrate; 0.5g protein; 0.5g fiber

panang curry paste

PREP + COOK TIME 20 MINS (+ STANDING) • MAKES 1 CUP

25 dried long red chilies
1 teaspoon ground coriander
2 teaspoons ground cumin
2 cloves garlic, quartered
8 green onions, chopped coarsely
2 x 4-inch sticks fresh lemon grass,
   sliced thinly

¾-inch piece fresh galangal,
   chopped finely
2 teaspoons shrimp paste
½ cup roasted unsalted peanuts
2 tablespoons peanut oil

1 Place chilies in small heatproof bowl, cover with boiling water; stand 15 minutes, drain.

2 Meanwhile, dry-fry ground coriander and cumin in small frying pan over medium heat, stirring until fragrant.

3 Blend or process chilies and spices with remaining ingredients until mixture forms a paste.

nutritional count per tablespoon 6.1g total fat (0.9g saturated fat); 69 cal; 1.3g carbohydrate; 1.9g protein; 0.9g fiber

massaman curry paste

PREP + COOK TIME 30 MINS • MAKES 1 CUP

20 dried red chilies
1 teaspoon ground coriander
2 teaspoons ground cumin
2 teaspoons ground cinnamon
½ teaspoon ground cardamom
½ teaspoon ground clove
5 cloves garlic, quartered
1 large brown onion,
   chopped coarsely

2 x 4-inch sticks fresh lemon grass,
   sliced thinly
3 fresh kaffir lime leaves,
   sliced thinly
1½-inch piece fresh ginger,
   chopped coarsely
2 teaspoons shrimp paste
1 tablespoon peanut oil

1 Place chilies in small heatproof bowl, cover with boiling water; stand 15 minutes. Drain; reserve chilies.

2 Meanwhile, dry-fry ground coriander, cumin, cinnamon, cardamom and clove in small frying pan, stirring, until fragrant.

3 Preheat oven to 325°F/320°F fan-forced.

4 Place chilies and roasted spices in small shallow baking dish with remaining ingredients. Roast, uncovered, in oven 15 minutes.

5 Blend or process roasted mixture until smooth.

nutritional count per tablespoon 6.7g total fat (1.2g saturated fat); 90 cal; 4.5g carbohydrate; 2.1g protein; 2.4g fiber

butter chicken

For a great pie filling, add 2 large cooked potatoes, chopped, and 3 ounces baby spinach leaves to the butter chicken. Spoon the filling into a deep pie dish and top with a sheet of puff pastry. Brush with beaten egg, snip two air holes in the top, and bake in a hot oven for 25 minutes or until the pastry is golden.

1 cup unsalted raw cashews
2 teaspoons garam masala
2 teaspoons ground coriander
½ teaspoon chili powder
3 cloves garlic, chopped coarsely
1½-inch piece fresh ginger, peeled, grated
2 tablespoons white vinegar
⅓ cup tomato paste
½ cup yogurt

2 pounds chicken thigh filets, halved
5 tablespoons butter
1 large brown onion, chopped finely
1 cinnamon stick
4 cardamom pods, bruised
1 teaspoon hot paprika
14-ounce can tomato puree
¾ cup chicken stock
¾ cup cream

1 Dry-fry nuts in small frying pan, stirring, until nearly brown. Add garam masala, coriander and chili, continue stirring, until nuts are browned lightly.

2 Blend or process nut mixture with garlic, ginger, vinegar, paste and half the yogurt until mixture forms a paste. Transfer to large bowl, stir in remaining yogurt and chicken. Cover; refrigerate 3 hours or overnight.

3 Melt butter in large saucepan; cook onion, cinnamon and cardamom, stirring, until onion is browned lightly. Add chicken mixture; cook, stirring, 10 minutes.

4 Stir in paprika, puree and stock; simmer, uncovered, 45 minutes, stirring occasionally.

5 Discard cinnamon and cardamom. Add cream; simmer, uncovered, 5 minutes.

nutritional count per serving 74g total fat (33.3g saturated fat); 990 cal; 20.8g carbohydrate; 59.3g protein; 6.5g fiber

Cardamom pods must be bruised (crushing with the side of a knife is the easiest way) to release their fragrance and warm subtle taste.

Fry the cashews in a small dry frying pan, shaking the pan and stirring until almost brown. Watch constantly—a moment's inattention here and the nuts will burn.

Blend or process the spiced nuts with ginger, garlic, vinegar, tomato paste and yogurt until smooth. Transfer the paste to a large bowl.

Know your spices

The trick with spices is to buy them fresh and never keep them for more than a year. Spices get stale and lose their sparkle, so buy them in small quantities and store them in airtight containers. Spices such as cinnamon, nutmeg and vanilla beans have the strongest and most intense flavor if bought whole.

RAS EL HANOUT
The name means "top of the shop" and the mixture varies from one merchant to another, but is always subtly savory with a touch of heat. Excellent with lamb or chicken.

FENUGREEK
The seeds of a herb of the pea family. Used in curry powder, good with seafood and in chutneys. The aroma of fenugreek is known for its characteristic of masking unpleasant odors.

SAFFRON
Expensive because it consists of the hand-gathered stigmas from a crocus flower. Buy it only from a reputable source. It colors food golden and has a bittersweet almondy taste.

STAR ANISE
The dried, star-shaped fruit of a small Asian tree with a pungent liquorice/clove/cinnamon flavor. Used whole or ground, it is the main spice in Chinese five-spice. Use sparingly with pork or duck or in a fruit compote.

ASAFOETIDA
The dried and ground resin of a giant fennel, notorious for its penetrating "rotten" smell but this is toned down in cooking. Its pungent flavor suggests fermented garlic. Use this spice sparingly with lentils and in fish and vegetable curries.

BAHARAT
A spice blend used throughout the Middle East. It typically includes ground paprika, black pepper, cumin, coriander, cassia, cloves, cardamom and nutmeg. Rub on fish, beef or lamb before cooking.

Q&A

Many curry recipes ask for the spice paste to be fried for several minutes "or until fragrant". What does this mean exactly and why do you have to do it?

You fry a spice paste to rid it of its "raw" taste. It needs about 5 minutes frying over gentle heat to develop a deeper, richer flavor and a noticeable "fragrance". If you use a curry paste, either homemade or purchased, without giving it this preliminary frying, you'll really notice the difference in taste.

SUMAC
A purple-red spice ground from the berries of a small Mediterranean tree. Adds a tart, lemony flavor to dips and dressings and goes well with meat, chicken, fish, tomato and avocado.

GARAM MASALA
The name simply means "spice blend" and the mixture varies, but is always savory with a touch of pepper bite. Used as a seasoning in Indian cooking and is sometimes sprinkled over the finished dish.

HARISSA
A fiery Tunisian paste made by pounding chili with spices, garlic and mint. Used to season meats such as kebabs and traditionally placed on the table as an all-purpose condiment.

KALONJI
Also called nigella, these are the seeds of a plant related to buttercups. The flavor is sharp/metallic (reduced by cooking), nutty, peppery. Used in or on Turkish and Indian breads, and in the Indian spice mix panch phora.

SICHUAN PEPPERCORNS
No relation to other peppercorns, Sichuan (also "Szechuan") peppercorns are the dried berries of a small tree native to the Sichuan province of south-west China, where highly spiced foods are much appreciated. They smell and taste peppery/lemony.

ZA'ATAR
A blend of roasted dried oregano, marjoram, thyme, sumac and sesame seeds found in the Lebanese and Syrian kitchen. Traditionally sprinkled on toast spread with ricotta, it's great tossed with roasted potato wedges too.

pork and vegetable vindaloo

This is often the hottest dish on a restaurant menu. To counteract the heat or "chili burn", drink milk or a lassi (yogurt drink).

2 teaspoons cumin seeds
2 teaspoons garam masala
1 teaspoon ground cinnamon
2 cloves garlic, quartered
4 fresh small red Thai chilies, chopped coarsely
¾-inch piece fresh ginger, peeled, sliced thinly
1 large brown onion, chopped coarsely
2 tablespoons white vinegar

2 tablespoons vegetable oil
2 pounds boneless pork shoulder, cut into ¾-inch pieces
2 cups beef stock
2 medium potatoes, cut into ¾-inch pieces
2 medium carrots, cut into ¾-inch pieces
5 ounces green beans, trimmed, chopped coarsely

1 Dry-fry spices in small frying pan, stirring, until fragrant; cool.

2 Blend or process spices, garlic, chili, ginger, onion and vinegar until mixture forms a smooth paste.

3 Heat half the oil in large saucepan; cook pork, in batches, until browned.

4 Heat remaining oil in same pan; cook paste, stirring, 5 minutes. Return pork to pan with stock; bring to a boil. Reduce heat; simmer, covered, 30 minutes. Add potato, carrot and beans; simmer, uncovered, about 30 minutes or until pork is tender and sauce thickens slightly.

nutritional count per serving 19.9g total fat (5.4g saturated fat); 398 cal; 13.6g carbohydrate; 39.3g protein; 3.8g fiber

tandoori chicken

The tandoori curry paste is spicy but not hot. Here it is mixed with yogurt and used as a marinade. Classically, it would then be baked on the wall of a tandoor, a round clay oven–it can be baked in an ordinary hot oven or, better still, baked and then finished on a barbecue.

7 ounces yogurt
1 medium brown onion, chopped coarsely
2 tablespoons lemon juice
1 tablespoon vegetable oil
¾-inch piece fresh ginger, grated
3 cloves garlic, crushed

2 teaspoons chili powder
1 teaspoon garam masala
1 teaspoon ground cumin
½ teaspoon red food coloring
3 pounds chicken pieces
1 cup loosely packed fresh coriander leaves

1 Blend or process yogurt, onion, juice, oil, ginger, garlic, spices and coloring until smooth. Combine paste with chicken in large bowl. Cover; refrigerate overnight.

2 Remove chicken from marinade; cook, covered, on heated oiled grill pan (or grill or barbecue) until cooked through. Serve chicken sprinkled with coriander leaves and with lemon wedges.

nutritional count per serving 26.5g total fat (7.7g saturated fat); 601 cal; 5.9g carbohydrate; 84g protein; 1.3g fiber

[opposite] pork and vegetable vindaloo

easy lamb curry

2 cloves garlic, crushed
2 long green chilies, chopped
2-inch piece fresh ginger,
  peeled, chopped
2 tablespoons vegetable oil or ghee
2 medium brown onions,
  chopped coarsely
1½ teaspoons turmeric

1 teaspoon ground cumin
3 teaspoons ground coriander
1 teaspoon ground chili powder
2 pounds diced lamb shoulder
1 teaspoon salt
14-ounce can peeled tomatoes
¼ cup coconut cream

1 Using a mortar and pestle (or small processor), pound garlic, chili and ginger to form a paste.

2 Heat oil or ghee in large saucepan; cook onion, stirring, about 10 minutes or until browned lightly. Add garlic paste; cook, stirring, over low heat, 3 minutes or until fragrant but not browned.

3 Blend spices with a little water to make a smooth paste, add to pan; cook, stirring, 5 minutes.

4 Add lamb to pan, in batches, cooking until browned. Return all lamb to pan with salt. Add undrained tomatoes; mix well.

5 Cook lamb curry, covered, stirring occasionally, about 50 minutes or until lamb is tender. Stir in coconut cream in the last 20 minutes of cooking time.

nutritional count per serving 26.9g total fat (10.6g saturated fat); 491 cal; 8.4g carbohydrate; 52.4g protein; 3g fiber

fish curry with lime and coconut

Coriander, also known as cilantro or Chinese parsley, is a bright-green-leafed herb with a pungent flavor. It is often stirred into or sprinkled over a dish just before serving for maximum impact. The stems and roots of coriander are also used in Thai cooking; wash well before chopping.

6 fresh small red Thai chilies,
  chopped coarsely
2 cloves garlic, quartered
10 shallots, chopped coarsely
4-inch stick fresh lemon grass,
  chopped coarsely
2-inch piece fresh galangal,
  peeled, quartered
¼ cup coarsely chopped fresh
  coriander root and stem mixture

¼ teaspoon ground turmeric
1 tablespoon peanut oil
2 x 14-ounce cans coconut milk
2 tablespoons fish sauce
4 fresh kaffir lime leaves, shredded
1 tablespoon lime juice
4 x 7-ounce kingfish or bass filets
½ cup loosely packed fresh
  coriander leaves

1 Blend or process chili, garlic, shallot, lemon grass, galangal, coriander root and stem mixture, turmeric and oil until mixture forms a smooth paste.

2 Cook paste in large frying pan, stirring, over medium heat, about 3 minutes or until fragrant. Add coconut milk, sauce and lime leaves; bring to a boil. Reduce heat; simmer, uncovered, about 15 minutes or until thickened slightly. Stir in juice.

3 Add fish to pan; simmer, uncovered, about 10 minutes or until cooked. Serve curry sprinkled with coriander leaves.

nutritional count per serving 50.6g total fat (38.5g saturated fat); 686 cal; 10.6g carbohydrate; 45.9g protein; 4.9g fiber

pork jungle curry

PREP + COOK TIME 40 MINS • SERVES 4

This fiery curry got its name from the originating cooks who, traveling through the jungle in Thailand's central plains, had to make do with what was available there. It has remained popular because it's easy to prepare and has such strong links to Thai history.

2 tablespoons peanut oil

¼ cup red curry paste (see page 412)

1½ pounds pork filet, sliced thinly

⅓ cup firmly packed fresh Thai basil leaves

1½ ounces pickled ginger, sliced thinly

5 ounces Thai eggplants, chopped coarsely

1 medium carrot, sliced thinly

4 ounces snake beans, chopped coarsely

8-ounce can bamboo shoots, rinsed, drained

2 x 2-inch stems pickled green peppercorns

2 fresh kaffir lime leaves, torn

1 quart vegetable stock

4 fresh small red Thai chilies, chopped coarsely

1 Place oil and curry paste in large saucepan; stir over heat until fragrant.

2 Add pork; cook, stirring, about 5 minutes or until browned all over.

3 Reserve about four large whole basil leaves for garnish. Add remaining basil leaves, ginger, eggplant, carrot, beans, bamboo shoots, peppercorns, lime leaves and stock to pan; bring to a boil. Reduce heat; simmer, uncovered, about 10 minutes or until vegetables are tender. Stir in chili.

4 Place curry in serving bowl; sprinkle with reserved Thai basil leaves.

nutritional count per serving 31.2g total fat (7.8g saturated fat); 496 cal; 6.5g carbohydrate; 45.3g protein; 5g fiber

beef massaman curry

Massaman curry is a staple in the Muslim communities in the south of Thailand close to the Malaysian border. It is a fragrant, hot curry with an acid note, showing the influence of traders who came from further west to that coast.

2 pounds skirt steak, cut into
    1-inch pieces
2 cups beef stock
5 cardamom pods, bruised
¼ teaspoon ground clove
2 star anise
1 tablespoon grated palm sugar
2 tablespoons fish sauce
2 tablespoons tamarind concentrate

2 x 14-ounce cans coconut milk
2 tablespoons massaman curry paste
    (see page 413)
8 baby brown onions, halved
1 medium sweet potato,
    chopped coarsely
¼ cup coarsely chopped roasted
    unsalted peanuts
2 green onions, sliced thinly

1 Place beef, 1½ cups of the stock, cardamom, clove, star anise, sugar, sauce, 1 tablespoon of the tamarind and half of the coconut milk in large saucepan; simmer, uncovered, about 1½ hours or until beef is almost tender.

2 Strain beef over large bowl; reserve braising liquid, discard solids. Cover beef to keep warm.

3 Cook curry paste in same pan, stirring, until fragrant. Add remaining coconut milk, tamarind and stock; bring to a boil. Cook, stirring, about 1 minute or until mixture is smooth. Return beef to pan with brown onion, sweet potato and 1 cup of the reserved braising liquid; simmer, uncovered, about 30 minutes or until beef and vegetables are tender.

4 Stir nuts and green onion into curry off the heat.

nutritional count per serving 52.7g total fat (39.5g saturated fat); 872 cal; 29.2g carbohydrate; 67.4g protein; 7.2g fiber

Place the beef in a large saucepan with the coconut milk and spices, and cook over low heat for about 1½ hours.

Strain the cooked beef over a bowl. Discard spices but reserve the cooking liquid.

Fry the massaman curry paste, stirring, for about 5 minutes until it becomes deliciously fragrant.

rogan josh

Rogan josh, traditionally made with lamb, is an Indian tomato-based curry, and literally means "meat in spicy red sauce". It is slightly milder than many curries due in equal part to the fairly large amount of tomato used and the very little chili found in the paste.

2 teaspoons ground cardamom
2 teaspoons ground cumin
2 teaspoons ground coriander
2 pounds boned leg of lamb, trimmed, diced into 1-inch pieces
2 tablespoons butter
2 tablespoons vegetable oil
2 medium brown onions, sliced thinly
1½-inch piece fresh ginger, peeled, grated
4 cloves garlic, crushed
2 teaspoons sweet paprika
½ teaspoon cayenne pepper
½ cup beef stock

15-ounce can crushed tomatoes
2 bay leaves
2 cinnamon sticks
7 ounces yogurt
¾ cup toasted slivered almonds
1 fresh long red chili, sliced thinly

cucumber raita

1 cup thick "country-style" yogurt
1 Lebanese cucumber, seeded, chopped finely
1 tablespoon finely chopped fresh mint
pinch ground cumin

1 Combine cardamom, cumin and coriander in medium bowl, add lamb; toss lamb to coat in spice mixture.

2 Heat butter and half of the oil in large deep saucepan; cook lamb, in batches, until browned all over. Remove from pan.

3 Heat remaining oil in same pan; cook onion, ginger, garlic, paprika and cayenne over low heat, stirring, until onion softens.

4 Return lamb to pan with stock, undrained tomatoes, bay leaves and cinnamon. Add yogurt, 1 tablespoon at a time, stirring well between each addition; bring to a boil. Reduce heat; simmer, covered, about 1½ hours or until lamb is tender.

5 Meanwhile, make cucumber raita.

6 Sprinkle lamb with nuts and chili off the heat; serve with raita and, if desired, warmed naan bread.

cucumber raita Combine ingredients in small bowl with salt and pepper to taste.

nutritional count per serving (incl. raita) 48.1g total fat (15.3g saturated fat); 770 cal; 15.7g carbohydrate; 68.9g protein; 5.5g fiber

panang fish curry

PREP + COOK TIME 45 MINS • SERVES 4

Panang is the English adaptation of the Thai word "phanoeng" or "panaeng" meaning curry. The paste is a complex, sweet and milder variation of an authentic Thai red curry paste, which is especially good with seafood. Kaffir lime leaves, aromatic leaves of a citrus tree, are used similarly to bay leaves or curry leaves. They are available from Asian food stores.

2 x 14-ounce cans coconut milk
¼ cup panang curry paste
  (see page 413)
¼ cup fish sauce
2 tablespoons grated palm sugar
4 fresh kaffir lime leaves, torn
2 tablespoons peanut oil
1 pound cod, cut into 1-inch pieces

1 pound medium king prawns
8 ounces scallops
7 ounces snake beans, chopped
½ cup loosely packed fresh
  Thai basil leaves
½ cup coarsely chopped roasted
  unsalted peanuts
2 fresh long red chilies, sliced thinly

1 Place coconut milk, paste, sauce, sugar and lime leaves in wok; simmer, stirring, about 15 minutes or until mixture reduces by a third.

2 Meanwhile, heat oil in large frying pan; cook seafood, in batches, until it just changes color. Drain on absorbent paper.

3 Add beans and seafood to curry mixture; cook, uncovered, stirring occasionally, about 5 minutes or until beans are just tender and seafood is cooked as desired.

4 Serve curry sprinkled with basil, nuts and chili.

nutritional count per serving 64.3g total fat (39.8g saturated fat); 889 cal; 18.3g carbohydrate; 57.1g protein; 7.2g fiber

green chicken curry

PREP + COOK TIME 50 MINS • SERVES 4

Green curry paste is one of the hottest of the Thai traditional pastes, but this doesn't stop it from being one of the favorite curries among non-Thai cooks and diners. Coconut milk tempers the fire but doesn't dilute the beautiful flavor of this curry. You can use ready-made green curry paste available in most supermarkets instead of making your own.

1 tablespoon peanut oil
¼ cup green curry paste
  (see page 412)
3 long green chilies, chopped finely
2 pounds chicken thigh filets,
  cut into 1-inch pieces
2 x 14-ounce cans coconut milk
2 tablespoons fish sauce
2 tablespoons lime juice

1 tablespoon grated palm sugar
5 ounces pea eggplants
1 large zucchini, sliced thinly
⅓ cup loosely packed fresh
  Thai basil leaves
¼ cup loosely packed fresh
  coriander leaves
2 green onions, chopped coarsely

1 Heat oil in large saucepan; cook paste and about two-thirds of the chili, stirring, about 2 minutes or until fragrant. Add chicken; cook, stirring, until browned.

2 Add coconut milk, sauce, juice, sugar and eggplants; simmer, uncovered, about 10 minutes or until eggplants are just tender.

3 Add zucchini, basil and coriander; simmer, uncovered, until zucchini is just tender.

4 Serve curry sprinkled with remaining chili and green onion.

nutritional count per serving 67.3g total fat (43.2g saturated fat); 889 cal; 17g carbohydrate; 52.9g protein; 6g fiber

[1] panang fish curry
[2] green chicken curry
[3] beef rendang [page 428]
[4] dhal and paneer vegetable curry [page 428]

beef rendang

Serve this curry with steamed jasmine rice, accompanied by combined finely chopped cucumber and finely sliced fresh red chili in rice vinegar.

You can make the curry a day or two before you need it.

3 pounds beef chuck steak, trimmed, cut into 1-inch cubes
14-ounce can coconut milk
½ cup water
4-inch stick fresh lemon grass, bruised
3 fresh kaffir lime leaves, torn

spice paste
2 medium red onions, chopped coarsely
4 cloves garlic, chopped coarsely
2-inch piece fresh ginger, peeled, chopped coarsely
2 fresh long red chilies, chopped coarsely
3 teaspoons grated fresh galangal
3 teaspoons ground coriander
1½ teaspoons ground cumin
1 teaspoon ground turmeric
1 teaspoon salt

1 Blend or process spice paste ingredients until combined.
2 Combine paste in wok with beef, coconut milk, the water, lemon grass and lime leaves; bring to a boil. Reduce heat; simmer, covered, stirring occasionally, about 2 hours or until mixture thickens and beef is tender.
nutritional count per serving 25.2g total fat (16.9g saturated fat); 467 cal; 6.1g carbohydrate; 52.9g protein; 2.5g fiber

dhal and paneer vegetable curry

The word dhal is the Hindi word for legumes and pulses; regarded as meat substitutes, they feature widely in Indian cooking because they are a good source of protein for this largely vegetarian nation.

2 tablespoons ghee
1 medium brown onion, chopped finely
2 cloves garlic, crushed
¾-inch piece fresh ginger, peeled, grated
2 teaspoons ground cumin
1 tablespoon ground coriander
1 teaspoon ground turmeric
2 teaspoons garam masala
2 cardamom pods, bruised
2 tablespoons mild curry paste

1 cup yellow split peas
28-ounce can crushed tomatoes
2 cups vegetable stock
2 cups water
8 ounces cabbage, chopped coarsely
2 medium carrots, cut into ¾-inch pieces
½ cup frozen peas
7 ounces paneer cheese, cut into ¾-inch pieces
⅓ cup loosely packed fresh coriander leaves

1 Heat ghee in large saucepan; cook onion, garlic and ginger, stirring, until onion softens. Add spices; cook, stirring, until fragrant. Add curry paste; cook, stirring, until fragrant.

2 Add split peas, undrained tomatoes, stock and the water; bring to a boil. Reduce heat; simmer, covered, 30 minutes, stirring occasionally. Uncover, add cabbage and carrot; cook, stirring occasionally, about 30 minutes or until split peas soften.

3 Add frozen peas and cheese; cook, uncovered, about 5 minutes or until cheese is heated through. Serve curry sprinkled with coriander.

nutritional count per serving 20.1g total fat (10g saturated fat); 460 cal; 39.6g carbohydrate; 23.4g protein; 14.2g fiber

chicken korma

PREP + COOK TIME 1 HOUR 10 MINS (+ REFRIGERATION) • SERVES 4

Also known as nigella, kalonji are angular purple-black seeds that are a creamy color inside and possess a sharp, nutty taste. They are the seeds sprinkled over the top of freshly made pide, Turkish bread, that give it a special sharp, peppery flavor. Kalonji are found in spice shops and Middle-Eastern and Asian food stores.

¼ cup unsalted cashews
1 teaspoon sesame seeds
16 ounces yogurt
3 cloves garlic, crushed
¾-inch piece fresh ginger, peeled, grated
1 teaspoon dried chili flakes
½ teaspoon ground turmeric
2 pounds chicken thigh filets, diced into 1-inch pieces
2 tablespoons vegetable oil
2 medium brown onions, sliced thinly

2 cardamom pods
2 whole cloves
½ teaspoon black cumin seeds
½ cinnamon stick
2 tablespoons lemon juice
⅓ cup flaked coconut
⅓ cup unsalted cashews, extra
2 teaspoons kalonji seeds
¼ cup loosely packed fresh coriander leaves

1 Process nuts and sesame seeds until ground finely. Combine nut mixture with yogurt, garlic, ginger, chili and turmeric in large bowl; add chicken, toss to coat in marinade. Cover; refrigerate 3 hours or overnight.

2 Heat oil in large saucepan; cook onion, stirring, until soft. Add chicken mixture. Reduce heat; simmer, uncovered, 40 minutes, stirring occasionally.

3 Using mortar and pestle, crush cardamom, cloves and cumin seeds.

4 Add spice mixture, cinnamon and juice to chicken mixture; cook, uncovered, about 10 minutes or until chicken is cooked through.

5 Meanwhile, dry-fry coconut and extra nuts in small frying pan, stirring, until browned lightly. Remove from heat; stir in kalonji seeds.

6 Discard cinnamon from curry; serve curry, sprinkled with coconut mixture and coriander, accompanied by steamed basmati rice, if desired.

nutritional count per serving 45.7g total fat (13.6g saturated fat); 698 cal; 13.2g carbohydrate; 58.1g protein; 3.7g fiber

squash and eggplant curry

2 tablespoons olive oil

1 medium brown onion, sliced thickly

1 clove garlic, crushed

¾-inch piece fresh ginger, grated

2 fresh small red Thai chilies, chopped finely

1 teaspoon ground cumin

½ teaspoon ground turmeric

¼ teaspoon ground cardamom

¼ teaspoon ground fennel

8 baby eggplants (1 pound), sliced thickly

2 pounds butternut squash, cut into ¾-inch pieces

14-ounce can diced tomatoes

14-ounce can coconut cream

1 cup vegetable stock

1 tablespoon tomato paste

14-ounce can chickpeas, rinsed, drained

½ cup coarsely chopped fresh mint

1 Heat oil in large saucepan; cook onion, garlic, ginger and chili, stirring, until onion softens. Add spices and eggplant; cook, stirring, 2 minutes.

2 Add pumpkin, undrained tomatoes, coconut cream, stock and paste; bring to a boil. Reduce heat; simmer, uncovered, 20 minutes. Add chickpeas; simmer, uncovered, about 10 minutes or until vegetables are tender.

3 Serve bowls of curry sprinkled with mint.

nutritional count per serving 22.3g total fat (13.6g saturated fat); 351 cal; 24.5g carbohydrate; 9.5g protein; 8.6g fiber

chicken tikka

Tikka paste is a mild paste which, in Indian cookery, is made to its maker's choice of spices and oils and sometimes tomatoes or coconut cream; it is frequently colored red. It is usually used for marinating or for basting the food as it cooks, rather than as an ingredient. It is most often used with chicken.

2 cups jasmine rice

2 tablespoons tikka masala paste

2 tablespoons mango chutney

2 pounds chicken thighs, sliced

⅓ cup vegetable stock

½ cup yogurt

½ cup loosely packed, coarsely chopped fresh coriander

2 teaspoons lime juice

1 red Thai chili, sliced thinly

1 Cook rice in large saucepan of boiling water, uncovered, until just tender; drain.

2 Meanwhile, combine paste, chutney and chicken in large bowl. Heat wok or large frying pan; stir-fry chicken mixture, in batches, until chicken is browned all over.

3 Add remaining ingredients to wok; bring to a boil. Reduce heat; simmer, uncovered, about 5 minutes or until chicken is cooked through. Serve with rice.

nutritional count per serving 23.4g total fat (6.8g saturated fat); 787 cal; 86.3g carbohydrate; 55.8g protein; 2.4g fiber

[opposite] squash and eggplant curry

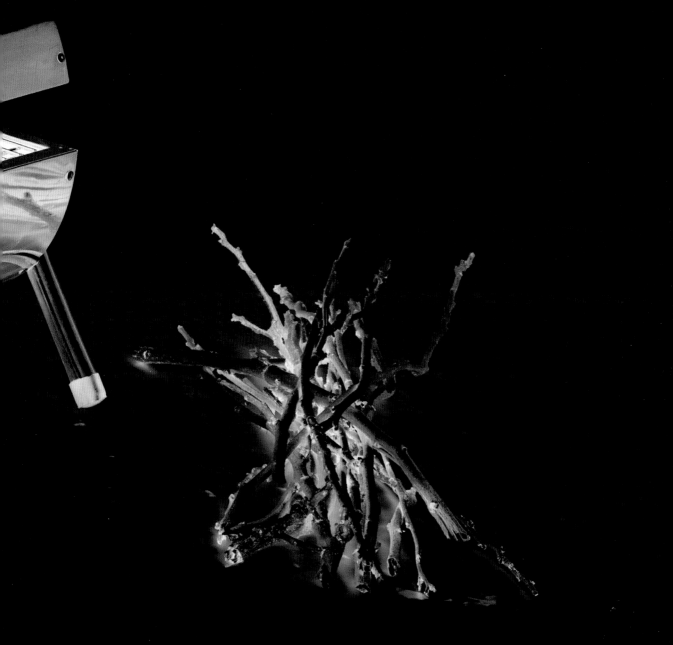

BARBECUES & GRILLS

Barbecues & grills

Barbecues are synonymous with summer, salads and languid meals spent around the outdoor table with family and friends. Few things say relaxed summer entertaining better than platters of steaming, char-grilled meat and fish, delivered straight from the barbecue to the outdoor table, alongside the salads.

People love the distinctive flavors and charming appearance of char-grilled foods. That's why we love barbecues and that's why we have embraced the arrival of grill pans, which allow you to cook food in a way similar to barbecuing, but indoors on your kitchen stove top, all year-round. And then, of course, there's the traditional broiler that is part of every kitchen: when it's Sunday night at home, and you don't want any fuss, nothing beats the humble broiler for a trusty grilled meal.

ON THE BARBECUE

Brush or spray food for barbecuing with oil or melted butter just before cooking. Also oil the grill, unless the manufacturer's instructions direct otherwise. Baste the food frequently with more oil (or with a marinade or sauce according to the recipe) while it is cooking.

STEAKS, CHOPS AND CHICKEN PIECES Cook the first side until browned to your liking, turn only once and cook the other side to your liking. Rest meat and chicken in the warmth next to the barbecue for 5 minutes before serving.

SAUSAGES Cook at a moderate heat, moving to the side of grill or plate if over-browning before they are cooked through. Or poach sausages beforehand, then brown them quickly on the barbecue.

ROASTS Follow the manufacturer's directions for roasting on your barbecue.

FISH Pay close attention to fish and remove it as soon as the flesh turns white (pink for salmon or trout). Whole fish is cooked when a skewer slides easily into the thickest part. For whole fish, slash sides two or three times before cooking and use a greased fish-shaped hinged wire basket to help turn it without breaking. If you don't have one, lift it carefully with two spatulas, one at each end.

UNDER THE BROILER

Broiling produces an even and deliciously browned surface on everything from lamb chops to an omelette. Housed in every wall oven or stove top, the broiler consists of a pierced tray or rack fitted over a shallow pan. Broiling is healthy because the fats and juices drip into the pan.

Pre-heat the broiler on high so that when the food goes under, it starts to brown immediately. Even if a recipe calls for medium heat, start with a hot broiler, then turn it down when you begin to broil.

If you're broiling small pieces of tender foods, broil on high heat, making sure you coat them with oil first. Larger items, like half a chicken, are usually cooked on medium-hot heat and may still be uncooked although they look golden-brown on the outside. If a recipe says to reduce the heat and continue cooking, it is best to lower the food away from the broiler rather than reduce the temperature. If this is too hard to do mid-broiling, then finish cooking it in a moderate oven.

BROILER CARE

High heat "cooks on" any food residue on a broiler tray. Soaking to loosen these bits is better for the tray than scouring it. Or, to minimize cleaning, cover the tray with heavy foil before use.

IN THE GRILL PAN

People love grill pans (which sit on the hotplate of your stove top) because they cook the food in a similar way to a barbecue—complete with those distinctive dark-barred markings, which are created by the ridges in the pan. The food chars where it makes contact with the very hot ridges, while the heat rising from the base of the pan cooks the parts in between. Char-grilling is a fast cooking method, best suited to small, tender items of food. It is a healthy way to cook because excess fat seeps off into the gutters between the ridges while the food is held above it. And it looks stylish and tastes marvelous.

GRILL PANS are available in round, square and rectangular shapes, in various sizes. They are made from a number of different materials including enameled cast iron, titanium, bare iron and toughened aluminum.

FOODS Char-grilling in a grill pan is suitable for a whole range of foods: seafood (thick, meaty fish filets); meat (steaks, filets, chops or cutlets); chicken thighs and breasts; vegetables, fruits and thickly-sliced breads.

GRILL PAN MUST-DOS

Grill pans can create smoky fumes so you need a strong exhaust fan, preferably ducted to the outside, to avoid a smoke-filled kitchen.

Brush both food and grill pan with melted butter or oil. Place food, slightly apart, across the ridges of the grill, pressing each piece down lightly with tongs to ensure it has full contact with the ridges. Allow the food to grill for a few minutes without moving it so that char marks will be clearly defined. Lift an edge to check when food is done to your liking and turn over. Turn food only once.

Seafood, thin steaks or cutlets may be nearly cooked by the time they are well marked on the first side. If so, cook them only briefly on the second side, then take them off the heat. Serve with the well-marked side up.

Thick foods, such as steak, may not be cooked through even when they look well-charred on the outside. Rather than continuing in the grill pan (which could scorch or dry it out), finish cooking in a moderate oven, turning it once, if necessary.

Coat fish in melted butter or oil before cooking to protect it and help it color quickly. All seafood should be removed from the grill pan while it is still a little underdone: its own heat will finish cooking it by the time it is served. Tuna and salmon are often served barely seared.

GRILL PAN CARE

After cooking, immediately plunge the grill pan into a sink of very hot water to loosen any food residue, then brush with a stiff brush (not metal). Dry with a cloth and place over very low heat for a few minutes to dry thoroughly.

BARBECUE CARE

CLEAN BARBECUE ACCORDING TO MANUFACTURER'S DIRECTIONS, OR CLEAN WHILE HOT—BUT TURNED OFF—WITH HOT WATER AND A WIRE BRUSH; DRY WITH A CLOTH AND LEAVE FOR AN HOUR OR TWO IN THE OPEN AIR TO DRY THOROUGHLY. SPRAY METAL PARTS WITH OIL AND WIPE OFF SURPLUS BEFORE COVERING.

garlic and rosemary smoked lamb

PREP + COOK TIME 1 HOUR (+ REFRIGERATION & SOAKING) • SERVES 6

2 pounds boned loin of lamb

4 cloves garlic, halved

8 fresh rosemary sprigs

1 teaspoon dried chili flakes

1 tablespoon olive oil

8 ounces smoking chips

When using indirect heat with a gas burner, place the food in a preheated, covered barbecue, then turn the burners off directly under the food while keeping the side burners on. With a charcoal barbecue, metal bars hold two layers of coals against the sides of the barbecue, leaving the center of the barbecue rack empty. A disposable aluminium baking dish can be placed here to catch fat drips.

Ask your butcher to bone the lamb loin for you.

1 Pierce lamb in eight places with sharp knife; push garlic and rosemary into cuts. Sprinkle lamb with chili; rub with oil. Roll and tie at intervals with kitchen string. Cover; refrigerate 3 hours or overnight.

2 Soak smoking chips in large bowl of water 2 hours.

3 Cook lamb, uncovered, on heated oiled barbecue until browned all over. Place drained smoking chips in smoke box on barbecue next to lamb. Cook lamb in covered barbecue, using indirect heat and following manufacturer's instructions, about 40 minutes or until cooked as desired.

nutritional count per serving 17.8g total fat (7.1g saturated fat); 299 cal; 0.2g carbohydrate; 35g protein; 0.3g fiber

TIP

• Smoking chips and smoke boxes are available from barbecue shops and home center stores.

Make eight slits in the lamb with a small sharp knife and insert the garlic and rosemary into the slits.

Smoking chips must be soaked in water for 2 hours before being used on the barbecue. This helps them to smolder slowly and prevents them from burning.

Drain the smoking chips and place them in the smoke box. Put the smoke box on the barbecue next to the lamb.

cajun chickens

A small chicken like this is also known as spatchcock (or poussin); they are no more than 6 weeks old and weigh a maximum of 1 pound. Spatchcock is also the cooking term to describe cutting a small chicken along the backbone and flattening it for grilling.

6 x 1-pound small chickens
2 tablespoons olive oil
1 small white onion,
   grated coarsely
2 cloves garlic, crushed
2 tablespoons sweet paprika
2 teaspoons ground cinnamon
2 teaspoons ground fennel
2 teaspoons dried oregano

spicy tomato salsa
6 large Roma tomatoes, halved
1 tablespoon olive oil
1 medium brown onion,
   chopped finely
2 cloves garlic, crushed
1 tablespoon sweet paprika
1 teaspoon smoked paprika
1 tablespoon red wine vinegar
1 fresh long red chili, chopped finely

1 Discard necks from chickens. Using scissors, cut along each side of each chicken's backbone; discard backbones. Turn chickens skin-side up; press down on breastbone to flatten.

2 Rub chickens all over with combined remaining ingredients. Cook chickens on heated oiled grill pan, turning midway through cooking time, about 1 hour or until cooked.

3 Meanwhile, make spicy tomato salsa.

4 Serve chickens with spicy tomato salsa.

spicy tomato salsa Cook tomato on heated oiled grill pan, turning, until softened; chop tomato coarsely. Heat oil in medium saucepan; cook onion and garlic, stirring, until onion softens. Add spices; cook, stirring, until fragrant. Stir in tomato, vinegar and chili; cook, uncovered, stirring occasionally, 20 minutes or until thickened.

nutritional count per serving 48.8g total fat (13.6g saturated fat); 657 cal; 4g carbohydrate; 50.6g protein; 2.1g fiber

salmon with dill and caper dressing

¼ cup sour cream
1 tablespoon drained tiny capers
2 teaspoons finely chopped fresh dill
2 teaspoons horseradish cream
1 teaspoon lime juice
4 small salmon filets (5-6 ounces each)

1 Combine sour cream, capers, dill, horseradish and juice in medium bowl.

2 Cook salmon on heated oiled grill pan (or grill or barbecue) until browned on both sides and cooked as desired.

3 Serve salmon with dill and caper dressing.

nutritional count per serving 13.8g total fat (4.5g saturated fat); 249 cal; 1.4g carbohydrate; 29.9g protein; 0.1g fiber

[opposite] cajun chickens

Know your mushrooms

There are a lot of mushroom varieties to choose from these days at farmers' markets, and many are even available from supermarkets. If your only experience with mushrooms has been button and field mushrooms, you're in for a culinary treat.

STRAW
These small and globe-shaped mushrooms have an internal stem and are so named for the straw on which they are grown. They are so fragile and deteriorate so quickly after harvesting that they are not a commercial proposition fresh so they are usually canned.

ENOKI
These cultivated mushrooms, also called enokitake, are tiny long-stemmed, pale mushrooms that grow and are sold in clusters; they can be used that way or separated by slicing off the base. They have a mild fruity flavor and are slightly crisp in texture.

FLAT
Large, white mushrooms that are fully open with gills exposed are more flavorful than smaller white varieties (buttons, caps). Earthy and rich, they are great for casseroles, stuffing or grilling; portobellos make a great substitute.

OYSTER
Also called abalone mushrooms when large. These fan-like shaped mushrooms are prized for their smooth texture and subtle, oyster-like flavor, making them ideal to combine with veal, seafood and poultry. They become unpleasantly slippery if cooked too long so should be added near the end of cooking.

PINE
Also called cep, these mushrooms are wild-picked in forests of introduced pine species. They are related to but not the same as the true European cep but their fruity scent and deep, earthy flavor explain the common name. They are best served simply: fried quickly or added in the last few minutes of cooking to a soup.

DRIED PORCINI
The richest-flavored mushrooms, also known as ceps. They are expensive but, because they are so strongly flavored, you only need to use a small amount for any particular dish. Rehydrate before use by soaking in hot water for 20-60 minutes, depending on the thickness of the caps. Strain the soaking water and use for soup or as stock for a risotto.

Q&A

I've always been a bit afraid of trying "new" types of mushrooms, worrying that they might be slimy or have a very strong taste. What's the best way to experiment with different types of mushrooms?

If you like mushrooms cooked in butter and cream, buy small quantities of enoki and cremini, as well as field and button mushrooms. Cook them all up together in butter with a little crushed garlic and some chopped parsley. It's a delicious combination. After that, experiment with other combinations until you find the ones you like the most.

DRIED CHANTERELLE
Also called girolles or pfifferling, this trumpet-shaped wild mushroom ranges in color from yellow to orange. The delicate flavor and chewy texture makes this a good all-around mushroom. Rehydrate before use by soaking in water for 15-20 minutes.

SHIMEJI
Also called beech mushrooms, these cultivated small oyster mushrooms grow and are sold in clumps. They have a delicate, sweet flesh with a nutty flavor and are suitable for stir-frying and pan-frying. When cooked, they are slightly crunchy in texture.

CREMINI
Also known as Roman or Swiss browns, cremini are light to dark brown in color with a full-bodied flavor. Their firm flesh means they hold their shape well when cooked so they are an excellent choice for use in risottos, casseroles or being stuffed and baked.

BUTTON
These are the youngest type of cultivated white mushrooms, and are tightly enclosed around the stem. The name refers to the shape and stage of its growth, not the size (cap and flat are the larger stages). They have a delicate flavor and fine texture that lends them to take on other flavors. When a recipe in this book calls for an unspecified type of mushroom, these are the ones to use.

CHESTNUT
These are cultivated mushrooms with a brown outer skin, a firm texture and a strong, nutty flavor. They are available infrequently. Cremini are a good substitute in recipes.

PORTOBELLO
Portobellos are fully mature creminis, larger and bigger in flavor. With an open, flat cap that can easily measure up to 6 inches in diameter, they are often served whole and grilled. Their stems are woody and should be removed.

grilled t-bone with three butters

PREP + COOK TIME 20 MINS (+ REFRIGERATION) • SERVES 8

8 large t-bone steaks (4 pounds)

peppercorn butter

6 tablespoons butter, softened

1 tablespoon canned drained
    green peppercorns

½ teaspoon mustard powder

mustard butter

6 tablespoons butter, softened

3 green onions, chopped finely

1 tablespoon wholegrain mustard

2 teaspoons lemon juice

satay butter

6 tablespoons butter, softened

1 small red pepper, chopped finely

⅓ cup salted peanuts,
    chopped finely

2 teaspoons light soy sauce

1 Make butters.

2 Cook steaks on heated oiled grill pan until cooked as desired.

3 Serve steaks with butters in small serving dishes.

butters Prepare each butter by combining ingredients in small bowl; mix well. Spoon each mixture onto a piece of foil; press each into triangle shape using two rulers or roll into sausage shape. Wrap foil firmly around butters to enclose; refrigerate 30 minutes or until firm.

nutritional count per serving 45.4g total fat (25.7g saturated fat); 553 cal; 2.3g carbohydrate; 34.7g protein; 0.7g fiber

piri piri chicken thigh filets

PREP + COOK TIME 45 MINS • SERVES 4

The Afro-Portuguese chili paste called piri piri seems made to enliven grilled poultry. The name originally came from the tiny, hot piri piri chili, which the Portuguese introduced to their former colonies of Angola and Mozambique.

4 fresh long red chilies, chopped coarsely

1 teaspoon dried chili flakes

2 cloves garlic, quartered

1 teaspoon sea salt

2 tablespoons olive oil

1 tablespoon apple cider vinegar

2 teaspoons brown sugar

8 x 4-ounce chicken thigh filets

1 Using mortar and pestle, grind fresh chili, chili flakes, garlic and salt to make piri piri paste.

2 Combine paste with oil, vinegar, sugar and chicken in medium bowl. Cook chicken on heated oiled grill pan (or grill or barbecue) until cooked through.

3 Serve chicken with lime wedges, if desired.

nutritional count per serving 27.2g total fat (6.8g saturated fat); 436 cal; 1.8g carbohydrate; 46.6g protein; 0.3g fiber

chili and honey barbecued steak

All grilled meat should be rested in a warm place, loosely covered with foil, for 5 minutes to allow the juices to settle and the meat to become more succulent.

2 tablespoons barbecue sauce

1 tablespoon Worcestershire sauce

1 tablespoon honey

1 fresh long red chili, chopped finely

1 clove garlic, crushed

4 x 7-ounce New York strip steaks

1 Combine sauces, honey, chili and garlic in large bowl, add steaks; turn to coat steaks in honey mixture.

2 Cook steaks on heated oiled grill pan (or grill or barbecue) until browned both sides and cooked as desired.

3 Serve steaks with coleslaw or warm potato salad.

nutritional count per serving 12.1g total fat (5g saturated fat); 324 cal; 11.7g carbohydrate; 42.4g protein; 0.3g fiber

cheeseburgers with caramelized onion

The first step in many recipes is to fry chopped onion slowly to a soft, golden mass, which takes about 20 minutes and needs frequent checking and stirring. A quicker way is to warm the butter or oil, stir in the onion until well coated, then barely cover with warm water; cook over high heat until the water has evaporated. Stir the now-softened onion on medium to low heat for a few minutes until it is golden, adding a little more butter or oil if needed.

1 pound ground beef

4 thin slices cheddar cheese

4 hamburger buns, split

1 small tomato, sliced thinly

8 large butter lettuce leaves

4 large dill pickles, sliced thinly

1 tablespoon yellow mustard

⅓ cup tomato sauce

caramelized onion

2 tablespoons olive oil

2 medium white onions, sliced thinly

1 tablespoon brown sugar

2 tablespoons balsamic vinegar

2 tablespoons water

1 Make caramelized onion.

2 Shape beef into four patties; cook on heated oiled grill pan (or grill or barbecue) until cooked through. Top each patty with cheese slices during the last minute of cooking time.

3 Meanwhile, toast buns, cut-sides down, on grill pan.

4 Place cheeseburgers, onion, tomato, lettuce and pickle between buns; serve with mustard and tomato sauce.

caramelized onion Heat oil in large frying pan; cook onion, stirring, until soft. Add sugar, vinegar and the water; cook, stirring, until onion is caramelized.

nutritional count per serving 23.6g total fat (7.4g saturated fat); 569 cal; 51.6g carbohydrate; 34.9g protein; 5g fiber

lemon-chili butterflied chicken

This shortcut to a perfect grilled chicken takes very little time but guarantees even cooking through the whole bird. To butterfly means, after you cut out and remove the backbone, you can open the chicken like a book (this shape rather resembles a butterfly) and press it flat. This easy technique will result in a grilled chicken that cooks faster and uniformly.

5 tablespoons butter, softened
½ teaspoon dried chili flakes
½ teaspoon cracked black pepper
1 tablespoon finely grated lemon rind
1 tablespoon finely chopped fresh rosemary

3-pound whole chicken
½ cup stale bread crumbs
2 teaspoons finely grated lemon rind, extra
¼ cup coarsely grated parmesan cheese

1 Move oven shelf to second-bottom position. Preheat broiler.

2 Combine butter, chili, pepper, rind and rosemary in small bowl.

3 Cut along each side of chicken's backbone; discard backbone. Turn chicken skin-side up; press down to flatten. Loosen and lift chicken skin; push butter mixture between skin and flesh.

4 Place chicken, skin-side down, on oiled wire rack in shallow flameproof roasting pan. Broil chicken 40 minutes. Turn chicken; cook about 10 minutes or until chicken is cooked.

5 Meanwhile, combine remaining ingredients in small bowl.

6 Remove chicken from pan; strain juices from pan into small heatproof pitcher. Return chicken to pan; sprinkle with crumb mixture, drizzle ¼ cup of the juices over crumb mixture.

7 Broil chicken about 5 minutes or until topping is browned lightly. Quarter chicken; serve with mixed green salad.

nutritional count per serving 50.5g total fat (21.9g saturated fat); 647 cal; 6g carbohydrate; 43.1g protein; 0.5g fiber

To butterfly the chicken, cut along each side of the backbone with poultry shears. Remove and discard the backbone.

Press down on the butterflied chicken with the heel of your hand to flatten it.

Gently loosen and lift the chicken skin and push the butter mixture between the flesh and the skin.

Know your seafood

Seafood that is freshly caught and simply cooked is one of life's great pleasures. But you need to know your seafood. Here are some of the more interesting varieties with information on how to prepare and cook them to bring out their best.

SCALLOPS
Available on the half-shell or shelled, their beautiful shell is sometimes used as part of the presentation. Often eaten raw or barely seared, they should never be cooked more than 30 seconds because they will lose their juicy tenderness and become tough.

ABALONE
This harvested single-shelled deep-water shellfish has a reputation for toughness so it's usually sliced and pounded before cooking. If bought live and used the same day by shelling, slicing and dropping into hot oil for seconds only, it tastes like lobster and is not tough.

BABY OCTOPUS
Usually tenderized before you buy them; both octopus and squid require either long slow cooking (usually for the large mollusks) or quick cooking over high heat (usually for the small mollusks)–anything in between will make the octopus tough and rubbery.

CRAYFISH
Crayfish, also called crawfish or crawdads, are a freshwater crustacean found throughout the Gulf states. They are found in creeks and dams, but those available commercially are now mostly farmed. Their fresh-tasting, moist meat is in the tail and claws.

LOBSTER
Found in virtually every ocean on earth, lobsters live near shorelines and are considered a delicacy. It is important to undercook, rather than overcook, lobster because they will continue cooking in residual heat. They are ideal to steam, poach, deep-fry, pan-fry, stir-fry, bake, grill or barbecue.

CLAMS
Clams, a species of bi-valve like oysters or scallops, burrow in the sand along the water's edge. Available from fish markets and large seafood outlets. They can be eaten raw from the shell with a squeeze of lemon juice, shelled and added to soup, or opened but left in the shell, to top a bowl of pasta. They can be substituted with manilas and cockles.

Q&A

Can you tell me about mussels? I've never cooked them but I believe they can make you sick if they're not prepared properly.

Mussels must be alive when cooked. The way you can tell is that their shells should be tightly closed when you buy them. Throw out any that have open shells–they're dead. Scrub them with a small scrubbing brush under running water and pull off their beard (the piece of string that protrudes from the shell), you'll need to give it a strong yank. Cook them in a large pan with a little liquid (wine or water)–not much because the mussels will lose some of their liquid as they cook. As soon as the mussels open, remove from the pan. Discard any that do not open–they are also dead.

MUSSELS

Mussels are found clustered on rocks or under jetties; the main varieties are the greenlip and black mussels. It is important to make sure fresh mussels are alive when you buy them, and equally important that they are still alive when you cook them.

FRESH SARDINES

Previously only available packed in oil, fresh sardines are now readily available in fish markets. Full of healthy omega-3 fatty acids, they can be grilled or broiled. Purchase them scaled and gutted and store them on ice until ready to cook. Use within one day.

BLUE SWIMMER CRAB

Also known as sand crab, blue manna crab, bluey, sand crab or sandy, this crab turns orange-red when cooked. Its fine-textured, sweet meat is found in the legs and claws. Can be substituted with lobster or crayfish

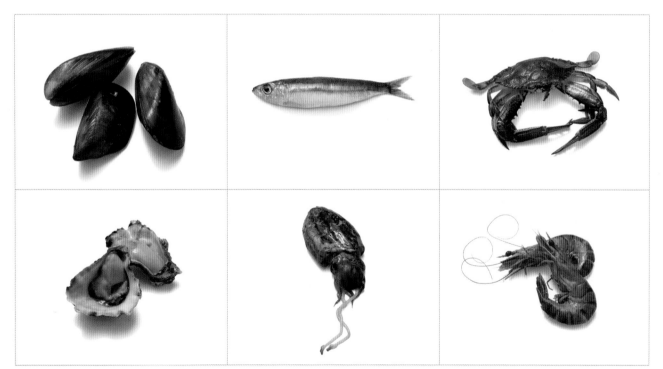

OYSTERS

With over 200 varieties of oysters grown in North America, each has a taste and texture of its own, depending on the ocean environment it comes from. Ideally, oysters should be bought alive in their closed shells and opened just before they are eaten, or they can also be bought shelled and packaged, which are useful for soups and stews.

SQUID

Also known as calamari, squid are shellfish without an external shell but with a long, bony "quill" inside. To prepare squid, gently pull the head and entrails away from the squid body, then remove and discard the quill. Cut the tentacles from the head just below the eyes, then remove the beak. Gently pull away the outer membrane from the hood and flaps, then wash the hood, tentacles and flaps well. You can also buy squid hoods to make preparation and cooking faster.

KING PRAWNS

These large prawns are also known as ocean king, blueleg, sand, western, and western king prawn. They have a sweet true-prawn flavor, moist firm flesh and are available uncooked (green) or cooked, with or without shells. When buying prawns, look for good color and luster and make sure shells are free of discoloration. They can be substituted with farmed tiger prawns.

lobster tails with garlic herbed butter

For many cooks, dealing with live lobsters at home can be challenging. Purchasing frozen tails brings the luxury home without the stress of live lobsters crawling around your kitchen. For best results, buy frozen cold-water tails from the North Atlantic, Australia or New Zealand, and thaw them in water in the refrigerator for 24 hours before cooking.

8 small lobster tails,
  6-8 ounces each
4 portobello mushrooms
3 ounces curly endive,
  chopped coarsely

garlic herbed butter
1 stick butter, softened
2 teaspoons finely grated lemon rind
2 tablespoons lemon juice
2 tablespoons finely chopped
  fresh chives
2 tablespoons coarsely chopped
  fresh flat-leaf parsley
2 tablespoons coarsely chopped
  fresh tarragon
1 clove garlic, crushed

1 Place lobster tails upside down on board. Using scissors, cut soft shell from underneath tails to expose meat. With a chef's knife, cut tails in half lengthwise. Discard back vein.

2 Make herbed butter.

3 Melt half the herb butter in small saucepan. Brush mushrooms with half the melted butter; cook on heated oiled grill pan until tender.

4 Brush tails with remaining melted butter mixture; cook on grill pan.

5 Serve endive and mushrooms with lobster halves; top with remaining herb butter.

garlic herbed butter Beat butter, rind and juice in small bowl with electric mixer until light and fluffy. Stir in herbs and garlic.

nutritional count per serving 27.1g total fat (17.1g saturated fat); 379 cal; 2.1g carbohydrate; 30.4g protein; 3.2g fiber

Cut the shell from underneath the tail to expose the flesh. It's best to do this with scissors or poultry shears. Cut the tails in half lengthwise.

There's a black vein down the center of the tails that should be removed before cooking them.

veal cutlets with green olive salsa

Because fingerling potatoes are small, they are quick and easy to cook on a barbecue. Prick the scrubbed potatoes, rub with butter or olive oil, then double-wrap individually in foil (with a sprig of herb or an unpeeled clove of garlic, if you like) and place directly on the coals. After about 30 minutes, stick a bamboo skewer through the foil to see if it's cooked through.

2 tablespoons olive oil
2 cloves garlic, crushed
1 tablespoon finely chopped fresh oregano
2 teaspoons finely grated lemon rind
1 tablespoon lemon juice
4 x 4-ounce veal cutlets

green olive salsa
1 tablespoon lemon juice
¼ cup coarsely chopped fresh flat-leaf parsley
½ cup finely chopped large green olives
1 small green pepper, chopped finely
1 tablespoon olive oil
1 clove garlic, crushed
1 tablespoon finely chopped fresh oregano

1 Make green olive salsa.
2 Combine oil, garlic, oregano, rind and juice in small bowl; brush mixture over veal. Cook veal on heated oiled grill pan (or grill or barbecue) until browned both sides and cooked as desired.
3 Serve veal with salsa and barbecued fingerling or mashed potatoes.
green olive salsa Combine ingredients in small bowl.
nutritional count per serving 16.3g total fat (2.7g saturated fat); 266 cal; 5.8g carbohydrate; 23.4g protein; 1.2g fiber
serving idea barbecued fingerling potatoes.

barbecued baby octopus

2-pound baby octopus
⅓ cup lemon juice
⅓ cup olive oil
2 cloves garlic, crushed
2 teaspoons dried oregano
1 medium lemon, cut into wedges

1 Clean octopus, remove eyes and beaks. Combine octopus with juice, oil, garlic and oregano in medium bowl. Cover, refrigerate 3 hours or overnight.
2 Drain octopus; discard marinade. Cook octopus on heated oiled barbecue (or grill or grill pan) until tender. Serve with lemon wedges.
nutritional count per serving 13.4g total fat (1.7g saturated fat); 235 cal; 1g carbohydrate; 27.6g protein; 0.2g fiber

texas-style spareribs

6 pounds pork spareribs (babybacks)
2 tablespoons sweet paprika
1 tablespoon ground cumin
1 teaspoon cayenne pepper
7 cups beer

1 cup barbecue sauce
¼ cup water
¼ cup maple syrup
¼ cup cider vinegar

1 Place ribs on large tray. Combine spices in small bowl, rub spice mixture all over ribs. Cover; refrigerate 3 hours or overnight.

2 Bring beer to a boil in medium saucepan. Reduce heat; simmer, uncovered, 20 minutes. Divide beer and ribs between two large shallow disposable baking dishes. Cook, covered, on barbecue, using indirect heat for 1¼ hours. Drain ribs; discard beer.

3 Meanwhile, combine sauce, the water, syrup and vinegar in small saucepan; bring to a boil. Reduce heat; simmer, uncovered, 5 minutes.

4 Cook ribs, in batches, directly on heated barbecue, turning and brushing with sauce occasionally, about 20 minutes until browned all over.

nutritional count per serving 17.5g total fat (6.1g saturated fat); 508 cal; 25.4g carbohydrate; 49.8g protein; 0.4g fiber

pork cutlet with fennel and apple salsa

To make crushed potatoes: boil, steam or microwave 2 pounds unpeeled new potatoes; drain. Mash half the potatoes with ½ cup sour cream and 3 tablespoons butter in a large bowl until smooth and stir in ¼ cup coarsely chopped flat-leaf parsley and 2 tablespoons chopped fresh dill. Roughly crush the remaining potatoes with the back of a fork until the skins burst and the flesh is just crushed; stir into herbed mash.

2 tablespoons cider vinegar
¼ cup olive oil
1 tablespoon dijon mustard
2 teaspoons superfine sugar
4 x 8-ounce pork cutlets
1 large unpeeled green apple, cored chopped finely

1 small red onion, chopped finely
1 medium fennel, trimmed, chopped finely

1 Whisk vinegar, oil, mustard and sugar in medium bowl; transfer 2 tablespoons of dressing to large bowl. Add pork to large bowl; turn to coat cutlets in dressing.

2 To make salsa, combine apple, onion and fennel in bowl with remaining dressing.

3 Meanwhile, cook drained pork on heated oiled grill pan (or grill or barbecue) until browned both sides and cooked as desired, brushing occasionally with dressing.

4 Serve pork with salsa, and with mashed potato or roasted potato wedges.

nutritional count per serving 31.2g total fat (7.9g saturated fat); 449 cal; 9.6g carbohydrate; 32g protein; 2.3g fiber

serving idea crushed potatoes.

grilled pork chops with apples

As always when buying meat, your best bet is a supplier you can trust. In general, pork should have fine-grained, pale pink flesh, white fat and thin, smooth skin. Avoid any that has waxy fat or is wet, meaning it has been badly handled and may be from an animal in poor condition.

2 medium apples

1 tablespoon olive oil

1 medium red onion, cut into thin wedges

4 x 8-ounce pork loin chops

½ cup plum sauce

¼ cup lemon juice

⅓ cup chicken stock

1 Cut each unpeeled, uncored apple horizontally into four slices. Heat oil in grill pan; cook apple and onion, turning, until softened.

2 Meanwhile, cook pork on heated oiled grill pan until cooked.

3 Stir sauce, juice and stock into apple mixture; simmer 1 minute.

4 Serve pork with sauce.

nutritional count per serving 29.7g total fat (9.1g saturated fat); 575 cal; 32g carbohydrate; 45g protein; 1.8g fiber

barbecued rib-eye filet

PREP + COOK TIME 1 HOUR 40 MINS (+ REFRIGERATION & STANDING) • SERVES 6

¼ cup barbecue sauce

2 tablespoons yellow mustard

4 cloves garlic, crushed

½ cup beer

3-pound piece rib-eye filet

1 Combine sauce, mustard, garlic and beer in large bowl, add beef; turn beef to coat in mixture. Cover; refrigerate 3 hours or overnight.

2 Place beef and marinade in oiled disposable aluminium baking dish. Cook, covered, on barbecue, using indirect heat, about 1½ hours or until cooked as desired. Cover; stand 15 minutes, slice thinly.

nutritional count per serving 14.2g total fat (5.9g saturated fat); 356 cal; 5.9g carbohydrate; 49.7g protein; 0.6g fiber

[1] grilled pork chops with apples
[2] barbecued rib-eye filet
[3] lemon and garlic kebabs
[page 454]
[4] barbecued whole snapper
[page 454]

lemon and garlic lamb kebabs

PREP + COOK TIME 30 MINS • SERVES 4

It's a good idea to pierce lamb with metal or bamboo skewers first to make threading the rosemary stalks easier.

8 x 6-inch stalks fresh rosemary
1½ pounds lamb filets, diced into 1-inch pieces
3 cloves garlic, crushed
2 tablespoons olive oil
2 teaspoons finely grated lemon rind
1 tablespoon lemon juice

1 Remove leaves from bottom two-thirds of each rosemary stalk; sharpen trimmed ends to a point.
2 Thread lamb onto rosemary skewers. Brush kebabs with combined garlic, oil, rind and juice. Cover; refrigerate until required.
3 Cook kebabs on heated oiled grill pan, brushing frequently with remaining garlic mixture, until cooked.
nutritional count per serving 16.4g total fat (4.5g saturated fat); 314 cal; 0.4g carbohydrate; 41.2g protein; 0.4g fiber

barbecued whole snapper

PREP + COOK TIME 1 HOUR • SERVES 8

We used snapper in this recipe, but a fish like salmon would work well, too–it may need slightly less cooking time, depending on how you like your salmon cooked.

1 whole snapper (4 pounds)
1 clove garlic, sliced thinly
3 sprigs fresh rosemary, cut into 1-inch lengths
1 medium lemon, sliced thinly
3 tablespoons butter
2 large zucchini
2 trimmed corn cobs, sliced thickly
2 medium red peppers, sliced thickly
1 large red onion, cut into wedges

lemon herb butter
10 tablespoons butter, softened
1 clove garlic, crushed
2 teaspoons finely grated lemon rind
2 teaspoons finely chopped fresh rosemary

1 Make lemon herb butter.

2 Meanwhile, place fish on board; score fish both sides through thickest part of flesh. Push garlic and rosemary into cuts; fill cavity with a third of the lemon slices.

3 Place a long piece of parchment paper on counter; place half of the remaining lemon slices on paper. Place fish on lemon; top with remaining lemon then butter. Fold paper over fish to completely enclose, then wrap tightly in foil.

4 Cook fish on heated oiled grill pan (or grill or barbecue) 20 minutes; turn, cook about 20 minutes.

5 Meanwhile, cut zucchini in half crosswise; cut each half lengthwise into six. Combine zucchini with remaining ingredients in large bowl. Place eight 12-inch foil squares on counter; divide vegetable mixture among foil squares. Gather corners of squares together; fold to enclose vegetables securely.

6 Cook packets on heated oiled grilled pan until vegetables are tender.

7 Open vegetable packets; top with slices of lemon herb butter. Serve with fish.

lemon herb butter Combine ingredients in small bowl. Place on piece of plastic wrap; shape into 2¼-inch log, wrap tightly. Freeze until firm; cut into eight slices.

nutritional count per serving 24.2g total fat (14.5g saturated fat); 398 cal; 12.4g carbohydrate; 30.9g protein; 4.2g fiber

grilled vegetables with garlic herb dressing   PREP + COOK TIME 1 HOUR • SERVES 4

1 medium red pepper
1 medium yellow pepper
¼ cup olive oil
1 clove garlic, crushed
1 teaspoon finely grated lemon rind
2 teaspoons finely chopped
   fresh rosemary
1 medium red onion,
   cut into wedges

2 small leeks, trimmed,
   cut into ¾-inch pieces
1 medium eggplant,
   sliced thickly
2 medium zucchini,
   sliced thickly
4 portobello mushrooms, quartered
3 cloves garlic, unpeeled
⅓ cup mayonnaise
1 tablespoon lemon juice

1 Quarter peppers, discard seeds and membranes. Roast under broiler or in very hot oven, skin-side up, until skin blisters and blackens. Cover pepper pieces in plastic or paper for 5 minutes; peel away skin, slice thickly.

2 Combine oil, crushed garlic, rind and half the rosemary in small bowl.

3 Brush onion, leek, eggplant, zucchini, mushrooms and unpeeled garlic with oil mixture; cook vegetables, in batches, on heated oiled grill pan until tender.

4 Squeeze cooked garlic into small bowl; discard skins. Whisk in remaining rosemary, mayonnaise and juice. Serve vegetables with dressing.

nutritional count per serving 22.8g total fat (2.9g saturated fat); 317 cal; 16.9g carbohydrate; 7.9g protein; 8.4g fiber

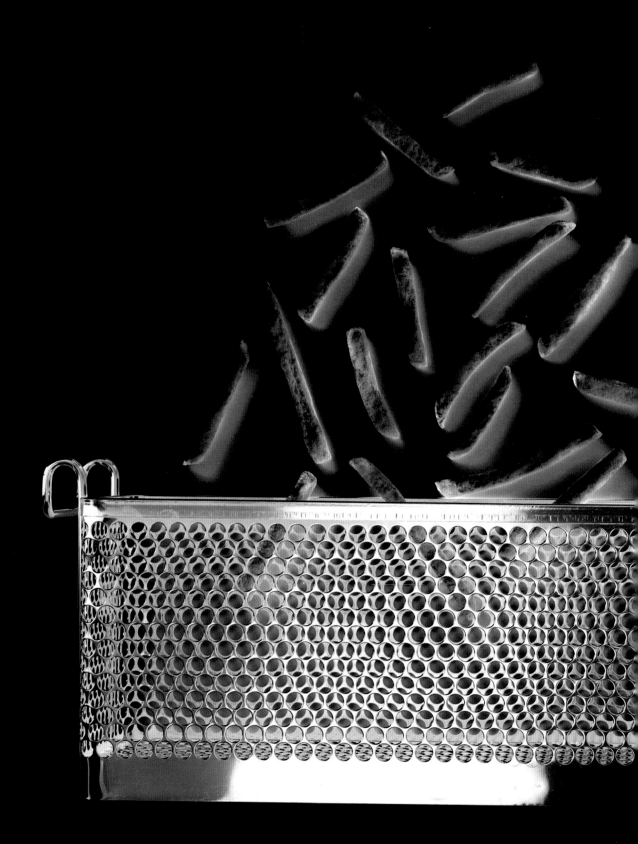

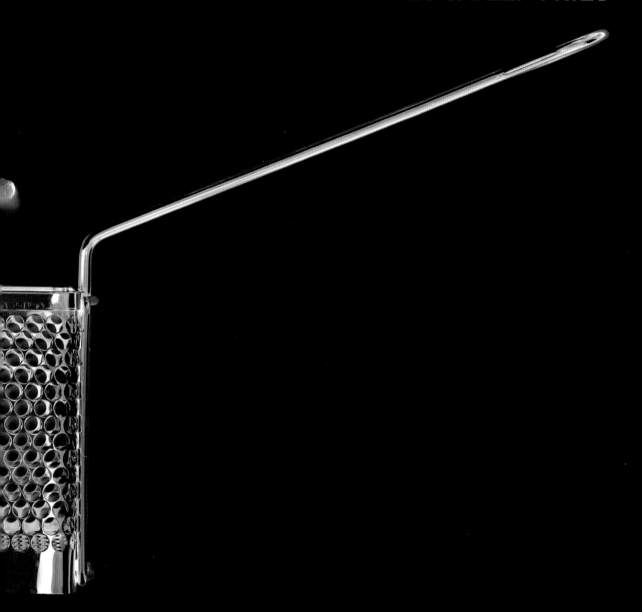

PAN-FRIES & DEEP-FRIES

Pan-fries & deep-fries

Pan-frying and deep-frying are like very different siblings: they share a common name and trait (they're both "dry cooking" methods that rely on hot oil to cook the food) but they operate differently, and produce different results.

PAN-FRYING

PAN-FRYING (ALSO CALLED SHALLOW FRYING) IS A COOKING METHOD IN WHICH FOOD IS FRIED IN A SHALLOW LAYER OF OIL IN A FRYING PAN. WITH PAN-FRYING, THE IDEA IS TO BROWN ONE SIDE FIRST, THEN TURN THE FOOD. THIS METHOD IS USED FOR DISHES SUCH AS CHICKEN SCHNITZEL AND BREADED LAMB CUTLETS.

Pan-frying produces a tasty, golden-brown crust around the food while also retaining the moisture inside. To ensure the food is moist inside, rather than greasy, the oil needs to be at a consistently medium-hot temperature. The amount of oil used in pan-frying can vary anywhere from a light coating on the base of the frying pan to half the height of the food.

TO PAN-FRY VEGETABLES Heat a little oil or butter, or a mixture of both, over medium heat until the oil shimmers or the butter stops sizzling. Fry the vegetables until browned and tender, turning once: remove with a slotted spoon or tongs and then drain on absorbent paper.

PAN-FRIED FOODS Food suitable for pan-frying includes tender cuts of meat, chicken, fish and vegetables. Meats are usually coated in bread crumbs before cooking; vegetables are not. All the foods must be cut thinly because they won't cook through if too thick (the surface will cook but the center will remain uncooked).

Place the food in the heated pan and cook until the first side is brown; turn and brown the other side. If cooking in batches, scoop out any errant food bits and add fresh oil in between batches.

Drain all pan-fried foods on absorbent paper.

THE FRYING PAN

A good frying pan is indispensable. A medium-sized one (7 to 8 inches across the base) is the most useful. If you think you require greater capacity, then a second medium-sized pan is more versatile than one huge one.

The key is to make sure your pan is solid and feels heavy. It should be thick so that it can take up and hold the heat, and made of a material that is a good conductor of heat—that is, it transmits heat rapidly and evenly to the whole cooking surface, and responds quickly when the heat is turned up.

WHAT TO LOOK FOR If money is no object, then you could invest in a titanium pan (which provides fast and even heat distribution and retention) but copper, aluminium, stainless steel or cast iron are more realistic options. Each of these has its advantages and disadvantages, and your decision should come down to performance, not looks. Make sure the handle is riveted or welded on, not just attached with screws, and a handle that can go into the oven makes it more versatile. A lid is also useful because browning is often only the first step in a recipe, followed by covered cooking.

DEEP-FRYING

THE GOAL OF DEEP-FRYING—PLUNGING FOOD INTO DEEP, HOT OIL—IS THAT THE FOOD GETS QUICKLY CRISPED ON THE OUTSIDE WHILE STEAMING ON THE INSIDE. FOR THIS TO HAPPEN, IT IS VITAL THAT THE OIL STAYS AT THE CORRECT TEMPERATURE (BETWEEN 350°F AND 375°F) THROUGHOUT COOKING. IF THE OIL IS NOT HOT ENOUGH, THE FOOD WILL BE SOGGY AND GREASY.

Deep-frying is a cooking method avoided by the health conscious although, in its defense, it doesn't (or shouldn't) make the food itself greasy or heavy if it is done properly. That said, no one can deny you're eating some oil when you're enjoying hot fish and chips: moderation is the order of the day as far as these foods go.

If the oil is too hot, the food will be burned on the outside by the time the interior is cooked. As long as the oil is hot enough and the food isn't immersed in it for too long, no oil will enter the interior and the food will remain light and digestible, encased in a crispy exterior.
Be careful not to overcrowd the deep fryer (or saucepan or wok) because this can lower the temperature of the oil, leading to greasy food. Fry in batches rather than in huge quantities.

DEEP-FRIED FOODS are usually coated with batter or egg and bread crumbs. After bread-crumbing, rest the pieces for about 20 minutes before frying to allow the egg to set. This ensures the coating adheres better during cooking. Pat off excess bread crumbs before placing the food in the oil.

OILS suitable for deep frying include peanut, safflower, sunflower and most blended oils.

Change the oil after every few batches or if it darkens.

Cut food pieces to a uniform size so they will cook at the same time

Fry in batches small enough for the pieces to float free without touching each other.

Drain the food after frying on absorbent paper.

WHAT YOU NEED

A DEEP PAN You need a container deep enough to cover your food with oil as it fries. You don't need to have an electric deep fryer: a saucepan or wok works perfectly well for this purpose.
A THERMOMETER For stove top deep-frying, use a special deep-frying thermometer with a clamp on it so you can attach it to the side of the pan. (Electric deep fryers have in-built thermostatic controls to keep the oil at a steady temperature.)
A SLOTTED SPOON OR LONG-HANDLED METAL TONGS In order to handle and remove items.
FRYING BASKET If you're deep-frying on the stove top on a regular basis, it's worth owning one of these to add and remove the food from the pan as a batch. Use a wire basket with a long handle.
OVEN GLOVES For handling the metal frying basket.

SAFETY

Deep-frying involves very hot oil so make sure children and pets are out of the way.

Avoid splashing hot oil: Place food items gently into the oil either in batches (using a basket) or individually using long tongs.

Never fill the pan or fryer more than half-full of oil because it bubbles up when the food is added.

Never lift or move the pan until it and the oil are completely cooled.

chicken schnitzel

The bread crumb mixture lends itself to the addition of extra flavors, such as grated parmesan, finely grated lemon rind, chopped thyme or rosemary, chili or mustard powder.

4 chicken breast filets (1½ pounds)
¼ cup all-purpose flour
2 eggs
1 tablespoon milk
2½ cups stale white bread crumbs
2 teaspoons finely grated lemon rind
2 tablespoons finely chopped fresh flat-leaf parsley
2 tablespoons finely chopped fresh basil
⅓ cup finely grated parmesan cheese
vegetable oil, for shallow-frying

1 Using meat mallet, gently pound chicken, one piece at a time, between sheets of plastic wrap until ¼-inch thick; cut each piece in half.
2 Whisk flour, eggs and milk in shallow bowl; combine bread crumbs, rind, herbs and cheese in another shallow bowl. Coat chicken pieces, one at a time, in egg mixture then bread crumb mixture.
3 Heat oil in large frying pan; shallow-fry chicken, in batches, until cooked. Drain on absorbent paper.
4 Serve chicken schnitzel with lemon wedges, if you like.
nutritional count per serving 41.5g total fat (9g saturated fat); 741 cal; 35.4g carbohydrate; 55.7g protein; 2.3g fiber

Dip the pounded-out chicken filets in a batter made from flour, eggs and milk.

Put the bread crumb mixture in a shallow dish and coat the chicken filets on both sides.

Heat enough oil to coat the bottom of the pan and shallow-fry the chicken schnitzels, turning once until golden brown and cooked through.

steak diane

No one really knows the origin of steak diane; chefs in the U.S., Australia and Brazil have all claimed to be its creators. The dish was extremely popular in restaurants in the 1950s and 1960s, often cooked at the table. Steak diane is popular on pub and bistro menus.

1 tablespoon olive oil

4 x 4-ounce beef filet steaks

⅓ cup brandy

2 cloves garlic, crushed

¼ cup Worcestershire sauce

1 cup cream

1 tablespoon finely chopped fresh flat-leaf parsley

1 Heat oil in large frying pan; cook steaks until cooked as desired. Remove from pan; cover to keep warm.

2 Add brandy to pan; bring to a boil. Add garlic, sauce and cream; cook, stirring, about 3 minutes or until sauce thickens slightly. Remove pan from heat; stir in parsley.

3 Serve steaks with sauce, and accompany with fries and a green salad, if you like.

nutritional count per serving 39.1g total fat (21.6g saturated fat); 2522 cal; 5.2g carbohydrate; 27.9g protein; 0.4g fiber

veal saltimbocca

Saltimbocca is a classic Italian veal dish that literally means "jump in the mouth"–just the sensation the wonderful flavors will produce with your first bite.

8 veal schnitzels (1½ pounds)

8 slices prosciutto

16 fresh sage leaves

3 tablespoons butter

1 cup dry white wine

1 tablespoon lemon juice

2 tablespoons coarsely chopped fresh sage

1 Top each piece of veal with prosciutto and sage leaves. Fold in half, prosciutto-side out, to secure filling; secure with toothpicks or small skewers.

2 Melt half the butter in large frying pan; cook veal, in batches, until cooked as desired. Cover to keep warm.

3 Add wine to pan; bring to a boil. Boil, uncovered, until reduced by half. Stir in remaining butter, juice and sage.

4 Serve saltimbocca with sauce, and accompany with steamed green beans and baby new potatoes, if you like.

nutritional count per serving 13g total fat (6.8g saturated fat); 361 cal; 0.5g carbohydrate; 50.3g protein; 0g fiber

[1] steak diane
[2] veal saltimbocca
[3] veal parmigiana [page 464]
[4] pork chops with apple and calvados [page 465]

veal parmigiana

PREP + COOK TIME 1 HOUR 45 MINS • SERVES 4

Veal comes from calves and may be milk-fed, meaning that the animal never ate grass, or grass-fed, meaning that the animal spent time in the pasture before slaughter. Milk-fed veal is very pale and delicate in flavor, and grass-fed is pink and fuller-flavored.

4 veal steaks (12 ounces)
¼ cup all-purpose flour
1 egg
1 tablespoon water
⅓ cup stale bread crumbs
2 tablespoons butter
⅓ cup olive oil
1½ cups coarsely grated mozzarella cheese
⅓ cup finely grated parmesan cheese

tomato sauce
1 tablespoon olive oil
1 medium brown onion, chopped finely
1 stalk celery, trimmed, chopped finely
1 medium red pepper, chopped finely
1 clove garlic, crushed
14-ounce can crushed tomatoes
2 teaspoons sugar
1 tablespoon tomato paste
1½ cups chicken stock
1 tablespoon finely chopped fresh flat-leaf parsley
1 tablespoon finely chopped fresh basil

1 Make tomato sauce.

2 Pound veal out thinly between layers of plastic wrap. Coat veal in flour; shake off excess. Dip veal in combined beaten egg and the water; press bread crumbs firmly onto veal. Refrigerate 10 minutes.

3 Preheat oven to 350°F/325°F fan-forced.

4 Heat butter and half the oil in large frying pan; cook veal, in batches, until browned on both sides. Place veal in large shallow ovenproof dish; top veal with mozzarella, drizzle with tomato sauce then sprinkle evenly with parmesan. Drizzle over remaining oil.

5 Bake parmigiana, in oven, about 20 minutes or until browned lightly. Serve with a green salad, if you like.

tomato sauce Heat oil in medium frying pan; cook onion, celery, pepper and garlic, stirring, until onion is soft. Remove pan from heat. Push undrained tomatoes through a sieve into the pan; discard solids. Add sugar, paste and stock. Cover; bring to a boil. Reduce heat; simmer, covered, 30 minutes. Uncover; simmer until sauce is thick. Stir in herbs.

nutritional count per serving 42g total fat (14.8g saturated fat); 620 cal; 21g carbohydrate; 37g protein; 3.7g fiber

pork chops with apples and calvados

Calvados is an expensive apple brandy–use brandy instead of calvados if you like.

4 x 10-ounce pork loin chops
3 tablespoons butter
2 medium apples, peeled, cored
    cut into thin wedges
4 shallots, sliced thinly

1 tablespoon all-purpose flour
½ cup calvados
1 cup cider vinegar
1 cup chicken stock
⅔ cup cream

1 Cook pork in heated oiled large frying pan until cooked as desired. Remove from pan; cover to keep warm. Drain and discard excess fat from pan.
2 Heat half the butter in pan; cook apples, stirring, until browned lightly. Remove from pan.
3 Heat remaining butter in pan; cook shallots, stirring, until soft. Add flour; cook, stirring, 1 minute. Add calvados; bring to a boil. Stir in cider, stock and cream; simmer, uncovered, until sauce thickens slightly. Return apples to pan; cook until heated through.
4 Serve pork topped with apples and sauce.
nutritional count per serving 47.5g total fat (25g saturated fat); 2705 cal; 18.1g carbohydrate; 35.7g protein; 1.4g fiber

salt and pepper squid

For a quick way to coat squid, place the flour, salt and pepper in a strong plastic bag with the squid; grip the bag tightly closed, then gently shake. Remove the squid from the bag; shake off any excess flour.

Tenderizing squid in coconut milk with 1 tablespoon fish sauce will impart a wonderful flavor. Drain well and pat dry with absorbent paper before tossing it in the flour.

1¼ pounds squid tubes, cleaned
¼ cup all-purpose flour
1½ teaspoons sea salt flakes
1½ teaspoons cracked black pepper
1 teaspoon dried chili flakes
vegetable oil, for deep-frying
1½ ounces baby arugula leaves
1 large tomato, seeded,
    chopped finely

lemon aïoli
2 egg yolks
1 teaspoon dijon mustard
⅔ cup extra light olive oil
⅓ cup olive oil
2 tablespoons lemon juice
2 cloves garlic, crushed

1 Make lemon aïoli.
2 Cut squid down center to open out; score the inside in a diagonal pattern. Halve squid lengthwise; slice halves crosswise into thick strips.
3 Combine flour, salt, pepper and chili in medium bowl, add squid; toss squid to coat in flour mixture. Shake off excess.
4 Heat oil in wok; deep-fry squid, in batches, until tender, drain.
5 Serve squid with arugula, tomato and aïoli.
lemon aïoli Whisk egg yolks and mustard in medium bowl. Gradually whisk in combined oils, in a thin, steady stream until thickened. Stir in juice and garlic.
nutritional count per serving 67.1g total fat (10.1g saturated fat); 746 cal; 8.2g carbohydrate; 28.6g protein; 1.6g fiber

steak sandwich

2 cloves garlic, crushed

2 tablespoons olive oil

4 thin beef rib-eye steaks (1 pound)

2 medium brown onions, sliced thinly

1 tablespoon brown sugar

1 tablespoon balsamic vinegar

8 thick slices white bread

1 baby romaine lettuce, leaves separated

2 dill pickles, sliced thinly

¼ cup tomato chutney

1 Combine garlic and half the oil in medium bowl, add steaks; rub both sides of steak with mixture.

2 Heat remaining oil in medium frying pan; cook onion over low heat, stirring occasionally, about 10 minutes or until soft. Add sugar and vinegar; cook, stirring, about 5 minutes or until caramelized. Remove from pan.

3 Meanwhile, cook steaks in heated oiled large frying pan.

4 Toast bread on both sides. Sandwich lettuce, steaks, onion, pickle and chutney between toast slices.

nutritional count per sandwich 20.5g total fat (5g saturated fat); 672 cal; 78.1g carbohydrate; 39.7g protein; 6.4g fiber

seared calves' liver with persillade

Persillade is a mixture of chopped garlic and parsley traditionally used either as a garnish or to flavor a sauce, as we have done here.

14-ounce piece calves' liver, sliced thinly

3 tablespoons butter

1 clove garlic, chopped finely

1 shallot, chopped finely

½ cup chicken stock

1 tablespoon lemon juice

⅓ cup finely chopped fresh flat-leaf parsley

1 Pat liver dry with absorbent paper. Melt about 1 tablespoon of the butter in large frying pan; cook liver quickly, in batches, over high heat until browned both sides and cooked as desired (do not overcook). Remove from pan; cover to keep warm.

2 To make persillade, heat remaining butter in same pan; cook garlic and shallot, stirring, until shallot softens. Add stock and juice; bring to a boil, stirring. Remove from heat; stir in parsley. Serve sliced liver with persillade.

nutritional count per serving 18g total fat (9.1g saturated fat); 1260 cal; 3g carbohydrate; 21.6g protein; 0.3g fiber

[opposite] steak sandwich

garlic prawns

Prawns are deveined because the vein, which is the gut, may contain grit as prawns are bottom-feeders.

2 pounds uncooked medium
   king prawns
4 cloves garlic, crushed
2 fresh small red Thai chilies,
   chopped finely
2 tablespoons olive oil
1 medium red pepper, sliced thinly

1 medium green pepper,
   sliced thinly
½ cup chicken stock
1¼ cups cream
1 tablespoon lemon juice
1 tablespoon finely chopped
   fresh flat-leaf parsley

1 Shell and devein prawns, leaving tails intact. Combine prawns, garlic and chili in medium bowl.

2 Heat half the oil in large frying pan; cook prawns, stirring, until changed in color. Remove from pan.

3 Heat remaining oil in same pan; cook peppers, stirring, until tender. Return prawns to pan with stock, cream and juice; bring to a boil. Reduce heat; simmer, uncovered, about 5 minutes or until sauce thickens slightly. Remove from heat; stir in parsley.

nutritional count per serving 42.6g total fat (22.9g saturated fat); 519 cal; 5.4g carbohydrate; 28.9g protein; 1.4g fiber

serving ideas good-quality bread, steamed rice, pasta.

breaded lamb cutlets

12 boneless lamb cutlets
   (1½ pounds)
¼ cup soy sauce
2 cloves garlic, crushed
½ cup all-purpose flour

2 eggs, beaten lightly
¼ cup milk
1 cup stale bread crumbs
1 cup packaged bread crumbs
vegetable oil, for shallow-frying

1 Trim excess fat from cutlets. Using meat mallet, pound each cutlet between sheets of plastic wrap until cutlets are flattened slightly.

2 Combine soy sauce and garlic in large dish, add cutlets. Cover; refrigerate, turning cutlets several times, 30 minutes.

3 Place flour in plastic bag; add cutlets; toss until cutlets are well coated. Dip cutlets in combined egg and milk, then coat with combined bread crumbs.

4 Heat oil in large frying pan; shallow-fry cutlets until cooked as desired. Drain on absorbent paper.

nutritional count per serving 63.7g total fat (22.4g saturated fat); 954 cal; 59.4g carbohydrate; 35g protein; 3.7g fiber

sausages with pea and bacon mash

It's not necessary to oil a frying pan when cooking bacon as the fat renders in the hot pan, creating its own frying medium.

3 strips bacon, chopped

1 tablespoon olive oil

2 medium onions, sliced thinly

8 thick beef sausages (1¼ pounds)

2 pounds potatoes, peeled, quartered

1 cup milk, warmed

3 tablespoons butter

½ cup frozen peas

1 Add the bacon to a heated frying pan, cook until browned and crisp; remove.
2 Heat oil in same pan, add onions and sausages; cook until onions are soft and the sausages are cooked through.
3 Meanwhile, boil or steam the potatoes until soft; drain. Mash potatoes with milk, butter and salt and pepper to taste.
4 Boil, steam or microwave peas until just tender; drain. Add peas and bacon to potatoes.
5 Serve mash topped with sausages and onion.

nutritional count per serving 60.5g total fat (28.8g saturated fat); 867 cal; 39.7g carbohydrate; 37.7g protein; 9.4g fiber

caramelized crispy-skin duck

4 duck breast filets

¼ cup brown sugar

1 teaspoon finely grated orange rind

2 tablespoons orange juice

1 fresh long red chili, chopped finely

¾-inch piece fresh ginger, peeled, grated

1 tablespoon balsamic vinegar

1 Cook duck, skin-side down, in heated large frying pan about 5 minutes or until skin is browned and crisp. Turn duck; cook about 5 minutes or until cooked as desired. Remove from pan; cover to keep warm.
2 Drain all but 2 tablespoons of duck fat from pan; reheat. Add sugar, rind, juice, chili, ginger and vinegar; bring to a boil. Reduce heat; simmer sauce, uncovered, 2 minutes.
3 Serve duck topped with sauce.

nutritional count per serving 29.1g total fat (8.7g saturated fat); 447 cal; 14.3g carbohydrate; 32.4g protein; 0.1g fiber

classic fish and chips

This dish is traditionally served with tartare sauce. To make your own, combine ⅔ cup whole-egg mayonnaise, ½ finely chopped small brown onion, 2 tablespoons finely chopped cornichons, 1 tablespoon finely chopped drained and rinsed capers, 1 tablespoon finely chopped fresh flat-leaf parsley and 1 tablespoon lemon juice in a medium bowl.

1 cup self-rising flour

1 cup dry ale

1 tablespoon sea salt

2 pounds potatoes, peeled

peanut oil, for deep-frying

4 x 5-ounce cod filets, halved lengthwise

1 Sift flour into medium bowl; whisk in beer and salt until smooth.

2 Cut potatoes lengthwise into ⅓-inch slices; cut each slice lengthwise into ⅓-inch batons; dry with absorbent paper.

3 Heat oil in large saucepan. Cook potatoes, in three batches, about 2 minutes or until tender but not brown. Drain on absorbent paper.

4 Dip fish in batter; drain away excess. Deep-fry fish, in batches, until cooked. Drain on absorbent paper.

5 Deep-fry potatoes, in three batches, until crisp and golden brown; drain on absorbent paper. Serve fish and chips with tartare sauce and lemon wedges.

nutritional count per serving 14.6g total fat (3.1g saturated fat); 541 cal; 55.1g carbohydrate; 39.6g protein; 4.8g fiber

Add beer to the flour and salt and whisk together until it becomes a smooth batter.

Dip the fish filets into the batter and shake off the excess.

Deep-fry the fish in batches until golden and cooked through. Drain the filets well on absorbent paper.

vegetable tempura

Adjust the size or thickness of slower-cooking vegetables (such as sweet potato and pumpkin) to ensure they cook at the same rate as faster-cooking vegetables (such as mushrooms). Always use fresh, clean oil and keep at a constant temperature during cooking. Optimum oil temperature for vegetables is fairly hot, about 350°F and for seafood slightly higher; seafood is usually cooked after vegetables.

Lotus root has a crisp texture and delicate flavor. It has small holes throughout its length, which, when sliced into rounds, looks like a flower. Fresh lotus root must be peeled and cooked before eating. Also available prepared and ready for cooking in cans, vacuum packs and frozen.

1 medium brown onion
1 small fresh or frozen lotus root
8 fresh shiitake mushrooms
2 sheets toasted seaweed
½ ounce cellophane noodles (harusame), cut in half
vegetable oil, for deep-frying
½ cup all-purpose flour
4-ounce piece pumpkin, sliced thinly
1½ ounces green beans, halved
1 small sweet potato, sliced thinly
1 baby eggplant, sliced thinly
1 small red pepper, cut into 1-inch pieces
1 medium carrot, sliced thinly, diagonally
8 ounces firm tofu, pressed, cut into ¾-inch cubes

batter
1 egg, beaten lightly
2 cups iced soda water
1 cup all-purpose flour
1 cup corn starch

dipping sauce
1 cup dashi or vegetable broth
⅓ cup mirin
⅓ cup light soy sauce
½ cup finely grated daikon
2-inch piece fresh ginger, peeled, grated finely

1 Make batter and dipping sauce.

2 Halve onion through root end. Insert toothpicks at regular intervals to hold onion rings together and slice crosswise in between.

3 Peel lotus root and slice. Place slices in water with a dash of vinegar to prevent browning. If using canned lotus, drain and slice. Remove and discard mushroom stems; cut a cross in the top of caps.

4 Cut one sheet seaweed into 2-inch squares, halve the other sheet and cut into ¾-inch-wide strips. Brush seaweed strips with water and wrap tightly around about 10 noodles, either at one end or in the middle; reserve noodle bunches.

5 Heat oil in wok or large saucepan. Toss vegetables in flour to coat; shake off excess flour. Dip seaweed squares and vegetables in batter, in batches; drain excess batter. Deep-fry ingredients, in batches, until browned lightly and crisp. Drain on absorbent paper. Deep-fry reserved noodle bunches.

6 Serve tempura with individual bowls of warm dipping sauce.

batter Combine egg in a bowl with iced water. Add sifted flours all at once, mixing lightly until just combined, but still very lumpy.

dipping sauce Place dashi, mirin and sauce in medium saucepan and heat gently; divide among four individual serving bowls. Shape daikon into four pyramid shapes. Place a pyramid in each serving bowl; top with even amounts of ginger.

nutritional count per serving 62g total fat (8.2g saturated fat); 1026 cal; 93.4g carbohydrate; 20.7g protein; 8.6g fiber

zucchini fritters

The smaller, the better is a good rule for buying zucchini and small squash, unless a certain size is required for stuffing. Whatever the size, they should be brightly colored with a sheen on the skin, and firm with no soft spots.

4 medium zucchini
2 teaspoons coarse cooking salt
peanut oil, for deep-frying

skordalia
4 slices stale white sandwich bread, crusts removed
4 cloves garlic, crushed
½ cup olive oil
1 tablespoon lemon juice
1 tablespoon water, approximately

batter
1 cup self-rising flour
¾ cup warm water
1 tablespoon olive oil
1 egg yolk

1 Make skordalia.
2 Cut zucchini into ⅓-inch diagonal slices. Place zucchini in colander, sprinkle with salt; stand 30 minutes. Rinse zucchini under cold water; drain zucchini on absorbent paper.
3 Make batter.
4 Heat oil in large saucepan. Dip zucchini into batter, carefully lower into hot oil; cook zucchini until browned and crisp. Drain on absorbent paper.
5 Serve zucchini fritters with skordalia.

skordalia Briefly dip bread into a bowl of cold water, then gently squeeze out the water. Blend or process bread and garlic until combined. With motor running, gradually add oil, juice and enough of the water, in a thin steady stream, until mixture is smooth and thick. Transfer to serving bowl.

batter Sift flour into medium bowl; whisk in combined remaining ingredients until smooth. Stand batter 10 minutes. If batter thickens too much, whisk in a little extra water to give it a coating consistency.

nutritional count per serving 28g total fat (4.2g saturated fat); 383 cal; 26.5g carbohydrate; 5.4g protein; 3g fiber

pan-seared scallops with anchovy butter

Scallops are often eaten raw or barely seared, and should never be cooked for more than about 30 seconds as they will lose their juicy tenderness and become tough. Cooked scallops are often served on the natural half-shells (which can be washed and used again) or on porcelain shell-shaped dishes.

2 teaspoons olive oil

12 sea scallops (10 ounces)

3 tablespoons butter

3 drained anchovy filets

2 cloves garlic, crushed

2 teaspoons lemon juice

1 tablespoon finely chopped fresh chives

1 Heat oil in large frying pan; cook scallops, both sides, until browned lightly. Remove from pan; cover to keep warm.

2 Add butter, anchovies and garlic to pan; cook, stirring, until garlic is browned lightly. Return scallops to pan with juice; cook until scallops are heated through. Serve scallops drizzled with anchovy butter and sprinkled with chives.

nutritional count per serving 9.1g total fat (4.8g saturated fat); 123 cal; 0.8g carbohydrate; 9.6g protein; 0.3g fiber

pancakes with lemon and sugar

This simple yet delicious combination makes a perfect Sunday breakfast or after-dinner treat. Use brown sugar in place of white for a more caramel flavor.

2 cups all-purpose flour

4 eggs, beaten lightly

2 cups milk, approximately

3 tablespoons butter

¼ cup lemon juice, approximately

2 tablespoons sugar, approximately

1 Place flour in medium bowl. Make well in center; gradually whisk or stir in egg and enough of the milk to make a thin, smooth batter. Transfer to a pitcher.

2 Heat large frying pan over high heat a few minutes. Place ½ teaspoon butter in pan; swirl around pan until greased all over. Pour ¼ cup of the batter from pitcher into center of pan; quickly tilt pan so that batter runs from center around edge.

3 When pancake is browned lightly underneath, turn and brown the other side. This can be done using a spatula or an egg slide, or pancake can be tossed and flipped over back into the pan; this takes a little practice.

4 Serve pancakes, as they are made, on warm plates; spread one side with a little of the butter. Drizzle with juice; sprinkle with sugar.

nutritional count per pancake 19.3g total fat (10.4g saturated fat); 537 cal; 69.7g carbohydrate; 19.2g protein; 2.9g fiber

[opposite] pan-seared scallops with anchovy butter

french toast

For a delicious alternative to powdered sugar, sprinkle french toast with vanilla or cinnamon sugar. Simply combine ¼ cup superfine sugar with the seeds of half a vanilla pod or a good pinch of ground cinnamon.

4 eggs
½ cup cream
¼ cup milk
1 teaspoon ground cinnamon
¼ cup superfine sugar
7 tablespoons butter, melted
8 thick slices white bread
2 tablespoons powdered sugar
⅓ cup maple syrup

1 Whisk eggs in medium bowl, then whisk in cream, milk, cinnamon and sugar.
2 Heat a quarter of the butter in medium frying pan. Dip two bread slices into egg mixture, one at a time; cook bread until browned both sides. Remove french toast from pan; keep warm.
3 Repeat step 2 to make a total of 8 slices.
4 Serve French toast dusted with sifted powdered sugar and drizzled with maple syrup. Top with sliced strawberries, if you like.
nutritional count per serving 42.2g total fat (24.8g saturated fat); 764 cal; 79.4g carbohydrate; 15.5g protein; 2.6g fiber

banana fritters

The word fritter comes from the Latin word "frictura", meaning fried. You can serve these fritters drizzled with pure maple syrup, sprinkled with chopped toasted pecans and topped with a scoop (or two) of vanilla ice cream. They are also delicious drizzled with coconut liqueur and sprinkled with toasted shredded coconut.

¼ cup powdered sugar
2 teaspoons ground cinnamon
1 egg, beaten lightly
¾ cup Japanese bread crumbs
vegetable oil, for deep-frying
4 large bananas, halved lengthwise

1 Combine sugar and cinnamon in shallow medium bowl. Beat egg in shallow medium bowl; place bread crumbs in another bowl.
2 Heat oil in medium saucepan.
3 Meanwhile, dip bananas in sugar mixture: shake off excess. Dip banana in egg, then in crumbs to coat.
4 Deep-fry bananas, in batches, until browned. Drain on absorbent paper.
nutritional count per serving 9.7g total fat (1.5g saturated fat); 318 cal; 49.2g carbohydrate; 6g protein; 3.9g fiber

[opposite] french toast

crêpes suzette

¾ cup all-purpose flour
3 eggs
2 tablespoons vegetable oil
¾ cup milk

orange sauce
1 stick unsalted butter
½ cup superfine sugar
1½ cups orange juice
2 tablespoons lemon juice
⅓ cup orange-flavored liqueur

TIPS

• Be very careful when igniting the sauce–use extra long matches, available from most supermarkets or camping stores. Igniting the sauce burns off the alcohol, leaving a more intense flavor. If you prefer, the sauce can be served as is, without first igniting it.

• Make sure overhead exhaust fans are turned off before igniting the orange sauce.

1 Sift flour into medium bowl, make well in center; add eggs and oil then gradually whisk in milk until smooth. Pour batter into large pitcher, cover; stand 1 hour.
2 Heat greased heavy-based crêpe pan or small frying pan; pour ¼ cup of batter into pan, tilting pan to coat base. Cook, over low heat, until browned lightly, loosening edge of crêpe with spatula. Turn crêpe; brown other side. Remove crêpe from pan; cover to keep warm. Repeat with remaining batter to make a total of 8 crêpes, greasing pan each time.
3 Make orange sauce.
4 Fold crêpes in half then in half again, place in sauce; warm over low heat. Remove crêpes to serving plates; pour hot sauce over crêpes. Serve with orange segments, if you like.

orange sauce Melt butter in large frying pan, add sugar; cook, stirring, until mixture begins to brown. Strain and add juices; bring to a boil. Reduce heat; simmer, uncovered, about 3 minutes or until a golden color. Remove from heat; add liqueur, ignite, and let stand until flame goes out.

nutritional count per serving 41g total fat (20.5g saturated fat); 727 cal; 66.9g carbohydrate; 10.3g protein; 1.3g fiber

Q&A

How do you cut orange segments so that they have no skin? They always look wonderful in photographs and I've had them in cafés too, but have never learned the trick myself.

It's harder (and probably takes longer) to describe than it would be to demonstrate. With a sharp knife, cut the peel away from the orange, leaving no white pith at all. Then, with a small very sharp knife, cut down through a segment to the center of the orange, and with a flicking movement, cut up the other side of the segment. The segment will fall out, minus its skin. (Do it over a bowl to catch the juices.) Continue all the way around the orange.

PULSES & GRAINS

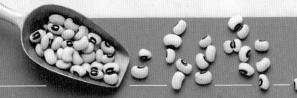

Pulses & grains

They used to be called "poor man's meats" because they were cheap and filling, but pulses (dried beans, peas and lentils) together with grains (such as couscous, polenta, rye and oats) are now prized around the world for their nutritional value and enjoyable eating. Collectively, they deliver rich supplies of protein, dietary fiber, vitamins and minerals and have little or no fat.

PULSES

OVER GENERATIONS, THESE HUMBLE INGREDIENTS HAVE BEEN TRANSFORMED INTO SOME OF THE WORLD'S MOST POPULAR DISHES SUCH AS ITALY'S FAMOUS MINESTRONE, FILLED WITH BEANS AND VEGETABLES; INDIA'S SOOTHING DHALS MADE FROM LENTILS; THE MIDDLE EAST'S CHICKPEA DIP, HUMMUS; AND MEXICO'S REFRIED BEANS, TO NAME A FEW.

BEANS Adzuki beans; black beans (turtle beans); black-eyed beans (black-eyed peas); borlotti beans; broad beans (fava beans); butter (lima) beans; chickpeas; flageolet beans; haricot beans (encompassing cannellini and navy beans, different varieties of mild-flavored white beans that are interchangeable with each other in recipes); kidney beans; mung beans (the bean usually used for sprouts); pinto beans and soybeans.

PEAS Blue boilers (whole peas, gray-green color, used for mushy peas, pea and ham soup); split peas (skinless, yellow or green, sweet, with a definite pea flavor).

LENTILS Are usually described by color:
• Brown lentils (also called green and continental lentils): pale brown to greenish in color, they come in various sizes, with their skin on. They have a warm, slightly spicy flavor.
• Red lentils: these tiny, orange-red lentils come skinned and split. They have a spicy flavor, and cook to a puree.
• Puy lentils (also called French green lentils): small, dark blue-green, and exceptionally fine in flavor and texture; originally from the Le Puy district in France.

SOAKING

Dried beans and peas are best soaked before cooking, but lentils don't need soaking.

LONG SOAKING Soak pulses in cold water, covered, for at least 6-8 hours. Chickpeas need up to 12 hours and broad beans need 24 hours. Refrigerate when soaking so they don't ferment.

QUICK SOAKING To quicken the soaking process, cover the pulses generously with cold water in a large saucepan, bring to the boil, then cover and cook for 2 minutes. Remove the pan from the heat and stand for an hour.

COOKING

Cover pulses with cold water and bring to a boil. Do not add salt, sugar or other flavoring as this will toughen them; add towards the end of cooking. Once boiling, cover, reduce heat to low and simmer until tender. Lentils may take 20 minutes or less to cook; beans and peas 1-2 hours or longer. When tender, drain and use. Store cooked pulses, covered, in the fridge for 2-3 days.

GRAINS

LIKE PULSES, GRAINS ARE INTEGRAL TO SOME OF THE WORLD'S GREAT DISHES AND THANKFULLY, THEY'RE NOW INGRAINED IN OUR OWN FOOD: WHERE WOULD WE BE WITHOUT OATS (EITHER IN MUESLI OR OATMEAL) AT BREAKFAST? OR THE CHEWY GOODNESS OF PEARL BARLEY IN OUR WINTER SOUPS? OR TABBOULEH SALAD IN SUMMER?

BARLEY Pearl barley is the type usually used for cooking. Delicious in soups, pearl barley has a robust, nutty flavor.

BUCKWHEAT Not a true grain, but the fruit of a plant related to rhubarb and sorrel. It is, however, used as a grain, cooked into a porridge or ground into a flour that is used for pancakes and noodles.

BULGUR The star of tabbouleh, bulgur is made from cracked wheat that is hulled, par-boiled or steamed, then dehydrated. Before use, it should be soaked in cold water to soften and swell the grains. Drain and squeeze as dry as possible and spread on a tea towel or absorbent paper to dry further.

COUSCOUS The staple cereal of North Africa, couscous is made from fine semolina (the first, grainy millings of the floury part of wheat grains), combined with flour, salt and water to make tiny pellets. Traditionally, couscous is first moistened to allow the grains to swell, then steamed over the pot in which the meat and vegetables for the meal are simmering. Pre-cooked "instant" couscous is also available.

OATS A very nutritious grain, oats are milled into oatmeal (of varying degrees of fineness) for various uses, including rolled oats, which are used in oatmeal, muesli and baking.

POLENTA The Italian name for cornmeal, polenta is made from dried corn ground to various degrees of fineness. It is prepared by boiling with water to make a porridge. It can be eaten like this (soft or wet polenta) or spread in a shallow pan, chilled to firm it, then brushed with oil and grilled, pan-fried or barbecued. Pre-cooked "instant" polenta is also available.

QUINOA Pronounced "keen-wa", this is a very nutritious South American cereal-like grain: the quality of its protein is equal to that of milk. It can be served instead of rice or couscous.

RYE A favorite grain in breads, including pumpernickel and rye crispbreads. Cracked whole rye, soaked overnight, can be made into porridge. Rye flakes can be used in the same way as rolled oats (for oatmeal, muesli and cooking).

STORING

IN STORAGE, PULSES HARDEN AND TAKE LONGER TO COOK, SO BUY FROM A SHOP WITH A HIGH TURNOVER. STORE IN AIRTIGHT CONTAINERS IN A COOL, DRY PLACE FOR NO MORE THAN A YEAR. MANY OF THE DRIED BEANS ARE AVAILABLE READY-COOKED IN CANS. THEY NEED TO BE DRAINED AND RINSED BEFORE USE. STORE GRAINS AWAY FROM HEAT OR LIGHT, IN LIDDED CONTAINERS TO PREVENT MOUSE OR INSECT DAMAGE.

grain and seed loaf

1 cup bulgur
1 tablespoon dry yeast
1 teaspoon sugar
¾ cup warm milk
¼ cup warm water
2¼ cups all-purpose flour

½ cup whole grain flour
1 teaspoon salt
2 tablespoons linseeds
2 teaspoons olive oil
1 tablespoon milk, extra
1 tablespoon sesame seeds

1 Place bulgur in medium heatproof bowl, cover with boiling water. Cover; stand 30 minutes. Rinse well; drain well.

2 Combine yeast, sugar, milk and the water in small bowl, whisk until yeast dissolves. Cover; stand in warm place about 10 minutes or until mixture is frothy.

3 Sift flours and salt into large bowl, add bulgur and linseeds. Stir in oil and yeast mixture; mix to a soft dough. Knead dough on floured surface about 10 minutes or until dough is smooth and elastic. Place dough in large oiled bowl; cover, stand in warm place about 1 hour or until dough has doubled in size.

4 Preheat oven to 425°F/400°F fan-forced. Oil 5½-inch x 8½-inch loaf pan.

5 Using fist, punch dough to expel air. Turn dough onto floured surface, knead until smooth. Divide dough into three pieces. Shape each piece into a 12-inch sausage. Braid sausages together, place into pan. Cover; stand in warm place about 30 minutes or until risen.

6 Brush dough with extra milk, sprinkle evenly with sesame seeds. Bake bread about 45 minutes; turn onto wire rack to cool.

nutritional count per slice 1.9g total fat (0.5g saturated fat); 129 cal; 22.3g carbohydrate; 4.1g protein; 2.8g fiber

Stand the yeast mixture in a warm place to allow it to become frothy. It's important that the spot you choose is warm, not hot. If it's too hot you'll kill the yeast.

Once the dough has doubled in size, punch it and knead it until it's smooth and elastic–you should be able to stretch the dough without breaking it.

Braid the three lengths of dough together loosely and place the dough in the oiled loaf pan.

Once the dough has risen above the top of the pan, brush it with milk and sprinkle with sesame seeds before baking.

hummus

Hummus can be served as a sauce with kebabs or meatballs or as a dip with pita bread. It is classically served in a shallow dish, drizzled with extra oil and sometimes sprinkled with paprika.

2 cups water

2 x 10-ounce cans chickpeas, rinsed, drained

¼ cup lemon juice

¼ cup olive oil

⅓ cup tahini

3 cloves garlic, crushed

1 tablespoon olive oil, extra

1 Place the water and chickpeas in medium saucepan; bring to a boil. Boil, uncovered, about 10 minutes or until tender. Strain chickpeas over medium bowl; reserve 1 cup cooking liquid.

2 Blend or process chickpeas and reserved cooking liquid with juice, oil, tahini and garlic until just smooth.

3 Serve hummus drizzled with extra oil.

nutritional count per ¼ cup 13.9g total fat (1.9g saturated fat); 180 cal; 7.2g carbohydrate; 5.2g protein; 3.8g fiber

falafel

These savory chickpea balls are a popular snack and street food in many parts of the Middle East, whether dipped in spices and yogurt, as in this recipe, or wrapped in pita bread with hummus and salad.

Dukkah is an Egyptian blend of nuts, spices and seeds, often mixed with oil or mayonnaise for a dip. You can make your own or buy it ready-made from specialty spice shops and delicatessens.

2 cups dried chickpeas

1 medium brown onion, chopped coarsely

2 cloves garlic, quartered

½ cup fresh flat-leaf parsley, chopped coarsely

2 teaspoons ground coriander

1 teaspoon ground cumin

1 teaspoon baking soda

2 tablespoons all-purpose flour

1 teaspoon salt

vegetable oil, for deep frying

1 Place chickpeas in large bowl, cover with cold water; stand overnight, drain.

2 Combine chickpeas, onion, garlic, parsley and spices in large bowl. Blend or process, in two batches, until almost smooth; return mixture to large bowl.

3 Add soda, flour and salt to chickpea mixture; knead on lightly floured surface for 2 minutes. Stand 30 minutes.

4 Roll level tablespoons of mixture into balls; stand 10 minutes.

5 Deep-fry balls in hot oil, in batches, until golden brown.

nutritional count per falafel 0.9g total fat (0.1g saturated fat); 19 cal; 1.8g carbohydrate; 0.7g protein; 0.6g fiber

serving ideas serve with separate bowls of dukkah and yogurt for dipping.

grilled parmesan polenta triangles

PREP + COOK TIME 25 MINS
(+ REFRIGERATION)
SERVES 4

1 quart water
1 cup polenta
2 tablespoons cold butter, chopped
1 cup finely grated parmesan cheese

Grilled polenta is made
by spreading soft polenta
into an even layer,
then chilling, cutting
into shapes, oiling and
grilling until crisp.

1 Oil deep 7½-inch square cake pan.
2 Bring the water to a boil in large saucepan. Gradually stir in polenta; simmer, stirring, about 10 minutes or until polenta thickens. Stir in butter and cheese.
3 Spread polenta into cake pan; cool 10 minutes. Cover; refrigerate 3 hours or until firm.
4 Turn polenta onto board. Cut polenta into four squares; cut squares into triangles. Cook polenta, both sides, in heated oiled grill pan (or grill or barbecue) until browned and heated through.
nutritional count per serving 11.4g total fat (6.9g saturated fat); 268 cal; 29.3g carbohydrate; 11.1g protein; 1.2g fiber

soft polenta

PREP + COOK TIME 40 MINS • SERVES 4

This goes beautifully
with meat casseroles,
especially those that
include red wine.

1 quart milk
1 large brown onion, quartered
4 bay leaves
4 cloves garlic, quartered
8 black peppercorns
1 cup instant polenta
3 tablespoons butter, chopped
1 cup finely grated parmesan cheese

1 Bring milk, onion, bay leaves, garlic and peppercorns to a boil in large saucepan. Strain milk mixture; discard solids. Return milk to same pan.
2 Gradually whisk in polenta; cook, stirring, over medium heat about 20 minutes.
3 Whisk in butter and cheese; season to taste with salt and freshly ground black pepper. Serve immediately.
nutritional count per serving 25.4g total fat (16.1g saturated fat); 494 cal; 44.5g carbohydrate; 20.5g protein; 2.4g fiber

mixed dhal

If you are unable to buy ghee, also known as "clarified butter", make your own. Heat some butter in a small pan until a white foamy layer appears on the surface; skim and discard. Pour off the butter leaving the sediment (milk solids) at the bottom of the pan; discard. Ghee will keep for several months in the fridge.

2 tablespoons ghee
1 medium brown onion, chopped finely
2 cloves garlic, crushed
1½-inch piece fresh ginger, grated
1½ tablespoons black mustard seeds
1 long green chili, chopped finely
1 tablespoon ground cumin
1 tablespoon ground coriander
2 teaspoons ground turmeric
½ cup brown lentils
⅓ cup red lentils
⅓ cup yellow split peas
⅓ cup green split peas
14-ounce can crushed tomatoes
2 cups vegetable stock
1½ cups water
4-ounce can coconut cream

1 Heat ghee in large saucepan; cook onion, garlic and ginger, stirring, until onion softens. Add seeds, chili and spices; cook, stirring, until fragrant.

2 Add lentils and peas to pan. Stir in undrained tomatoes, stock and the water; simmer, covered, stirring occasionally, about 1 hour or until lentils are tender.

3 Just before serving, add coconut cream; stir over low heat until heated through.

nutritional count per serving 18.4g total fat (12.5g saturated fat); 454 cal; 42.6g carbohydrate; 23.3g protein; 12.7g fiber

split pea and vegetable tagine

Like the word "casserole", the word "tagine" means both the food and the pot in which it is cooked, an attractive pottery vessel with a shallow circular base and a tall, conical lid that collects and condenses the steam so that it drips or slides back into the food in a continuous cycle.

2 tablespoons olive oil
1 large red onion, sliced thinly
¾ cup yellow split peas
2 cloves garlic, crushed
2-inch piece fresh ginger, grated
3 teaspoons ground coriander
2 teaspoons ground cumin
2 teaspoons sweet paprika
1 teaspoon caraway seeds
1 quart vegetable stock
14-ounce can diced tomatoes
1½ pounds butternut squash, cut into ¾-inch pieces
12 ounces yellow patty pan squash, quartered
7 ounces green beans, trimmed, halved crosswise
½ cup water
½ cup coarsely chopped fresh coriander

1 Heat oil in large saucepan; cook onion, stirring, until softened. Add peas, garlic, ginger, spices and seeds; cook, stirring, until fragrant.

2 Add stock and undrained tomatoes; bring to a boil. Reduce heat; simmer, uncovered, stirring occasionally, 15 minutes. Add squash; simmer 15 minutes or until peas are tender. Stir in yellow squash, beans and the water, cover; cook 5 minutes or until vegetables are tender.

3 Serve tagine sprinkled with chopped coriander.

nutritional count per serving 8.3g total fat (1.6g saturated fat); 256 cal; 27.8g carbohydrate; 13.5g protein; 7.9g fiber

[1] mixed dhal
[2] split pea and vegetable tagine
[3] baked lima beans [page 490]
[4] black bean, corn and chipotle stew [page 490]

baked lima beans

Also known as butter beans, lima beans are small and pale green if picked young or large, flat and white if picked when fully grown.

The baked beans are even better if made a day in advance as this allows the flavors to develop.

1½ cups dried lima beans
2 cups vegetable stock
½ cup polenta
1 tablespoon dijon mustard
½ cup finely grated
   parmesan cheese
2 tablespoons finely chopped
   fresh flat-leaf parsley

2 teaspoons olive oil
1 large brown onion,
   chopped finely
2 cloves garlic, crushed
14-ounce can crushed tomatoes
1 tablespoon tomato paste
2 tablespoons brown sugar
1½ cups vegetable stock, extra

1 Place beans in medium bowl, cover with water; soak overnight, drain. Rinse under cold water; drain. Place beans in medium saucepan of boiling water; return to a boil. Reduce heat; simmer, covered, 15 minutes or until beans are just tender. Drain.

2 Preheat oven to 400°F/350°F fan-forced. Oil 7½-inch square loaf pan; line base with baking paper.

3 Bring stock to a boil in medium saucepan. Gradually add polenta, stirring constantly. Reduce heat; simmer, stirring, 10 minutes or until polenta thickens. Stir in mustard, cheese and parsley. Spread polenta into pan; cover, refrigerate about 3 hours or until firm.

4 Heat oil in large flameproof pan; cook onion and garlic, stirring, until onion softens. Add beans, undrained tomatoes, paste, sugar and extra stock; bring to a boil. Cook, uncovered, in oven about 40 minutes or until sauce thickens.

5 Preheat broiler.

6 Turn polenta onto board; trim edges. Cut into four squares, cut each square into two triangles. Broil polenta until browned both sides. Serve polenta with bean mixture.

nutritional count per serving 8.4g total fat (3g saturated fat); 404 cal; 55.3g carbohydrate; 25.2g protein; 15.8g fiber

black bean, corn and chipotle stew

PREP + COOK TIME
2 HOURS 15 MINS
(+ STANDING)
SERVES 4

1½ cups dried black beans
2 dried chipotle chilies
½ cup boiling water
1 tablespoon cumin seeds
2 cobs corn, shucked, cleaned
2 teaspoons olive oil
1 large brown onion,
   chopped finely
28-ounce can crushed tomatoes
8 small white corn tortillas

salsa
1 small red onion,
   chopped coarsely
1 small tomato,
   chopped coarsely
½ cup coarsely chopped
   fresh coriander
1 Lebanese cucumber,
   chopped coarsely
1 tablespoon olive oil
2 tablespoons lemon juice

1 Place beans in medium bowl, cover with water; stand overnight, drain. Rinse under cold water; drain. Place beans in medium saucepan of boiling water; return to a boil. Reduce heat; simmer, uncovered, about 15 minutes or until beans are just tender.

2 Preheat oven to 400°F/375°F fan-forced.

3 Place chilies and the boiling water in small bowl; stand 15 minutes. Discard stalks; blend or process chili and its soaking liquid until smooth.

4 Meanwhile, dry-fry cumin seeds in small frying pan, stirring, until fragrant.

5 Cook corn on heated oiled grill pan (or grill or barbecue) until browned lightly and just tender. When cool enough to handle, cut kernels from cobs with sharp knife.

6 Heat oil in large flameproof pan; cook onion, stirring, until soft. Add drained beans, chili mixture, cumin, undrained tomatoes and half of the corn; bring to a boil. Cook, uncovered, in oven about 20 minutes or until sauce thickens.

7 Meanwhile, heat tortillas according to manufacturer's instructions.

8 Combine remaining corn with salsa ingredients in medium bowl.

9 Serve stew with tortillas and salsa.

nutritional count per serving 10.4g total fat (1.3g saturated fat); 440 cal; 61.3g carbohydrate; 26.2g protein; 19.5g fiber

pumpernickel bread

PREP + COOK TIME 1 HOUR 15 MINS (+ STANDING) • MAKES 24 SLICES

This pumpernickel is milder in flavor than the classic version, which uses rye flour only, but still has the characteristic sweet-sour tang of this popular German bread.

2 teaspoons dried yeast
1 teaspoon superfine sugar
1 cup warm water
3 tablespoons butter, melted
1 tablespoon molasses
1 tablespoon caraway seeds

½ cup polenta
1½ cups rye flour
1 cup all-purpose flour
2 tablespoons cocoa powder
1 teaspoon salt

1 Whisk yeast, sugar and the water in large bowl until yeast dissolves, cover; stand in warm place about 10 minutes or until mixture is frothy.

2 Stir in butter and molasses, then seeds, polenta and sifted flours, cocoa and salt. Turn dough onto floured surface; knead about 10 minutes or until smooth. Place dough into large greased bowl, cover; stand in warm place about 2 hours or until dough has doubled in size.

3 Grease 3¼-inch x 10¼-inch bar cake pan; line sides of pan with baking paper, extending 2 inches above edge. Turn dough onto floured surface; knead until smooth. Press dough into pan, cover loosely; stand in warm place about 45 minutes or until dough has risen to top of pan.

4 Preheat oven to 350°F/325°F fan-forced. Cover pan with foil.

5 Bake 15 minutes. Uncover; bake about 30 minutes. Turn onto wire rack to cool.

nutritional count per slice 2.1g total fat (1.2g saturated); 80 cal; 12.3g carbohydrate; 2.2g protein; 1.4g fiber

lentil and bean burger

The relish is best made a day or two ahead and stored, covered, in the refrigerator to allow the flavors to blend. You can add a finely chopped, fresh red chili to the mixture if you want it hotter.

1 cup red lentils
15-ounce can four-bean mix, rinsed
1 egg
4 green onions, chopped coarsely
2 tablespoons coarsely chopped
   fresh coriander
½ cup stale whole wheat
   bread crumbs
4 hamburger buns
8 butter lettuce leaves
1½ ounces bean sprouts
1½ ounces snow pea sprouts,
   trimmed
1 Lebanese cucumber, sliced

chili tomato relish
2 medium tomatoes,
   chopped coarsely
1 small brown onion,
   chopped finely
1 clove garlic, crushed
⅓ cup sweet chili sauce
2 tablespoons malt vinegar

Process the cooked lentils, canned beans and egg until the mixture is smooth.

Divide the mixture into four portions and, using floured hands, shape them into flattened patties.

1 Make chili tomato relish.

2 Meanwhile, cook lentils in medium saucepan of boiling water until tender; drain. Cool 10 minutes.

3 Blend or process lentils, beans and egg until smooth. Combine in medium bowl with onion, coriander and bread crumbs; season to taste. Cover; refrigerate 1 hour.

4 Using floured hands, shape lentil mixture into four patties; cook patties in large heated lightly oiled non-stick frying pan until browned both sides and heated through. Remove from pan; cover to keep warm.

5 Split buns in half; toast cut-sides of buns. Spread buns with relish; sandwich lettuce, sprouts, cucumber, patties and remaining relish between buns.

chili tomato relish Cook tomato, onion and garlic in small saucepan, stirring, about 10 minutes or until tomato has softened. Add sauce and vinegar; bring to a boil. Reduce heat; simmer, uncovered, stirring occasionally, about 10 minutes or until relish thickens. Cool 15 minutes.

nutritional count per serving 6.5g total fat (1.2g saturated fat); 546 cal; 82g carbohydrate; 29.4g protein; 19.1g fiber

dhansak with caramelized onion rice

PREP + COOK TIME
2 HOURS 55 MINS
(+ STANDING)
SERVES 8

1 cup yellow split peas
½ cup dried chickpeas
½ cup red lentils
⅓ cup vegetable oil
2 pounds diced lamb
1 large eggplant, chopped
1½ pounds pumpkin, chopped coarsely
5 medium tomatoes, peeled, chopped coarsely
2 pounds medium brown onions, sliced

garam masala
1 tablespoon ground coriander
2 teaspoons ground cumin
2 teaspoons ground turmeric
½ teaspoon ground cinnamon
½ teaspoon ground cardamom
½ teaspoon black mustard seeds
¼ teaspoon ground clove

masala paste
6 dried small red chilies
6 long green chilies, seeded
1½-inch piece fresh ginger, peeled, chopped coarsely
6 cloves garlic, quartered
½ cup firmly packed fresh mint leaves
½ cup firmly packed fresh coriander leaves
¼ cup hot water

caramelized onion rice
2½ cups basmati rice
5 cups water
2 tablespoons vegetable oil
2 tablespoons butter
4 medium brown onions, sliced thinly

Dhansak, a lentil and meat stew, is a tantalizingly complex mixture of traditional Persian and Indian food. It is always served with "brown" rice—white rice cooked with caramelized onion until it changes color.

1 Place split peas and chickpeas in large bowl, cover with water; stand overnight, drain. Rinse under cold water; drain. Rinse lentils under cold water; drain. Combine lentils, split peas and chickpeas in large saucepan of boiling water; return to a boil. Reduce heat; simmer, uncovered, 40 minutes or until chickpeas are tender.

2 Meanwhile, make garam masala and masala paste.

3 Heat half of the oil in large frying pan; cook lamb, in batches, until just browned. Remove from pan; cover to keep warm.

4 Drain pea mixture through sieve over large bowl. Return 1 quart cooking liquid to same pan, discard remainder. Reserve pea mixture in same bowl.

5 Place eggplant, pumpkin, tomato and about a third of the sliced onion in pan with reserved cooking liquid, cover; bring to a boil. Reduce heat; simmer dhansak, covered, 10 minutes, stirring occasionally. Drain vegetable mixture through sieve over another large bowl; reserve 2 cups of the cooking liquid, discard remainder.

6 Combine half of the split pea mixture and half of the vegetable mixture in large bowl; mash until smooth.

7 Heat same cleaned pan; dry-fry garam masala and masala paste, stirring, until fragrant. Add mashed and whole split pea and vegetable mixtures, lamb and reserved cooking liquid to pan; bring to a boil. Reduce heat; simmer, uncovered, 45 minutes, stirring occasionally.

8 Meanwhile, make caramelized onion rice.

9 Heat remaining oil in large frying pan; cook remaining sliced onion, stirring, about 15 minutes or until softened and caramelized lightly. Sprinkle onion over dhansak; serve with rice, and lemon wedges.

garam masala Combine all ingredients in small bowl.

masala paste Blend or process ingredients until mixture forms a smooth paste.

caramelized onion rice Wash rice in strainer under cold water until water runs clear; drain. Heat oil and butter in medium saucepan; cook onion, stirring, about 15 minutes or until softened and lightly caramelized. Carefully add the water to pan; bring to a boil. Stir in rice; return to a boil. Reduce heat; simmer rice, partially covered, about 10 minutes or until steam holes appear on the surface. Cover rice tightly, reduce heat to as low as possible; steam 10 minutes (do not remove lid). Remove from heat; stand 10 minutes without removing lid. Fluff with fork before serving.

nutritional count per serving 18g total fat (3.5g saturated fat); 623 cal; 87.9g carbohydrate; 20.4g protein; 12.3g fiber

chickpea and vegetable gratin

PREP + COOK TIME 1 HOUR • SERVES 6

2 tablespoons olive oil
1 large brown onion,
　chopped finely
4 cloves garlic, crushed
½ teaspoon ground allspice
½ teaspoon chili flakes
2 x 14-ounce cans diced tomatoes
2 large red peppers
2 medium eggplants, cut into
　2-inch slices

3 medium zucchini,
　cut into 2-inch slices
2 x 14-ounce cans chickpeas,
　rinsed, drained
½ cup coarsely chopped fresh
　flat-leaf parsley
⅓ cup coarsely chopped fresh basil
1 teaspoon fresh thyme leaves
1 teaspoon sugar
1 cup finely grated
　parmesan cheese

1 Heat half the oil in medium saucepan; cook onion, stirring, until softened. Add garlic, allspice and chili; cook, stirring, until fragrant. Add undrained tomatoes; simmer, uncovered, about 15 minutes or until sauce thickens slightly.

2 Meanwhile, quarter peppers; discard seeds and membranes. Roast under preheated broiler or in very hot oven, skin-side up, until skin blisters and blackens. Cover pepper pieces with plastic or paper 5 minutes; peel away skin then cut pepper into 1-inch pieces.

3 Combine eggplant, zucchini and remaining oil in large bowl; place vegetables in single layer on two oven trays, broil both sides until tender.

4 Preheat oven to 400°F/350°F fan-forced.

5 Stir chickpeas, herbs and sugar into tomato sauce. Place half the combined pepper, eggplant and zucchini in shallow 2½-quart ovenproof dish; pour half the chickpea sauce over vegetables. Repeat layering; sprinkle with cheese. Cook, uncovered, about 20 minutes or until browned lightly.

nutritional count per serving 13.3g total fat (3.9g saturated fat); 310 cal; 26.4g carbohydrate; 15.8g protein; 11.2g fiber

Beans, peas & grains

Beans, peas and grains, collectively called pulses, are some of the most nutritious foods we can eat. Unfortunately they have a reputation for being bland and boring. This is simply not the case—some of the world's great dishes are made from pulses.

ADZUKI BEANS
Small russet beans with a cream stripe. Thin-skinned and sweet, they are used in Japan in a paste for desserts and cakes, and are also good in stews and for sprouting.

BLACK BEANS
Also called turtle beans. Their big, savory flavor makes them the stars of Caribbean and Latin-American cooking, famously for black-bean soup. Not the same as chinese black beans, which are salted, fermented soybeans.

BLACK-EYED BEANS
Also called black-eyed peas or cow peas. Mild-flavored and thin-skinned, so they cook faster than most other beans. Often served in the south with pork and corn bread.

HARICOT BEANS
The haricot bean family includes navy beans for Boston baked beans and Great Northern for French cassoulet as well as cannellini. All are mild-flavored white beans which can be interchanged with each other.

BULGUR
Best-known in the refreshing Middle Eastern salad, tabbouleh, bulgur is hulled, steamed or par-boiled and dried cracked wheat ground to various degrees of fineness. Before use, it is soaked briefly in water to soften and swell the grains, then squeezed dry.

PUY LENTILS
From the Le Puy district in southern France, these tiny dark gray-green lentils are delicious and very expensive. Local versions are available, sold under the name of French green or bondi lentils.

Q&A

I'm a vegetarian and I've read that we should eat pulses and grains to make up the nutrients we are missing by not eating meat. Is this right?

Vegetarians should make a particular point of eating pulses and grains—when eaten together they form a complete protein. Interestingly many cultures have always known this: tacos and beans; dhal and rice, even baked beans on toast are all combinations of grains and pulses.

BROAD BEANS
Also called fava beans. Large and mealy-textured, found fresh and dried. Used with chickpeas for falafel. Fresh broad beans are labor-intensive, but well worth it; they must be boiled briefly to remove the waxy peel.

SPLIT PEAS
Yellow or green varieties, both with a sweet, strong pea flavor. Best known for pea and ham soup and for traditional pease pudding (mashed with butter, mint, parsley and eggs, then steamed) to serve with corned beef.

CHICKPEAS
Also called garbanzos, channa or hummus, prized for their full, nutty flavor and crisp texture. Essential for the Italian soup pasta e ceci, and for the Middle Eastern hummus bi tahini.

POLENTA
Also known as cornmeal, made from dried corn ground to various degrees of fineness. It is boiled with water to a porridge (soft polenta), which may also be chilled, cut into shapes, oiled and grilled.

COUSCOUS
The staple cereal of North Africa, made from fine semolina. It is steamed over the pot in which the meat and vegetables are cooking, or, for sweet couscous, over water, then mixed with sugar, nuts and fruits.

CANNELLINI BEANS
Small, white Italian members of the haricot bean family. Used in minestrone and other soups and in Tuscan dishes such as beans baked with pancetta and garlic or chilled beans with tuna.

bircher muesli

PREP TIME 20 MINS (+ REFRIGERATION) • SERVES 6

Try to find plain full-cream yogurt, sometimes called country-style or Greek-style yogurt, for this recipe. Other types, especially the low-fat kind, are not suitable. Additional milk can be added if the muesli is too thick. Use a tart, crisp green apple, such as a granny smith, for this recipe.

2 cups rolled oats

1¼ cups apple juice

1 cup Greek yogurt

2 medium apples

¼ cup toasted slivered almonds

¼ cup currants

¼ cup toasted shredded coconut

1 teaspoon ground cinnamon

½ cup Greek yogurt, extra

1 Combine oats, juice and yogurt in medium bowl. Cover; refrigerate overnight.

2 Peel, core and coarsely grate one apple; stir into oat mixture with nuts, currants, coconut and cinnamon.

3 Core and thinly slice remaining apple. Serve muesli topped with extra yogurt and apple slices.

nutritional count per serving 10.4g total fat (4.1g saturated fat); 284 cal; 37g carbohydrate; 8.2g protein; 4.3g fiber

roasted muesli with dried fruit and honey

PREP + COOK TIME 30 MINS • SERVES 6

Oats have a tendency to go rancid more quickly than other grains because they contain more oils. Therefore, only make enough muesli to last a couple of weeks. Keep muesli in a sealed container in a cool place; it will keep longest if stored in the refrigerator.

2 cups rolled oats

1 cup rolled rice

¼ cup unprocessed wheat bran

¼ cup pepitas

1 teaspoon ground cinnamon

⅓ cup honey

1 tablespoon vegetable oil

¾ cup flaked coconut

⅓ cup coarsely chopped dried apricots

⅓ cup coarsely chopped dried apples

⅓ cup golden raisins

¼ cup dried cranberries, chopped coarsely

1 Preheat oven to 350°F/325°F fan-forced.

2 Combine oats and rice in large bowl, then spread evenly between two oven trays. Roast, uncovered, in oven 5 minutes.

3 Stir bran, pepitas and cinnamon into oat mixtures, then drizzle evenly with combined honey and oil; stir to combine. Roast, uncovered, 5 minutes. Stir in coconut. Roast, uncovered, 5 minutes.

4 Remove trays from oven; place muesli mixture in same large bowl, stir in remaining ingredients. Serve with milk or yogurt.

nutritional count per serving 16.1g total fat (4.8g saturated); 423 cal; 52.8g carbohydrate; 7.3g protein; 11.1g fiber

[opposite] bircher muesli

white bean puree

This recipe calls for white beans, a generic term we use for canned or dried cannellini, haricot, navy or great northern beans which are all of the same family, *phaseolus vulgaris*, and are all interchangeable.

2 tablespoons butter
1 small brown onion, chopped finely
1 clove garlic, crushed
¼ cup dry white wine
¾ cup chicken stock
2 x 14-ounce cans white beans, rinsed, drained
2 tablespoons cream

1 Melt butter in medium frying pan; cook onion and garlic, stirring, until onion softens. Add wine; cook, stirring, until liquid is reduced by half.
2 Add stock and beans; bring to a boil. Reduce heat; simmer, uncovered, about 10 minutes or until liquid is almost evaporated.
3 Blend or process bean mixture and cream until smooth.

nutritional count per serving 8.9g total fat (5.8g saturated fat); 131 cal; 4.9g carbohydrate; 4.2g protein; 3.1g fiber

semolina slice

Known in Middle Eastern and North African countries as basboosa, namoura or harisi, these sweets are appreciated for their lovely orange perfume. Cover the slice loosely with foil if it starts to overbrown while cooking.

2 pounds coarsely ground semolina
2½ cups sugar
1 cup milk
1 stick butter
¼ cup blanched almonds

sugar syrup
3 cups water
2 teaspoons lemon juice
1½ cups superfine sugar
2 teaspoons orange flower water

1 Make sugar syrup.
2 Preheat oven to 325°F/300°F fan-forced. Grease 8-inch x 12-inch cake pan.
3 Combine semolina and sugar in large bowl. Place milk and butter in small saucepan; stir over low heat until butter melts. Pour into semolina mixture; stir to combine.
4 Spread semolina mixture into pan; smooth the top with a wet hand. Score batter into 1½-inch diamond shapes; center one almond on each diamond. Bake about 1 hour 20 minutes or until slice is golden brown and slightly firm to the touch.
5 Cut through diamond shapes to bottom of cake; gradually pour cooled syrup over hot cake. Cool in pan.

sugar syrup Bring the water, juice and sugar to a boil in medium saucepan. Reduce heat; simmer, uncovered, about 20 minutes or until syrup reduces to about 2½ cups. Cool to room temperature. Add orange flower water, cover; refrigerate 3 hours or overnight.

nutritional count per piece 5.2g total fat (2.8g saturated fat); 293 cal; 55.6g carbohydrate; 4.4g protein; 1.3g fiber

[opposite] semolina slice

DESSERTS

Desserts

When you're eating dessert, it's impossible to have anything but pleasant thoughts. For most of us, eating dessert is not an everyday occurrence but rather a little luxury we reserve for dinner parties and special family meals, and we relish every blissful mouthful.

THE RECIPES IN THIS CHAPTER ARE BELOVED CLASSICS AND ALL-TIME FAVORITES. SOME ARE SIMPLE AND QUICK TO CREATE. OTHERS ARE MORE COMPLICATED AND TIME-CONSUMING, BUT WORTH IT. SOME ARE IMPRESSIVE STATEMENTS THAT COMMAND CENTER STAGE AT A DINNER PARTY, OTHERS FIT MORE COMFORTABLY WITH A QUIET FAMILY DINNER. TRY THEM ALL, FROM THE SUMPTUOUS SUMMER PUDDING, TO THE ELEGANT CHOCOLATE TART, TO THE UNMATCHED PAVLOVA AND THE SIMPLE BREAD AND BUTTER PUDDING LIKE YOUR GRANDMOTHER USED TO MAKE.

BAKING TIPS

It's important to get to know your oven. Every nuance and quirk will have an impact on your baking. Every oven bakes differently, but as a general rule, it's good to position the dish so the top of the dessert is at the center of the oven.

Check the accuracy of your oven's temperature gauge with an oven thermometer. Most domestic ovens have hotspots, so don't be nervous about opening the oven door to reposition the dish. But any dessert or cake full of air, like a soufflé or sponge, should be treated carefully–they might deflate if moved at the wrong time.

A WATER BATH is used to insulate baked desserts, making the baking process gentler. The water also adds humidity, which can prevent the top of the dessert from cracking. If the recipe calls for a water bath, place the dessert dish in a larger baking dish and pour boiling water into the larger dish until the water comes halfway up the side(s) of the dessert dish. Do this while they are on a shelf in the oven–it's safer than trying to get both dishes in the oven. While baking, keep an eye on the water level–if it looks low, top it up.

MERINGUE DESSERTS

Everyone needs to make a pavlova at least once in their lives–that wonderful symphony of melt-in-your-mouth meringue, cream and strawberries. Lemon meringue is another family favorite with its memorable combination of tangy lemon custard crowned by meringue.

The main point to watch when making meringue is that all utensils are dry and free of grease, and that egg whites are completely free of yolk, as even a hint of grease or a speck of yolk will prevent the whites from whipping up properly.

TO MAKE THE MERINGUE Beat egg whites only until soft peaks form before you start adding the sugar: if you beat the whites until they are stiff and dry, the sugar will take longer to dissolve. If the sugar doesn't dissolve properly, the meringue can "weep" droplets of moisture during and after baking.

The meringue case for pavlova can be made up to 4 days ahead and stored in an airtight container at room temperature. Fill with cream and fruit about an hour before serving.

CHEESECAKES

No wonder cheesecakes are so wonderful: they had their genesis in ancient Greek times, so we've had time to perfect them. Back then, a combination of cheese and honey was served on an oat crust. Today's cheesecakes can be baked or fridge-set, and many countries claim to have the supreme recipe. Our baked New York cheesecake combining a creamy, not-too-sweet filling with a crunchy crust is hard to surpass.

You'll need a springform pan for cheesecakes: these are special round pans that come in two parts—the base and the ring—that attach and detach using a special catch on the side of the ring. Springform pans eliminate all the uncertainties of turning out the cheesecake: you simply release the ring and it slips off the dessert.

For a smooth-textured filling, be sure the cream cheese and all other ingredients are at room temperature before you start to mix.

You need fine, evenly-sized crumbs to make a good crust. This can be achieved by using a blender or a food processor, or by crushing them in a plastic bag with a rolling pin. When the crust mixture is made, you'll need about one third of it for the base and the rest for the side.

> DON'T OVER-BEAT MIXTURES THAT CONTAIN CREAM AND MASCARPONE CHEESE AS THE MIXTURE CAN CURDLE

For an extra smooth side to an unbaked "crust-base only" cheesecake, you can line the pan with plastic wrap: remove the base of the pan, then drape a piece of plastic wrap over the lightly greased side of the pan. Position and secure the base back into the pan, stretching the wrap neatly and leaving a little of the wrap hanging over the edge.

Follow cooking times carefully and don't overcook.

Leave the cheesecake to cool in the oven: this will allow it to cool slowly and avoid shrinking, sinking in the middle or cracking as it cools.

To cut cheesecakes easily, run a large sharp knife under hot water until warmed; wipe the knife dry with a towel, and cut the cake by slicing through to the crust.

FROZEN DESSERTS

HOMEMADE ICE CREAM, LIKE THE VANILLA BEAN ICE CREAM IN THIS CHAPTER, SHOULD BE STORED IN THE FREEZER TO ALLOW IT TO DEVELOP (LET THE FLAVORS BECOME STRONGER) FOR AT LEAST AN HOUR AFTER IT IS MADE. IT IS BEST EATEN WITHIN 48 HOURS OF BEING MADE. HOMEMADE ICE CREAM IS HARDER THAN COMMERCIAL ICE CREAM AND SHOULD BE TRANSFERRED FROM THE FREEZER TO THE FRIDGE ABOUT HALF AN HOUR BEFORE SERVING, SO IT CAN SOFTEN.

crème caramel

There is a great sense of achievement once you've mastered crème caramel. Home cooks are usually concerned about the caramel, but it's not as tricky as you think. Use a heavy pan and stir the sugar and water over medium heat. Once the sugar has been dissolved and the mixture starts to boil, watch it carefully. As soon as it starts to brown, tilt the pan until the brown areas merge. Keep tilting and turning the pan until the caramel is a rich golden color. Remove the pan from the heat, let the bubbles subside, then pour caramel over the base of the cake pan. There is no need to coat the side of the pan, or even grease it. An aluminum cake pan gives the best results for even baking of the custard. Refrigerating the crème caramel overnight breaks down and liquifies the caramel, which will make it easier to turn the crème caramel out of the pan. When you're ready to serve, use your fingers to ease the custard away from the side of the pan, gently shake the pan and you'll "feel" the custard floating on the caramel. Put the serving plate on top of the cake pan and quickly invert.

¾ cup superfine sugar

½ cup water

6 eggs

1 teaspoon vanilla extract

⅓ cup superfine sugar, extra

1¼ cups cream

1¾ cups milk

1 Preheat oven to 350°F/325°F fan-forced.

2 Combine sugar and the water in medium heavy-based saucepan; stir over heat, without boiling, until sugar dissolves. Bring to a boil; boil, uncovered, without stirring, until mixture is a deep caramel color. Remove from heat; allow bubbles to subside. Pour caramel into a deep 8-inch round cake pan; cool completely.

3 Whisk eggs, extract and extra sugar in large bowl.

4 Combine cream and milk in medium saucepan; bring to a boil. Whisking constantly, pour hot milk mixture into egg mixture. Strain mixture into cake pan.

5 Place pan in baking dish; add enough boiling water to come halfway up side of pan. Bake, in oven, about 40 minutes or until set. Remove custard from baking dish, let stand until cool, cover; refrigerate overnight.

6 Gently ease crème caramel from side of pan; invert onto deep-sided serving plate.

nutritional count per serving 22.3g total fat (13.3g saturated fat); 365 cal; 33.8g carbohydrate; 7.5g protein; 0g fiber

All the sugar needs to be dissolved when you're making caramel. Some sugar will stick to the sides of the pan – brush these off using a dampened pastry brush.

When the caramel is a deep, rich brown, pour it into the base of a deep 8-inch cake pan.

Put the custard into a baking dish and pour enough boiling water around the cake pan to come halfway up its side.

apple pie

Make sure your cooked apples are drained well and cooled to room temperature. Brushing the inside of the pastry case with egg white will also help to stop the apples from making the pastry soggy.

10 medium apples (3 pounds)
½ cup water
¼ cup superfine sugar
1 teaspoon finely grated lemon rind
¼ teaspoon ground cinnamon
1 egg white
1 tablespoon superfine sugar, extra

pastry
1 cup all-purpose flour
½ cup self-rising flour
¼ cup corn starch
¼ cup custard powder or instant vanilla pudding mix
1 tablespoon superfine sugar
6 tablespoons cold butter, chopped coarsely
1 egg yolk
¼ cup iced water

1 Make pastry.

2 Peel, core and slice apple thickly. Place apple and the water in large saucepan; bring to a boil. Reduce heat; simmer, covered, about 10 minutes or until apples soften. Drain; stir in sugar, rind and cinnamon. Cool.

3 Preheat oven to 425°F/400°F fan-forced. Grease deep 10-inch pie dish.

4 Divide pastry in half. Roll one half between sheets of parchment paper until large enough to line dish. Lift pastry into dish; press into base and side. Spoon apple mixture into pastry case; brush edge with egg white.

5 Roll remaining pastry large enough to cover filling; lift onto filling. Press edges together; trim away excess pastry. Brush pastry with egg white; sprinkle with extra sugar.

6 Bake pie 20 minutes. Reduce oven to 350°F/325°F fan-forced; bake an additional 25 minutes or until golden brown. Serve with vanilla cream sauce or scoops of vanilla ice cream, if you like.

pastry Process dry ingredients with butter until crumbly. Add egg yolk and the water; process until combined. Knead on floured surface until smooth. Cover; refrigerate 30 minutes.

nutritional count per serving 11.4g total fat (7g saturated fat); 344 cal; 53.9g carbohydrate; 4.3g protein; 3.7g fiber

Q&A

What are the best apples to use for an apple pie?

Granny smiths are the traditional apple-pie apple because they have just enough tartness to complement the sweet pastry, and they soften beautifully. For tarte tartin and other open-faced apple tarts, golden delicious are a better choice because they keep their shape even when they're fully cooked.

baked custard

We heat the milk to decrease the baking time. The milk should be hot, not boiling, but certainly much more than warm. Be careful to avoid overcooking. The custard is done when it still looks and feels a bit wobbly in the middle. The heat within the custard will continue to cook and thicken the rest of the custard as it cools down.

6 eggs
1 teaspoon vanilla extract
⅓ cup superfine sugar
1 quart hot milk
¼ teaspoon ground nutmeg

1 Preheat oven to 325°F/300°F fan-forced. Grease shallow 1½-quart ovenproof dish.

2 Whisk eggs, extract and sugar in large bowl; gradually whisk in hot milk. Pour custard mixture into dish; sprinkle with nutmeg.

3 Place dish in larger baking dish; add enough boiling water to come halfway up sides of dish. Bake, uncovered, about 45 minutes. Remove custard from water bath; stand 5 minutes before serving.

nutritional count per serving 11.8g total fat (5.9g saturated fat); 238 cal; 20.7g carbohydrate; 12.3g protein; 0g fiber

golden syrup steamed pudding

Honey or molasses can be substituted for the golden syrup here. Make sure the parchment paper and foil (pleated to allow room for the pudding to expand) are tied tightly around the bowl.

½ stick butter
¼ cup golden syrup
½ teaspoon baking soda
1 cup self-rising flour
2 teaspoons ground ginger
½ cup milk
1 egg

syrup
⅓ cup golden syrup
2 tablespoons water
3 tablespoons butter

1 Grease 1½-quart steamed pudding mold.

2 Stir butter and syrup in small saucepan over low heat until smooth. Remove from heat, stir in soda; transfer mixture to medium bowl. Stir in sifted dry ingredients, then combined milk and egg, in two batches.

3 Spread mixture into mold. Cover with pleated parchment paper and foil; secure with lid. Place pudding steamer in large saucepan with enough boiling water to come halfway up side of mold; cover pan with tight-fitting lid. Boil 1 hour, replenishing water as necessary to maintain level. Stand pudding 5 minutes before turning onto serving plate.

4 Meanwhile, make syrup.

5 Serve pudding topped with syrup and, if desired, cream.

syrup Stir ingredients in small saucepan over heat until smooth; bring to a boil. Reduce heat; simmer, uncovered, 2 minutes.

nutritional count per serving 14.3g total fat (9g saturated fat); 327 cal; 44.5g carbohydrate; 4.5g protein; 1g fiber

[1] baked custard
[2] golden syrup steamed pudding
[3] vanilla bean ice cream [page 512]
[4] chocolate self-saucing pudding [page 512]

vanilla bean ice cream

PREP + COOK TIME 25 MINS (+ REFRIGERATION, CHURNING & FREEZING) SERVES 8

2 vanilla beans
1⅔ cups milk
2½ cups heavy cream
8 egg yolks
¾ cup superfine sugar

When you want to finish freezing ice cream in a hurry, remove it from your ice cream churn when it's only partially frozen, spread it into a thin layer in a loaf pan, cover it well with foil, and put it in your freezer. It will become solidly frozen in about an hour.

1 Split vanilla beans lengthwise; scrape out seeds into medium saucepan. Add pods, milk and cream; bring to a boil.

2 Meanwhile, whisk egg yolks and sugar in medium bowl until creamy; gradually whisk into hot milk mixture. Stir over low heat, without boiling, until mixture thickens slightly.

3 Strain mixture into medium heatproof bowl; discard pods. Cover surface of custard with plastic wrap; refrigerate about 1 hour or until cold.

4 Pour custard into ice cream maker, churn according to manufacturer's instructions (or place custard in shallow container, such as an aluminium cake pan, cover with foil; freeze until almost firm). Place ice cream in large bowl, chop coarsely, then beat with electric mixer until smooth. Pour into deep container, cover; freeze until firm. Repeat process two more times.

nutritional count per serving 35.5g total fat (21.4g saturated fat); 444 cal; 25.5g carbohydrate; 6.5g protein; 0g fiber

chocolate self-saucing pudding

PREP + COOK TIME 55 MINS • SERVES 6

½ stick butter
½ cup milk
½ teaspoon vanilla extract
¾ cup superfine sugar
1 cup self-rising flour

1 tablespoon cocoa powder
¾ cup firmly packed light brown sugar
1 tablespoon cocoa powder, extra
2 cups boiling water

1 Preheat oven to 350°F/325°F fan-forced. Grease 1½-quart baking dish.

2 Melt butter with milk in medium saucepan. Remove from heat; stir in extract and superfine sugar then sifted flour and cocoa.

3 Spread pudding mixture into dish. Sift brown sugar and extra cocoa over mixture; gently pour boiling water over mixture.

4 Bake pudding about 40 minutes or until center is firm. Stand 5 minutes before serving.

nutritional count per serving 9.7g total fat (6.2g saturated fat); 401 cal; 73.4g carbohydrate; 3.8g protein; 1.1g fiber

chocolate tart

Use unsalted butter and good-quality chocolate for this tart. Dust lightly with good-quality cocoa powder just before serving. A small dollop of cream on each serving, despite its added richness, somehow cuts through the rich chocolate filling.

2 eggs
2 egg yolks
¼ cup superfine sugar
8 ounces bittersweet chocolate, melted
1¾ sticks butter, melted

pastry
1½ cups all-purpose flour
½ cup superfine sugar
9 tablespoons cold butter, chopped
1 egg, beaten lightly

1 Make pastry.

2 Grease 8-inch removable-bottom tart pan. Roll dough between sheets of parchment paper until large enough to line pan. Lift pastry into pan, ease into base and side; trim edge, prick base all over with fork. Refrigerate 30 minutes.

3 Preheat oven to 400°F/375°F fan-forced.

4 Place pan on oven tray. Line pastry case with parchment; fill with dried beans or rice. Bake 10 minutes. Remove paper and beans; bake 5 minutes. Cool.

5 Reduce oven to 350°F/325°F fan-forced.

6 Whisk eggs, egg yolks and sugar in medium heatproof bowl over medium saucepan of simmering water about 15 minutes or until light and fluffy. Gently whisk chocolate and butter into egg mixture; pour into pastry shell.

7 Bake tart 10 minutes or until filling is set; cool 10 minutes. Refrigerate 1 hour.

pastry Process flour, sugar and butter until crumbly. Add egg; process until ingredients come together. Knead pastry on floured surface until smooth. Wrap in plastic wrap; refrigerate 30 minutes.

nutritional count per serving 32g total fat (21.8g saturated fat); 467 cal; 39.4g carbohydrate; 5.2g protein; 1.7g fiber

chocolate mousse

TIP

• The eggs must be at room temperature for success with this recipe.

7 ounces bittersweet chocolate, chopped coarsely
3 tablespoons unsalted butter
3 eggs, separated
1¼ cups heavy cream, whipped to soft peaks

1 Melt chocolate and butter in large glass heatproof bowl over large saucepan of simmering water (do not allow water to touch base of bowl). Remove from heat. Stir in egg yolks; cool.

2 Beat egg whites in small bowl with electric mixer until soft peaks form.

3 Meanwhile, fold cream into chocolate mixture; fold in egg whites in two batches.

4 Spoon mousse mixture into serving dishes; refrigerate 3 hours or overnight.

nutritional count per serving 34.8g total fat (21.4g saturated fat); 425 cal; 22.5g carbohydrate; 6.1g protein; 0.4g fiber

serving ideas top mousse with whipped cream and chocolate curls.

lemon meringue pie

Use a rolling pin to gently ease the pastry into the tart pan, being careful not to stretch it.

Spread the lemon filling evenly into the cooked and cooled pie shell. A spatula is the best implement to use for this.

Roughen the surface of the lemon filling before you spread the meringue on top. This will help prevent the meringue from shrinking away from the filling as it cooks.

½ cup corn starch
1 cup superfine sugar
½ cup lemon juice
1¼ cups water
2 teaspoons finely grated lemon rind
½ stick unsalted butter, chopped
3 eggs, separated
½ cup superfine sugar, extra

pastry
1½ cups all-purpose flour
1 tablespoon powdered sugar
9 tablespoons cold butter, chopped
1 egg yolk
2 tablespoons cold water

1 Make pastry.

2 Grease 8-inch removable-bottom tart pan. Roll pastry between sheets of parchment until large enough to line pan. Ease pastry into pan, press into base and side; trim edge. Cover; refrigerate 30 minutes.

3 Preheat oven to 450°F/425°F fan-forced.

4 Place pan on oven tray. Line pastry case with baking paper; fill with dried beans or rice. Bake 15 minutes; remove paper and beans carefully from pie shell. Bake about 10 minutes; cool pie shell, turn oven off.

5 Meanwhile, combine corn starch and sugar in medium saucepan; gradually stir in juice and the water until smooth. Cook, stirring, over high heat, until mixture boils and thickens. Reduce heat; simmer, stirring, 1 minute. Remove from heat; stir in rind, butter and egg yolks. Cool 10 minutes.

6 Spread filling into pie shell. Cover; refrigerate 2 hours.

7 Preheat oven to 450°F/425°F fan-forced.

8 Beat egg whites in small bowl with electric mixer until soft peaks form; gradually add extra sugar, beating until sugar dissolves.

9 Roughen surface of filling with fork before spreading with meringue mixture. Bake about 2 minutes or until browned lightly.

pastry Process flour, powdered sugar and butter until crumbly. Add egg yolk and the water; process until ingredients come together. Knead dough on floured surface until smooth. Cover; refrigerate 30 minutes.

nutritional count per serving 18.9g total fat (11.6g saturated fat); 424 cal; 57.7g carbohydrate; 5g protein; 0.9g fiber

Tropical fruit

Tropical fruit is considered by many to be the closest thing to heaven that food can provide. All tropical fruits are at their best served ripe and just as they are–it seems a sacrilege to mess with perfection.

RAMBUTAN
A relative of the lychee, with similar luscious, perfumed, grape-like flesh. To remove the leathery, tendril-covered shell, break open with a fingernail and peel like an egg.

GOLDEN BANANA
These are small, golden-skinned bananas from Asia. The flesh is sweet and creamy. These bananas are usually sold in bunches in Asian food shops. Do not store in the refrigerator as the skin will turn black.

STAR FRUIT
Also called carombola and belimbing (a smaller variety). Some ripen to yellow or pinky yellow, most to a yellow-green. Very crisp and juicy, with a mild sweet flavor.

LYCHEE
Its juicy, translucent flesh tastes like a more luscious, perfumed grape. Will keep, unshelled, for weeks in the fridge. Refreshing eaten on its own, in fruit salads or as a touch of delicate sweetness in a duck salad.

JACKFRUIT
A huge fruit containing numerous seeds surrounded by golden, richly flavored, sharp-sweet flesh. Used in fruit salads, ice cream, milk drinks and soups. The seeds are edible boiled, then roasted in a pan with a little oil.

DRAGON FRUIT
The fruit of a pitaya cactus. The flesh, eaten raw, is tasty and mildly sweet, a little like the flavor of kiwi. Scoop the flesh and seeds out of the chilled fruit with a teaspoon.

Q&A

Many recipes call for green papaya and green mango. Are they a different fruit from the ones we normally see in the greengrocer?

No, the green fruit are simply unripe. They are both used, usually grated, in Thai and Vietnamese salads. Served with a spicy, lime juice-laden dressing, they are refreshing and really delicious. And it's reassuring to know that green papaya and green mango won't give you a stomach ache.

GREEN MANGO
This is the unripe fruit of the mango tree. The flesh is deliciously tart. Used raw in many Asian salads or as a vegetable; it can also be bought pickled or dried.

MANGO
Paradise flavor, texture and fragrance–wonderful alone, in desserts and also with curries. Buy fully colored but not oversoft, or with a touch of green, then ripen at room temperature.

PAPAYA
The papaya family includes both the yellow-fleshed fruit called pawpaw and the pink-fleshed fruit called papaya. Their mild, sweet flavor is best with a squeeze of lime.

PASSIONFRUIT
A member of the berry family, this fruit is filled with tart-sweet pulp with small black seeds. To extract the pulp for desserts or drinks, slice the passionfruit in half, scoop out the seeds and pulp with a spoon, and press it with a spatula through a fine sieve.

MANGOSTEEN
The shiny, purple-brown skin peels to reveal segments of white flesh with refreshing, sweet-sour flavor reminiscent of pineapple. Delicious peeled and eaten raw in segments, like an orange, or chilled and mixed with other tropical fruits.

DURIAN
Famous as the fruit that "smells like hell and tastes like heaven". One recommendation for enjoying the taste without the smell is to cut the flesh into pieces and soak for a day in coconut milk.

tarte tatin

Be prepared for a bit of work if you're going to make this sensational dessert. Golden delicious apples are the best apples to use, granny smith the second best.

7 tablespoons unsalted butter, chopped

6 large apples, peeled, cored, quartered

1 cup firmly packed light brown sugar

2 tablespoons lemon juice

pastry

1 cup all-purpose flour

2 tablespoons superfine sugar

5 tablespoons cold unsalted butter, chopped

2 tablespoons sour cream

1 Melt butter in large heavy-based frying pan; add apples, sprinkle evenly with sugar and juice. Cook, uncovered, over low heat, about 40 minutes, turning apples as they caramelize.

2 Meanwhile, make pastry.

3 Preheat oven to 400°F/375°F fan-forced.

4 Place apples, rounded-sides down, in 9-inch pie dish, packing tightly to ensure there are no gaps; drizzle with 1 tablespoon of the caramel in pan. Reserve remaining caramel.

5 Roll pastry between sheets of parchment until large enough to cover apples. Peel away one sheet of baking paper; cut pastry to fit dish. Remove remaining paper. Place pastry carefully over hot apples; tuck pastry around apples.

6 Bake tarte tatin about 30 minutes or until pastry is browned. Carefully turn onto serving plate, apple-side up; drizzle apple with reheated reserved caramel.

pastry Process flour, sugar, butter and sour cream until ingredients just come together. Knead on floured surface until smooth. Cover; refrigerate 30 minutes.

nutritional count per serving 21.1g total fat (13.7g saturated fat); 445 cal; 59.5g carbohydrate; 2.7g protein; 2.9g fiber

Place the caramelized apples, rounded-side down, in the pie dish. Remember, this is an upside-down pie, so be careful to arrange the apples in a decorative pattern.

Cut the pastry round to fit snugly into the pie dish and place it over the hot apples.

Tuck the pastry carefully and evenly down the sides of the dish—this will form the pastry base when the pie is inverted.

Turn the pie out onto the serving plate, apple-side up and drizzle the tart with the reheated reserved caramel.

classic trifle

3-ounce packet raspberry gelatin
8 ounces sponge cake, cut into
   1-inch pieces
¼ cup sweet sherry
¼ cup custard powder
¼ cup superfine sugar

½ teaspoon vanilla extract
1½ cups milk
28-ounce can sliced peaches, drained
¼ cup heavy cream
2 tablespoons sliced almonds,
   toasted

1 Make gelatin according to directions on packet; pour into shallow container. Refrigerate 20 minutes or until gelatin is almost set.

2 Arrange cake in 3-quart bowl; sprinkle with sherry.

3 Blend custard powder, sugar and extract with a little of the milk in small saucepan; stir in remaining milk. Stir over heat until mixture boils and thickens. Cover surface with plastic wrap; cool.

4 Pour gelatin over cake; refrigerate 15 minutes. Top with peaches. Stir a third of the cream into custard; pour over peaches.

5 Whip remaining cream; spread over custard, sprinkle with nuts. Refrigerate 3 hours or overnight.

nutritional count per serving 19.7g total fat (10.9g saturated fat); 404 cal; 47g carbohydrate; 7.1g protein; 1.6g fiber

plum clafoutis

This is a rustic dessert from the Limousin region of central France; in the local dialect it translates as "brimming over". It is usually made in the cherry season, when a baking dish is filled with the ripe fruit and a sweet batter is poured over and baked. Other stone fruits or plumped prunes can be used instead of cherries. We have used plums in this recipe but you could use apricots, peeled peaches or caramelized apple instead.

10 small plums, halved,
   pitted
1 cinnamon stick, halved
¼ cup water
¼ cup light brown sugar
⅔ cup milk

⅔ cup cream
1 teaspoon vanilla extract
4 eggs
½ cup superfine sugar
¼ cup all-purpose flour

1 Preheat oven to 400°F/375°F fan-forced. Grease shallow 2½ quart ovenproof dish.

2 Place plums in saucepan with cinnamon and the water; sprinkle with brown sugar. Cook about 15 minutes or until plums soften.

3 Remove cinnamon from dish and add to medium saucepan with milk, cream and extract; bring to a boil. Cool; remove cinnamon stick.

4 Whisk eggs and sugar in medium bowl until light and frothy; whisk in flour then whisk mixture into cream mixture.

5 Place drained plums in shallow ovenproof dish; pour cream mixture over plums. Bake about 30 minutes or until browned lightly. Serve dusted with powdered sugar.

nutritional count per serving 16.1g total fat (9.3g saturated fat); 339 cal; 46.2g carbohydrate; 7.1g protein; 2.4g fiber

new york cheesecake

We've added some orange rind as well as the lemon rind to this famous cheesecake. If you prefer the lemon flavor, you can increase the amount of finely grated lemon rind up to 1 tablespoon and leave the orange rind out completely–or add 1 teaspoon vanilla extract instead of the orange rind for that lovely lemon/vanilla combination.

8 ounces plain sugar cookies
1 stick butter, melted
1½ pounds cream cheese, softened
2 teaspoons finely grated orange rind
1 teaspoon finely grated lemon rind
1 cup superfine sugar
3 eggs
¾ cup sour cream
¼ cup lemon juice

sour cream topping
1 cup sour cream
2 tablespoons superfine sugar
2 teaspoons lemon juice

1 Process cookies until fine. Add butter, process until combined. Press mixture over base and side of 9½-inch springform pan; place on oven tray. Refrigerate 30 minutes.
2 Preheat oven to 350°F/325°F fan-forced.
3 Beat cheese, rinds and sugar in medium bowl with electric mixer until smooth. Beat in eggs, one at a time, then cream and juice. Pour filling into pan.
4 Bake cheesecake 1¼ hours. Remove from oven; cool 15 minutes.
5 Make sour cream topping by combining ingredients in small bowl; spread topping over cheesecake.
6 Bake cheesecake 20 minutes; cool in oven with door ajar. Refrigerate 3 hours or overnight.
nutritional count per serving 39.3g total fat (24.4g saturated fat); 543 cal; 38.9g carbohydrate; 9.2g protein; 0.4g fiber

apple crumble

5 large apples
¼ cup superfine sugar
¼ cup water

crumble
½ cup self-rising flour
¼ cup all-purpose flour
½ cup firmly packed
    light brown sugar
7 tablespoons cold butter, chopped
1 teaspoon ground cinnamon

1 Preheat oven to 350°F/325°F fan-forced. Grease deep 1½-quart baking dish.
2 Peel, core and quarter apples. Cook apples, sugar and the water in large saucepan over low heat, covered, about 10 minutes. Drain; discard liquid.
3 Meanwhile, make crumble.
4 Place apples in dish; sprinkle with crumble. Bake about 25 minutes.
crumble Blend or process ingredients until combined.
nutritional count per serving 21g total fat (13.6g saturated fat); 537 cal; 80.7g carbohydrate; 3.6g protein; 4.5g fiber

summer pudding

Mix and match the berries and the jam to suit your tastes. You can use fresh berries instead of frozen, if you like. A combination of fresh and frozen is good too.

⅓ cup superfine sugar
½ cup water
2 cups frozen blackberries
3⅓ cups frozen mixed berries
10 thick slices stale white bread
¼ cup blackberry jam

1 Bring sugar and the water in medium saucepan to a boil. Stir in berries; return to a boil. Reduce heat; simmer, uncovered, until berries soften. Strain over medium bowl; reserve syrup and berries separately.

2 Line 5-cup pudding bowl with plastic wrap, extending wrap 4 inches over side of bowl. Remove crust from bread. Place two slices of bread on top of each other, then cut into a rounded wedge shape (see step, pic 2, below); repeat with another two slices of bread. Cut a round from another slice of bread to fit the base of the bowl. Cut remaining bread into 4-inch long strips.

3 Place small bread round in base of bowl; use bread strips to line side of bowl.

4 Pour ⅔ cup of the reserved syrup into small pitcher; reserve. Fill pudding bowl with berries; cover with remaining syrup, top with rounded wedge shapes. Cover pudding with overhanging plastic wrap, weight pudding with saucer; refrigerate 3 hours or overnight.

5 Stir jam and 2 tablespoons of the reserved syrup in small saucepan until heated through. Turn pudding onto serving plate; brush with remaining reserved syrup then jam mixture. Serve with extra fresh berries and whipped cream.

nutritional count per serving 3.5g total fat (0.5g saturated fat); 444 cal; 84.6g carbohydrate; 12.8g protein; 8.9g fiber

Line the bowl with plastic wrap to make it easier to remove the pudding from the bowl and to help keep its shape.

Line the bottom and sides of the bowl with bread slices, overlapping slightly and making sure there are no gaps for the filling to ooze out.

Fill the bread-lined bowl with fruit and pour the syrup over it. Top with bread slices until completely covered.

Cover the pudding with a saucer that will fit inside the bowl and place weights (cans of food are good) on top. This compresses the pudding.

bread and butter pudding

Change the bread in this classic dish for something different— good-quality fruit cake, croissants or panettone. You can also add chunks of chocolate to the mixture, any dried fruit you like, or even jam. Try using brown instead of white sugar, or replacing some of the sugar with maple syrup, honey or golden syrup. For a richer pudding you might also substitute cream or coconut cream for some of the milk—the variations are endless.

6 slices white bread
3 tablespoons butter, softened
½ cup raisins
¼ teaspoon ground nutmeg

custard
1½ cups milk
2 cups cream
⅓ cup superfine sugar
1 teaspoon vanilla extract
4 eggs

1 Preheat oven to 325°F/300°F fan-forced. Grease shallow 2-quart ovenproof dish.

2 Make custard.

3 Trim crust from bread. Spread each slice with butter; cut into four triangles. Layer bread, overlapping, in dish; sprinkle with raisins. Pour custard over bread; sprinkle with nutmeg.

4 Place ovenproof dish in large baking dish; add enough boiling water to come halfway up side of ovenproof dish.

5 Bake pudding about 45 minutes or until set. Remove pudding from baking dish; stand 5 minutes before serving. Serve dusted with sifted powdered sugar, if you like.

custard Combine milk, cream, sugar and extract in medium saucepan; bring to a boil. Whisk eggs in large bowl; whisking constantly, gradually add hot milk mixture to egg mixture.

nutritional count per serving 48.6g total fat (30.4g saturated fat); 684 cal; 49.3g carbohydrate; 12.4g protein; 1.8g fiber

lemon pudding

This is the all-time best lemon pudding. It needs to be served straight from the oven or the pudding will sink and absorb all the sauce.

1 stick butter, melted
2 teaspoons finely grated lemon rind
1½ cups superfine sugar
3 eggs, separated

½ cup self-rising flour
⅓ cup lemon juice
1⅓ cups milk

1 Preheat oven to 350°F/325°F fan-forced. Grease six 1-cup ovenproof dishes; place in large baking dish.

2 Combine butter, rind, sugar and yolks in large bowl. Whisk in sifted flour then juice. Gradually whisk in milk; mixture should be smooth and runny.

3 Beat egg whites in small bowl with electric mixer until soft peaks form; fold into lemon mixture in two batches.

4 Divide lemon mixture among dishes. Add enough boiling water to baking dish to come halfway up side of ovenproof dishes. Bake about 30 minutes or until puddings have risen and are a light golden color.

nutritional count per serving 22g total fat (13.5g saturated fat); 495 cal; 67.1g carbohydrate; 6.7g protein; 0.5g fiber

[1] bread and butter pudding
[2] lemon delicious pudding
[3] marshmallow pavlova [page 526]
[4] tiramisu [page 526]

marshmallow pavlova

4 egg whites
1 cup superfine sugar
½ teaspoon vanilla extract
¾ teaspoon white vinegar

¼ cups heavy cream
8 ounces strawberries, halved
¼ cup passionfruit pulp

1 Preheat oven to 250°F/225°F fan-forced. Line oven tray with foil; grease foil, dust with corn starch, shake away excess. Mark 7-inch circle on foil.
2 Beat egg whites in small bowl with electric mixer until soft peaks form; gradually add sugar, beating until sugar dissolves. Beat in extract and vinegar until combined.
3 Spread meringue into circle on foil, building up at the side to 3 inches in height. Smooth side and top of pavlova gently. Using spatula blade, mark decorative grooves around side of pavlova; smooth top again.
4 Bake pavlova about 1½ hours. Turn oven off; cool pavlova in oven with door ajar.
5 Cut around top edge of pavlova (the crisp meringue top will fall on top of the marshmallow center). Top with whipped cream, strawberries and passionfruit.
nutritional count per serving 14g total fat (9.2g saturated fat); 262 cal; 30g carbohydrate; 3.3g protein; 1.7g fiber

tiramisu

People are often confused about whether to regard mascarpone as a cheese or a thick cream. It is, in fact, a fresh triple-cream cheese originating in Italy's Lombardy region, and probably first became known to us when tiramisu was the dessert du jour in the mid-1980s.

Like most wonderful things, there is no real substitute for mascarpone, but some recipes can be adapted to use soft cream cheese, sour cream or ricotta— or blends of all three.

2 tablespoons ground espresso coffee
1 cup boiling water
½ cup marsala
8-ounce packet soft ladyfingers
1¼ cup heavy cream

¼ cup powdered sugar
2 cups mascarpone cheese
2 tablespoons marsala, extra
2 teaspoons cocoa powder

1 Combine coffee and the water in coffee plunger; stand 2 minutes before plunging. Combine coffee mixture and marsala in medium heatproof bowl; cool 10 minutes.
2 Place half the ladyfingers, in single layer, over base of deep 2-quart dish; drizzle with half the coffee mixture.
3 Beat cream and sifted sugar in small bowl until soft peaks form; transfer to large bowl. Fold in combined mascarpone cheese and extra marsala.
4 Spread half the cream mixture over ladyfingers in dish. Submerge the remaining ladyfingers, one at a time, in coffee mixture, being careful they do not become so soggy that they fall apart; place over cream layer. Top ladyfinger layer with the remaining cream mixture. Cover; refrigerate 3 hours or overnight.
5 Serve tiramisu dusted with sifted cocoa.
nutritional count per serving 45g total fat (29.9g saturated fat); 572 cal; 25.8g carbohydrate; 6.5g protein; 0.5g fiber

sticky date pudding

PREP + COOK TIME 1 HOUR 10 MINS (+ STANDING) • SERVES 6

Both the pudding and sauce can be made a day ahead and stored, separately, covered, in the fridge. You can freeze the pudding for up to 3 months. Defrost and warm in a microwave oven while making the butterscotch sauce. Or freeze wedges of the pudding, thaw in a microwave oven for about 30 seconds– an instant dessert to have with cream or ice cream, with or without the sauce.

1¼ cups pitted dried dates
1¼ cups boiling water
1 teaspoon baking soda
3 tablespoons butter, chopped
½ cup firmly packed light brown sugar
2 eggs, beaten lightly
1 cup self-rising flour
butterscotch sauce
¾ cup firmly packed light brown sugar
1¼ cups cream
9 tablespoons butter

1 Preheat oven to 350°F/325°F fan-forced. Grease deep 8-inch round cake pan; line base and side with parchment paper.

2 Combine dates and the water in medium heatproof bowl. Stir in baking soda; stand 5 minutes.

3 Blend or process date mixture with butter and sugar until pureed. Add eggs and flour; blend or process until just combined. Pour mixture into pan.

4 Bake cake about 1 hour. Stand in pan 10 minutes; turn onto serving plate.

5 Meanwhile, make butterscotch sauce.

6 Serve cake warm with butterscotch sauce.

butterscotch sauce Stir ingredients in medium saucepan over low heat until smooth.

nutritional count per serving 41.5g total fat (26.6g saturated fat); 734 cal; 82g carbohydrate; 6.5g protein; 4.2g fiber

Q&A

Why is it that every time I make a pavlova the results are different?

There are many factors that contribute to the success, or perceived failure, of the perfect pav. There are huge variations in the egg whites themselves and then there's the weather, which affects the sugar in the pavlova. As soon as the weather becomes wet or humid, the sugar absorbs the extra moisture in the air and your pav begins to weep, forming sticky condensation droplets on the surface. The best you can do is to follow a good recipe–make sure every grain of sugar is dissolved, bake the pavs carefully and thoroughly, and resign yourself to the idea that every pav you make will be slightly different–and still edible, no matter what happens.

CAKES

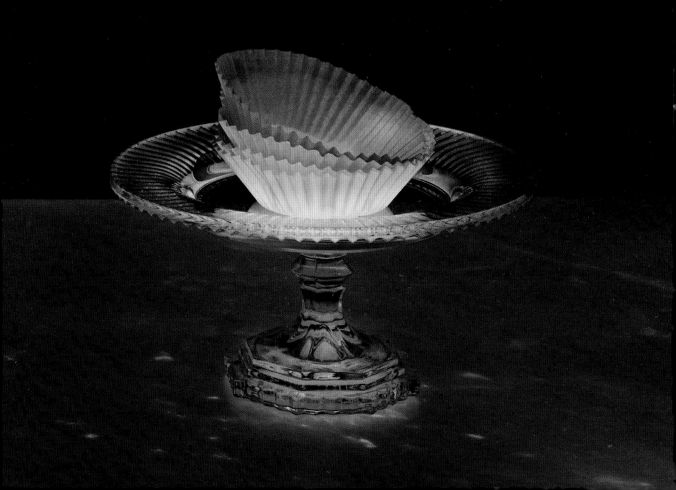

Cakes

There is something incredibly heartening about the smell of a freshly baked cake. And eating it, perhaps still slightly warm, is one of life's unequivocal pleasures. In this chapter, we've assembled recipes for all the classic and impressive cakes you need to have in your repertoire.

THE BASICS

Take cold ingredients out of the refrigerator ahead of cooking so they have time to come to room temperature for baking.

Follow recipes closely and always use the size and shape of cake pan directed by the recipe: using a different size or shape requires a different oven temperature or baking time.

To grease a pan, either spray it with a light, even coating of cooking oil or brush melted butter lightly over the base and side(s). If a recipe calls for a greased and floured pan: brush the pan with melted butter and let it set for a minute before sprinkling a little flour evenly over the surface. Tap it to remove any excess flour.

Cakes that are high in sugar or contain golden syrup or molasses tend to stick to the pan; we recommend lining the pan with parchment paper.

Spoon and cup measurements should be leveled off with a knife or spatula. Be exact about leveling measuring spoons when measuring ingredients like honey: more is not better in this case.

As a rule, we don't mix cakes in a food processor: use an electric mixer to mix the cake then a spatula or spoon to work in the other ingredients.

COOLING

Once cooked, stand the cake in its pan for 5 to 10 minutes. Turn the cake onto a wire rack to cool: the easiest way to do this is to hold the cake pan firmly and shake it, gently, to loosen the cake. Turn the cake upside down onto a wire rack, then turn the cake top-side up immediately using a second rack. Fruit cakes are the exception to this cooling process. Fruit cakes should be covered with foil and left to cool completely in the pan.

STORING

• Most cakes keep well for 2 to 3 days depending on the climate and type of cake. Generally, the higher the sugar content, the longer the cake will keep.
• The cake needs to be at room temperature before placing it in an airtight container.
• Most cakes will freeze well: unfilled and un-iced is best. Wrap or seal in plastic wrap or a freezer bag.
• Thaw a whole cake overnight in the refrigerator; slices of frozen cake need only 10 or 15 minutes at room temperature.

TYPES OF CAKES

BUTTER CAKES

Butter cakes are also called pound cakes–a term derived from the traditional balance of the main ingredients: a "pound" each of butter, eggs, flour and sugar.

• When combining the dry ingredients and the liquid, be careful: there is a tendency to overmix and this will toughen the mixture. Add half the dry ingredients and half the liquid then beat on low speed until just combined. Add the remaining ingredients, beating on low speed until just combined, then increase the speed, beating for about 30 seconds, until mixture is smooth.

HOW DO YOU TEST IF A BUTTER CAKE IS COOKED?

Take the cake out of the oven, push a skewer gently through the thickest part of the cake to the bottom of the pan. Pull the skewer out slowly: if the skewer is clean the cake is done: if the skewer has uncooked mixture on it, cook the cake further. For cupcakes: you can usually tell if they're cooked through simply by looking at them and touching them. If in doubt, use a skewer as you would a butter cake.

CHOCOLATE CAKES

The secret to a great chocolate cake rests in the quality of the chocolate you use. The better quality the chocolate, the better the results. The more bitter the chocolate, the higher the content of cocoa solids and more intense the chocolate flavor.

In most of our recipes, like the mud cake in this chapter, we recommend using good-quality eating chocolate. Generally, try to avoid anything labeled compound chocolate (the cheaper chocolates) in which some of the cocoa butter is replaced with other vegetable fats such as palm, coconut or soy oil. Exceptions to this rule are when the recipe calls for chocolate chips or chunks: these are sometimes specified for particular recipes because they keep their shape when baked.

HOW DO YOU TEST IF A CHOCOLATE CAKE IS COOKED?

Use the same method as for butter cakes above.

SPONGE CAKES

• Most recipes insist on triple-sifting the dry ingredients to aerate the flour as much as possible.
• Use an electric mixer to beat the eggs. Start beating at a low speed and, as they thicken, increase to moderately high.
• When adding the sugar, add it a tablespoon at a time: keep the mixer beating until the grains dissolve after each addition and continue until all the sugar is used.
• The best way to fold in the dry ingredients of a sponge mixture is to use your hands: with fingers splayed like a rake, drag the flour up through the egg mixture, wiping the side of your hand around the edge of the bowl. You can also use a metal spoon, or a plastic or rubber spatula.
• A deep-sided cake pan gives the best results for a sponge–the high side(s) protect it from developing a crisp crust.

HOW DO YOU TEST IF A SPONGE IS COOKED?

Assess a sponge cake by its appearance and feel–piercing with a skewer will deflate it. Toward the end of baking time, open the oven gently: it should be well-risen, browned and not shrunken from the side of the pan. Feel the top of the cake–it should be slightly springy. Turn sponges out immediately as they continue to cook and dry out if left in the pan. Turn onto a wire rack, then quickly turn the right way up to prevent the wire racks from indenting the surface.

FRUIT CAKES

• Be guided by the recipe's cooking time, but check every half hour or so–it might need turning.
• Once you think your cake is cooked, feel the top with your fingers: there should be a feeling of a firm crust.

HOW DO YOU TEST IF YOUR FRUIT CAKE IS COOKED?

Rich fruit cakes are best tested using the blade of a sharp, pointed knife. The blade gives you a larger area to see and feel what's going on inside the cake. Push the knife into the center of the cake and look at the blade: if it has uncooked mixture on it, continue baking; if the blade is shiny and feels clean, the cake is done.

Preparing cake pans

It's important to grease, flour and line your cake pans with care. It would be a sad thing to go to all the trouble of making a wonderful cake only to have it break into pieces when you try to remove it from the pan.

GREASING WITH COOKING-OIL SPRAY
Hold the cake pan up with the base vertical, then spray lightly with cooking-oil spray, evenly coating the base and side(s). Ideally, do this by an outside door to avoid oil falling onto kitchen equipment.

GREASING WITH BUTTER
Melt butter and, with a pastry brush, brush it evenly over base and sides of pan. If butter collects in corners or where sides meet base, go back and dab with brush to even it out, or use your fingers.

FLOURING A PAN (1)
First grease the pan with cooking-oil spray or butter, as described previously, then sprinkle lightly but evenly with a little flour, tilting pan to flour the side evenly too.

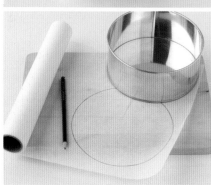

LINING A ROUND PAN (1)
Place round cake pan on parchment paper (close to the edge to minimize waste) and trace around it with a pencil.

LINING A ROUND PAN (2)
Cut out the circle you have traced, cutting just inside the pencil line to allow for the thickness of the pan so it will fit the inside base exactly.

LINING A ROUND PAN (3)
Cut a strip of baking parchment paper so that it's long enough to go around the pan with a little overlap, is wide enough to allow for a ¾-inch turn-up, and extends 2 inches above the rim of the pan.

Q&A

if you're using parchment paper to line a cake pan, do you have to grease the paper?

No. In fact you don't really need to grease the pan when you're using parchment. The only reason you do it is to make the baking stick to the pan so you can smooth it out evenly.

FLOURING A PAN (2)
After flouring, hold pan upside down and tap firmly to shake out excess flour. This ensures that the cake browns evenly and there is no flour "band" around the base of cake after baking.

LINING A RECTANGULAR OR SQUARE PAN
Mark width of pan on parchment and cut a strip of this width, long enough to line pan end-to-end with overhang. Mark length and cut another strip to line side-to-side with some overhang. Place strips in pan, overlapping.

LINING A BAR COOKIE PAN
Mark pan width on parchment, and cut a strip of this width, long enough to line pan end-to-end and extend over. Place in pan with equal overhang at each end, smoothing to fit.

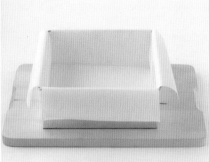

LINING A ROUND PAN (4)
Fold over long side of paper about ¾ inch from the edge, run a finger along to make a crease; open out and use scissors to make diagonal cuts, about ¾ inch apart, across the folded strip from edge to crease.

LINING A ROUND PAN (5)
Place paper around inside of pan, with the snipped edge flat on the base, securing it to the side or base, as needed, with melted butter or cooking-oil spray.

LINING A ROUND PAN (6)
Place the cut-out circle of paper into the pan and smooth it out, covering the snipped edges of the side lining, to fit neatly.

lemon syrup cake

Lemon syrup cake is probably the most well-known and popular of all. We love this recipe for its tangy taste and velvety texture.

1 stick butter, softened
3 teaspoons finely grated lemon rind
⅔ cup superfine sugar
2 eggs
⅔ cup buttermilk
2 tablespoons lemon juice
1½ cups self-rising flour

lemon syrup
⅓ cup lemon juice
¼ cup water
¾ cup superfine sugar

1 Preheat oven to 350°F/325°F fan-forced. Grease 9-inch baba pan or deep 9-inch round cake pan.

2 Beat butter, rind and sugar in small bowl with electric mixer until light and fluffy. Beat in eggs, one at a time. Transfer mixture to large bowl; fold in buttermilk, lemon juice and sifted flour, in two batches. Spread mixture into pan.

3 Bake cake about 30 minutes if using baba pan or about 40 minutes if using round pan. Stand cake 5 minutes; turn onto wire rack set over tray.

4 Meanwhile, make lemon syrup. Pour hot syrup over hot cake; serve warm.

lemon syrup Stir ingredients in small saucepan over heat, without boiling, until sugar dissolves. Simmer, uncovered, without stirring, 5 minutes.

nutritional count per serving 11.9g total fat (7.3g saturated fat); 323 cal; 48.8g carbohydrate; 4.4g protein; 0.9g fiber

A baba pan has a pretty fluted base, which becomes the top of the cake. Grease it well with softened butter.

Beat the butter, lemon rind and sugar in a small bowl with an electric mixer until it is light and fluffy.

Place the warm cake and wire rack on an oven tray (to catch the drips) then pour the hot syrup over it. Serve warm.

hummingbird cake

This cake will keep for several days in an airtight container.

15-ounce can crushed pineapple in syrup
1 cup all-purpose flour
½ cup self-rising flour
½ teaspoon baking soda
½ teaspoon ground cinnamon
½ teaspoon ground ginger
1 cup firmly packed light brown sugar
½ cup dried coconut
1 cup mashed banana
2 eggs, beaten lightly
¾ cup vegetable oil

cream cheese frosting
3 tablespoons butter, softened
2 ounces cream cheese, softened
1 teaspoon vanilla extract
1½ cups powdered sugar

TIPS

• You need about 2 large overripe bananas for this recipe.

1 Preheat oven to 350°F/325°F fan-forced. Grease deep 9-inch square cake pan, line base with parchment paper.
2 Drain pineapple over medium bowl, pressing with spoon to extract as much syrup as possible. Reserve ¼ cup syrup.
3 Sift flours, soda, spices and sugar into large bowl. Using wooden spoon, stir in drained pineapple, reserved syrup, coconut, banana, egg and oil; pour into pan.
4 Bake cake about 40 minutes. Stand in pan 5 minutes; turn, top-side up, on wire rack to cool.
5 Meanwhile, make cream cheese frosting. Spread cold cake with frosting.
cream cheese frosting Beat butter, cream cheese and extract in small bowl with electric mixer until light and fluffy; gradually beat in powdered sugar.
nutritional count per serving 21.1g total fat (6.6g saturated fat); 450 cal; 59.5g carbohydrate; 4.5g protein; 2.2g fiber

Q&A

Tell me about hummingbird cake. Where did it come from?

Hummingbird cake is rich and sweet. The simple one-bowl recipe first appeared in *Southern Living* magazine in the late 1970s and has been a crowd favorite ever since. The cake is made from pineapple, bananas, spices and coconut, and usually comes thickly iced with cream cheese frosting. It's the perfect cake to serve at parties or large gatherings because a little goes a long way.

3 cups sugar

2 sticks butter, chopped

2 cups water

⅓ cup cocoa powder

1 teaspoon baking soda

3 cups self-rising flour

4 eggs

fudge frosting

6 tablespoons butter

½ cup sugar

⅓ cup water

1½ cups powdered sugar

⅓ cup cocoa powder

1 Preheat oven to 350°F/325°F fan-forced. Grease deep 10½-inch x 13-inch cake pan; line base with parchment paper.

2 Stir sugar, butter, the water and sifted cocoa and soda in medium saucepan over heat, without boiling, until sugar dissolves; bring to a boil. Reduce heat; simmer, uncovered, 5 minutes. Transfer mixture to large bowl; cool to room temperature.

3 Add flour and eggs to bowl; beat with electric mixer until mixture is smooth and pale in color. Pour mixture into pan.

4 Bake cake about 50 minutes. Stand in pan 10 minutes; turn, top-side up, onto wire rack to cool.

5 Meanwhile, make fudge frosting. Spread cold cake with frosting.

fudge frosting Stir butter, sugar and the water in small saucepan over low heat, without boiling, until sugar dissolves. Sift powdered sugar and cocoa into small bowl then gradually stir in hot butter mixture. Cover; refrigerate about 20 minutes or until frosting thickens. Beat with wooden spoon until spreadable.

nutritional count per serving 15.8g total fat (9.8g saturated fat); 432 cal; 67.3g carbohydrate; 4.3g protein; 1g fiber

Q&A

I know flourless chocolate cakes are extremely moist and I love them, but they're very expensive. Is there a recipe for a moist chocolate cake that won't cost me a fortune?

This moist chocolate cake is an excellent family cake. The mixture is boiled before it is baked, which gives the cake a lovely dense texture. And it's not all that expensive to make, using cocoa instead of chocolate.

orange cake

When making any cake by the quick-mix, one-bowl method, you should start by having the butter, eggs and milk at room temperature. You might also like to bake this cake in a loaf pan; line the pan base and bake the cake about 50 minutes.

10 tablespoons butter, softened
1 tablespoon finely grated orange rind
⅔ cup superfine sugar
3 eggs
1½ cups self-rising flour
¼ cup milk
¾ cup powdered sugar
1½ tablespoons orange juice

1 Preheat oven to 350°F/325°F fan-forced. Grease deep 8-inch round cake pan.

2 Beat butter, rind, sugar, eggs, flour and milk in medium bowl with electric mixer at low speed until just combined. Increase speed to medium, beat about 3 minutes or until mixture is smooth.

3 Spread mixture into pan; bake about 40 minutes. Stand cake 5 minutes; turn, top-side up, onto wire rack to cool.

4 Combine sifted powdered sugar and juice in small bowl; spread over cake.

nutritional count per serving 12g total fat (7.3g saturated fat); 270 cal; 36.3g carbohydrate; 3.8g protein; 0.7g fiber

boiled fruit cake

Cover the cake loosely with foil during baking if it starts to overbrown; and give the cake quarter turns several times during baking if it is browning unevenly. This cake can be made up to 3 months ahead. Store in an airtight container in a cool, dry place, or refrigerate if the weather is humid.

2¾ cups mixed dried fruit
½ cup water
1 cup firmly packed light brown sugar
1 stick butter, chopped
1 teaspoon pie spice
½ teaspoon baking soda

½ cup sweet sherry
1 egg
1 cup all-purpose flour
1 cup self-rising flour
⅓ cup blanched almonds
2 tablespoons sweet sherry, extra

1 Combine fruit, the water, sugar, butter, spice and soda in large saucepan. Stir over low heat, without boiling, until sugar dissolves and butter melts; bring to a boil. Reduce heat; simmer, covered, 5 minutes. Remove from heat; stir in sherry. Cool to room temperature.

2 Preheat oven to 325°F/300°F fan-forced. Grease deep 8-inch round cake pan; line base and side with two layers of parchment, extending paper 2 inches above side.

3 Stir egg and sifted flours into fruit mixture. Spread mixture into pan; decorate with almonds. Bake about 1½ hours. Brush top of hot cake with extra sherry. Cover cake with foil, cool in pan.

nutritional count per serving 12.2g total fat (6.1g saturated fat); 411 cal; 64.6g carbohydrate; 5g protein; 3.7g fiber

[1] orange cake
[2] boiled fruit cake
[3] genoise sponge [page 540]
[4] mississippi mud cake [page 540]

genoise sponge

This classic sponge relies totally on the air incorporated into the egg mixture for its leavening. Beat the egg mixture well, and fold the flour in gently, being careful not to deflate the fluffy eggs.

4 eggs
½ cup superfine sugar
⅔ cup all-purpose flour
½ stick butter, melted, cooled
1¼ cup heavy cream

1 tablespoon powdered sugar
¼ cup strawberry jam, warmed
1 pound strawberries, sliced thinly
1 tablespoon powdered sugar, extra

1 Preheat oven to 350°F/325°F fan-forced. Grease deep 8-inch round cake pan; line base with parchment paper.

2 Combine eggs and sugar in large heatproof bowl, place over saucepan of simmering water (do not allow water to touch base of bowl); beat with electric mixer about 10 minutes or until mixture is thick and creamy. Remove bowl from saucepan; beat mixture until it returns to room temperature.

3 Sift half the flour over egg mixture; carefully fold in flour. Sift remaining flour into bowl, fold into mixture. Working quickly, fold in melted butter.

4 Pour mixture into pan; bake about 20 minutes. Turn immediately, top-side up, onto parchment-paper-covered wire rack to cool.

5 Beat cream and sifted powdered sugar in small bowl with electric mixer until soft peaks form. Split sponge in half; place one half, cut-side up, on serving plate. Spread with jam and cream; top with strawberries, then remaining sponge. Decorate cake with extra sifted powdered sugar, and strawberries, if you like.

nutritional count per serving 22.9g total fat (14g saturated fat); 376 cal; 35.1g carbohydrate; 6.6g protein; 2g fiber

mississippi mud cake

2 sticks butter, chopped
5 ounces bittersweet chocolate, chopped coarsely
2 cups sugar
1 cup hot water
⅓ cup coffee liqueur
1 tablespoon instant coffee granules
1½ cups all-purpose flour
¼ cup self-rising flour
¼ cup cocoa powder
2 eggs, beaten lightly

dark chocolate ganache
½ cup cream
7 ounces bittersweet chocolate, chopped coarsely

1 Preheat oven to 325°F/300°F fan-forced. Grease deep 8-inch round cake pan; line base and side with parchment paper.

2 Combine butter, chocolate, sugar, the water, liqueur and coffee granules in medium saucepan. Using wooden spoon, stir over low heat until chocolate melts.

3 Transfer mixture to large bowl; cool 15 minutes. Whisk in combined sifted flours and cocoa, then egg. Pour mixture into prepared pan.

4 Bake cake about 1½ hours. Stand cake in pan 30 minutes before turning, top-side up, onto wire rack to cool.

5 Meanwhile, make dark chocolate ganache; spread over top of cake.

dark chocolate ganache Bring cream to a boil in small saucepan. Pour hot cream over chocolate in medium heatproof bowl; stir until smooth. Stand at room temperature until spreadable.

nutritional count per serving 23.7g total fat (14.9g saturated fat); 457 cal; 53.6g carbohydrate; 4.3g protein; 1g fiber

flourless chocolate and almond torte

PREP + COOK TIME
1 HOUR 15 MINS
(+ COOLING & STANDING)
SERVES 14

5 ounces dark chocolate, chopped
10 tablespoons unsalted butter, diced
5 eggs, separated
¾ cup superfine sugar
1 cup ground almonds
⅔ cup sliced almonds, toasted, chopped coarsely

⅓ cup coarsely grated bittersweet chocolate
1 cup candied almonds
dark chocolate ganache
4 ounces dark chocolate, chopped
⅓ cup heavy cream

Flourless (making this recipe gluten-free) cakes have a delightful texture and are now very popular in restaurants. They are simple to make, we're not sure why more home cooks don't make them. Serve slim wedges of cake with whipped cream and some berries of your choice.

1 Preheat oven to 350°F/325°F fan-forced. Grease deep 9-inch round cake pan; line the base and side with two layers of parchment paper.

2 Stir chopped chocolate and butter in small saucepan over low heat until smooth; cool to room temperature.

3 Beat egg yolks and sugar in small bowl with electric mixer until thick and creamy. Transfer mixture to large bowl; fold in chocolate mixture, ground almonds, sliced almonds and grated chocolate.

4 Beat egg whites in small bowl with electric mixer until soft peaks form; fold into chocolate mixture, in two batches. Pour mixture into pan.

5 Bake cake about 45 minutes. Stand cake in pan 15 minutes before turning, top-side up, onto wire rack to cool.

6 Meanwhile, make dark chocolate ganache.

7 Spread ganache over cake, decorate with candied almonds; stand 30 minutes before serving.

dark chocolate ganache Stir ingredients in small saucepan over low heat until smooth.

nutritional count per serving 36.9g total fat (13.5g saturated fat); 503 cal; 32.6g carbohydrate; 9.7g protein; 2.9g fiber

date and walnut rolls

If you can't buy new nut roll tins, look around in some second-hand shops or garage sales, you might be lucky. They will rust if they're not cared for properly because they're made from tin.

½ stick butter

1 cup boiling water

1 cup finely chopped dried dates

½ teaspoon baking soda

1 cup firmly packed light brown sugar

2 cups self-rising flour

½ cup coarsely chopped walnuts

1 egg, beaten lightly

1 Preheat oven to 350°F/325°F fan-forced. Grease two 3-inch x 7½-inch nut roll tins; line bases with parchment paper. Place tins upright on oven tray.

2 Stir butter and the water in medium saucepan over low heat until butter melts. Remove from heat; stir in dates and soda, then remaining ingredients. Spoon mixture into tins; replace lids.

3 Bake rolls about 50 minutes. Stand rolls in tins 5 minutes; remove ends (top and bottom), shake tins gently to release rolls onto wire rack to cool. Serve rolls sliced with butter.

nutritional count per serving 5g total fat (1.9g saturated fat); 168 cal; 27.4g carbohydrate; 2.5g protein; 1.6g fiber

TIPS

• It is important that you do not fill nut roll tins with too much mixture. The nut rolls rise surprisingly high; both because the tin is narrow and because the cooking method approximates that of steaming. As a rough guide, the tins should be filled just a little over halfway.

• Some nut roll tins open along the side; be certain these are closed properly before baking.

• Some lids have tiny holes in them to allow steam to escape; make sure these are not used on the bottom of the tins.

Using a pastry brush, grease the nut roll tins generously with very soft butter. Place a round of parchment paper inside the top and bottom lids.

Spoon the cake mixture into the tins, filling them to just above halfway.

When the rolls are cooked, remove both top and bottom lids and shake the tins gently to release the rolls. Cool them on a wire rack.

jelly roll

This filled and rolled sponge cake has long been a favorite here and in the UK. Quick and easy to make, yet very impressive-looking, slices of the roll are good served warm or at room temperature with a dollop of whipped cream.

3 eggs, separated
½ cup superfine sugar
2 tablespoons hot milk
¾ cup self-rising flour
¼ cup superfine sugar, extra
½ cup jam, warmed

1 Preheat oven to 400°F/350°F fan forced. Grease 10-inch x 12-inch jelly roll pan; line base with parchment paper, extending paper 2 inches over short sides.
2 Beat egg whites in small bowl with electric mixer until soft peaks form; add sugar, 1 tablespoon at a time, beating until dissolved between additions. With motor running, add egg yolks, one at a time, beating until mixture is pale and thick; this will take about 10 minutes.
3 Pour hot milk down side of bowl; add triple-sifted flour. Working quickly, use plastic spatula to fold milk and flour through egg mixture. Pour mixture into pan, gently spreading evenly into corners.
4 Bake cake about 8 minutes.
5 Meanwhile, place a piece of parchment paper cut the same size as pan on counter; sprinkle evenly with extra sugar.
6 Turn cake immediately onto sugared paper; peel away lining paper. Use serrated knife to trim crisp edges from all sides of cake.
7 Using paper as a guide, gently roll warm cake loosely from one of the short sides. Unroll; spread evenly with jam. Reroll cake from same short side. Cool.
nutritional count per serving 1.9g total fat (0.6g saturated fat); 196 cal; 40.5g carbohydrate; 3.3g protein; 0.6g fiber

Place the cake on a piece of sugared baking paper and gently peel away the lining paper, using a spatula to press down on the paper. The weight of the spatula will prevent the sponge from breaking.

Using a serrated knife, trim away the crisp edges from all sides of the cake.

With no filling, and using the sugared baking paper as a guide, gently roll the warm cake loosely. You do this so that once you've spread it with jam, it will roll up easily.

carrot cake with lemon cream cheese frosting

PREP + COOK TIME
1 HOUR 25 MINS
SERVES 12

TIP

• You need about 3 large carrots for this recipe.

3 eggs

1⅓ cups firmly packed light
    brown sugar

1 cup vegetable oil

3 cups firmly packed, coarsely
    grated carrot

1 cup coarsely chopped walnuts

2½ cups self-rising flour

½ teaspoon baking soda

2 teaspoons pie spice

lemon cream cheese frosting

3 tablespoons butter, softened

3 ounces cream cheese, softened

1 teaspoon finely grated lemon rind

1½ cups powdered sugar

1 Preheat oven to 350°F/325°F fan-forced. Grease deep 9-inch round cake pan; line base with parchment paper.

2 Beat eggs, sugar and oil in small bowl with electric mixer until thick and creamy. Transfer mixture to large bowl; stir in carrot and nuts then sifted dry ingredients. Pour mixture into pan.

3 Bake cake about 1¼ hours. Stand in pan 5 minutes; turn, top-side up, onto wire rack to cool.

4 Meanwhile, make lemon cream cheese frosting. Spread cold cake with frosting.

lemon cream cheese frosting Beat butter, cream cheese and rind in small bowl with electric mixer until light and fluffy; gradually beat in powdered sugar.

nutritional count per serving 32.1g total fat (6.1g saturated fat); 578 cal; 64.2g carbohydrate; 7g protein; 2.7g fiber

lamingtons

PREP + COOK TIME 1 HOUR • MAKES 16

Lamingtons are tasty little cake cubes coated in chocolate and rolled in coconut. They are a favorite treat in Britain and Australia, but there are many commercial types available here in the U.S. as well.

6 eggs

⅔ cup superfine sugar

⅓ cup corn starch

½ cup all-purpose flour

⅓ cup self-rising flour

2 cups dried coconut

icing

4 cups confectioners sugar

½ cup cocoa powder

1 tablespoon butter, melted

1 cup milk

1 Preheat oven to 350°F/325°F fan-forced. Grease 8-inch x 10-inch high-sided sheet pan; line with parchment paper, extending paper 2 inches over long sides.

2 Beat eggs in large bowl with electric mixer about 10 minutes or until thick and creamy; gradually beat in sugar, dissolving between additions. Fold in triple-sifted flours. Spread mixture into pan.

3 Bake cake about 35 minutes. Turn cake immediately onto a parchment-covered wire rack to cool.

4 Meanwhile, make icing.

5 Cut cake into 16 pieces; dip each square in icing, drain off excess. Toss squares in coconut. Place lamingtons onto wire rack to set.

icing Sift powdered sugar and cocoa into medium heatproof bowl; stir in butter and milk. Set bowl over medium saucepan of simmering water; stir until icing is of a coating consistency.

nutritional count per lamington 10.4g total fat (1.8g saturated fat); 359 cal; 59.6g carbohydrate; 5.1g protein; 1.9g fiber

strawberry jelly cakes

PREP + COOK TIME 50 MINS (+ REFRIGERATION) • MAKES 15

These jelly cakes are a popular variation of the traditional lamington. Experiment with other flavored gelatins such as passionfruit, lime, raspberry or cherry.

6 eggs
⅔ cup superfine sugar
⅓ cup corn starch
½ cup all-purpose flour
⅓ cup self-rising flour
3-ounce packet strawberry gelatin
2 cups dried coconut
1¼ cups heavy cream, whipped to soft peaks

1 Preheat oven to 350°F/325°F fan-forced. Grease 8-inch x 10-inch high-sided sheet pan; line base and long sides with parchment, extending paper 2 inches over sides.

2 Beat eggs in large bowl with electric mixer about 10 minutes or until thick and creamy; gradually add sugar, beating until dissolved between additions. Triple-sift flours; fold into egg mixture.

3 Spread mixture into pan; bake about 35 minutes. Turn cake immediately onto parchment-covered wire rack to cool.

4 Meanwhile, make gelatin as per packet instructions; refrigerate until set to the consistency of unbeaten egg white.

5 Trim all sides of cake. Cut cake into 15 squares; dip squares into gelatin, drain off excess. Place coconut into medium bowl; toss squares in coconut. Refrigerate 30 minutes. Halve cakes horizontally; sandwich cakes with whipped cream.

nutritional count per cake 16.6g total fat (11.7g saturated fat); 260 cal; 22.2g carbohydrate; 5g protein; 1.9g fiber

marble cake

Pink, green and white also make a pretty marble cake. If this is your preference, omit the cocoa powder and extra milk from this recipe, and add a few drops of green food coloring into the mixture instead.

2 sticks butter, softened
1 teaspoon vanilla extract
1¼ cups superfine sugar
3 eggs
2¼ cups self-rising flour
¾ cup milk
pink food coloring
2 tablespoons cocoa powder
2 tablespoons milk, extra

butter frosting
1 stick butter, softened
2 cups powdered sugar
2 tablespoons milk

1 Preheat oven to 350°F/325°F fan-forced. Grease deep 9-inch round or 7½-inch square cake pan; line base with parchment paper.

2 Beat butter, extract and sugar in medium bowl with electric mixer until light and fluffy. Beat in eggs, one at a time. Stir in sifted flour and milk, in two batches.

3 Divide mixture among three bowls; tint one mixture pink. Blend sifted cocoa with extra milk in a cup; stir into second mixture; leave remaining mixture plain. Drop alternate spoonfuls of mixtures into pan. Pull a skewer backwards and forwards through cake mixture.

4 Bake cake about 1 hour. Stand cake in pan 5 minutes before turning, top-side up, onto wire rack to cool.

5 Make butter frosting. Spread frosting over top and side of cake.

butter frosting Beat butter in small bowl with electric mixer until light and fluffy; beat in sifted powdered sugar and milk, in two batches.

nutritional count per serving 28.3g total fat (18g saturated fat); 562 cal; 70.8g carbohydrate; 5.6g protein; 1.1g fiber

Tint one third of the cake mixture pink using a few drops of pink food coloring. Stir in only a drop or two of coloring at a time–overcoloring produces an unattractive cake.

To flavor the chocolate third of the cake mix, combine cocoa powder with a little milk and stir into the mixture.

Drop alternate spoonfuls of each cake mixture into the pan.

Use a skewer to "marble" the cake by pulling it backward and forward through the mixture.

madeira cake

1½ sticks butter, softened
2 teaspoons finely grated lemon rind
⅔ cup superfine sugar
3 eggs

¾ cup all-purpose flour
¾ cup self-rising flour
⅓ cup chopped candied citrus
¼ cup slivered almonds

1 Preheat oven to 325°F/300°F fan-forced. Grease deep 8-inch round cake pan; line base with parchment.

2 Beat butter, rind and sugar in small bowl with electric mixer until light and fluffy; beat in eggs, one at a time. Transfer mixture to large bowl, stir in sifted flours.

3 Spread mixture into pan; bake 20 minutes. Remove cake from oven; sprinkle with citrus and nuts. Return to oven; bake about 40 minutes. Stand cake 5 minutes; turn, top-side up, onto wire rack to cool.

nutritional count per serving 15.5g total fat (8.6g saturated fat); 272 cal; 28.7g carbohydrate; 4.3g protein; 1.1g fiber

pound cake

Many cooks believe the butter or pound cake to be the mother of all cakes and indeed it has been around so long and spawned so many variations that it deserves the title. The term "pound cake" comes from the balance of major ingredients – a pound of each.

2 sticks butter, softened
1 cup superfine sugar
1 teaspoon vanilla extract
4 eggs
½ cup self-rising flour
1 cup plain flour

1 Preheat oven to 350°F/325°F fan-forced. Grease deep 8-inch round cake pan; line base with parchment paper.

2 Beat butter, sugar and extract in small bowl with electric mixer until light and fluffy. Beat in eggs, one at a time. Transfer mixture to large bowl; fold in sifted flours in two batches.

3 Spread mixture into pan; bake about 1 hour. Stand cake in pan 5 minutes before turning, top-side up, onto wire rack to cool. If you like, serve with whipped cream and strawberries, and dust with sifted powdered sugar.

nutritional count per serving 19.1g total fat (11.8g saturated fat); 317 cal; 31.9g carbohydrate; 4.3g protein; 0.7g fiber

[1] madeira cake
[2] pound cake
[3] one-bowl raisin loaf [page 552]
[4] vanilla patty cakes with glacé icing [page 552]

one-bowl raisin loaf

Loaf pans come in slightly different sizes and depths, also in different materials and finishes. The most common size is 5½ inches x 8½ inches inside-top measurement and about 2 inches deep.

1 stick butter, melted
1½ pounds raisins
½ cup firmly packed
  light brown sugar
2 tablespoons marmalade
2 eggs, beaten lightly

¼ cup sweet sherry
¾ cup all-purpose flour
¼ cup self-rising flour
1 ounce blanched almonds
2 tablespoons apricot jam

1 Preheat oven to 300°F/275°F fan-forced. Grease 6-inch x 10-inch loaf pan; line base with parchment paper.

2 Beat butter, raisins, sugar, marmalade, egg, sherry and flours in large bowl using a wooden spoon until combined. Spread mixture into pan; decorate top with blanched almonds.

3 Bake loaf about 1½ hours. Cover cake with foil; cool in pan. Brush cold cake with warmed strained apricot jam

nutritional count per serving 16.8 g total fat (9g saturated fat); 628 cal; 106.7g carbohydrate; 7.1g protein; 5.3g fiber

vanilla patty cakes with glacé icing

You can make glacé icing without butter (or oil) but a tiny amount of butter will add gloss to the icing and make it easy to cut neatly–without butter, glacé icing tends to shatter when you cut it.

1 stick butter, softened
1 teaspoon vanilla extract
⅔ cup superfine sugar
3 eggs
1½ cups self-rising flour
¼ cup milk

glacé icing
1½ cups powdered sugar
1 teaspoon butter
2 tablespoons milk, approximately

1 Preheat oven to 350°F/325°F fan-forced. Line two deep 12-hole cupcake pans with paper cases.

2 Beat butter, extract, sugar, eggs, flour and milk on low speed in medium bowl with electric mixer until ingredients are combined. Increase speed to medium; beat about 3 minutes or until mixture is smooth and paler in color.

3 Drop slightly rounded tablespoons of mixture into paper cases.

4 Bake cakes about 20 minutes. Turn cakes, top-side up, onto wire racks to cool.

5 Meanwhile, make glacé icing. Top cool cakes with icing.

glacé icing Sift powdered sugar into small heatproof bowl; stir in butter and enough milk to give a firm paste. Place bowl over small saucepan of simmering water; stir until icing is spreadable.

nutritional count per patty cake 5.4g total fat (3.2g saturated fat); 150 cal; 23.1g carbohydrate; 1.9g protein; 0.4g fiber

banana cake

1 stick butter, softened
¾ cup superfine sugar
2 eggs
1 cup mashed banana
1 teaspoon baking soda
2 tablespoons hot milk
1 cup all-purpose flour
⅔ cup self-rising flour

TIP

• You need about 2 large overripe bananas for this recipe.

1 Preheat oven to 350°F/325°F. Grease deep 8-inch round cake pan; line base and side with parchment paper.

2 Beat butter and sugar in small bowl with electric mixer until light and fluffy. Beat in eggs, one at a time. Transfer to large bowl; stir in banana.

3 Combine soda and milk in small bowl; stir into banana mixture then stir in sifted flours. Spread mixture into pan.

4 Bake cake about 50 minutes. Stand cake in pan 5 minutes before turning, top-side up, onto wire rack to cool. Serve dusted with sifted powdered sugar, if you like.

nutritional count per serving 11.8g total fat (7.2g saturated fat); 291 cal; 40.8g carbohydrate; 4.5g protein; 1.5g fiber

cinnamon teacake

The secret to making a perfect cinnamon teacake is to beat the butter, sugar and egg mixture in a small bowl until it's as light and white as possible.

½ stick butter, softened
1 teaspoon vanilla extract
⅔ cup superfine sugar
1 egg
1 cup self-rising flour

⅓ cup milk
1 tablespoon butter, melted, extra
1 teaspoon ground cinnamon
1 tablespoon superfine sugar, extra

1 Preheat oven to 350°F/325°F fan-forced. Grease deep 8-inch round cake pan; line base with parchment paper.

2 Beat butter, extract, sugar and egg in small bowl with electric mixer until light and fluffy, this will take about 10 minutes. Stir in sifted flour and milk. Spread mixture into pan.

3 Bake cake about 30 minutes. Turn cake onto wire rack then turn top-side up; brush top with extra butter, sprinkle with combined cinnamon and extra sugar. Serve warm with butter, if you like.

nutritional count per serving 6.8g total fat (4.2g saturated fat); 184 cal; 27.8g carbohydrate; 2.5g protein; 0.6g fiber

TEATIME

Teatime

When friends drop by for a visit, it's nice to welcome them with a home-baked treat. A plate of still-warm scones or crunchy cookies will always hit the spot. Watch the treats disappear while you chat, laugh and solve the world's problems. This chapter contains a selection of sweet sentimental favorites to accompany that freshly brewed pot of tea or coffee. It's always handy to have a supply in the freezer (or cookie jar) for such an occasion.

SCONES & MUFFINS

WELCOME YOUR GUESTS WITH OPEN ARMS, WITH WARM MUFFINS AND SCONES. YOU CAN WHIP UP A BATCH BETWEEN THE TIME YOU RECEIVE THE CALL TO SAY "WE THOUGHT WE MIGHT DROP BY" AND WHEN YOUR SMILING GUESTS SHOW UP AT YOUR DOOR.

FOR SCONES

Use a round-ended knife to "cut" the milk through the flour and butter mixture. The finished dough should be soft and sticky, just holding its shape. If you need to add a little flour when you turn it onto the floured working surface, be sparing.

You can freeze uncooked scones and then bake them straight from the freezer.

It's easy to tell if scones are done. They should be well-risen and even in color. Scones don't take long to cook through because they're small and are baked at a high temperature. The best test is to tap them with your finger: they have a distinctive hollow sound. Test the scones in the center of the batch because the ones on the outside will have cooked first. Slide the scones onto a wire rack and cover them loosely to cool.

FOR MUFFINS

Muffins are quick and easy, and most only require a single bowl for mixing. Use a large metal spoon or fork, and mix with the edge, in a cutting motion, in as few strokes as possible. Stop when the dry ingredients are just moistened–the mixture should still be coarse and lumpy.

Muffins are cooked when risen, browned, firm to touch and beginning to shrink from the sides of the pan. Turn them onto a rack to cool.

STORAGE AND FREEZING SCONES AND MUFFINS ARE BEST EATEN THE DAY THEY ARE MADE, IDEALLY SOON AFTER THEY COME OUT OF THE OVEN. THEY CAN BE KEPT IN AN AIRTIGHT CONTAINER FOR 2 DAYS AND FROZEN FOR UP TO 2 MONTHS.

COOKIES

- Don't overbeat the butter and sugar mixture: stop when they are well combined but still firm. Overbeating makes the mixture too soft, causing cookies to spread.
- When baking, it's important to use the correct trays. These should be flat, with little or no sides, to allow the heat to circulate and ensure even browning. Lightly coat trays with cooking-oil spray or brush with melted butter.
- If you bake two or more trays at once, swap the trays mid-way through baking and rotate them as well, to help with even browning.
- Cookies should develop a crust, but still feel slightly soft to the touch when you remove them from the oven. They will firm up as they cool.
- Don't stack cookies on top of each other when cooling; most cookies need air circulating around them to crisp.
- If the cookies are too brown underneath, the tray may have been overgreased; incorrect oven position and temperature could also be the cause.

SLICES

Slices are halfway between a cake and a tart–they can be made of one mixture, or can combine a crust (cookie or pastry) covered with a topping and/or a filling.

- Use aluminium trays: pans made from tin and stainless steel don't conduct heat as evenly.
- Preheating the oven is important for slices as they require less than 30 minutes of baking. Preheat for around 10 minutes before placing the food in the oven.

STORING AND FREEZING MOST SLICES KEEP FOR 2 TO 3 DAYS IN AN AIRTIGHT CONTAINER. REFRIGERATE THOSE CONTAINING DAIRY PRODUCTS. MOST SLICES CAN BE FROZEN FOR UP TO 2 MONTHS BUT THOSE WITH ICING AND CREAM FILLINGS MAY CRACK AND CHANGE IN APPEARANCE AS THEY THAW.

FINANCIER

Financier (French for small cakes) are perfect little morsels when you want a bite that is small and stylish but not too rich. One of their many charms is that they can be made very quickly. You can make them in muffin pans, but if you plan to serve them often, there are sweet little oval or rectangular financier pans available. You can buy these pans separately or in the form of 6-, 8-, 9- or 12-hole pans from good kitchen and cookware shops.

STORAGE AND FREEZING FINANCIER ARE BEST EATEN THE DAY THEY ARE MADE, BUT CAN BE STORED IN AN AIRTIGHT CONTAINER FOR 2 DAYS. THEY ALSO FREEZE WELL.

basic scones

The fear-of-failure-factor surrounding scones is very high. But once you've got the hang of them, you'll find them incredibly easy to make. Home-bakers seem to fall into two categories, those who can, and those who can't make scones. Read on for some tips to help you become an expert and a much-admired scone-maker.

4 cups self-rising flour
2 tablespoons powdered sugar
½ stick butter
1½ cups milk
¾ cup water, approximately

1 Preheat oven to 425°F/ 400°F fan-forced. Grease 8-inch x 12-inch sheet pan.
2 Sift flour and sugar into large bowl; rub in butter with fingertips.
3 Make a well in center of flour mixture; add milk and almost all the water. Use knife to "cut" the milk and water through the flour mixture, mixing to a soft, sticky dough. Knead dough on floured surface until smooth.
4 Press dough out to ¾-inch thickness. Dip 1¾-inch round cutter in flour; cut as many rounds as you can from piece of dough. Place scones, side by side, just touching, in pan.
5 Gently knead scraps of dough together; repeat pressing and cutting of dough, place in same pan. Brush tops with a little extra milk.
6 Bake scones about 15 minutes or until just browned and they sound hollow when tapped firmly on the top with fingers. Serve with jam and cream.
nutritional count per scone 2g total fat (1.2g saturated fat); 81 cal; 13.2g carbohydrate; 2.1g protein; 0.7g fiber

VARIATIONS

raisin and lemon Add ½ cup raisins and 2 teaspoons finely grated lemon rind to mixture after butter has been rubbed in.
blueberry and ginger Add 3 teaspoons ground ginger and ½ cup fresh or frozen blueberries to mixture after butter has been rubbed in.

Rub the butter into the sifted flour and sugar mixture using your fingertips.

Add the milk and water to the bowl and, using a flat-bladed knife, slice through the flour mixture, mixing until the dough is soft and sticky.

Place the dough on a floured surface and knead until smooth. Press the dough out to a ¾-inch thickness with your fingertips.

Brush the tops of the scones with the extra milk. The scones should be arranged so they are sitting side by side in the pan and just touching.

almond financier

These delicious tea cakes got their name in France, where they were originally baked in tiny, gold-bar shaped pans. You can buy these traditionally shaped pans individually from specialty kitchen stores or as baking dishes with multiple holes from most supermarkets. You might also choose to make tiny cakes containing a single berry or piece of fruit using a mini-muffin pan, or larger ones in a regular muffin pan.

6 egg whites
1½ sticks butter, melted
1 cup ground almonds
1½ cups powdered sugar
½ cup all-purpose flour

1 Preheat oven to 400°F/350°F fan-forced. Grease 12 x ½-cup pans; stand on oven tray.

2 Place egg whites in medium bowl; whisk lightly with fork until combined. Using wooden spoon, stir in remaining ingredients until just combined. Divide mixture among pans.

3 Bake cakes about 25 minutes. Stand cakes in pans 5 minutes; turn onto wire rack. Serve dusted with extra sifted powdered sugar.

nutritional count per financier 18.5g total fat (8.7g saturated fat); 286 cal; 25g carbohydrate; 4.6g protein; 1.2g fiber

VARIATIONS

raspberry and white chocolate Stir 3½ ounces coarsely chopped white chocolate into the egg-white mixture. Top cakes with 3½ ounces fresh or frozen raspberries.

lime coconut Stir 2 teaspoons finely grated lime rind, 1 tablespoon lime juice and ¼ cup dried coconut into the egg-white mixture; sprinkle unbaked cakes with ⅓ cup flaked coconut.

rhubarb and custard muffins

2 cups self-rising flour
½ cup all-purpose flour
¾ cup superfine sugar
7 tablespoons butter, melted
1 cup milk
1 egg
3 cups finely chopped rhubarb
1 tablespoon demerara sugar

custard
2 tablespoons custard powder
  or vanilla pudding mix
¼ cup superfine sugar
1 cup milk
1 teaspoon vanilla extract

1 Make custard.

2 Preheat oven to 400°F/375°F fan-forced. Line 12-hole (⅓-cup) muffin pan with paper cases.

3 Sift flours and sugar into large bowl. Stir in butter, milk and egg. Do not over-mix. Stir in half of the rhubarb.

4 Spoon half of the mixture into cases; top with custard. Spoon in remaining mixture to cover custard. Sprinkle with remaining rhubarb and demerara sugar.

5 Bake muffins about 20 minutes. Stand muffins in pan 5 minutes; turn, top-side up, onto wire rack to cool.

custard Combine custard powder and sugar in small saucepan; gradually stir in milk. Stir custard over medium heat until mixture boils and thickens. Stir in extract. Cool.

nutritional count per muffin 9.3g total fat (5.8g saturated fat); 295 cal; 45.7g carbohydrate; 5.7g protein; 1.9g fiber

berry muffins

Buttermilk, despite its luscious-sounding name, is low-fat. It adds a unique quality to muffins, scones and cakes. Try it and taste the difference.

2½ cups self-rising flour

6 tablespoons cold butter, chopped

1 cup superfine sugar

1¼ cups buttermilk

1 egg, beaten lightly

7 ounces fresh or frozen mixed berries

1 Preheat oven to 350°F/325°F fan-forced. Grease 12-hole (⅓-cup) muffin pan.

2 Sift flour into large bowl; rub in butter. Stir in sugar, buttermilk and egg. Do not overmix; mixture should be lumpy. Add berries; stir through gently. Spoon mixture into pan holes.

3 Bake muffins about 20 minutes. Stand muffins 5 minutes; turn, top-side up, onto wire rack to cool.

nutritional count per muffin 7.5g total fat (4.6g saturated fat); 262 cal; 42.4g carbohydrate; 5.1g protein; 1.6g fiber

VARIATIONS

lemon poppy seed Omit berries. Add 2 teaspoons lemon rind and 2 tablespoons poppy seeds with the sugar.

date and orange Omit berries. Add 1½ cups pitted, chopped dried dates and 2 teaspoons finely grated orange rind with the sugar.

chocolate chip and walnut Omit berries. Add ¾ cup dark chocolate chips and 1 cup coarsely chopped walnuts with the sugar.

chocolate fudge brownies

Despite the richness of these seriously chocolatey brownies, nobody can stop at one. It's great to think that something so good is so easy to make—all in one pan. If you like your brownies really fudgy, bake them for less time. Dust the brownies with a little sifted cocoa powder or powdered sugar, or both.

10 tablespoons butter, chopped
10 ounces bittersweet chocolate, chopped
1½ cups firmly packed light brown sugar
3 eggs

1 teaspoon vanilla extract
¾ cup all-purpose flour
¾ cup dark chocolate chips
½ cup sour cream
¾ cup roasted macadamias, chopped coarsely

1 Preheat oven to 350°F/325°F fan-forced. Grease 7½-inch x 11½-inch rectangular cake pan; line base with parchment, extending paper 2 inches over sides.
2 Stir butter and chocolate in medium saucepan over low heat until smooth. Cool 10 minutes.
3 Stir in sugar, eggs and extract, then sifted flour, chocolate chips, sour cream and nuts. Spread mixture into pan.
4 Bake brownies 40 minutes. Cover pan with foil; bake an additional 20 minutes Cool in pan. Serve dusted with sifted cocoa powder, if you like.
nutritional count per serving 24.8g total fat (12.7g saturated fat); 412 cal; 42.8g carbohydrate; 4.2g protein; 1g fiber

chocolate caramel slice

½ cup self-rising flour
½ cup all-purpose flour
1 cup dried coconut
1 cup firmly packed brown sugar
1 stick butter, melted
2 tablespoons golden syrup

13-ounce can sweetened condensed milk
3 tablespoons butter, extra
7 ounces bittersweet chocolate, chopped coarsely
2 teaspoons vegetable oil

1 Preheat oven to 350°F/325°F fan-forced. Grease 8-inch x 12-inch shallow cake pan; line with parchment paper, extending paper 2 inches over long sides.
2 Combine sifted flours, coconut, sugar and butter in medium bowl; press mixture evenly over base of pan. Bake about 15 minutes or until browned lightly.
3 Meanwhile, make caramel filling by combining syrup, condensed milk and extra butter in small saucepan. Stir over medium heat about 15 minutes or until caramel mixture is golden brown; pour over base. Bake 10 minutes; cool.
4 Make topping by combining chocolate and oil in small saucepan; stir over low heat until smooth. Pour warm topping over caramel. Refrigerate 3 hours or overnight.
nutritional count per piece 17.7g total fat (11.8g saturated fat); 357 cal; 44.6g carbohydrate; 4.1g protein; 1.2g fiber

[1] chocolate fudge brownies
[2] chocolate caramel slice
[3] date slice [page 564]
[4] portuguese custard tarts [page 564]

date slice

This recipe works just as well with prunes, instead of dates–or a combination of both dates and prunes would also be good.

1½ cups all-purpose flour
1¼ cups self-rising flour
10 tablespoons cold butter, chopped
1 tablespoon honey
1 egg
⅓ cup milk, approximately
2 teaspoons milk, extra
1 tablespoon sugar

date filling
3½ cups dried pitted dates, chopped coarsely
¾ cup water
2 tablespoons finely grated lemon rind
2 tablespoons lemon juice

1 Grease 8-inch x 12-inch shallow cake pan; line base with parchment paper, extending paper 2 inches over long sides.
2 Sift flours into large bowl; rub in butter until mixture is crumbly. Stir in combined honey and egg and enough milk to make a firm dough. Knead on floured surface until smooth. Cover; refrigerate 30 minutes.
3 Meanwhile, make date filling.
4 Preheat oven to 400°F/350°F fan-forced.
5 Divide dough in half. Roll one half large enough to cover base of pan; press into pan, spread filling over dough. Roll remaining dough large enough to cover filling. Brush with extra milk; sprinkle with sugar. Bake about 20 minutes; cool in pan.
date filling Cook ingredients in medium saucepan, stirring, about 10 minutes or until thick and smooth. Cool to room temperature.
nutritional count per piece 5.7g total fat (3.6g saturated fat); 181 cal; 28.2g carbohydrate; 2.6g protein; 2.7g fiber

portuguese custard tarts

Use a vegetable peeler to peel a strip of rind– about 2 inches long and ⅓-inch wide– from a washed and dried lemon. Avoid the white pith, and use a rough-skinned lemon for the best flavor.

½ cup superfine sugar
2 tablespoons corn starch
4 egg yolks
1¼ cups cream
⅓ cup water
1-inch strip lemon rind
1 teaspoon vanilla extract
1 sheet puff pastry

1 Preheat oven to 425°F/400°F fan-forced. Grease 12-hole (⅓-cup) muffin pan.

2 Combine sugar and corn starch in medium saucepan; whisk in egg yolks, cream and the water. Add rind; stir over medium heat until mixture comes to a boil. Remove from heat; discard rind. Stir extract into custard.

3 Cut pastry sheet in half; place halves on top of each other. Roll pastry tightly (like a jelly roll) from one short side; cut roll into twelve ⅓-inch rounds.

4 Place pastry rounds, cut-sides up, on floured surface; roll each into a 4-inch round. Push rounds into pan holes; spoon in custard.

5 Bake tarts about 20 minutes. Stand 5 minutes before transferring to wire rack to cool.

nutritional count per tart 14.3g total fat (8.3g saturated fat); 203 cal; 16.5g carbohydrate; 2.4g protein; 0.2g fiber

tangy lemon squares

PREP + COOK TIME 50 MINS • MAKES 16

Wonderful for an afternoon tea with a pot of earl grey. These squares are also delicious made with orange or mandarin rind and juice.

1 stick butter
¼ cup powdered sugar
1¼ cups all-purpose flour
3 eggs
1 cup superfine sugar
2 teaspoons finely grated lemon rind
½ cup lemon juice

1 Preheat oven to 350°F/325°F fan-forced. Grease shallow 9-inch square pan; line base and sides with parchment, extending paper ¾ inch above edges of pan.

2 Beat butter and powdered sugar in small bowl with electric mixer until smooth. Stir in 1 cup of the flour. Press mixture evenly over base of pan.

3 Bake base about 15 minutes or until browned lightly.

4 Meanwhile, whisk eggs, superfine sugar, remaining flour, rind and juice in bowl until combined. Pour egg mixture over hot base.

5 Bake about 20 minutes or until firm. Cool in pan on a wire rack before cutting. Dust with extra sifted powdered sugar, if you like.

nutritional count per square 7.5g total fat (4.5g saturated fat); 179 cal; 24.9g carbohydrate; 2.6g protein; 0.5g fiber

vanilla slice

It's best to store any leftover slice in large pieces, so if you think it won't all be eaten or you want to save some for later, keep a portion without cutting it into squares or bars. Keep the piece of slice as airtight as possible in a resealable plastic bag or an airtight container, and cut it when you're going to serve it.

2 sheets puff pastry
½ cup superfine sugar
½ cup corn starch
¼ cup custard powder
2½ cups milk
3 tablespoons butter
1 egg yolk
1 teaspoon vanilla extract
¾ cup heavy cream

passionfruit icing
1½ cups powdered sugar
1 teaspoon soft butter
¼ cup passionfruit pulp

1 Preheat oven to 475°F/425°F fan-forced. Grease deep 9-inch square cake pan; line with foil, extending foil 4 inches over sides of pan.

2 Place each pastry sheet on separate greased oven trays. Bake about 15 minutes; cool. Flatten pastry with hand; place one pastry sheet in pan, trim to fit if necessary.

3 Meanwhile, combine sugar, corn starch and custard powder in medium saucepan; gradually add milk, stirring until smooth. Add butter; stir over heat until mixture boils and thickens. Simmer, stirring, about 3 minutes or until custard is thick and smooth. Remove from heat; stir in egg yolk and extract. Cover surface of custard with plastic wrap; cool to room temperature.

4 Make passionfruit icing.

5 Whip cream until firm peaks form. Fold cream into custard, in two batches. Spread custard mixture over pastry in pan. Top with remaining pastry, trim to fit if necessary; press down slightly. Spread pastry with passionfruit icing; refrigerate 3 hours or overnight.

passionfruit icing Place sifted powdered sugar, butter and pulp in small heatproof bowl over small saucepan of simmering water; stir until icing is spreadable.

nutritional count per piece 12.6g total fat (7.6g saturated fat); 237 cal; 37.2g carbohydrate; 3.1g protein; 0.8g fiber

Once cooled, flatten each baked pastry sheet with your hands.

Add egg yolk and vanilla extract to the custard, stirring with a wooden spoon to combine.

Fold the whipped cream into the custard, in two batches.

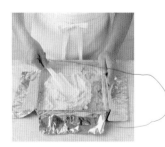

Spread the custard mixture over the pastry in the cake pan. Smooth out the surface to make it even.

traditional shortbread

Shortbread is the national cookie of Scotland and, for some, making shortbread has become a serious competition, featured as a category at the annual Scottish Highland Games.

2 sticks butter, softened
⅓ cup superfine sugar
1 tablespoon water
2 cups all-purpose flour
½ cup rice flour
2 tablespoons white sugar

1 Preheat oven to 325°F/300°F fan-forced. Grease oven trays.

2 Beat butter and superfine sugar in medium bowl with electric mixer until light and fluffy; stir in the water and sifted flours, in two batches. Knead on floured surface until smooth.

3 Divide mixture in half; shape each, on separate trays, into 8-inch rounds. Mark each round into 12 wedges; prick with fork. Pinch edges of rounds with fingers; sprinkle with white sugar.

4 Bake shortbread about 40 minutes; stand 5 minutes. Using sharp knife, cut into wedges along marked lines. Cool on trays.

nutritional count per piece 8.8g total fat (5.7g saturated fat); 154 cal; 17g carbohydrate; 1.7g protein; 0.6g fiber

vanilla kisses

Custard powder is a mix of cornstarch and flavorings used to make pudding for fillings and cakes. It is commonly used in British desserts, and can be found in the international aisle of the supermarket. Instant vanilla pudding mix is a good substitute.

1 stick butter, softened
½ cup superfine sugar
1 egg
⅓ cup all-purpose flour
¼ cup self-rising flour
⅔ cup corn starch
¼ cup custard powder

vienna cream
½ stick butter, softened
½ teaspoon vanilla extract
¾ cup powdered sugar
2 teaspoons milk

1 Preheat oven to 400°F/350°F fan-forced. Grease oven trays; line with parchment.

2 Beat butter, sugar and egg in small bowl with electric mixer until light and fluffy. Stir in sifted dry ingredients, in two batches.

3 Spoon mixture into piping bag fitted with ⅓-inch star tip. Pipe 1-inch rosettes about 1 inch apart on trays.

4 Bake cookies about 10 minutes; cool on trays.

5 Meanwhile, make vienna cream. Sandwich cookies with vienna cream.

vienna cream Beat butter and extract in small bowl with electric mixer until as white as possible; gradually beat in sifted powdered sugar and milk, in two batches.

nutritional count per kiss 8g total fat (5.1g saturated fat); 155 cal; 20g carbohydrate; 0.9g protein; 0.2g fiber

chocolate chip cookies

Don't overbeat the butter, sugar and egg mixture or the cookies will spread too much during baking. You can use dark or white chocolate in place of the milk chocolate if you like—or a mixture of any type of chocolate.

2 sticks butter, softened
1 teaspoon vanilla extract
¾ cup sugar
¾ cup firmly packed light brown sugar
1 egg
2¼ cups all-purpose flour
1 teaspoon baking soda
13 ounces dark chocolate chunks, chopped coarsely

1 Preheat oven to 350°F/325°F fan-forced. Grease oven trays.
2 Beat butter, extract, sugars and egg in small bowl with electric mixer until light and fluffy. Transfer mixture to large bowl; stir in sifted flour and baking soda, in two batches. Stir in chocolate. Cover; refrigerate 1 hour.
3 Roll level tablespoons of mixture into balls; place about 1 inch apart on trays.
4 Bake cookies about 12 minutes; cool on trays.
nutritional count per cookie 8.2g total fat (6g saturated fat); 159 cal; 19.5g carbohydrate; 1.5g protein; 0.8g fiber

almond macaroons

Macaroons can be stored in an airtight container for up to 2 days.

For coconut macaroons, replace ground almonds with ¾ cup dried coconut and ¾ cup shredded coconut; replace almond extract with vanilla extract; omit blanched almonds.

2 egg whites
½ cup superfine sugar
1¼ cups ground almonds
½ teaspoon almond extract
2 tablespoons all-purpose flour
¼ cup blanched almonds

1 Preheat oven to 300°F/275°F fan-forced. Grease oven trays.
2 Beat egg whites in small bowl with electric mixer until soft peaks form; gradually add sugar, beating until dissolved between additions. Gently fold in ground almonds, extract and sifted flour, in two batches.
3 Drop level tablespoons of mixture about 2 inches apart on trays; press one nut onto each macaroon.
4 Bake macaroons about 20 minutes or until firm and dry; cool on trays.
nutritional count per macaroon 4.8g total fat (0.3g saturated fat); 78 cal; 6.1g carbohydrate; 2.2g protein; 0.8g fiber

1½ sticks butter, softened
1 teaspoon vanilla extract
½ cup firmly packed
   light brown sugar
1 egg
1¼ cups self-rising flour
¾ cup all-purpose flour
¼ teaspoon baking soda
⅔ cup dried coconut
⅓ cup raspberry jam

vienna cream
½ stick butter
½ teaspoon vanilla extract
¾ cup powdered sugar
2 teaspoons milk

1 Preheat oven to 400°F/375°F fan-forced. Grease oven trays; line with parchment paper.

2 Beat butter, extract and sugar in small bowl with electric mixer until just combined; beat in egg. Stir in sifted flours, baking soda and coconut, in two batches.

3 Roll 2 level teaspoons of mixture into ovals; place on trays about 2 inches apart. Flatten slightly; use back of fork to roughen surface.

4 Bake cookies about 7 minutes.

5 Meanwhile, make vienna cream.

6 Transfer cookies to wire rack to cool. Sandwich biscuits with vienna cream and jam.

vienna cream Beat butter, extract and sifted powdered sugar in small bowl with electric mixer until fluffy; beat in milk.

nutritional count per monte carlo 8.5g total fat (5.7g saturated fat);157 cal; 18.3g carbohydrate; 1.5g protein; 0.7g fiber

Q&A

When I bake cookies at home, I always make a few varieties and then store them in a clean, dry airtight container, yet some of them turn soft and soggy within two days. What could I be doing wrong?

If cookies are stored properly, they should retain their freshly baked taste and texture longer than two days. You may be combining soft and crisp-textured cookies in the jar. If so, you need to store them in separate containers, otherwise the soft cookies will make the crisp ones soft. Crisp cookies can be stored in an airtight container—it's important to eliminate as much air as possible from inside the container too, either by keeping it full of cookies or using smaller containers. Cookies with dairy-based centers should be assembled just before serving.

pistachio and cranberry biscotti

PREP + COOK TIME 1 HOUR
(+ REFRIGERATION &
COOLING) • MAKES 60

½ stick unsalted butter, softened
1 teaspoon vanilla extract
1 cup superfine sugar
2 eggs
1¾ cups all-purpose flour
½ teaspoon baking soda

1 cup dried cranberries
¾ cup coarsely chopped
   toasted pistachios
1 egg, extra
1 tablespoon water
2 tablespoons superfine sugar, extra

Serve these biscotti with fruit tea, good strong coffee, or at the end of dinner with a tiny glass of limoncello (lemon-flavored liqueur). For a change, use slivered almonds instead of pistachios.

1 Beat butter, extract and sugar in medium bowl until combined. Beat in eggs, one at a time. Stir in sifted flour and soda then cranberries and nuts. Cover dough; refrigerate 1 hour.

2 Preheat oven to 350°F/325°F fan-forced. Grease oven tray.

3 Knead dough on floured surface until smooth but still sticky. Halve dough; shape each half into 12-inch log. Place logs on oven tray.

4 Combine extra egg with the water in small bowl. Brush egg mixture over logs; sprinkle with extra sugar. Bake 20 minutes or until firm; cool 3 hours or overnight.

5 Preheat oven to 325°F/300°F fan-forced.

6 Using serrated knife, cut logs diagonally into ⅓-inch slices. Place slices on ungreased oven trays. Bake about 15 minutes or until dry and crisp, turning halfway through baking time; cool on wire racks.

nutritional count per biscotti 2.1g total fat (0.7g saturated fat); 62 cal; 9.2g carbohydrate; 1.2g protein; 0.4g fiber

anzacs

PREP + COOK TIME 35 MINS • MAKES 25

1 cup rolled oats
1 cup all-purpose flour
1 cup firmly packed
   light brown sugar
½ cup dried coconut

1 stick butter
2 tablespoons golden syrup
1 tablespoon water
½ teaspoon baking soda

1 Preheat oven to 325°F/300°F fan-forced. Grease oven trays; line with parchment paper.

2 Combine oats, sifted flour, sugar and coconut in large bowl.

3 Stir butter, syrup and the water in small saucepan over low heat until smooth; stir in soda. Stir syrup mixture into dry ingredients.

4 Roll level tablespoons of mixture into balls; place about 2 inches apart on trays, flatten slightly.

5 Bake cookies about 20 minutes; cool on trays.

nutritional count per biscuit 5.5g total fat (2.8g saturated fat); 124 cal; 17g carbohydrate; 1.2g protein; 0.7g fiber

[opposite] pistachio and cranberry biscotti

CHRISTMAS & OTHER CELEBRATIONS

Christmas & other celebrations

Around the world, food is at the heart of all rituals and celebrations: when there is a special occasion in our lives, we love to celebrate it with special food.

Some foods might represent a specific important occasion, such as a wedding cake, while other foods may be simply part of a family tradition, like a celebration fruit cake. And other foods might signify "party": delicious, tasty little morsels eaten off roaming platters at a great cocktail party.

Some food traditions are deeply ingrained, while others can change over time: the classic Christmas dinner consisting of roast beef and Yorkshire pudding has relaxed over the years. Many opt for a simple buffet of meats, cheeses, seafood platters and sweets rather than going to the trouble of preparing a multi-course sit-down meal. In this chapter, we have assembled a glorious assortment of festive foods to accompany some of the special occasions in your life: perhaps there is a recipe here that echoes, with some subtle changes, a favorite tradition in your family. Or perhaps you will create a tradition of your own.

PLANNING

Whatever the occasion—a small soiree with a few friends or a big party—the key to running a smooth event is in the planning. Without it, you can feel fretful instead of fabulous when you open your doors to your guests.

In the case of a big party, you should have a plan of action drawn up weeks in advance. A small party requires at least a week of planning.

It's a time for making lists. Put together a list of the food and drink shopping that needs to be done. List all the equipment you'll need for the occasion (everything from extra cutlery pieces to extra chairs and napkins) and assess whether you need to buy, borrow or hire anything ahead of time.

MENU PLANNING

Make a list detailing all the foods you're aiming to cook, and when you plan to cook them. Think about whether the food will be competing for counter space and fridge and/or freezer space.

If you're organizing a big party, think about which foods you can cook ahead of time and those suitable for freezing. Defrosting foods is much less stressful than cooking them all on the day.

On the day of your event, think about what can be done ahead of time—from preparing vegetables to making dressings. If you're hosting a traditional Christmas lunch then you will need to start roasting the meat early in the morning, and the steamed pudding will have been made weeks ahead.

KEEP IT MANAGEABLE THE FIRST RULE OF ENTERTAINING IS TO BE REALISTIC ABOUT HOW MUCH YOU CAN DO WITHOUT GETTING TOO FRAZZLED. YOU WANT TO SOCIALIZE, NOT JUST SPEND YOUR TIME IN THE KITCHEN OR PLAYING FOOD SERVER FOR THE ENTIRE EVENT.

FINGER FOOD

HAVING A REPERTOIRE OF DELICIOUS MORSELS THAT CAN BE EATEN IN ONE OR TWO MOUTHFULS IS A VALUABLE ASSET WHEN ENTERTAINING. YOU CAN EITHER HAND AROUND PLATTERS OF FINGER FOODS OR PLACE THEM STRATEGICALLY AROUND THE ROOM FOR GUESTS TO HELP THEMSELVES.

HOME-MADE AND BOUGHT

When it comes to finger foods, don't worry about striving for a smorgasbord of offerings: just a few kinds will keep your guests happy. And don't think that you must make everything yourself: combine a few homemade appetizers with quality bought items (see Starters, page 74).

If you tend to host impromptu gatherings, then it's wise to keep some provisions on hand in the freezer: most savory pastries and items such as pizzas or blini can be frozen and then half-thawed in the microwave.

EQUIPMENT

GLASSES Have an abundant supply of suitable, clean glasses on hand: classic wine glasses, champagne flutes, V-shaped, stemmed cocktail glasses and straight-sided tumblers will cover most needs. Chilling them before-hand (30 minutes in the refrigerator; 10 minutes in the freezer, space permitting) is a nice touch.

ICE You will need plenty of ice. Fill a large tub, such as a laundry tub, with ice and use it as a cooler for bottles and cans.

GARNISHES A fresh garnish adds color and party glamor even to a glass of mineral water: slices of lemon or lime placed on the rim of a glass; strawberries (cut in half with a slit to slide onto the rim of a glass); a pair of joined cherries dangling over the rim; or a sprig of mint, all look wonderful.

QUANTITIES

WHETHER IT'S A COCKTAIL PARTY OR LOW-KEY STAND-AROUND AFFAIR, ALLOW FOUR TO FIVE PIECES OF FINGER FOOD PER PERSON FOR THE FIRST HOUR, THEN FOUR PIECES FOR EACH HOUR AFTER THAT. FOR A FULL AFTERNOON OR EVENING, ALLOW 12 TO 14 PIECES PER PERSON FOR THE WHOLE PARTY.

COCKTAIL PARTY DRINKS

While wine and beer are perfect party drinks, the offer of cocktail drinks elevates your event into a special occasion. You don't have to provide a full menu of cocktails, just a couple of crowd pleasers–like a champagne cocktail, bellini or a cosmopolitan, as we've included in this chapter. Make sure you practice making them beforehand and–ideally–ask a friend or family member if they could be your cocktail makers for the occasion.

Alternatively, you could pre-make a punch, which still says "special event" and can be made ahead of time. Because cocktails are very powerful, it's important to offer enough food to help absorb the alcohol that's being consumed. Elegant finger food is the perfect match. It's customary to offer cocktails for only the first hour or so, then switch to wine, beer, mineral water and perhaps a freshly-squeezed juice.

QUANTITIES Ten guests will consume about 20 drinks at a cocktail party. If it's a full afternoon or evening affair, this increases to 40 drinks. Have a modest reserve of wine and beer and a larger one of non-alcoholic drinks.

CHAMPAGNE Champagne and other sparkling drinks should be chilled in a tub of ice or in the refrigerator (not the freezer) until needed. To pour champagne, add a little at a time to each glass so they don't overflow.

WINE Glasses for both still and sparkling wines should be filled only half-full so that the bouquet (aroma) will collect in the top of the glass.

champagne cocktail

Use a little less than ⅔ cup of champagne for each cocktail and you will be able to make five cocktails from one bottle of champagne.

2-inch strip orange rind
1 sugar cube
5 drops Angostura bitters
⅔ cup chilled champagne

1 Slice rind thinly.
2 Place sugar cube in champagne glass; top with bitters then champagne. Garnish with rind.
nutritional count per serving 0g total fat (0g saturated fat); 126 cal; 6.9g carbohydrate; 0.3g protein; 0.1g fiber

bellini

2 medium peaches, chopped coarsely
½ cup peach schnapps
750ml bottle chilled champagne
8 sugar cubes

1 Blend or process peach and schnapps until smooth. Combine peach mixture with champagne in large pitcher.
2 Place 1 sugar cube in each of eight champagne glasses; top with bellini mixture.
nutritional count per serving 0.1g total fat (0g saturated fat); 133 cal; 12.6g carbohydrate; 0.5g protein; 0.4g fiber

sparkling burgundy and cranberry punch

PREP TIME 15 MINS
(+ STANDING &
REFRIGERATION)
SERVES 8

1¼ cups cranberry juice
1 cup sugar
1 black-leaf tea bag
4 ounces raspberries

8 ounces strawberries, quartered
4 ounces blueberries
2 cups ice cubes
750ml bottle sparkling burgundy

1 Combine juice and sugar in small saucepan; stir over heat until sugar dissolves. Bring to a boil, remove from heat. Add tea bag; stand 15 minutes; discard tea bag, cool tea.
2 Combine berries in a large punch bowl. Stir in ice cubes and cranberry mixture; refrigerate 2 hours. Stir in burgundy before serving.
nutritional count per serving 0.3g total fat (0g saturated fat); 211 cal; 35.2g carbohydrate; 1.6g protein; 1.8g fiber

cosmopolitan

This refreshingly tart concoction is a favorite summer cocktail. You can double the quantities to make two at a time.

1½ ounces vodka
1 ounce cointreau
2 tablespoons cranberry juice

1 teaspoon lime juice
1 cup ice cubes

1 Place ingredients in cocktail shaker; shake vigorously.
2 Strain into 7-ounce chilled martini glass.
nutritional count per serving 0.1g total fat (0g saturated fat); 237 cal; 17.4g carbohydrate; 0.2g protein; 0g fiber

caipiroska

See page 581 for garnishing tips on making a curl with citrus peel.

1 lime, cut into eight wedges
2 teaspoons superfine sugar
1½ ounces vodka
½ cup crushed ice

1 Place lime wedges in cocktail shaker. Using muddler, crush lime with sugar. Add vodka and ice; shake vigorously.
2 Pour into 8-ounce old-fashioned glass. Garnish with a curl of lime rind.
nutritional count per serving 0.1g total fat (0g saturated fat); 140 cal; 13.7g carbohydrate; 0.4g protein; 1.4g fiber

piña colada

This recipe makes 1½ cup of sugar syrup. Store any remaining syrup in an airtight container in the refrigerator for up to 1 month.

See page 580 for tips on garnishing with pineapple.

1 cup ice cubes
1 ounce white rum
1 ounce dark rum
⅓ cup pineapple juice
4 teaspoons coconut cream
dash Angostura bitters

sugar syrup
1 cup superfine sugar
1 cup water

1 Make sugar syrup.
2 Blend ice, rums, juice, 2 teaspoons syrup, coconut and bitters until smooth.
3 Pour into 14-ounce tulip glass. Garnish with pineapple piece and leaves.
sugar syrup Stir sugar and the water in small saucepan over low heat, until sugar dissolves; bring to a boil. Reduce heat; simmer, uncovered, 5 minutes. Cool.
nutritional count per serving 8.4g total fat (7.3g saturated fat); 282 cal; 19.8g carbohydrate; 1g protein; 0.7g fiber

Drink garnishes

These are the final flourishes that make drinks memorable. For a party, prepare garnishes ahead of time and refrigerate in covered containers.

CHERRIES
Choose pairs of ripe black, red or white cherries joined by their stems. Hang over the rim of a tall glass of any fruity or creamy drink.

CITRUS SLICE
Cut a slit in a slice of lemon or lime (or both together) and place on the rim of a glass; for larger fruit, such as orange or blood orange, use half-slices, slit from the center.

PINEAPPLE
Pull small leaves from a pineapple top, slit in half at the bottom end and place on the rim of a glass. A small wedge of pineapple can be placed alongside.

 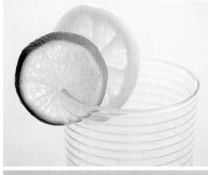 

 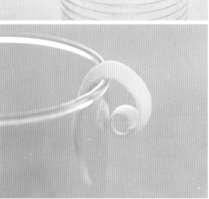 

DECORATED ICE CUBES
Fill an ice-cube tray half-full of water and freeze. Dip herb leaves, citrus-slice segments, edible flowers, etc., in iced water, place on top of the cubes and freeze until firm. Top with iced water and freeze.

COCONUT CURLS
Bake a whole coconut in a moderate oven for about 10 minutes, then split by hitting it with a hammer. Remove the flesh and, using a very sharp knife, pare off thin peelings to make curls to hang on the rim of a glass.

FROSTING
Hold a glass upside down and wipe the outside of the rim with a cut lemon until evenly moistened, then dip the rim into a saucer filled with salt or sugar. Shake away excess.

Q&A

What is a frappé and how do I make one?

A frappé is a mixture of fresh fruit and crushed ice. You need a heavy-duty blender to crush the ice. Half-fill a blender with ice cubes and blend on high until crushed. Add whatever fruits you like, cut into chunks (unless they're berries). The most famous frappés are mango, pineapple, strawberry (or a mixture of berries) or you can make your own tropical mixture using whatever fruit you like. You must drink a frappé soon after it's made or it will separate. You can add iced water to a frappé if you feel it needs thinning.

STRAWBERRY
Choose firm, ripe strawberries with fresh green tops; slit almost in half from the point, or make a few slits and fan out. Place on the glass rim.

CELERY STICK
Cut celery into sticks about 1½ inches longer than the glasses to be used, leaving the leafy tops on if fresh and undamaged. Place in a bloody mary or vegetable juice as a stirrer.

MELON BALLS
Use a melon-baller to cut balls from melons of different colors. Thread alternately onto cocktail sticks and place in drinks in short glasses.

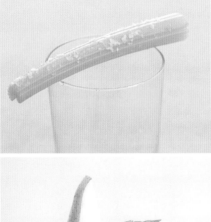

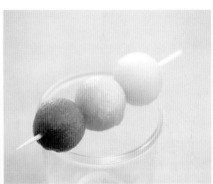

CUCUMBER
Using Lebanese cucumbers, thinly slice the unpeeled cucumber. More than just a fresh garnish, these are also useful stirrers.

PEAR AND MINT
Cut a thin slice of pear and cut a slit from the bottom of the slice to the center. Gently press a small fresh mint sprig into the pear and place in a drink.

CITRUS PEEL
Peel the rind from citrus fruit in a spiral. Place in a drink, hooking one end over the rim; or slice straight strips into narrow "strings", tie in knots and drop into drinks.

kingfish carpaccio

Specify sashimi-grade tuna, kingfish, bream, mackerel or yellowtail when purchasing, and only buy from a reputable fish market. Wrap the fish tightly in plastic wrap and freeze until just firm. Immediately on removing from the freezer and unwrapping, use a heavy, sharp knife to slice the fish as thinly as possible.

14-ounce piece sashimi grade kingfish or yellowtail
¼ cup lemon juice
2 tablespoons olive oil
1 small red onion, sliced thinly
1 cup loosely packed fresh flat-leaf parsley leaves
2 tablespoons drained baby capers, rinsed

1 Tightly wrap kingfish in plastic wrap; freeze 1 hour or until firm. Unwrap fish; slice as thinly as possible.

2 Arrange slices on platter; drizzle fish with juice. Cover; refrigerate 1 hour.

3 Combine oil, onion, parsley and capers in medium bowl. Drain juice from fish; serve with onion mixture.

nutritional count per serving 5.7g total fat (1g saturated fat); 98 cal; 0.9g carbohydrate; 10.5g protein; 0.5g fiber

blini with chili crab salad

You can buy cooked crab meat at the local fish markets or supermarket. Alternatively, buy fresh crabs and cook them (blue swimmer crabs are good). To tell if crabs are meaty, look at the claws; if they are pointy and sharp it means they have a new shell and don't have much meat. If the claws are rounded, they have an older shell and will have more meat.

⅔ cup whole wheat flour
¼ cup self-rising flour
1 tablespoon all-purpose flour
½ teaspoon cayenne pepper
2 eggs
¾ cup buttermilk
2 green onions, sliced finely
3 tablespoons butter, melted

chili crab salad
5 ounces cooked crab meat
1 tablespoon finely chopped fresh mint
1 tablespoon finely chopped fresh Vietnamese mint
1 teaspoon finely grated lime rind
2 tablespoons lime juice
2 teaspoons fish sauce
½ Lebanese cucumber, seeded, chopped finely
1 fresh small red Thai chili, sliced thinly

1 Sift flours and pepper into medium bowl; whisk in eggs and buttermilk until smooth. Stir in onion and butter.

2 Heat oiled large frying pan; cook level tablespoons of blini mixture, in batches, until golden on both sides; cool on wire racks.

3 Meanwhile, make chili crab salad.

4 Serve blinis topped with salad.

chili crab salad Combine ingredients in medium bowl; season to taste.

nutritional count per piece 2.1g total fat (1.1g saturated fat); 48 cal; 4.6g carbohydrate; 2.5g protein; 0.6g fiber

[1] kingfish carpaccio
[2] blini with chili crab salad
[3] tomato tarts [page 584]
[4] peppered beef and blue cheese canapés [page 584]

tomato tarts

Chervil is a delicate, lacy herb with a fresh, slightly anise flavor. It is one the four fines herbes (the others are parsley, tarragon and chives) that flavor a classic omelette aux fines herbes. It is good used as a garnish or sprinkled on salads, fish, cream soups or cooked vegetables. Chervil is available for much of the year but is at its best in spring.

4 medium vine-ripened tomatoes, peeled, quartered, seeded
1 tablespoon brown sugar
1 tablespoon balsamic vinegar
½ sheet puff pastry
16 sprigs fresh chervil

1 Preheat oven 425°F/400°F fan-forced.
2 Combine tomato, sugar and vinegar in small baking dish; roast, uncovered, about 20 minutes or until tomato is soft.
3 Meanwhile, cut pastry sheet in half lengthwise, cut each half into 4 squares; cut each square into triangles (you will have 16). Place pastry triangles on oiled oven tray; top with another oiled oven tray (the second tray stops the pastry from puffing up). Bake pastry, alongside tomato, about 10 minutes or until crisp.
4 Place a tomato piece on each pastry triangle. Serve topped with chervil.
nutritional count per tart 1.2g total fat (0.6g saturated fat); 28 cal; 3.4g carbohydrate; 0.7g protein; 0.5g fiber

peppered beef and blue cheese canapés

Use a soft creamy blue cheese for the blue cheese mousse; the mousse can be made a day ahead and kept, covered, in the fridge. It's best to cook the beef as close to serving time as possible.

1 pound beef tenderloin, trimmed
¼ cup olive oil
2 tablespoons finely cracked black pepper
6 ounces lavash crispbreads or crackers
1 small bunch watercress
blue cheese mousse
3½ ounces blue cheese, softened
3½ ounces packaged cream cheese, softened
¼ cup cream

1 Halve beef lengthwise; rub with oil and pepper. Cook beef on heated oiled grill pan (or grill or barbecue) until cooked to your liking, turning beef once. Cover beef; stand 10 minutes before slicing thinly.
2 Meanwhile, make blue cheese mousse.
3 Serve lavash topped with beef, a spoonful of mousse, and sprigs of watercress.
blue cheese mousse Stir ingredients together until smooth; season to taste.
nutritional count per piece 4.2g total fat (1.8g saturated fat); 65 cal; 2.5g carbohydrate; 4g protein; 0.8g fiber

barbecued seafood platter

16 uncooked medium king prawns
1 teaspoon finely grated lemon rind
½ teaspoon dried chili flakes
1 clove garlic, crushed
1 tablespoon finely chopped
   fresh oregano
2 tablespoons olive oil
8 slices prosciutto
8 butterflied sardines
10-ounce baby octopus, quartered

7 ounces squid tubes, sliced
   into rings
2 tablespoons balsamic vinegar
¼ cup coarsely chopped fresh
   flat-leaf parsley
1 pound small black mussels,
   cleaned and debearded
¼ cup lemon juice
1 medium tomato, seeded,
   chopped finely

1 Remove and discard prawn heads. Cut prawns lengthwise, three-quarters of the way through (and down to ⅓ inch before the tail), leaving shells intact; press down on prawns on board to flatten.

2 Combine prawns, rind, chili, garlic, oregano and half the oil in medium bowl. Cover; refrigerate 1 hour.

3 Wrap a prosciutto slice firmly around each sardine.

4 Cook octopus and squid on heated oiled grill pan (or grill or barbecue). Combine octopus and squid in medium heatproof bowl with remaining oil, vinegar and 2 tablespoons of the parsley. Cover to keep warm.

5 Cook prawns and sardines on heated oiled grill pan (or grill or barbecue).

6 Meanwhile, cook mussels, covered, in heated oiled skillet about 5 minutes or until mussels open (discard any that do not). Place mussels in medium heatproof bowl; drizzle with juice, sprinkle with tomato and remaining parsley. Serve seafood with lemon wedges, if you like.

nutritional count per serving 8.7g total fat (1.7g saturated fat); 200 cal; 1.3g carbohydrate; 28.5g protein; 0.4g fiber

Q&A

I'd like to buy more fresh fish and other types of seafood, but I'm not sure how to tell if they've been sitting there for days or just arrived that morning. How do I know that the seafood I'm buying is fresh?

Fresh seafood (fish and shellfish) should always be bought from seafood markets or a reputable fisherman. All seafood should look fresh and have a fresh "sea" smell–any seafood that smells "fishy" is no good to eat. Whole fish should have firm, not spongy, flesh with red gills; the skin should be shiny with close-fitting scales and the eyes should be clear and bright. Fish filets and cutlets should have moist flesh with a firm texture; there should be no signs of discoloration or dryness. Any bones should be firmly attached to the flesh. Crustaceans and mollusks should have brightly colored shells or flesh, and the tentacles, heads, flesh or shells should be plump, firm and intact. Shells should be closed, or should close when tapped on a bench. There should also be no discoloration of the joints.

smoked salmon and dilled sour cream crêpe cakes

**PREP + COOK TIME
1 HOUR (+ STANDING &
REFRIGERATION)
MAKES 16**

½ cup all-purpose flour
2 eggs
2 teaspoons vegetable oil
1 cup milk
2 tablespoons drained capers,
    rinsed, chopped coarsely

2 tablespoons finely chopped fresh dill
1 tablespoon grated lemon rind
2 teaspoons lemon juice
1 clove garlic, crushed
1 cup sour cream
1 pound sliced smoked salmon

For a vegetarian
version, combine
8 ounces spreadable
feta cheese,
2 tablespoons
chopped fresh mint,
2 teaspoons finely
grated lemon rind,
2 teaspoons lemon
juice and 1 crushed
garlic clove. Spread
over crêpes; top with
thin slices of roasted
red pepper, char-grilled
eggplant, 1½ ounces
chopped kalamata
olives and 1½ ounces
chopped semi-dried
tomatoes.

1 Line base and side of deep 8-inch round cake pan with plastic wrap.
2 Place flour in medium bowl. Make well in center; gradually whisk in combined eggs, oil and milk. Strain into large pitcher; stand 30 minutes.
3 Heat oiled 7½-inch frying pan; pour ¼ cup of the batter into pan, tilting pan to coat base. Cook over low heat, loosening around edge with spatula until browned lightly. Turn; brown other side. Remove from pan; repeat with remaining batter to make a total of five crêpes.
4 Combine capers, dill, rind, juice, garlic and sour cream in small bowl. Place a crêpe in cake pan; spread with ⅓ cup of sour cream mixture, cover with a quarter of the salmon. Continue layering with remaining crêpes, sour cream mixture and salmon, finishing with a crêpe. Cover; refrigerate overnight.
5 Gently turn crêpes cake onto chopping board; discard plastic wrap. Using sharp knife, carefully trim cake into a square; discard trimmings. Cut into 1½-inch squares; top squares with a little extra sour cream and dill, if you like.
nutritional count per piece 9.3g total fat (4.9g saturated fat); 140 cal; 4.8g carbohydrate; 9.4g protein; 0.3g fiber

Pour ¼ cup of the batter into a frying pan (a crêpe or omelette pan is perfect). Tilt the pan so the mixture evenly coats the base.

Cook crêpes lightly on both sides and stack one on top of the other (they won't stick).

Place one crêpe in a plastic-wrap-lined cake pan and spread with sour cream mixture, top with smoked salmon slices, then another crêpe.

Remove the crêpe cake from the pan and cut into a square, then cut into 1½-inch squares for serving.

chicken and mayonnaise finger sandwiches

2 cups coarsely shredded rotisserie chicken

2 tablespoons drained capers, chopped coarsely

2 tablespoons finely chopped fresh chives

⅓ cup whole-egg mayonnaise

8 slices brown bread

1 Lebanese cucumber, sliced thinly

1 Combine chicken, capers, chives and ¼ cup of the mayonnaise in medium bowl.

2 Spread chicken mixture over four bread slices; top with cucumber. Spread remaining mayonnaise over remaining bread; place on top of cucumber.

3 Remove and discard crusts; cut sandwiches into three strips.

nutritional count per finger 4.3g total fat (0.7g saturated fat); 101 cal; 9.9g carbohydrate; 5.7g protein; 1.2g fiber

chermoulla prawn skewers

Soak bamboo skewers in water for at least an hour to prevent splintering or scorching during cooking.

16 uncooked medium king prawns

1 tablespoon olive oil

2 tablespoons finely chopped fresh flat-leaf parsley

2 tablespoons finely chopped fresh mint

2 tablespoons finely chopped fresh coriander

2 cloves garlic, crushed

2 teaspoons finely grated lemon rind

1 tablespoon lemon juice

1 teaspoon ground allspice

1 teaspoon caraway seeds

1 Shell and devein prawns, leaving tails intact.

2 Combine prawns with oil and remaining ingredients in medium bowl.

3 Preheat grill.

4 Thread prawns, tail-end first, onto 16 small bamboo skewers or strong toothpicks; grill prawns about 5 minutes or until they change in color.

nutritional count per skewer 1.3g total fat (0.2g saturated fat); 31 cal; 0.1g carbohydrate; 4.7g protein; 0.1g fiber

sticky pork on betel leaves

Use a splatter guard while deep-frying pork; these are handy to have and are available from supermarkets. The pork becomes sticky during the second cooking (stir-frying), so use a non-stick pan to make cleaning up easier. Use scissors to finely shred kaffir lime leaves.

2½ pounds pork belly, skin and bones removed
⅓ cup fish sauce
2 tablespoons grated palm sugar
1 star anise
⅓-inch piece fresh ginger, peeled, sliced thinly
2 cloves garlic, bruised
1 quart water
vegetable oil, for deep-frying

1½ teaspoons white peppercorns
½ cup coarsely chopped fresh coriander root
8 green onions, chopped coarsely
½ cup grated palm sugar, extra
¼ cup fish sauce, extra
48 betel leaves
4 fresh kaffir lime leaves, shredded finely

1 Cut pork into ½-inch cubes. Place pork in medium saucepan with sauce, sugar, star anise, ginger, garlic and the water; bring to a boil. Reduce heat; simmer, covered, about 25 minutes or until pork is tender. Drain pork; discard liquid and spices. Dry pork well with absorbent paper

2 Heat oil in wok, deep-fryer or deep wide saucepan; deep-fry pork, in batches, until golden brown. Drain on absorbent paper.

3 Meanwhile, dry-fry peppercorns in small frying pan until fragrant. Using mortar and pestle, grind peppercorns until fine. Add coriander and onion, grind until smooth. Add extra sugar and extra sauce; grind until sugar is dissolved.

4 Stir-fry pork with coriander mixture in oiled wok over high heat until pork is crisp.

5 Place betel leaves on a serving platter, top with pork mixture and lime leaves.

nutritional count per leaf 6.9g total fat (2.1g saturated fat); 91 cal; 2.6g carbohydrate; 4.9g protein; 0.2g fiber

Q&A

What are betel leaves and where can I find them? If they're not available what can I use as a substitute?

Betel leaves are mostly used as a little wrap or a tiny plate–the filling is placed on top and the diner picks up a leaf, folds it over the filling, and pops it into his mouth. They are available at some greengrocers and most Asian food stores. If you can't find them, endive leaves or soft lettuce cups would work well.

2 sticks butter, softened
1¼ cups firmly packed
    light brown sugar
4 eggs
2 tablespoons orange marmalade
3 pounds mixed dried fruit,
    chopped finely
1½ cups all-purpose flour
½ cup self-rising flour
2 teaspoons pie spice
½ cup sweet sherry
¼ cup blanched whole almonds
2 tablespoons sweet sherry, extra

decorations
½ cup powdered sugar
1½ pounds ready-made fondant
½ cup orange marmalade,
    warmed, strained
luster dust

TIPS

• If your oven won't hold three sets of muffin pans, it's fine to leave the mixture standing at room temperature while the first batch bakes.

• Use an embossed rolling pin or plastic doily to mark the icing. These are available from craft and cake-decorating shops.

• We used three cake stands stacked on top of each other to display the cakes. They measured 7 inches, 10 inches and 13 inches in diameter. Mix and match the colors of the plates, cakes and flowers to suit the occasion.

1 Preheat oven to 300°F/ 275°F fan-forced. Line three 12-hole (⅓-cup) muffin pans with silver foil and paper cases.

2 Beat butter, sugar and eggs in small bowl with electric mixer until just combined. Transfer mixture to large bowl, add marmalade and fruit; mix well.

3 Sift flours and spice over mixture, add sherry; mix well. Place 2 level tablespoons of mixture into each case; smooth surface.

4 Bake cakes about 50 minutes. Remove cakes from oven; brush tops with extra sherry. Cover pan tightly with foil; cool cakes in pan.

5 On surface dusted with sifted powdered sugar, knead fondant until smooth. Roll out to a thickness of ⅛ inch. With an embossed rolling pin, gently press over icing to make a pattern. Using a 3-inch round fluted cutter, cut out 36 rounds.

6 Brush cakes with marmalade; top with icing rounds. Carefully brush silver luster dust over pattern on icing.

nutritional count per cupcake 7g total fat (4g saturated fat); 326 cal; 58.7g carbohydrate; 3.4g protein; 3.6g fiber

Knead the icing with the heel of your hand on a surface dusted with powdered sugar until the icing is smooth.

Roll out the icing until it is about ⅛ inch thick. Then, using an embossed rolling pin, gently roll over the icing to make a pattern.

Cut out 36 rounds of icing using a 3-inch round fluted cutter.

Carefully remove the scraps of icing between the rounds and lift the rounds on top of the marmalade-brushed cakes.

fruit mince pies

Mince pies will keep well in an airtight container for up to two weeks. Make double the quantity of fruit mince to bottle for gifts.

5 ounces dried figs, chopped finely
½ cup dried cranberries
½ cup raisins, chopped coarsely
¼ cup mixed candied citrus peel
¼ cup finely chopped candied ginger
¼ cup finely chopped dried peach
1 medium apple, grated
½ cup firmly packed light brown sugar
2 tablespoons fig jam
1 teaspoon finely grated orange rind
2 tablespoons orange juice
1 cinnamon stick, halved
1 teaspoon pie spice
⅓ cup brandy
3 sheets refrigerated pie crust
1 egg white

pastry
2 cups all-purpose flour
⅓ cup superfine sugar
10 tablespoons cold butter, chopped coarsely
1 egg, beaten lightly

1 Combine fruit, sugar, jam, rind, juice, spices and brandy in medium bowl. Cover, stand for a week or up to a month; stir mixture every two or three days.
2 Make pastry.
3 Grease 24 mini tartlet molds (2½-inch diameter) and put on a baking tray. Divide pastry in half; roll one portion of dough between parchment sheets to ⅛-inch thickness; cut 12 x 3-inch rounds from pastry. Repeat with remaining pastry. Press rounds into tartlet molds; pricks bases with fork, refrigerate.
4 Preheat oven to 400°F/375°F fan-forced.
5 On a floured surface, cut a pie crust sheet into ¼-inch wide strips. Arrange the strips into a tight lattice pattern and lightly roll over the pastry with a rolling pin to adhere them. With a 2½-inch cutter, cut 8 rounds from the lattice sheet. Repeat with remaining crusts.
6 Discard cinnamon from mince, spoon mince into pastry cases; top with lattice pastry rounds. Press edges to seal; brush pastry with egg white.
7 Bake pies about 20 minutes. Dust with a sifted powdered sugar before serving.
pastry Blend or process flour, sugar and butter until crumbly. Add egg; process until combined. Knead pastry on floured surface until smooth. Cover; refrigerate 30 minutes.
nutritional count per pie 8.5g total fat (5g saturated fat); 238 cal; 34.7g carbohydrate; 2.9g protein; 2.1g fiber

rich chocolate christmas cakes

PREP + COOK TIME
2 HOURS 15 MINS
(+ STANDING & COOLING)
MAKES 8

1 cup pitted prunes

1 cup pitted dried dates

1 cup raisins

½ cup muscat raisins

1 cup dried figs

5 glacé orange slices

1½ cups Irish whiskey

1½ cups firmly packed
   dark brown sugar

1½ sticks butter, softened

3 eggs

½ cup ground hazelnuts

1½ cups all-purpose flour

2 tablespoons cocoa powder

1 teaspoon pie spice

½ teaspoon ground nutmeg

½ teaspoon baking soda

5 ounces bittersweet chocolate,
   chopped finely

¼ cup water

5 ounces champagne grapes, optional

2 tablespoons cocoa powder, extra

These cakes make fabulous Christmas gifts and you can make them weeks ahead—except for the decoration—and store them in airtight containers. Store the whiskey syrup in a screw-top jar, then stand the jar in hot water to thin it again when glazing grapes.

1 Chop all fruit finely. Combine fruit and ¾ cup of the whiskey in large bowl. Cover with plastic wrap; stand overnight.

2 Preheat oven to 250°F/225°F fan-forced. Line eight deep 3-inch round cake pans with two thicknesses of parchment paper, extending paper 2 inches above sides of pans.

3 Stir remaining whiskey and ¾ cup of the sugar in small saucepan over heat until sugar dissolves; bring to a boil. Remove from heat; cool syrup 20 minutes.

4 Meanwhile, beat butter and remaining sugar in small bowl with electric mixer until combined; beat.in eggs, one at a time. Add butter mixture to fruit mixture; mix well. Mix in ground hazelnuts, sifted dry ingredients, chocolate and ½ cup of the cooled syrup. Spread mixture into pans.

5 Bake cakes about 1¾ hours.

6 Bring remaining syrup and the water to a boil in small saucepan; boil for 3 minutes or until thickened slightly. Brush hot cakes with half of the hot syrup, cover cakes with foil; cool in tins.

7 Divide grapes into eight small bunches; place bunches in remaining cooled syrup. Stand in syrup 5 minutes, drain.

8 Dust cakes with extra sifted cocoa, top with grape bunches.

nutritional count per cake 31.5g total fat (16.9g saturated fat); 975 cal; 132.5g carbohydrate; 10.9g protein; 10.4g fiber

Sprinkle flour onto the boiled pudding cloth and spread it out to cover an area of about 16 inches.

Gather pudding cloth evenly around pudding, avoiding deep pleats then pat the mixture into a round shape.

TIPS

• You need a 24-inch square of unbleached heavy linen for the pudding cloth. If linen has not been used before, soak in cold water overnight; next day, boil it for 20 minutes then rinse in cold water.

• To store pudding: remove cloth, then allow pudding to come to room temperature, wrap it in plastic wrap and seal tightly in a freezer bag or airtight container. Pudding can be stored in refrigerator up to 2 months or frozen up to 12 months.

• To reheat: thaw frozen pudding 3 days in refrigerator; remove from fridge 12 hours before reheating. To reheat in microwave oven: cover whole pudding with plastic wrap; microwave on medium (55%) about 15 minutes or until hot.

1½ cups raisins
1½ cups golden raisins
1 cup dried currants
¾ cup mixed candied citrus peel
1 teaspoon finely grated lemon rind
2 tablespoons lemon juice
2 tablespoons brandy
2 sticks butter, softened

2 cups firmly packed
light brown sugar
5 eggs
1¼ cups all-purpose flour
½ teaspoon ground nutmeg
½ teaspoon pie spice
4 cups stale bread crumbs

1 Combine fruit, rind, juice and brandy in large bowl. Cover tightly with plastic wrap; store in a cool, dark place overnight or up to a week, stirring every day.

2 Beat butter and sugar in large bowl with electric mixer only until combined. Beat in eggs, one at a time, beat only until combined between each addition. Add butter mixture to fruit mixture then sifted dry ingredients and bread crumbs; mix well.

3 Fill stock pot three-quarters full of hot water, cover; bring to a boil. Have ready 8 feet of kitchen string and an extra ½ cup of flour. Wearing thick rubber gloves, dip pudding cloth in boiling water; boil 1 minute then remove and carefully squeeze excess water from cloth. Working quickly, spread hot cloth on counter, rub flour into center of cloth to cover an area about 16 inches in diameter, leaving flour a little thicker in center of cloth where "skin" on the pudding needs to be thickest.

4 Place pudding mixture in center of cloth. Gather cloth evenly around mixture, avoiding any deep pleats; then pat into round shape. Tie cloth tightly with string as close to mixture as possible. Pull ends of cloth tightly to ensure pudding is as round and firm as possible. Knot two pairs of corners together to make pudding easier to remove.

5 Lower pudding into boiling water; tie free ends of string to handles of pot to suspend pudding. Cover with tight-fitting lid, boil for 6 hours, replenishing water as necessary to maintain level.

6 Untie pudding from handles; place wooden spoon through knotted cloth loops to lift pudding from water. Do not put pudding on counter; suspend from spoon by placing over rungs of upturned stool or wedging handle in drawer. Pudding must be suspended freely. Twist ends of cloth around string to avoid them from touching pudding. If pudding has been cooked correctly, cloth will dry in patches within a few minutes; hang 10 minutes.

7 Place pudding on counter; cut string, carefully peel back cloth. Turn pudding onto a plate then carefully peel cloth away completely; cool. Stand at least 20 minutes or until skin darkens and pudding becomes firm.

nutritional count per serving 15.5g total fat (9.1g saturated fat); 500 cal; 79.7g carbohydrate; 7g protein; 3.3g fiber

These cookies make the perfect wedding gift, or treat for your guests to take home after the big day. Drop a little food coloring into your royal icing if you want a variation to the all-white decorations we've used here—pastel pink or yellow would look sweet.

⅓ cup dried mixed fruit
2 tablespoons brandy
1 stick butter, softened
1 teaspoon finely grated orange rind
⅓ cup superfine sugar
1 tablespoon golden syrup
1 cup self-rising flour
⅔ cup all-purpose flour
½ teaspoon pie spice

fondant icing
10 ounces ready-made fondant, chopped coarsely
1 egg white
½ teaspoon lemon juice
royal icing
1½ cups powdered sugar
1 egg white

1 Process fruit and brandy until smooth.

2 Beat butter, rind, sugar and syrup in small bowl with electric mixer until combined. Stir in sifted dry ingredients and fruit puree, in two batches.

3 Knead dough on floured surface until smooth; roll dough between sheets of parchment until ¼ inch thick. Cover; refrigerate 30 minutes.

4 Preheat oven to 350°F/325°F fan-forced. Grease oven trays; line with baking paper.

5 Using 4-inch wedding cake cutter, cut 12 shapes from dough. Place about 2 inches apart on oven trays. Bake about 12 minutes. Cool on wire racks.

6 Make fondant icing. Use a metal spatula, dipped in hot water, to spread icing quickly over cookies; set at room temperature.

7 Make royal icing. Decorate cookies with royal icing.

fondant icing Stir fondant in small heatproof bowl over small saucepan of simmering water until smooth. Add egg white and juice; beat until smooth.

royal icing Sift powdered sugar through fine sieve. Beat egg white until foamy in small bowl with electric mixer; beat in powdered sugar, a tablespoon at a time. Cover surface tightly with plastic wrap.

nutritional count per serving 8.8g total fat (5.7g saturated fat); 372 cal; 67.1g carbohydrate; 3.2g protein; 1.5g fiber

[1] wedding cake cookies
[2] white christmas ice-cream puddings [page 598]
[3] celebration fruit cake [page 598]
[4] steamed christmas pudding [page 599]

white christmas ice-cream puddings

**PREP + COOK TIME
1 HOUR (+ COOLING &
REFRIGERATION)
MAKES 8**

1 vanilla bean
1¾ cups milk
2½ cups cream
6 ounces white chocolate,
   chopped coarsely
8 egg yolks

¾ cup superfine sugar
1 cup dried cranberries
2 tablespoons brandy
1 cup unsalted pistachios
2 teaspoons vegetable oil

It is considered that
the black specks from
the vanilla bean in
a dish give it cachet
as they show that the
real thing has been
used. Each bean can
be washed, dried and
re-used several times,
and then be put into
a jar of sugar to scent
it to be used in cakes
and desserts.

1 Split vanilla bean lengthwise; scrape seeds into medium saucepan. Add pod, milk, cream and 1½ ounces of the chocolate; bring to a boil.

2 Meanwhile, whisk egg yolks and sugar in medium bowl until thick and creamy; gradually whisk into hot milk mixture. Stir custard over low heat, without boiling, until thickened slightly. Cover surface of custard with plastic wrap; cool 20 minutes.

3 Strain custard into shallow container, such as a plastic food container, cover with foil; freeze until almost firm.

4 Place ice cream in large bowl, chop coarsely; beat with electric mixer until smooth. Pour into deep container, cover; freeze until firm. Repeat process two more times.

5 Meanwhile, place cranberries and brandy in small bowl; stand 15 minutes.

6 Stir cranberry mixture and nuts into ice cream. Spoon ice cream into eight ¾-cup molds. Cover; freeze 3 hours or until firm.

7 Stir remaining chocolate and oil in small saucepan over low heat until smooth.

8 Dip each mold, one at a time, into a bowl of hot water for about 1 second. Turn ice cream onto serving plates; top with warm chocolate mixture.

nutritional count per pudding 57.7g total fat (30.4g saturated fat); 785 cal; 53.1g carbohydrate; 11.5g protein; 2.3g fiber

celebration fruit cake
PREP + COOK TIME 4 HOURS 10 MINS (+ STANDING & COOLING) • SERVES 20

3 cups golden raisins
1¾ cups raisins, halved
1¾ cups dried dates, chopped finely
1 cup dried currants
⅔ cup mixed candied citrus peel
⅔ cup glacé cherries, halved
¼ cup coarsely chopped
   glacé pineapple
¼ cup coarsely chopped
   glacé apricots

½ cup dark rum
2 sticks butter, softened
1 cup firmly packed
   light brown sugar
5 eggs
1½ cups all-purpose flour
⅓ cup self-rising flour
1 teaspoon pie spice
2 tablespoons dark rum, extra

1 Combine fruit and rum in large bowl. Cover tightly with plastic wrap. Store mixture in cool, dark place overnight or up to a week, stirring every day.

2 Preheat oven to 300°F/275°F fan-forced. Line deep 9-inch round cake pan with three thicknesses of parchment paper, extending paper 2 inches above side.

3 Beat butter and sugar in small bowl with electric mixer until just combined. Add eggs, one at a time, beating only until combined between additions.

4 Add butter mixture to fruit mixture; mix well. Mix in sifted dry ingredients; spread mixture evenly into pan.

5 Bake cake, uncovered, about 3½ hours. Brush cake with extra rum. Cover hot cake, in pan, tightly with foil; cool overnight.

nutritional count per serving 12g total fat (7.2g saturated fat); 465 cal; 77.2g carbohydrate; 4.9g protein; 4.5g fiber

steamed christmas pudding

PREP + COOK TIME
7 HOURS 45 MINS
(+ STANDING & COOLING)
SERVES 12

4 cups mixed dried fruit
½ cup dark rum
2 sticks butter, chopped
2½ cups firmly packed
   dark brown sugar
1 tablespoon molasses

4 eggs
1 cup all-purpose flour
1 teaspoon pie spice
4 cups stale bread crumbs
1 large apple, grated coarsely

This pudding can be made up to 3 months ahead and kept refrigerated, or made up to one year ahead and frozen. If the pudding was made in an aluminium steamer, remove the pudding from the steamer and wrap in plastic wrap before storing.

1 Combine fruit and rum in large bowl. Cover; stand overnight or up to a week, stirring every day.

2 Beat butter, sugar and molasses in small bowl with electric mixer until just combined. Beat in eggs, one at a time. Add butter mixture to fruit mixture, then stir in sifted flour and spice, then bread crumbs and apple; mix well.

3 Grease 2-quart pudding steamer; line base with parchment paper. Spoon pudding mixture into steamer.

4 Place 12-inch x 16-inch sheet of foil on counter, grease foil; top with a sheet of parchment. Fold 2-inch pleat crosswise through center of both sheets. Place sheets, paper-side down, over steamer; secure with string or lid. Make a handle with excess string. Crush excess foil and paper firmly around the rim to help form a good seal; trim any excess.

5 Place pudding in large pot with enough boiling water to come halfway up side of steamer. Cover with tight-fitting lid, boil 6–7 hours, replenishing water as necessary to maintain level. Stand pudding 15 minutes before turning onto a plate; cool.

6 Wrap pudding in plastic wrap, then place in an airtight container or freezer bag.

nutritional count per serving 20.4g total fat (12.2g saturated fat); 686 cal; 108.3g carbohydrate; 8.4g protein; 5.3g fiber

Cheeses

This is just a small sample of the many cheeses available to us today. Even supermarkets now carry a range of exceptional cheeses. Soft cheeses such as brie and camembert should be taken out of the refrigerator half an hour or so before you serve them to allow their full flavors to develop.

BOCCONCINI
Italian for "little mouthfuls", bocconcini are bite-sized balls of fresh mozzarella. A delicate-flavored, semi-soft cheese, traditionally made from buffalo milk but now mostly made from cow's milk. Sold fresh, it will only keep, refrigerated in brine, for 1-2 days.

BRIE
A soft-ripened cow's milk cheese with a delicate, creamy texture and a rich, sweet taste. After a brief period of aging, brie should have a bloomy white rind and creamy, voluptuous center, which becomes runny on ripening. Best served at room temperature.

CAMEMBERT
A luscious, buttery cow's milk cheese with a thin edible, aromatic rind. It is probably the most famous and most popular soft French cheese in the world. For the best flavor, eat it at room temperature.

GOAT'S CHEESE (CHEVRE)
Made from goat's milk, this cheese has a very earthy, strong taste. It is available in soft, crumbly and firm textures, in various shapes and sizes, and is sometimes covered in a layer of edible ash (pictured), or herbs.

COTTAGE CHEESE
Its name comes from the description of where it is thought to have been made originally–in cottages from any milk left over after making butter. This mild, fresh, unripened curd product has a grainy consistency and a fat content of 15 to 55 percent.

EDAM
Instantly recognizable from the coating of red paraffin wax on exported products, edam is a semi-hard Dutch cheese made from part-skimmed cow's milk. It is mild in flavor and supple in texture when young, but becomes dry and hard when mature.

Q&A

I recently tried haloumi cheese in a restaurant. What a delicious cheese it is. Can you tell me a simple recipe for using it please?

Place torn arugula leaves in a bowl. Cut some snow peas into thin strips and microwave briefly (1 minute), then plunge into cold water. Drain and add these to the greens. Cut some baby eggplants into rounds and fry on both sides in olive oil–watch these carefully, they burn easily. Fry halved plum tomatoes in olive oil until soft. Lastly, fry slices of haloumi on both sides in olive oil. Drain all the fried ingredients on absorbent paper and pat with more paper to remove excess oil. Mix the salad together and sprinkle with a little balsamic vinegar. Serve warm.

FETA
A crumbly textured goat- or sheep-milk cheese, with a sharp, salty taste. Originally from Greece, other countries, including Denmark, now produce it with cow's milk. Ripened and stored in salted whey, it is particularly good tossed into salads.

FONTINA
A smooth, firm Italian cow's milk cheese with a creamy, nutty taste and brown or red rind. It is ideal for melting or grilling. The original fontina from Italy is fairly pungent and quite intense, while fontina produced in other countries tends to be much milder.

GORGONZOLA
Named after the Italian village, Gorgonzola, in Milan, where it was first made, this creamy blue-veined cheese has a mild, sweet taste. It is good as an accompaniment to fruit or used to flavor sauces (especially for pasta or gnocchi).

GRUYERE
A hard-rind cow's milk cheese named after the town of Gruyères in Switzerland. It is sweet but slightly salty, with a flavor that varies widely with age–often described as creamy and nutty when young, it becomes more assertive, earthy and complex with age. It is a popular cheese for soufflés.

HALOUMI
This Greek Cypriot cheese has a semi-firm, spongy texture and very salty sweet flavor, and is ripened and stored in salted whey. Best grilled or fried, it holds its shape well on being heated. Eat while still warm as it becomes tough and rubbery on cooling.

HAVARTI
Originating in Denmark, this traditional, creamy, semi-hard cow's milk cheese is washed-rind. It is very mild in flavor and dotted with small holes and irregularities.

PRESERVES

Preserves

Don't dismiss preserving. Yes, it might have been something your Great Aunt did, but like a lot of those lovely, homespun notions we've returned to in recent years, there's a lot of wisdom in the practice. Preserving was a way of ensuring that the household had summer fruits all year round. These days, there isn't the urgency to stock up, but it's deeply rewarding nonetheless.

FOR ALL THE SAME REASONS THAT KNITTING HAS ENJOYED A COMEBACK, YOU SHOULD CONSIDER PRESERVING: IT'S A GENTLE ANTIDOTE TO OUR HECTIC TIMES AND A COUPLE OF HOURS IN THE KITCHEN ABSORBED IN THE CALM PLEASURE OF CREATING A JEWEL-LIKE JAM OR A TANGY CHUTNEY COULD BE JUST THE THERAPEUTIC OUTLET YOU'RE LOOKING FOR.

READY, SET?

JAM OR JELLY IS READY FOR TESTING when a candy thermometer reads 220°F. If you don't have a candy thermometer, dip a wooden spoon into the jam, hold it horizontal above the pan, and tilt the bowl of the spoon towards you. When the mixture falls from the spoon in heavy drops, it is ready for testing.

TO TEST WHEN JAM IS READY remove the pan from the heat, allow the bubbles to subside, and drop a teaspoon of mixture on a freezer-chilled plate. Return the plate to the freezer briefly to cool the jam to room temperature. When it has cooled, test the consistency: smooth jam should be of a spreadable consistency, jam with pieces of fruit should form a skin and wrinkle when pushed with a finger; jelly should be a firm mass.

If the mixture hasn't achieved the desired consistency, boil for a few more minutes and test again. Always take the jam or jelly off the heat and wait until it stops bubbling before testing.

JARS FOR BOTTLING

Use ultra-clean, just-sterilized glass jars without chips or cracks. Sterilize jars and metal funnels in one of the following ways:

DISHWASHER In the dishwasher, on the rinse cycle, without detergent, at the hottest temperature.

STOVE TOP Cover with cold water in a large saucepan, put the lid on, bring to a boil and boil for 20 minutes. Remove the jars, drain well and stand right-side up on a board (they'll dry by evaporation).

OVEN Stand the jars right-side up, not touching each other, on an oven tray in a cold oven. Heat the oven to 275°F and leave for 30 minutes.

SAVORY JOYS

A LITTLE RELISH OR CHUTNEY, OR SOME PICKLES, CAN LIVEN UP A SANDWICH AND SUDDENLY MAKE A SNACK OF LEFTOVER COLD MEATS ANYTHING BUT ORDINARY.

PICKLES are vegetables, and occasionally fruits, that are preserved in vinegar, brine or a mixture of the two, usually with flavorings like herbs or spices and sugar or mustard. The best-known pickles are pickled onions, pickled cucumbers (called dill pickles or gherkins), and mixed mustard pickles. Pickles are assertive, sharp and spicy in flavor.

RELISHES Usually based on a single vegetable such as corn or tomatoes, relishes are cooked on the stove top and simmered for about an hour. Relishes are milder than pickles; they are sweet/savory and tangy rather than strong and sharp. These usually only keep for a few weeks, stored in the refrigerator.

CHUTNEYS Similar to relishes, they encompass a variety of spicy, sweet and tangy fruit and/or vegetable mixtures that have been cooked to a thickened texture. Often combining ingredients as diverse as tomatoes, apples, mustard powder and raisins, chutney mixtures are brought to a boil, then simmered for about an hour. The most famous of these is mango chutney, which is superb with curries.

SAVORY JAMS Onion and chili jams are delicious, deep-flavored accompaniments to meats and seafood or can be used to flavor a casserole or soup.

SWEET DELIGHTS

THERE IS SOMETHING SUBLIME ABOUT A DOLLOP OF CRIMSON JAM FILLED WITH REAL CHUNKS OF FRUIT: THE PERFECT PARTNER TO A PIECE OF TOAST OR A SCONE.

JAMS are made with small pieces of fruit. The fruit is cooked until tender, then sugar is added and the mixture is cooked until it's of a spreadable but set consistency, achieved by the action of pectin, a substance in the cell walls of fruit. Fruits vary greatly in their pectin content–high-pectin ones include apples, citrus, plums, quinces and black or red currants. Low-pectin fruits such as cherries, figs, peaches, pears, pineapples, rhubarb, strawberries and raspberries can be mixed with high-pectin fruits to make jam set well.

CONSERVES are made with whole pieces of fruit, such as cherries or strawberries, or large pieces of fruits such as peaches or apricots.

MARMALADES are clear, bittersweet jams usually made from one or more citrus fruits. The bitterness comes from the pieces of citrus peel that are cooked into the jam with the fruit.

JELLIES are clear, candy-colored mixtures made from cooked fruit that is strained overnight through a jelly strainer. The clear juice is boiled with sugar until it reaches a consistency that will gel. Jelly strainers are available from kitchen shops or you can make your own from a cheesecloth.

STORING

HOMEMADE PRESERVES, OR HOME-STYLE ONES FROM SMALL PRODUCERS AT FARMERS' MARKETS, CAN BE STORED AT ROOM TEMPERATURE AWAY FROM SUNLIGHT UNTIL THEY'RE OPENED, AND THEN THEY NEED TO BE REFRIGERATED AND USED WITHIN A MONTH OR TWO.

spicy mustard pickles

This is an old-fashioned pickle that is splendid with cold roast lamb or cheddar cheese. For a delicious snack, mix it with grated cheese, pile it on toast and broil.

¼ medium head cauliflower, chopped coarsely

8 ounces green beans, trimmed, chopped coarsely

3 medium brown onions, sliced thickly

1 medium red pepper, sliced thickly

¼ cup coarse cooking salt

2 teaspoons dry mustard

2 tablespoons whole grain mustard

3 teaspoons curry powder

¼ teaspoon ground turmeric

2 cups white vinegar

1 cup firmly packed light brown sugar

2 tablespoons all-purpose flour

1 Combine vegetables and salt in large bowl. Cover; stand overnight.

2 Rinse vegetables; drain. Stir vegetables, mustards, curry powder, turmeric, 1¾ cups of the vinegar and sugar in large saucepan over heat, without boiling, until sugar dissolves; bring to a boil. Reduce heat; simmer, uncovered, about 10 minutes or until vegetables are just tender.

3 Stir in blended flour and remaining vinegar; stir over heat until mixture boils and thickens. Pour into hot sterilized jars; seal.

nutritional count per tablespoon 0.1g total fat (0g saturated); 27 cal; 5.7g carbohydrate; 0.6g protein; 0.5g fiber

Place the salted vegetables in a pan with the spices, vinegar and brown sugar. Stir over low heat until sugar dissolves, then boil until vegetables are tender.

Add blended flour and vinegar to the cooked vegetables and stir over heat until the mixture boils and thickens.

Spoon the hot pickle mixture into hot, sterilized jars. Seal the jars while mixture is still hot.

tomato chutney

Tomato chutney makes a great addition to casseroles, rice dishes, burgers and pot roasts.

10 medium ripe tomatoes (3 pounds), peeled, chopped coarsely
2 large apples, peeled, chopped coarsely
2 medium brown onions, chopped coarsely
1 cup firmly packed light brown sugar
1½ cups cider vinegar
¼ teaspoon chili powder
½ teaspoon dry mustard
¾ cup golden raisins
1 clove garlic, crushed
2 teaspoons curry powder
2 teaspoons ground allspice

1 Stir ingredients in large saucepan over heat, without boiling, until sugar dissolves; bring to a boil. Reduce heat; simmer, uncovered, stirring occasionally, about 1 hour or until mixture is thick.
2 Pour chutney into hot sterilized jars; seal immediately.
nutritional count per tablespoon 0g total fat (0g saturated fat); 24 cal; 5.3g carbohydrate; 0.3g protein; 0.5g fiber

orange marmalade

PREP + COOK TIME
1 HOUR 40 MINS
(+ STANDING & COOLING)
MAKES 7 CUPS

5 large seville oranges (3 pounds)
5 cups water
5 cups sugar, approximately
2 tablespoons lemon juice

Seville oranges have a short season in winter, and they make a superb bittersweet marmalade. The seeds and pith are reserved because they contain high levels of pectin, which will help the marmalade to set.

1 Peel oranges; cut rind into thin strips. Remove pith from all oranges; reserve half, discard remaining pith. Chop flesh coarsely, reserve seeds.
2 Combine flesh and rind in large bowl with the water. Tie reserved pith and seeds in muslin; add to bowl. Stand at room temperature overnight.
3 Place orange mixture and muslin bag in large saucepan; bring to a boil. Reduce heat; simmer, covered, 35 minutes or until rind is soft. Discard bag.
4 Measure fruit mixture; allow 1 cup sugar for each cup of mixture.
5 Return mixture to pan with sugar and juice; stir over heat, without boiling, until sugar dissolves. Boil, uncovered, about 30 minutes or until marmalade gels when tested.
6 Pour marmalade into hot sterilized jars; seal immediately.
nutritional count per tablespoon 0g total fat (0g saturated fat); 78 cal; 18.8g carbohydrate; 0.2g protein; 0.5g fiber

[opposite] tomato chutney

dark plum jam

When cooking jam, be sure to use a large wide-topped saucepan that allows for the necessary evaporation, otherwise you will end up with runny jam. Usually about half the liquid has to evaporate before the jam will gel.

28 medium red plums (4 pounds)
1 quart water
⅓ cup lemon juice
6 cups sugar

1 Cut plums into quarters; discard pits. Place plums and the water in large saucepan; bring to a boil. Reduce heat; simmer, covered, 1 hour.

2 Add juice and sugar, stir over heat, without boiling, until sugar dissolves. Boil, uncovered, without stirring, 20 minutes or until jam gels when tested.

3 Pour into hot sterilized jars; seal immediately.

nutritional count per tablespoon 0g total fat (0g saturated fat); 61 cal; 14.7g carbohydrate; 0.1g protein; 0.4g fiber

apricot jam

Fruit for jam-making should be barely ripe, as overripe fruit results in a jam or jelly that does not set well. Remove any bruised or damaged pieces before you start.

25 medium apricots (2 pounds)
1½ cups water
5 cups sugar, approximately

1 Halve apricots; discard pits. Combine apricots and the water in large saucepan; bring to a boil. Reduce heat; simmer, covered, about 15 minutes or until apricots are soft.

2 Measure fruit mixture, allow 1 cup sugar to each cup of fruit mixture. Return fruit mixture and sugar to pan; stir over heat, without boiling, until sugar is dissolved. Bring to a boil; boil, uncovered without stirring, about 15 minutes or until jam gels when tested.

3 Pour jam into hot sterilized jars; seal immediately.

nutritional count per tablespoon 0g total fat (0g saturated fat); 80 cal; 9.3g carbohydrate; 0.1g protein; 0.3g fiber

quince paste

It is really important that the puree and sugar mixture is cooked until it turns a deep rose color. The cooking times may vary, depending on the pectin content of the individual fruit. If you have a food processor, puree cooked quinces in seconds, rather than using a sieve.

4 large quinces (4 pounds)
¼ cup lemon juice
1¾ cups water
5 cups superfine sugar, approximately
¼ cup shelled pistachios, chopped coarsely

1 Oil 6-inch x 10-inch loaf pan. Peel, quarter and core quinces; chop coarsely. Place in large saucepan with juice and the water, simmer, covered, about 40 minutes or until soft; cool.
2 Push quince mixture through sieve into medium bowl. Measure puree, for each cup allow 1 cup sugar. Stir puree and sugar in medium saucepan over heat 20 minutes or until thick and red; stir in nuts. Spread into pan; smooth top. Stand, uncovered, 24 hours.
nutritional count per slice 0.5g total fat (0.1g saturated fat); 129 cal; 29g carbohydrate; 0.4g protein; 2.7g fiber

apple jelly

Try adding ½ cup passionfruit pulp to this jelly just before bottling; it's delicious.

5 medium sour green apples, chopped coarsely
1½ quarts water
4 cups sugar, approximately

1 Place apples (seeds, skin, cores and all) and the water in large saucepan; bring to a boil. Simmer, covered, 1 hour. Strain mixture through cheesecloth; discard pulp.
2 Measure apple liquid; allow 1 cup of sugar for each cup of liquid.
3 Place apple liquid and sugar in large saucepan; stir over heat, without boiling, until sugar dissolves. Bring to a boil; boil, uncovered, 15 minutes or until jelly sets.
4 Pour jelly into hot sterilized jars; seal immediately.
nutritional count per tablespoon 0g total fat (0g saturated fat); 107 cal; 26.2g carbohydrate; 0.1g protein; 0.3g fiber

3 pounds strawberries, hulled
5 cups sugar
1 cup lemon juice

TIPS

• You will need about 3 medium lemons to get the amount of juice needed for this recipe.

1 Gently heat berries in large saucepan, covered, 5 minutes to extract juice from berries. Transfer berries with slotted spoon to large bowl; reserve.

2 Add sugar and lemon juice to strawberry juice in pan, stir over heat, without boiling, until sugar dissolves; bring to a boil. Boil, uncovered, without stirring, 20 minutes. Return reserved berries to pan; simmer, uncovered, without stirring, 25 minutes or until jam gels when tested.

3 Pour hot jam into hot sterilized jars; seal immediately.

nutritional count per tablespoon 0g total fat (0g saturated fat); 67 cal; 15.9g carbohydrate; 0.4g protein; 0.5g fiber

Add lemon juice to the sugar and strawberry juice in the pan. (The lemon adds pectin to help the jam set.)

The way to test whether a jam is set is to put a spoonful of it onto a freezer-chilled saucer. Push the jam with your finger; if it wrinkles, the jam is set. If it doesn't wrinkle, cook for a little longer then test again.

Pour the hot jam into hot sterilized jars, taking the mixture right up to the top. Seal the jars while the jam is still hot.

TEACHING KIDS TO COOK

Teaching kids to cook

Children love to help in the kitchen, and it's wonderful to find the time to harness their enthusiasm. After all, food preparation and eating is a major part of our lives and it's natural for children to want to be a part of it.

The key is to choose a cooking project that's interesting and uncomplicated. You also need to accept that your assistant chef might create a little extra mess on the kitchen counter–and go with it.

Sharing the counter with an enthusiastic helper takes patience and time, but it can be deeply rewarding for all parties: not only is there the simple joy of creating food together, but you get to see your little person grow up with a love of good food and a respect for the ways of the kitchen.

Bringing them into the kitchen also de-mystifies it for them, and they are more likely to follow the safety rules you lay down–they need to sit or stand safely at the counter; they shouldn't go near the stove top, etc. There are many lessons to be learned in the kitchen, but more than anything, teaching kids to cook needs to be fun, not stressful. The learning just happens. It's important for children to realize that cooking is more than getting food to the table: it's about creating healthy meals, sharing, passion and creativity.

HYGIENE

The first lesson for any budding young chef is in personal hygiene. They need to understand that they cannot begin to help you in the kitchen until they wash their hands carefully with warm water and soap. It's wise to get girls into the habit of tying back long hair too.

Perhaps you could buy your child a special cooking apron of their own. Not only will it help to protect clothes, but donning the apron can be part of the ritual of helping in the kitchen: they can only put on their apron once they've washed their hands.

REMINDER Clean hands are especially important when handling uncooked food, and everyone should wash their hands again after touching uncooked meat, seafood or poultry.

SAFETY

When there is a child in the kitchen, everyone needs to be extra cautious and aware of potential dangers lurking within the reach of darting, inquisitive hands.

Keep sharp knives and other pointy utensils out of reach. If there are pots on the stove top, make sure they are on the back burners, with handles facing towards the back wall.

If a tea kettle has recently boiled, make sure it is out of arm's reach.

Never, ever leave a young child alone in the kitchen–not even for a moment. Give children clear rules about what they can touch and what is strictly out of bounds.

A TACTILE EXPERIENCE

While safety is the priority, don't forget that cooking is an activity filled with sights, smells and sounds. Let your child feel the ingredients: encourage them to compare textures like sugar and flour; touch a cold raw chicken filet; smell a cut onion, as well as herbs and spices. Let them taste the ingredients too, if they want to: teach about sweet and sour and bitter and "sharp" tastes. And of course, get them into the good habit of washing their hands before proceeding.

START WITH THE SIMPLE THINGS

You don't want to tackle a complicated recipe with your four-year-old in tow. Start with simple foods they love to eat like pizza or nachos. Let them stir the ingredients and spread the tomato paste. Encourage older children to read the recipe out loud. Talk through the steps of the instructions, what ingredients and utensils are needed: encourage your child to find the equipment and measure out the quantities.

FAMILIARIZATION

As part of your child's orientation around the kitchen, it's important to explain the workings of the appliances in the room, and the utensils you're using–graters, whisks, beaters, measuring spoons, spatulas, pastry brushes, chopping boards, etc.–and where they live in the kitchen. The next time you're cooking together, you can ask your child to help you find the utensils (as long as they're safely located), which gives them a greater sense of involvement.

DEFROSTING MEAT

If you're working with meat, make sure you impart lessons on meat care as you go. Meat, seafood and poultry always needs to be thawed in the refrigerator, so if your menu calls for any of these, be sure you've thawed them ahead of time, making sure to place a tray under the meat to prevent drips. It's not ideal to defrost any of these items in the microwave because sometimes the outside edges of the meat can actually cook.

CLEANING UP

THIS IS THE PART WHERE YOUR LITTLE HELPERS, WHILE ENTHUSIASTIC, SUDDENLY LOSE INTEREST IN THE KITCHEN, BUT IT'S IMPORTANT FOR THEM TO KNOW THAT PACKING UP IS A PART OF THE PROCESS OF COOKING, TOO. EXPLAIN TO THEM THE IMPORTANCE OF CAREFULLY PUTTING AWAY ANY UNUSED FOOD. IF YOU'RE PUTTING AWAY UNUSED MEAT OR VEGETABLES, MAKE SURE THEY'RE PLACED IN A SEALED CONTAINER OR RESEALABLE PLASTIC BAG.

TIDY UP AS YOU GO

Keep the counter and the rest of the preparation area clean and tidy as you work. Wipe up any spills or grease spots when they happen.

Use one cloth for wiping the counter and a separate one for wiping spills on the floor. And use another cloth altogether for wiping hands. Rinse cloths constantly in hot soapy water.

Wash–or at least rinse–the equipment you're using after each use: don't let the food cement itself to the bottom of the bowls or pans.

TASTE-TESTING

This is the part where there is usually never any problem recruiting help. It's good to taste-test the food you're making, and children love to learn about the flavors they're creating.

REMEMBER Don't taste from the stirring spoon and return it to the saucepan or mixing bowl. Use clean cutlery each time you taste.

ham and pineapple pizza

2 teaspoons olive oil

⅓ cup prepared tomato pasta sauce

2 cups coarsely grated
pizza cheese

3½ ounces sliced ham,
chopped coarsely

⅔ cup coarsely chopped drained
canned pineapple pieces

pizza dough

2 teaspoons dried yeast

1 teaspoon sugar

½ teaspoon salt

¾ cup warm water

2½ cups all-purpose flour

2 tablespoons olive oil

1 Make pizza dough.

2 Preheat oven to 500°F/450°F fan-forced.

3 Carefully lift each dough round onto oiled pizza pans or oven trays; using a pastry brush, brush oil over pizza crust. Spoon tomato pasta sauce on crusts, using back of large spoon to spread sauce all over base.

4 Sprinkle half of the cheese over sauce, then top with ham and pineapple. Sprinkle remaining cheese over pizzas.

5 Bake pizzas, uncovered, 20 minutes. Serve cut into slices.

pizza dough Combine yeast, sugar, salt and the warm water in small bowl, cover; stand in warm place about 20 minutes or until mixture is frothy. Combine flour and oil in large bowl; stir in yeast mixture, mix to a soft dough. Knead dough on floured surface about 5 minutes or until smooth and elastic. Place dough in large oiled bowl, cover; stand in warm place about 1 hour or until dough doubles in size. Turn dough onto floured surface; knead until smooth. Divide dough in half; using rolling pin, flatten dough and roll each half out to a 12-inch round.

nutritional count per serving 12.2g total fat (4.6g saturated fat); 324 cal; 36.8g carbohydrate; 15.2g protein; 2.5g fiber

Place the yeast, sugar, salt and warm water in a bowl and allow to stand for 20 minutes or until the mixture becomes frothy.

Set the dough mixture aside for about an hour or until it is well risen. The dough should double in size.

Divide the kneaded dough in half. Roll out each half to a 12-inch round with a rolling pin. Drape the dough over the rolling pin and place onto the oiled pizza pans.

Sprinkle grated pizza cheese evenly over the tomato sauce, then top with chopped ham and pineapple pieces.

noodle and vegetable rice paper rolls

The rolls can be made at the table or prepared ahead of time and stored in the fridge for up to 3 hours. Cover them with a damp clean tea towel to keep them moist.

2 ounces rice vermicelli noodles
1 small carrot, grated coarsely
7 ounces Napa cabbage, shredded finely
1 tablespoon fish sauce
1 tablespoon brown sugar
¼ cup lemon juice
12 x 7-inch square rice paper sheets
12 fresh mint leaves

1 Place noodles in medium heatproof bowl, cover with boiling water; stand about 10 minutes or until just tender, drain. Using kitchen scissors, cut noodles into random lengths.

2 Place noodles in same cleaned bowl with carrot, cabbage, sauce, sugar and juice; toss gently to combine.

3 To assemble rolls, place one sheet of rice paper in medium bowl of warm water until just softened; lift sheet carefully from water, placing it on a tea-towel-covered board with a corner point facing towards you. Place a little of the vegetable filling horizontally in center of sheet, top with one mint leaf. Fold corner point facing you up over filling; roll sheet to enclose filling, folding in sides after first complete turn of roll. Repeat with remaining sheets, filling and mint.

nutritional count per roll 0.2g total fat (0g saturated fat); 31 cal; 6g carbohydrate; 1.1g protein; 0.6g fiber

serving idea sweet chili sauce for dipping.

With a corner pointing towards you, carefully lift a softened rice paper sheet onto a clean board covered with a tea towel.

Place a little of the filling in the middle of the sheet, then top with one mint leaf. Fold the corner point facing you over the filling and roll the sheet to enclose the filling.

As you roll the rice paper sheet over to enclose the filling, tuck in the sides after the first complete turn. Continue rolling the sheet to form a roll. Repeat for the remaining sheets and filling.

veggie nachos

Serve nachos straight from the oven so the corn chips remain crunchy and the cheese is nice and oozy.

1 tablespoon olive oil
1 medium brown onion, chopped finely
1 clove garlic, crushed
14-ounce can chopped tomatoes
15-ounce can pinto beans, drained, rinsed
8-ounce bag corn chips
1 cup grated cheddar cheese
½ cup sour cream
1 tablespoon chopped fresh coriander

1 Preheat oven to 400°F/350°F fan-forced.
2 Heat oil in medium frying pan; cook onion and garlic, stirring, about 5 minutes or until onion softens. Stir in undrained tomatoes and beans.
3 Bring mixture to a boil; reduce heat, simmer, uncovered, 15 minutes, stirring constantly, until mixture thickens slightly.
4 Place corn chips onto large ovenproof plate; spoon bean mixture over chips, then sprinkle with cheese. Bake, uncovered, about 10 minutes or until cheese is melted. Serve topped with sour cream and coriander.
nutritional count per serving 43.4g total fat (21.3g saturated fat); 686 cal; 49.3g carbohydrate; 20.5g protein; 13.3g fiber

Add the onion and garlic to a heated, oiled frying pan and cook, stirring, until onion is soft.

Add tomatoes and beans to the pan with the onion mixture. Simmer, stirring constantly, for 15 minutes, until the mixture becomes thick.

Spoon the cooked bean mixture over the corn chips, arranged on an ovenproof plate.

meatballs napoletana

The combination of ground pork and veal gives these meatballs a deliciously rich quality that you won't get with ground beef.

1 pound ground pork and veal
1 egg
½ cup packaged bread crumbs
¼ cup finely grated
   parmesan cheese
¼ cup finely chopped fresh
   flat-leaf parsley
1 tablespoon olive oil

1 small brown onion,
   chopped finely
1 clove garlic, crushed
3 cups prepared tomato pasta sauce
½ cup frozen peas
¼ cup coarsely chopped fresh basil
½ cup pitted green olives

1 Combine meat, egg, bread crumbs, cheese and parsley in medium bowl. Roll level tablespoons of meat mixture into balls.

2 Heat half the oil in large frying pan; cook meatballs until browned and cooked through. Remove meatballs from pan.

3 Heat remaining oil in same pan; cook onion and garlic, stirring, until onion softens. Add sauce; bring to a boil. Add meatballs, reduce heat; simmer, uncovered, about 10 minutes or until sauce thickens slightly.

4 Add peas and basil to meatball mixture; simmer, uncovered, until peas are tender. Add olives to meatball mixture, season to taste; stir until heated through.

nutritional count per serving 18.2g total fat (5.7g saturated fat); 438 cal; 30.5g carbohydrate; 35.3g protein; 5.4g fiber

serving idea serve meatballs with spaghetti.

In a medium bowl, combine the pork and veal, egg, bread crumbs, cheese and parsley, using clean hands.

Take a level tablespoon of meat mixture and roll it in your hands to form a ball. Repeat until you have used up all the meat.

Add the cooked meatballs to the pasta sauce and simmer, uncovered, for 10 minutes or until the sauce thickens slightly.

mango and raspberry parfait

If mangoes are in season, you can use one large fresh mango weighing about 1¼ pounds for this recipe. Peel the mango over a small bowl to catch as much of the juice as possible, then cut off mango cheeks; slice cheeks thinly. Squeeze as much juice as possible from around the mango pit into the bowl with other juice; add enough cold water to make 1 cup of liquid to be added to the mango gelatin (see step 2).

15-ounce can sliced mango
3-ounce packet mango gelatin
2 cups boiling water
5 ounces raspberries
3-ounce packet raspberry gelatin
1 cup cold water
1¼ cup heavy cream

1 Drain mango in sieve over small bowl; reserve liquid. Measure ¼ cup mango slices and reserve. Divide remaining mango slices among eight 6-ounce glasses.

2 Combine mango gelatin with 1 cup of the boiling water in medium pitcher, stirring until it dissolves; stir gelatin into reserved mango liquid. Divide evenly among glasses over mango, cover; refrigerate about 2 hours or until gelatin sets.

3 Divide raspberries among glasses over gelatin. Combine raspberry gelatin and remaining cup of the boiling water in medium pitcher, stirring until it dissolves; stir in the cold water. Divide evenly among glasses over raspberries. Cover; refrigerate about 2 hours or until gelatin sets.

4 Beat cream in small bowl with electric mixer until soft peaks form. Using rubber spatula, spread equally among glasses; top with reserved mango.

nutritional count per serving 13.9g total fat (9.1g saturated fat); 246 cal; 26.8g carbohydrate; 2.9g protein; 1.5g fiber

Drain the mango in a sieve over a bowl and reserve the syrup.

Add the gelatin mixture to the reserved mango syrup, stirring constantly to combine.

Carefully pour the raspberry mixture over the raspberries and mango in each glass. Cover glasses and chill until set.

butterfly cakes

Use whatever jam you like, or some pureed fruit. Stewed fruit such as apple or stone fruits also make a lovely variation—it helps if they are not too thin in consistency though. Lemon curd is another popular filling.

1 stick butter, softened
1 teaspoon vanilla extract
⅔ cup superfine sugar
3 eggs
1½ cups self-rising flour
¼ cup milk
½ cup jam
1¼ heavy cream, whipped

1 Preheat oven to 350°F/325°F fan-forced. Line two 12-hole (2 tablespoons) deep mini muffin tins with paper cases.

2 Beat butter, extract, sugar, eggs, sifted flour and milk in small bowl on low speed with electric mixer until ingredients are just combined. Increase speed to medium; beat about 3 minutes or until mixture is smooth and pale in color.

3 Drop slightly rounded tablespoons of mixture into paper cases.

4 Bake cakes about 20 minutes. Stand cakes in pans 5 minutes before turning, top-sides up, onto wire racks to cool.

5 Using sharp, pointed vegetable knife, cut a circle from the top of each cake; cut circle in half to make two "wings". Fill cavities with jam and whipped cream; position wings on top of cakes.

nutritional count per cake 9.8g total fat (6.2g saturated fat); 168 cal; 17.8g carbohydrate; 2.2g protein; 0.4g fiber

serving idea dust butterfly cakes with sifted powdered sugar just before serving.

Beat together the butter, vanilla extract, sugar, eggs, sifted flour and milk with an electric mixer until the mixture is smooth and pale in color.

Place tablespoons of cake mixture into the paper cases.

Cut a circle out of the top of each cake, using a pointed vegetable knife. Cut each circle in half to form two wings.

Fill the cavity of each cake with jam, then top with the whipped cream, before placing the two wings on top.

gingerbread men

You obviously need a gingerbread-man cutter to make this shape, but any decorative cutter– a star, diamond, heart or whatever shape you may already have in your kitchen–can be used for this recipe.

TIPS

• If the mixture in step 3 is dry and crumbly, add a little more beaten egg–enough to make it feel like playdough.

• To make a quick piping bag, cut off a corner of a small plastic bag.

1 stick butter
⅓ cup firmly packed
    light brown sugar
½ cup golden syrup or honey
3 cups all-purpose flour
2 teaspoons ground ginger
2 teaspoons ground cinnamon
½ teaspoon ground clove
2 teaspoons baking soda
1 egg, beaten lightly
1 teaspoon vanilla extract

royal icing
1 egg white
1 cup powdered sugar
food coloring

1 Preheat oven to 350°F/325°F fan-forced. Grease oven trays.

2 Heat butter, sugar and golden syrup, in small microwave-safe bowl, uncovered, on HIGH (100%) in microwave oven about 1 minute or until butter has melted. Using oven mitts, remove bowl from microwave oven; cool butter mixture 5 minutes.

3 Sift combined flour, spices and baking soda into large bowl; add butter mixture, egg and extract, stir with wooden spoon until combined.

4 Divide dough in half; knead each portion of dough on floured surface. Using rolling pin, roll dough out to ¼-inch thickness. Using gingerbread-man cutter, cut out shapes; place on oven trays.

5 Bake gingerbread men about 10 minutes or until golden brown. Cool on trays.

6 Make royal icing. Decorate gingerbread men with royal icing.

royal icing Beat egg white in small bowl with electric mixer until just frothy; gradually add sifted powdered sugar, beating between additions, until stiff peaks form. Tint icing as desired, using food coloring.

nutritional count per gingerbread man 5.7g total fat (3.5g saturated fat); 273 cal; 51.4g carbohydrate; 3.2g protein; 0.9g fiber

decorating ideas you could also use colored dragees or mini candies to make buttons or other patterns.

Using a rolling pin, roll each portion of biscuit dough out to a thickness of ¼ inch.

Cut out shapes from the dough, using a gingerbread-man cutter.

Arrange the biscuits on an oven tray, leaving space between each one.

Pipe tinted royal icing onto gingerbread men. You can also use dragees or candies to decorate.

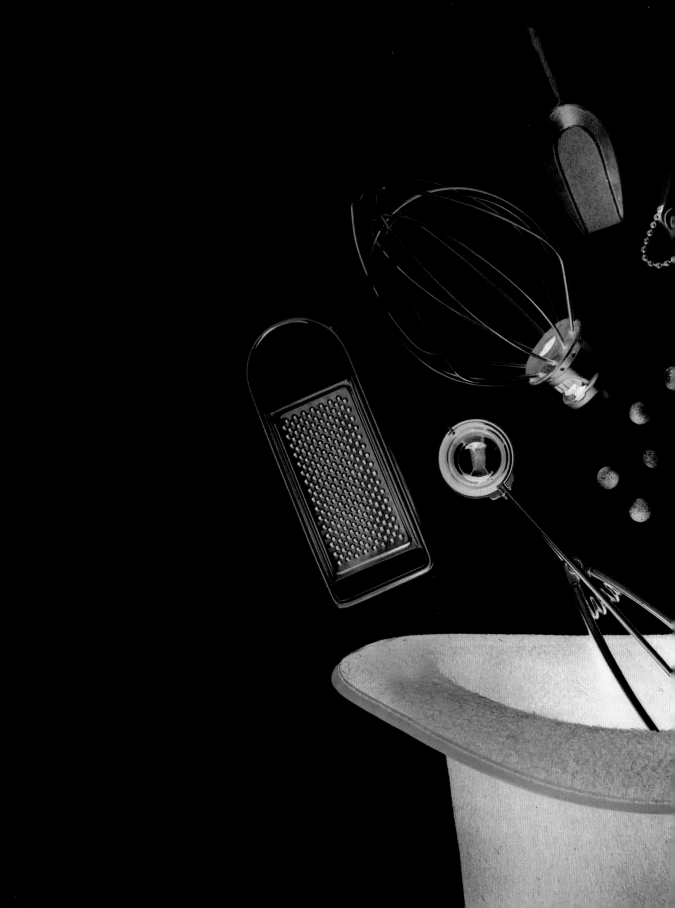

TRICKS OF THE TRADE

Tricks of the trade

Even if you're a veteran cook, there are always new tricks that you can learn to improve your cooking. Here are some tips and techniques from the experts that will get you cooking like a professional and eating like a king or queen.

EGGS

ALWAYS CRACK EGGS INTO A SMALL BOWL OR CUP ONE AT A TIME, IN CASE THERE IS ONE THAT IS NOT FRESH.

TO TEST THE FRESHNESS OF EGGS, PLACE IN A BOWL OF WATER. ANY THAT FLOAT ARE NOT FRESH AS THEY HAVE A LARGER AIR SAC IN THEM (THE AIR SAC GETS BIGGER AS THE EGG AGES). THOSE THAT SINK ARE FRESHER.

WHEN POACHING EGGS, PLACE A TEASPOON OF VINEGAR IN THE WATER. THIS HELPS TO QUICKLY COAGULATE THE EGG WHITE, PREVENTING IT FROM SPREADING. ALSO CREATE A WHIRLPOOL IN THE WATER USING A SPOON. ADD THE EGG TO THE CENTER OF THE WHIRLPOOL, THIS HELPS THE EGG TO KEEP A ROUND SHAPE.

TO MAKE PERFECT MASHED POTATOES

BOIL THE POTATOES UNTIL COMPLETELY TENDER, THEN DRAIN THEM WELL. TURN OFF THE BURNER. RETURN THE POTATOES TO THE SAUCEPAN AND THE PAN TO THE SAME BURNER FOR 1 MINUTE TO EVAPORATE ANY REMAINING LIQUID. THIS ALSO ALLOWS THE STARCH IN THE POTATOES TO DRY, MAKING THEM READY TO ABSORB HOT MILK WHEN MASHED.

ALL ABOUT BAKING

Store vanilla beans in a jar of white sugar. The sugar creates an airtight environment for the beans, keeping them fresh and you'll produce vanilla sugar that can be used in a variety of dishes.

When adding citrus rinds to cakes, always cream with the butter and sugar. This helps to release natural oils in the rind, giving more flavor.

Make sure the water is icy cold when making pastry. The key to flaky dough is suspending fat deposits of butter and shortening, rather than fully incorporating them into the dough. The colder the fat remains, the easier it is to turn out the ultimate pie.

To test if bread or scones are cooked, tap the bottom; if it sounds hollow, it's cooked through.

To prevent meringues from "weeping" a liquid, sticky substance, ensure the sugar is dissolved properly in the meringue mixture. Beat whites to soft peaks, then gradually add sugar, beating well between additions. To test if the sugar is dissolved, rub a little of the meringue between your fingers. If it's still grainy, continue beating.

When making cakes such as sponges, the fresher the eggs, the more volume you will get when whipping them, resulting in a light cake. Always have eggs at room temperature before whipping, you will get more volume.

When melting chocolate, stir with a metal spoon, if you use a wooden spoon, any moisture in the wood might cause the chocolate to seize.

When whipping egg whites, rub a cut lemon over the inside of the bowl before adding the egg whites. This neutralizes any fat or grease that might be in the bowl. Fat prevents the whites from whipping.

If you don't have a pastry bag and need one for a recipe, take a resealable plastic bag and cut one of the corners off for an instant makeshift pastry bag.

Cooling a baked cheesecake in the oven with the door slightly ajar will prevent it from cracking on the surface. Cracks occur when the cheesecake is removed hot from the oven–the cold air causes the protein in the eggs to seize, and the cheesecake to shrink and crack.

THE PERFECT SAUCE

When you make a sauce and use a starchy thickener like a roux (butter and flour mix), you have to be careful of one crucial thing that will prevent lumping of the starch–you need to heat the starch evenly. What happens then is that the starch granules will swell up at the same time and eventually burst and release the starch particles into the sauce and thicken it. But if you don't heat the starch evenly, the granules will become sticky on the outside and start to aggregate with other starches. So what you need to do is simple: add the hot liquid sauce to the roux at a slow rate and make sure to stir at all times. Cook up the sauce between each addition. If you still get some lumps, you can always strain the sauce through a fine sieve.

If your hollandaise or béarnaise sauce looks like it's about to split (curdle), whisk in a tablespoon of boiling water to emulsify it.

If a creamy sauce looks like it is splitting during cooking, add a little cold cream, this will make it smooth again.

STORAGE

STORE FRESH HERBS WRAPPED IN DAMP ABSORBENT PAPER IN AN AIRTIGHT CONTAINER IN THE FRIDGE, THIS KEEPS THEM FRESHER FOR LONGER.

TO RIPEN FRUITS, WRAP THEM IN NEWSPAPER OR A BROWN PAPER BAG AND PUT IN A WARM PLACE FOR 2-3 DAYS. THE ETHYLENE GAS THEY EMIT WILL MAKE THEM RIPE.

BUTTER AND OIL

Melt butter and oil together when pan-frying. The butter adds flavor and the oil prevents the butter from burning.

To test if oil is hot enough for deep-frying, add a cube of bread to see if oil sizzles, or stand the end of a wooden spoon in oil. If the oil around the spoon sizzles, it means any moisture in the wood is reacting with the oil, meaning the oil is hot enough.

Peanut oil is the best oil to fry with because it has a high smoking/heating point.

THE GOODNESS OF GARLIC

WHEN A RECIPE CALLS FOR CRUSHED GARLIC, CHOP THE GARLIC INTO SMALL PIECES. ADD A LITTLE PINCH OF SALT THEN CONTINUE TO CHOP, THEN MASH WITH THE BACK OF YOUR KNIFE. IT'S WORTH CRUSHING A LARGE QUANTITY AND PLACING IT IN ICE CUBE TRAYS WITH A LITTLE WATER, THEN COVER AND FREEZE. WHENEVER YOU NEED CRUSHED GARLIC, PLACE A CUBE STRAIGHT FROM THE FREEZER INTO THE PAN.

FRUIT

To prevent apples from browning when cutting a lot for pies, place peeled, cut apple in a bowl of cold water with 2 tablespoons of lemon juice. The acid prevents the enzymes that make the apple brown from reacting.

Freeze overripe bananas in a freezer bag. Defrost and use in banana cakes.

When squeezing a lemon or lime, first roll the fruit around on a work surface with your hands to start releasing some of the juices or you can place it in the microwave for about 30 seconds. Then cut the fruit in half and squeeze cut-side up so the seeds don't get into what you're doing. You can also stick a fork in the fruit to help squeeze without getting all the seeds everywhere.

VEGETABLES

To store a cut avocado, squeeze a little lemon on the cut surface then wrap in plastic wrap—this prevents the avocado from browning.

To stop your eyes from weeping when cutting onions, place peeled onions in water for about 20 minutes before chopping... or wear goggles!

When sautéing onions, add salt after the onions have started to turn brown or the salt will slow down the caramelization process.

MEAT AND FISH

How to know if fish is fresh? There are several things to look for. One, the skin should be shiny. Two, the eyes should be clear and not opaque. Three, the gills should be pink-red. And four, the smell should be pleasant and not too fishy. Seawater fish should smell like the ocean coast, and freshwater fish should have a grassy smell.

An easy way to devein peeled prawns is to bend the prawn, exposing the vein down the back. Insert a skewer or toothpick through the skin and behind the vein, then lift, this will pull out the vein. Rub a cut lemon on your hands before washing with warm soapy water to remove the prawn smell.

Salt salmon skin before pan-frying, then cook skin-side down first to get a crispy skin. The salt helps draw any moisture out of the skin to make it crisp.

When cooking steaks or fish, only turn once during pan-frying. Place the best side down first in the pan, this will be the presentation side. Cook until browned nicely, then turn and cook until desired. Turning only once prevents any juices from the food from being lost and making the food dry.

To test the doneness of a steak, insert a skewer for 30 seconds, then place on your bottom lip. If the steak is medium, the skewer will be warm and juices that run out will be bloody, if it's well done, the skewer will be hot and juices will be clear. Or do the finger test, the firmer the steak, the more cooked it is.

GENERAL

TO PREVENT WOODEN SKEWERS FROM SCORCHING DURING COOKING, SOAK THEM IN WATER BEFORE USING THEM.

PLACE PLASTIC WRAP OVER THE SURFACE OF CUSTARD WHEN STORING TO PREVENT A SKIN FROM FORMING.

WHEN MEASURING A REALLY STICKY SUBSTANCE SUCH AS HONEY OR MOLASSES, COAT THE UTENSIL OR MEASURING CUP WITH A LITTLE COOKING-OIL SPRAY–THE HONEY WILL SLIDE RIGHT OUT, LEAVING NOTHING BEHIND.

IF YOU NEED SOUR CREAM BUT DON'T HAVE ANY ON HAND, YOU CAN ALWAYS IMPROVISE. TAKE NORMAL CREAM AND ADD SOME LEMON JUICE TO IT. STIR THE MIXTURE AND USE IN THE RECIPE AS SOUR CREAM.

TO KEEP SALT FROM CLUMPING TOGETHER IN YOUR SALT SHAKER, ADD SOME UNCOOKED RICE TO IT.

WHEN COOKING PANCAKES, THEY ARE READY TO TURN WHEN BUBBLES APPEAR ON THE SURFACE OF THE PANCAKE.

IF YOU HAVE BURNED THE BASE OF A FRYING PAN OR SAUCEPAN, ADD WATER AND BAKING SODA AND BRING TO A BOIL. BOIL FOR 5 MINUTES. THE SODA HELPS TO SOFTEN THE BURNED BITS.

KNOW YOUR SPUDS

THERE ARE A NUMBER OF VARIETIES AVAILABLE SO CHOOSING WHICH TYPE TO USE CAN BE CONFUSING. GENERALLY POTATOES CAN BE DIVIDED INTO FLOURY AND WAXY VARIETIES. FLOURY VARIETIES SUCH AS RUSSET, RUSSET BURBANK AND IDAHO ARE LOW IN MOISTURE AND HIGH IN STARCH, MAKING THEM PERFECT FOR BAKING, FRYING AND MASHING. WAXY VARIETIES SUCH AS YELLOW FINN, RED BLISS, WHITE ROSE AND PURPLE PERUVIAN ARE LOWER IN STARCH AND HIGHER IN MOISTURE, AND WILL BOIL BEAUTIFULLY AND CUT INTO CLEAN SLICES FOR SALAD. YUKON GOLD AND CRESCENT ARE ALL-PURPOSE VARIETIES THAT WILL BOIL, BAKE, FRY AND MASH WELL.

USING LEFTOVERS

SOUPS, FRITTATAS AND PASTA SAUCES ARE WONDERFUL WAYS TO USE UP LEFTOVER BITS AND PIECES. ANY LEFTOVER VEGGIES LIKE A FLORET OF BROCCOLI, A FEW MUSHROOMS OR A PIECE OF PEPPER CAN EASILY BE CHOPPED UP AND SAUTEED WITH SOME ONION AND MADE INTO A VEGGIE FRITTATA, ADDED TO A SOUP OR TURNED INTO A LOVELY HEALTHY PASTA SAUCE.

BREAD

BREAD IS ALWAYS BEST WHEN FRESH, BUT FEW OF US CAN GET THROUGH A WHOLE LOAF AT ONCE. IF YOU'RE ONLY STORING IT FOR A DAY OR TWO, KEEP IT IN A BREAD BOX OR PAPER BAG TO PREVENT IT FROM DRYING OUT. YOU MAY STILL NEED TO SLICE OFF AND THROW OUT THE EXPOSED SURFACE, BUT THE BREAD UNDER THAT SHOULD STILL BE OK. STORING BREAD IN THE FRIDGE MAKES IT TURN STALE VERY QUICKLY. BREAD FREEZES VERY WELL, SO IF YOU WANT TO STORE A FRESH LOAF FOR A LONGER PERIOD, CUT IT INTO SLICES, SEPARATE SLICES WITH PARCHMENT PAPER, AND FREEZE THEM IN SEALED PLASTIC BAGS.

PASTRY PERFECT

TO LINE A PIE OR TART PAN WITH BUTTER-RICH PASTRY, COARSELY GRATE THE PASTRY STRAIGHT INTO THE PAN AND PRESS DOWN WITH YOUR FINGERTIPS. THIS HELPS TO MAKE SURE THAT THE PASTRY IS NOT OVERWORKED, WHICH CAN EASILY HAPPEN WHEN ROLLING IT. WHEN PASTRY IS OVERWORKED, IT WILL TOUGHEN AND SHRINK DURING COOKING.

REFRESHING VEGETABLES

SOME VEGETABLES, IN PARTICULAR GREEN BEANS, SNOW PEAS AND SUGAR SNAP PEAS, TEND TO LOSE THEIR BRIGHT GREEN COLOR AND CRUNCHY TEXTURE AFTER THEY'RE COOKED. TO PREVENT THIS, PLUNGE THEM INTO A BOWL OF ICED WATER STRAIGHT AFTER COOKING. THIS WILL STOP THEM FROM CONTINUING TO COOK AND KEEP THEM BRIGHT AND CRUNCHY.

PASTA PERFECT

IT IS A MYTH THAT ADDING OIL TO THE COOKING WATER WILL PREVENT THE PASTA FROM STICKING TOGETHER, AS IT SIMPLY SITS ON THE SURFACE. INSTEAD, MAKE SURE THAT YOU HAVE PLENTY OF RAPIDLY BOILING, WELL-SALTED WATER. ADD THE PASTA, GIVE IT A GOOD STIR AND REPLACE THE LID OF THE POT ONLY UNTIL THE WATER COMES BACK TO A BOIL, THEN REMOVE THE LID. STIR THE PASTA FREQUENTLY AND DRAIN WHEN IT IS AL DENTE. TOSS HOT PASTA WITH HOT SAUCE QUICKLY WITHOUT RINSING IT.

YOU SHOULD ALWAYS RESERVE A CUP OR TWO OF THE PASTA COOKING WATER TO ADD TO THE PASTA AT A LATER STAGE, AS THE PASTA WILL ABSORB THE SAUCE YOU ARE SERVING IT WITH AND MAY DRY OUT. THE PASTA COOKING WATER, WHICH IS FLAVORED BY THE SALT AND ENRICHED STARCH FROM THE PASTA, WILL REFRESH THE PASTA.

CHEESE PLEASE

CHEESE SHOULD ALWAYS BE EATEN AT ROOM TEMPERATURE, NOT STRAIGHT OUT OF THE FRIDGE, SO REMOVE IT FROM THE FRIDGE AN HOUR OR TWO BEFORE USING.

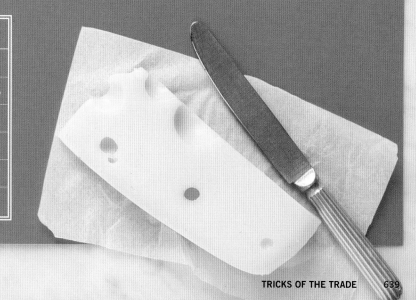

Conversion chart

MEASURES

All cup and spoon measurements are level. The most accurate way to measure dry ingredients is to use a spoon to fill the measuring cup, without packing or scooping with the cup, and leveling off the top with a straight edge.

When measuring liquids, use a clear glass or plastic liquid measuring cup with markings on the side.

We use large eggs with an average weight of 2 ounces. Do not substitute with extra large eggs, as the higher amount of protein and volume of the whites can make baked goods tough and affect the outcome of recipes.

.

DRY MEASURES

METRIC	IMPERIAL
15g	½oz
30g	1oz
60g	2oz
90g	3oz
125g	4oz (¼lb)
155g	5oz
185g	6oz
220g	7oz
250g	8oz (½lb)
280g	9oz
315g	10oz
345g	11oz
375g	12oz (¾lb)
410g	13oz
440g	14oz
470g	15oz
500g	16oz (1lb)
750g	24oz (1½lb)
1kg	32oz (2lb)

LIQUID MEASURES

METRIC	IMPERIAL
30ml	1 fluid oz
60ml	2 fluid oz
100ml	3 fluid oz
125ml	4 fluid oz
150ml	5 fluid oz
190ml	6 fluid oz
250ml	8 fluid oz
300ml	10 fluid oz (½ pint)
500ml	16 fluid oz
600ml	20 fluid oz (1 pint)
1000ml (1 litre)	1¾ pints

LENGTH MEASURES

METRIC	IMPERIAL
3mm	⅛in
6mm	¼in
1cm	½in
2cm	¾in
2.5cm	1in
5cm	2in
6cm	2½in
8cm	3in
10cm	4in
13cm	5in
15cm	6in
18cm	7in
20cm	8in
23cm	9in
25cm	10in
28cm	11in
30cm	12in (1ft)

OVEN TEMPERATURES

These oven temperatures are only a guide for conventional ovens. For fan-forced ovens, check the manufacturer's manual.

	°C (CELSIUS)	°F (FAHRENHEIT)	GAS MARK
Very slow	120	250	½
Slow	150	275-300	1-2
Moderately slow	160	325	3
Moderate	180	350-375	4-5
Moderately hot	200	400	6
Hot	220	425-450	7-8
Very hot	240	475	9

Glossary

ALLSPICE
Also called pimento or Jamaican pepper; tastes like a combination of nutmeg, cumin, clove and cinnamon. Available whole or ground.

ALMONDS
Flat, pointy-tipped nuts with a pitted brown shell enclosing a creamy white kernel that is covered by a brown skin.
blanched brown skins removed.
candied toffee-coated almonds.
sliced paper-thin slices.
ground also known as almond meal; nuts are powdered to a coarse flour-like texture.
slivered small pieces cut lengthwise.

ARROWROOT
A starch made from the rhizome of a Central American plant, used mostly as a thickening agent.

ARUGULA
Also called rocket, rugula and rucola; peppery green leaf eaten raw in salads or used in cooking. Baby leaves are smaller and less peppery. See also page 107.

ARTICHOKES
globe large flower-bud of a member of the thistle family; it has tough petal-like leaves, and is edible in part when cooked. See also page 216.
hearts tender center of the globe artichoke; can be harvested from the plant after the prickly choke is removed. Cooked hearts can be bought from delicatessens or canned in brine.
Jerusalem neither from Jerusalem nor an artichoke, this crunchy brown-skinned tuber tastes a bit like a water chestnut and belongs to the sunflower family. Eat raw in salads or cooked like potatoes. See also page 218.

ASAFOETIDA
The dried and ground resin of a giant fennel, notorious for its penetrating "rotten" smell, which is toned down in cooking. Its pungent flavor suggests fermented garlic. Use this spice sparingly with lentils and in fish and vegetable curries. See also page 416.

BAHARAT
An aromatic spice blend, includes some or all of the following: ginger, black pepper, allspice, dried chili flakes, paprika, coriander seeds, cinnamon, clove, sumac, nutmeg, cumin seeds and cardamom seeds. It is used through the Middle East; here, it is often sold as Lebanese seven-spice, and can be found in Middle Eastern food stores and some delicatessens. See also page 416.

BAKING POWDER
A rising agent consisting mainly of two parts cream of tartar to one part baking soda. See also gluten-free baking powder.

BAKING SODA
Leavening agent for baking.

BANANA LEAVES
Used to line steamers and wrap food; sold in bundles in Asian food shops, greengrocers and supermarkets. Cut leaves, on both sides of center stem, into required sized pieces then immerse in hot water or hold over a flame until pliable enough to wrap or fold over food; secure with kitchen string, toothpicks or skewers.

BARLEY
A nutritious grain used in soups and stews. Hulled barley, the least processed, is high in fiber. Pearl barley has had the husk removed and then has been steamed and polished so that only the "pearl" of the original grain remains, much the same as white rice.

BAY LEAVES
Aromatic leaves from the bay tree available fresh or dried; adds a strong, slightly peppery flavor.

BEANS
adzuki small russet beans with a cream stripe. Thin-skinned and sweetish, they are used in Japan in a paste for desserts and cakes, and are also good in stews and for sprouting. See also page 496.
black also called turtle beans or black kidney beans; an earthy-flavored dried bean completely different from the better-known Chinese black beans (fermented soybeans). Used mostly in Mexican and South American cooking. See also page 496.
black-eyed also called black-eyed peas or cow peas. Mild-flavored and thin-skinned so they cook faster than most other beans. Often served in the southern states with pork and cornbread. See also page 496.
borlotti also called Roman beans or pink beans, can be eaten fresh or dried. Interchangeable with pinto beans due to their similarity in appearance–pale pink or beige with dark red streaks. See also page 216.
broad also called fava, windsor and horse beans; available dried, fresh, canned and frozen. Fresh should be peeled twice (discarding both the outer long green pod and the beige-green tough inner shell); the frozen beans have had their pods removed but the beige shell still needs removal. See also pages 216 and 497.
butter cans labeled butter beans are, in fact, cannellini beans. Confusingly butter is also another name for lima beans, sold both dried and canned; a large beige bean with a mealy texture and mild taste.

cannellini small white bean similar in appearance and flavor to other *phaseolus vulgaris* varieties (great northern, navy or haricot). Available dried or canned. See also page 497.

green also known as french or string beans (although the tough string they once had has generally been bred out of them), this long thin fresh bean is consumed in its entirety once cooked. See also page 216.

haricot the haricot bean family includes navy beans and cannellini. All are mild-flavored white beans that can be interchangeable. See also page 496.

kidney medium-sized red bean, slightly floury in texture yet sweet in flavor; sold dried or canned, it's found in bean mixes and is used in chili con carne.

lima large, flat kidney-shaped, beige dried and canned beans. Also known as butter beans.

snake long (about 15 inches), thin, round, fresh green beans, Asian in origin, with a taste similar to green or french beans. Used most frequently in stir-fries, they are also known as yard-long beans because of their length. See also page 216.

soy the most nutritious of all legumes; high in protein and low in carbohydrate and the source of products such as tofu, soy milk, soy sauce, tamari and miso. Also available dried and canned.

sprouts tender new growths of assorted beans and seeds germinated for consumption as sprouts.

white a generic term for canned or dried cannellini, haricot, navy or great northern beans belonging to the same family, *phaseolus vulgaris*.

BEEF

chuck inexpensive cut from the neck and shoulder area; good ground and slow-cooked.

corned beef usually top round or brisket; little fat, cut from the upper leg and

cured. Sold cryovac-packed in brine.

gravy boneless stewing beef from shin; slow-cooked, imbues stocks, soups and casseroles with gelatin richness. Cut crosswise, with bone in, is osso buco.

ground very finely chopped.

New York cut boneless striploin steak.

oxtail a flavorful cut originally from the ox but today more likely to be from any beef cattle; requires long, slow cooking so it is perfect for curries and stews.

rib eye cut from the muscle running behind the shoulder along the spine. Also known as cube roll, cuts include standing rib roast and prime rib.

rump boneless tender cut from the upper part of the round (hindquarter). Cut into steaks, good for barbecuing; as one piece, great as a roast.

skirt steak lean, flavorful coarse-grained cut from the inner thigh. Needs slow-cooking; good for stews or casseroles.

tenderloin filet fine texture, most expensive and extremely tender.

topside roast a cut from the rump; commonly used for making roast beef.

t-bone sirloin steak with bone in and filet eye attached.

BEETS

Firm, round root vegetable. See also page 216.

BELL PEPPER

Always discard seeds and membranes before use.

BESAN

See flour.

BETEL LEAVES

Grown and consumed in India and throughout Southeast Asia, betel leaves are used raw as a wrap, cooked as a vegetable, or chopped and used as both a herb and a medicine. They are available at some greengrocers and most Asian food stores, especially

those specializing in Vietnamese produce. See also page 349.

BLACK BEAN SAUCE

An Asian cooking sauce made from salted and fermented soybeans, spices and wheat flour; used most often in stir-fries.

BOK CHOY

Also known as buk choy, pak choi, Chinese white cabbage or Chinese chard; has a fresh, mild mustard taste. Use stems and leaves, stir-fried or braised. Baby bok choy, also called pak kat farang or shanghai bok choy, is much smaller and more tender. Its mildly acrid, distinctively appealing taste has made it one of the most commonly used Asian greens. See also page 348.

BREAD CRUMBS

fresh bread, usually white, processed into crumbs.

Japanese also called panko; available in two kinds: larger pieces and fine crumbs; have a lighter texture than Western-style ones. Available from Asian food stores and some supermarkets.

packaged prepared fine-textured but crunchy white bread crumbs; good for coating foods that are to be fried.

stale crumbs made by grating, blending or processing 1- or 2-day-old bread.

BRIOCHE

French in origin; a rich, yeast-leavened, cake-like bread made with butter and eggs. Available from bakeries or specialty bread shops.

BROCCOLINI

A cross between broccoli and Chinese kale; long asparagus-like stems with a long loose floret, both completely edible. Resembles broccoli but is milder and sweeter in taste. See also page 217.

BUCKWHEAT
A herb in the same plant family as rhubarb; not a cereal so it is gluten-free. Available as flour; ground (cracked) into coarse, medium or fine granules (kasha) and used similarly to polenta; or groats, the whole kernel sold roasted as a cereal product.

BULGUR
Also called burghul wheat; hulled steamed wheat kernels that, once dried, are crushed into various sized grains. Used in Middle Eastern dishes such as falafel, kibbeh and tabbouleh. Is not the same as cracked wheat. See also page 496.

BUTTER
We use salted butter unless stated otherwise; 1 stick is equal to 4 ounces. Butter is basically churned pasteurized cream. Salted is the most popular one sold in supermarkets. Unsalted or "sweet" butter has no salt added and is perhaps the most popular butter among pastry chefs.

BUTTER LETTUCE
Small, round, loosely formed heads with a sweet flavor; its soft, buttery-textured leaves range from pale green on the outer leaves to pale yellow-green inner leaves.

BUTTERMILK
See milk.

CAPERBERRIES
Olive-sized fruit formed after the buds of the caper bush have flowered; they are usually sold pickled in a vinegar brine with stalks intact.

CAPERS
The grey-green buds of a warm climate (usually Mediterranean) shrub, sold either dried and salted or pickled in a vinegar brine; tiny young ones, called baby capers, are also available both in brine or dried in salt. Their pungent taste adds piquancy to a tapenade, sauces and condiments.

CARAWAY SEEDS
The small, half-moon-shaped dried seed from a member of the parsley family; adds a sharp anise flavor when used in both sweet and savory dishes. Used widely in foods such as rye bread, harissa and the classic Hungarian fresh cheese, liptauer.

CARDAMOM
A spice native to India and used extensively in its cuisine; can be purchased in pod, seed or ground form. Has a distinctive aromatic, sweetly rich flavor and is one of the world's most expensive spices.

CASHEWS
Plump, kidney-shaped, golden-brown nuts with a distinctive sweet, buttery flavor and containing about 48 percent fat. Because of this high fat content, cashews should be kept, sealed tightly, under refrigeration to avoid becoming rancid. We use roasted unsalted cashews in this book, unless otherwise stated; they're available from health-food stores and most supermarkets. Roasting cashews brings out their intense nutty flavor.

CAYENNE PEPPER
A thin-fleshed, long, extremely hot dried red chili, usually purchased ground.

CELERIAC
Tuberous root with bumpy brown skin, white flesh and a celery-like flavor. Keep peeled celeriac in acidulated water to stop it from discoloring. It can be grated and eaten raw in salads; used in soups and stews; boiled and mashed like potatoes; or sliced thinly and deep-fried. See also page 217.

CHAR SIU
Also called Chinese barbecue sauce; a paste-like ingredient dark-red-brown in color with a sharp sweet and spicy flavor. Made with fermented soybeans, honey and various spices; can be diluted and used as a marinade or brushed onto grilling meat.

CHEESE
blue mold-treated cheeses mottled with blue veining. Varieties include firm and crumbly stilton types and mild, creamy brie-like cheeses.
bocconcini from the diminutive of "boccone", meaning mouthful in Italian; walnut-sized, baby mozzarella, a delicate, semi-soft, white cheese traditionally made from buffalo milk. Sold fresh, it spoils rapidly so will only keep, refrigerated in brine, for 1 or 2 days at the most. See also page 600.
brie soft-ripened cow-milk cheese with a delicate, creamy texture and a rich, sweet taste that varies from buttery to mushroomy. Best served at room temperature after a brief period of aging, brie should have a bloomy white rind and creamy, voluptuous center, which becomes runny with ripening. See also page 600.
camembert a luscious, buttery cheese with a thin edible, aromatic rind; it is probably the most famous and most popular soft French cheese in the world. It is best eaten at room temperature. See also page 600.
cottage fresh, white, unripened curd cheese with a grainy consistency and a fat content of 15 to 55 percent. See also page 600.
cream a soft cow-milk cheese, its fat content ranges from 14 to 33 percent.
edam a semi-hard Dutch cheese made from part-skimmed cow's milk. Mild

in flavor and supple in texture when young, it becomes stronger, dry and hard when mature. See also page 600.

feta Greek in origin; a crumbly textured goat- or sheep-milk cheese with a sharp, salty taste. Ripened and stored in salted whey; particularly good cubed and tossed into salads. See also page 601.

fontina a smooth, firm Italian cow-milk cheese with a creamy, nutty taste and brown or red rind; an ideal melting or grilling cheese. See also page 601.

fromage frais a light, fresh French cheese that has the consistency of thick yogurt with a refreshing, slightly tart taste. Low fat varieties are available.

goat's made from goat's milk, has an earthy, strong taste. Available in soft, crumbly and firm textures, in various shapes and sizes, and sometimes rolled in ash or herbs. See also page 600.

gorgonzola a creamy Italian blue cheese with a mild, sweet taste; good as an accompaniment to fruit or used to flavor sauces (especially pasta). See also page 601.

gruyère a hard-rind Swiss cheese with small holes and a nutty, slightly salty flavor. A popular cheese for soufflés. See also page 601.

haloumi a Greek Cypriot cheese with a semi-firm, spongy texture and very salty sweet flavor. Ripened and stored in salted whey; best grilled or fried, and holds its shape well on being heated. Eat while still warm as it becomes tough and rubbery on cooling. See also page 601.

havarti a traditional, creamy, semi-hard cow's milk cheese from Denmark. This washed-rind cheese is mild in flavor and peppered with small holes and irregularities. See also page 601.

mascarpone an Italian fresh cultured-cream product made in much the same way as yogurt. Whiteish to creamy yellow in color, with a buttery-rich, luscious texture. Soft, creamy

and spreadable, it is used in Italian desserts and as an accompaniment to fresh fruit.

mozzarella soft, spun-curd cheese; originating in southern Italy where it was traditionally made from water-buffalo milk. Now generally made from cow's milk, it is the most popular pizza cheese because of its low melting point and elasticity when heated.

parmesan also called parmigiano; a hard, grainy cow-milk cheese originating in the Parma region of Italy. The curd for this cheese is salted in brine for a month, then aged for up to 2 years in humid conditions. Reggiano is the best parmesan, aged for a minimum 2 years and made only in the Italian region of Emilia-Romagna.

pecorino the Italian generic name for cheeses made from sheep milk. This family of hard, white to pale-yellow cheeses, traditionally made in the Italian winter and spring when sheep graze on natural pastures, have been matured for 8 to 12 months. They are classified according to the area in which they were produced–romano from Rome, sardo from Sardinia, toscano from Tuscany, etc. If you can't find it, use parmesan.

pizza cheese a commercial blend of varying proportions of processed grated mozzarella, cheddar and parmesan.

provolone a mild stretched-curd cheese similar to mozzarella when young, becoming hard, spicy and grainy the longer it's aged. Golden yellow in color, with a smooth waxy rind, provolone is a good all-purpose cheese used in cooking, for dessert with cheese, and shredded or flaked.

ricotta a soft, sweet, moist, white cow's milk cheese with a low fat content (8.5 percent) and a slightly grainy texture. The name roughly translates as "cooked again" and refers to ricotta's manufacture from a whey that is itself a by-product of other cheese-making.

roquefort considered the "king of cheeses", this is a blue cheese with a singularly pungent taste; made only from the milk of specially bred sheep and ripened in the damp limestone caves found under the village of Roquefort-sur-Soulzon in France. Has a sticky, bone-colored rind and, when ripe, the sharp, almost metallic-tasting interior is creamy and almost shiny.

Swiss generic name for a variety of slightly firm to hard Swiss cheeses, among them emmentaler and gruyère.

CHICKEN

barbecued we use cooked whole barbecued chickens weighing about 2 pounds apiece in our recipes. Skin discarded and bones removed, this size chicken provides 4 cups shredded meat or about 3 cups coarsely chopped meat.

breast filet breast halved, skinned and boned.

drumette small fleshy part of the wing between shoulder and elbow, trimmed to resemble a drumstick.

drumstick leg with skin and bone intact.

maryland leg and thigh still connected in a single piece; bones and skin intact.

small chicken also called spatchcock or poussin; no more than 6 weeks old, weighing a maximum of 1 pound. Spatchcock is also a cooking term to describe splitting a small chicken open, flattening then grilling.

tenderloin thin strip of meat lying just under the breast; good for stir-frying.

thigh skin and bone intact.

thigh cutlet thigh with skin and center bone intact; sometimes found skinned with bone intact.

thigh filet thigh with skin and center bone removed.

CHICKPEAS

Also called garbanzos or channa; an irregularly round, sandy-colored legume used extensively in

Mediterranean, Indian and Hispanic cooking. Firm texture even after cooking, a floury mouth-feel and robust nutty flavor; available canned or dried (reconstitute for several hours in cold water before use). See also page 497.

CHILI

Use rubber gloves when seeding and chopping fresh chilies because they can burn your skin. Whole chopped chilies with the seeds are spicier, so use less in recipes unless you remove the seeds before chopping.

ancho mild, dried chilies commonly used in Mexican cooking.

chipotle pronounced cheh-pote-lay. The name used for jalapeño chilies once they've been dried and smoked. With a deep, intensely smoky flavor, rather than a searing heat, chipotles are dark brown, almost black in color and wrinkled in appearance.

flakes also sold as crushed chili; dehydrated deep-red extremely fine slices and whole seeds.

green any unripened chili; also some particular varieties that are ripe when green, such as jalapeño, habanero, poblano or serrano.

jalapeño pronounced hah-lah-pain-yo. Fairly hot, medium-sized, plump, dark green chili; available pickled, sold canned or bottled, and fresh, from greengrocers.

long red available both fresh and dried; a generic term used for any moderately hot, long, thin chili (about 2½ to 3 inches long).

powder the Asian variety is the hottest, made from dried ground Thai chilies; can be used instead of fresh in the proportion of ½ teaspoon chili powder to 1 medium chopped fresh red chili.

sauce, sweet comparatively mild, fairly sticky and runny bottled sauce made from red chilies, sugar, garlic and white vinegar; used in Thai cooking.

Thai also known as "scuds"; tiny, very hot and bright red in color.

CHINESE BARBECUED DUCK
See duck

CHINESE BARBECUED PORK
See pork

CHINESE COOKING WINE
Also called hao hsing or Chinese rice wine; made from fermented rice, wheat, sugar and salt with a 13.5 percent alcohol content. Inexpensive and found in Asian food shops; can be replaced with mirin or sherry.

CHOCOLATE

baking chocolate also called compounded chocolate; good for cooking because it doesn't require tempering, and sets at room temperature. Made with vegetable fat instead of cocoa butter so it lacks the rich, buttery flavor of eating chocolate. Cocoa butter is the most expensive component in chocolate so the substitution of a vegetable fat means that baking chocolate is much cheaper to produce.

bittersweet also known as luxury chocolate; made of a high percentage of cocoa liquor and cocoa butter, and little added sugar. Unless stated otherwise, we use bittersweet chocolate in this book because it's ideal for use in desserts and cakes.

chocolate chips also called chocolate morsels; available in milk, white and dark chocolate. Made of cocoa liquor, cocoa butter, sugar and an emulsifier, these hold their shape in baking and are ideal for decorating.

couverture a term to describe a fine quality, very rich chocolate high in both cocoa butter and cocoa liquor. Requires tempering when used to coat but not if used in baking, mousses or fillings.

melts small disks of compounded milk, white or dark chocolate ideal for melting and molding.

milk most popular eating chocolate, mild and very sweet; similar in make-up to dark with the difference of the addition of milk solids.

white contains no cocoa solids but derives its sweet flavor from cocoa butter. Very sensitive to heat.

CHOCOLATE HAZELNUT SPREAD
Also known as Nutella; made of cocoa powder, hazelnuts, sugar and milk.

CHAYOTE
Choko or christophine are the other names for this South American tuber. Some describe its taste as bland, others say it is subtle. It can be used like a potato in recipes, but the skin has a sticky sap, so wear gloves when peeling it. Available early winter. See also page 217.

CHORIZO
Sausage of Spanish origin, made of coarsely ground pork and highly seasoned with garlic and chili.

CHOY SUM
Also known as pakaukeo or flowering cabbage, a member of the bok choy family; easy to identify with its long stems, light green leaves and yellow flowers. Stems and leaves are both edible, steamed or stir-fried. See also page 348.

CIABATTA
In Italian, the word means slipper, the traditional shape of this popular crisp-crusted, open-textured white sourdough bread. Often used for bruschetta.

CINNAMON
Available both in the piece (sticks or quills) and ground; one of the world's

most common spices, used universally as a sweet, fragrant flavoring in sweet and savory foods.

CLOVES
Dried flower buds of a tropical tree; can be used whole or in ground form. They have a strong scent and taste so should be used sparingly.

COCOA POWDER
Also known as unsweetened cocoa; cocoa beans (cacao seeds) that have been fermented, roasted, shelled, ground into powder, then cleared of most of the fat content.

COCONUT
cream obtained commercially from the first pressing of the coconut flesh alone, without the addition of water; the second pressing (less rich) is sold as coconut milk. Available in cans and cartons at most supermarkets.
dried concentrated, unsweetened and finely shredded coconut flesh.
extract synthetically produced from flavoring, oil and alcohol.
flaked dried flaked coconut flesh.
milk not the liquid found inside the fruit, which is called coconut water, but the diluted liquid from the second pressing of the white flesh of a mature coconut (the first pressing produces coconut cream). Available in cans and cartons at most supermarkets.
shredded thin strips of dried coconut flesh; can be sweetened or unsweetened.

COINTREAU
See liqueurs.

COOKING-OIL SPRAY
See oil.

CORAL LETTUCE
A soft-leafed lettuce with either red or green tightly crinkled leaves. Its leaves

have a delicate, sweet flavor so they're perfect with a mixture of lettuces. You'll often find coral as part of a mesclun mix. Use within two days of purchase and dress lightly. See also page 106.

CORN STARCH
Also known as cornflour. Available made from corn or wheat (wheat starch, gluten-free, gives a lighter texture in cakes); used as a thickening agent in cooking.

CORNICHON
French for gherkin, a very small variety of cucumber. Pickled, they are a traditional accompaniment to pâté, and are also served with fondue or raclette.

COUSCOUS
A fine, grain-like cereal product made from semolina, from the countries of North Africa. A semolina flour and water dough is sieved then dehydrated to produce minuscule even-sized pellets; it is rehydrated by steaming or adding a warm liquid and swells to three or four times its original size; eaten like rice with a tagine, as a side dish or salad ingredient. See also page 497.

CRANBERRIES
Available dried and frozen; with a rich, astringent flavor and can be used in cooking sweet and savory dishes. The dried version can usually be substituted for or with other dried fruit.

CREAM
heavy also known as pure cream. It has no additives and contains a minimum fat content of 35 percent. If a recipe here calls for an unspecified cream, this is the one we use.
light similar to half and half with a fat content between 18–30 percent.
sour cream a thick, commercially-cultured sour cream with a minimum fat content of 35 percent.

CREAM OF TARTAR
The acid ingredient in baking powder; added to confectionery mixtures to help prevent sugar from crystallizing. Keeps frostings creamy and improves volume when beating egg whites.

CREME FRAICHE
A mature, naturally fermented cream (minimum fat content 35 percent) with a velvety texture and slightly tangy, nutty flavor. Crème fraîche, a French variation of sour cream, can boil without curdling and is used in sweet and savory dishes.

CUCUMBER, LEBANESE
Short, slender and thin-skinned cucumber. Probably the most popular variety because of its tender, edible skin, tiny, yielding seeds, and sweet, fresh and flavorful taste.

CUMIN
Also known as comino; resembling caraway in size, cumin is the dried seed of a plant related to the parsley family. Its spicy, almost curry-like flavor is essential to the traditional foods of Mexico, India, North Africa and the Middle East. Available dried as seeds or ground. Black cumin seeds are smaller than standard cumin, and dark brown rather than true black; they are mistakenly confused with kalonji.

CURLY ENDIVE
Also known as frisée, curly endive belongs to the chicory family and has its characteristic bitterness played against grassy freshness. Particularly good with beets and also used in mesclun. It will keep in the refrigerator, unwashed, for five days. See also page 106.

CURRANTS, DRIED
Tiny, almost black raisins so-named after a grape variety that originated in Corinth, Greece.

CURRY PASTES

Make your own with the recipes found in this book or purchase the ready-made pastes from the supermarket. The heat intensity of ready-made pastes may differ from brand to brand, so adjust the amount used according to your taste.

green hottest of the traditional Thai pastes; particularly good in chicken and vegetable curries, and a great addition to stir-fry and noodle dishes.

korma a classic north Indian sauce with a rich yet delicate coconut flavor and hints of garlic, ginger and coriander.

massaman rich, spicy flavor reminiscent of Middle Eastern cooking; favored by southern Thai cooks for use in hot and sour stew-like curries and satay sauces.

panang based on the curries of Penang, an island off the northwest coast of Malaysia, close to the Thai border. A complex, sweet and milder variation of red curry paste; good with seafood and for adding to soups and salad dressings.

red probably the most popular Thai curry paste; a hot blend of different flavors that complements the richness of pork, duck and seafood. Also works well stirred into marinades and sauces.

rogan josh a paste of medium heat, from the Kashmir region of India, made from fresh chilies or paprika, tomato and spices, especially cardamom. It sometimes has red beet added to make it a dark red.

tikka in Indian cooking, the word "masala" loosely translates as paste and the word "tikka" means a bite-sized piece of meat, poultry or fish, or sometimes a cutlet. Tikka paste is any maker's choice of spices and oils, mixed into a mild paste, frequently colored red. Used for marinating or for brushing over meat, seafood or poultry, before or during cooking instead of as an ingredient.

vindaloo a Goan combination of vinegar, tomatoes, pepper and other spices that exemplifies the Portuguese influence on this part of India's coast.

yellow one of the mildest Thai pastes; similar in appearance to Indian curries as they both include yellow chili and fresh turmeric. Good blended with coconut in vegetable, rice and noodle dishes.

CURRY POWDER

A blend of ground spices used for making Indian and some southeast Asian dishes. Consists of some of the following spices: dried chili, cumin, cinnamon, coriander, fennel, mace, fenugreek, cardamom and turmeric. Available mild or hot.

CUSTARD POWDER

Instant mixture used to make pouring custard; similar to flavored instant pudding mixes.

DAIKON

Also called white radish; an everyday fixture at the Japanese table, this long, white horseradish has a wonderful, sweet flavor. After peeling, eat it raw in salads or shredded as a garnish; also great when sliced or cubed and cooked in stir-fries and casseroles. The flesh is white but the skin can be either white or black; buy those that are firm and unwrinkled from Asian food shops. See also page 219.

DASHI

The basic fish and seaweed stock that accounts for the distinctive flavor of many Japanese dishes, such as soups and various casserole dishes. Made from dried bonito (a type of tuna) flakes and kombu (kelp); instant dashi (dashi-no-moto) is available in powder, granules and liquid concentrate from Asian food shops.

DATES

Fruit of the date palm tree, eaten fresh or dried. About 1½ inches in length, oval and plump, thin-skinned, with a honey-sweet flavor and sticky texture.

DRAGÉES

Minuscule metallic-looking but edible confectionery balls used in cake decorating; available in silver, gold or various colors.

DRAGON FRUIT

The fruit of a pitaya cactus. The flesh, eaten raw, is tasty and mildly sweet, a little like the flavor of kiwifruit. Scoop the flesh and seeds out of the chilled fruit with a teaspoon. See also page 516.

DRIED CHINESE SAUSAGE

Also called lap cheong; highly spiced, bright red, thin pork sausages. The meat is preserved by the high spice content and can be kept at room temperature.

DUCK

We use whole ducks in some recipes; available from specialty markets and some supermarkets.

breast filets boneless whole breasts, with the skin on.

Chinese barbecued traditionally cooked in special ovens in China; dipped into and brushed during roasting with a sticky sweet coating made from soy sauce, sherry, ginger, five-spice, star anise and hoisin sauce. Available from Asian food shops as well as dedicated Chinese barbecued meat shops.

maryland thigh and drumstick still connected, skin on.

DUKKAH

An Egyptian specialty spice mixture made up of roasted nuts, seeds and an array of aromatic spices.

DURIAN

Famous as the fruit that "smells like hell and tastes like heaven". To enjoy the taste without the smell, cut the sweet, aromatic flesh into pieces and soak in coconut milk for a day. See also page 517.

EGGPLANT
Also called aubergine. Ranging in size from tiny to very large and in color from pale green to deep purple. Can also be purchased char-grilled, packed in oil, in jars.

baby also called finger or Japanese eggplant; very small and slender, it can be used without disgorging.

pea tiny, about the size of peas; sometimes known by their Thai name, "makeua puang". Sold in clusters of 10 to 15 eggplants, similar to vine-ripened cherry tomatoes; very bitter in flavor, a quality suited to balance rich, sweet coconut-sauced Thai curries. Available in Asian greengrocers and food shops, fresh or pickled.

Thai found in a variety of different sizes and colors, from a long, thin, purplish-green one to a hard, round, golf-ball size with a white-streaked pale-green skin. This last looks like a small unripe tomato and is the most popular eggplant used in Thai and Vietnamese curries and stir-fries.

EGGS
We use large chicken eggs weighing an average of 2 ounces unless stated otherwise in the recipes in this book. If a recipe calls for raw or barely cooked eggs, exercise caution if there is a salmonella problem in your area, particularly in food eaten by children and pregnant women.

ENDIVE
Also known as belgian endive; related to and confused with chicory. A versatile vegetable, it tastes as good cooked as it does eaten raw. Grown in darkness like white asparagus to prevent it from becoming green; looks somewhat like a tightly furled, cream-

to very light-green cigar. The leaves can be removed and used to hold a canapé filling; the whole vegetable can be opened up, stuffed then baked or casseroled; and the leaves can be tossed in a salad with other vegetables. See also page 107.

FENNEL
Also called finocchio or anise; a crunchy green vegetable slightly resembling celery that's eaten raw in salads; fried as an accompaniment; or used as an ingredient in soups and sauces. Also the name given to the dried seeds of the plant, which have a stronger licorice flavor. See also page 218.

FENUGREEK
Hard, dried seed usually sold ground as an astringent spice powder. Good with seafood and in chutneys, fenugreek helps mask unpleasant odors. See also page 416.

FISH SAUCE
Called naam pla if Thai-made, nuoc naam if Vietnamese; the two are almost identical. Made from pulverized salted fermented fish (most often anchovies); has a pungent smell and strong taste. Available in varying degrees of intensity, so use according to your taste.

FIVE-SPICE POWDER
Although the ingredients vary from country to country, five-spice is usually a fragrant mixture of ground cinnamon, cloves, star anise, sichuan pepper and fennel seeds. Used in Chinese and other Asian cooking; available from most supermarkets or Asian food shops.

FLOUR
besan also called chickpea flour or gram; made from ground chickpeas so it's gluten-free and high in protein. Used in Indian cooking to make dumplings, noodles and chapati; for a

batter coating for deep-frying; and as a sauce thickener.

buckwheat see buckwheat.

all-purpose unbleached wheat flour is the best for baking: the gluten content ensures a strong dough, which produces a light result.

rice very fine, almost powdery, gluten-free flour; made from ground white rice. Used in baking, as a thickener, and in some Asian noodles and desserts. Another variety, made from glutinous sweet rice, is used for chinese dumplings and rice paper.

self-rising all-purpose flour with baking powder and salt added; make it yourself in the proportion of 1 cup flour to 2 teaspoons baking powder.

whole wheat also known as whole grain flour; milled with the wheat germ so it's higher in fiber and more nutritional than all-purpose flour.

FOOD COLORING
A vegetable-based substance available in liquid, paste or gel form. Used to color icings, cake mixtures or sugar.

FRENCH BREAD STICK
A long, narrow cylindrical loaf with a crisp brown crust and a light chewy interior. Also called French loaf.

FROMAGE FRAIS
See cheese.

GAI LAN
Also called gai larn, chinese broccoli and chinese kale; green vegetable appreciated more for its stems than its coarse leaves. Can be served steamed and stir-fried, in soups and noodle dishes. One of the most popular Asian greens, best known as a dish with dim sum, where it's steamed then sprinkled with a mixture of oyster sauce and sesame oil. See also page 349.

GALANGAL
Also known as ka or lengkaus if fresh and laos if dried and powdered; a root, similar to ginger in its use. It has a hot-sour ginger-citrusy flavor; used in fish curries and soups.

GARAM MASALA
Literally meaning blended spices in its northern Indian place of origin; based on varying proportions of cardamom, cinnamon, cloves, coriander, fennel and cumin, roasted and ground together. Black pepper and chili can be added for a hotter version. See also page 417.

GELATIN
A thickening agent. We use dried (powdered) gelatin; it's also available in sheet form known as leaf gelatin. Three teaspoons of dried gelatin (¼ ounce or one packet) is about the same as four leaves. The two types are interchangable but leaf gelatin gives a much clearer mixture than dried gelatin.

GHEE
Clarified butter; with the milk solids removed, this fat has a high smoking point so it can be heated to a high temperature without burning. Used as a cooking medium in Indian recipes.

GINGER
candied fresh ginger root preserved in sugar. It is used in baked goods and eaten as a treatment for nausea.
fresh also called green or root ginger; the thick gnarled root of a tropical plant. Can be kept, peeled, covered with dry sherry in a jar and refrigerated, or frozen in an airtight container.
ground also called powdered ginger; used as a flavoring in baking but cannot be substituted for fresh ginger.
pickled pink or red colored; available, packaged, from Asian food shops. Pickled paper-thin shavings of ginger

in a mixture of vinegar, sugar and natural coloring; used in Japanese cooking.

GLACE CHERRIES
Also called candied cherries; boiled in heavy sugar syrup and then dried.

GLACE FRUIT
Fruit such as peaches, pineapple and orange cooked in heavy sugar syrup and then dried.

GLUCOSE SYRUP
Also known as liquid glucose, made from wheat starch; used in jam and confectionery making. Available at health food stores and supermarkets.

GLUTEN-FREE BAKING POWDER
Used as a leavening agent in bread, cake, pastry or pudding mixtures. Suitable for people with an allergic response to gluten or seeking an alternative to everyday baking powder. See also baking powder.

GOLDEN SYRUP
A by-product of refined sugarcane; pure maple syrup or honey can be substituted. Golden syrup and treacle (a thicker, darker syrup not unlike molasses), also known as flavor syrups, are similar sugar products made by partly breaking down sugar into its component parts and adding water. Treacle is more viscous, and has a stronger flavor and aroma than golden syrup (which has been refined more and contains fewer impurities so it's lighter in color and more fluid). Both can be used in baking and for making certain confectionery items.

GOW GEE WRAPPERS
See wrappers.

GRAND MARNIER
See liqueurs.

GRAPEVINE LEAVES
From early spring, fresh grapevine leaves can be found in most specialty greengrocers. Alternatively, cryovac-packages containing about 60 leaves in brine can be found in Middle Eastern food shops and some delis; these must be rinsed well and dried before using. Used as wrappers of savory fillings for Mediterranean foods.

GREEN PAPAYA
See Papaya. See also page 348.

HARISSA
A North African paste made from dried red chilies, garlic, olive oil and caraway seeds; can be used as a rub for meat, an ingredient in sauces and dressings, or eaten as a condiment. It is available from Middle Eastern food shops and some supermarkets. See also page 417.

HAZELNUTS
Also called filberts; plump, grape-sized, rich, sweet nut having a brown skin that is removed by rubbing heated nuts together vigorously in a tea towel.
ground also called hazelnut meal; is made by grounding the hazelnuts to a coarse flour texture for use in baking.
oil a mono-unsaturated oil, made in France, extracted from crushed hazelnuts.

HERBS
basil *holy* also called kra pao or hot basil; different from Thai and sweet basil, having an almost hot, spicy flavor similar to clove. Used in many Thai dishes, especially curries; distinguished from Thai basil by tiny "hairs" on its leaves and stems.
sweet the most common type of basil; used extensively in Italian dishes and one of the main ingredients in pesto. See also page 229
Thai also called horapa; different from

holy basil and sweet basil in both look and taste, with smaller leaves and purplish stems. It has a slight aniseed taste and is one of the identifying flavors of Thai food. See also page 229.

chervil also called cicily; mildly fennel-flavored member of the parsley family with curly dark-green leaves. Available fresh and dried but, like all herbs, is best used fresh; like coriander and parsley, its delicate flavor diminishes the longer it's cooked. See also page 228.

chives related to the onion and leek; has a subtle onion flavor. Used more for flavor than as an ingredient; chopped finely, they're good in sauces, dressings, omelettes or as a garnish. *garlic chives* also known as Chinese chives; are strongly flavored, have flat leaves and are eaten as a vegetable, usually in stir-fries. See also page 228.

coriander also called cilantro, pak chee or Chinese parsley; bright-green-leafed herb with both pungent aroma and taste. Used as an ingredient in a wide variety of cuisines. Often stirred into or sprinkled over a dish just before serving for maximum impact as, like other leafy herbs, its characteristics diminish with cooking. Both the stems and roots of coriander are used in Thai cooking: wash well before chopping. Coriander seeds are dried and sold either whole or ground, and neither form tastes remotely like the fresh leaf. See also page 228.

dill also called dill weed; used fresh or dried, in seed form or ground. Its anise/celery sweetness flavors the food of Scandinavian countries, Germany and Greece. Its feathery, frond-like fresh leaves are grassier and more subtle than the dried version or the seeds (which slightly resemble caraway in flavor). Use dill leaves with smoked salmon and sour cream, poached fish or roast chicken; use the seeds with simply cooked vegetables, or home-baked dark breads. See also page 228.

marjoram closely related to and similar in flavor to oregano, but milder and sweeter. Delicious in herb mixtures for omelettes, stuffings, herb scones and herb and cream cheese sandwiches. As with oregano, many chefs prefer dried marjoram to fresh. See also page 229.

mint the most commonly used variety of mint is spearmint; it has pointed, bright-green leaves and a fresh flavor.

oregano a herb, also known as wild marjoram; has a woody stalk and clumps of tiny, dark-green leaves. Has a pungent, peppery flavor. See also page 228.

parsley a versatile herb with a fresh, earthy flavor. There are about 30 varieties of curly parsley; the flat-leaf variety (also called continental or Italian parsley) is stronger in flavor and darker in color. See also page 229.

rosemary pungent herb with long, thin pointy leaves; use large and small sprigs, and the leaves are usually chopped finely.

sage pungent herb with narrow, grey-green leaves; slightly bitter with a slightly musty mint aroma. Refrigerate fresh sage wrapped in a paper towel and sealed in a plastic bag for up to 4 days. Dried sage comes whole, crumbled or ground. It should be stored in a cool, dark place for no more than three months. See also page 229.

tarragon French tarragon, with its subtle aniseed flavor, complements chicken, eggs and veal, and is perfect in a béarnaise sauce. It is also one of the herbs that make up the French fines herbs. Russian and Mexican tarragons are slightly coarser in taste. See also page 229.

thyme a basic herb of French cuisine it's widely used in Mediterranean countries to flavor meats and sauces. A member of the mint family, it has tiny grey-green leaves that give off a

pungent minty, light-lemon aroma. Dried thyme comes in both leaf and powder form. Dried thyme should be stored in a cool, dark place for no more than three months. Fresh thyme should be stored in the refrigerator, wrapped in a damp paper towel and placed in a sealed bag for no more than a few days.

Vietnamese mint not a mint at all, but a pungent and peppery narrow-leafed member of the buckwheat family. Not confined to Vietnam, it is also known as Cambodian mint, pak pai (Thailand), laksa leaf (Indonesia), daun kesom (Singapore) and rau ram in Vietnam. It is a common ingredient in Thai foods, particularly soups, salads and stir-fries. See also page 228.

HOISIN SAUCE
A thick, sweet and spicy Chinese barbecue sauce made from salted fermented soybeans, onions and garlic; used as a marinade or baste, or to accent stir-fries and barbecued or roasted foods. From Asian food shops and supermarkets.

HONEY
Look for artisinal honeys for baking; the type in squeeze bottles can be too thin for recipes.

HORSERADISH
A vegetable with edible green leaves but mainly grown for its long, pungent white root. Occasionally found fresh in specialty greengrocers and some Asian food shops, but commonly purchased in bottles at the supermarket in two forms: prepared horseradish and horseradish cream. These cannot be substituted one for the other in cooking but both can be used as table condiments. Horseradish cream is a commercially prepared creamy paste consisting of grated horseradish, vinegar, oil and sugar,

while prepared horseradish is the preserved grated root.

IRISH CREAM
See liqueurs.

JACKFRUIT
A huge fruit containing numerous seeds surrounded by golden, richly flavored, sharp-sweet flesh. Used in fruit salads, ice cream, milk drinks and soups. The seeds are edible boiled, then roasted in a pan with a little oil. See also page 516.

JERUSALEM ARTICHOKE
Crunchy brown-skinned tuber with a taste and texture like water chestnut. Eat raw in salads or cooked like potatoes. See also page 218.

JUNIPER BERRIES
Dried berries of an evergreen tree; it is the main flavoring ingredient in gin.

KAFFIR LIME
Also known as magrood, leech lime or jeruk purut. The wrinkled, bumpy-skinned green fruit of a small citrus tree originally grown in South Africa and Southeast Asia. As a rule, only the rind and leaves are used.

KAFFIR LIME LEAVES
Also known as bai magrood and looks like two glossy dark green leaves joined end to end, forming a rounded hourglass shape. Used fresh or dried in many Southeast Asian dishes, they are used like bay leaves or curry leaves, especially in Thai cooking. Sold fresh, dried or frozen, the dried leaves are less potent so double the number if using them as a substitute for fresh; a strip of fresh lime peel may be substituted for each kaffir lime leaf. See also page 349.

KAHLUA
See liqueurs

KALE
This strong-flavored member of the cabbage family is very high in antioxidants. It can be sauteed, boiled, braised, added to stews or used like cabbage. Kale is best during winter. The summer variety is paler and thinner. See also page 218.

KALONJI
Also called nigella or black onion seeds. Tiny, angular seeds, black on the outside and creamy within, with a sharp nutty flavor that is enhanced by frying briefly in a dry hot pan before use. Typically sprinkled over Turkish bread immediately after baking or as an important spice in Indian cooking, kalonji can be found in most Asian and Middle Eastern food shops. Often erroneously called black cumin seeds. See also page 417.

KANG KONG
Also known as water spinach, this delicate green vegetable has long, hollow stems and thin leaves. Use the leaves and top half of the stems, cut into 2-inch lengths. Stir-fry, dip in batter and deep-fry, or serve steamed with kecap manis or a curry paste. See also page 349.

KECAP ASIN
A thick, dark, salty Indonesian soy sauce.

KECAP MANIS
A dark, thick sweet soy sauce used in most Southeast Asian cuisines. Depending on the manufacturer, the sauce's sweetness is derived from the addition of either molasses or palm sugar when brewed.

KIRSCH
See liqueurs.

KIWI
Also known as Chinese gooseberry; it has a brown, somewhat hairy skin and bright-green flesh with a unique sweet-tart flavor. Used in fruit salads, desserts and eaten as is.

KOHLRABI
This round purple or green globe is a member of the cabbage family and develops a bulbous stem above ground. The bulb has a delicate cauliflower/turnip flavor and can be added to soups and casseroles, or used like potatoes. It comes into season in winter. See also page 218.

LADYFINGERS
Also called savoiardi, savoy biscuits or sponge fingers, they are Italian-style crisp fingers made from sponge cake mixture.

LAMB
chump Cut from just above the hind legs to the mid-loin section; can be used as a piece for roasting or cut into chops.
cutlet small, tender rib chop; sometimes sold french-trimmed, with all the fat and gristle at the narrow end of the bone removed.
diced cubed lean meat.
filets fine texture, most expensive and extremely tender.
ground very finely chopped lamb.
leg cut from the hindquarter; can be boned, butterflied, rolled and tied, or diced.
loin sometimes called backstrap; the larger filet from a row of loin chops or cutlets. Tender, best cooked rapidly: barbecued or pan-fried.
rolled shoulder boneless section of the forequarter, rolled and secured with string or netting.

shank forequarter leg; sometimes sold as drumsticks or frenched shanks if the gristle and narrow end of the bone are discarded and the remaining meat trimmed.

shoulder large, tasty piece with a lot of connective tissue so it is best pot-roasted or braised. Makes the best ground lamb.

LAMB'S LETTUCE
Also known as mâche or corn lettuce, this salad green has long, spoon-shaped dark leaves that resemble the shape of a lamb's tongue. They have a distinctive, tangy flavor and work best with a light dressing. They can also be cooked. Available in the cooler months. See also page 106.

LEEKS
A member of the onion family, the leek resembles a green onion but is much larger and more subtle in flavor. Tender baby or pencil leeks can be eaten whole with minimal cooking but adult leeks are usually trimmed of most of the green tops then chopped or sliced and cooked as an ingredient in stews, casseroles and soups.

LEMON GRASS
Also known as takrai, serai or serah. A tall, clumping, lemon-smelling and tasting, sharp-edged aromatic tropical grass; the white lower part of the stem is used, finely chopped, in many Southeast Asian dishes. Can be found, fresh, dried, powdered and frozen, in supermarkets, greengrocers and Asian food shops. See also page 348.

LENTILS (RED, BROWN, YELLOW)
Dried pulses often identified by and named after their color. Eaten by cultures all over the world, most famously perhaps in the dhals of India, lentils have high food value.

French green lentils are a local cousin to the famous (and very expensive) French lentils du puy; green-blue, tiny lentils with a nutty, earthy flavor and a hardy nature that allows them to be rapidly cooked without disintegrating. See also page 496.

LIMONCELLO
See liqueurs

LINSEED
The seed from the flax plant. Mostly used to produce linseed oil, the grain is also used in breads.

LIQUEURS
cointreau citrus-flavored liqueur.

Grand Marnier orange liqueur based on cognac-brandy.

Irish cream we used Baileys, a smooth and creamy natural blend of fresh Irish cream, the finest Irish spirits, Irish whiskey, cocoa and vanilla.

kahlua coffee-flavored liqueur.

kirsch cherry-flavored liqueur.

limoncello Italian lemon-flavored liqueur; originally made from the juice and peel of lemons grown along the Amalfi coast.

rum we use a dark lower-alcohol-content rum for a more subtle flavor in cooking. White rum is almost colorless, sweet and used mostly in mixed drinks.

Tia Maria coffee-flavored liqueur.

LOTUS ROOT
The crisp, delicately-flavored root of a waterlily. Crosswise slices are patterned with holes arranged like a flower. To prepare, simply peel and slice as the recipe directs, dropping the slices into acidulated water (water with lemon juice) to prevent them from browning. It is available canned or frozen and sometimes fresh.

LYCHEES
A small fruit from China with a hard shell and sweet, juicy flesh. The white flesh has a gelatinous texture and musky, perfumed taste. Discard the rough skin and seed before using in salads or as a dessert fruit. Also available canned in a sugar syrup. See also page 516.

MACADAMIAS
Native to Australia; fairly large, slightly soft, buttery rich nut. Used to make oil and macadamia butter; equally good in salads or cakes and pastries; delicious eaten on their own. Should always be stored in the refrigerator to prevent their high oil content from turning them rancid.

MANGO
Tropical fruit originally from India and Southeast Asia. With skin color ranging from green to yellow and deep red; fragrant, deep yellow flesh surrounds a large flat seed. Slicing off the cheeks, cross-hatching them with a knife then turning them inside out shows the sweet, juicy flesh at its best. Mangoes can also be used in curries and salsas, or pureed for ice cream, smoothies or mousse. Mango slices in light syrup are available canned. Sour and crunchy, green mangoes are just the immature fruit that is used as a vegetable in salads, salsas and curries. See also page 517.

green this is the unripe fruit of the mango tree. The flesh is deliciously tart. Used raw in many Asian salads or as a vegetable; it can also be bought pickled or dried. See also page 517.

MANGOSTEEN
The shiny, purple-brown skin peels to reveal segments of white flesh with a refreshing, sweet-sour flavor reminiscent of pineapple. Delicious peeled and eaten raw, like an orange,

or chilled and mixed with other tropical fruits. See also page 517.

MAPLE-FLAVORED SYRUP
Made from sugar cane and also known as golden or pancake syrup. It is not a substitute for pure maple syrup.

MAPLE SYRUP
Distilled from the sap of sugar maple trees found only in Canada and about ten states in the U.S. Most often eaten with pancakes or waffles, but also used as an ingredient in baking or in preparing desserts. Maple-flavored syrup or pancake syrup is not an adequate substitute for the real thing.

MARSALA
A fortified Italian wine produced in the region surrounding the Sicilian city of Marsala; recognizable by its intense amber color and complex aroma. Often used in cooking.

MAYONNAISE, WHOLE-EGG
Commercial mayonnaise of high quality made with whole eggs. Must be refrigerated once opened.

MERGUEZ SAUSAGES
A small, spicy sausage believed to have originated in Tunisia but eaten in North Africa, France and Spain; is traditionally made with lamb meat and is easily recognized because of its chili-red color. Can be fried, grilled or roasted; available from many butchers, delis and specialty sausage stores.

MESCLUN
Sold as a pre-mixed pile or bouquet of baby greens, which may include coral, mignonette, oak-leaf or butter lettuce, arugula, spinach, curly endive, mizuna and/or radicchio. If buying loose, grab more than you need and discard the tired-looking leaves. See also page 107.

MIGNONETTE LETTUCE
This is a small, soft-leafed lettuce, but crisper and glossier than coral or oak-leaf. It has a good grassy flavor with just a delicate suggestion of bitterness. Its leaves vary from red to green. See also page 107.

MILK
We use whole homogenized milk unless otherwise specified in recipes.
buttermilk in spite of its name, buttermilk is actually low in fat, varying between 0.6 percent and 2 percent per ¼ cup. Originally the term given to the slightly sour liquid left after butter was churned from cream, today it is intentionally made from no-fat or low-fat milk to which specific bacterial cultures have been added during the manufacturing process. It is readily available from the dairy department in supermarkets. Because it is low in fat, it's a good substitute for dairy products such as cream or sour cream in some baking and salad dressings.
evaporated unsweetened canned milk from which water has been extracted by evaporation. Evaporated skim or low-fat milk has 0.3 percent fat content.
sweetened condensed a canned milk product consisting of milk with more than half the water content removed and sugar added to the remaining milk.
whole milk powder instant powdered milk made from whole cow 's milk with liquid removed and emulsifiers added.

MIRIN
A Japanese champagne-colored cooking wine, made of glutinous rice and alcohol. It is used just for cooking and should not be confused with sake. A seasoned sweet mirin, manjo mirin, made of water, rice, corn syrup and alcohol, is used in dipping sauces.

MISO
Fermented soybean paste. There are many types of miso, each with its own aroma, flavor, color and texture; it can be kept, airtight, for up to a year in the fridge. Generally, the darker the miso, the saltier the taste and denser the texture. Salt-reduced miso is available. Buy in tubs or plastic packs.

MIXED DRIED FRUIT
A combination of golden and black raisins, currants, mixed candied citrus and cherries.

MIZUNA
A mustard green from Japan where it is traditionally used in soups and other cooked main dishes. It's often found in a mesclun, but its mild, aromatic jagged green leaves can also stand alone. Refrigerate in a plastic bag, unwashed, for up to five days. See also page 106.

MOLASSES
A thick, dark brown syrup, the residue from the refining of sugar; available in light, dark and blackstrap varieties. Its slightly bitter taste is an essential ingredient in cooking, found in foods such as gingerbread, shoofly pie and Boston baked beans.

MORTAR AND PESTLE
A cooking tool with a design that has remained the same over the centuries: the mortar is a bowl-shaped container and the pestle a rounded, bat-shaped tool. Together, they grind and pulverize spices, herbs and other foods. The pestle is pressed against the mortar and rotated, grinding the ingredient between the two surfaces. Essential for curry pastes and crushing spices.

MOULI
Also known as food mill; an essential kitchen tool in terms of versatility, ease

of use and multi-task function. It's a rotary grater large enough to fit over a saucepan or bowl that comes with variety of interchangeable plates for processing different textures; it strains, pulps, rices, mashes, purees and even dices. Unlike a blender or processor, it separates the peel, seeds, cores, etc., from the puree and allows the cook a degree of control over the final texture.

MUESLI
Also known as granola; a combination of grains (mainly oats), nuts and dried fruits. Can also be toasted in oil and honey, adding crispness and calories.

MUSCAT GRAPES
Also known as muscatel; used to make the sweet dessert wine of the same name. This grape variety is superb eaten fresh; when dried, its distinctively musty flavor goes well with cheese, chocolate, pork and game.

MUSHROOMS
button small, cultivated white mushrooms with a mild flavor. When a recipe in this book calls for an unspecified type of mushroom, use button. See also page 441.

chanterelle also called girolles or pfifferling; a trumpet-shaped wild mushroom ranging in color from yellow to orange. It has a delicate flavor and a chewy texture. Also available dried. See also page 441.

chestnut are cultivated mushrooms with a firm texture and strong flavor. They are available only irregularly. See also page 441.

cremini also known as Roman or Swiss brown. Light to dark brown mushrooms with full-bodied flavor; suited for use in casseroles or being stuffed and baked. See also page 441.

dried porcini the richest-flavored mushrooms, also known as cèpes. Expensive, but because they're so

strongly flavored, only a small amount is required. See also page 440.

enoki cultivated mushrooms also called enokitake; are tiny long-stemmed, pale mushrooms that grow and are sold in clusters, and can be used that way or separated by slicing off the base. They have a mild fruity flavor and are slightly crisp in texture. See also page 440.

flat large, flat mushrooms with a rich earthy flavor, ideal for filling and barbecuing. They are sometimes misnamed field mushrooms, which are wild mushrooms. See also page 440.

oyster also called abalone; gray-white mushrooms shaped like a fan. Prized for their smooth texture and subtle, oyster-like flavor. Also available pink. See also pages 348 & 440.

pine also called the Australian cep, are wild-picked in forests of introduced pine species in autumn and early winter. They are related to but not the same as the true European cep, but their fruity scent and deep, earthy flavor explain the common name. They are best served simply: fried quickly or added in the last few minutes of cooking to a soup. See also page 440.

portobello are mature, fully opened cremini; they are larger and bigger in flavor. See also page 441.

shiitake *fresh*, are also called Chinese black, forest or golden oak mushrooms. Although cultivated, they have the earthiness and taste of wild mushrooms. Large and meaty, they can be used as a substitute for meat in some Asian vegetarian dishes. See also page 349. *dried* also called donko or dried Chinese mushrooms; have a unique meaty flavor. Rehydrate before use.

shimeji cultivated mushrooms also called beech mushrooms, grow and are sold in clumps; are nutty in flavor and slightly crunchy. See also page 441.

straw so named for the straw on which they are grown; are small and globe-shaped with internal stems. They are cultivated but are so fragile

and deteriorate so quickly after harvesting that they are not a commercial proposition fresh so are usually canned. See also page 440.

MUSLIN
Inexpensive, undyed, finely woven cotton fabric called for in cooking to strain stocks and sauces; if unavailable, use disposable coffee filter papers.

MUSTARD
dijon also called French. Pale brown, creamy, distinctively flavored, fairly mild French mustard.

English traditional hot, pungent, deep yellow mustard. Serve with roast beef and ham; wonderful with hard cheeses.

Japanese hot mustard available in ready-to-use paste in tubes or powder form from Asian food shops.

wholegrain also known as seeded. A French-style coarse-grain mustard made from crushed mustard seeds and dijon-style French mustard. Works well with cold meats and sausages.

yellow bright yellow in color, a sweet mustard containing mustard seeds, sugar, salt, spices and garlic. Serve with hot dogs and hamburgers.

MUSTARD SEEDS
black also called brown mustard seeds, they are more pungent than the white variety; used frequently in curries.

white also called yellow mustard seeds; used ground for mustard powder and in most prepared mustards.

NAAN
The rather thick, leavened bread associated with the tandoori dishes of Northern India, where it is baked pressed against the inside wall of a heated tandoor (clay oven). Now made by commercial bakers and sold in most supermarkets.

NAPA CABBAGE

Also called Chinese cabbage or Peking cabbage; elongated in shape with pale green, crinkly leaves, it's the most common cabbage in Southeast Asia. Can be shredded or chopped and eaten raw or braised, steamed or stir-fried. See also page 349.

NOODLES

bean thread also called cellophane or glass noodles, these are made from a paste of water and mung bean flour. To soften bean thread noodles, it is best to soak them in hot water as they lose texture when boiled. They can also be fried directly from the pack until puffed. See also page 192.

dried rice noodles also called rice stick noodles. Made from rice flour and water, available flat and wide or very thin (vermicelli). Must be soaked in boiling water to soften.

fresh egg also called ba mee or yellow noodles; made from wheat flour and eggs, sold fresh or dried. Range in size from very fine strands to wide, spaghetti-like pieces as thick as a shoelace. See also page 193.

fresh rice also called ho fun, khao pun, sen yau, pho or kway tiau, depending on the country of manufacture; the most common form of noodle used in Thailand. Can be purchased in strands of various widths or large sheets weighing about 1 pound that are to be cut into the desired noodle size. Chewy and pure white, they do not need pre-cooking before use. See also page 193.

fried also known as crispy noodles, these wheat flour and egg noodles have been deep-fried until crisp, then dried and packaged. Add directly to a stir-fry or place in boiling water for one minute before using. Often used for the popular Chinese dish sang choy bow. See also page 192.

hokkien also called stir-fry noodles; fresh wheat noodles resembling thick, yellow-brown spaghetti needing no pre-cooking before use. See also page 192.

ramen popular Japanese wheat noodles, sold in dried, fresh, steamed and instant forms. A popular fast food in the many ramen houses of Japan, these noodles are also a diet staple for students. See also page 192.

rice stick also called sen lek, ho fun or kway teow; especially popular southeast Asian dried rice noodles. They come in different widths (thin used in soups, wide in stir-fries), but all should be soaked in hot water to soften. The traditional noodle used in pad thai which, before soaking, measures about ¼ inch in width. See also page 193.

rice vermicelli also called sen mee, mei fun or bee hoon. Used throughout Asia in spring rolls and cold salads; similar to bean threads, only longer and made with rice flour instead of mung bean starch. Before using, soak the dried noodles in hot water until softened, boil them briefly, then rinse with hot water. Vermicelli can also be deep-fried until crunchy and used in salad or as a garnish or bed for sauces. See also page 193.

Shanghai fresh thick, round wheat noodles, similar to hokkien but paler in color, and usually sold unoiled. Also available as dried thin white noodles, which need to be boiled for up to 15 minutes, or until soft; often used in stir-fries. See also page 192.

Singapore pre-cooked wheat noodles best described as a thinner version of hokkien; sold, packaged, in the refrigerated section of supermarkets.

soba thin, pale-brown noodle originally from Japan; made from buckwheat and varying proportions of wheat flour. Available dried and fresh, and in flavored (for instance, green tea) varieties; eaten in soups, stir-fries and, chilled, on their own. See also page 192.

somen extremely thin noodles made from hard wheat–if eggless, they are labeled somen and tamago if made with egg. These Japanese noodles are traditionally eaten in cold dishes but can be served in warm broth. Avoid overcooking, as they become sticky. See also page 193.

udon available fresh and dried. These broad, white, wheat Japanese noodles are similar to the ones used in homemade chicken noodle soup. See also page 193.

NORI

A type of dried seaweed used in Japanese cooking as a flavoring, garnish or for sushi. Sold in thin sheets, plain or toasted (yaki-nori).

NUTMEG

A strong and pungent spice ground from the dried nut of an evergreen tree native to Indonesia. Usually found ground but the flavor is more intense from a whole nut, available from spice shops, so it's best to grate your own. Used most often in baking and milk-based desserts, but also works nicely in savory dishes. Found in pie spice mixtures.

OAK-LEAF LETTUCE

The curly leaves vary from reddish-brown to pale green and resemble the shape of oak leaves. This popular variety of lettuce has a soft texture with a sweet, mild flavor. It is an ideal lettuce to grow because the leaves can be harvested one at a time. See also page 107.

OATMEAL

Also sold as oatmeal flour, is made from milled oat kernels; not the same product as rolled oats or oat bran. It is available at health food stores.

OIL

cooking spray we use a cholesterol-free cooking spray made from canola oil.

grapeseed comes from grape seeds; available from supermarkets.

hazelnut oil see hazelnuts.

macadamia oil see macadamias.

olive made from ripened olives. Extra virgin and virgin are the first and second press, respectively, of the olives and are therefore considered the best; the "extra light" or "light" name on other types refers to taste not fat levels.

peanut pressed from ground peanuts; the most commonly used oil in Asian cooking because of its high smoke point (capacity to handle high heat without burning).

sesame made from roasted, crushed, white sesame seeds; a flavoring rather than a cooking medium.

vegetable any of a number of oils sourced from plant rather than animal fats.

OKRA

A green, ridged, oblong pod with a furry skin. Native to Africa, this vegetable is used in Indian, Middle Eastern and South American cooking. Can be eaten on its own; as part of a casserole, curry or gumbo; used to thicken stews or gravies. See also page 218.

ONIONS

brown strongly-flavored onions with a brown skin and creamy flesh; they are the most commonly used onion in cooking.

fried onion served as a condiment on Asian tables to be sprinkled over just-cooked food. Found in cellophane bags or jars at all Asian grocery shops; once opened, they will keep for months if stored tightly sealed. Make your own by frying thinly sliced peeled baby onions until golden and crisp. See also shallots.

green also called scallion; an immature onion picked before the bulb has formed, has a long, bright-green edible stalk.

red also known as purple or bermuda onion; a sweet-flavored, large, purple-red onion.

spring crisp, narrow green-leafed tops and a round sweet white bulb larger than green onions.

white milder than brown onions, these white-skinned and white-fleshed onions are suitable in salads as well as cooking.

ORANGE FLOWER WATER

Concentrated flavoring made from orange blossoms.

OYSTER SAUCE

Asian in origin, this thick, richly flavored brown sauce is made from oysters and their brine, cooked with salt and soy sauce, and thickened with starches. Use as a condiment.

vegetarian mushroom a "vegetarian" oyster sauce made from blended mushrooms and soy sauce.

PANCETTA

An Italian unsmoked bacon, pork belly cured in salt and spices then rolled into a sausage shape and dried for several weeks. Used, sliced or chopped, as an ingredient rather than eaten on its own; can also be used to add taste and moisture to tough or dry cuts of meat.

PAPAYA

The papaya family includes both the yellow-fleshed fruit called pawpaw and the pink-fleshed fruit called papaya. Their mild, sweet flavor is best with a squeeze of lime. See also page 517.

green are available at Asian food stores; look for one that is hard and slightly shiny, proving it is freshly picked. Papaya will soften rapidly if not used within a day or two. See also page 348.

PAPRIKA

Ground dried sweet red pepper (bell pepper); there are many grades and types available, including sweet, hot, mild and smoked.

PARSNIP

Their nutty sweetness is especially good when steamed and dressed with a garlic and cream sauce or in a curried parsnip soup, or simply baked. Can be substituted for potatoes. Available all year but the cold develops their sweet/savory flavor in winter. See also page 218.

PASSIONFRUIT

A member of the berry family, this fruit is filled with tart-sweet pulp with small black seeds. It is used in desserts and the juice is extracted from the seeds and pulp.

PASTA

conchiglie "shellfish" or "shells" have concave, ridged shapes that hold sauces well. A dried type, great in hearty soups like minestrone, or added to a vegetable salad. Available in different sizes: conchigliette (small), conchiglioni (larger). See also page 146.

farfalle bow-tie shaped short pasta; sometimes known as butterfly pasta. See also page 146.

fettuccine fresh or dried ribbon pasta made from durum wheat, semolina and egg. Also available plain or flavored. See also page 146.

fresh lasagne sheets thinly rolled wide sheets of plain or flavored pasta; they do not need par-boiling before being used in cooking. See also page 146.

fusilli "Little spindles", also called

corkscrews, are a dried spiral pasta. Fusilli can be topped with any sauce, makes a great addition to casseroles or can be turned into a wonderful salad. Also comes in a longer, coil-like shape, called *fusilli col buco*. See also page 147.

gnocchi Italian "dumplings" made of potatoes, semolina or flour; can be cooked in boiling water or baked with sauce. See also page 147.

macaroni tube-shaped pasta available in various sizes; made from semolina and water, does not contain eggs.

orecchiette "little ears" are named after their shape, resembling tiny human ears. It's a chewy pasta that's traditional in southern Italy's Puglia region, where it is made from semolina. See also page 147.

pappardelle from the Italian verb *pappare*, meaning "to gobble up", pappardelle are broad, flat or frilly, ribbons of pasta. Go well with red meat sauces (rabbit is a Tuscan favorite), chunky tomato and mushroom sauces as in *pappardelle boscaiola*, or with cream. See also page 147.

penne Italian for "pen", this dried pasta resembles a quill, and has angled ends and ridges to hold chunky sauces. Penne are also available in a smooth variety to complement finer sauces. See also page 146.

ravioli "little turnips", squares of pasta stuffed with cheese, vegetables or meat. Usually made from fresh pasta either by hand or in molds. Ravioli are a match for tomato-based sauces, including bolognese, or they can be served with butter, olive oil or cream. See also page 147.

rigatoni Italian for "large, ridged", this dried ribbed, tubular pasta is perfect with any sauce, from cream or cheese (especially ricotta) to the chunkiest meat sauces. Rigatoni is also good for pasta bakes. See also page 147.

risoni small rice-shape pasta; very similar to another small pasta, orzo.

spaghetti long, thin solid strands of pasta.

tagliatelle long, flat strips of wheat pasta, slightly narrower and thinner than fettuccine.

tortellini circles of fresh plain pasta that are stuffed with a meat or cheese filling, and then folded into little hats. See also page 146.

PASTRY

filo or phyllo is unique in that no fat or margarine is added to the dough. The dough is very elastic in texture and not rolled like other pastries, but stretched to the desired thickness. This gives it its delicate, tissue-thin sheets. It is best brushed with butter or margarine before baking.

sheets packaged sheets of refrigerated ready-made pie crust dough. Available in the dairy section of supermarkets.

PEANUTS

Also known as groundnut, not in fact a nut but the pod of a legume. We mainly use raw (unroasted) or unsalted roasted peanuts.

oil See oil.

PEARL BARLEY

See barley.

PEAS

green also known as garden peas, must be shelled and their pods never eaten. Peas in the pod will yield just under half their weight of shelled peas; 2 pounds will serve 4. Peas in the pod are available fresh; shelled peas, frozen. See also page 219.

snow a variety of garden pea, eaten pod and all (although you may need to string them). Used in stir-fries or eaten raw in salads. Snow pea sprouts are available from supermarkets or greengrocers and are usually eaten raw in salads or sandwiches. See also page 219.

sugar snap also known as honey snap peas; fresh small pea that can be eaten, whole, pod and all, similarly to snow peas. See also page 219.

PECANS

Native to the U.S., pecans are golden brown, buttery and rich. Good in savory as well as sweet dishes; walnuts are a good substitute.

PEPITAS

Are the pale green kernels of dried pumpkin seeds; they can be bought plain or salted.

PIE SPICE

A classic spice mixture generally containing cardamom, allspice, cinnamon, nutmeg and ginger, although other spices can be added. It is used with fruit and in cakes.

PINE NUTS

Also known as pignoli; not a nut but a small, cream-colored kernel from pine cones. They are best roasted before use to bring out the flavor.

PIRI PIRI SAUCE

A Portuguese chili sauce made from red chilies, ginger, garlic, oil and various herbs.

PISTACHIOS

Green, delicately flavored nuts inside hard off-white shells. Available salted or unsalted in their shells; you can also get them shelled.

PITA BREAD

Also known as Lebanese bread. A wheat-flour pocket bread sold in large, flat pieces that separate into rounds. Also available in small pieces called pocket pita.

PLUM SAUCE
A thick, sweet and sour dipping sauce made from plums, vinegar, sugar, chilies and spices.

POLENTA
Also called cornmeal; a flour-like cereal made of dried corn (maize). Also the dish made from it. See also page 497.

POMEGRANATE
Dark-red, leathery-skinned fresh fruit about the size of an orange filled with hundreds of seeds, each wrapped in an edible crimson pulp with a unique tangy sweet-sour flavor.

POMEGRANATE MOLASSES
Not to be confused with pomegranate syrup or grenadine (used in cocktails); pomegranate molasses is thicker, browner and more concentrated in flavor–tart, sharp, slightly sweet and fruity. Brush over grilling or roasting meat, seafood or poultry, add to salad dressings. Buy from Middle Eastern food stores or specialty food shops.

POPPY SEEDS
Small, dried, bluish-gray seeds of the poppy plant, with a crunchy texture and a nutty flavor. Can be purchased whole or ground in most supermarkets.

PORK
american-style spareribs or baby backs well-trimmed mid-loin ribs.
belly fatty cut sold in slices or in a piece, with or without rind or bone.
chinese barbecued roasted pork filet with a sweet, sticky coating. Available from Asian food shops or specialty stores.
cutlets cut from ribs.
filet skinless, boneless eye-filet cut from the loin.
ground very finely chopped pork.
ham hock the shank of the leg, which does not form part of the ham but is salted and smoked in the same way.
neck sometimes called pork collar, boneless cut from the foreloin.
shoulder joint sold with bone in or out.
speck smoked pork.

POTATOES
crescent a type of fingerling; thin-skinned and waxy but moist flesh. Longer and thinner than russet, it is grown in white and pink varieties. A good all-purpose potato, it can be mashed with the skin on, or boiled and sliced for salads. Also great roasted with skin on.
fingerling heirloom variety with a long stubby, finger-like shape. Fully mature when harvested; they are typically halved lengthwise and roasted or grilled and hold their shape well due to their low starch content. Varieties include ruby crescent, Russian banana and rose finn.
new potato an immature variety of any potato; commonly found with both red and yellow thin skins. Starch content increases as potatoes mature so their low-starch flesh is great for boiling. Particularly good for salads or chowders as they hold their shape well.
red bliss very firm, round, waxy potato with low starch content. Holds its shape when cooked so perfect for boiling and slicing or cubing for salads. Also a good choice for roasting or grilling; thin skinned, so can be eaten with skin on.
russet also known as a baking potato or Idaho, long and oval, rough tan skin with shallow eyes and white flesh. Floury variety with high starch content, it is great for mashing, baking whole, or cut and deep-fried for classic French fries.
sweet potato a variety of tuber from the same family as the morning glory climbing flower, they are a distant cousin to the potato. Extremely high in antioxidants and vitamins, they are called a "superfood" and are best mashed or boiled. Also can be fried, but do not hold crispness due to their low starch and high sugar content.
Yukon gold lower in starch than russets, but mealier flesh than waxy potatoes. Great all-purpose potato; creamy yellow sweet flesh delicious for mashing, roasting, or frying.

PRESERVED LEMON
Whole or quartered salted lemons preserved in olive oil and lemon juice and occasionally clove, cinnamon and coriander. A North African specialty, added to casseroles and tagines to impart a rich, salty-sour acidic flavor; also added to dressings or yogurt. Available from delis and specialty food shops. Use the rind only and rinse well under cold water before using.

PRESERVED TURNIP
Also called hua chai po or cu cai muoi, or dried radish because of its similarity to daikon. Sold packaged whole or sliced, is very salty and must be rinsed and dried before use.

PROSCIUTTO
A kind of unsmoked Italian ham; salted, air-cured and aged, it is usually eaten uncooked.

QUAIL
Related to the pheasant and partridge; a small, delicate-flavored farmed game bird ranging from 8 to 10 ounces.

QUINCE
Yellow-skinned fruit with hard texture and astringent, tart taste; eaten cooked or as a preserve. Long, slow cooking makes the flesh a deep rose pink.

RADICCHIO
A red-leafed Italian chicory with a refreshing bitter taste that's eaten raw and grilled. Comes in varieties named after their places of origin, such as round-headed Verona or long-headed Treviso. See also page 107.

RAITA
Yogurt that is whipped and seasoned with salt, pepper and one or two piquant spices; often has mint stirred through it. Served as a condiment, it possesses cooling properties to help temper the heat of a curry.

RAMBUTAN
A relative of the lychee, with similar luscious, perfumed, grape-like flesh. To remove the leathery, tendril-covered shell, break open with a fingernail and peel like an egg. See also page 516.

RAS EL HANOUT
The name means "top of the shop" and the spice mixture varies from one merchant to another, but is always subtly savory with a touch of heat. See also page 416.

RHUBARB
A plant with long, green-red stalks; becomes sweet and edible when cooked.

RICE
arborio small, round grain rice that absorbs a large amount of liquid; the high level of starch makes it especially suitable for risottos for its classic creaminess. See also page 173.
basmati a white, fragrant long-grained rice; the grains fluff up when cooked. It should be washed several times before cooking. See also page 172.
black also called purple rice, black rice is unmilled, leaving the dark husk in place, coloring the grain when cooked. It has a nutty taste and crunchy texture.

There are hundreds of varieties across Asia, from Chinese black rice to Thai black sticky rice. See also page 173.
brown retains the high-fiber, nutritious bran coating that's removed from white rice when hulled. It takes longer to cook than white rice and has a chewier texture. Once cooked, the long grains stay separate, while the short grains are soft and stickier. See also page 172.
calrose a medium-grain white rice developed as an all-purpose rice; it gives different results according to how it is cooked. Calrose brown rice is also available. See also page 173.
glutinous also known as sticky rice, this variety is a stickier version of short-grain rice. Its plump, distinctively flavored grains cling together when cooked so they can be easily formed into small balls for dipping into savory dishes and soaking up the sauce. See also page 173.
jasmine or Thai jasmine, is a long-grain white rice recognized around the world as having a perfumed aromatic quality; moist in texture, it clings together after cooking. Sometimes substituted for basmati rice. See also page 172.
koshihikari small, round-grain white rice. Substitute white short-grain rice and cook by the absorption method. See also page 173.
long-grain elongated grains that remain separate when cooked; this is the most popular steaming rice in Asia. See also page 172.
nishiki a Japanese variety that's often sold as medium-grain rice, but is actually a slightly longer short-grain rice. Like koshihikari, nishiki cooks to the tender and lightly clinging texture that is right for sushi. This light, fresh-tasting grain is also grown in California. See also page 173.
short-grain fat, almost round grain with a high starch content; tends to clump together when cooked.
white is hulled and polished rice,

can be short- or long-grained.
wild not a member of the rice family but the seed of an aquatic grass native to the cold regions of North America. Wild rice has a strong nutty taste and can be expensive, so is best combined with brown and white rices in pilafs, stuffings and salads. See also page 172.
wild rice blend a packaged blend of white long-grain rice and wild rice. With its dark brown, almost black grains, crunchy, resilient texture and smokey-like flavor, wild rice contrasts nicely with mild-tasting white rice. Perfect with lentils, fish, in pilaf or added to soups. See also page 172.

RISONI
See pasta.

ROLLED OATS
Flattened oat grain rolled into flakes and traditionally used for porridge. Instant oats are also available, but use traditional oats for baking.

ROLLED RICE
Flattened rice grain rolled into flakes; looks similar to rolled oats.

ROLLED RYE
Flattened rye grain rolled into flakes and similar in appearance to rolled oats.

ROMAINE LETTUCE
Also known as cos lettuce; the traditional caesar salad lettuce. Long, with leaves ranging from dark green on the outside to almost white near the core; the leaves have a stiff center rib giving a slight cupping effect to the leaf on either side. See also page 106.

ROSEWATER
Extract made from crushed rose petals; used for its aromatic quality in many candies and desserts.

RUM
See liqueurs.

SAFFRON
The dried stamen of the crocus family, available ground or in strands; imparts a yellow-orange color to food once infused. The quality can vary greatly; the best is the most expensive spice in the world. See also page 416.

SAMBAL OELEK
Also called ulek or olek; an Indonesian salty paste made from ground chilies and vinegar.

SASHIMI
Fish sold as sashimi has to meet stringent guidelines regarding handling. Seek advice from seafood organizations before eating any raw seafood.

SAVOY CABBAGE
Large, heavy head with crinkled dark-green outer leaves; a fairly mild tasting cabbage.

SEAFOOD
abalone is a harvested single-shelled deep-water shellfish with a reputation for toughness, it is usually sliced and pounded before cooking. Tastes like lobster. See also page 446.
blue-eye also called deep sea trevalla or trevally and blue-eye cod; thick, moist white-fleshed fish.
blue swimmer crab also known as sand crab, blue manna crab, bluey, sand crab or sandy. Substitute with lobster or crayfish. See also page 447.
bream (yellowfin) also known as silver or black bream, seabream or surf bream; soft, moist white flesh. Substitute with snapper or ocean perch.
clams a species of bivalve, clams burrow into the sand along the water's edge. Can be eaten raw on the half shell with lemon or shelled and added

to soups and stews. Small varieties like manila or cockles are more tender and best for pastas and soups. See also page 446.
fish filet use your favorite firm-fleshed white fish filet.
fresh sardines now readily available in fish markets whole or already cleaned. Full of healthy omega-3 fatty acids, they can be grilled or broiled; purchase them scaled and gutted, and store them on ice until ready to cook. Use within one day. See also page 447.
king prawns large shrimp, usually found with the head and shell on. Sweet, firm flesh good for steaming and boiling. Shells can be used for flavoring stocks and soups. Can be substituted with tiger prawns. See also page 447.
lobster found in virtually every ocean on earth, lobsters live near the shoreline and are considered a delicacy. It is important to undercook, rather than overcook, lobster as they will continue cooking in residual heat. See also page 446.
mussels should only be bought from a reliable fish market: they must be tightly closed when bought, indicating they are alive. Before cooking, scrub shells with a strong brush and remove the beards; do not eat any that do not open after cooking. Varieties include black and green-lip. See also page 447.
ocean trout a farmed fish with pink, soft flesh. From the same family as the Atlantic salmon; one can be substituted for the other.
octopus usually tenderized before you buy them; both octopus and squid require either long slow cooking (usually for the large mollusks) or quick cooking over high heat (usually for the small mollusks)–anything in between will make the octopus tough and rubbery. See also page 446.
oysters over 200 varieties of oysters are grown in North America, each with a taste and texture of its own depending on the environment it was grown in.

Purchase while still alive and open the shells just prior to eating. See also page 447.
salmon red-pink firm flesh with few bones; moist delicate flavor.
scallops a type of bivalve; often eaten raw or barely seared, they should never be cooked more than 30 seconds as they will lose their juicy tenderness and be tough. See also page 446.
squid also known as calamari; a type of mollusk. Buy squid hoods to make preparation and cooking faster. See also page 447.
swordfish also known as broadbill. Substitute with yellowfin or bluefin tuna or mahi mahi.
tuna reddish, firm flesh; slightly dry. Varieties include bluefin, yellowfin, skipjack or albacore; substitute with swordfish.
white fish means non-oily fish; includes bream, flathead, whiting, snapper, dhufish, redfish and ling.

SEMOLINA
Coarsely ground flour milled from durum wheat; the flour used in making gnocchi, pasta and couscous.

SESAME SEEDS
Black and white are the most common of this small oval seed, however there are also red and brown varieties. The seeds are used as an ingredient and as a condiment. Toast the seeds in a heavy-based frying pan over low heat.

SEVEN-SPICE MIX (SHICHIMI TOGARASHI)
A Japanese blend of seven ground spices, seeds and seaweed. The mix varies but includes hot and aromatic flavors. Used as a seasoning with noodles and cooked meats and fish.

SHALLOTS
Also called french shallots, golden shallots or eschalots. Small and elongated, with a brown skin, they

grow in tight clusters similar to garlic.

fried can be purchased at Asian grocery stores; once opened, fried shallots will keep for months if stored in a tightly sealed glass jar. See also onions.

purple also known as asian shallots; related to the onion but resembling garlic (they grow in bulbs of multiple cloves). Thin-layered and intensely flavored, they are used in cooking throughout southeast Asia.

SHERRY
Fortified wine consumed as an aperitif or used in cooking. Sold as fino (light, dry), amontillado (medium sweet, dark) and oloroso (full-bodied, very dark).

SHRIMP PASTE
Also called kapi, trasi and blanchan; a strong-scented, very firm preserved paste made of salted dried shrimp. Used sparingly as a pungent flavoring in many southeast Asian soups, sauces and rice dishes. It should be chopped or sliced thinly then wrapped in foil and roasted before use.

SICHUAN PEPPERCORNS
Also called szechuan or Chinese pepper, native to the Sichuan province of China. A mildly hot spice that comes from the prickly ash tree. Although it is not related to the peppercorn family, small, red-brown aromatic sichuan berries look like black peppercorns and have a distinctive peppery-lemon flavor and aroma. See also page 417.

SKEWERS
Metal or bamboo skewers can be used: rub oil onto metal skewers to stop meat sticking; soak bamboo skewers in water for at least 1 hour to prevent them splintering or scorching during cooking.

SOPRESSATA
A salami from the north of Italy, can be found in both mild and chili-flavored varieties. If you can't find it easily, you can use any hot salami, but the taste won't be exactly the same.

SOUR CREAM
See cream.

SOY SAUCE
Also called sieu; made from fermented soybeans. Several variations are available in supermarkets and Asian food stores; we use Japanese soy sauce unless indicated otherwise.

dark deep brown, almost black in color; rich, with a thicker consistency than other types. Pungent but not particularly salty; good for marinating.

Japanese an all-purpose low-sodium soy sauce made with more wheat content than its Chinese counterparts; fermented in barrels and aged. Possibly the best table soy and the one to choose if you only want one variety.

light fairly thin in consistency and, while paler than the others, the saltiest tasting; used in dishes in which the natural color of the ingredients is to be maintained. Not to be confused with salt-reduced or low-sodium soy sauces.

SPECK
See pork.

SPINACH
Also called English spinach and incorrectly, silver beet. Baby spinach leaves are best eaten raw in salads; the larger leaves should be added last to soups, stews and stir-fries, and should be cooked until barely wilted.

SPLIT PEAS
Yellow or green varieties, both with a sweet, strong pea flavor. They are usually pre-soaked but may be cooked without soaking. See also page 497.

SPRING ROLL WRAPPERS
Also known as egg roll wrappers; they come in various sizes and can be purchased fresh or frozen. Made from a delicate wheat-based pastry, they can be used for making gow gee and samosas as well as spring rolls. See also wrappers.

STAR ANISE
A dried star-shaped pod, the seeds have an astringent aniseed flavor; commonly used to flavor stocks and marinades. See also page 416.

STAR FRUIT
Also known as carambola, five-corner fruit or chinese star fruit; pale green or yellow color, it has a clean, crisp texture. Flavor may be either sweet or sour, depending on the variety and when it was picked. There is no need to peel or seed it and it's slow to discolor. See also page 516.

SUGAR
We use coarse, granulated table sugar in these recipes unless specified.

brown a soft, finely granulated sugar retaining molasses for its characteristic color and flavor.

demerara small-grained golden-colored crystal sugar.

muscovado a fine-grained, moist sugar that comes in two types, light and dark. Light muscovado has a light toffee flavor and is good for sticky toffee sauce and caramel ice cream. Dark muscovado is used in sweet and spicy sauces.

palm also called nam tan pip, jaggery, jawa or gula melaka; made from the sap of the sugar palm tree. Light brown to black in color and usually sold in rock-hard cakes; use brown sugar if unavailable.

powdered also known as confectioners' sugar or icing sugar; pulverized granulated sugar crushed together with a small amount of corn starch.

raw natural brown granulated sugar.

superfine also known as caster or finely granulated table sugar.

SUMAC
A purple-red, astringent spice ground from berries growing on shrubs that flourish wild around the Mediterranean; adds a tart, lemony flavor to dips and dressings and goes well with barbecued meat. Can be found in Middle Eastern food stores. See also page 417.

SUNFLOWER SEEDS
Grey-green, slightly soft, oily kernels; a nutritious snack.

SWISS CHARD
Also called silver beet and, incorrectly, spinach; has fleshy stalks and large leaves, both of which can be prepared as for spinach. See also page 217.

TAHINI
Sesame seed paste; found in Middle Eastern food stores and in the health food section of most supermarkets.

TAMARI
Similar to but thicker than Japanese soy; very dark in color with a distinctively mellow flavor. Good used as a dipping sauce or for basting.

TAMARIND
The tamarind tree produces clusters of hairy brown pods, each of which is filled with seeds and a viscous pulp, which are dried and pressed into the blocks of tamarind found in Asian food shops. Gives a sweet-sour, slightly astringent taste to marinades, pastes, sauces and dressings.

TAMARIND CONCENTRATE (OR PASTE)
The commercial result of the distillation of tamarind juice into a condensed, compacted paste.

TAT SOI
Also known as pak choy and Chinese flat cabbage, tat soi is a variety of bok choy. Its dark green leaves are cut into sections rather than separated and used in soups, braises and stir-fries. Available from some supermarkets and greengrocers. See also page 348.

TIA MARIA
See liqueurs.

TOFU
Also called soybean curd or bean curd; an off-white, custard-like product made from the "milk" of crushed soybeans. Refrigerate fresh tofu in water (changed daily) for up to 4 days.
firm made by compressing bean curd to remove most of the water. Good in stir-fries as it can be tossed without disintegrating. Can also be flavored, preserved in rice wine or brine.
fried packaged pieces of deep-fried soft bean curd; the surface is brown and crunchy and the inside almost totally dried out. Add to soups and stir-fries at the last minute so they don't soak up too much liquid.
sheets also called dried bean curd skins or yuba. Manufactured product made from the sweet, stiffened skin that forms on warm soybean liquid as it cools. Reconstitute before use.
silken not a type of tofu but reference to the manufacturing process of straining soybean liquid through silk; this denotes best quality.
soft delicate texture; does not hold its shape when overhandled. Can be used as a dairy substitute in ice cream etc.

TOMATOES
canned whole peeled tomatoes in natural juices; available crushed, chopped or diced. Use undrained.
cherry also called tiny tim or tom thumb tomatoes; small and round.
jarred pasta sauce a prepared sauce; a blend of tomatoes, herbs and spices.
paste triple-concentrated tomato puree used to flavor soups, stews and sauces.
plum also called Roma, smallish, oval-shaped tomatoes commonly used in Italian cooking or salads.
puree canned pureed tomatoes (not tomato paste).
semi-dried partially dried tomato pieces in olive oil; softer and juicier than sun-dried, these are not a preserve thus do not keep as long as sun-dried.
sun-dried tomato pieces that have been dried with salt; this dehydrates the tomato and concentrates the flavor. We use sun-dried tomatoes packaged in oil, unless otherwise specified.
truss small vine-ripened tomatoes with vine still attached.

TURKISH BREAD
Also called pide. Sold in long (18-inch) flat loaves and individual rounds; made from wheat flour and sprinkled with black onion seeds.

TURMERIC
Also called kamin; it's a rhizome related to galangal and ginger. Must be grated or pounded to release its acrid aroma and pungent flavor. Known for the golden color it imparts, fresh turmeric can be substituted with the more commonly found dried powder.

VANILLA
bean dried, long, thin pod from a tropical golden orchid; the minuscule black seeds inside the bean are used to impart a vanilla flavor in baking and desserts. Place a whole bean in a jar of sugar to make the vanilla sugar often called for in recipes; a bean can be used three or four times.
extract obtained from vanilla beans infused in water; a non-alcoholic version of essence.

VEAL

osso buco also called veal shin, usually cut into 1½- to 2-inch thick slices and used in the famous Italian slow-cooked casserole of the same name.

rack row of small chops or cutlets.

scaloppine a piece of lean steak hammered with a meat mallet until almost see-through; cook over high heat for as little time as possible.

schnitzel thinly sliced steak.

VERMOUTH

A wine flavored with a number of different herbs, mostly used as an aperitif and for cocktails.

VINEGAR

balsamic originally from Modena, Italy, there are now many balsamic vinegars on the market ranging in pungency and quality depending on how, and for how long, they have been aged. Quality can be determined up to a point by price; use the most expensive sparingly.

brown malt made from fermented malt and beech shavings.

cider made from fermented apples.

rice a colorless vinegar made from fermented rice and flavored with sugar and salt. Also called seasoned rice vinegar; sherry can be substituted.

white made from distilled grain alcohol.

WALNUTS

As well as being a good source of fiber and healthy oils, nuts contain a variety of vitamins, minerals and other beneficial plant components called phytochemicals. Walnuts contain the beneficial omega-3 fatty acids.

WASABI

Also called wasabe; an Asian horseradish used to make the pungent, green-colored paste traditionally served with Japanese raw fish dishes; sold in powdered or paste form.

WATER CHESTNUTS

Resemble true chestnuts in appearance, hence the English name. Small brown tubers with a crisp, white, nutty-tasting flesh. Their crunchy texture is best fresh; however, canned water chestnuts are more easily obtained and can be kept for about a month in the fridge, once opened. Used, rinsed and drained, in salads and stir-fries.

WATERCRESS

One of the cress family, a large group of peppery greens used raw in salads, dips and sandwiches, or cooked in soups. Highly perishable, so it must be used as soon as possible after purchase. See also page 106.

WOK CHAN

A long-handled, metal mini-shovel used in stir-frying to lift, toss and stir food in a wok. Invest in a wooden chan if you use a non-stick wok so that you don't scratch its surface.

WORCESTERSHIRE SAUCE

Thin, dark-brown spicy sauce developed by the British when in India; used as a seasoning for meat, gravies and cocktails, and as a condiment.

Japanese there are two types available, one similar to normal worcestershire and the other somewhat blander; both are made from varying proportions of vinegar, tomatoes, onions, carrots, garlic and spices.

WRAPPERS

Wonton wrappers and gow gee or spring roll pastry sheets, made of flour, egg and water, are found in the refrigerated or freezer section of Asian food shops and many supermarkets. These come in different thicknesses and shapes. Thin wrappers work best in soups, while the thicker ones are best for frying; and the choice of round or square, small or large is dependent on the recipe. See also spring roll wrappers.

YEAST (DRIED AND FRESH)

Rising agent used in dough-making. Granular (¼-ounce packets) and fresh compressed (7-ounce blocks) yeast can almost always be substituted one for the other when yeast is called for.

YOGURT

We use plain full-cream yogurt unless specifically noted otherwise. If a recipe in this book calls for low-fat yogurt, we use one with a fat content of less than 0.2 percent.

ZA'ATAR

A Middle Eastern herb and spice mixture that varies but always includes thyme (for which it gets its Arabic name), with ground sumac and, usually, toasted sesame seeds. It is sprinkled on yogurt and flatbreads and can be used as a rub on lamb or chicken to grilled or roasted. See also page 417.

ZUCCHINI

Small, pale- or dark-green or yellow vegetable of the squash family. Harvested when young, its edible flowers can be stuffed and deep-fried. See also page 219.

Index

DELISH

Elizabeth Shepard   Executive Director

This title was previously published as *The AWW Cooking School* by ACP books, Sydney Australia

Chapter Openers, Special Features and Step-by-Steps
Photographer   Louise Lister
Stylist   Kate Nixon
Photochefs   Nicole Dicker, Lucy Nunes
Assistant Photochef   Tessa Immens

Additional Photos:
Page 446: Crayfish: Nata-Lia/Shutterstock.com; Lobster: Isantilli/Shutterstock.com
Page 447: Sardine: Picturepartners/Shutterstock.com

Library of Congress Cataloging-in-Publication Data Available Upon Request

10 9 8 7 6 5 4 3 2 1

Published by Hearst Books
A division of Sterling Publishing Co., Inc.
387 Park Avenue South, New York, NY 10016

Delish is a registered trademark of Hearst Communications, Inc.

www.delish.com

For information about custom editions, special sales, premium and corporate purchases, please contact Sterling Special Sales Department at 800-805-5489 or specialsales@sterlingpublishing.com.

Distributed in Canada by Sterling Publishing
C/o Canadian Manda Group, 165 Dufferin Street
Toronto, Ontario, Canada M6K 3H6

Manufactured in China

Sterling ISBN 978-1-58816-930-3